THE GOOD HOTEL GUIDE 2007

THE GOOD HOTEL GUIDE 2007

Great Britain & Ireland

Editors:

DESMOND BALMER
AND ADAM RAPHAEL

Editor in Chief:
Caroline Raphael

Founding Editor:
Hilary Rubinstein

Contributing Editors:
Bill Bennett
Nicola Davies
Sarah Mitchell
Lottie Moggach

The Good Hotel Guide Ltd

Please send reports on hotels to
The Good Hotel Guide
50 Addison Avenue, London W11 4QP
or (if posted in UK)
Freepost PAM 2931, London W11 4BR
Tel/fax: 020-7602 4182
Email: Goodhotel@aol.com
Website: www.goodhotelguide.com

The Good Hotel Guide Ltd

This edition first published in 2006 by
The Good Hotel Guide Ltd

1 3 5 7 9 10 8 6 4 2

Copyright © 2006 Adam and Caroline Raphael
Maps © 2006 David Perrott
Illustrations © 2006 David Brindley

Design: Mick Keates
Production: Hugh Allan
Text editor: Daphne Trotter
Managing editor: Alison Wormleighton
Computer consultant: Gwyn Evans

A CIP catalogue record for this book may be found in the British Library.

ISBN-10 0-9549404-1-5
ISBN-13 978-0-9549404-1-6

Typeset from authors' disks by
MATS Typesetters, Southend-on-Sea, Essex
Printed and bound in Great Britain by
Creative Print and Design (Wales), Ebbw Vale

Contents

The truly independent guide

This is the leading independent guide to hotels in Great Britain and Ireland. Hotels cannot buy their entry as they do in most rival guides. No money changes hands, and the editors and inspectors do not accept free hospitality on their anonymous visits to hotels. The only vested interest is that of the reader seeking impartial advice to find a good hotel.

Our hotels are as independent as we are. Most are small, family owned and family run. They are places of character where the owners and their staff spend time looking after their guests, rather than reporting to an area manager. We look for a warm welcome, with friendly and flexible service. We like hotels where early-departing guests are offered breakfast before the kitchen officially opens, and arriving visitors are given a cup of tea and home-made cake. We don't like rules, which are written for the convenience of the hotel, not the guest.

We recognise that one size doesn't fit all: each traveller has individual requirements. This explains the diversity of choice in our selection. An entry for a grand country house might be followed by a simple B&B. We describe some of our favourite places as guest houses; they may not have the full range of facilities, but the welcome will be warm. Our B&Bs, never with fewer than three bedrooms, often provide a better breakfast than some five-star hotels. There are some chain hotels, especially in the larger cities; each one will have met our criteria of high standards of service.

Our readers play a crucial role by reporting on existing entries as well as recommending new discoveries. Reader reports, written on the forms at the back of the book or sent by email, bring our entries to life, and give the *Guide* a unique 'word-of-mouth' quality. Many join our Readers' Club (see page 58). The editors make a balanced judgment based on these reports, backed up where necessary by an anonymous inspection.

Annual updates give the *Guide* an added edge. We drop a hotel if there has been a change of owner, if this year's reports are negative, or in rare cases where there has been no feedback. About 80 hotels fall by the wayside every year; a similar number are introduced, often interesting new discoveries.

Introduction

None too soon, the craze for designer hotels is ending as guests question their emphasis on style over service. We welcome a return to the values that have sustained this guide since it was first published 30 years ago. We like sharp design, and welcome genuine innovation. Indeed, we have given a *César* award this year to one of the best of the breed. But our award looks beyond style. We celebrate good service, a warm welcome, the feeling that the guest comes first. Too often, reviews of hotels focus on decor and design, forgetting that it is the people who are the most important. A waiter may look smart in an Armani suit, but it is how he engages with the guest and serves at table that matters.

The need to balance good design with guest comfort was highlighted this year by an architect whose first impressions of a boutique hotel were good. Then guests for a wedding party started to change for the evening. 'The corridors are lined with wood, floors covered in timber or sea-grass matting with little soundproofing, so that every noise was amplified and we could hear every word said,' he told us.

The menace of the wedding parties

Weddings and other celebrations have been a recurring theme in reports from readers and inspectors this year. A regular visitor to a Birmingham hotel was told he would have to dine alone in his bedroom because the restaurant was fully booked for a celebration dinner. Clearly, he wasn't receiving the levels of service he had every right to expect. Other readers, visiting other hotels, have been banished to a small side room for dinner when a wedding party took over the restaurant, and have complained of crowded bars and late-night noise. A hotel can be an excellent venue for a wedding party, and functions are an important source of revenue, but small hotels should not accept other guests when hosting a wedding party, and larger hotels should channel the celebrations to areas that do not impact on other guests. It can be done. A reader nominating a hotel on Skye this year told us: 'A wedding reception was handled without any adverse effect on the services provided to residents.'

The personal touch works both ways

A cautionary tale for those who use the Internet to book a hotel. A *Guide* inspector in Ireland was among those who ran foul of a wedding party this year. When he emailed the hotel to complain, the manager apologised with easy Irish charm: 'As your booking was made through our website and not over the phone, we missed the opportunity to advise you of the wedding party that would be taking place at the time of your stay.'

The Internet might be a good tool for buying a budget airline ticket, but we recommend direct contact with a hotel before booking a room. The tone of the reply alone should indicate whether it is a place you will enjoy, and you can ask about the details that matter to you: perhaps sheets and blankets rather than duvets, road noise, whether children are catered for.

Our cautionary tale had a happy ending. The hotel manager offered a free night's stay as compensation 'for not being able to enjoy the house in all its glory'.

The wrong kind of guest

We enjoyed a report this year from a hotel-reservation company that alerted four- and five-star hotels to the dangers of attracting 'the wrong kind of guests' when offering discounted rates on websites. The company's managing director warned that regular clients accustomed to these hotels are bound 'to be a touch snobbish towards cut-price customers who can be socially out of their depth, and be badly behaved. For high net-worth individuals, the status of fellow guests matters as much as the decor or cuisine.' He misses the point. What customers require are warnings about the wrong kind of *hotel*, especially those that worry about the social status of their guests.

Good service knows no boundaries

The manager of a hotel in the Lake District took us to task over a quotation from a reader's report in our 2006 entry that 'staff (foreign) were attentive'. 'I have tried to employ local staff,' she wrote. 'Despite incentives and a salary well above the minimum, the response has been poor.' She found our comment derogatory. This was not our intention. We understand that hotels have difficulty in recruiting local staff. We applaud good service whatever the nationality of the staff, but we owe it to our readers to give an idea of what to expect: you might not have a very 'Scottish experience' in a hotel in Scotland, thanks to the predominance of young Eastern European, Antipodean or South African staff. Staff are a crucial part of any hotel, so we often mention if they are local or otherwise. No criticism is implied. There have been many tributes this year to the level of service achieved by hard-working young people from around the world. 'What would we do without the Poles?' one inspector wrote. We leave the last word to the Lake District manager: 'These "foreigners" are well educated, some speaking three or four languages, extremely courteous, very rarely ill, and *never* hung over.'

The perils of tip and pin

Chip-and-pin technology has created a new variation on an old malpractice. Hotels and restaurants used to leave a space on credit card slips for customers to add a gratuity. They have found new ways of testing our generosity. We decry the practice of those places which incorporate a facility on the new portable terminals for customers to key in a tip before they complete the transaction. Inevitably, the process has to be explained by the staff member ('press Y or N, and then the amount, before hitting the green button'). Some hoteliers, like John Jenkinson of *The Evesham Hotel*, reject tipping altogether, pointing out that service is an essential component of the experience the guest is paying for.

A rip-off

Recently visiting a hotel that caters largely for business visitors, *Guide* inspectors were amazed to read a notice stating that guests would be charged for the use of Wi-Fi: £5 an hour or £20 a day. This is robbery, since providing Wi-Fi costs the hotel virtually nothing. Please tell us if you encounter similar rip-offs.

Dress codes

The insistence that men should wear a jacket and tie in hotel restaurants continues to baffle foreign visitors of all ages as well as natives under 40. A minority of hotels in the *Guide* continue to require formal dress in the evening. We believe they are fighting a losing battle. Fair enough if hotels require both men and women to wear smart casual wear: we are not in favour of sawn-off, tattered blue jeans or other attire which would be better suited to the beach. But sometimes you have to acknowledge that the world has moved on.

We liked the common sense of the note in the brochure of *Corse Lawn House*: 'We prefer that you wear smart casual in the restaurant. Should you wish to relax in T-shirt and jeans or similar, you will probably be more comfortable in our bistro.'

A question of contract

A particular area of contention is the deposit that some hotels require at the time of booking. Small businesses can be severely affected by late cancellations, so we have no quarrel with hoteliers trying to protect themselves by requiring a non-refundable deposit. But it is vital that the policy on deposits and cancellations be spelt out at the time of booking and confirmed in writing. This leads to fewer disputes and is in the interests of both hotels and their guests.

Whatever happened to silence?

A reader asked this question over a decade ago, and since then complaints about piped music have increased each year. Sometimes it is now so loud that it cannot be described as background music. Daniel Barenboim, in his 2006 Reith lectures, got it right. He described muzak as 'absolutely offensive', something that people 'hear without listening to'. While soft music can ease the awkwardness of a near-empty dining room, the guests should be consulted about whether or not they want it. One hotelier told us: 'I have six CDs which I play in rotation, as they will probably like at least one of them.' No thanks. Worse perhaps than CDs is Classic FM with its inane chat between numbers. The *Guide* will continue to campaign against what Julian Lloyd Webber, the cellist, has described as 'incontinent aural pollutant'.

A guide written by its readers

The *Guide* turns 30 this year. Other guides come and go, but we have somehow soldiered on. There are a few changes this year – more concise entries, expanded Hotelfinder and Shortlist – which we hope make it more user-friendly.

As ever, we would welcome comments. There would be no *Good Hotel Guide* without the support of our readers. This is not just because they buy the *Guide*: we salute all the correspondents who have written to us about the hotels they have visited. Their reports add the ingredient that gives our entries their focus and allows us to be the guide that speaks up for the guest. We have a close relationship with our readers, many of whom have been in contact for years. But we are not a closed circle; we have been encouraged this year by hearing from a new generation of readers who equally share our enthusiasm for finding a hotel that delivers warmth and personal service. Many thanks to you all. Please keep sending reports.

DESMOND BALMER AND ADAM RAPHAEL

July 2006

THE 2007 CÉSAR AWARDS

Our *César* awards, named after César Ritz, the most celebrated of all hoteliers, are the accolade that hoteliers most want to win. Every year we nominate ten hotels that stand out for their excellence. But our laurel wreaths are not given for grandeur. We champion independent hotels of all sizes and budgets. The following special places caught our eye this year. Each has a distinct character; what they have in common is an attitude to service that puts the customer first.

Previous *César* winners, provided that they are still in the same hands and are as good as ever, are indicated in the text by the symbol of a small laurel leaf.

COUNTRY HOTEL OF THE YEAR

Combe House, Gittisham

In a glorious setting of woodland and pastures, this Elizabethan manor house has been beautifully restored by Ruth and Ken Hunt, thoughtful hosts. Philip Leach's contemporary cooking, using local suppliers and home-grown vegetables, is judged exceedingly good.

 NEWCOMER OF THE YEAR

The Dartmoor Inn, Lydford

On the west side of Dartmoor, this ancient inn has been renovated in charismatic style by Karen and Philip Burgess, who show flair, dedication and talent. His cooking (with Andrew Honey) is much admired; the service is impeccable.

 LAKELAND HOTEL OF THE YEAR

Swinside Lodge, Newlands

At the foot of Cat Bells, Eric and Irene Fell's traditional Regency house has been decorated and furnished in immaculate style. She is a charming host; his exceptional cooking is enjoyed in a candlelit dining room.

 CITY HOTEL OF THE YEAR

Hart's Hotel, Nottingham

All is well thought out at Tim Hart's purpose-built designer hotel on the site of a medieval castle. Reception is impeccable, and the staff are attentive in the all-day *Park Bar*; the excellent *Hart's* restaurant has a happy atmosphere.

 WELSH RESTAURANT-WITH-ROOMS OF THE YEAR

The Drawing Room, Cwmbach

Everything is stylishly done at Colin and Melanie Dawson's very personally run Georgian building, beautifully restored. He is the chef, she the *sous-chef* and front-of-house for the restaurant, where the cooking is thought delicious, the service professional.

Scottish hotel of the year
Isle of Eriska, Eriska

On a 300-acre private island, brothers Beppo and Chay Buchanan-Smith ensure outstanding service and attention to detail at their Scots baronial mansion. Robert MacPherson's well-liked six-course dinner is served in impeccable style in the formal dining room.

 ### Inn of the year
Ardeonaig Hotel, Killin

Pete and Sara Gottgens have created a feel of South Africa at their white-painted old inn whose grounds stretch down to Loch Tay. The welcome is warm, the atmosphere is unstuffy and the host's cooking is much admired.

 ### Island hotel of the year
Hotel Petit Champ, Sark

On a headland above a secluded beach on car-free Sark's west coast, Caroline and Chris Robins's delightful small hotel wins regular praise for the warm welcome and old-fashioned values. Local lobster and crab feature on Tony Atkins's interesting menus.

 ### Irish restaurant-with-rooms of the year
The Mill, Dunfanaghy

Beside a lake on the Donegal coast, Susan Alcorn, a vivacious hostess, welcomes guests with pleasing informality to her late grandfather's 19th-century house. Her husband, Derek, is an excellent cook; his imaginative menus are greatly enjoyed.

For utterly enjoyable mild eccentricity
Clow Beck House, Croft-on-Tees

On a working farm, David and Heather Armstrong are exceptional hosts at their fascinating and unusual hotel. The bedrooms can be flamboyant; in the beautiful garden a game of cricket by a miniature team has been in progress for some years.

Hotelfinder

A visit to a hotel ought to be a special occasion.
This section is to help you find a good hotel that
matches your mood, whether it would be
for romance, or sport, or to entertain the children.
Don't forget to turn to the full entry
for the bigger picture.

DISCOVERIES

There are 80 new hotels
in the *Guide* this year.
Here are some of the most
interesting finds

The Town House, Arundel

'No dress code; stuffiness is taboo,'
say Lee and Katie Williams, who
have turned a Grade II listed
building on the high street into a
restaurant-with-rooms. 'Charming
service, stunning food'.;
'housekeeping faultless.'
Read more: page 86.

The Castle Inn, Castle Combe

By the market cross of a much
photographed village, this inn has
been cobbled together from several
buildings, some 12th-century.
Friendly new owners Charles and
Lisa Bullock have filled it with
antiques. There are fireside nooks,
cosy corners, rambling corridors,
low beams. Enjoyable meals are
served without pretension.
Read more: page 138.

Fritton House, Fritton

On his family's traditional farming
estate, the Hon. Hugh Crossley
has turned a 16th-century inn near
a lake into a relaxing, contemporary hotel/restaurant. The welcome
is warm. Fresh flowers everywhere;
interesting artwork, comfy sofas in

a lounge with a large fireplace.
Estate produce supplies the
kitchen for the good meals served
in the restaurant.
Read more: page 175.

Combe House, Holford

In a valley leading to the
Quantock hills, this 17th-century
tannery, still with its waterwheel,
has been revamped by Andrew
Ryan and Ray Fox-Cumming.
Artwork and pottery abound.
Beautiful hand-made furniture in
the restaurant. The food is a
highlight: unusual lunch menus,
delicious cream teas; for dinner,
Laurence Pratt's seasonal menu
uses home-grown organic
ingredients.
Read more: page 196.

The Moody Goose at The Old Priory, Midsomer Norton

Stephen and Victoria Shore have
moved their *Michelin*-starred
restaurant from Bath to a beautiful
building in this market town. It is
one of the oldest houses in
Somerset (dating in part to 1152);
there are antiques in the bedroom,
bathrooms are modern. The

cooking is contemporary English: the reasonably priced *table d'hôte* menu is recommended, with dishes interchangeable from the *carte*.
Read more: page 237.

The Mistley Thorn, Mistley

With panoramic views down the Stour estuary, this Georgian inn has been given a 'seasidey' freshness by Sherri Singleton, from California, and her husband, David McKay. Sage-green panelling throughout, uncluttered bedrooms in taupe and cream. Wooden tables, basket-weave chairs, modern artwork in the busy restaurant where the menus place an emphasis on seafood and seasonal local produce. Excellent value.
Read more: page 241.

Zanzibar Hotel, St Leonards-on-Sea

Max O'Rourke, charming and helpful, has opened an exotic small hotel in a Victorian town house in this seaside resort outside Hastings. Bedrooms are themed (Morocco, India, etc). Antarctica, on the second floor facing the sea, is done in white, cream and chrome. Breakfast is served in the bedroom or the Grand Salon, which has sofas, newspapers, and 'extravagant flowers'. A fish restaurant is planned.
Read more: page 289.

Isle of Colonsay Hotel, Colonsay

On an 'idyllic' Hebridean island, this 'unpretentious old inn' has been transformed into a 'cool, stylish' hotel by the local laird, his wife, and two partners. They promise 'simple rooms, luxurious beds, sea views, whisky galore'. The 'modern, but not flamboyant' food has a 'strong local accent'.
Read more: page 357.

Neuadd Lwyd, Penmynydd

In large grounds with 'wonderful views' towards the Snowdonia mountains, this Victorian rectory has been turned into an upmarket guest house by Susannah and Peter Woods. Our inspectors were enchanted by the Welsh atmosphere, the lovely house and the 'superb' cooking. 'When we left, everyone came out to say goodbye.'
Read more: page 435.

Stella Maris, Ballycastle

Bought as a near ruin by Frances Kelly and her American husband, Terence McSweeney, this 19th-century coastguard station has been fully restored. The highlight is a 100-foot conservatory facing the sea. 'All you hear is the wind and the waves,' said the nominator. The hosts are 'convivial'; she is an 'accomplished cook'.
Read more: page 456.

ROMANCE

Get in the mood for love
by treating your chosen
one to a night at one of these
romantic hotels

The Portobello, London

Favoured by pop stars and actors,
this bohemian little hotel in
Notting Hill has some sexy
themed bedrooms. Share the
oversized bath in a Japanese
water garden basement suite, or
try out the round bed in the
Round Room, which has a
freestanding Edwardian bathing
machine. Residents get a discount
at nearby *Julie*'s restaurant.
Read more: page 74.

Amberley Castle, Amberley

'A tranquil place for a special
treat,' says a fan of this luxury
hotel, a Grade I listed monument
surrounded by a 60-foot wall
and a dry moat. Choose a room
to match your taste; perhaps
Chichester, on the second floor of
the manor house, with a huge bath
on a marble pedestal; or Pevensey,
which has direct access to the
battlements.
Read more: page 82.

Tor Cottage, Chillaton

Guests at Maureen Rowlatt's
upmarket B&B in a secluded
Devon valley are welcomed with a
trug containing sparkling wine,
home-made truffles and fresh fruit.
Laughing Waters, a clapboard
cabin by a stream, is in a private
corner of the garden; it has a log
fire, private terrace, hammock,
barbecue area, and its own
gypsy caravan.
Read more: page 145.

Cross House Lodge at the Star Inn, Harome

Linger over dinner at this
Michelin-starred North Yorkshire
inn where 'original modern
cooking' is served in an atmospheric bar and elegant dining
room. Then stay in the lodge, a
medieval longhouse, perhaps in
Room 1, which has a bath at the
end of the bed, and a shower big
enough for two; or Room 7, in the
ground-floor annexe, with its large
spa bath 'for sociable bathing'.
Read more: page 186.

Lavenham Priory, Lavenham

There are five spacious bedchambers at this sympathetically
restored 13th-century priory, later
an Elizabethan merchant's house.
They have sloping, beamed

ceilings, oak floor; some unusual beds (four-poster, polonaise or 'sleigh'); the Great Chamber has a slipper bath. Warning: one *Guide* reader was moved to propose marriage here (he was accepted).
Read more: page 211.

Swinton Park, Masham

In landscaped grounds, this creeper-clad 17th-century castle is now a luxury hotel with a spa. Sleep in the circular Turret suite with rooms on three floors linked by a steep, curved staircase: there's a fabulous view from the shower room, and a freestanding rain bath on the top floor.
Read more: page 232.

The Old Railway Station, Petworth

An unusual B&B, this disused Victorian railway station has been restored with flair. The biggest bedrooms are in the station building, but you may prefer one of the 'well-designed' Pullman cars: they have 'particularly comfortable' beds. 'My surprised boyfriend was speechless,' said a reader.
Read more: page 264.

driftwood hotel, Porthscatho

Popular with romantic adults as well as funky parents with their children, this contemporary hotel stands above a quiet cove on the Roseland peninsula. Opt for the privacy of the two-roomed cabin on a hillside overlooking the private beach. 'Tremendous fun.'
Read more: page 269.

Isle of Eriska, Eriska

Run in country house style, this Scottish baronial mansion is on a private island north of Oban. The tower room has a 'fantastic view, well worth climbing 54 stairs'. Or choose one of the spa suites in the grounds: each has a conservatory and private garden with hot tub.
Read more: page 368.

Ardanaiseig, Kilchrenan

A new room for lovers has been created in a converted boat shed on the shore of peaceful Loch Awe, in the grounds of this baronial mansion. Double-height windows open on to a deck above the water. The bedroom, in shades of blue, is on a mezzanine level; a balustrade allows uninterrupted views across the loch to Ben Lui. A golf buggy will take you to the main building – or will carry room service to the lakeside.
Read more: page 378.

FAMILY

All too rare in Britain, these are places parents can relax, knowing that their children are genuinely welcome

The Evesham Hotel, Evesham

'We just treat children as part of the human race, an approach that is sadly rare in British hotels,' say John and Sue Jenkinson, whose quirky hotel has lots to keep them happy. 'Fun things' in the garden include a trampoline and slides; there's an indoor swimming pool, a junior *à la carte* menu and a games room. The Alice in Wonderland suite is popular with families.
Read more: page 165.

Moonfleet Manor, Fleet

Part of the Luxury Family Hotels Group, this sprawling Georgian manor house behind the Fleet lagoon has 'excellent' facilities for children of all ages. These include a swimming pool, computer games, ping-pong, indoor tennis and a supervised nursery. Parents can pack as many offspring as they can tolerate into their bedroom. Children take high tea or dine with their parents.
Read more: page 171.

Fowey Hall, Fowey

High above the sailing and fishing port, this Victorian mansion is part of the Luxury Family Hotels group. Bedrooms are named after characters from *The Wind in the Willows*. There is a crèche for children under 7, baby-listening devices and babysitting. Older children have a games room and lots of activities. The beach at Readymoney cove is a short walk away.
Read more: page 174.

Fritton House, Fritton

The Hon. Hugh Crossley has turned an old inn, on his family's Somerleyton estate, into a contemporary hotel. There is much for children to do on the estate: rowing boats and pedalos on a lake; assault courses and aerial slides at an adventure playground; giant board games and slides; and a model farmyard. The hotel is 'comfortable, relaxing'.
Read more: page 175.

Seaview Hotel, Seaview

'Children are welcomed, not merely tolerated', at this small hotel/restaurant in a seaside village on the Isle of Wight. Plenty to do on the island: beaches with rock pools abound; access to a

local sports club, with swimming pool, tennis, etc. Young children have high tea at 5 pm. Much redevelopment this year at a 'comfortable, cheerful, and popular' place.
Read more: page 296.

Calcot Manor, Tetbury

'The best holiday I have had as a parent,' reports a visitor this year to this conversion of a 14th-century Cotswold farmhouse, cottages and outbuildings. It has baby listening, an Ofsted-registered crèche and a Playzone in a converted tithe barn. Suites have a bedroom for parents, and a sitting room with bunk beds or sofa beds for the young.
Read more: page 313.

The Priory Inn, Tetbury

Parents of young children themselves, David and Tanya Kelly welcome families to their hotel/gastropub/coffee bar/pizza takeaway in this charming market town on the River Avon. High chairs, baby monitors, changing facilities, special menus are provided. Children's toys, leather sofas and newspapers in the coffee bar.
Read more: page 314.

Glenfinnan House, Glenfinnan

Fans of the Harry Potter movies will recognise Glenfinnan viaduct, which can be seen from this family-friendly, handsome, Victorian mansion on the shores of Loch Shiel. You can also see Ben Nevis, and the monument on the spot where Bonnie Prince Charlie raised his standard. Children under 12 are accommodated free; they have special menus and a playground.
Read more: page 373.

Porth Tocyn Hotel, Abersoch

'Our children enjoyed their stay, making new friends and exploring the hotel and grounds,' say visitors to this traditional family hotel above Cardigan Bay. Several bedrooms are interconnecting, and bunk beds are available. Parents can relax on sunbeds in the pretty garden while the children enjoy the many activities.
Read more: page 414.

The Druidstone, Broadhaven

'A fantastic family-friendly establishment with bags of character' (this year's tribute), the Bell family's 19th-century house stands on cliffs above 'one of the best beaches in Britain'. It is liked for the 'relaxed atmosphere plus real sense of comfort'. The hotel's own fisherman catches mackerel and sea bass before breakfast.
Read more: page 417.

CITY CHIC

At these designer hotels you can expect decent standards of service as well as cutting-edge urban style

One Aldwych, London

Opposite Waterloo Bridge, Gordon Campbell Gray's impressive conversion of the Edwardian offices of the *Morning Post:* muted tones, white pillars and a giant statue of an oarsman in the double-height lobby; trendy flower arrangements and 400 pieces of contemporary art. Even the smaller bedrooms are stylish. All bedrooms have the latest technology and an elegant granite bathroom. Service is 'impeccable'.
Read more: page 72.

drakes, Brighton

Signage is discreet (an etched opaque-glass panel) at Andy Shearer's luxury designer hotel on the seafront, an expensive conversion of two 19th-century town houses. There is a touch of the orient about the style. Bedrooms have bamboo wood floors, shutters. Some have a wet room.
Read more: page 125.

Hotel du Vin & Bistro, Henley-on-Thames

Close to the river, the former Brakspear's Brewery, 'brilliantly converted', has many of the Hotel du Vin trademarks: airy interiors, white walls, exposed beams, sisal floor covering. In buildings encircling the old brewery yard, each bedroom, sponsored by a wine company, has a huge bed, deluxe bedding, good lighting; a powerful shower and a freestanding bath in the modern bathroom. Lively bistro and bar.
Read more: page 191.

42 The Calls, Leeds

Regarded as a pioneer designer hotel, this conversion of an old mill on the River Aire in the city centre retains its 'flair for design and decor'. It has hundreds of original paintings and drawings, bold fabrics, stylish public rooms. Bedrooms are 'fully kitted out for the business traveller' with Wi-Fi, etc. Beds are 'supremely comfortable'. Attractive weekend rates.
Read more: page 211.

Eleven Didsbury Park, Manchester

The 'simple stylishness' and 'relaxed, efficient staff' are liked at Eamonn and Sally O'Loughlin's converted Victorian town house in a conservation area in a fashionable suburb. White walls, large steel-framed mirrors, coffee tables made from old trunks in the public rooms. Modern bedrooms and bathrooms. A leisurely breakfast.
Read more: page 228.

Malmaison, Newcastle upon Tyne

In 'buzzy area, full of bars and restaurants' opposite the Millennium Bridge, this former warehouse has been converted 'with flair', making it 'one of the best examples of the group'. An Art Deco-style canopy over the entrance, ground-floor lobby with mirrors; strong colours, bold prints. Handmade furniture in bedrooms.
Read more: page 250.

Hart's Hotel, Nottingham

On the site of a medieval castle, Tim Hart's purpose-built designer hotel has curved buttresses, lots of glass, limestone floors. It is liked for 'first-class service', 'comfortable' bedrooms (most have 'breathtaking' views), 'efficient' bathrooms. Interesting snacks, and wine and champagne by the glass in the 'crisp, bright' bar.
Read more: page 256.

Old Bank, Oxford

An elegant conversion of three buildings, one a former bank on the High. The owner, Jeremy Mogford, displays his collection of modern art in the public rooms and bedrooms, which have 'many extras and nice bathroom'. The old banking hall houses *Quod*, a lively bar/restaurant with wooden tables, stone floors and a zinc-topped bar.
Read more: page 259.

Malmaison, Glasgow

'Unfussy' contemporary decor in conversion of a former Greek Orthodox church in the city's financial district. There is a magnificent Art Nouveau staircase, and a champagne bar in the atrium. Bedrooms have bold colours and stripes. There are big beds, 'all the usual goodies'. 'Big Yin' suite has roll-top bath on platform of pebbles in living area.
Read more: page 372.

The Clarence, Dublin

Catch the city's youthful *zeitgeist* at this 19th-century warehouse on the lively 'left bank', restored with 'minimalist designer chic' by Bono and The Edge, of rock group U2. Wi-Fi Internet access in all public areas; modern bedrooms; upmarket toiletries in the tiled bathroom. French/Irish cooking in the large-windowed restaurant.
Read more: page 472.

ACCESS

These hotels provide better-than-average facilities for visitors with impaired mobility or who use a wheelchair

Rothay Manor, Ambleside

Two bedrooms at the Nixon family's Lake District Georgian house are adapted for disabled visitors. One, on the ground floor next to Reception, has a fully equipped bathroom. The other is a suite in an annexe: it has its own lounge, and paved access to the house, where there is full wheelchair access to the dining rooms and lounges.
Read more: page 83.

The Leathes Head Hotel, Borrowdale

'Wheelchair access is excellent throughout the ground floor and gardens,' says a visitor to Roy and Janice Smith's gabled Edwardian house in wooded grounds outside Borrowdale. There are three ground-floor bedrooms which can be accessed without steps; one has a square bathroom with a shower stand, lavatory frame, etc.
Read more: page 114.

Clow Beck House, Croft-on-Tees

The bedrooms at this 'fascinating and unusual' hotel on a working farm are in stone outbuildings. One, with its own reserved parking, is fully equipped for visitors in wheelchairs. There is ramped access on a paved pathway to the dining room. Braille menus are available. A disabled information pack is supplied on request.
Read more: page 152.

Castle House, Hereford

The Dutch owner, Albert Heijn, a wheelchair user, has ensured that this luxury hotel, a sensitive conversion of two listed town houses, is disabled friendly. The Cavalier suite, on the ground floor, has been adapted and equipped for guests with mobility difficulties; the king-size bed has an electric mattress; the doorways are wheelchair wide; there are French doors on to the gardens.
Read more: page 192.

Bedruthan Steps Hotel, Mawgan Porth

A newly refurbished suite on the ground floor is suitable for guests with limited mobility, and for those using a wheelchair, at this large modern hotel on a slope in a north Cornwall village. The three main floors are accessible by lift, but 'we are not able to make all areas totally accessible at the moment', says the hotel, which offers 'the help of our team' to overcome difficulties.
Read more: page 233.

Kilworth House, North Kilworth

Two ground-floor bedrooms have been built specifically for wheelchair access at this magnificent Victorian country house, now a luxury hotel set in 38-acre grounds. 'The whole of the ground floor is accessible to wheelchairs, as is much of the surrounding gardens, including the terrace adjacent to the *Orangery* restaurant,' the hotel says.
Read more: page 252.

The Rose & Crown, Snettisham

Two new bedrooms, on the ground floor of this 'very relaxed' 14th-century inn, are adapted for guests with mobility problems. They are 'well appointed, smaller than some of the other rooms, but very comfortable'. One of the dining rooms is accessible from these bedrooms, but not all areas of the old building, which has twisting passages and low beams, are fully accessible.
Read more: page 299.

New Lanark Mill, Lanark

Five of the 40 bedrooms at this converted 18th-century cotton mill near the Falls of Clyde are equipped for disabled guests. They have grab rails and a wheel-in shower; panic buttons beside the beds. There are two lifts to every floor. The bar, lounge and restaurant are all accessible. The hotel is part of a World Heritage Site, owned and run by a conservation trust. The visitor centre has full wheelchair access.
Read more: page 384.

Cringletie House, Peebles

Guests in wheelchairs may stay without needing assistance at this luxury Borders hotel which has been given a disability award by VisitScotland. The hotel promises that less mobile guests will enjoy the same experience as other visitors: there is an outside ramp, a wheelchair lift and a specially adapted bedroom.
Read more: page 392.

Trefeddian Hotel, Aberdyfi

Disabled guests are 'marvellously catered for' at the Cave family's popular Edwardian hotel over-looking Cardigan Bay. In an 'access statement' on the hotel website, Peter Cave, the managing director, provides a detailed check-list of facilities and services for visitors with special needs.
Read more: page 413.

COUNTRY HOUSE

Bastions of old-fashioned service, these offer sumptuous rooms and lots of pampering

Hartwell House, Aylesbury

King Louis XVIII of France held court in exile at this stately home, with Jacobean front and Georgian rear, in 90 acres of landscaped parkland. Magnificent public rooms; 'flooded with light' thanks to high ceilings, tall windows. 'Nothing forbidding or gloomy'; antiques, 'to be used not just admired'. Jacket and tie no longer 'obligatory' in dining rooms.
Read more: page 91.

Farlam Hall, Brampton

Approached up a sweeping drive, this manorial house stands in an 'immaculate' landscaped garden with a large ornamental lake. 'Wonderful, fun and friendly', it has been run by the Quinion and Stevenson families since 1975. Public rooms are ornate, with open fires; bedrooms are traditionally furnished. 'Very enjoyable' country house cooking.
Read more: page 122.

Gravetye Manor, East Grinstead

The 'aroma of polish and pot-pourri' pervades the oak-panelled hall and staircase of this creeper-clad Elizabethan manor in peaceful grounds. It has 'blossomed' under new owners, Andrew Russell and Mark Raffan (also the chef: *Michelin* star for his traditional cooking), and their 'enthusiastic young brigade'. 'Personal touches, kindness and courtesy are even more in evidence.'
Read more: page 162.

Stock Hill House, Gillingham

In landscaped, tree-lined grounds, with terraced lawns and a small lake fed by a stream, Peter and Nita Hauser's small luxury hotel is much liked. The Victorian building has a 'splendid formal lounge', and a 'cosy snug with log fire'. The bedrooms have antiques and curios. In the formal dining room, the 'delicious' cooking reflects the host's Austrian heritage.
Read more: page 177.

Hambleton Hall, Hambleton

In a 'memorable' setting on a peninsula jutting into Rutland Water, Tim Hart's Victorian

mansion has classic interiors designed by his wife, Stefa, with Nina Campbell: fine fabrics, antiques, good paintings, open fires. The welcome is praised: bags whisked to the rooms, cars parked. 'Approachable service' and modern cooking 'worth saving up for'.
Read more: page 185.

Sharrow Bay, Ullswater

The grand old lady of country house hotels has a spectacular setting on Lake Ullswater. Now owned by von Essen Hotels, it still has many long-serving staff 'attentive to the last detail'. Rooms are 'exceptionally comfortable', with 'thoughtful provision of books and games'. Colin Akrigg's elaborate six-course dinner is 'perhaps the best feature'. Breakfast is 'wonderful', too.
Read more: page 322.

Gilpin Lodge, Windermere

'No weddings or conferences here, just the art of relaxation,' say John and Christine Cunliffe whose Lakeland house is surrounded by moors, woodlands and 20-acre grounds. They run it informally (no reception area or bar). Afternoon teas are 'a work of art'. 'Carefully cooked modern British dishes' are served in four 'lovely' dining rooms. There is a lengthy breakfast menu.
Read more: page 336.

Kinloch House, Blairgowrie

'It feels nothing like a hotel; the impression is of an elegant country house with pastoral views.' This grand 19th-century Scottish mansion (with oak-panelled hall, *objets d'art*, a portrait gallery) is run by the Allen family. Graeme Allen 'presides affably but not intrusively, supported by superbly trained staff'.
Read more: page 353.

Kinnaird, Dunkeld

Once the dower house to Blair Castle, this creeper-covered mansion stands in woodland on a vast Perthshire estate. Sumptuously furnished, it has family portraits, antiques, billiards. A chambermaid brings tea to the bedroom on a tray in the morning. Formal dining in the elegant frescoed restaurant, with many home-produced ingredients.
Read more: page 360.

Cashel House, Cashel Bay

In wild Connemara country, the McEvilly family's 19th-century manor house is a civilised place. Kay McEvilly is 'always in evidence, charming and efficient'; her husband, Dermot, oversees the kitchen, which serves 'beautifully prepared and presented' Irish/French dishes.
Read more: page 464.

GOURMET

Savour the pleasures of the table at these hotels and restaurants-with-rooms without having to drive home

Little Barwick House, Barwick

'Cuisine comes first' at Tim and Emma Ford's 'relaxed' restaurant-with-rooms in Georgian dower house in quiet countryside. He cooks 'delicious modern dishes' (saddle of wild roe deer with a crispy confit of pork belly, beetroot purée, rösti); she is 'attentive front-of-house'. Well-spaced tables in an airy dining room.
Read more: page 94.

Fischer's Baslow Hall, Baslow

In a Derbyshire manor house on the edge of the Chatsworth estate, Max and Susan Fischer's restaurant-with-rooms is highly praised. Vegetables from the kitchen garden are used for the well-sourced modern cuisine. 'Excellent' tasting menu; 'good value' *menu du jour* with dishes like slow-braised pork belly, caramelised apple, celeriac purée.
Read more: page 95.

Cross House Lodge at the Star Inn, Harome

'A certain northern rootedness' inspires Andrew Pern's original modern cooking at this Yorkshire inn, once a medieval longhouse. In the 'elegant' small dining room, readers this year enjoyed duck liver pâté accompanied by sloe gin and soda; monkfish on mash and mussels. 'Mix of rustic and modern' in bedrooms in a building opposite.
Read more: page 186.

Mr Underhill's, Ludlow

In a beautiful setting on the banks of the River Teme below Ludlow Castle, Christopher and Judy Bradley's restaurant-with-rooms maintains 'high standards', say old and new fans this year. His cooking is 'excellent, well presented'. The set menu might start with 'a doll's-house portion of butternut squash soup'; monkfish with cep pasta and jus, with girolle and cep.
Read more: page 225.

The Yorke Arms, Ramsgill-in-Nidderdale

'It is rare to experience such quality,' say visitors this year to this creeper-clad old inn beside a village green of this North Yorkshire village. The 'superb'

cooking of Frances Atkins is praised: 'Stunning food, the best I have had for a long time. A main course of belly pork and pork loin with borlotti beans and tomatoes was a delight.'
Read more: page 274.

The Castle at Taunton, Taunton

Kit and Louise Chapman have nurtured no fewer than four chefs to a *Michelin* star at their elegant, castellated hotel. The latest, Richard Guest, serves inventive modern British dishes, eg, baked organic egg with white truffle cream; a celebration of British beef. The 'kindness, skill and care' of the staff impressed this year.
Read more: page 309.

The Stagg Inn, Titley

'Atmosphere relaxing, food superb, rooms excellent,' say inspectors nominating Steve and Nicola Reynolds's ancient inn for the *Guide*. 'This must be the most unpretentious and laid-back *Michelin*-starred establishment in Europe.' Virtually all ingredients are sourced locally for the 'modern pub cooking'. Sample dish: venison with cumin and wild mushrooms.
Read more: page 316.

Summer Isles Hotel, Achiltibuie

Mark and Gerry Irvine's hotel/restaurant has 'sublime views' over the Summer Isles to match the much admired cooking. Almost everything is home produced or locally caught for Chris Firth-Bernard's five-course meals, eg, Summer Isles langoustines and spiny lobsters with hollandaise sauce; 'stupendous pudding trolley'.
Read more: page 346.

Ynyshir Hall, Eglwysfach

At this small luxury hotel on the Dovey estate, Adam Simmonds's cooking is 'up there with the best in the country'. 'Expensive, but a short step from heaven.' His dishes, 'arranged with panache', use seafood from Cardigan Bay, local venison and game, Welsh farmhouse cheeses. Service is also praised.
Read more: page 423.

Ballymaloe House, Shanagarry

The Allen family's ivy-covered Georgian hotel/restaurant and cookery school is an enduring *Guide* favourite. Myrtle Allen still presides; one daughter-in-law is manager; another runs the cookery school. Jason Fahy's five-course dinner is served in five small dining rooms. 'Roast duck the best any of us had ever tasted,' reported a visitor this year. The farm in the 40-acre grounds supplies the kitchen.
Read more: page 500.

GASTROPUBS

You can expect interesting cooking and a lively atmosphere in these revitalised old inns and pubs

The Masons Arms, Branscombe

In the centre of a National Trust village; this popular old inn is now owned by Carol and Colin Slaney, 'calm and authoritative'. Richard Reddaway uses local ingredients for his English cooking in the bar (try trio of sausages with crispy bubble and squeak), and the restaurant (king prawn and scallop brochette).
Read more: page 123.

The Sun Inn, Dedham

'Coaching inn meets small boutique hotel,' says owner/chef Piers Baker of his refurbishment of this 15th-century building. It has oak floorboards and beams in the public rooms; neutral fabrics in the bedrooms. His daily-changing menu features modern dishes 'with Mediterranean overtones', eg, linguini with clams, tomatoes and garlic.
Read more: page 159.

The Nobody Inn, Doddiscombsleigh

In a remote Devon hamlet, Nick Borst-Smith's 16th-century inn is a haven for wine and whisky lovers (over 600 wines, 240 whiskies). There are inglenook fireplaces, antique settles, carriage lanterns in the lounge. 'The locally sourced ingredients, from cheeseboard to marmalade, were delicious.' The seasonal menu has some old favourites, eg, roast duck with orange sauce ('on the menu since the 1960s, and we dare not take it off'). 'Food and wine excellent. Good value.'
Read more: page 159.

The Royal Oak, East Lavant

On the edge of the South Downs, Nick and Lisa Sutherland's listed Georgian stone inn is popular with locals as well as overnight guests, who stay in six modern bedrooms in a converted barn. The restaurant, with a *carte* and blackboard specials, opens seven nights a week; the style is 'Mediterranean, French, modern English', eg, confit of twice-cooked pork belly.
Read more: page 163.

The Museum Inn, Farnham

Owners Mark Stephenson and Vicky Elliot have given this

thatched 17th-century inn a bright modern look while retaining original features. Meals are served at wooden tables in the bar and, at weekends, in the *Shed* restaurant. The bistro-style cooking of the chef, Daniel Turner, is praised: 'Good goat's cheese starter, spicy crab cakes, excellent rhubarb crumble tart.'
Read more: page 169.

The Angel Inn, Hetton

An institution as a dining pub in the Yorkshire Dales, this old coaching inn has five bedrooms in a converted barn across the road. The bar/brasserie, which has cosy alcoves, panelling and beams, has its own menu with blackboard specials. Modern English dishes, eg, poached haunch of venison, wild mushroom and horseradish mousse, are served off a *carte* in the restaurant.
Read more: page 193.

The Howard Arms, Ilmington

On the green of a quiet village south of Stratford-upon-Avon, Robert and Gill Greenstock's expanded 400-year-old pub is 'sophisticated and quintessentially English'. The menu combines modern and traditional dishes, eg, beef, ale and mustard pie; roast cod, spinach, potato and chorizo. 'Copious and interesting.'
Read more: page 202.

The Felin Fach Griffin, Felin Fach

Between the Brecon Beacons and the Black Mountains, this terracotta-coloured inn is 'relaxed, civilised'. The Dutch chef, Ricardo Van Ede, uses local ingredients for his award-winning cooking, 'piping hot, stylishly presented', perhaps cep mushroom risotto with basil foam; roasted partridge, muscat grapes, braised puy lentils.
Read more: page 424.

The Bell at Skenfrith, Skenfrith

'An unpretentious pub that's also a terrific restaurant' is this year's verdict on Janet and William Hutchings's 17th-century inn facing a ruined castle in the Monmow valley. Chef David Hill serves 'well-constructed and pres-ented' modern British dishes, eg, fillet of Brecon beef, rösti potatoes, spinach and celeriac, red wine jus.
Read more: page 438.

Bushmills Inn, Bushmills

On Northern Ireland's dramatic Causeway coast, this ancient coaching inn stands on the main street of the village which gave its name to the world's oldest distil-lery. Booking is essential for the restaurant; the cooking is 'classical/ new Irish', eg, well-aged peppered beef flambéed in Bushmills whiskey; sticky toffee pudding.
Read more: page 460.

SEASIDE

Pack your buckets and spades and be ready to get sand in your shoes at these special coastal places

The Place, Camber

Opposite one of the finest sandy beaches in the south-east, this single-storey former motel has been transformed into a smart restaurant-with-rooms. 'Cheerful, think Scandinavia or New England.' Bedrooms are 'amazingly quiet'; the admired brasserie is popular with locals. Camber Sands, 2½ miles long and half a mile wide at low tide, is popular with families, kite surfers and windsurfers.
Read more: page 135.

Bedruthan Steps, Mawgan Porth

By this large, modern hotel is a wide beach with Atlantic waves for surfers, and coves and rock pools for explorers. If children tire of the beach, they can enjoy 'fantastic play areas', indoor and outdoor swimming pools, children's clubs, and 'water fun sessions'. There are 'amazing sea views', coastal walks, and a spa for recovery.
Read more: page 233.

driftwood hotel, Portscatho

In a 'marvellous position' above a quiet cove, this contemporary hotel has superb sea views from most bedrooms. Steep steps through woodland lead down to a private beach; there is good walking on the coastal paths. The modern interiors with a 'simple white background and shades of blue' are in keeping with the seaside theme.
Read more: page 269.

St Martin's on the Isle, St Martin's

The only hotel on this 'charming' small island (just 30 houses and a population of 100). Built in the 1980s to resemble a row of fisher-men's cottages, it stands by a beach, and other sandy stretches can be found on the island. Many bedrooms face the sea; the best views are from the dining room on the first floor.
Read more: page 289.

Soar Mill Cove Hotel, Soar Mill Cove

In an 'idyllic' setting, this single-storey stone and slate building stands in grounds that slope down to a beautiful beach. All around is National Trust land. The beach, framed by cliffs, is regularly swept. Glorious views from the restaurant; sea-facing rooms, with patios in front, get the afternoon sun. Children are genuinely welcomed (high tea, high chairs, etc).
Read more: page 300.

The Wellington Hotel, Ventnor

'Grandstand views of waves' can be enjoyed from the balconies, terraces and large sun deck of this 'smart, stylish' hotel on the south side of the Isle of Wight. It is built into cliffs, a minute's walk from a 'safe and friendly' sandy beach, and five minutes' walk from the town centre. All but two bedrooms face the sea. 'The only noise at night is the sound of the waves.'
Read more: page 324.

Port Charlotte Hotel, Port Charlotte

You can reach a sandy beach from the garden of this small hotel on the water's edge of a pretty conservation village of whitewashed cottages on the Isle of Islay. There are lovely views across the water. A popular spot for bird- and wildlife watchers.
Read more: page 396.

Trefeddian Hotel, Aberdyfi

The Cave family's large Edwardian hotel on Cardigan Bay stands above a 'fantastic' four-mile beach of golden sand, good for surfing, swimming, kite-flying, etc. 'Having brought my children, I'm now back with my grandchildren,' says a visitor. Even in busy half-term weeks, the hotel 'absorbed all the children and kept cool'.
Read more: page 413.

The White House, Herm

On the approach by boat, visitors to this tiny, car-free island see a long stretch of sand that unfolds into three beaches – Bear's, Fisherman's and Harbour. Over the hill is Shell Beach, rich in colour from tiny shells. *The White House*, a long, low, white building by a beach, is the island's only hotel. 'As you dine, you watch the sun setting over Guernsey.'
Read more: page 446.

Rathmullan House, Rathmullan

On a golden two-mile sandy beach (safe bathing) on Lough Swilly, an inlet of the sea, the Wheeler family's hotel has a wide range of facilities. There are tennis courts in the one-acre grounds, and a croquet lawn. On rainy days, you can swim in the indoor pool.
Read more: page 496.

GARDENS

Glorious gardens and beguiling landscapes make each of these hotels a destination in its own right

Lindeth Fell, Bowness-on-Windermere

Superb views over the water from the gardens of this Edwardian house up a tree-lined drive on hills above Lake Windermere. The 'extensive, well-tended' gardens, filled with rhododendrons, azaleas and specimen trees, are best in spring and early summer, when open to public. Lawns are laid for bowls, croquet. On warm days, tea and drinks are served on the grass.
Read more: page 118.

Hob Green, Markington

In a secluded setting, this 18th-century house, now a traditional hotel, has huge grounds with farm, woodlands and award-winning gardens. Walkways and paths lead through extensive herbaceous borders to feature lawns, a rockery. There's a large greenhouse and a walled kitchen garden. 'We enjoyed the total absence of noise and disturbance.'
Read more: page 230.

Meudon, Mawnan Smith

In wooded countryside on the south Cornish coast, the Pilgrim family's traditional hotel stands at the head of a valley leading to a beach. It has a fine example of a Cornish 'hanging garden', with specimens from early RHS expeditions to Yangtze and Himalayas; rare shrubs, plants, trees. Giant Australian tree ferns were brought as ballast by packet ships to Falmouth, and thrown overboard in the bay. 'A delight; peace reigns eternal.'
Read more: page 235.

Moccas Court, Moccas

One of Herefordshire's finest buildings, this stately home stands above the River Wye. Capability Brown designed the large park, which has his characteristic sweeping views, interrupted only by a stream that meanders to the river. Humphry Repton created the gardens and terracing in front of the house.
Read more: page 242.

Stone House, Rushlake Green

In unspoilt rural Sussex, Jane and Peter Dunn offer a 'quintessentially English country experience' at their 15th-century house which stands in huge grounds. Guests are encouraged to enjoy the 'wonderful' 5½-acre garden, which has an ornamental lake, gazebos, a rose garden, 100-foot herbaceous border, and a walled and brick-pathed herb, vegetable and fruit garden.
Read more: page 281.

Spread Eagle Inn, Stourton

In the middle of one of the great gardens of England, Stourhead (National Trust), this famous old country inn has been reopened and restored. The landscaped gardens, designed by Henry Hoare II between 1741 and 1780, have classical temples around a central lake; a series of vistas; exotic trees in mature woodland. *Read more: page 304.*

The Island Hotel, Tresco

The only hotel on this small private island famed for its sub-tropical 17-acre Abbey Gardens. The designer, Augustus Smith, built tall windbreaks and walled enclosures to allow species from 80 countries to flourish in terraces around the priory ruins. The hotter, drier terraces at the top suit South African and Australian plants; those at the bottom provide the humidity that favours flora from South America and New Zealand. There are more than 20,000 exotic plants, 300 in flower at winter equinox. *Read more: page 318.*

Rampsbeck, Watermillock

On the shores of Lake Ullswater, this white-walled 18th-century country house has spectacular views of lake and fells across 18-acre grounds. 'The best hotel

gardens I have ever seen, combined with a superb situation.' Many of the bedrooms have lake and garden views; the best have a balcony. *Read more: page 328.*

Ladyburn, Maybole

In a lovely Ayrshire valley, Jane Hepburn's home ('guests are treated as members of the family') has large wild and formal gardens. Rhododendrons, bluebells, azaleas grow in spring. Guests may also walk in the grounds of the 'magnificent' neighbouring Kilkerran estate. *Read more: page 387.*

Cashel House, Cashel Bay

The McEvilly family's 19th-century manor house is set in 50 acres of Connemara countryside. A previous owner, Jim O'Mara, parliamentarian and keen botanist, developed 'lively and interesting gardens', with exotic flowering shrubs (many from Tibet), camellias and rare magnolias; woodland walks. *Read more: page 464.*

GOLF

Golfers and golf widows alike can enjoy these hotels, well placed for some of the best courses on these islands

Highbullen Hotel, Chittlehamholt

Club selection is the key to a good round at the 18-hole par-68 course at the Neil family's 'hotel, golf and country club'. Set in wooded parkland, it is protected by bunkers and water (especially on the par-3s); there are splendid views towards Exmoor and Dartmoor.
Read more, page 147.

Budock Vean, Mawnan Smith

In an area of outstanding natural beauty, the attractive nine-hole parkland course at the Barlow family's traditional hotel is a good place to brush up your game. David Short runs three- and four-day golf schools, less intensive tuition breaks, and competition weeks for all handicaps, over five local courses.
Read more, page 234.

St Enodoc, Rock

On the north Cornish coast, this contemporary hotel offers golf breaks at the adjacent St Enodoc links and other nearby courses. Don't miss the Church Course at St Enodoc, a fine traditional links designed by James Braid, with trademark undulating fairways, blind shots and firm greens. The course passes the sandy graveyard where John Betjeman is buried.
Read more, page 277.

Blackford Hotel, Blackford

A 'small but beautifully formed' hotel, two miles from Gleneagles and its famous course, to which it is affiliated. Golf can be arranged there, or at any of 50 courses within an hour's drive. Don't miss Killin, a nine-holer in Glen Lochay, described as Scotland's most scenic course: 'the best excuse for not keeping the head down when playing golf'.
Read more page 352.

2 Quail, Dornoch

'We are undoubtedly the smallest golf hotel and restaurant in Scotland,' say Michael and Kerensa Carr, keen members of Royal Dornoch. Golf has been played on these famous links since 1616; the course is popular with top American golfers preparing for the Open. The hospitality at

2 *Quail* is 'outstanding'; Michael Carr's cooking is judged 'superb'.
Read more page 359.

Roxburghe Hotel & Golf Course, Heiton

The Duke of Roxburghe, an avid golfer, commissioned Dave Thomas to build this championship course which opened in 1997 in the grounds of his castellated Borders country house. From the elevated 14th tee, you can see the River Teviot, which hugs the left of the fairway. The course hosts the Scottish Seniors Open.
Read more page 376.

Stella Maris, Ballycastle

Terence McSweeney, who runs this converted 19th-century coastguard station in north Mayo with his wife, Frances Kelly, works for the US PGA in Florida during the winter. Golf memorabilia and photographs are on the walls. He can guide golfers to the world-class links at Enniscrone and Carne and, further afield, Rosses Point and Westport.
Read more page 456.

St Ernan's House, Donegal

A small historic house hotel on a wooded tidal island, a few minutes' drive from the magnificent Donegal course at Murvagh. The fifth hole, known as the Valley of Tears, is a vicious 200-yard par-3,

with high banks to the left of the hole, pot bunkers on the right. The reward, on the sixth tee, is a panorama of sea and hillside.
Read more page 469.

Moy House, Lahinch

Golfing talk may be heard in the bar of Antoin O'Looney's hotel which overlooks Lahinch Bay, famous for its championship links created in 1927 by Dr Alister MacKenzie, one of the great golf course designers. Nature dictates the shape of the holes; fairways follow the dunes, and the greens follow the natural fall of the land.
Read more page 486.

Admiralty Lodge, Miltown Malbay

The south-west coast of Ireland is ringed by magnificent links courses. Greg Norman's new course along the beach and dunes at Doonbeg is close to Pat O'Malley's Georgian country house. For a genuine links experience at a fraction of the cost (and no need for a handicap certificate), try the nine-hole Spanish Point just minutes away.
Read more page 491.

FISHING

No need to cast around for the best beats; these hotels all have private access to rivers and lakes

The Arundell Arms, Lifton

Anne Voss-Bark, an expert fly-fisher, offers fishing courses at all levels at the creeper-covered sporting hotel she has run for 45 years. She has 20 miles of fishing (salmon and brown trout in season) on the Tamar and its four tributaries, 'wild' rivers which rise on Dartmoor. There is a three-acre stocked lake with rainbow trout all year round. Saltwater fly-fishing instruction is also arranged.
Read more: page 215.

The Sportsman's Arms, Wath-in-Nidderdale

Popular with sporting visitors, this unpretentious but smart Dales pub has 'a wonderful friendly atmosphere'. It is reached across an old packhorse bridge on the River Nidd on which it has fishing rights. The nearby Gouthwaite reservoir has wild brown trout. Good shooting, walking and birdwatching, too.
Read more: page 329.

Kinnaird, Dunkeld

Spoil yourself at this luxurious country house hotel, a creeper-covered mansion in woodland on a vast Perthshire estate with the River Tay flowing through. Guests may fish for salmon and trout on the Tay, and for trout in *Kinnaird*'s three lochs. The hotel, the former dower house to Blair Castle, has its own smokehouse. Acclaimed chef Trevor Brooks uses home-produced or locally sourced produce wherever possible for the three-course set dinners.
Read more: page 360.

Tomdoun Sporting Lodge, Invergarry

'An authentic Highland lodge experience' was enjoyed at this simple sporting hotel overlooking the Upper Garry river on the old road to Skye. *Tomdoun* offers fishing on 25,000 acres of water spanning four lochs and more than three miles of the river. Fly-fishing tuition in summer; ghillies available and seven boats for hire.
Read more: page 377.

Gliffaes, Crickhowell

The trout- and salmon-laden River Usk runs through the large wooded grounds of this smart sporting hotel, which owns a stretch of 2½ miles. Ghillies are available, and three-day fly-fishing courses for beginners are offered. The best bedrooms have a river view and balcony. Only 'environmentally responsible' fish are served in the dining room. *Read more: page 421.*

Tynycornel, Talyllyn

A fishing hostelry since 1800, this white-fronted inn has a superb location on the shore of 222-acre Lake Talyllyn (which it owns), one of few remaining natural brown-trout fisheries south of Scotland. Tuition, tackle, picnic lunches are available. There is a drying room and freezing facilities. 'Esoteric fly-fishing stories in bar.' *Read more: page 440.*

Ballyvolane House, Castlelyons

Justin Green's 'family heritage home', a Georgian house in the Blackwater valley. He has four beats on a 24-mile stretch of the Blackwater, the best salmon fishing river in Ireland; these are available at all times in season, and others can be arranged. When conditions on the river are impossible, there is fly fishing for rainbow trout on three lakes in the grounds. *Read more: page 466.*

Delphi Lodge, Leenane

Fishing is the main pursuit at Peter Mantle's sporting lodge (built for the Marquis of Sligo) by a lake in gloriously remote upland country north of Connemara. Advance booking is required for Mantle's fishery, famous for salmon and sea-trout fishing; courses and ghillies available. There is much fishing talk at the communal dinner (the cooking is 'eclectic' and the wine list 'serious') around a big oak table. *Read more: page 487.*

Newport House, Newport

On an estuary looking towards Achill Island, this Georgian mansion is run 'like a large private home' by Thelma and Kieran Thompson. They have eight miles of fishing on the River Newport for spring salmon, grilse and sea trout; also fishing on Lough Beltra West, one of the few fisheries in Ireland where salmon can be fished from a boat. *Read more: page 494.*

Currarevagh House, Oughterard

The Hodgson family's country house has a 'glorious setting of lake, lawns and woodland'. They have their own boats and ghillies on Lough Corrib, 'probably the best wild brown-trout lake in Europe' (also pike, perch and a small run of salmon from May to July). *Read more: page 494.*

WALKING

Your boots are meant for walking at these hotels for serious ramblers and casual walkers alike

Biggin Hall, Biggin-by-Hartington

An unpretentious small hotel in the Peak District national park, 'ideal for walkers', with footpaths in all directions over beautiful countryside. The 17th-century stone house has antiques, mullioned windows, 'a marvellous fire in the living room'. Rooms in a barn conversion have an outdoor porch. Hearty cooking.
Read more: page 108.

The Leathes Head Hotel, Borrowdale

Roy and Janice Smith offer 'warm, personal service' at their Edwardian house, high up in wooded grounds outside Borrowdale, popular with serious walkers and climbers. Tea, drinks served in a sunroom; 'quite ambitious' daily-changing four-course dinner; breakfast ranges from healthy to full English.
Read more: page 114.

Seatoller House, Borrowdale

At the head of the beautiful Borrowdale valley, well away from the main tourist areas, this 350-year-old building is an unpretentious guest house, much liked by hikers and ramblers for its homely atmosphere, camaraderie and good value. Non-stop coffee (can be taken out in flasks) and honesty bar. Traditional meals 'with a twist' taken at communal oak tables. Big breakfasts.
Read more: page 114.

Old Dungeon Ghyll, Great Langdale

This 'unique Victorian mountain hotel' has long welcomed fell walkers and serious climbers. Owned since 1928 by the National Trust, and run since 1984 by Neil and Jane Walmsley, it is in a green

valley on the approach to England's highest mountain, Scafell Pike. Traditional food; children welcome.
Read more: page 182.

Lydgate House, Postbridge

There is good walking from the door at Peter and Cindy Farrington's unassuming Victorian country house near a famous clapper bridge over the River Dart. A 'warm welcome' from 'civilised owners'. 'Excellent, unfussy food' from daily-changing menu. Picnics available. 'Well-behaved' dogs welcomed, but not children under 12.
Read more: page 270.

Howtown Hotel, Ullswater

'Out on a limb, good for walkers', Jacquie Baldry's popular guest house on the eastern shore of Lake Ullswater has fields and garden on one side, wooded hills on the other. 'Traditional food', generous breakfasts. Picnics provided.
Read more: page 322.

Wasdale Head Inn, Wasdale Head

Popular with climbers and hikers, this informal inn, seven miles up a dead-end road, has mountains on three sides. Howard Christie, who owns it with his wife, Kate, sometimes helps rescue lost walkers. The inn has its own micro-brewery. Traditional dishes 'with lighter touches' in the restaurant. 'Outstanding' breakfast. Packed lunches, cream teas available.
Read more: page 328.

Pear Trees Country House, West Haddon

'Walkers are spoiled for choice,' say Carolyn and Brian Hyde whose small guest house in an 18th-century building is on the Jurassic Way and near the Grand Union Canal. 'He is a wonderful host, she is an excellent cook.' Optional evening meal (bring your own drinks).
Read more: page 330.

The Airds Hotel, Port Appin

Local walks at Shaun and Jenny McKivragan's old ferry inn include the Clach Thoull circular route starting at the front door; the more adventurous head for Glencoe. Paul Burns serves award-winning modern menus; excellent breakfasts.
Read more: page 395.

Pen-y-Gwryd Hotel, Nant Gwynant

Brian and Jane Pullee's eccentric, low-priced inn at the foot of Snowdonia is not for everyone, but those who love it, really love it. Long popular with mountaineers, it has a slate-floored bar filled with climbing gear; this was the training base for the 1953 Everest expedition. Substantial packed lunches.
Read more: page 433.

GREEN

Enjoy a guilt-free stay at these hotels and restaurants which take active measures to protect the environment

The Austwick Traddock, Austwick

The kitchen at this informally run Georgian house in the Yorkshire Dales national park has been certified as 100% organic by the Soil Association and was named organic restaurant of the year for 2006. Of the 60 wines, 20 are organic. An organic malt whisky and an organic port are now offered.
Read more: page 89.

The Place, Camber

'We care passionately about the ingredients used in our menu,' says Matthew Wolfman, founder of this smart restaurant-with-rooms, the first in south-east England to have Marine Stewardship Council certification for sourcing supplies from well-managed and sustainable fisheries. Local organic produce used 'where sensible'.
Read more: page 135.

The Chilgrove White Horse, Chilgrove

'We are lucky to live and work in a very old building (1765) in beautiful countryside. We want to share that with our guests now, and to leave it in a good state for generations to come,' write Charles and Carin Burton. Members of the Green Tourism Business Scheme, they have implemented a 14-point environmental policy at their South Downs coaching inn.
Read more: page 145.

Bedruthan Steps, Mawgan Porth

'We aim to make the *Bedruthan* as environmentally friendly as possible,' say the owners of this family-friendly north Cornish hotel, winner of the Cornish Tourist Board's Sustainable Tourism award in 2005. Guests are asked to help by recycling newspapers, magazines, cans and plastic bottles. They are also offered a free 'real nappy kit'. Low-energy lighting has been installed.
Read more: page 233.

Milden Hall, Milden

Juliet and Christopher Hawkins promote 'the environmental benefits of sensitively farmed Suffolk countryside' at their listed 16th-century farmhouse. They promise to buy local produce and goods 'that are not over-packaged', to recycle and compost as much as possible, to be energy efficient, and to 'minimise the use of the car'. Gadgets and fittings are being changed to reduce energy consumption.

Read more: page 238.

Primrose Valley Hotel, St Ives

The eco-friendly owners of this Edwardian villa above the Blue Flag Porthminster Beach have raised more than £1,500 to go towards Cornish marine conservation initiatives, thanks to an optional £1 charge on bills. 'We champion local, organic and Fairtrade produce where possible,' they say. Ethical guidelines are followed in the supply of fish.

Read more: page 288.

Innsacre Farmhouse, Shipton Gorge

'In a quiet way, we try to damage the environment as little as possible,' say Sydney and Jayne Davies, who are committed to local produce, organic where possible, at their 17th-century Dorset farmhouse. They have planted 3,000 trees to sustain broadleaf indigenous species. They promise: 'Injunctions in the rooms about waste and recycling are authentic rather than formulaic.'

Read more: page 297.

Strattons, Swaffham

At their Palladian-style villa in this market town, Vanessa and Les Scott have won awards for their environmental initiatives. They strictly control 'waste streams', and support local suppliers, buying organic produce. 'Throughout the development of *Strattons*, we have stuck to our personal commitment to the environment,' they say.

Read more: page 306.

Auchendean Lodge, Dulnain Bridge

Owners Ian Kirk and Eric Hart are proud of their green credentials at their Spey valley Edwardian hunting lodge. Laundry is washed in bleach-free powder and line-dried; everything possible is recycled; no foods are pre-packaged. Stale beer keeps down the snails in the organic garden. Low-wattage bulbs; firewood from felled local forests.

Read more: page 360.

Argyll Hotel, Iona

On the 'spiritual' island of Iona, Daniel Morgan and Claire Bachellerie have a strong ecological ethos at their small hotel in a row of 19th-century houses. Most of their produce is organically home grown, local or Fairtrade. They are committed recyclers and users of environmentally friendly products. Vegetarians and vegans are catered for.

Read more: page 377.

EN ROUTE

Break up those long drives by treating yourself to a stopover at a good hotel along the way

TO SCOTLAND

Homelands Guest House, Barnard Castle

Irene Williamson's Victorian house in a Teesdale market town is 'a favourite stopover on journeys to the far north'. 'Welcoming hosts'; 'superb for a B&B'. Five 'extremely comfortable' bedrooms (some compact; all redecorated this year). No evening meals; 'helpful advice' on local restaurants. Large choice of 'well-cooked dishes' at breakfast.
Read more: page 92.

Crosby Lodge, Crosby-on-Eden

Just five minutes' drive from the M6, near Carlisle and the Scottish border, Michael and Patricia Sedgwick's early 19th-century Grade II listed country house is liked for its 'generous northern hospitality'. 'A bit old-fashioned (not unhappy with that),' said a visitor this year. Food 'excellent'.
Read more: page 154.

Temple Sowerby House, Temple Sowerby

'A welcome stopover between south and north,' say visitors to Paul and Julie Evans's old farmhouse in a village on the A66 in the Eden valley (a bypass is being built). Cosy lounges, 'excellent bedrooms'. Modern British dishes served in the conservatory-style restaurant.
Read more: page 312.

Hart Manor, Eskdalemuir

Between the A74(M) and A7 in border country, Kath and John Leadbeater's unpretentious hotel stands in a picturesque hamlet in the lovely Esk valley. A former shooting lodge, it is decorated in contemporary style. The owners are 'industrious, helpful, hospitable'. Her traditional farmhouse cooking is liked. Afternoon tea on arrival. Breakfasts include daily-changing specials such as kedgeree.
Read more: page 369.

TO THE SOUTH-WEST

Little Barwick House, Barwick

In quiet countryside on the Somerset/Dorset border just outside Yeovil, Tim and Emma Ford run their Georgian dower house as a restaurant-with-rooms. Much liked, it is 'relaxed, and beautifully kept'. Complimentary tea and home-made cake on arrival; 'delicious' modern dishes in the dining room; 'stylishly arranged' breakfast.
Read more: page 94.

Bindon Country House, Langford Budville

Amid formal and woodland gardens in rural Somerset, five miles from the M5, Lynn and Mark Jaffa's hotel is 'friendly, unpretentious, well organised'. It is dedicated to the Duke of Wellington, who took his title from the nearby town. 'A particularly fine breakfast with personal service.'
Read more: page 208.

TO THE ISLES OF SCILLY

Mount Prospect, Penzance

Five minutes' drive from the heliport for flights to the Isles of Scilly, this 'very pleasant small hotel' looks over Mount's Bay to St Michael's Mount (many bedrooms have the view). 'Excellent' cooking. 'A good atmosphere throughout.'
Read more: page 262.

TO THE CHANNEL ISLANDS

The Priory, Wareham

By the River Frome between Poole and Weymouth (ports for Channel Island crossings), this former 16th-century priory is a much praised luxury hotel. Staff 'particularly friendly'. Christopher Lee's cooking is enjoyed.
Read more: page 326.

TO AND FROM IRELAND

Belcamp Hutchinson, Dublin

Near Dublin airport, this 18th-century mansion is a good base for travellers on a late or an early flight: good road links in all directions. It is run as a guest house by Count Karl Waldburg and Doreen Gleeson, 'a charming hostess'. 'She gave us printed instructions for our route to Tipperary and a two-euro coin for the motorway toll.'
Read more: page 471.

Viewmount House, Longford

In the geographical centre of Ireland, Jim and Beryl Kearney's informal B&B in a handsome Georgian house is a popular stopover for visitors driving west from Dublin. 'Welcoming, comfortable, homely.' A 'superb' breakfast.
Read more: page 489.

DOGS

No need to leave your best
friend at home when visiting
these hotels where dogs
command special treatment

The Cottage in the Wood, Braithwaite

A ground-floor room at this refurbished 17th-century coaching inn
on Whinlatter Pass, in the Lake
District national park, is designated
for pet owners. It has 'a useful
door which allowed us to take our
dog outside without disturbing
other guests'. Dogs are allowed in
the bar, but not in other public
rooms. 'Our dogs felt right at
home,' guests reported.
Read more: page 121.

Corse Lawn House, Corse Lawn

Dogs are welcomed at Baba Hine's
'easy, comfortable' Grade II listed
Queen Anne building set back
from the green and road in a
village south-west of Tewkesbury.
A grateful owner writes: 'A path is
mowed in adjacent fields to make
it easier for owners to exercise
their dogs.'
Read more: page 150.

Knocklayd, Dartmouth

'Strongly recommended for dog
lovers', Susan and Jonathan
Cardale's large, rambling house 'is
very much a home; not for those

who prefer a sanitised atmosphere'.
Visiting dogs are welcomed; they
sleep in the utility room or in the
kitchen. The Cardales have two
elderly Labradors, Jack and Jessie,
and Molly, a 'woolly little hearing
dog for the deaf (retired)'.
Read more: page 156.

Overwater Hall, Ireby

No need to apologise for your
pet at this castellated Grade II
listed Georgian mansion in
18-acre grounds flanked by
Skiddaw and surrounding fells in
the Lake District national park.
They advise owners: 'Dogs are
very welcome here, and at no
extra charge – we even have a
lounge area for you to sit with
your dogs (no dogs on chairs,
please), and our grounds are
always open for you and your
dog to enjoy.' Dogs may run
unleashed in the garden. Good
walking from the door; 'your
dogs will love it, too'.
Read more: page 203.

Meaburn Hill Farmhouse, Maulds Meaburn

'The most blissfully relaxing place
in the world; even our dog was

welcome to chill out in front of the fire.' Praise for this guest house in a 16th-century farmhouse in a 'peaceful and beautiful' village near Penrith. Dogs are allowed in public rooms 'if acceptable to other guests'; there's a dog-walking area in the garden. Plenty of good walks locally.

Read more: page 233.

Yew Tree Cottage, Northleach

Visiting dogs are 'positively encouraged' at Vivien Burford's home, a cottagey old stone building in a peaceful Cotswolds hamlet. They have a 'real canine B&B treat' with accommodation in a 'super-deluxe kennel suite', but are not allowed in the house. Mrs Burford has two black Labradors of her own.

Read more: page 255.

The Boar's Head, Ripley

'Dogs are welcome providing they bring with them well-trained owners' at Sir Thomas and Lady Ingilby's old inn in a model village on their castle estate. Hotel guests have access to the 150-acre castle grounds. The courtyard rooms, where dog-owners stay, may be smallish, but a 'turn-down Bono is placed in the dogs' baskets, and water bowls are provided'. £10 charge for dogs.

Read more: page 277.

Prince Hall Hotel, Two Bridges

'This is a genuinely dog-friendly hotel,' say John and Anne Grove of their 18th-century house in the middle of Dartmoor. You can walk from the grounds straight on to the moor. The Groves' dog, Bosun, a friendly black Labrador, sets the tone, warmly welcoming visitors.

Read more: page 321.

Willowburn Hotel, Clachan Seil

At Jan and Chris Wolfe's 'highly rated' small hotel on a little island on the shores of Clachan Sound, the dogs of prospective guests get a letter from Sisko the 'food-guided' Labrador, Laren the 'non-stop play machine' collie, and Odo the cat, outlining their attitude to canine visitors. The Wolfes are 'kind hosts', and the atmosphere is friendly.

Read more: page 356.

Rathmullan House, Rathmullan

One of the recently added courtyard rooms at the Wheeler family's handsome white mansion has a 'room within a room, complete with pooch's own bed'. The house stands in a well-tended garden on a two-mile sandy beach on Lough Swilly, one of Donegal's finest.

Read more: page 497.

THE WEST COUNTRY

Dorset, Devon and Cornwall are hot spots for good *Guide* establishments

Abbey House, Abbotsbury

In a 'delightful' garden with wide lawns that slope down to a mill-pond and a Benedictine watermill, this 15th-century building, on the site of an 11th-century abbey, is run as an unpretentious guest house by Jonathan and Maureen Cooke, who are 'gentle and kind'. The house has flagstone floors, panelled doors, original windows; a 'cosy lounge with plenty of books', 'lots of chintz and knick-knacks'. Evening meals for house parties only.
Read more: page 80.

Blagdon Manor, Ashwater

In a 'deeply rural' setting, Steve and Liz Morey's rambling 17th-century manor house is the 'kind of hotel the *Guide* was invented for'. She is an 'attentive' front-of-house, he the 'excellent' chef serving traditional dishes 'with Mediterranean hints'. Original features are retained in the house; fresh flowers and open fires in the bar and lounge. Bedrooms are 'spotless'.
Read more: page 88.

The Henley, Bigbury-on-Sea

On a cliff above the tidal Avon estuary ('great views'), Martyn Scarterfield and Petra Lampe's small, unpretentious hotel has many fans. Public rooms have dark red walls, Lloyd Loom chairs. Bedrooms are 'spick and span'; some bathrooms are small but all have fluffy towels. The 'excellent' short menu offers a choice of two dishes ('you always want to eat both').
Read more: page 108.

Mill End Hotel, Chagford

'We wanted peace and quiet, and found it here,' said visitors this year to Keith Green's white-walled former mill. There are large grounds to explore; the River Teign runs at the bottom of the garden. The ambience is 'pleasant' and service is universally praised. 'Dinner was something to look forward to; the lobster ravioli was outstanding.'
Read more: page 140.

Mount Haven Hotel & Restaurant, Marazion

In a village opposite St Michael's Mount, this former coach house has been refurbished to create a 'bright and airy contemporary hotel'. There are fresh flowers, silks from Mumbai, tapestries from Jaipur, modern paintings and pastel shades. The food is 'first

class and generous'. Holistic treatments are given.
Read more: page 229.

Porlock Vale House, Porlock Weir

In a fold of ancient woodland on the lower slopes of Exmoor, Helen and Kim Youd's small country hotel is best known in equestrian circles; non-horsey guests come for 'relaxation and comfort'. Public rooms have a hunting-lodge atmosphere; most look over the Bristol Channel, as do many bedrooms. The 'homely' cooking is enjoyed.
Read more: page 267.

Port Gaverne Hotel, Port Isaac

A classic Cornish inn in a quiet cove north of the busy fishing village of Port Isaac. Unpretentious, it has 'bags of character' and a lovely setting looking across to the tiny port. The popular bar has slate floors, wooden beams, local artwork. The meals here, and in the restaurant, are enjoyed.
Read more: page 268.

Rosevine Hotel, Portscatho

Down a narrow road above a cove on the Roseland peninsula, this traditional, child-friendly hotel is liked for the 'warm welcome', friendly staff and good food. Some bedrooms have a balcony overlooking the semi-tropical garden.

'Why go abroad when there's a spot like this?' asked a reader.
Read more, page 270.

Prince Hall Hotel, Two Bridges

You can walk on to the moor from the grounds of John and Anne Grove's small hotel near a packhorse bridge with panoramic views over the West Dart valley. The 18th-century house is 'nicely proportioned, not over-fancy'. They are 'welcoming hosts'; the service is 'attentive'. Best bedrooms, like the lounge and bar, face the moor.
Read more: page 321.

The Nare, Veryan-in-Roseland

In gardens above a lovely bay in the Roseland peninsula, Toby Ashworth's unashamedly old-fashioned hotel is loved by a host of regular visitors: 'Such a good atmosphere throughout.' 'Perfect as usual.' In the dining room, dinner is an event, jacket and tie preferred for men, with hors d'oeuvres and sweet trolleys. Afternoon tea is 'unmissable'.
Read more: page 325.

LAKE DISTRICT

In the magnificent setting of lakes and mountains, these are some of our favourite hotels for a variety of budgets

Rothay Manor, Ambleside

You can walk across fields to the head of Lake Windermere from the attractive grounds of the Nixon brothers' white-fronted Georgian house, which has been in every edition of the *Guide*. It is 'warm and welcoming', 'comfortable and civilised'. 'You feel relaxed and cosseted taking afternoon tea by a real fire.' The traditional British/French cooking is admired.
Read more: page 83.

The Drunken Duck Inn, Barngates

There are breathtaking views of the surrounding fells from this inn on a hillside between Ambleside and Hawkshead. The lounge has squashy sofas, board games and a resident cat. Nick Foster's 'delicious' cooking is enjoyed in the busy dining rooms, and an informal area of the bar.
Read more: page 93.

Lindeth Fell, Bowness-on-Windermere

On the hills above Lake Windermere, Pat and Diana Kennedy's traditional hotel is thought 'unpretentious but gracious, with just the right blend of formality and informality'. 'Stunning' views of the lake from the dining room and one lounge; Philip Taylor serves modern dishes on a daily-changing menu.
Read more: page 118.

The Cottage in the Wood, Braithwaite

Within Britain's only mountain forest, Liam and Kath Berney's 17th-century coaching inn looks down the valley to the Skiddaw mountain range. 'We had a superb welcome,' says a report this year. The 'cosy' sitting room has an open fire, plants, magazines and books. Local suppliers are used for the meals; breads, pasta and ice cream are home made.
Read more: page 121.

Aynsome Manor, Cartmel

Between fells and the sea in the Vale of Cartmel, in the south of Cumbria, this traditional Lakeland hotel has been run for 25 years by the Varley family. It has views towards a Norman priory, meadowlands and woods. Regular

visitors 'marvel at the high standard of food, hospitality and friendship'. Men are asked to wear a jacket and tie for dinner in the oak-panelled restaurant.
Read more: page 137.

The Punch Bowl, Crosthwaite

Stephanie Barton, who owns *The Drunken Duck Inn*, Barngates (see opposite), has renovated this 300-year-old inn beside St Mary's church in the Lyth valley. *Guide* inspectors were impressed at the 'smartly formal' atmosphere. A 'good choice of brasserie dishes' is served in the bar, and a modern *carte* in the low-ceilinged restaurant. There are two terraces for alfresco meals.
Read more: page 155.

New House Farm, Lorton

In a lovely valley in the northwest corner of the Lake District national park, this 'well-organised country guest house' is run 'almost single-handed' by the owner, Hazel Thompson. The whitewashed 17th-century farmhouse has period features (oak beams, flagged floors). The traditional no-choice meals are enjoyed. Marvellous views in all directions.
Read more: page 222.

The Old Rectory, Torver

A 20-minute stroll from Coniston Water, Paul and Elizabeth Mitchell's unpretentious 19th-century house stands in gardens and woods in farmland beneath the peaks of Coniston Old Man. 'Excellent hospitality, outstanding home-made food and beautiful decor,' says a visitor this year. The bedrooms are 'spotlessly clean'.
Read more: page 317.

Rampsbeck, Watermillock

On the shores of Lake Ullswater, with spectacular views of lake and fells, Tom and Marion Gibb's white-fronted 18th-century house is liked for its 'wonderful setting, good food and friendly service'. The best bedrooms have lake views, and a balcony where a continental breakfast can be taken. The elegant lounges have large bay windows, high ceilings and elaborate mouldings.
Read more: page 328.

Holbeck Ghyll, Windermere

In large grounds that slope down to the lake, David and Patricia Nicholson's luxurious hotel (built as a hunting lodge for Lord Lonsdale) has 'wonderful' lake and mountain views. The public rooms have stained glass, open fires, wood panelling, antiques. The chef, David McLaughlin, has a *Michelin* star for his refined cooking, served in two dining rooms.
Read more: page 337.

EAST ANGLIA

Whether you are seeking a seascape or a country hide-away, the *Guide* has a wide choice in Norfolk and Suffolk

The Wentworth, Aldeburgh

Overlooking fishing huts and boats on Aldeburgh's shingle beach, this family-run seaside hotel is 'old-fashioned in the nicest sense'. Antiques, books, plants, Russell Flint prints in the lounges; sea views from the best bedrooms. Chef Graham Reid serves 'generous', 'well-cooked and presented' dishes.
Read more: see page 80.

The White Horse, Brancaster Staithe

In a 'spectacular location', Cliff Nye's popular inn has wide views over the sea and salt marshes of Brancaster Bay. At high tide the sea reaches the bottom of the garden. Bedrooms are light and spacious, decorated in blues and yellows 'in keeping with the serene seascape'. 'Wonderful food', modern English

with a traditional twist, is served in a large conservatory.
Read more: see page 123.

Field House, Hindringham

A modern flint and brick cottage with wide country views near the north Norfolk coast, run by Wendy and Graham Dolton as a small guest house. They 'have the knack of being friendly but not intrusive'. She cooks a 'delicious' four-course dinner. 'The peace and quiet, birdsong and fresh air delighted us Londoners.'
Read more: see page 194.

The Great House, Lavenham

Chef/patron Régis Crépy and his wife, Martine, run this restaurant-with-rooms in professional French style. The imposing part-Tudor, part-Georgian house stands on the marketplace of the old wool town. Four of the five bedrooms are suites, with antiques, old beams, modern bathroom. Classic French cooking is enjoyed in an oak-beamed dining room or a courtyard.
Read more: see page 210.

Morston Hall, Morston

In an area of outstanding natural beauty on the north Norfolk coast, this flint and brick Jacobean house is run as a restaurant-with-rooms by Tracy and Galton Blackiston. He has a *Michelin* star for his accomplished cooking on a four-course menu. 'Lovely atmosphere, not a jot of pretension.'
Read more: see page 243.

Beechwood, North Walsham

Once Agatha Christie's Norfolk hideaway, this creeper-clad Georgian house (with Victorian character) is now a small hotel. Lindsay Spalding and Don Birch are 'hands-on' owners/managers. 'We guarantee a restful stay because we don't take large groups,' they say. Steven Norgate's modern cooking is admired.
Read more: see page 254.

The Crown and Castle, Orford

Cookery writer Ruth Watson and her husband, David, run this red-brick inn in a peaceful Suffolk village. Bedrooms are 'stylish, well-equipped'; those in the garden are decorated in cool stone and beige; each has a small terrace. In the restaurant, Ruth Watson and Max Dougal have a *Michelin Bib Gourmand* for their dishes based on seasonal produce.
Read more: see page 258.

The Bell Hotel, Saxmundham

Liked for its 'great value', this old coaching inn on the high street of the old market town is owned and managed by Andrew Blackburn (the chef) and his French wife, Catherine. Real ale in the public bar (open all day, popular locally). Spacious bedrooms have been redecorated. 'Excellent' modern/traditional English cooking
Read more: see page 294.

Titchwell Manor, Titchwell

Facing dunes and salt marshes near Titchwell nature reserve, this small hotel/restaurant (built as a farmhouse in 1890) has been refurbished by Margaret and Ian Snaith, who have added 12 new rooms in a herb garden. Mosaic-tiled floors, dark woodwork. Seafood is a speciality.
Read more: see page 315.

The Saracen's Head, Wolterton

Ask for directions when you book: this popular eating place set amid fields calls itself the 'lost inn'. Its 'hands-on' owner/chef Robert Dawson-Smith has presided for 17 years. It is liked for the 'excellent welcome and service; wide choice of first-class food', ordered from a blackboard menu that changes with each meal.
Read more: see page 339.

THE COTSWOLDS

Enjoy beautiful towns and villages whose wealth was built on the wool trade

Bibury Court, Bibury

William Morris described Bibury as 'the most beautiful village in England'. On its edge, this impressive manor house stands in lovely grounds on the River Colne. Readers this year praised the 'excellent service' and 'hard work' of Robert Johnson, who has taken it over from his parents. 'Full of character'; many bedrooms have a four-poster; some have a Victorian bath.
Read more: page 106.

Dial House, Bourton-on-the-Water

The River Windrush runs through the centre of this pretty village, popular with day-trippers and coach parties. This 17th-century house, now a sophisticated small hotel, is set back from the bustle and touristy shops; its garden is 'a delightful retreat'. The house has beams, inglenook fireplaces, monk's chairs. 'Good value in a pricey region' is one verdict.
Read more: page 117.

The Malt House, Broad Campden

In this small village, Judi Wilkes is a 'warmly welcoming', 'perfection-ist' hostess at her 16th-century listed malt house, an upmarket B&B liked for its 'charm and tranquillity'. Three of the bedrooms have their own entrance on to the garden, where teas and evening drinks are served in warm weather. From the gate you can walk on to the Cotswold Way.
Read more: page 126.

Russell's Restaurant, Broadway

In a lovely old village, this listed building has been given a 'smart modern look' as a restaurant with seven bedrooms. Beams, inglenook fireplaces and Arts and Crafts oak banisters have been retained. 'First-class food' is served in the bistro-style restaurant.
Read more: page 127.

Jonathan's at the Angel, Burford

A short walk from Burford's High Street, this 16th-century coaching inn has been transformed by Jonathan and Josephine Lewis into an informal brasserie-with-rooms. 'They are down-to-earth hosts who really know how to look after their guests.' The cooking is

eclectic, using 'extraordinarily good ingredients'. The three bedrooms are themed.
Read more: page 132.

Cotswold House, Chipping Campden

The exterior of Ian and Christa Taylor's Regency house, which dominates the main square of this lovely old town, may be traditional, but inside are striking modern design and furnishings. The bedrooms are 'ultra-chic Italian-style dens, with deep dark colours, many stylish touches'. Two eating options: a formal restaurant, and a brasserie.
Read more: page 146.

The Grey Cottage, Leonard Stanley

Many original features have been retained at Rosemary Reeves's little stone guest house which continues to win plaudits from readers. Arriving guests are greeted with biscuits and leaf tea. Bedrooms have 'wonderful touches'. 'Sumptuous' no-choice dinners; bring your own bottle (no corkage charge). Excellent value.
Read more: page 213.

The Redesdale Arms, Moreton-in-Marsh

Travellers on the Fosse Way have been welcomed at this old coaching inn, on the wide main street of a market town, since the reign of Charles II. It has a 'pleasant, informal atmosphere', and 'courteous, cheerful' staff. Country-style rooms have fresh flowers, a decanter of sherry. The bar is popular with locals; the cooking is thought 'excellent'.
Read more: page 243.

Yew Tree Cottage, Northleach

In a peaceful hamlet, Vivien Burford's old stone home captivated visitors this year with its 'real cottage feel, lovely rooms, great food'. Cream teas with home baking are served in the garden in warm weather; 'farmhouse plus' dinners are provided by arrangement. Mrs Burford is 'incredibly helpful with itinerary planning', even transporting guests to local pubs.
Read more: page 255.

Wesley House, Winchcombe

On the main street of this old wool town on the North Cotswold Edge, Matthew Brown's restaurant-with-rooms 'jostles successfully between things medieval and things 21st century'. The half-timbered building dates from the 15th century; the cooking in the striking two-tiered restaurant is modern. Bedrooms, up a steep beamed staircase, are 'stylish' if small.
Read more: page 334.

Join the *Good Hotel Guide* Readers' Club

Send us a review of your favourite hotel.

As a member of the club, you will be entitled to:

1. Pre-publication discount offers

2. Personal advice on hotels

3. Advice if you are in dispute with a hotel

The 12 best reviews will win a bottle of champagne.

Send your review via:

our website: www.goodhotelguide.com

or email: Goodhotel@aol.com

or fax: 020-7602 4182

or write to:

Good Hotel Guide
Freepost PAM 2931
London W11 4BR
(no stamp is needed in the UK)

or, from outside the UK:

Good Hotel Guide
50 Addison Avenue
London W11 4QP
England

How to use the *Good Hotel Guide*

We have introduced several new features this year to make the *Guide* easier to use.

Hotelfinder is for those looking for ideas: we suggest hotels to match your mood or interests, perhaps romance or sport, for a family or for gourmets. Ten hotels are highlighted in each of 20 categories, with a short profile, and a cross-reference to the main entry.

Main entries carry our considered judgments, based on anonymous inspections and reader reports, of those hotels we consider to be the best of their type. Hotels are listed alphabetically by country, under the name of the town or village. If you remember a hotel's name but not where it is, please consult the alphabetical hotel list at the end of the book.

Italic entries These short entries describe hotels which are worth considering, but for various reasons – lack of information, recent change of ownership, mixed reports – do not merit a full entry.

The Shortlist suggests alternatives, especially in areas where we have a limited choice. These short entries have not been subjected to the same rigorous tests as the main entries; standards may be variable.

The maps Each hotel's location is marked. A small house indicates a main entry, a triangle a Shortlist one. We give the map number and grid reference at the top of the hotel's entry.

Reading the entries

Information panels We have simplified the way we present details for each hotel. We give the number of bedrooms without detailing the type of room (the distinction between a single room and a small double for single use, a standard or a superior double, a junior or a senior suite varies widely between hotels). We give the geographical location, but not detailed driving directions. As with room types, these are best discussed with the hotel when booking; directions are often found on a hotel's website.

Prices We give each hotel's estimated prices for 2007, or the 2006 prices, which applied when the *Guide* went to press. The figures indicate the range from off-season to high season. A 'set lunch/dinner' can be no-choice or *table d'hôte*. The 'full alc' price is the cost per person of a three-course meal with a half bottle of wine; 'alc' indicates the price excluding wine. These figures cannot be guaranteed. *You should always check prices when booking.*

Symbols The label 'New' at the top of an entry identifies a hotel making its first appearance in the *Guide*, or one returning after an absence. The 'Budget' label indicates a hotel which offers, for a reasonable part of the year, B&B for £35 per person or less, or D,B&B at around £55 or less. We say 'Unsuitable for &' when a hotel tells us that it cannot accommodate wheelchair-users. We do not have the resources to inspect such facilities or to assess the even more complicated matter of facilities for the partially disabled. You will have to discuss such details directly with the hotel.

Names We give the names of the readers who have nominated or endorsed a hotel in brackets at the end of each entry. We do not name inspectors, correspondents who ask to remain anonymous, or those who have written critical reports.

Facilities We give an outline of the facilities offered by each hotel. We suggest that you check in advance if specific items (tea-making equipment, trouser press, sheets and blankets instead of duvets) are important to you.

Changes We try to ensure that the details we provide are correct, but inevitably they are subject to change. Small hotels sometimes close at short notice off-season.

Vouchers Hotels which join our voucher scheme (identified by a *V*) have agreed to give readers a discount of 25% off their normal bed-and-breakfast rate for one night only. You will be expected to pay the full price for other meals and all other services. *You should request a voucher reservation at the time of booking,* but hotels may refuse to accept them at busy periods. The six vouchers in the centre of the book are valid until the publication of the next edition of the *Guide.*

Traveller's tales These horror stories are taken from reports from readers. None of the hotels mentioned is included in the *Guide*, and the stories have *no connection* with the entry immediately above.

Reviews of the *Good Hotel Guide*

The *Guide* is unique, written with wit and evocative style... The perfect guide for people who care about where they stay.' *The American*, 2003

'A bible for the discerning traveller.' *Sunday Independent*, Dublin 2003

'The most rigorous is the *Good Hotel Guide* which relies on a small, unpaid army of inspectors who always stay overnight.' *Independent on Sunday*, 2003

'The travel writers' bible.' *Executive Woman*, 2003

What hotels say:

'We are huge fans of your guide – it is great that inclusion can't be bought. It makes it such a reliable guide to use.' Emma Stratton, *Bedruthan Steps Hotel*, Mawgan Porth

'The *Good Hotel Guide* is consistently the primary source of new business for the hotel and brings such lovely guests to our door.' Nigel Crapper, *Amerdale House*, Arncliffe

'It is the inclusions that cannot be bought which are the really prestigious ones.' Chris Dobbins, *Beaufort Lodge*, Norwich

'The *Good Hotel Guide* is by far the best and most objective guide there is.' Peter McKay, *The Gore*, London

'To us the only guide that matters is the *Good Hotel Guide*. We are honoured to have our hotel included in it.' Carolyn and Brian Hyde, *Pear Trees Country House*, West Haddon

'The *Good Hotel Guide* is consistently our third highest source of business (after word of mouth and company bookings) exceeding Johansens, AA, and the Internet.' Francis Young, *The Pear Tree at Purton*, Purton

'We have long regarded the *Guide* as the bible of the industry.' Christopher and Alison Davy, *The Rose and Crown*, Romaldkirk

What readers say:

'In an era of increasingly greater homogeneity, it's fabulous to have a guide to unique hotels and inns that have a sense of place, and specific personality.' Vicki C Smith

'No one in their right mind would go near a hotel without your advice.' David Taylor

'Thank you for providing us – the public – with such an essential piece of kit. A *Gray's Anatomy* of information, but more pleasant reading.' John Field

'We have been using the *Guide* for over 16 years and have never been disappointed.' R Flaherty

'The only truly reliable guide to interesting, largely family-run hotels. Paid-for guides simply do not publish the downsides of a property.' Oliver Schick

'As ever, the *Guide* is priceless. Or, in words often heard here in the Deep South, now taken generically as referring to the book, its editors and its contributors: "You da MAN!"' John Stege

'My husband can't understand why I spend so much time writing reports [for you], but your guide is still by far the best way to find a hotel, so I feel an obligation. And it's fun too!' Susan Hanley

'I have spent many a happy hour armchair travelling. Often I feel I don't actually need to visit the hotel: I know it already.' Lesley Abbott

'Without the *Guide*, we would not have had the marvellous holidays we have had.' Alice and JM Sennett

'It is the one guide that I and my family have used and relied on for over 20 years.' Sandy Dunbar

British Isles maps

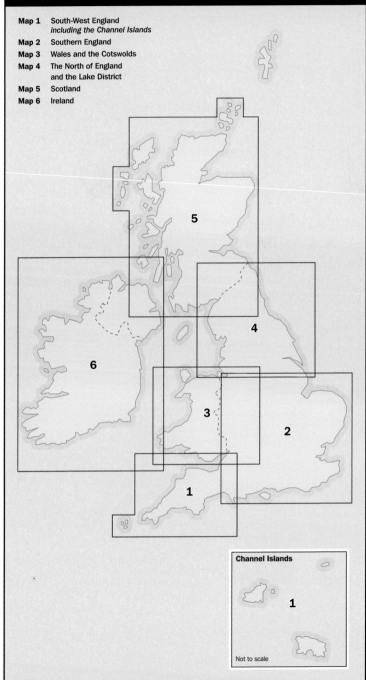

Channel Islands

Not to scale

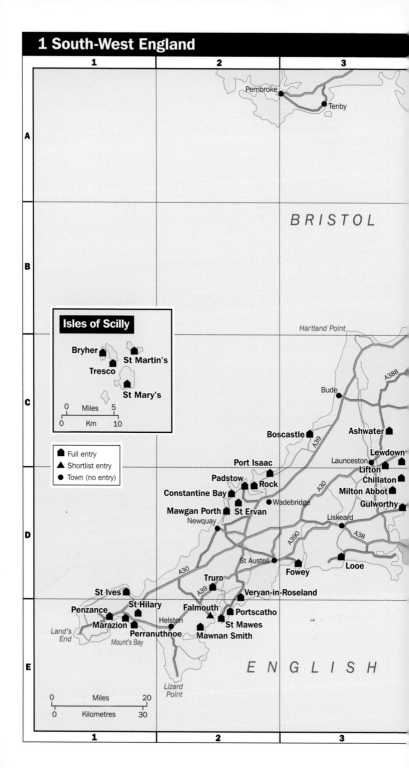

1 South-West England

Isles of Scilly

Bryher
St Martin's
Tresco
St Mary's

Miles 5
Km 10

▮ Full entry
▲ Shortlist entry
● Town (no entry)

BRISTOL

Hartland Point

Pembroke
Tenby

Bude

Boscastle
Ashwater
Lewdown
Launceston
Lifton
Chillaton
Port Isaac
Milton Abbot
Padstow
Rock
Gulworthy
Constantine Bay
Wadebridge
Mawgan Porth
St Ervan
Newquay
Liskeard
St Austell
Fowey
Looe
Truro
Veryan-in-Roseland
St Ives
Penzance
St Hilary
Falmouth
Portscatho
Marazion
Helston
St Mawes
Perranuthnoe
Mawnan Smith
Land's End
Mount's Bay

ENGLISH

Lizard Point

Miles 20
Kilometres 30

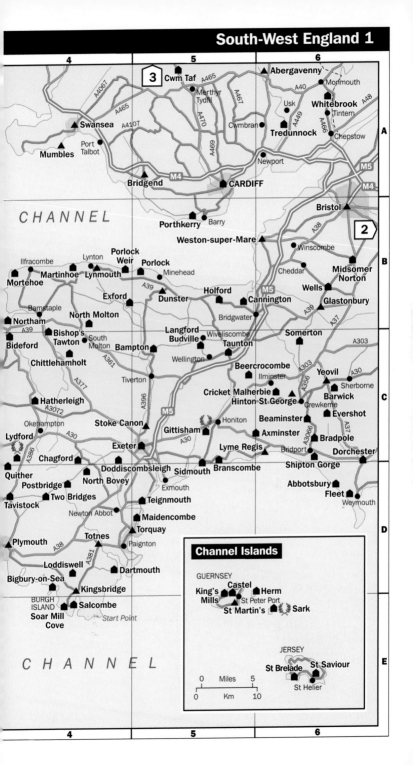

South-West England 1

CHANNEL

CHANNEL

Channel Islands

GUERNSEY

King's Mills
Castel
Herm
St Peter Port
St Martin's
Sark

JERSEY

St Brelade
St Saviour
St Helier

0   Miles   5

0   Km   10

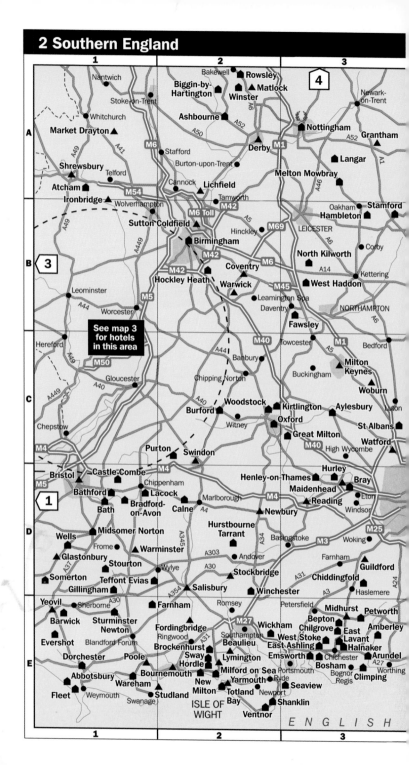

2 Southern England

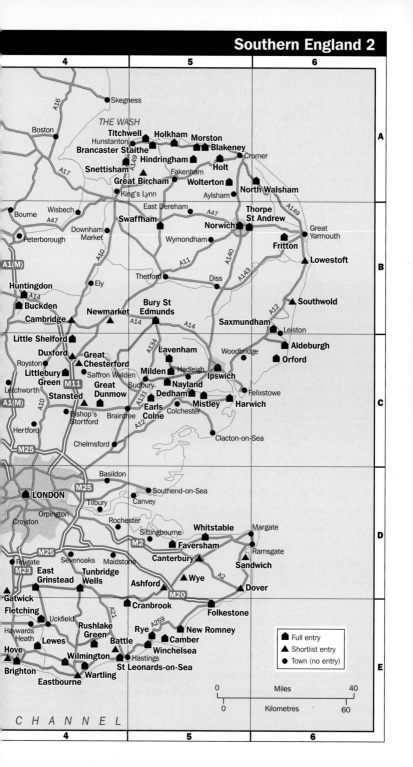

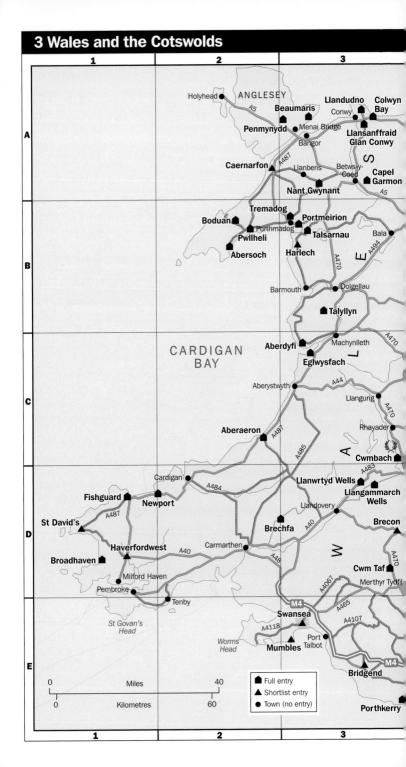

3 Wales and the Cotswolds

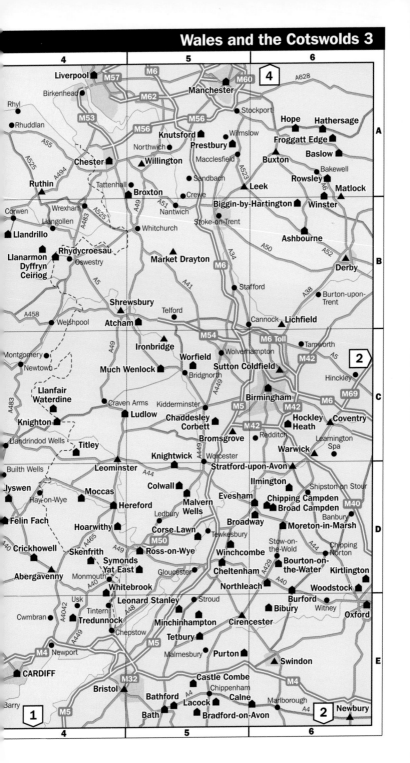

4 The North of England and the Lake District

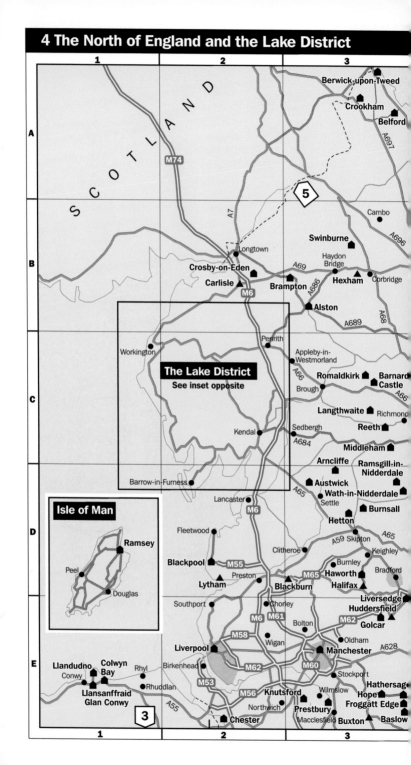

Berwick-upon-Tweed
Crookham
Belford

Cambo

SCOTLAND

M74

M6

A7

A697

A696

5

Swinburne
Haydon Bridge
Hexham
Corbridge

Longtown
Crosby-on-Eden
Carlisle
Brampton
A69
A686
Alston
A689
A68

Workington
Penrith
Appleby-in-Westmorland
A66
Romaldkirk
Barnard Castle
A66

The Lake District
See inset opposite

Brough
Langthwaite
Richmond
Reeth

Kendal
Sedbergh
A684
Middleham

Arncliffe
Ramsgill-in-Nidderdale
Austwick
Wath-in-Nidderdale
Barrow-in-Furness
A65
Burnsall
Hetton

Lancaster
Settle

Isle of Man
Ramsey
Peel
Douglas

M6
A59
Skipton
A65
Keighley
Fleetwood
Clitheroe
Bradford
Burnley
Haworth

Blackpool
M55
Preston
M65
Blackburn
Halifax
Lytham

Liversedge
Huddersfield
Southport
Chorley
M6
M61
Bolton
Golcar
M58
Wigan
Oldham
A628

Liverpool
M62
Manchester
Birkenhead
M60
Stockport
Hathersage
Llandudno
Colwyn Bay
Rhyl
M53
Wilmslow
Hope
Conwy
Rhuddlan
M56
Knutsford
Prestbury
Froggatt Edge
Llansanffraid
Glan Conwy
A55
Northwich
Macclesfield
Buxton
Baslow

3

Chester

1   2   3

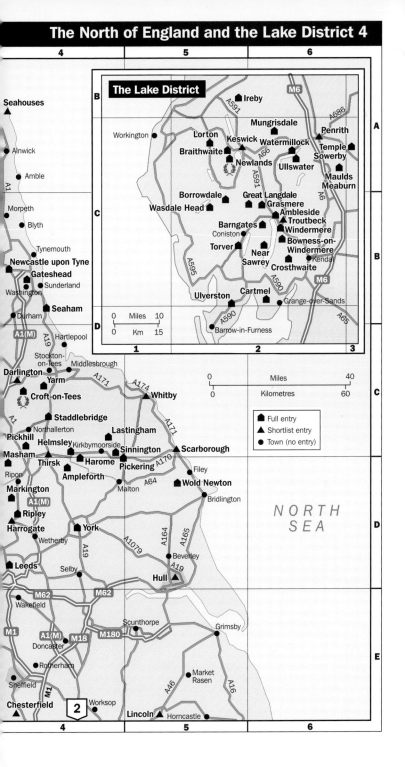

The Lake District

Ireby
Mungrisdale
Lorton
Keswick
Watermillock
Penrith
Braithwaite
Temple Sowerby
Workington
Newlands
Ullswater
Maulds Meaburn
Borrowdale
Great Langdale
Grasmere
Wasdale Head
Ambleside
Barngates
Troutbeck
Coniston
Windermere
Torver
Bowness-on-Windermere
Near Sawrey
Crosthwaite
Kendal
Ulverston
Cartmel
Grange-over-Sands
Barrow-in-Furness

0 Miles 10
0 Km 15

Seahouses
Alnwick
Amble
Morpeth
Blyth
Tynemouth
Newcastle upon Tyne
Gateshead
Sunderland
Washington
Seaham
Durham
Hartlepool
Stockton-on-Tees
Middlesbrough
Darlington
Yarm
Whitby
Croft-on-Tees
Staddlebridge
Northallerton
Lastingham
Pickhill
Helmsley
Kirkbymoorside
Sinnington
Scarborough
Masham
Thirsk
Harome
Pickering
Filey
Ampleforth
Wold Newton
Ripon
Markington
Malton
Bridlington
Ripley
York
Harrogate
Wetherby
Beverley
Leeds
Selby
Hull
Wakefield
Scunthorpe
Grimsby
Doncaster
Market Rasen
Rotherham
Sheffield
Chesterfield
Worksop
Lincoln
Horncastle

NORTH SEA

0 Miles 40
0 Kilometres 60

■ Full entry
▲ Shortlist entry
● Town (no entry)

5 Scotland

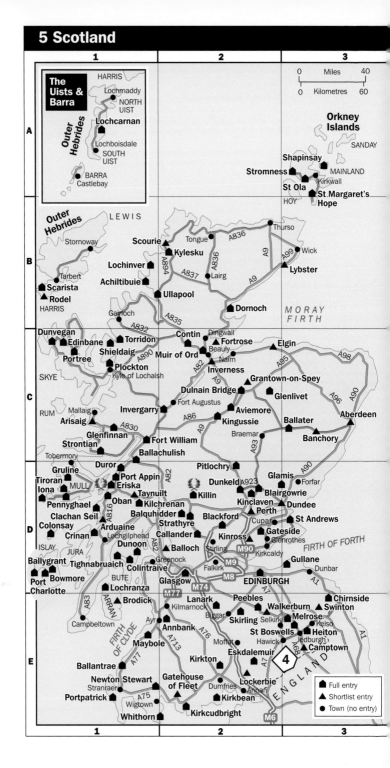

The Uists & Barra

Outer Hebrides

HARRIS
Lochmaddy
NORTH UIST
Lochcarnan
Lochboisdale
SOUTH UIST
BARRA
Castlebay

Orkney Islands

Miles 0 — 40
Kilometres 0 — 60

SANDAY
MAINLAND
Shapinsay
Stromness
St Ola
Kirkwall
St Margaret's Hope
HOY

Outer Hebrides
LEWIS
Stornoway
Tarbert
Scarista
Rodel
HARRIS

Scourie
Kylesku
Lochinver
Achiltibuie
Ullapool
Tongue
Laing
Thurso
Wick
Lybster

Gairloch
MORAY FIRTH
Dornoch

Dunvegan
Edinbane
Portree
SKYE
Torridon
Shieldaig
Plockton
Kyle of Lochalsh
Contin
Dingwall
Fortrose
Beauly
Muir of Ord
Nairn
Inverness
Elgin
Grantown-on-Spey
Glenlivet
Aberdeen

RUM
Mallaig
Arisaig
Glenfinnan
Strontian
Tobermory
Invergarry
Fort Augustus
Dulnain Bridge
Aviemore
Kingussie
Braemar
Ballater
Banchory
Fort William
Ballachulish

Gruline
Tiroran
Iona
MULL
Pennyghael
Clachan Seil
Colonsay
Arduaine
Crinan
Duror
Port Appin
Eriska
Oban
Taynuilt
Kilchrenan
Balquhidder
Strathyre
Callander
Lochgilphead
Dunoon
Balloch
Pitlochry
Dunkeld
Killin
Blackford
Kinross
Stirling
Glamis
Forfar
Blairgowrie
Kinclaven
Perth
Dundee
St Andrews
Cupar
Gateside
Glenrothes
Kirkcaldy
FIRTH OF FORTH

ISLAY
JURA
Ballygrant
Tighnabruaich
Colintraive
Greenock
Falkirk
Gullane
Dunbar

Port Charlotte
Bowmore
BUTE
Lochranza
Glasgow
EDINBURGH

ARRAN
Brodick
Campbeltown
Ayr
Kilmarnock
Lanark
Biggar
Annbank
Maybole
Kirkton
Peebles
Skirling
Selkirk
Walkerburn
Melrose
Kelso
St Boswells
Hawick
Jedburgh
Heiton
Camptown
Chirnside
Swinton

Ballantrae
Newton Stewart
Stranraer
Portpatrick
Gatehouse of Fleet
Eskdalemuir
Moffat
Dumfries
Annan
Lockerbie
Kirkbean
Wigtown
Whithorn
Kirkcudbright
ENGLAND

■ Full entry
▲ Shortlist entry
● Town (no entry)

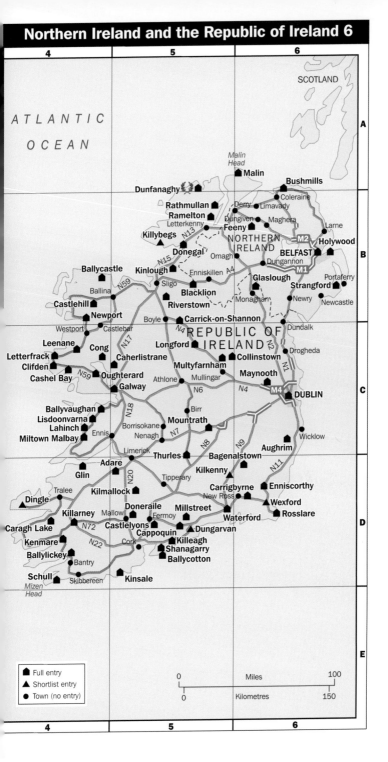

SCOTLAND

ATLANTIC

OCEAN

Malin Head

Malin

Bushmills

Dunfanaghy

Coleraine

Rathmullan

Derry

Limavady

Ramelton

Letterkenny

Dungiven

Maghera

Larne

Killybegs

N13

Feeny

NORTHERN

Holywood

Donegal

IRELAND

BELFAST

Omagh

Dungannon

N15

M2

M1

Kinlough

Enniskillen

A4

Glasslough

Portaferry

Ballycastle

Sligo

Blacklion

Strangford

Ballina

N59

Riverstown

Monaghan

Newry

Newcastle

Castlehill

Boyle

Carrick-on-Shannon

Dundalk

Newport

Castlebar

N4

REPUBLIC OF

Westport

N17

Longford

IRELAND

Drogheda

Leenane

Cong

Caherlistrane

Collinstown

N1

Letterfrack

Multyfarnham

Maynooth

Clifden

N59

Oughterard

Athlone

Mullingar

M4

Cashel Bay

Galway

N6

N4

DUBLIN

N18

Birr

Ballyvaughan

Borrisokane

Mountrath

Lisdoonvarna

Nenagh

N7

Lahinch

Ennis

Wicklow

Miltown Malbay

Limerick

N8

N9

Aughrim

Adare

Thurles

Bagenalstown

N11

Glin

Tipperary

Kilkenny

Kilmallock

N20

Carrigbyrne

Enniscorthy

Tralee

Mallow

Doneraile

New Ross

Wexford

Dingle

Killarney

Fermoy

Millstreet

Rosslare

N72

Castlelyons

Waterford

Caragh Lake

Cappoquin

Dungarvan

Kenmare

N22

Cork

Killeagh

Ballylickey

Shanagarry

Bantry

Ballycotton

Schull

Skibbereen

Kinsale

Mizen Head

■ Full entry

▲ Shortlist entry

● Town (no entry)

Miles

0   100

0   150

Kilometres

LONDON

Chain hotels, sometimes efficient but often faceless,
dominate the London scene. Fortunately, there are
still some places with the kind of character
and warmth that comes from individual or family
ownership and hands-on management. Some of our
entries in this chapter belong to small chains,
but in these, too, the owners are able to set
the style and establish the character.

Durrants, London

LONDON   Map 2:D4

The Capital   *Tel* 020-7589 5171
22–24 Basil Street   *Fax* 020-7225 0011
London SW3 1AT   *Email* reservations@capitalhotel.co.uk
                              Website www.capitalhotel.co.uk

A 'discreet bolthole', owned and run by the Levin family for 35 years, on a busy little street between Knightsbridge and Sloane Square. They have, says David Levin, commissioned 'every piece of furniture, work of art, and accoutrement'. Enthusiastic reports came in 2006. 'An oasis of civilised calm. Seriously high standards. Staff attentive without mock obsequiousness.' 'From the moment of arrival (greeting and valet parking by the doorman), it's clear this is going to be good (and expensive) service.' The decor is traditional, understated. The bedrooms have heavy fabrics, flowers, double glazing and air conditioning, a marble bathroom; thick cotton sheets (no duvets). 'Friendly, efficient staff contributed to an impression that everybody here was nice,' say visitors to the intimate restaurant. 'The food was superb, the wine list extensive.' Breakfasts are thought good, and 'the afternoon tea was of impeccable country house standard'. The chef, Eric Chavot, has two *Michelin* stars for dishes like langoustine and pork belly with sweet spice. Henrik Muehle is the manager. Under the same ownership is the simpler *L'Hotel*, almost next door (*qv*). (*Peter Jowitt, John and Jane Holland, JJ and MR*)

49 bedrooms. Knightsbridge. (Underground: Knightsbridge.) Private car park (£5 an hour, £28 a day). Lift. Sitting room, bar, restaurant; 2 private dining rooms; business facilities. No background music. Only restaurant suitable for &. No smoking in restaurant. No dogs. All major credit cards accepted. Room: single £210, double £285, suite £435. Breakfast £18.50. Set lunch £29.50, dinner £55; full alc £100.

The Draycott   *Tel* 020-7730 6466
26 Cadogan Gardens   *Fax* 020-7730 0236
London SW3 2RP   *Email* info@draycotthotel.com
                              Website www.draycotthotel.com

Composed of three Edwardian buildings, this 'delightful hotel', Union flag flying at its entrance, is part of the South African Mantis Collection ('hence the cosmopolitan feel'). It is managed by John Hanna. The location, in a quiet street near Sloane Square, is thought 'gorgeous'. The bedrooms are named after authors and actors; some overlook a private garden square. The suites are spacious. Some double rooms have an adjacent single. 'As a sole female traveller, I felt very safe in mine (Ellen Terry), tiny but very comfortable; theatrical memorabilia combined with modern-day items. The bathroom was perfect.' In the 'lovely' breakfast room there are 'excellent coffee, jams and pastries'. The lounges, with their paintings, flowers and chandeliers, are 'grand and attractive'. There is afternoon tea at 4 pm, champagne at 6. A full meal can be ordered from the 'imaginative' 24-hour room service menu. Seven steps to the building's front door make wheelchair access awkward. (*WA*)

35 bedrooms. Central, behind Peter Jones store. NCP nearby. (Underground: Sloane Sq.) 2 lounges, breakfast room; small conference room. No background music. 1-acre garden. Unsuitable for &. No smoking in 1 lounge. All major credit cards accepted. Room [2006] (*excluding VAT*): single £120–£125, double £170–£290, suite £250–£390. Breakfast £15.50–£19.50. Full alc £45.

Durrants

George Street
London W1H 5BJ

Tel 020-7935 8131
Fax 020-7487 3510
Email enquiries@durrantshotel.co.uk
Website www.durrantshotel.co.uk

'Quite an old-fashioned air about it – you rather expect to see Miss Marple walking through the door at any moment,' wrote a *Guide* hotelier on a visit to one of London's few privately owned hotels. 'I was well looked after; the staff are friendly and efficient.' The attractive row of four terraced houses with a Georgian facade, in an excellent location behind Oxford Street, has been run for the last 86 years by the Miller family: Ian McIntosh is its manager. Its character is traditional: small panelled lounges with leather settees and chairs; original paintings, prints and engravings; antique furniture. The larger bedrooms at the front may get some traffic noise; quieter rooms at the back might be disturbed by early-morning deliveries. 'My room had good lighting and a comfortable bed; the soft furnishings were tired.' Another visitor in 2006 had a 'pleasant if sparsely furnished' room, but 'the experience lost its shine when the heating failed to work, a problem that wasn't properly remedied'. The chef, Mauro Battaglia, serves 'generous portions' of international dishes. Differing views on breakfast: 'Good choices, nice fresh juice, eccentric service'; 'rather poor, especially the toast'. (*Yvonne Howes, also David Craig, and others*)

92 bedrooms. Some air conditioned. 7 on ground floor. Off Oxford Street. (Underground: Bond St, Baker St.) Restaurant closed for dinner 25 Dec. 2 lifts, ramp. 3 lounges, bar, breakfast room, restaurant; function rooms. No background music. No smoking: breakfast room, bar, lounge, restaurant. Guide dogs only. Amex, MasterCard, Visa accepted. Room [2006]: single £105–£125, double £145–£175. Breakfast from £10.50. Full alc £40 (*excluding 12½% 'optional' service charge*).

The Gore
190 Queen's Gate
London SW7 5EX

Tel 020-7584 6601
Fax 020-7589 8127
Email reservations@gorehotel.co.uk
Website www.gorehotel.com

A £25 million refurbishment has created some larger bedrooms and added air conditioning and Wi-Fi to Peter McKay's idiosyncratic hotel in a tree-lined street near the Royal Albert Hall and Kensington Gardens. This 'heaven for lovers of Victoriana' (say inspectors who enjoyed 'one of those rare hotel visits where almost everything felt right') contains a collection of antiques, pictures and books, wood panelling and heavy drapes. Some bedrooms are named after celebrity guests (Judy Garland, Dame Nellie Melba, etc). One has linenfold panelling, an open fire, a minstrels' gallery, and a secret panel leading to the bathroom. 'Our room, richly decorated, had expensively framed pictures and a glass chandelier. We loved the entry in the information pack: "Mosquitoes. These are unknown in London. For homesick dwellers in warmer climates, an irritating buzz can be arranged."' In the hotel's *Bistrot 190* restaurant 'food was excellent [eg, braised oxtail; smoked haddock fish cakes]. We asked the waiter to turn off the thudding music. He was reluctant but turned the volume down. Later we insisted it be switched off.' The bar, open till late, serves snacks, cocktails, etc. *Hazlitt's* (*qv*) and *The Rookery* (see Shortlist) are under the same ownership.

46 bedrooms. Central. Meter parking. (Underground: South Kensington, Gloucester Rd.) Lift. Lounge, bar, restaurant ('urban funk' music); private dining/conference rooms. Unsuitable for &. Civil wedding licence. No smoking: restaurant, some bedrooms. No dogs. All major credit cards accepted. Room (*Excluding VAT*): double £171, suite £252. Breakfast £16.95. Full alc £30. Weekend breaks. Christmas/New Year packages. **'V'**

The Goring
Beeston Place
Grosvenor Gardens
London SW1W 0JW

Tel 020-7396 9000
Fax 020-7834 4393
Email reception@goringhotel.co.uk
Website www.goringhotel.co.uk

Ω *César award in 1994*

Jeremy Goring, the fourth generation of the family to run this traditional hotel, has been making his mark in his first year in charge. The dining room has been redesigned to critical acclaim by (Viscount) David Linley, and a new veranda has extended the lounge bar and terrace into the hotel's private garden (open to guests). David Morgan-Hewitt has taken over from William Cowpe as managing director, and Graham Copeman has joined as general manager. 'It must be the only great hotel of tradition and character left in London,' says a regular visitor this year. 'A proper hotel,' says another, 'an oasis of rare sumptuosity in a desert of corporate hospitality.' Other comments: 'Good old-fashioned ambience and personal service in bright, well-kept surroundings.' 'Not cheap, but how do you put a price on perfection?' Many bedrooms face the garden; some have a balcony. Eccentric touches include large replica sheep which migrate between public rooms and bedrooms. The restaurant may have a new look, but it remains a mobile phone-free haven, and Derek Quelch's menu is traditionally British. Breakfast has 'a mind-boggling selection of fruits'. 'The best kipper this fan of fish has tasted.' (*Becky and Selwyn Goldsmith, Brian Pullee*)

71 bedrooms. 2 suitable for &. All air conditioned. Near Victoria Station (front rooms double glazed). Garage, mews parking. (Underground: Victoria.) Lift, ramps. Lounge bar (pianist in evening), terrace room, restaurant; function facilities. No background music. Free access to nearby health club. Civil wedding licence. Guide dogs only. All major credit cards accepted. Room [2006] (*Excluding VAT*): single £180–£275, double £200–£430, suite £295–£530. English breakfast £23. Bar meals. Full alc £48. Weekend breaks. Christmas/New Year packages. ***V***

Hazlitt's   *Tel* 020-7434 1771
6 Frith Street   *Fax* 020-7439 1524
London W1D 3JA   *Email* reservations@hazlitts.co.uk
       Website www.hazlittshotel.com

Q *César award in 2002*

Named after the essayist who once lived here, this quirky B&B hotel occupying three Soho houses is owned by Peter McKay. It is popular with people in film, fashion, music and publishing: writers who stay here leave signed copies of their books. The bedrooms, named after William Hazlitt's friends (Jonathan Swift, Lady Frances Hewitt, etc), have prints, plants, an 18th- or 19th-century bed (many are four-poster or half-tester), and good linen. They have restored wood panelling, antique furniture, sloping floors, dramatic drapes. Most are light, though some at the back overlook an inner courtyard. Bathrooms combine classic 19th-century fittings (a claw-footed freestanding bath in many) with modern plumbing. The only public room is a small lounge; a continental breakfast is brought to the bedroom on a tray. No lift, but air conditioning, modem points, etc. A simple room service menu is available from 11 am to 10.30 pm. *The Gore* (*qv*), in South Kensington, and *The Rookery*, Clerkenwell (see Shortlist), are under the same ownership. More reports, please.

23 bedrooms. Soho (windows triple glazed; rear rooms quietest). NCP nearby. (Underground: Tottenham Court Rd, Leicester Sq.) Sitting room. No background music. 3 small courtyard gardens. Unsuitable for &. No smoking in some bedrooms. All major credit cards accepted. Room [2006] (*Excluding VAT*): single from £175, double from £205, suite from £300. Breakfast £9.75. Special breaks.

L'Hotel

28 Basil Street
London SW3 1AS

Tel 020-7589 6286
Fax 020-7823 7826
Email reservations@lhotel.co.uk
Website www.lhotel.co.uk

Cultivating 'a French rural ambience', David Levin's relatively inexpensive but upmarket B&B operates without a large staff, and has minimal facilities (no residents' lounge; reception at night is shared with *The Capital* (*qv*) next door but one, also owned by Mr Levin). Isabel Murphy is the manager. Visitors generally like the 'friendly service' and the country-style decor. Bedrooms have pale colours, patterned wallpaper, pine furniture, wooden shutters, good fabrics; also kettle, crockery and fridge. Naive paintings hang on bathroom walls. Some rooms are interconnecting. Cots and babysitters are available. One guest this year would have liked air conditioning in summer; Ms Murphy tells us that air conditioning is planned in a future refurbishment. A continental or English breakfast ('lovely pastries'; 'real orange juice') is available between 7.30 and 11.30 am in the basement wine bar, *Le Metro*. From 12 to 9.30 pm, it serves bistro dishes. Some wines come from *The Capital*'s own French vineyard; some good ones are sold by the glass. (*M and BH, and others*)

12 bedrooms. 1 on ground floor. 1 suitable for &. Knightsbridge. Rear rooms quietest. NCP opposite. (Underground: Knightsbridge, Harrods exit.) *Metro* closed 25/26 Dec, 1 Jan. Lift. Wine bar/breakfast room (background music: 'jazz during day, funkier in evening'). Access to gym and swimming pool in nearby *Carlton Towers* (£10 per day). No smoking in bedrooms. Small dogs only, by arrangement. All major credit cards accepted. B&B [2006] (*Excluding VAT*): single £155, double £155–£170, suite £190. Full alc £25.

Knightsbridge Green Hotel

159 Knightsbridge
London SW1X 7PD

Tel 020-7584 6274
Fax 020-7225 1635
Email reservations@thekghotel.com
Website www.thekghotel.co.uk

Close to Hyde Park, the Marler family's unpretentious B&B hotel is liked by regular visitors for its value in an expensive part of London. Paul Fizia has been manager for a decade. Signalled by a discreet canopy, it has limited facilities: complimentary tea and coffee is served in a small lounge. Reception is staffed from 7.30 am to 10.30 pm; porters are generally on duty between 7 am and 8 pm. The bedrooms vary in size and quality. All have secondary double glazing, thick curtains, a beverage tray, mineral water and biscuits, and (new this year) Wi-Fi Internet access. The suites (some are spacious) have a double bedroom and sitting room. Some have been refurbished and given new furniture. Inspectors had a small, unrefurbished one that faced a dark courtyard. 'Decor of lime green, an orange and lime bedspread. Its lounge, with sofa, small wooden table and chairs and oldish TV, was not a space to spend time in.' Breakfast is from 7.30 am on weekdays, 8 to 10 on Sunday. Delivered to the room, it comes as 'express' (croissant and coffee), continental ('a disappointing basket of thin sliced toast and croissants, small packets of butter, preserves in jars; the best thing was the fresh orange juice') or cooked. (*MT-S, G and JD, and others*)

28 bedrooms. All air conditioned. Knightsbridge. NCP nearby. (Underground: Knightsbridge.) Closed 24/25 Dec. Lift. Reception (background music), lounge; office (Internet access). Access to nearby health club. No smoking. No dogs. All major credit cards accepted. Room: single £105–£120, double £140–£160, suite £160–£185. Breakfast: express £4, continental £7.50, English £12.

Number Sixteen   *Tel* 020-7589 5232
16 Sumner Place   *Fax* 020-7584 8615
London SW7 3EG   *Email* sixteen@firmdale.com
                      Website www.numbersixteenhotel.co.uk

With a pretty garden with a fountain, this white stucco, mid-Victorian, terraced building has a 'great location with a neighbourhood feel'. It is owned by Kit and Tim Kemp; the manager is Marianne Clave. Visitors like 'the warm welcome', and the 'smart and helpful staff'. The bedrooms 'vary in size and desirability': the quietest overlook the garden; some have a private courtyard. Bathrooms 'have granite galore and good lighting', but some may be small. The drawing room has neutral coloured walls; fabrics are checked and striped. Breakfast, tea and drinks are served in the garden in fine weather; there is a 24-hour room-service menu. Children are welcomed (babysitters can be arranged). Restaurants of all sorts are close by.

42 bedrooms. South Kensington. Pay parking 5 mins' walk. (Underground: South Kensington.) Lift. Drawing room, library with honesty bar, conservatory. No background music. Small garden. Limited access for ♿. No dogs. Amex, MasterCard, Visa accepted. Room [To 31 Mar 2007] (*Excluding VAT*): single £100–£135, double £175–£250. Full breakfast from £14.50. Christmas/New Year/summer packages.

Please always send a report if you stay at a *Guide* hotel, even if it's only to endorse the existing entry.

One Aldwych
1 Aldwych
London WC2B 4RH

Tel 020-7300 1000
Fax 020-7300 1001
Email reservations@onealdwych.com
Website www.onealdwych.com

꒰ *César award in 2005*

The Edwardian offices of the old *Morning Post*, opposite Waterloo Bridge, have been 'impressively' converted by Gordon Campbell Gray into this ultra-modern luxury hotel. Over 400 pieces of contemporary art are displayed throughout. The double-height lobby, with bar, has huge arched windows, white pillars, a giant statue of an oarsman, muted tones and 'trendy flower arrangements'. Our inspectors wrote of 'impeccable service' by the young staff. Bedrooms have 'all the latest technology' (flat-screen TVs this year). Granite surfaces, 'elegant taps' and an ecological 'vacuum-based waste water system' are in the bathrooms. 'Beds truly luxurious: the plumpest of pillows. Our huge windows looked over rooftops.' Even the smaller rooms are stylish. In the 'relaxed' *Indigo* restaurant, on the balcony, organic ingredients are sourced for 'delicious meals'. Classic European dishes are served in the more formal *Axis*, on the lower ground floor. The *Cinnamon Bar* serves soups, sandwiches, fruit juice cocktails, tapas and wine by the glass. There is a gym, and a narrow swimming pool with underwater music. Personal trainers are available; two suites have a private gym. Breakfast is continental, healthy or English. During the week, many clients are on business; at weekends there are reduced rates, and children are welcomed.

105 bedrooms. Some no-smoking. 6 adapted for ♿. All air conditioned. Strand (windows triple glazed). Valet parking. (Underground: Covent Garden, Charing Cross, Waterloo.) *Axis* closed Easter, Christmas, bank holidays. Lifts. 2 bars, 2 restaurants (*Axis* has background music Tues and Wed evenings); private dining rooms; function facilities; screening room; newsagent, florist; health club: 60-ft swimming pool, sauna, gym. Civil wedding licence. No smoking in some bedrooms. Guide dogs only. All major credit cards accepted. Room [2006] (*Excluding VAT*): double £179–£415, suite £385–£1,050. Breakfast £21.25. Set lunch/dinner (*Axis*) £19.75; full alc £50. Weekend breaks. 1-night bookings sometimes refused in high season.

Parkes Hotel
41 Beaufort Gardens
London SW3 1PW

Tel 020-7581 9944
Fax 020-7581 1999
Email info@parkeshotel.com
Website www.parkeshotel.com

Guests are welcomed by a hand-written note from the manager, Susan Shaw (née Burns), at Bertil Nygren's conversion of three Victorian houses in a quiet Knightsbridge street. 'Staff show the same attention to detail, making a point of learning your name, and using it,' says one visitor. 'Our suite had a small, comfortable bedroom, a separate living room with a little kitchen, and a swish bathroom with acres of green marble, and powerful hand-held and ceiling showers.' There are tapestry curtains and sofas; colours are rich red and saffron. Some rooms have a large balcony facing the leafy square. New flat-screen TVs have been installed in all rooms, with movies on demand. Residents have a lounge; breakfast, continental or cooked, is served until 10.30 am. No restaurant, but 'a thoughtful information folder has local recommendations, and lists restaurants which deliver'. 'Highly recommended; it is our London home,' writes a self-confessed 'picky hotel customer'. (*SL*)

33 bedrooms. Some on ground floor. Knightsbridge (windows double glazed). Meter parking. (Underground: Knightsbridge.) Lobby, lounge, breakfast room; background music. Access to nearby health club. Unsuitable for &. No smoking in some bedrooms. Dogs by arrangement. All major credit cards accepted. Room [2006] (*Excluding VAT*): single £195, double £240–£290, suite £325–£415. Breakfast from £10.

The Pelham
15 Cromwell Place
London SW7 2LA

Tel 020-7589 8288
Fax 020-7584 8444
Email pelham@firmdale.com
Website www.pelhamhotel.co.uk

Opposite South Kensington underground station, Tim and Kit Kemp's large, white Victorian terraced building is liked for its location, and 'competent concierge and desk staff'. 'An excellent choice for a London stay,' said one reader. Wood panelling, brass chandeliers, gilt-framed paintings, antiques, china ornaments and elaborate flower arrangements are in the elegant public rooms. Spacious suites have a high ceiling, and original features; there are a large bed and antique furnishings in the larger bedrooms; smaller rooms are in the eaves. All rooms have business facilities, and 24-hour room service. *Kemps*, the basement restaurant, is popular with locals; Mark Hollyer is its new chef this year – we would welcome reports on his modern European cooking. Children are welcomed. Hyde Park is near; so are the Knightsbridge shops.

52 bedrooms. South Kensington, opposite tube station (windows double glazed). Meter parking; public car park nearby. Lift. Drawing room, library, bar, restaurant/ bar (background music); 3 private dining/meeting rooms. Gym. Access to nearby health club. Limited access for &. No dogs. Amex, MasterCard, Visa accepted. Room [To 28 Feb 2007] (*Excluding VAT*): single from £160, double £180–£250, suite £450–£690. Breakfast from £14.50. Set meal £12.95; full alc £31. Special rates Christmas/New Year, summer.

The Portobello
22 Stanley Gardens
London W11 2NG

Tel 020-7727 2777
Fax 020-7792 9641
Email info@portobello-hotel.co.uk
Website www.portobello-hotel.co.uk

Opened in 1971 as a guest house for the music industry, this bohemian little hotel, in a Victorian terrace in residential Notting Hill, remains the choice for pop stars and actors. Tim and Cathy Herring own it with managing partner Johnny Ekperigin. Our inspector liked 'the happy atmosphere, quite un-London-like', and the engaging service. The quirky interior has gilt mirrors, military pictures, marble fireplaces, potted palms, Edwardiana, etc. The more modest double rooms are small, with a tiny bathroom. Themed 'special rooms' offer more eccentric accommodation: the Round Room has a large, freestanding Edwardian bathing machine and a round bed; there are two Japanese water garden basement suites, each with an oversized bath. Eight bathrooms have been renovated this year. The simple continental breakfast has croissants, toast; the *à la carte* version includes smoked salmon with scrambled eggs, champagne, fresh fruit, yogurt, etc. The small basement restaurant/bar, open day and night, also serves a snack menu. For more serious food, try *Julie's*, the restaurant/bar/café under the same ownership, in nearby Clarendon Cross (the hotel's residents get a discount). Parking is awkward. Portobello Road, with its famous Saturday market, is close by.

24 bedrooms. Notting Hill. Meter parking. (Underground: Notting Hill Gate.) Closed 5 days at Christmas. Lift. Foyer/lounge, restaurant. No background music. Access to nearby health club. Unsuitable for &. Smoking discouraged in restaurant. No dogs in public rooms. All major credit cards accepted. B&B [2006]: single £135, double £180–£200, 'special' £230–£350. English breakfast £12. Full alc £30–£40.

Report forms (Freepost in UK) are at the end of the *Guide*.

thequeensgate
54 Queens Gate
London SW7 5JW

Tel 020-7761 4000
Fax 020-7761 4040
Email enquiries@thequeensgate.com
Website www.the queensgate.com

With a 'discreet, minimalist style' and 'youthful feel', this member of Alan Corlett's small Niche Hotels group has an 'excellent setting' opposite the Natural History Museum. Bedrooms have contemporary light colours, wooden floors and furnishings. 'Our smallish double had a high ceiling; the compact furnishings made clever use of the space; large bed, bright spotlights, black marble in the bathroom. A lovely view across Queensgate to the museum, though some traffic noise was inevitable.' The only public room is the bar/lounge decorated in brown, beige and gold and with wooden floors, sofas. A simple continental breakfast is served here until 10.30 am. Many restaurants are nearby, and meals can be delivered. More reports, please.

26 bedrooms. South Kensington. Meter parking; public car park nearby. (Underground: South Kensington, Gloucester Rd.) Ramp (24 hrs' notice), lift. Bar/lounge/breakfast room ('easy listening' music all day). Terrace. Unsuitable for &. No smoking: breakfast room 7 am to 11 pm, 20 bedrooms. No dogs. Amex, MasterCard, Visa accepted. B&B [2006]: single £110, double £160, suite £260.

---

22 Jermyn Street
22 Jermyn Street
London SW1Y 6HL

Tel 020-7734 2353
Fax 020-7734 0750
Email office@22jermyn.com
Website www.22jermyn.com

Q *César award in 1996*

Managed by Laurie Smith, Henry Togna's town house hotel is in one of London's most fashionable streets, near Piccadilly Circus and the Royal Academy. Most of the accommodation is in suites (some can be turned into two or three bedrooms). A disadvantage for some: no public rooms, and 'little downstairs space'. But fans appreciate the 'amenities, decor and service: they personalise your visit, remembering preferences. Staff have a wealth of knowledge, and are well connected when it comes to booking tables or tickets.' Each suite has a fridge/bar, multi-channel TV, DVD-player, two direct-dial telephones, broadband and Wi-Fi Internet access. A newsletter provides information on restaurants, entertainment, shopping and the arts. Room sizes vary from 'comfortable' to 'palatial', but 'all echo the same attention to detail'. Breakfast, brought to the room, includes fresh orange juice, cooked dishes *à la carte* (good porridge, eggs, etc). Light room-service meals (salads, pasta, sandwiches and so on) are available. Guests may use the sporting facilities at a nearby club, borrow a mountain bike, go jogging in St James's Park. Children and pets are welcomed. More reports, please.

18 bedrooms. In St James's. Car park nearby. Valet parking (expensive). (Underground: Piccadilly Circus.) Air conditioning. 24-hour room service. Lift. Reception (background music); small conference facilities. Access to health club. All major credit cards accepted. Room: double £258.50, suite £364.25–£411.25. Breakfast £12.65. Full alc £30–£45.

The Victoria
10 West Temple Sheen
London SW14 7RT

Tel 020-8876 4238
Fax 020-8878 3464
Email reservations@thevictoria.net
Website www.thevictoria.net

In a quiet residential street in leafy south-west London, this unpretentious gastropub is a 'friendly, relaxing place to stay'. It is owned by Mark Chester with his business partner, the chef, Darren Archer. Adèle Stebbings is manager. The bedrooms are in an annexe at the back: two (No. 4 and No. 7) are large. They have free broadband Internet access, Egyptian cotton bedlinen. 'Ours was compact, simple, perhaps even plain, but comfortable, warm and peaceful,' say visitors in 2006. Other comments: 'In our downstairs room (No. 2) we heard every movement in the room above.' 'The bar and restaurant have a lively, friendly ambience. The food is first class, well presented and full of flavour.' The style is modern European, eg, roast halibut with a laverbread stovie, spinach and bouillabaisse sauce. Service from the front desk was 'attentive; the lady who greeted us insisted on carrying my bag even though I was twice her size'. Breakfast has fresh juices, 'DIY toast from good bread, home-made marmalade, tea in mugs (bag in)'. Parties and receptions are catered for in the conservatory. 'Central London is just 20 minutes away by frequent trains; we prefer here to any central hotel.' (*Andy Aitken and Carole Sheppard, Richard and Joanna Hobson, and others*)

7 bedrooms. 3 on ground floor. Near Richmond. Train: Mortlake (5 mins' walk) to Waterloo/Clapham Jct. Car park. Restaurant closed 4 days over Christmas. Ramp. Bar (background music), restaurant, conservatory. Garden: children's play area. Unsuitable for &. No smoking: restaurant, bedrooms. No dogs. Amex, MasterCard, Visa accepted. B&B [2006] £54.25 per person. Full alc £34.50.

The terms printed in the *Guide* are only a rough indication of the size of the bill to be expected at the end of your stay. Always check the tariffs when booking.

The Zetter
86–88 Clerkenwell Road
London EC1M 5RJ

Tel 020-7324 4444
Fax 020-7324 4445
Email info@thezetter.com
Website www.thezetter.com

In fashionable Clerkenwell, this five-storey 19th-century warehouse has been turned into an informal modern hotel by Mark Sainsbury and Michael Benyan. A glass front door opens into a lobby with a pink Murano chandelier and white walls; cocktails and snacks are served in the bar in a five-floor central atrium. 'Service is on the ball,' wrote one visitor. 'Staff are exceptionally friendly.' Bedrooms are done in bright colours; there are duck-down duvets, raindance showers, second-hand Penguin classics and 'the latest gadgetry'. 'My "superior" room was small and a bit stark, but stylish. Lighting was great, with a pink option; the oblong granite basin was smart but awkward to use.' The seven rooftop studios each have a patio and panoramic views. Vending machines on each floor produce drinks, disposable cameras, champagne, etc. In the busy crescent-shaped restaurant, whose floor-to-ceiling windows face St John's Square, modern Italian dishes are served, eg, pappardelle with pork ragout. *The Zetter* 'has an environmental conscience', (sustainable materials and energy-efficient technology). (*JH*)

59 bedrooms. Some with access. In Clerkenwell. NCP garage, 5 mins' walk. (Underground: Farringdon.) 2 lifts, ramps. Cocktail bar, restaurant; background music in all public areas daily until 10 pm; 2 function/meeting rooms. No smoking in bedrooms. No dogs. Amex, Visa accepted. Room [2006]: £140–£229, studio £264–£329. Breakfast £9.50–£15. Full alc £30. Weekend breaks. Christmas/New Year packages.

See also SHORTLIST

Organisations in London offering B&B in private homes include:
At Home in London, 70 Black Lion Lane, London W6 9BE. *Tel* 020-8748 1943, *fax* 020-8748 2701, *email* info@athomein london.co.uk, www.athomeinlondon.co.uk. B&B in over 90 private homes in central and west London. All close to public transport. B&B (min. 2 nights): single £29–£74, double £57–£92.
Uptown Reservations, 8 Kelso Place, London W8 5QD. *Tel* 020-7937 2001, *fax* 020-7937 6660, *email* inquiries@uptownres.co.uk, www.uptownres.co.uk. Upmarket accommodation in private homes in central London. B&B: single from £72, double from £95. Family rooms, studios, 1-bedroom apartments also available.

ENGLAND

You have to look beyond the label to understand
the diversity in our selection of English hotels.
It is a broad church, with traditional city or country
hotels listed alongside some distinctly un-hotel-like
places: restaurants or pubs with rooms, simple but
affordable B&Bs, guest houses with limited facilities.
The common factors are the warmth of the welcome,
the concentration on looking after the guest and
a distinct character almost always provided
by a hands-on owner or manager.

Combe House, Gittisham

ABBOTSBURY Dorset   Map 1:D6

Abbey House   **BUDGET**   *Tel* 01305 871330
Church Street   *Email* info@theabbeyhouse.co.uk
Abbotsbury DT3 4JJ   *Website* www.theabbeyhouse.co.uk

In 'one of the most beautiful settings ever', this unpretentious guest house
is a 15th-century building on the site of an 11th-century abbey. It has
flagstone floors, panelled doors, original windows, 'cosy lounge with plenty
of books'; 'lots of chintz and knick-knacks'. The 'gentle, kind' owners,
Jonathan and Maureen Cooke, 'run it impeccably, yet find time to chat'.
The 'delightful' garden has flowerbeds, wide lawns that slope down to a
millpond, and the only surviving Benedictine watermill in the country.
Beyond is a huge, ancient tithe barn. Light alfresco lunches and cream teas
are served in summer, and operas are sometimes performed. The 'cottagey'
bedrooms vary in size and style: two have a king-size brass antique bed;
another has 'a comfortable four-poster'. There's a 'romantic, private' room
at the top. Breakfasts, served with damask tablecloths, are 'very good'.
Evening meals are available only for house parties. '*Abbey House* has a
comprehensive list of eating places, but all involve a drive. The local
Ilchester Arms is not to be recommended,' say inspectors. The village is
famed for its swannery (established by monks over 600 years ago), and its
subtropical gardens. (*Janet and John Wylie, Ken and Liz Bartlett, Ray and Janet
Anstis, and others*)

5 bedrooms. On B3157 halfway between Weymouth and Bridport. Tea room open
midday Apr–Oct; closed at night, except for house parties. Reception (background
music sometimes), lounge, breakfast/tea room. 1½-acre garden: stage for opera. Sea
15 mins' walk. Unsuitable for &. No smoking. No dogs. No credit cards. B&B
£35–£40 per person. Full alc £35. 1-night bookings sometimes refused Sat.

ALDEBURGH Suffolk   Map 2:C6

The Wentworth   *Tel* 01728-452312
Wentworth Road   *Fax* 01728-454343
Aldeburgh IP15 5BD   *Email* stay@wentworth-aldeburgh.co.uk
                              Website www.wentworth-aldeburgh.com

'I'm glad to see *The Wentworth* getting the praise it deserves,' comments a
regular visitor to this seaside hotel which overlooks fishing huts and boats
on Aldeburgh's shingle beach. It is 'old-fashioned (in the nicest sense)'.
Announcing a revamp of the Garden Lounge, it promises: 'The style will
be verging on the more contemporary, but nothing for traditionalists to be

alarmed about.' The conservatory restaurant and six bedrooms have also been refurbished this year. Michael Pritt is the third generation of his family in charge; his manager is the 'warm, pleasant' Jolyon Gough. In the lounges are antiques, books, plants, fresh flowers and Russell Flint prints. Each bedroom has a copy of Kathleen Hale's *Orlando the Marmalade Cat* (her 'Owlbarrow' is Aldeburgh). 'Our suite was well furnished, and had excellent sea views.' The annexe, *Darfield House*, has large rooms, but no sea views. The chef, Graham Reid, serves 'generous' dishes: 'A good range of choices, invariably well cooked and presented, without overdoing the sauces. Ice-cream sundaes to die for.' Light lunches and cream teas are served in a conservatory (with fireplace) or on a terrace. Musicians and actors often stay here during the Aldeburgh Festival. (*Patricia Darby, John and Sheila Cotton*)

35 bedrooms. 7 in annexe, *Darfield House.* 5 on ground floor. On seafront, 5 mins' walk from centre. Parking. Train: Saxmundham, 8 miles. Ramps. 2 lounges, bar, restaurant; private dining room; conference room. No background music. Small sunken terrace. Shingle beach 200 yds. No smoking: restaurant, bedrooms, 1 lounge. All major credit cards accepted. B&B £45–£102 per person. Set dinner £15.50–£18.50. Weekend, midweek breaks; special events. Christmas/New Year packages. 1-night bookings refused Sat.

See also SHORTLIST

ALSTON Cumbria   Map 4:B3

Lovelady Shield   *Tel* 01434-381203
Nenthead Road   *Fax* 01434-381515
nr Alston CA9 3LF   *Email* enquiries@lovelady.co.uk
                            Website www.lovelady.co.uk

Set against a background of trees, and with the River Nent running through its large grounds, this secluded country hotel is approached by a long, tree-lined drive. Visitors returning this year found it 'still very good', and the food 'very tasty'. An earlier comment: 'It oozes content-ment and relaxation.' 'A silent hotel' (no muzak), write the owners, Peter and Marie Haynes, who run it 'with a touch of eccentricity and masses of charm'. The early 19th-century house was built on the site of a 13th-century convent. All bedrooms and bathrooms were recently refurbished. 'Ours was comfortable, and had plenty of storage space.' Early morning tea is brought to the room (for a charge), or tea-making equipment can be provided. Both sitting rooms are smoke-free; one is a 'cosy library stuffed full of books and games for rainy days'. Chef Barrie Garton, who describes his style as 'British with continental excursions', offers a daily-changing four-course menu with choices, eg, Dublin Bay prawn clafoutis; griddled veal loin steak with thyme roasted tomato. There is good walking from the door, and the Pennine Way and Hadrian's Wall are within easy reach. (*GC; also Kelvin Juba*)

12 bedrooms. 2½ miles E of Alston. 2 lounges, bar, restaurant. No background music. 3-acre grounds: river, fishing, croquet, woodland walks. Unsuitable for &. Civil wedding licence. Smoking in bar only. No dogs in public rooms. Amex, MasterCard, Visa accepted. B&B £85 per person; D,B&B £105 (reductions for 2/3 nights). Set dinner £37.50. Christmas/New Year packages. **•V•**

AMBERLEY West Sussex   Map 2:E3

Amberley Castle	*Tel* 01798-831992
Amberley	*Fax* 01798-831998
nr Arundel BN18 9LT	*Email* info@amberleycastle.co.uk
	Website www.amberleycastle.co.uk

Owned by Martin and Joy Cummings since 1988, this luxury hotel (Relais & Châteaux) is a Grade I listed monument surrounded by a 60-foot wall and a dry moat. It stands on a bend of the River Arun at the foot of the South Downs. In its 'immaculate' grounds are 'lots of flowers' and a tree house. 'A tranquil place for a special treat,' one visitor wrote. The bedrooms and suites are in the castle, the stone-built *Bishopric* in the moat, and a manor house: the ones with direct access to the battlements are particularly liked. Rooms vary greatly in size, but all have antiques, fine fabrics, spa bath, flat-screen TV, DVD-player and a fluffy toy. 'There was also fine china, fresh milk, a cheese platter with biscuits, grapes, dates and apricots.' 'Housekeeping standards are high.' James Peyton's 'traditional English, with a touch of modern' menu might include mosaic of game with mushrooms; monkfish osso bucco with seafood and saffron risotto. Men must wear jacket and tie for dinner, but 'smart casual' is accepted at lunchtime. Breakfast has freshly squeezed orange juice and home-baked bread. A popular venue for weddings and social events. (*Mrs JRP, and others*)

19 bedrooms. 5 in *Bishopric*, outside walls. SW of village, 4 miles N of Arundel. Hall, 3 lounges, 2 restaurants; function facilities. No background music. 12-acre grounds: gardens, tennis, 18-hole putting, croquet, ponds, wildlife. Helipad. Civil wedding licence. Unsuitable for &. Smoking in 1 lounge only. No children under 12. Guide dogs only. All major credit cards accepted. Room £77.50–£187.50 per person; D,B&B (2 nights min.) £230–£475. Breakfast £16. Set lunch £23, dinner £43–£50; full alc £68. Min. 2-night booking weekends. Christmas/New Year packages.

AMBLESIDE Cumbria   Map 4: inset C2

The Regent by the Lake
Waterhead Bay
Ambleside LA22 0ES

Tel 015394-32254
Fax 015394-31474
Email info@regentlakes.co.uk
Website www.regentlakes.co.uk

Renamed this year, this 'welcoming' hotel ('good value, good food, pleasant ambience,' says a regular visitor) stands opposite a slipway on to Lake Windermere. Mrs Hewitt, who runs it with sons Andrew and Jason, now offers more flexible eating: a 'Dine around Ambleside' option gives guests deals at restaurants; a picnic hamper in the bedroom is available for those wanting 'a cosy night in'. And breakfast, always liked ('you can order anything in any form'), is served until midday. In the split-level restaurant, Nick Martin's daily-changing dinner menu includes 'tender meats, fish with delicious sauces', but the dessert menu may be 'a bit repetitive'. 'The new, smaller wine list did not restrict choice.' The restaurant and lounges have a modern decor of pale browns and cream. As to bedrooms, a garden room, in a separate building, was liked: 'Spacious, with patio doors on to a small wooden deck; a table for clutter, and a comfy bed. No traffic noise. The path to the hotel not ideal for high heels.' A courtesy car will meet visitors from the train or bus, and a 'Jeeves' package with chauffeur collects guests who don't fancy a long drive from home. (*Shirley Tennent, and others*)

30 bedrooms. 10 in courtyard. 5 in garden. 7 on ground floor. 1 suitable for &. On A591, S of centre, at Waterhead Bay. Train: Windermere, 5 miles. Closed Christmas. Ramp. Lounge, sun lounge, bar, restaurant; classical background music at night; 50-ft heated swimming pool. Courtyard. ½-acre garden. On Lake Windermere: sailing, waterskiing, fishing. No smoking. MasterCard, Visa accepted. B&B [2006] £57–£78 per person. Set lunch £25. Special breaks. **°V°**

Rothay Manor
Rothay Bridge
Ambleside LA22 0EH

Tel 015394-33605
Fax 015394-33607
Email hotel@rothaymanor.co.uk
Website www.rothaymanor.co.uk

Q *César award in 1992*

'Such a special place; not big, flash or pretentious, but warm and wel-coming.' Owned by the Nixon brothers, Nigel and Stephen, this 'very comfortable, civilised', white-fronted, listed Georgian house has been in every edition of the *Guide*. A comment this year: 'You feel relaxed and cosseted taking afternoon tea sitting by a real fire.' The house is at the junction of several busy roads, but is surrounded by trees and attractive gardens. 'Traffic noise is unobtrusive by day and virtually non-existent at night.' Bedrooms are 'well furnished' (many are large); quietest ones face the garden; four are in an annexe joined to the main building by a covered walkway. 'Sitting in the sun on our balcony was idyllic.' Children are welcomed: there are family rooms, special menus, cots, high chairs and baby-listening. The long-serving chefs, Colette Nixon and Jane Binns, offer much choice on a daily-changing 'traditional British/French' menu. 'Delicious food: good vegetables and super sweets.' The 'excellent' breakfasts have freshly squeezed orange juice, 'eggs perfectly cooked', 'very good toast, butter and marmalade'; 'prunes served in champagne glasses'. You can walk across fields to Lake Windermere, and many local villages can be reached on foot. (*Barbara E Wood, MB, and others*)

19 bedrooms. 2 in annexe, 20 yds. 2 suitable for &. ¼ mile SW of Ambleside. Open 26 Jan–3 Jan. Ramp. 2 lounges, bar, 2 dining rooms; meeting/conference facilities. No background music. 1-acre garden: croquet. Access to local leisure centre. No smoking. No dogs. All major credit cards accepted. B&B [2006] £65–£97.50 per person; D,B&B £90–£127.50. Set menus £18–£40. Christmas/New Year packages. 1-night bookings refused Sat.

AMPLEFORTH North Yorkshire   Map 4:D4

Shallowdale House
West End, Ampleforth
nr York, YO62 4DY

Tel 01439-788325
Fax 01439-788885
Email stay@shallowdalehouse.co.uk
Website www.shallowdalehouse.co.uk

Q *César award in 2005*

'Four happy nights' were enjoyed this year by new visitors to Phillip Gill and Anton van der Horst's small guest house in an area of outstanding natural beauty on the edge of the North York Moors national park. 'We have nothing but praise for their hospitality and friendliness; we have booked to return.' A regular visitor is equally fervent: 'They seem really to like their guests, their welcome is warm, and they always ask how the day has been.' The architect-designed building (1963) is on a sheltered slope of the Hambleton Hills. 'The view from the dining room and bedrooms is panoramic, and of incredible beauty and restfulness.' The ground-floor drawing room has an open fire in winter. Here, and in the first-floor sitting room, guests can take complimentary tea with 'wonderful home-made delights'. Two of the three bedrooms are spacious; the third, slightly smaller, has a private bathroom across a corridor. A four-course set dinner, by arrangement, is served at separate candlelit tables: 'The food is superb, with first-class ingredients.' 'A good wine list, though the house red has a high alcohol content.' The traditional breakfast includes dry-cured bacon, Whitby kippers, home-made preserves. (*Christine Moore, Richard Creed*)

3 bedrooms. At W end of Ampleforth. Closed Christmas/New Year, occasionally in winter. Drawing room, sitting room, dining room. No background music. 2½-acre grounds. Unsuitable for &. No smoking. No children under 12. No dogs. MasterCard, Visa accepted. B&B: single £67.50–£77.50, double £85–£105. Set dinner £32.50. 1-night bookings usually refused weekends.

ARNCLIFFE North Yorkshire   Map 4:D3

Amerdale House   *Tel* 01756-770250
Arncliffe, Littondale   *Fax* 01756-770266
Skipton BD23 5QE   *Email* amerdalehouse@littondale.com
                                   Website www.amerdalehouse.co.uk

Q *César award in 1995*

'An irresistible destination.' 'Satisfaction guaranteed every time.' So write regular visitors to Nigel and Paula Crapper's small hotel, liked for its 'lovely setting' and 'quiet, friendly ambience'. The Victorian manor house stands peacefully in large gardens in a small village. It is 'comfortable rather than luxurious'; bedrooms vary in size; some are small; three are on the second floor (no lift). 'They have all one needs and more: huge bath towels, plenty of hot water, etc.' Nigel Crapper's daily-changing four-course dinner menus 'have changed little over the years; modern fads are ignored; his high standards never falter'. Wines are reasonably priced. Vegetarians should give advance notice. 'Apart from the sound of lambs in the surrounding fields, there was just a murmur of gentle conversation as guests enjoyed their leisurely meal.' 'Superb' breakfasts include black pudding and Cumberland sausage, freshly squeezed orange juice, copious tea or coffee. There is good walking all around: maps, guidebooks and picnic lunches are provided; also a boot box in the porch, and help with drying clothes. *Amerdale House* is still on the market, but the Crappers say they expect to carry on for some time yet. (*Trevor Lockwood, and others*)

11 bedrooms. 1 in converted stables. 17 miles NW of Skipton. Mid-Mar–end Oct. Restaurant closed midday. Lounge, library, bar, restaurant. No background music. 2-acre grounds. Unsuitable for &. No smoking in restaurant. No dogs. MasterCard, Visa accepted. D,B&B £82–£90 per person. Set dinner £34. 1-night bookings refused bank holidays, high-season weekends.

Hotels do not pay to be included in the *Guide*.

ARUNDEL West Sussex   Map 2:E3

Arundel House	*Tel* 01903-882136
11 High Street	*Email* mail@arundelhouseonline.com
Arundel BN18 9AD	*Website* www.arundelhouseonline.com

At the foot of Arundel's high street, near the castle and a bridge over the River Arun, this bow-windowed 19th-century merchant's town house has been turned by Billy Lewis-Bowker and Luke Hackman (the chef) into a restaurant-with-rooms. The decor of 'stylish simplicity' is by the former's artist wife, Emma, whose paintings hang throughout the building. 'Very good value,' reported our inspector. 'Superb food.' The restaurant, in two rooms, one on each side of the entrance hall, serves dishes that are 'classic English with an occasional modern twist', eg, confit belly of pork; seared fillet of roe deer with a savoury fig tart. The wine list is thought good, and breakfast is enjoyed too. Some visitors disliked the background music, and there is no lounge. The bedrooms have flat-screen TV, wireless Internet access and power shower. 'Our second-floor room, decorated in white and rich cream, had raspberry striped blinds.' There is a choice between duvet and blankets (best specify when you book). The house is on a short one-way system: no car park, but you can draw up outside to unload, and vouchers are given for the large, safe municipal car park opposite the castle entrance.

5 bedrooms. All with power shower. On High Street. Municipal car park 200 yds. Closed 25–29 Dec. Restaurant closed Sun. Restaurant (background music). Unsuitable for &. No smoking. No children under 16. Guide dogs only. Amex, MasterCard, Visa accepted. B&B £30–£80 per person; D,B&B £58–£112. Set meal £28–£34. 1-night bookings refused bank holidays. ***V***

The Town House	**NEW**	*Tel* 01903-883847
65 High Street		*Email* enquiries@thetownhouse.co.uk
Arundel BN18 9AJ		*Website* www.thetownhouse.co.uk

At the top of Arundel's high street, this Grade II listed building was turned by owner/chef Lee Williams and his wife, Katie, into a restaurant-with-rooms when they bought it in December 2005. 'No dress code,' they write. 'Stuffiness is taboo.' Visitors who called for lunch in 2006 were enchanted by the 'beautiful building' and the 'amazing 16th-century carved Florentine ceiling' in the dining room. 'Service was charming; food stunning.' We sent inspectors who report: 'Our second-floor room, Rosemary, newly decorated (beige and white), had a short lobby and an amazing amount of intricate plasterwork and furniture mouldings. Plenty of wardrobe space, sash windows looking across the road to the castle. Duvets only, but the owner said he would get a blanket and sheets in case anyone else asked for them. Adequate bathroom. Housekeeping was faultless, so was the food: shellfish bisque; smoked haddock and leek risotto; scallops with pea purée, crisp Parma ham. Cheeses excellent and in perfect condition. Wine prices reasonable. Home-made fudge with coffee. Breakfast the usual continental or full English with additions. Excellent scrambled eggs and smoked salmon. A good experience: relaxed and informal.' No lounge or grounds, so probably best for a short stay. (*Richard Furn, and others*)

5 bedrooms. On High St, next to 'Arundel Ghost Experience'. Municipal car park nearby. Closed 2 weeks Jan, 2 weeks Oct. Restaurant (closed Sun/Mon; background music). Unsuitable for &. No smoking. No dogs. All major credit cards accepted. B&B double £65–£100 per person. Set lunch £12.50–£16, dinner £22–£25. **'V'**

ASHBOURNE Derbyshire   Map 3:B6

Callow Hall   NEW   *Tel* 01335-300900
Mappleton   *Fax* 01335-300512
Ashbourne DE6 2AA   *Email* reservations@callowhall.co.uk
                                 Website www.callowhall.co.uk

In its own conservation area above the valley of the River Dove and its tributary, the Bentley Brook, this Grade II listed Victorian mansion is at the southern edge of the Peak District national park. It was put on the market last year by its owners, the Spencer family, David, Dorothy, Anthony and Emma, but they have now decided to carry on. They have refurbished half the bedrooms and many public areas. There are rugs on polished floors, stags' heads, large flower arrangements. Most *Guide* readers remain strongly in favour. 'Good as ever. Lovely old house, beautifully furnished. Staff always near if needed.' 'Run with warmth and profession-alism. Breakfast first class. Well-sourced dinners, satisfying without ventur-ing into *haute cuisine*.' Mrs Spencer and her daughter run front-of-house; son Anthony and his father are in the kitchen. Butchery, smoking and baking are done on site. 'Interesting starters, beautifully cooked roasts, home-made puddings.' The bedrooms, up a wooden staircase, vary greatly: the larger ones are 'worth the extra money'; some others are 'small, with no view'. Maintenance may not always be perfect. Biscuits, fruit and mineral water are replenished daily. Children are welcomed. Functions are sometimes held. (*Kathleen and Jim Craddock, David and Kate Wooff, David Grant, and others*)

16 bedrooms. 2 on ground floor. 1 suitable for &. ¾ mile from Ashbourne, off A515 to Buxton. Train: Derby, 13 miles. Closed 25/26 Dec, 1 Jan, occasionally for a week in Feb. Restaurant closed for lunch except Sun. Lounge, bar, restaurant; function/ conference facilities. No background music. 42-acre grounds: walled garden, woodland, farm, stables; river, fishing (tuition available). No smoking: restaurant, bedrooms (throughout building from mid-2007). No dogs in public rooms. All major credit cards accepted. B&B [2006] £70–£120 per person. Set menu £42; full alc £43.50. Weekend/midweek breaks. *V*

ASHFORD Kent *See SHORTLIST*   Map 2:D5

ASHWATER Devon   Map 1:C3

Blagdon Manor	*Tel* 01409-211224
Ashwater EX21 5DF	*Fax* 01409-211634
	Email stay@blagdon.com
	Website www.blagdon.com

Ω *César award in 2006*

'The kind of hotel the *Guide* was invented for,' writes a reporter endorsing last year's *César* award for this 'wonderful' small country hotel. The Grade II listed, 17th-century, rambling manor house ('more gentleman-farmer than lord-of-the-manor'), retains many original features (oak beams, slate flagstones, etc). Visitors find the owners, Steve and Liz Morey, 'charming and hard-working'. She is a 'most attentive front-of-house', he an 'excellent chef'. Their staff are 'well trained, and very nice'. The setting is 'idyllic', 'deeply rural', midway between the north and south Devon coasts: southern views are across lawns and countryside to Dartmoor. The bedrooms, which vary in size and style, are spotless. 'My bed was big and firm.' Fresh flowers and open fires are in the bar and lounge. Books, ornaments and striped fabrics abound. The cooking, 'traditional with Mediterranean hints', is 'imaginative and exquisitely presented'. 'The highlight was a galantine of quail and grouse with a smooth, buttery brioche.' Some ingredients are home grown. Breakfast (with exotic fruits, 'delicious porridge, perfect scrambled eggs') and lunch are taken in a spacious conservatory. The Moreys have two 'gorgeous' chocolate Labradors and some cats. Guests' dogs are welcomed (*RC, GC, and others*)

7 bedrooms. 8 miles NE of Launceston. Closed New Year, 2 weeks Jan, 2 weeks Oct. Ramps. Lounge, library, bar, conservatory, restaurant; private dining room. No background music. 20-acre grounds: 3-acre gardens, croquet, giant chess, gazebo, pond. Sea 12 miles. Unsuitable for &. Smoking in bar and garden only. No children under 12. No dogs in restaurant. MasterCard, Visa accepted. B&B £60–£85 per person. Set lunch £17–£21, dinner £32–£35. 1-night bookings refused at Christmas.

ATCHAM Shropshire   Map 3:B5

The Mytton & Mermaid Hotel
Atcham, nr Shrewsbury
SY5 6QG

Tel 01743-761220
Fax 01743-761292
Email admin@myttonandmermaid.co.uk
Website www.myttonandmermaid.co.uk

A blend of 'modern and traditional', a 'roaring log fire', and 'service without pomp' prevail at Ann and Danny DiTella's hotel. The Grade II listed building (1735) has a 'great setting', in a village on the River Severn. It faces a magnificent National Trust property, Attingham Park. 'Great food using local suppliers,' was one comment. 'Everyone very friendly. Large superior room with fab views and full breakfast (smoked haddock with poached egg).' 'Corridors and stairways look tired', however. Bar meals are available, and there are menus for vegetarians and for children. The chef, Adrian Badland, describes his cooking as 'modern British with a twist': perhaps spiced Shropshire rump of lamb with lamb and cherry wontons. The bar, where a jazz evening is held every Sunday, is named after a notorious local squire, 'Mad Jack' Mytton, famed for his excesses. The best bedrooms are in the main house (some have a 'Gothic' bed); there are six bedrooms more suitable for people of limited mobility, in converted stables. 'A little noisy: nearby busy road.' (*Conrad Barnard, AM*)

18 bedrooms. 6 in courtyard. Also 4-bedroom cottage. 3 miles SE of Shrewsbury. Closed 25 Dec. Ramps. Riverside drawing room with TV, *Mad Jack's Bar* (jazz all day), restaurant. 1-acre garden on River Severn (fishing rights). Civil wedding licence. No smoking: restaurant, bedrooms. Dogs in courtyard rooms only. All major credit cards accepted. B&B [2006] £47.50–£77.50 per person. Set dinner £27.50; full alc £33. New Year package. ***V***

AUSTWICK North Yorkshire   Map 4:D3

The Austwick Traddock
Austwick, via Lancaster
LA2 8BY

Tel 01524-251224
Fax 01524-251796
Email info@austwicktraddock.co.uk
Website www.austwicktraddock.co.uk

In a village in the Yorkshire Dales national park (despite the Lancashire postal address), this substantial Georgian house is informally run by Bruce and Jane Reynolds. 'Highly recommended for comfort and happy service,' said inspectors. Other visitors wrote of 'helpful owners' and 'well-motivated staff'. In winter there are log fires in the lounge. In summer, drinks are served on the deck facing the garden. The bedrooms (three were redecorated this year) are 'comfortably furnished in restrained country style' (patterned wallpaper, plain fitted carpets, 'fine country antiques'; also sherry and 'a profusion of good magazines'). 'Our small bathroom was well equipped, but lacked storage space.' The kitchen has been certified as 100% organic by the Soil Association: chef James Stocks serves modern dishes, eg, lamb rump with potato fondant and roasted root vegetables. 'We enjoyed everything we ate,' says a report in 2006. Another visitor thought 'a stronger managerial touch' was needed in the candlelit, stone-walled dining room, and commented that the menu did not change during a three-night stay. 'Wonderful breakfast: toast made from home-made bread, lovely jams and an array of cooked dishes.' Children are welcomed; so are 'well-behaved pets'. Good walking from the door. (*Alison Davies, J and SB, and others*)

10 bedrooms. 3 miles NW of Settle. Train: Settle; bus. Large lounge, front lounge, bar, dining room, breakfast room; occasional background music; function facilities. 1½-acre grounds: sun deck. Only public rooms accessible to &. Smoking in bar only. No dogs in public rooms. Amex, MasterCard, Visa accepted. B&B £65–£85 per person. Set meals £24–£30. Activity breaks. Christmas/New Year packages. 1-night bookings refused Fri/Sat. ***V***

AXMINSTER Devon   Map 1:C6

Kerrington House
Musbury Road
Axminster EX13 5JR

Tel 01297-35333
Fax 01297-35345
Email enquiries@kerringtonhouse.com
Website www.kerringtonhouse.com

In landscaped gardens on the edge of this old market town, Hilary and Jim Reaney's late Victorian family house, with grey stone walls and bay windows, is thought 'a pleasant place to stay; comfortable, stylish, impeccable and fresh'. There are antique furnishings, and a spacious lounge in an Art Nouveau extension (originally built as a music room); this has views of the lovely garden (with pond) and terrace, and of a modern estate on the hill opposite. *Guide* inspectors reported: 'After escorting us to our room, Mrs Reaney offered tea and delicious home-made biscuits. In the evening, fronting the house was by very polite youngsters.' The pastel decor is 'relaxing, and gives light in darker areas'. There is background music at mealtimes in the lounge and in the restaurant, which is open on Thursday, Friday and Saturday – light suppers can be prepared for residents on other nights. Dishes based on local ingredients, on a short menu, include smoked salmon blinis; lamb fillet with roast parsnips. The 'small but excellent wine list' is 'reasonably priced'. Smoked fish and kedgeree are offered at breakfast as well as full English or continental. Bedrooms are all different, and there are 'lovely, well-equipped bathrooms'. House parties are catered for.

5 bedrooms. ½ mile SW of Axminster. Restaurant closed midday and Sun–Wed (light meal available for residents). Lounge, dining room; background CDs at mealtimes. ½-acre garden. Unsuitable for &. No smoking. No dogs. MasterCard, Visa accepted. B&B [2006] £50–£75 per person; D,B&B £78–£103. Set dinner £28. 1-night bookings refused Sat in summer.

AYLESBURY Buckinghamshire   Map 2:C3

Hartwell House
Oxford Road
nr Aylesbury HP17 8NR

Tel 01296-747444
Fax 01296-747450
Email info@hartwell-house.com
Website www.hartwell-house.com

'Unstinting praise. There is nothing forbidding or gloomy about this stately pile,' writes a visitor to Richard Broyd's 'gracious' Historic House Hotel (with a Jacobean front and a Georgian rear). 'I can't fault hotel, staff or food.' Set in a huge park, it has been managed by the 'admirable' Jonathan Thompson for many years. 'The ceilings are so high, the windows so tall and wide, that the place is full of light. It has been furnished with priceless antiques, there to be used, not just admired. Our bedroom in *Hartwell Court*, the converted stable block, was attractively decorated in green and white, and had a six-foot-square bed and a dressing table with good lighting.' Bedrooms in the main house vary in size and layout; 'all are covetable'. Dinner was 'enjoyed enormously; it satisfied the tastebuds, without a sign of pretentiousness' (eg, roast partridge with fondant potato). This year the dress code has been eased: 'Smart please, although jacket and tie are not obligatory. No trainers, tracksuits or shorts.' Light meals are available in the buttery. 'Our dog was made welcome, not a guilty secret.' Mr Broyd also owns *Middlethorpe Hall*, York, and *Bodysgallen Hall*, Llandudno, Wales (*qqv*). (*Pat Fenn; also Nick Chapman, Martin and Jane Bailey*)

46 bedrooms. 16 in stable block. Some on ground floor. 2 miles S of Aylesbury. Lift, ramp. 4 drawing rooms, bar, 3 dining rooms, buttery; conference facilities; spa: 55-ft swimming pool, whirlpool, sauna, beauty salon, bar/buttery. No background music. Pianist in vestibule, Fri/Sat evening. 90-acre grounds: tennis, croquet, lake (fishing), jogging track, woodlands. Civil wedding licence. No smoking: dining room, morning room, drawing room, spa, main house and some other bedrooms. No children under 6. No dogs: public rooms, main house bedrooms. Amex, MasterCard, Visa accepted. B&B £140–£190 per person; D,B&B £190–£210. Cooked breakfast £6. Set lunch from £25; full alc £46. Christmas/New Year packages. ***V*** (Sun–Thurs)

BAMPTON Devon   Map 1:C5

The Bark House   *Tel* 01398-351236
Oakfordbridge   *Email* bark.house.hotel@btinternet.com
nr Bampton EX16 9HZ   *Website* www.barkhouse.co.uk

♔ *César award in 2006*

'Sensitive personal service, superb food and facilities.' 'We made two visits,
in winter and autumn. Each time was a delight.' This year's praise for
Alastair Kameen's wisteria-covered 18th-century stone house, which he
runs with Justine Hill. The small, 'simple but upmarket' guest house has a
lovely location in the 'prettiest stretch of the Exe valley'. Other praise: 'An
admirable small hotel – one of the best I have encountered.' In a garden
(on several levels) across the busy road, guests can look across the valley
to a wooded hillside. Several more bedrooms have been refurbished this
year, and some bathrooms upgraded. Drinks are served, with generous
canapés, in the candlelit dining room at 7 pm; dinner, cooked by Mr
Kameen and served by Ms Hill at 7.30, is a set menu (preferences discussed
when booking or on arrival), with a choice of starter and dessert.
'Imaginative, beautifully cooked and presented.' The short wine list is
admired. Morning tea and juice are brought to the bedrooms. Breakfasts are
'the best': the provenance of each ingredient is listed. Traffic noise could
be a problem. As we went to press, *The Bark House* was put on the market.
An early sale is not expected, but you should check the position before
booking. (*WHM Davies, Jill McLaren, Gwyn Morgan, and others*)

5 bedrooms. 2-bedroom self-catering cottage. In hamlet 3 miles W of Bampton, on
A396. Open 'most of the year': occasional closures during quiet spells. Lounge, dining
room (background music in evening). 1½-acre garden: croquet. Cycling, horse riding,
fishing, birdwatching nearby. Bedrooms unsuitable for ♿. No smoking: bedrooms,
restaurant ('we prefer guests not to smoke in the hotel'). 'Children of considerate
parents only; no "free-range" children.' No dogs in public rooms. No credit cards.
B&B £47.50–£59.50 per person. Set dinner £29.50. Christmas/New Year packages.
1-night bookings occasionally refused.

BARNARD CASTLE Co. Durham   Map 4:C3

Homelands Guest House   <kbd>BUDGET</kbd>   *Tel* 01833-638757
85 Galgate   *Email* enquiries@homelandsguesthouse.co.uk
Barnard Castle DL12 8ES   *Website* www.homelandsguesthouse.co.uk

'Very welcoming hosts; everything well run and spotless.' 'Superb for just
a B&B.' Readers continue to lavish praise on Irene Williamson's spacious

Victorian town house in a residential area of this Teesdale market town. It is a 'favourite stop-over on journeys to the far north'. This year all five of the 'extremely comfortable' bedrooms have been redecorated. Some are 'compact', with a small shower room. The house stands on a road that is busy by day but quiet at night (windows are double glazed). The quietest room is in the 'exquisitely tended' garden. Breakfast has cereals, fruit, etc, from a buffet; and 'a large choice of well-cooked dishes' including kippers, and scrambled egg with smoked bacon muffin. No evening meals: 'Mrs Williamson offers helpful advice on local restaurants.' *Homelands* is within easy walking distance of the 'fabulous' Bowes Museum and the 'interesting ruined castle' from which the town takes its name. (*MC and GR Bradshaw, Kelvin Juba*)

5 **bedrooms.** 1 in garden. Central. No private parking. Closed Christmas/New Year. Lounge, breakfast room ('easy listening' background music). Garden. Unsuitable for &. No smoking. No children under 6. Guide dogs only. MasterCard, Visa accepted. B&B £29–£35 per person. 1-night bookings refused bank holidays.

BARNGATES Cumbria   Map 4: inset C2

The Drunken Duck Inn
Barngates, nr Ambleside
LA22 0NG

Tel 015394-36347
Fax 015394-36781
Email info@drunkenduckinn.co.uk
Website www.drunkenduckinn.co.uk

& *César award in 2006*

On a hillside between Ambleside and Hawkshead, this white-fronted inn (named after ducks that drank from a leaking cask) has breathtaking views of the surrounding fells. Stephanie Barton, the owner, has 'a sure touch with the decor', said our inspectors who admired the 'imaginative modern design'. But a visitor in 2006 found her bedroom's cream walls 'drab' and its beige carpet 'slightly grubby'. All agree about the 'delicious' cooking, served in the busy dining rooms and an informal area of the bar. Nick Foster, the chef, uses local ingredients of quality, many of them organic, in his 'modern British' dishes (eg, Cumbrian air-dried ham; Swaledale lamb). Bread is home baked. Nick Munford, the manager for 15 years, leads a friendly staff. The beamed garden room has floor-length windows and a large balcony above the garden. In the lounge are squashy sofas, a stove, board games and a resident cat. 'There are beautiful, wide wooden floor-boards; interesting prints, cartoons and architectural engravings hang throughout.' Bedrooms have 'lots of goodies: fruit, water, high-quality toiletries'. A 'superb' breakfast has freshly squeezed juice, leaf tea, good toast and 'lavish cooked dishes'. Afternoon teas are served alfresco in summer. The inn has its own fly-fishery. Its new sister hotel, *The Punch Bowl*, Crosthwaite, enters the *Guide* this year.

16 bedrooms. 8 across small courtyard. Some on ground floor. 3 miles SW of Ambleside. Closed Christmas. Residents' lounge, bar, 3 dining rooms. No background music. 1-acre garden in 60-acre grounds. Fly-fishery 50 yds. No smoking. Dogs in bar only. Amex, MasterCard, Visa accepted. B&B [2006] £45–£110 per person. Full alc £37.50. New Year package.

BARWICK Somerset   Map 1:C6

Little Barwick House	*Tel* 01935-423902
Barwick, nr Yeovil	*Fax* 01935-420908
BA22 9TD	*Email* reservations@barwick7.fsnet.co.uk
	Website www.littlebarwickhouse.co.uk

Q *César award in 2002*

'Relaxed, and beautifully kept', Tim and Emma Ford's restaurant-with-rooms is in a Georgian dower house in 'delightful quiet countryside' near the Somerset/Dorset border. Most reports continue favourable. 'Cuisine comes first,' all agree. 'Tim's cooking is excellent'; his wife is the 'attentive front-of-house'; she and her staff are 'welcoming in every way'. Prospective visitors appreciated 'a phone call asking whether we prefer duvet or blanket and sheets'. Complimentary tea with 'fabulous' home-made cake and shortbread greets arrivers; it is served by a log fire in a cosy lounge, or in the garden. Some bedrooms were refurbished this year. 'Our large room had king-size bed, turned down during dinner; functional bathroom with good power shower.' 'Our high-ceilinged room was tastefully decorated.' But Room 4's shower was 'pathetic'. Tables are well spaced in the 'large, airy' dining room with a conservatory extension. 'Delicious' modern dishes include sardines on thyme toast; saddle of wild rabbit on butternut squash risotto. One visitor thought the young staff 'lacked an experienced firm hand'; another was impressed by their efficiency when a party of 16 arrived. The 'stylishly arranged' breakfast has fresh juices, fruit compote, 'melt-in-the-mouth croissants'. (*Jane Legate, Simon Bennett and Terri Clark, J Rochelle, Mrs KA Winslow, Chris Ball, and others*)

6 bedrooms. ¾ mile outside Yeovil. Closed New Year, 2 weeks Jan. Restaurant closed Sun/Mon evenings, Tues lunch. Ramp. 2 lounges, restaurant, conservatory. No background music. 3½-acre garden: terrace, pond, paddock. Unsuitable for &. No smoking: restaurant, 1 lounge, bedrooms. No children under 5. No dogs in public rooms. MasterCard, Visa accepted. B&B [2006] £63–£110 per person; D,B&B £84–£100. Set lunch £18.95–£20.95, dinner £34.95; full alc £40. 2-night breaks. 1-night bookings sometimes refused Fri/Sat.

BASLOW Derbyshire   Map 3:A6

The Cavendish
Church Lane
Baslow DE45 1SP

Tel 01246-582311
Fax 01246-582312
Email info@cavendish-hotel.net
Website www.cavendish-hotel.net

♥ *César award in 2002*

A traditional country hotel 'that has the ability to relax a visitor immediately on entering': returning visitors this year confirm the 'usual high
standard'. Within the grounds of the Duke of Devonshire's Chatsworth
estate, it is leased to the 'ever elegant, charming' Eric Marsh. The 'helpful'
staff are much liked for their ability 'to take on any role – it was the
breakfast waiter who carried our bags to the car'. 'Our bedroom had two
large windows with beautiful views of the estate. There was a large,
comfortable bed and a very good bathroom and shower.' This year, a
further seven bedrooms have been redecorated. For meals, you can choose
between 'nearly formal' in the *Gallery* restaurant ('really stunning, more like
a drawing room') and 'relaxed' in the redecorated conservatory *Garden
Room*. The cooking style is 'English with flair. We had an excellent
"Celebration of Derbyshire Beef", which was a beef and mushroom pie, a
beef sausage and a piece of seared calf's liver.' Breakfast, not included in
the room price, was also thought 'excellent'. Eric Marsh owns *The George
Hotel* in nearby Hathersage (*qv*). (*Kay and Peter Rogers, LM Mayer-Jones, John
and Padi Howard, John and Jackie Tyzack*)

24 bedrooms. On A619, in Chatsworth grounds. Restaurant closed 25 Dec to non-
residents. Lounge, bar, 2 restaurants (classical background music); 2 private dining
rooms. ½-acre grounds: putting. River fishing nearby. Civil wedding licence. No
smoking. No dogs. All major credit cards accepted. Room [2006]: single £105–£145,
double £138–£182, suite £220. Breakfast £14.95. Set menus £30–£55 (*5% 'service levy'
added to all accounts*). 1-night bookings sometimes refused weekends.

Fischer's Baslow Hall
Calver Road
Baslow DE45 1RR

Tel 01246-583259
Fax 01246-583818
Email m.s@fischers-baslowhall.co.uk
Website www.fischers-baslowhall.co.uk

♥ *César award in 1998*

Occupying a typical Derbyshire manor house, on the edge of the
Chatsworth estate, Max and Susan Fischer's restaurant-with-rooms wins
more praise this year from *Guide* readers: 'We really enjoyed our stay, the
garden was delightful, staff very pleasant.' But the main attraction is

the food. Mr Fischer is chef/*patron*, with Rupert Rowley as head chef; their well-sourced modern cuisine has a *Michelin* star for dishes like roast saddle and braised shoulder of Derbyshire lamb with tomato and thyme jus. Vegetables from the kitchen garden are used whenever possible. The early *menu du jour* is 'good value', and the tasting menu (served to a whole table) is thought 'excellent'. Residents must book for the elegant dining room; smart casual dress is required. Bedrooms in the Grade II listed manor house are 'very chintzy'; some may be 'a little cramped', with a small bathroom. The rooms in the *Garden House* have a contemporary style and good bathroom, and are commended for the 'peace and quiet'. Fresh-squeezed juice, a wide range of teas, and 'good fruit salad' appear at breakfast. 'The gardens are a joy.' The Fischers and Rupert Rowley have now opened a gastro pub, *Rowley's Restaurant & Bar*, down the road. (*AJ Ward, John and Jackie Tyzack, Peter Halliwell*)

11 bedrooms. 5 in *Garden House.* Edge of village on A623. Closed 25/26 and 31 Dec. Restaurant closed to non-residents Sun night. Lounge, bar, breakfast room, 3 dining rooms; function facilities. No background music. 5-acre grounds. Unsuitable for &. Civil wedding licence. No smoking. No children under 12 in restaurant after 7 pm. No dogs. All major credit cards accepted. B&B [2006]: single £100–£130, double £140–£180. English breakfast £9.50. Set dinner £35–£65. 1-night bookings refused at weekends in season.

BATH Somerset   Map 2:D1

Apsley House   *Tel* 01225-336966
141 Newbridge Hill   *Fax* 01225-425462
Bath BA1 3PT   *Email* info@apsley-house.co.uk
                              Website www.apsley-house.co.uk

Just a five-minute drive from the city centre, this elegant Georgian house has been 'lovingly restored' by 'delightful' owners, Nicholas and Claire Potts, to create 'the feel of a private house'. Guide readers praise its 'wonderful atmosphere' and the welcome. Built by the Duke of Wellington in 1830 as a country home for a mistress, and set in its own garden, it retains many period features and is furnished with fine antiques and paintings. There is a smart drawing room (with open fire and grand piano), and a small bar. Some bedrooms are large; two can be a family suite; one has an immense bathroom, a fireplace, and French windows opening on to the garden, where tables and chairs stand on the lawn. 'We had a good room on the first floor, comfortable, though lighting was a bit weak.' This year a new garden room, with four-poster, is available. Breakfast 'is a feast', says 'possibly the longest-staying resident' (a year and a half). It can include 'nice chunks of melon and pineapple' as well as 'a good fry'. Mrs Potts serves sandwich platters and light suppers by arrangement. (*John B Adams, Ann H Edwards, Barrie Price-Davies*)

11 bedrooms. 1 mile W of centre. Closed 23–28 Dec. Drawing room, bar, dining room; background radio (Classic FM) most of the time. ¼-acre garden. Unsuitable for &. No smoking. No dogs. Amex, MasterCard, Visa accepted. B&B: single £55–£140, double £70–£120, suite £90–£200. 1-night bookings refused Sat in peak season. ***V*** (not weekends or peak times)

The Bath Priory
Weston Road
Bath BA1 2XT

Tel 01225-331922
Fax 01225-448276
Email mail@thebathpriory.co.uk
Website www.thebathpriory.co.uk

'Blissful,' says a regular correspondent about this luxury hotel set in land-scaped gardens close to the city centre; 'perfect, expensive but worth it'. Built as a private residence in 1835 on land once owned by the priory of Bath Abbey, the listed building is owned by Andrew Brownsword, owner of Bath Rugby Club, who also owns *Gidleigh Park*, Chagford (closed for renovation at the time of writing). Sue Williams manages both. This year, guest reception rooms and some bedrooms have been redecorated and a total no-smoking policy has been introduced. The drawing room and library have 'classic soft furnishings' in country house style, fresh flowers and log fires. Bedrooms vary in size; 'premier deluxe' ones are 'seriously comfortable'; all have antiques and also the latest technology (satellite TV, ISDN, voicemail, modem point, etc); but some get traffic noise. The chef, Chris Horridge, who took over in 2005, has this year earned his first *Michelin* star for his 'creative' cooking (eg, salad of quail with garden flowers and beetroot soup). But one couple reported long delays at dinner during a Christmas package. Good health and beauty facilities. The city centre is reached by a short bus ride, or a walk through Victoria Park. (*JS Rutter, JD, and others*)

31 bedrooms. Some in adjacent house. Some on ground floor. 1½ miles W of centre. Ramps. Library, drawing room, 2 dining rooms, private dining rooms; wine room; conference facilities. Spa: indoor heated swimming pool, gym, sauna, beauty treatments. No background music. 4-acre grounds: heated swimming pool (35 by 15 ft), croquet. Civil wedding licence. No smoking. No children under 8 at dinner. No dogs. All major credit cards accepted. B&B £122.50–£212.50 per person; D,B&B £177.50–£267.50. Set lunch £25; full alc £63.50. Christmas/New Year packages. 1-night bookings refused Sat. ***V***

For details of the Voucher scheme see page 60.

County Hotel   *Tel* 01225-425003
18–19 Pulteney Road   *Fax* 01225-466493
Bath BA2 4EZ   *Email* reservations@county-hotel.co.uk
                              Website www.county-hotel.co.uk

With views over the cricket ground and Bath Abbey, this grey-stone
building near the Pulteney Bridge has a bonus for Bath: parking with a
night-watchman. It is owned by Maureen Kent, her son James (the
manager) and her sister Sandra Masson. They are 'friendly not fawning',
say regular visitors who report 'everything up to its usual high standard'. A
dissenting view came from a visitor in 2006 who was unhappy with
maintenance of her small bedroom. The decor is traditional, with flowery
fabrics and heavy drapes. 'Our room was spacious, nicely furnished.
Luxurious towelling robes. At night we liked watching the city light up.'
Tea, coffee and drinks can be served in the reading room, and private
dining is available in the conservatory. Breakfast (8–9 am on weekdays,
8–9.45 at weekends) has choices of cheese, ham, fruit, croissants and the
usual cereals, as well as a full English. The road is busy by day, but quiet
at night. (*Wendy and Nick Chapman, and others*)

22 bedrooms. 5 mins' walk from centre. Station 1 mile. Car park. Open 10 Jan–
22 Dec. Bar area (background music), lounge/reading room, conservatory, breakfast
room. Patio (seating). Unsuitable for &. Smoking in bar only. No children under 13.
No dogs. All major credit cards accepted. B&B [2006] £55–£90 per person. Special
breaks. 1-night bookings refused Sat.

Harington's Hotel   NEW   *Tel* 01225-461728
8–10 Queen Street   *Fax* 01225-444804
Bath BA1 1HE   *Email* post@haringtonshotel.co.uk
                             Website www.haringtonshotel.co.uk

Now owned by Melissa Pritchard and Peter O'Sullivan who have completely refurbished it, this small hotel is in the city centre, near the abbey
and Pump Room. Composed of a group of 18th-century houses on a
cobbled street, it has been described as 'a haven of quiet in the centre of
a busy city', though there was one complaint about noisy seagulls. A
visitor this year liked 'the fantastic location, lots of nice touches'. She
found the family bedroom 'though well decorated, best for miniature
people', but added: 'Staff courtesy made up for minor gripes. The evening
receptionist was incredibly helpful.' Some bedrooms are up a steep spiral
staircase (no lift; listed building). The café/bar, open all day, serves light
meals until 8 pm ('a very passable and cheap chicken fillet and risotto').
There is free wireless broadband access, and guests may browse on the

house laptop computer. Reserved parking is within five minutes' walk (you may stop on the double yellow lines outside the hotel for unloading). (*Rebecca Leach*)

13 bedrooms. Central, near Queen Sq. Reserved parking with security cameras nearby. Coffee lounge, bar, restaurant. Background music 7 am–12 pm. Small patio. Unsuitable for &. Smoking in bar only. No dogs. Amex, MasterCard, Visa accepted. B&B: single £68–£118, double £88–£138. Full alc £26. Christmas/New Year packages. 1-night bookings usually refused Sat.

Haydon House
9 Bloomfield Park
Bath BA2 2BY

Tel 01225-444919
Fax 01225-427351
Email stay@haydonhouse.co.uk
Website www.haydonhouse.co.uk

In a residential area above the city, this B&B, a semi-detached stone Edwardian house fronted by a dovecote, is a long-time *Guide* favourite. Visitors returning in 2006 were delighted to find it unchanged. 'It feels loved, and so friendly. On a bleak day, we were warmly received, and given tea and shortbread.' The owners, Gordon and Magdalene Ashman-Marr, say they have made some 'quiet improvements': public areas refurbished and wireless broadband access provided for guests. The comfortable lounge is crammed with family photos, ornaments, plants and dried flowers. 'Our room (No. 2, probably the best) was immaculate, and so attractive.' The communal breakfast is served by the host ('eccentricity personified'), using good china, silver and crystal. It includes eggs Benedict; whisky or rum porridge; scrambled eggs with smoked salmon; home-made marmalade; raisin and cinnamon French toast. There are vegetarian and vegan options, and a continental breakfast can be taken in the bedroom. Guests may sit in the colourful rear garden (with statues), which is floodlit at night. There is 'masses of unrestricted free parking' on surrounding streets; the city centre is an easy walk down; a steepish walk or a bus ride back. (*Brian and Eve Webb, and others*)

5 bedrooms. 1 suitable for a family. 1 mile from centre. Sitting room, study/library, breakfast room (soft classical background music); terrace. ½-acre garden, sun terrace. Sports/leisure centre/boat trips/fishing nearby. 'Not really suitable for &, but they are welcome by prior arrangement.' No smoking. Children by arrangement. No dogs. Amex, MasterCard, Visa accepted. B&B £40–£80 per person. 1-night bookings occasionally refused weekends. ***V***

We ask for more reports on a hotel if we haven't received feedback from readers for some time. Do send an endorsement if you think a hotel should remain in the *Guide*.

Paradise House   *Tel* 01225-317723
86–88 Holloway   *Fax* 01225-482005
Bath BA2 4PX   *Email* info@paradise-house.co.uk
                         Website www.paradise-house.co.uk

In a 'sensational' position above the city, David and Annie Lanz's listed
Georgian house, with Victorian extensions, has 'fabulous views' from the
secluded garden, where, say inspectors, 'roses were being pruned on a dark
February day'. Since June 2005, Glyn and Megumi Moulson, 'an engaging
young couple, eager to please', have been resident managers. Most bedrooms are spacious and well appointed. 'Ours, on the ground floor, was
compact, but with a big bed which had proper sheets and blankets.
Furnished to a high standard (except for the captive hangers).' At the back
of the house is a 'classic drawing room', with floor-to-ceiling arched
windows. Here, drinks are served, and newspapers supplied. Breakfast, taken
in a bright room and at busy times in the drawing room too, has good
cooked items (including Wiltshire bacon and sausages), 'proper toast', good
tea and coffee. Continental breakfast can be served in the bedroom. No restaurant, but a list of eating places, with sample menus, is provided. The
house is on a quiet cul-de-sac on the ancient Fosse Way; it's a seven-minute
walk down a steep hill to the city centre (a little longer on the way back).

11 bedrooms. 2 on ground floor. Off Wells Road, close to city centre. Closed
Christmas. Lounge with bar (background music all day), breakfast room. ½-acre
garden: *boules.* Unsuitable for ♿. No smoking. No dogs. MasterCard, Visa accepted.
B&B £65–£95 per person. 1-night bookings sometimes refused Sat.

The Queensberry   *Tel* 01225-447928
4–7 Russel Street   *Fax* 01225-446065
Bath BA1 2QF   *Email* reservations@thequeensberry.co.uk
                         Website www.thequeensberry.co.uk

Visitors to this 'wonderfully located, very handsome' hotel this year found
it 'very comfortable and well run' with an 'easy-going atmosphere'. 'A
proper small town hotel,' was an inspector's earlier verdict. Composed of
four adjoining town houses, it is in a quiet residential street just off the
Circus (the centrepiece of Bath's Georgian architecture). It was designed
by John Wood for the Marquis of Queensberry in 1772. A glass roof and
white paint create a light feel, and a rabbit warren of corridors leads to
bedrooms of varying sizes. Owners Laurence and Helen Beere have
continued to redecorate the rooms to 'create a more contemporary style'.
Four terraced gardens, on different levels at the rear, have been replanted:
with their shrubs and garden furniture, they are 'nice for aperitifs in

summer'. In the *Olive Tree* restaurant, which occupies three rooms in the basement, staff are 'efficient and welcoming', but some guests find the muzak irritating. Marc Salmon is the chef, cooking in 'modern British' style. A visitor with dietary problems was willingly catered for. Light meals and a continental breakfast can be brought to the bedrooms. (*Nicholas Crace, EM Anderson, and others*)

29 bedrooms. Some on ground floor. Close to Assembly Rooms. Lift. 2 drawing rooms, bar, restaurant (background music); meeting room. 4 linked courtyard gardens. Unsuitable for &. No smoking: restaurant, bedrooms. Guide dogs only. Amex, MasterCard, Visa accepted. Room [2006] £110–£300. Breakfast £9.50–£14. Full alc £44.50. 1-night bookings refused weekends. ***V***

Tasburgh House	*Tel* 01225-425096
Warminster Road	*Fax* 01225-463842
Bath BA2 6SH	*Email* hotel@bathtasburgh.co.uk
	Website www.bathtasburgh.co.uk

In large grounds that slope down to the Kennet and Avon canal, this red brick Victorian house has panoramic views towards the city: the centre is a short walk away via the canal towpath, or a five-minute bus ride. The owner, Susan Keeling, is a dedicated gardener, and 'the chief glory of *Tasburgh House*', say inspectors, 'is its lovely grounds: a terrace with pots of flowers (where drinks can be served) leads to a lawn with elegant wooden tables and chairs, then a meadow with the odd urn or sculpture'. Charlie, the parrot in Reception, provides entertainment. Mirrors and chandeliers abound. The bedrooms, each named after an English author (Eliot, Dickens, etc), vary in size: some have a four-poster; all were recently renovated. 'Ours had attractive original watercolours, small shower room, amazingly generous storage space. All was immaculate. Breakfast included good home-made muesli, a vegetarian option, choice of eggs, kippers, etc.' Small groups and 'special occasions' (hen parties, etc) are catered for; dinner can be served to groups of six or more. Help is given with sight-seeing and dinner reservations. The house stands on a busy road, 'but once inside, we didn't notice the traffic'.

12 bedrooms. 2 on ground floor. On A36 to Warminster, ½ mile E of centre. Closed Christmas. Drawing room, dining room; background radio/music all day; conservatory; terrace. 7-acre grounds: canal walks, mooring. Unsuitable for &. No smoking. No dogs. Amex, MasterCard, Visa accepted. B&B £47.50–£70 per person. 1-night bookings refused Sat.

See also SHORTLIST

BATHFORD Somerset   Map 2:D1

Eagle House   BUDGET   *Tel* 01225-859946
Church Street   *Fax* 01225-859430
Bathford BA1 7RS   *Email* jonap@eagleho.demon.co.uk
                                                     Website www.eaglehouse.co.uk

'A little charmer, with a Jane Austen atmosphere', this listed Georgian
mansion is run as an informal and child-friendly B&B by its 'helpful
owners', John and Rosamund Napier. Bath city centre is easily reached
from the village by regular buses. There are toys and games in the
drawing room, and a large garden with croquet lawn, grass tennis court,
sandpit and tree house. The Napiers are pet-friendly too, and guests'
dogs are welcome by arrangement. 'Old furniture (good, but not too
smart) and family possessions are everywhere,' one guest wrote. The
handsome drawing room has a marble fireplace (log fires on winter
evenings) and a moulded ceiling. A curving staircase leads up from the
hall to some of the bedrooms; two others are in a cottage in the 'romantic'
garden. Glasses and ice are provided for guests who bring their own
drinks. Continental breakfast (yogurt, fruit, etc), served until 10 am, is
included in the price; for other items (eg, an egg), there is an extra charge.
(*A and M de P, BA*)

8 bedrooms. 2 in cottage with sitting room, kitchen, walled garden. 3 miles E of
Bath. Closed 16 Dec–8 Jan. Drawing room, breakfast room. No background music.
2-acre garden: tennis, croquet, sandpit, tree house, swings. Unsuitable for &. No
smoking: breakfast room, some bedrooms. Dogs by arrangement. MasterCard, Visa
accepted. B&B [2006] £27–£68 per person. Cooked breakfast £4.80. 1-night bookings
often refused Sat, bank holidays. ***V*** (not weekends)

BATTLE East Sussex *See SHORTLIST*   Map 2:E4

BEAMINSTER Dorset   Map 1:C6

The Bridge House   *Tel* 01308-862200
Prout Bridge   *Fax* 01308-863700
Beaminster DT8 3AY   *Email* enquiries@bridge-house.co.uk
                                                     Website www.bridge-house.co.uk

In an attractive old town, this small hotel/restaurant stands on a busy road
by a bridge but is backed by a large walled garden. Once a priest's house,
it has thick walls, mullioned windows, old beams and inglenook fireplaces.

Mark and Joanna Donovan (new to the hotel trade), who took it over in 2004, have continued with refurbishment. Public areas and the bedrooms have been redecorated; wireless broadband has been installed; smoking has been banned throughout. One visitor this year was enthusiastic. 'Our ground-floor bedroom had three comfortable chairs and reasonable storage. Helpful staff. Two good and interesting dinners.' Other guests had reservations about housekeeping, but would nevertheless return. Their bedroom, overlooking the garden, was 'bright, well furnished, spacious'; they thought the food 'excellent and good value', but felt that the restaurant staff were not adequately supervised. In the panelled dining room, with a conservatory extension, chef Linda Paget serves dishes 'rooted in Dorset produce', eg, seared West Bay scallops; medallions of organic pork with fresh figs. Breakfast and light lunches are taken in another conservatory; summer meals can be served in the garden. Tea is taken by a fire in winter. (*LM Mayer-Jones, and others*)

14 bedrooms. 5 in coach house. 5 on ground floor. 100 yards from centre. Train: Crewkerne, 8 miles. Restaurant closed Mon–Wed in winter. Hall/reception, lounge, bar, 2 conservatories, restaurant; patio. No background music. ¼-acre walled garden. Civil wedding licence. No smoking. No dogs in public rooms, or unattended in bedrooms. Amex, MasterCard, Visa accepted. B&B £64–£91 per person; D,B&B £94–£123. Set dinner £32.50; full alc £48. 2-night breaks. Winter discounts for returning guests. Christmas/New Year packages. 1-night bookings refused weekends and peak season.

BEAULIEU Hampshire *See SHORTLIST*   Map 2:E2

BEERCROCOMBE Somerset   Map 1:C5

Frog Street Farm   `BUDGET`   *Tel/Fax* 01823-480430
Beercrocombe, Taunton TA3 6AF

♛ *César award in 1988*

'Enthusiastically endorsed' by a reader who found last year's *Guide* entry 'spot on', Veronica and Henry Cole's small 15th-century house stands amid farm land in the Somerset countryside between Taunton and Ilminster. The 'delightful old building' has beamed ceilings, Jacobean panelling and inglenook fireplaces: 'At night there is absolute silence and the sky is unpolluted by city light,' say visitors. 'Mrs Cole's welcome was warm, her cooking first rate. We are vegetarians, and she produced excellent meals for us.' Other guests, who also met with a 'warm welcome', thought the house 'a bit shabby', and 'the surrounding farm buildings were derelict'. Dinner, by arrangement, at 7 pm, is generally at separate tables, but communal if guests choose. Mr Cole breeds steeplechasers (his horses can be seen in the fields around the house) and 'grows all the vegetables and fruit'. 'Our bedroom was comfortable and spotless,' said one couple. A double-aspect room was 'enormous, with an equally large bathroom'. The farm can be difficult to find: Mrs Cole will talk visitors in by mobile phone. (*PE Carter, and others*)

3 bedrooms. 4 miles NW of Ilminster. Open Apr–Oct. 2 lounges, dining room. No background music. 150-acre working farm: garden, trout stream. Unsuitable for &. No smoking. Children by arrangement; not under 11. No dogs. No credit cards. B&B £30–£40 per person. Set dinner £24. Reductions for 4 or more nights.

BELFORD Northumberland   Map 4:A3

Waren House   *Tel* 01668-214581
Waren Mill, Belford   *Fax* 01668-214484
NE70 7EE   *Email* enquiries@warenhousehotel.co.uk
                                Website www.warenhousehotel.co.uk

'Guests feel wanted' at Anita and Peter Laverack's Georgian house, which stands in wooded grounds above the natural birdlife sanctuary of Budle Bay. 'It is very comfortable,' say this year's visitors. 'Our suite, Rose, in a semi-detached cottage reached by a stone path, was delightful: fully carpeted, spacious.' Once owned by the third Lord Derwentwater, *Waren House* is just two miles from Bamburgh Castle and beach, and has good views towards Holy Island. The owners have decorated with enthusiasm, 'cramming the reception area with antique dolls; bits and pieces on any vacant surface. The walls of every room are covered with old oil paintings, watercolours and antique mirrors. The smoking area has heavy leather chairs which swallow anyone so unwise as to sit in them.' It is not to everyone's taste: a dissenter thought it 'too dark, too ornate, too many plates on the mantelpiece'. Drinks and 'lovely' canapés are served in the drawing room from 6.30 pm and, in the long, narrow dining room, dishes were 'skilfully cooked and attractively presented; we hadn't expected such good food'. (*Dr and Mrs G Collingham, RC, and others*)

13 bedrooms. 1 with & access. 15 miles SE of Berwick-upon-Tweed. Drawing room, library, dining room. 6-acre garden. Golf nearby. Smoking in library only. No children under 14. No dogs in public rooms. All major credit cards accepted. B&B £54–£96.50 per person; D,B&B (2 nights min.) £79.50–£126. Set dinner £31. Christmas/New Year packages. 1-night bookings sometimes refused weekends, public holidays.

BEPTON West Sussex   Map 2:E3

Park House   *Tel* 01730-819000
Bepton, nr Midhurst   *Fax* 01730-819099
GU29 0JB   *Email* reservations@parkhousehotel.com
                           Website www.parkhousehotel.com

In a recognised area of outstanding natural beauty (good walking, riding, etc), this Victorian house stands in well-maintained grounds in a sleepy village at the foot of the South Downs. It was recently extensively restored 'to the highest standards' by the O'Brien family owners (who turned it into a hotel in 1948), in traditional style, combining antique furniture and contemporary art. Seamus and Kate O'Brien run it with manager Rebecca Crowes. 'The atmosphere is relaxed, unfussy, with attentive, but not over-attentive, staff,' said one impressed visitor. 'Bedrooms are tastefully decorated, bathrooms luxurious in every respect.' The public rooms have 'just as tasteful decor, comfortable places to sit, a sense of warmth everywhere'. 'Fresh, wholesome food, with some contemporary options' is served in the dining room or a conservatory. Breakfast has a choice of five juices, 'inviting bowls of stewed fruit and muesli', home-made jams. A 'delightful' lounge overlooking the pretty terrace has an honesty bar and 'an unusually good selection of books'. Most bedrooms are spacious; some are in cottages in the garden. There is a small converted barn for conferences and functions. (*AB*)

15 bedrooms. Some in 2 cottages. 1 on ground floor. 2½ miles SW of Midhurst. Lounge, bar, dining room, conservatory. No background music. 9-acre grounds: tennis, croquet, heated 40-ft swimming pool, pitch-and-putt golf. Civil wedding licence. No smoking: dining room, bedrooms. MasterCard, Visa accepted. B&B [2006] double £125–£290; D,B&B £100–£175 per person. Set lunch £18, dinner £30. Winter breaks.

BERWICK-UPON-TWEED Northumberland Map 4:A3

No. 1 Sallyport   NEW   *Tel/Fax* 01289-308827
1 Sallyport   *Email* info@sallyport.co.uk
Berwick-upon-Tweed TD15 1EZ   *Website* www.sallyport.co.uk

Near the River Tweed and the medieval walls, this luxury B&B is a 17th-century Grade II listed town house with a contemporary decor. 'Quiet yet central', it stands down a cobbled lane once painted by LS Lowry. 'Lovely room, friendly service,' writes this year's nominator. The 'very good breakfast' (which includes kippers, waffles and kedgeree) is taken at a communal table in the kitchen, by a large stone fireplace. And an evening meal ('rustic French Provençal cooking') is available by arrangement. 'You can have your own personal chef to cook your requirements,' writes the 'effortlessly chic' owner, Elizabeth Middlemiss, who 'knows when to leave you in peace', according to another visitor. The three suites, each with its own lounge, have plasma TV, contemporary works of art, a big bed. Outdoor shoes are banned on the upper floors. (*Roger Down, and others*)

5 bedrooms. Central. Garage, car park. Kitchen/breakfast room. Patio. Background radio/CDs. Unsuitable for &. No smoking. MasterCard, Visa accepted. B&B £60–£70 per person. Set dinner £35 (bring your own wine: £3 corkage). Christmas/ New Year packages. 1-night bookings refused at weekends. ***V***

West Coates   **NEW**   *Tel/Fax* 01289-309666
30 Castle Terrace   *Email* karenbrownwestcoates@yahoo.com
Berwick-upon-Tweed TD15 1NZ   *Website* www.westcoates.co.uk

Set in a mature garden in this interesting border town, Karen Brown's 'superb small establishment' is warmly recommended: 'Beautifully furnished bedrooms, with everything one could want, including home-made cake on the hospitality tray each day. Wonderful breakfast (smoked salmon and scrambled eggs, porridge, yogurt, etc).' Mrs Brown, who also runs a cookery school, is 'an accomplished cook'. The no-choice four-course dinners are thought 'fabulous' (eg, langoustines with herb butter; duck with caramelised oranges). And 'the Brown family are lovely, friendly people'. The indoor swimming pool is also appreciated. (*Susan Kettell*)

3 bedrooms. 10 mins' walk from centre. Parking. Closed Christmas/New Year. Sitting/dining room (background music at mealtimes). 40-ft indoor swimming pool; hot tub. 2½-acre garden: croquet. Unsuitable for &. No smoking. No dogs in house. MasterCard, Visa accepted. B&B from £50 per person; D,B&B from £85. ***V***

See also SHORTLIST

BIBURY Gloucestershire   Map 3:E6

Bibury Court   *Tel* 01285-740337
Bibury   *Fax* 01285-740660
nr Cirencester GL7 5NT   *Email* info@biburycourt.com
                                   Website www.biburycourt.com

In a famous Cotswolds village, this impressive manor house (part Tudor, mainly 17th-century) stands in large, beautiful grounds on the River

Coln. 'It is full of character; a little fading, but this adds to the charm.' In October 2005, Robert Johnston, with his business partner Sam Pearman, took it over from his parents. 'They are working very hard,' reports a returning visitor. 'The service is excellent.' Other visitors praise the 'welcoming and helpful staff', and the 'very good' cooking of the new chef, Antony Ely. In the small, 'rather dark' restaurant and the 'lovely' conservatory, he serves 'traditionally English' dishes, eg, warm salad of wood pigeon; crisp roast Bibury trout. 'A little rich,' was another comment. Afternoon tea can be taken in the drawing room, or on the terrace in the summer. Many bedrooms have a four-poster; some have a large Victorian bath. 'Our large double room looked out over the front lawn to the Coln valley beyond.' Other rooms have views of the gardens and a part-Saxon church. (*BA and P Orman, Dr and Mrs James Stewart, Diane Moss*)

18 bedrooms. 1 on ground floor. Village centre, behind church. Lounge, bar, restaurant, conservatory, billiard room. No background music. 6-acre grounds. On River Coln (fishing). Civil wedding licence. Unsuitable for &. No smoking: restaurant, conservatory. All major credit cards accepted. B&B £62.50–£125 per person; D,B&B £90–£150. Set dinner £35. Christmas/New Year packages. 1-night bookings sometimes refused weekends. *V*

BIDEFORD Devon   Map 1:C4

The Mount   NEW/BUDGET   *Tel* 01237-473748
Northdown Road   *Fax* 01237-373813
Bideford EX39 3LP   *Email* andrew@themountbideford.fsnet.co.uk
                        Website www.themount1.cjb.net

'Well run, spotless', and with 'very friendly' proprietors, Andrew and Heather Laugharne, this Georgian guest house, fronted by creepers and plants in pots, is a short walk from the centre and the River Torrington. Inside are bright colours: red walls to the staircase, pink in the lounge which has an open fire and a licence to sell alcohol, blue in the room where the 'excellent breakfasts' are served. 'The bedrooms are tastefully furnished, and the beds are large and comfortable,' says one of many regular visitors. And guests have access to a pretty garden. Discounts are available at the Royal North Devon Golf Club. (*Judith Ross, Pat Goddard, Wendy Snell*)

8 bedrooms. Some family. 1 on ground floor. 5 mins' walk from centre. Parking. Train: Barnstaple. Closed Christmas. Lounge, breakfast room; background music 'as the mood suits me'. Walled garden. No smoking. No dogs. Amex, MasterCard, Visa accepted. B&B £31–£35 per person.

BIGBURY-ON-SEA Devon   Map 1:D4

The Henley   *Tel/Fax* 01548-810240
Folly Hill   *Email* enquiries@thehenleyhotel.co.uk
Bigbury-on-Sea TQ7 4AR   *Website* www.thehenleyhotel.co.uk

Q *César award in 2003*

'Still one of our favourite spots for food, location, relaxation,' say returning
guests to this small, unpretentious hotel on a cliff above the tidal Avon
estuary ('great views'). 'Charming atmosphere; an idyllic place,' was another
comment. Martyn Scarterfield and Petra Lampe, now married, are owner/
managers: he the chef, she front-of-house. Guests gather in the lounge at
7 pm for drinks while she recites the short menu. His cooking is thought
'excellent'. 'The choice is small, between two dishes, but you always want
to eat both': perhaps Gruyère-glazed fillet beef with Provençal sauce, or
roast monkfish with king prawns, garlic and butter sauce. Bedrooms are
'spick and span': another has been revamped. Some bathrooms may be
small, but all have 'fluffy towels'. The public rooms have dark red walls,
well-polished old furniture, Lloyd Loom chairs. Books, magazines and
binoculars are provided. At breakfast, 'you are asked when you want toast.
Good coffee and tea, replenished when you wish; excellent bacon and
sausages.' The 'delightfully unfussy' garden, 'quite spectacularly precipi-
tous', has 'many sheltered nooks with seating'. A black Labrador, Kasper,
'adds to the fun'. Guests' dogs are welcomed. (*Stephen and Jane Savery,
Jennifer and Colin Beales, Mrs G Smith, E Lake*)

6 bedrooms. 5 miles S of Modbury. Open Mar–Oct. 2 lounges, bar, conservatory
dining room; jazz/classical background music at night. Small garden; steps to beach.
Golf, sailing, fishing, Coastal Path nearby. Unsuitable for &. No smoking. No
children under 12. No dogs in public rooms. MasterCard, Visa accepted. B&B [2006]
£45–£62 per person; D,B&B (4 nights or more) £73–£90. Light lunch available. Set
dinner £28. Off-season reductions. 1-night bookings sometimes refused at weekends.

BIGGIN-BY-HARTINGTON Derbyshire   Map 3:B6

Biggin Hall   **BUDGET**   *Tel* 01298-84451
Biggin-by-Hartington   *Fax* 01298-84681
Buxton SK17 0DH   *Email* enquiries@bigginhall.co.uk
                                Website www.bigginhall.co.uk

High in the Peak District national park, this unpretentious small hotel is
'ideal for walkers': close by are 'footpaths in all directions over beautiful
countryside'. One path starts at the side of the house; disused railway tracks

provide flat walking. Owned by James Moffett, the 17th-century Grade II* listed building has antiques, narrow mullioned windows and 'a marvellous fire in the living room'. A recent visitor liked her bedroom in a barn conversion; it had 'a porch for hanging outdoor clothes, a small settee and a large bed'. Other rooms, including the master suite (with beams and a four-poster), are in the main house, where 'the welcome is warm, and the seating encourages a friendly atmosphere'. Mark Wilton's 'traditional English' cooking is hearty, eg, roast pork with apple and stuffing stacks; Bakewell tart. The 'very good cheeseboard and home-made rolls' are also enjoyed. The continental breakfast has self-service cereals, home-made croissants, DIY toast. A cooked version is available for an extra £3.80, and a 'decent' packed lunch can be had from £2.50. The winter 'Icebreaker Special' includes a full English breakfast with porridge; and Glühwein in the evening. More reports, please.

20 bedrooms. 12 in annexes. Some on ground floor. 8 miles N of Ashbourne. Sitting room, library, dining room (classical background music); meeting room. 7-acre grounds: croquet. River Dove 1½ miles. Unsuitable for &. No smoking. No children under 12. No dogs in main house. Amex, MasterCard, Visa accepted. B&B [2006] £35–£80 per person; D,B&B £47–£92. English breakfast £3.80. Set dinner £18.50. Christmas/New Year packages. 1-night bookings sometimes refused. *V*

BIRMINGHAM West Midlands   Map 2:B2

Copperfield House   BUDGET   *Tel* 0121-472 8344
60 Upland Road, Selly Park   *Fax* 0121-415 5655
Birmingham B29 7JS   *Email* info@copperfieldhousehotel.fsnet.co.uk
     Website www.copperfieldhousehotel.fsnet.co.uk

An imposing red brick Victorian house, now a 'warm, comfortable' hotel, in secluded, mature grounds in a residential area south-west of the centre. The owner, Jeremy Thomas, is 'a mine of local information', according to regular visitors. A classically trained chef, he oversees the kitchen. His wife, Daphne, 'an excellent hostess with an astonishing memory', supervises breakfast ('fresh juices and fruit, tasty full English'). The lounge has an honour bar. 'Friendly staff made me feel at home; my room was warm and quiet,' was one comment. Some bedrooms have garden views, and those at the front now have double glazing. The daily-changing dinner menu was 'short and predictable, but much more interesting than I expected, particularly good steak; delicious house wine – the list is reasonably priced'. Vegetarians are catered for. One guest was put out to be told on arrival that his dinner would be brought to his bedroom as the dining room was fully booked for a celebration: 'It was nicely presented, but a complimentary glass of wine would have inclined me to feel more charitable.' The university is near, also the BBC Pebble Mill studios ('staying at *Copperfield House* you might at times feel you were in the cast of *The Archers*').

17 bedrooms. Some on ground floor. 2 miles SW of centre. Closed 24 Dec–2 Jan. Restaurant closed Sat/Sun. Ramp. Lounge, bar, restaurant; background music at night. Garden. No smoking and no dogs in restaurant. Amex, MasterCard, Visa accepted. B&B £32.50–£79.50 per person. Full alc £28.

Hotel du Vin & Bistro
25 Church Street
Birmingham B3 2NR

Tel 0121-200 0600
Fax 0121-236 0889
Email info@birmingham.hotelduvin.com
Website www.hotelduvin.com

In the revitalised jewellery quarter, close to shops, waterways, art galleries and theatres, this is the largest of the Hotel du Vin group, an ornate early Victorian building, formerly the Birmingham eye hospital. The imposing entrance has giant pillars, *trompe l'œil* stonework and a ceiling fresco. Inside, original features include a magnificent sweeping staircase and granite pillars. The 'Bubble Lounge' has plump sofas and a choice of 50 champagnes; the basement bar has leather seating and jazz. The bedrooms, each sponsored by a wine producer, are on five floors around a central courtyard. All have air conditioning, Egyptian cotton sheets, CD-player, etc. Colours tend to be greys and beige. A report in 2006, following the arrival of the new manager, Mark Huntley, is enthusiastic. 'Staff, a mix of local, French and middle European, were friendly, efficient. Huge bedroom, huge bathroom with superb power shower.' Some rooms get noise (lift, kitchen fans and so on). The 'relaxed' bistro has wooden floors and tables, and a menu with a Mediterranean bias: the food is thought 'interesting, properly cooked, good value'. The 'formidable' wine list, mainly French, 'has few bottles under £20', but it includes 'great delights'. 'Breakfasts, both continental and cooked, were substantial.' (*John Crisp, and others*)

66 bedrooms. 5 suitable for &. Central, near St Philip's Cathedral (quietest rooms face courtyard). Valet parking (£10 a night). Ramp, lift. Bistro, 2 bars ('chill-out' music in cellar bar at night); billiard room; spa; courtyard. Civil wedding licence. No smoking: bistro, some bedrooms. Guide dogs only. Amex, MasterCard, Visa accepted. Room [2006]: single/double £135–£165, suite £205–£375. Breakfast £9.50–£13.50. Full alc £30. Spa breaks. Christmas/New Year packages.

Hotels will often try to persuade you to stay for two nights at the weekend. Resist this pressure if you want to stay only one night.

Simpsons   NEW

20 Highfield Road, Edgbaston
Birmingham B15 3DU

Tel 0121-454 3434
Fax 0121-454 3399
Email info@simpsonsrestaurant.co.uk
Website www.simpsonsrestaurant.co.uk

Birmingham has two *Michelin*-starred restaurants (*Jessica's* is the other). This one, a converted Georgian mansion in a leafy suburb, has four bedrooms and is admired for the cooking, 'based on classic French principles', of chefs/*patrons* Andreas Antona and Luke Tipping. 'It is superb,' says a visitor in 2006. 'I arrived tired and late to be met by Alison Antona. She greeted me and sent a glass of wine to my room. Just what I needed. It set the tone for the rest of my stay.' The bedrooms are themed: French (the best: plaster mouldings, hand-painted cream and gold French furniture), Venetian (antique bed, lots of velvet, reds and golds), Oriental (silk-lined, with dark lacquered furniture), Colonial (browns and beige, dark wood furniture). Bathrooms are 'bright'. In a series of dining rooms, the atmosphere is 'relaxed', the waiters are efficient, and the menus include fillet of halibut, asparagus risotto, sevruga caviar cream; pot-roast rabbit, crispy ravioli, dried fruit, fennel, chicory jus. The petits-fours trolley is 'laden with treats like chocolate lollipops'. There are menus for children and vegetarians. Drinks are served in an orangery that faces the secluded garden, and in summer you can dine alfresco. (*Kelvin Juba*)

4 bedrooms. 1 mile from centre. Closed bank holidays. Lounge, restaurant; private dining room; cookery school. No background music. Garden (alfresco dining). No smoking: restaurant, bedrooms. Guide dogs only. Amex, MasterCard, Visa accepted. B&B double £160–£225. Set menus £27.50–£30; full alc £65.

See also SHORTLIST

BISHOP'S TAWTON Devon   Map 1:C4

Halmpstone Manor

Bishop's Tawton
nr Barnstaple EX32 0EA

Tel 01271-830321
Fax 01271-830826
Email charles@halmpstonemanor.co.uk
Website www.halmpstonemanor.co.uk

'Everything that a small country hotel should be; comfortable accommodation, good food and friendly proprietors.' A warm endorsement for Charles and Jane Stanbury's manor house in the garden of a working farm in north Devon. 'The house is beautifully furnished, as are the well-equipped bedrooms.' 'Our room had a good-size bathroom, lots of extras, such as sherry, fruit and bottled water', and 'additional heaters are available if required'. Views are 'magnificent, looking south towards Dartmoor where Hay Tor can be seen on the horizon'. Help with luggage is offered to arriving guests to whom complimentary tea with cake is served in the 'relaxing' lounge. There are log fires, deep sofas, 'flowers and family photos everywhere'. The four-course dinner (by arrangement only), served in a 'lovely wood-panelled room', is thought 'good – starters and sweets particularly'. No choice until dessert, but 'you are consulted at breakfast about likes and dislikes'. 'Splendid breakfasts, especially the porridge, made with plentiful cream.' You need a car to visit the nearby attractions. (*SP, and others*)

4 bedrooms. 4 miles SE of Barnstaple. Open 1 Mar–20 Dec. Lounge, bar, dining room. No background music. ½-acre garden. Unsuitable for &. No smoking: dining room, lounge, some bedrooms. No dogs in restaurant. MasterCard, Visa accepted. B&B [2006] £50–£70 per person. Set dinner £30.

BLACKBURN Lancashire *See SHORTLIST*   Map 4:D3

BLACKPOOL Lancashire   Map 4:D2

Raffles Hotel & Tea Room   BUDGET   *Tel* 01253-294713
73–77 Hornby Road, Blackpool   *Fax* 01253-294240
FY1 4QJ   *Email* enquiries@raffleshotelblackpool.fsworld.co.uk
Website www.raffleshotelblackpool.co.uk

Within walking distance of all of Blackpool's sights, this small, flower-fronted, bay-windowed hotel is thought 'quirky, friendly, and superb value for money'. The owners, Ian Balmforth (the chef) and Graham Poole, are 'amazingly cheery, helpful hosts', providing 'down-to-earth service'. Furnishings are 'of the highest quality'; bedroom lighting is 'brilliant'; housekeeping is 'exemplary'. 'My double room, though small, lacked nothing; every square inch was put to good use,' one visitor wrote. From 11 am to 6 pm, the traditional English tea room next door serves teas with home-made cakes, toasties, sandwiches, soups, jacket potatoes and hot dishes like liver and onions, fried scampi or beef chilli. Breakfast is 'well cooked and presented'. More reports, please.

19 bedrooms. 2 on ground floor. Central. Tea room closed Mon, and weekdays in winter. No telephone. Ramp. Lounge, bar, tea room; background music all day. Sea, safe bathing 200 yds. No smoking: tea room, some bedrooms. No dogs in public rooms. MasterCard, Visa accepted. B&B [2006] £28–£65 per person. Christmas/ New Year packages. 1-night bookings refused high-season bank holidays.

See also SHORTLIST

BLAKENEY Norfolk   Map 2:A5

The Blakeney Hotel   *Tel* 01263-740797
Blakeney   *Fax* 01263-740795
nr Holt NR25 7NE   *Email* reception@blakeney-hotel.co.uk
                                     Website www.blakeney-hotel.co.uk

A large, traditional hotel in this north Norfolk holiday village; it is popular with families and, off-season, retired couples. 'We had a lovely few days here in the summer,' reports a regular *Guide* correspondent. Another visitor wrote: 'I found the staff most obliging, polite and helpful; the accommodation was satisfactory, the food good.' Owned by Michael Stannard, the hotel stands above the National Trust harbour. The bar and the first-floor sun lounge look across the estuary and salt marshes to Blakeney Point as do many bedrooms: others have garden views. This year, six bedrooms have been added in the granary annexe; 21 bedrooms have been refurbished. The swimming pool will remain open through the winter of 2006/7 during refurbishment. Light lunches are served on weekdays; there is a choice of roasts on Sunday. Wines are 'fairly priced'. Local smoked kippers appear at the 'excellent' breakfast. Rooms in a modern annexe have a patio overlooking the garden. Six rooms in the main building are being refurnished this year. (*Minda Alexander, Trevor Lee, and others*)

64 bedrooms. 16 in annexe opposite. Some on ground floor. On quay. Lift, ramps. Lounge, sun lounge, bar, restaurant; function facilities; indoor swimming pool (37 by 17 ft), spa bath, sauna, mini-gym; games room. No background music. ¼-acre garden: table tennis, swings. Sailing, fishing, water sports, golf, tennis nearby. Smoking in bar only. No dogs in public rooms, some bedrooms. All major credit cards accepted. B&B £77–£129 per person; D,B&B (min. 2 nights) £84–£142. Set dinner £22.50; full alc £40. Christmas/New Year packages. 1-night bookings usually refused Fri/Sat.

If you dislike piped music, why not join Pipedown, the campaign for freedom from piped music? They can be reached at 1 The Row, Berwick St James, Salisbury SP3 4TP. *Tel:* 01722-790622, www.pipedown.info.

BORROWDALE Cumbria   Map 4: inset C2

The Leathes Head Hotel
Borrowdale
Keswick CA12 5UY

Tel 017687-77247
Fax 017687-77363
Email enq@leatheshead.co.uk
Website www.leatheshead.co.uk

'A well-run hotel, run by hard-working owners.' Set back from the road in spacious gardens, Roy and Janice Smith's gabled Edwardian house stands high up in wooded grounds outside Borrowdale. With 'lovely views of the valley', it is popular with serious walkers and climbers. The house is furnished in keeping with its age; stained glass, old fireplaces and plasterwork are retained. Tea and drinks are served in a sunroom with wicker armchairs: it overlooks the garden and has a powerful telescope. 'Wheelchair access is excellent throughout the ground floor and garden.' Three bedrooms have been redecorated this year. 'Ours was not large, but more than adequate and with a good view. It's worth paying extra for a superior room.' Dinner (four courses with choice for each), prepared by David Jackson, is mostly praised, though one visitor would have liked more vegetables. 'Quite ambitious now.' 'Amazing.' 'Food puts this hotel a cut above many others.' The packed lunches are warmly recommended. Breakfast ranges from healthy to full English: 'Must be one of the best anywhere.' Guests have access, for a small fee, to a nearby leisure club. (*MC and GR Bradshaw, S Finch, CL Hodgkin, Frank G Millen*)

12 bedrooms. 3 on ground floor. 1 suitable for &. 3½ miles S of Keswick. Open mid-Feb–end Nov. Ramp. Lounge, sun lounge, bar lounge, restaurant (light classical background music at night). 3-acre grounds: sun terrace, woodland. Temporary membership of leisure club. No smoking. No children under 9. No dogs. MasterCard, Visa accepted. D,B&B £58.95–£85.95 per person. Set dinner £30. 1-night bookings sometimes refused. ***V***

Seatoller House   **BUDGET**
Borrowdale
Keswick CA12 5XN

Tel 017687-77218
Fax 017687-77189
Email seatollerhouse@btconnect.com
Website www.seatollerhouse.co.uk

At the head of the beautiful Borrowdale valley, this 350-year-old building is an unpretentious guest house, popular with hikers and ramblers. It is owned by a private company, The Lake Hunts Ltd; Daniel Potts and Lynne Moorehouse have been managers since 2004. Recent praise from frequent visitors: 'They have raised standards to new heights of comfort, cuisine, and warmth of welcome. No request, however bizarre, is beyond them.' The homely atmosphere is liked: oak panelling, creaky floorboards, cosy chairs, cushioned window seats and a piano in the sitting room. Non-stop coffee is available in the tea bar (it can also be taken out in flasks); there is an honesty bar, and a self-help fridge. Lynne Moorehouse serves a no-choice menu at 7 pm at communal oak tables; her style is traditional 'with a twist', eg, garlic-stuffed mushrooms; pork fillet with apple, walnut and smoked cheese stuffing. On Tuesday a light supper of soup, bread and cheese is substituted. Breakfast, between 8 and 8.30 am, is hearty. The simple bedrooms are warm in cold weather; all have private facilities, though some are not *en suite*. (*S and GW*)

10 bedrooms. 2 on ground floor. 1 in garden bungalow. All with shower. On B5289, 8 miles S of Keswick. Train: Penrith; regular buses. Open 9 Mar–25 Nov. Dining room closed midday. Lounge, library, tea bar, dining room; drying room. No background music. ¾-acre grounds: beck. Unsuitable for &. No smoking. No children under 5 (unless full-house booking). No dogs in public rooms. MasterCard, Visa accepted. B&B £38–£49 per person; D,B&B £48–£59. Set dinner £17. Reductions for longer stays. 1-night bookings refused Fri/Sat.

BOSCASTLE Cornwall   Map 1:C3

The Old Rectory   *Tel/Fax* 01840-250225
St Juliot, nr Boscastle   *Email* sally@stjuliot.com
PL35 0BT   *Website* www.stjuliot.com

The writer Thomas Hardy, an architect at the time, met Emma Gifford at this house in March 1870; they fell in love and were married in 1874. The rectory was later immortalised in Hardy's novel *A Pair of Blue Eyes*. Now it is the family home of Chris and Sally Searle, who run it as a B&B. Fairtrade tea and coffee, free-range eggs and locally produced bacon and sausage appear at breakfast; the rest of the menu changes with the seasons as the 'warmly welcoming' owners select 'the best produce we have in the garden'. In August this might be home-grown peaches, loganberries and goose-berries. The conservatory described by the novelist still stands, and Mr Hardy's, which has an antique carved double bed, is one of the three bedrooms in the house. Two rooms share a bathroom; the third has a shower and the original thunderbox loo. There is also a double room, with a wood stove, in 'wonderfully restored' stables. Guest have their own sitting room. More reports, please.

4 bedrooms. 1 in stables (linked to house). 2 miles NE of Boscastle. Open March–Nov. Sitting room, breakfast room. No background music. 3-acre garden:

croquet lawn, 'lookout'. Unsuitable for ♿. No smoking. No children under 12. Dogs in stable room only (£6 per stay). MasterCard, Visa accepted. B&B [2006] £30–£54 per person. 1-night bookings sometimes refused weekends, bank holidays.

See also SHORTLIST

BOSHAM West Sussex   Map 2:E3

The Millstream	*Tel* 01243-573234
Bosham Lane	*Fax* 01243-573459
Bosham, nr Chichester	*Email* info@millstream-hotel.co.uk
PO18 8HL	*Website* www.millstream-hotel.co.uk

'One of a handful of hotels to which I return every year; it goes from strength to strength,' writes one fan of this converted small manor house and 18th-century malt house cottage. 'A most comfortable haven', it is 'seriously pretty outside', with manicured gardens, the eponymous mill-stream and a gazebo. The general manager, Antony Wallace, has run it for many years and achieves a 'consistent standard of service', with his 'hard-working staff'. 'As soon as you arrive, you feel relaxed.' 'We were enthusiastically welcomed with a glass of sherry.' The public rooms are pleasant and spacious. But one visitor complained of 'too much, too loud muzak'. Bedrooms, with conventional decor, vary in size and have 'thoughtful details' (ironing board, CD-player, flat-screen TV, etc). The previously criticised noisy fridges have been replaced with new, silent models, and Room 19 has been enlarged, following a *Guide* comment that it was 'poky'. Food and service in the restaurant are thought 'excellent': the chef, Bev Boakes, produces 'well-varied' menus, with plenty of choice: 'Chicken breast stuffed with herb mousse was full of flavour and beautifully prepared. High standards maintained at breakfast – not always the case elsewhere. And of course the location must be mentioned: the tidal creek at Bosham and the whole Chichester harbour area to explore.' Guests attending the Chichester theatre can have an early supper. (*Mrs JR Parker, HJM Tucker, and others*)

35 bedrooms. 2 in cottage. 7 on ground floor, 1 equipped for ♿. 4 miles W of Chichester. Lounge (pianist Fri and Sat evenings), bar, restaurant (2 parts); classical background music 10.30 am–10.30 pm; conference room. 1½-acre garden: stream, gazebo. Chichester Harbour (sailing, fishing) 300 yards. Civil wedding licence. No smoking. Guide dogs only. All major credit cards accepted. B&B [2006] £69–£104 per person; D,B&B (min. 2 nights) £79–£124. Set lunch £20, dinner £29. Christmas/New Year packages. 1-night bookings refused Sat.

BOURNEMOUTH Dorset *See SHORTLIST*   Map 2:E2

BOURTON-ON-THE-WATER   Map 3:D6
Gloucestershire

Dial House NEW	*Tel* 01451-822244
High Street	*Fax* 01451-810126
Bourton-on-the-Water GL54 2AW	*Email* info@dialhousehotel.com
	Website www.dialhousehotel.com

In a very pretty, if touristy, small Cotswold town on the River Windrush, Jane and Adrian Campbell-Howard have turned their 17th-century house (complete with beams, inglenook fireplaces and monks' chairs) into a sophisticated small hotel. Our inspectors found much to admire: 'Lovely atmosphere in the main house (but intrusive muzak); keen young waiters; smartly presented food with well-judged portions (slow-cooked lamb with delicious couscous); first-rate breakfast served at table. Garden a delightful retreat. Our coach-house room (reasonably sized; huge bed; French grey trimmings) faced the car park but was quiet.' 'Good value in a pricey region' was another verdict. The best bedrooms are in the main house (one has an oak four-poster). A single, though very small, was thought well designed. For computer buffs, there is 'access to state-of-the-art communications links'.

13 bedrooms. 5 in coach house. Town centre. Car park. Train: Kingham. Lounge, 2 dining rooms (background music always). 1-acre garden. No smoking. No children under 12. All major credit cards accepted. B&B £45–£110 per person; D,B&B £70–£135. Full alc £42. Christmas/New Year packages. 1-night bookings refused weekends. *V*

The *V* sign at the end of an entry indicates a hotel that has agreed to take part in our Voucher scheme and to give *Guide* readers a 25% discount on their room rates for a one-night stay, subject to the conditions explained on page 60 and listed on the back of the vouchers.

BOWNESS-ON-WINDERMERE   Map 4: inset C2
Cumbria

Fayrer Garden House	*Tel* 015394-88195
Lyth Valley Road	*Fax* 015394-45986
Bowness-on-Windermere	*Email* lakescene@fayrergarden.com
LA23 3JP	*Website* www.fayrergarden.com

Since arriving in 2004, Claire and Eric Wildsmith have carried out a major refurbishment of this extended Edwardian house. Its manager is Mark Jones. Set in large grounds half a mile above Lake Windermere, it has superb views of lake and mountain: one lounge, the dining room, the spacious terrace and some bedrooms face the water. The long-serving head chef, Eddie Wilkinson, serves modern English dishes based on local produce, eg, chicken supreme on a leek and wild mushroom tart with Madeira sauce. 'The hotel has been much improved by the extension of the lounge area. The cuisine was as good as ever, and service was excellent,' wrote one returning visitor. Other praise: 'We were pampered. Staff were delightful. Amenities very good. We never saw cleaners, but each day after breakfast we returned to our room to find that it had been serviced. The owners joined their guests for dinner and mingled throughout the evening.' (*Trevor Lee, Derek Penkeith*)

29 bedrooms. 5 in cottage. 1 on ground floor. 1 mile S of Bowness on A5074. Closed 1st 2 weeks Jan. 2 lounges, lounge bar (background music), restaurant. 5-acre grounds. Civil wedding licence. No smoking. No children under 5. No dogs in public rooms. MasterCard, Visa accepted. D,B&B £73–£140 per person. Christmas/New Year packages. 1-night bookings sometimes refused Sat.

Lindeth Fell	*Tel* 015394-43286
Lyth Valley Road	*Fax* 015394-47455
Bowness-on-Windermere	*Email* kennedy@lindethfell.co.uk
LA23 3JP	*Website* www.lindethfell.co.uk

At the top of a tree-lined drive, on hills above Lake Windermere, this Edwardian house, owned by Pat and Diana Kennedy, has superb views over the water. The 'extensive, well-tended' gardens, filled with rhododendrons, azaleas and specimen trees, are open to the public in spring and early summer. The hotel is traditional, 'unpretentious but gracious, with just the right blend of formality and informality', say visitors this year. 'Mrs Kennedy made me and two young grandsons so welcome, and put us in a large, well-equipped family room.' Another comment: 'Single guests in hotels are sometimes ignored, but not here.' The dining rooms and one lounge have 'stunning' views of the lake. There are patterned carpets in public areas, log fires, watercolours, bric-a-brac, books and magazines in the spacious lounges; flowery or patterned fabrics and wallpaper in the bedrooms. 'Our bed was large and comfortable; washbasin in the room, shower/WC *en suite*.' Cooking, by chef Philip Taylor, is in the modern English style (eg, baked cod with a tomato and basil sauce; savoury mushroom risotto) and the four-course menu changes daily. On warm days, tea and drinks are served on a terrace. (*Robert Gower, Dorothy Brining, and others*)

14 bedrooms. 1 on ground floor. 1 mile S of Bowness on A5074. Closed 3 weeks Jan. Ramp. Hall, 2 lounges, dispense bar, 3 dining rooms. No background music. 7-acre grounds: gardens, croquet, putting, bowls, tarn. Fishing permits. Smoking in 1 lounge only. No dogs. MasterCard, Visa accepted. B&B [2006] £40–£80 per person; D,B&B £65–£105. Set dinner £35. Christmas/New Year packages. 1-night bookings sometimes refused Sat. *V*

Linthwaite House

Crook Road
Bowness-on-Windermere
LA23 3JA

Tel 015394-88600
Fax 015394-88601
Email stay@linthwaite.com
Website www.linthwaite.com

In a superb location, looking across landscaped grounds towards Lake Windermere, Mike Bevans's timbered, creeper-covered white and stone house was enjoyed again by *Guide* readers. 'Our stay was really good, despite poor weather. We were warmly welcomed by staff, and had a room with a fabulous view.' 'Mr Bevans spends a great deal of time making sure all is running smoothly.' The public rooms, 'warm and welcoming', have an Edwardian decor, with oriental rugs, potted plants, cabin trunks and memorabilia. A new, enclosed veranda with lake views opened in 2006. The bedrooms vary greatly: rooms 14 and 15 (each with king-size bed and lake views) have been admired. 'Ours was on the small side, but well equipped; cleanliness was faultless. Superb scenery.' The chef, Simon Bolsover, offers six choices for each of the four courses ('all beautifully presented') on his modern menu (eg, line-caught sea bass and scallop with smoked tomato ratatouille). 'Desserts were to die for.' Guests may fish in a tarn in the grounds. (*JH, CB*)

27 bedrooms. Some on ground floor. ¾ mile S of Bowness off B5284. Ramp. Lounge/bar, conservatory, 2 dining rooms; background music. 14-acre grounds: croquet, tarn (fly-fishing). Civil wedding licence. No smoking. No children under 7 at dinner. Dogs in grounds only (kennels), except guide dogs. Amex, MasterCard, Visa accepted. B&B £75–£157 per person; D,B&B £89–£180. Set dinner £46. Christmas/New Year/Easter packages. 1-night bookings refused weekends, bank holidays. *V*

BRADFORD-ON-AVON Wiltshire   Map 2:D1

Woolley Grange	*Tel* 01225-864705
Woolley Green	*Fax* 01225-864059
Bradford-on-Avon	*Email* info@woolleygrangehotel.com
BA15 1TX	*Website* www.luxuryfamilyhotels.com

The accent at this Jacobean stone manor, in big grounds on the edge of the medieval wool town, is on keeping children busy while their parents relax. It is part of the Luxury Family Hotels group, which was bought by von Essen Hotels in December 2005. Clare Hammond stays on as manager, and Adie Ware has been promoted to head chef. We received mixed reports this year while the sale was taking place ('a good atmosphere, though with an underlying sense of chaos just around the corner'; 'excellent facilities for children; dreary food'). The ethos is unchanged: guests pay by the room, sharing with as many children as they can tolerate. The very young are catered for in the Woolley Bears' Den; older children have the run of the Hen House (with games galore). Children take high tea, while their parents enjoy a candlelit dinner. We would welcome reports on *Woolley Grange*, and the other group members, *Fowey Hall*, Fowey, and *Moonfleet Manor*, Fleet (*qqv*). (*GH, and others*)

26 bedrooms. 9 in courtyard, 3 in pavilion in grounds. 1 on ground floor. 1 mile NE of Bradford-on-Avon on B3105. Train: Bath/Bradford-on-Avon/Chippenham. Ramps. 2 lounges, TV room, 2 restaurants, dispense bar, conservatory; children's nursery, games rooms. No background music. 14-acre grounds: heated swimming pool (40 by 20 ft), tennis, badminton, croquet, children's play area. Cycling, riding, golf, fishing, hot-air ballooning nearby. No smoking in restaurant. All major credit cards accepted. B&B [2006]: single £95–£125, double £120–£160, suite £200–£245; D,B&B £85–£212.50 per person. Light meals available. Full alc £45. Winter/7-night breaks. Midweek breaks. Gardening/cookery weeks for children. Christmas/New Year packages. 1-night bookings refused weekends.

BRADPOLE Dorset   Map 1:C6

Orchard Barn	**NEW**	*Tel/Fax* 01308-455655
Bradpole		*Email* reservations@lodgeatorchardbarn.co.uk
nr Bridport DT6 4AR		*Website* www.lodgeatorchardbarn.co.uk

Nigel and Margaret Corbett, who for many years ran the much-loved *Summer Lodge*, Evershot, now own and run this small B&B (it will have a third bedroom in 2007). Built on the site of an old Dorset farm, it stands in an apple orchard. The River Asker runs by (you might spot a kingfisher or trout). 'Delightful. We could not have been better cared for,' says the nominator. 'Margaret does the cooking. Nigel looks after front-of-house with tremendous zest. The comfortable bedrooms are simple, but with everything one needs: fine linen, no awful captive coat-hangers, good lighting, bottled water, tea/coffee facilities and home-made shortcake. Above all warm: temperature controlled from the room.' The guest lounge has a log fire and gallery. There are 'flowers everywhere', and a collection of cheese dishes. Home-made marmalade and jams appear at the 'five-star' breakfast which also includes 'extra-large glasses of orange juice', free-range eggs in many forms, local bacon and sausages, 'delicious and unusual yogurts' and organic wholemeal toast. A snack supper is available, served in the lounge and ranging from a tureen of soup to quiches and salads. Many eating places are within a ten-minute drive. (*Brian and Eve Webb*)

3 bedrooms. 1 on ground floor. Closed Christmas/New Year. Dining room closed midday. Off A35, via Lee Lane, in village adjoining Bridport. Train: Dorchester; bus to Bridport. Lounge, dining room. No background music. ¼-acre garden: river. Sea 2 miles. No smoking. Dogs in public rooms subject to other guests' approval. Some credit cards to be accepted in 2007. B&B £42.50–£65. Snack supper £5–£12.50. 1-night bookings occasionally refused weekends.

BRAITHWAITE Cumbria   Map 4: inset C2

The Cottage in the Wood	**BUDGET**	*Tel* 017687-78409
Whinlatter Pass		*Email* info@thecottageinthewood.co.uk
Braithwaite CA12 5TW		*Website* www.thecottageinthewood.co.uk

On Whinlatter Pass, in the Lake District national park and within Britain's only mountain forest, this 17th-century coaching inn looks down the valley to the Skiddaw mountain range. 'We had a superb welcome from the owners, Liam and Kath Berney,' says a report this year. 'They met us in the car park, brought coffee and biscuits by a lovely fire.' Refurbishment of the bedrooms continues. Oak and Sycamore now have a large sleigh bed, and 'what used to be our family attic' (Spruce) has a roll-top bath and separate shower *en suite*. Other rooms are smaller, including a ground-floor one (not yet renovated) designated for pet owners. The 'cosy' sitting room has an open fire, plants, 'lots of walking magazines and books'. In the dining room which, though comparatively large, 'retains a cottagey feel', the cooking is thought 'absolutely delicious' (eg, wild salmon fillet on spinach and saffron mash). Local suppliers are used, and breads, pasta and ice cream are home made. Breakfast includes fresh grapefruit, yogurts and fruit, and a full Cumbrian cooked platter. 'Full marks for everything.' 'Our dogs felt right at home.' (*Kenneth and Mary Moore, Michael and Alison Garraway*)

9 bedrooms. 5 miles NW of Keswick. Mid-Feb–Dec. Restaurant closed midday, and Mon night. Lounge, bar, restaurant; background radio/CDs at mealtimes. 4½-acre grounds: terraced garden. No smoking. No children under 7. Dogs in 1 designated bedroom only; not in public rooms except bar. MasterCard, Visa accepted. B&B £32–£52.50 per person; D,B&B £54–£80. Set dinner £22.50–£27.50. Christmas/New Year packages. 1-night bookings sometimes refused peak weekends.

BRAMPTON Cumbria   Map 4:B3

Farlam Hall
Brampton CA8 2NG

Tel 01697-746234
Fax 01697-746683
Email farlam@relaischateaux.com
Website www.farlamhall.co.uk

♙ *César award in 2001*

Owned and run by the Quinion and Stevenson families since 1975, this 'warm and welcoming' place (Relais & Châteaux) has seen many changes since it was built in the late 16th century as a manorial house. A listed building, it was last transformed in 1860 and has retained its Victorian character. Approached up a sweeping drive, it stands in an 'immaculate' landscaped garden, with a large ornamental lake, tall trees, a stream and a paddock. 'Wonderful, fun and friendly. Our favourite hotel owners in England.' Ornate public rooms ('perhaps a bit over the top') have an open fire, patterned wallpaper, fresh flowers, and ornaments. Bedrooms are priced according to size (best ones have a whirlpool bath). 'Ours had windows on two sides; the bathroom was warm but the room was gloomy, having badly designed lighting. Traditional furnishings; good bed; plenty of reading materials.' Drinks are served in the lounge (no bar). In the dining room, which reminded one reader of 'the type found in hotels of the 1940s', Barry Quinion's 'competent English country house' cooking was found 'very enjoyable'. (*Charlie Nairn, CD, and others*)

12 bedrooms. 1 in stables. 2 on ground floor. On A689, 2½ miles SE of Brampton (*not* in Farlam village). Closed 24–30 Dec. Restaurant closed midday (light lunches for residents by arrangement). Ramps. 2 lounges, restaurant. No background music. 10-acre grounds: croquet lawn. Unsuitable for &. No smoking. No children under 5. Amex, MasterCard, Visa accepted. D,B&B £137.50–£167.50 per person. Set dinner £38–£39.50. New Year package. ***V***

****

> **Traveller's tale** When booking, we were offered a 'country room'. On arrival, we discovered that it faced the car park. (*Hotel in Devon*)

****

BRANCASTER STAITHE Norfolk   Map 2:A5

The White Horse   *Tel* 01485-210262
Main Road   *Fax* 01485-210930
Brancaster Staithe   *Email* reception@whitehorsebrancaster.co.uk
PE31 8BY   *Website* www.whitehorsebrancaster.co.uk

'An absolutely delightful restaurant and hotel in a spectacular location.'
More praise this year for Cliff Nye's popular inn, which has wide views
over the sea and salt marshes of Brancaster Bay. The conservatory and
dining room have been redecorated this year, and there has been more
work on the bedrooms and bathrooms. The rooms, with their decor of soft
blues and yellows, 'are light and spacious', 'tastefully decorated, in accord
with the serene seascape'. The 'Room at the Top' (which carries a £15
supplement, and is thought 'worth every penny') has split-level facilities
and a viewing balcony with telescope. Room 9 gets some noise from the
kitchen below. The open-plan public area includes the bar (with sepia
photographs, bar billiards, wall settles, modern unvarnished tables, 'all neat
and tidy'), and an adjacent area with 'comfy' sofas and chairs. The
restaurant, in a large conservatory, serves 'wonderful food'. The cooking of
chef Nicholas Parker, who has worked for the Roux brothers, is 'modern
English with a traditional twist'. 'We enjoyed succulent mussels, harvested
within sight of the building.' At high tide, the sea reaches the bottom of the
garden, alongside the Norfolk Coastal Path. (*Mrs E Tyrrell, John and Sheila
Cotton, and others*)

15 bedrooms. 8 in annexe. 2 with facilities for &. Centre of village just E of
Brancaster. 2 lounge areas, public bar, conservatory restaurant, dining room; light
classical background music 'at quiet times'. ½-acre garden. Harbour sailing. No
smoking: restaurant, some bedrooms. Dogs in annexe rooms and bar only (£5 per
night). Diners, MasterCard, Visa accepted. B&B £45–£80 per person. Full alc £37.
Off-season breaks.

BRANSCOMBE Devon   Map 1:C5

The Masons Arms   `BUDGET`   *Tel* 01297-680300
Branscombe EX12 3DJ   *Fax* 01297-680500
                                Email reception@masonsarms.co.uk
                                 Website www.masonsarms.co.uk

Carol and Colin Slaney, who bought this popular creeper-covered inn
(Grade II listed) in the centre of a National Trust village in March 2005,
have created a new reception and a 'waterfall' lounge, and added a second
dining room. They run it 'with notable calm and authority, helped by a

charming young staff', says one visitor. Many bedrooms are in cottages across the road; others have views across the valley. 'I was much taken with our room with its spacious, irregular walls, so full of character.' Other guests had 'a lovely room with exposed beams open to the eaves, windows on three sides, stable door opening to a tiny flower-filled balcony; big four-poster, antique chest of drawers; pink-tiled bathroom with lots of hot water'. Rooms in the main building may hear some noise from the bar and kitchen, or other rooms. Richard Reddaway is the chef; his English cooking uses local ingredients wherever possible, eg, seared West Country scallops; smoked Dartmouth duck breast. 'Breakfast was excellent.' 'There is a wide choice of dishes in both restaurant and bar. Portions are large.' Booking is advised for both the restaurant and the pub. (*MB, PE Carter, and others*)

19 bedrooms. 14 in cottages. Village centre. Parking. Ramps. Lounge, 2 bars, 2 dining rooms. No background music. Large garden, terrace. Pebble beach ½ mile. Unsuitable for &. No smoking: 5 bedrooms, 1 bar, restaurant. No dogs: restaurant, some bedrooms. MasterCard, Visa accepted. B&B £30–£140 per person; D,B&B £55–£165. Set menu £25; full alc £35. Christmas/New Year packages. 1-night bookings refused weekends.

BRAY Berkshire   Map 2:D3

The Waterside Inn   *Tel* 01628-620691
Ferry Road   *Fax* 01628-784710
Bray SL6 2AT   *Email* reservations@waterside-inn.co.uk
                         Website www.waterside-inn.co.uk

In a wealthy Berkshire village, Michel Roux has run his Thames-side inn (Relais & Châteaux) for 34 years, and for 21 years has had three *Michelin* stars for his classic French cuisine. Visiting hoteliers were impressed: 'Very professional. Lots of attentive staff. We stayed in a suite which had fresh flowers and stunning views of the river.' All bedrooms have access to a kitchenette, and the two best rooms, La Terrasse and La Tamise, open on to a terrace. This year there is an additional suite and a new bedroom apartment. In the 'opulent' dining room, M. Roux's son Alain serves food that is 'very professionally' prepared and cooked. 'Wine selection was superb.' At dinner, the *carte* has dishes like smoked haddock and dill soufflé; grilled and roasted Challandais duck. Drinks can be taken in a summer house or on an electric launch. Breakfast, served after 8 in the bedroom, is a large wicker tray with fresh orange juice, yogurt, croissants, etc; 'good coffee'. The restaurant attracts corporate visitors, which can affect the atmosphere, but fans wrote of 'a cosseting dining experience'. (*David and Heather Armstrong, NB, and others*)

11 bedrooms. 3 in cottage, 30 yds. On Thames, 3 miles SE of Maidenhead. Closed 26 Dec–1 Feb, also bank holidays and Mon/Tues (except Tues evenings June–Aug). Restaurant; private dining room (with drawing room and courtyard garden). Riverside terrace; launch for drinks/coffee. No background music. Unsuitable for &. Civil wedding licence. No smoking: restaurant, bedrooms. No children under 12. Guide dogs only. All major credit cards accepted. B&B £90–£330 per person. Set 3-course lunch: Wed–Sat £40, Sun £56; full alc £125 (*Excluding 'optional' 12½% service charge on meals*).

BRIGHTON East Sussex   Map 2:E4

drakes	*Tel* 01273-696934
43/44 Marine Parade	*Fax* 01273-684805
Brighton BN2 1PE	*Email* info@drakesofbrighton.com
	Website www.drakesofbrighton.com

Two 19th-century town houses have been expensively converted 'with a touch of the Orient' to create this luxury design hotel; Andy Shearer is the owner, Richard Hayes the manager. Signage is discreet, an etched, opaque glass panel in the setting-down area; reception is in the small bar/lounge. Some rooms face the ocean; others have a 'city view', mainly of the back gardens of nearby houses. 'Our smallish second-floor room was up an attractive hanging staircase (quite steep; no lift),' said our inspector. 'Done in cream, shades of brown and natural wood, it was fresh and well designed, and had air conditioning, flat-screen TV, DVD-player, Internet access, etc. The bed was comfortable, lighting excellent; limited shelving and almost no hanging space; not good for a long stay.' The basement *Gingerman* restaurant (separately managed) is popular locally: hotel guests should reserve a table when booking their room. Ben McKellar's modern cooking is thought 'outstanding and reasonably priced'. Typical dishes: apple and beech-smoked eel; squab pigeon on potato rösti. 'The atmosphere is informal, "smart casual" predominated over jacket and tie. Breakfast adequate, no cooked fruit or yogurt, but the waiter offered to make fruit salad.'

20 bedrooms. 2, on ground floor, suitable for &, but no & access to restaurant. 3 miles from centre. Station 20 mins' walk. Parking arrangement with Marina, 1 mile. Ramp. Lounge/bar/reception, restaurant (separately owned); background music all day; meeting room. Sea across road. No smoking: bedrooms, restaurant until 10 pm. Guide dogs only. Amex, MasterCard, Visa accepted. Room [2006]: single £95–£125, double £115–£145, suite £245–£295. Breakfast £10–£12.50. Set dinner £32. 1-night bookings refused weekends.

All our inspections are paid for, and carried out anonymously.

Hotel du Vin & Bistro   *Tel* 01273-718588
2–6 Ship Street   *Fax* 01273-718599
Brighton BN1 1AD   *Email* info@brighton.hotelduvin.com
                          Website www.hotelduvin.com

'Great accommodation,' say visitors to this branch of the Hotel du Vin
chain (it is managed by Lora Strizic). 'For a special occasion we splashed
out on the Cristal suite. Very impressive, huge bed and TV, and a shower
big enough for a rugby team.' Once a nightclub, the mock-Tudor building
is in a 'superb location' in a one-way street between the Lanes area and the
seafront. Each bedroom is sponsored by a wine company; there are
'fantastic, comfortable beds, high-quality furnishings and fittings'. 'We could
not fault service or housekeeping. But the restaurant, busy and buzzy on a
Saturday night, simply could not cope with the capacity; dishes were given
to the wrong people. They were apologetic and didn't charge for the main
courses.' Breakfast (which costs extra) has 'good fresh juice in large glasses';
buffet tables laden with cereals, fruit, etc; fresh toast and cooked dishes
brought to the table. Limited parking is available: phone beforehand.
(*Caroline and Chris Wainman, and others*)

37 bedrooms. Some in courtyard. 2, on ground floor, suitable for &. 50 yds from
beachfront. Lounge/bar ('easy listening' background music all day), bistro. No
smoking: restaurant, bedrooms. No dogs in public rooms. All major credit cards
accepted. Room [to Oct 2007]: double £140–£180, suite £245–£400. Breakfast from
£9.95. Full alc £40. 1-night bookings refused Fri/Sat.

See also SHORTLIST

BRISTOL *See SHORTLIST*   **Map 1:B6**

BROAD CAMPDEN Gloucestershire   **Map 3:D6**

The Malt House   *Tel* 01386-840295
Broad Campden   *Fax* 01386-841334
nr Chipping Campden   *Email* info@malt-house.co.uk
GL55 6UU   *Website* www.malt-house.co.uk

'Standards remain high,' according to a returning visitor to Judi Wilkes's
16th-century Grade II listed malt house (with two adjacent cottages)
in a small, honey-stone Cotswold village. The 'warmly welcoming',

'perfectionist' hostess has created an upmarket B&B with 'excellent taste', say fans who appreciate the 'charm and tranquillity'. In the sitting rooms are log fires, low-beamed ceilings, antiques, *objets trouvés*, and flowers. Three bedrooms have their own entrance to the garden. One room has a fireplace, one a small sitting room. 'Ours had good lighting, nice fabrics, a huge magnolia tree outside the window, fresh milk for tea-making, current magazines by the bed.' 'Utter peace and quiet.' At the 'delicious' breakfasts, the non-cooked part (freshly squeezed orange juice, fruit, home-made preserves, etc) is 'as satisfying as the cooked dishes'. In warm weather, teas (with home-made biscuits) and evening drinks are served in the summer house in the garden. Meals may be served, by arrangement for groups of 12 or more, and house parties are catered for. From the gate you can walk on to the Cotswold Way. (*BB, Zara Elliott*)

7 bedrooms. 1 on ground floor. 1 mile S of Chipping Campden. Car park. Train: Moreton-in-Marsh, 5 miles. Closed Christmas. Ramp. 2 lounges, dining room. No background music. 3-acre garden: croquet, orchard, stream. Unsuitable for &. No smoking. Dogs in 1 bedroom only; not in public rooms. Amex, MasterCard, Visa accepted. B&B £70–£85 per person. 1-night bookings refused Apr–Oct weekends. *V*

BROADWAY Worcestershire   Map 3:D6

Russell's Restaurant	*Tel* 01386-853555
The Green, 20 High Street	*Fax* 01386-853964
Broadway WR12 7DT	*Email* info@russellsofbroadway.com
	Website www.russellsofbroadway.co.uk

Ω *César award in 2006*

'Terrific: comfortable, stylish and with wonderful attention to detail,' runs this year's tribute to Barry Hancox and Andrew Riley's restaurant-with-rooms in a listed building in this lovely old Cotswold village. A reporter thought the bedrooms 'sensationally good' (three more have been added this year, along with a private dining room). A 'smart, modern look' has been created, while beams, inglenook fireplaces and Arts and Crafts oak banisters have been retained. 'Our room had a window seat with its own reading light, and there was even a magnifying make-up mirror.' Some rooms face the village, but windows are double glazed, and 'all is quiet at night'. The bistro-style restaurant has a comfortable sitting area and well-spaced wooden tables with grey slate mats. Matthew Laughton, head chef since June 2005, serves an inexpensive fixed-price menu at midday and from 6 to 7 pm; later, guests eat *à la carte*. 'First-class food: superbly tender partridge and an excellent Chianti Classico; charming service, welcoming owners.' Alfresco meals are served on the heated patio when weather permits. 'The *Russell's* experience was managed with panache, and was great value.' (*Margaret Coombes, BB, and others*)

7 bedrooms. 2 on ground floor. Village centre. Restaurant closed Sun night. Ramp. Residents' lobby, bar, restaurant (background music); private dining room. Patio (heating; meal service). No smoking. No dogs in public rooms. Amex, MasterCard, Visa accepted. B&B £52.50–£175 per person. Set meal £17.95; full alc £35. ***V***

BROCKENHURST Hampshire   Map 2:E2

The Cloud Hotel	*Tel* 01590-622165
Meerut Road, Brockenhurst	*Fax* 01590-622818
SO42 7TD	*Email* enquiries@cloudhotel.co.uk
	Website www.cloudhotel.co.uk

April Owton (a former Tiller Girl) is 'very much a hands-on owner/ manager' at this traditional hotel, comprising four white-painted houses, on the fringe of a village in the New Forest. 'She was pleasantly in evidence most of the time,' says a visitor this year. The decor has a theatrical flavour, with a 'safety curtain' that comes down over the swagged bar when it is closed, and walls lined with Tiller Girl photographs. Lounges and entrance hall were recently refurbished. Many of the bedrooms (modern, with pastel colours and pine furniture) have views over New Forest heathland, with its wild horses and cattle. 'We enjoyed lovely afternoon teas in the garden, with good scones and jam and a generous amount of cream.' The cooking, by chef Stephen Gates, is 'English traditional', eg, roast loin of pork with stuffing and apple sauce. Breakfast is 'standard English, with good cooked dishes'. There is a terrace for alfresco meals. (*Joan Burton, and others*)

17 bedrooms. 2 on ground floor. 1 mile N of centre. Open 12 Jan–27 Dec. Ramps. 2 lounges, bar lounge, restaurant (background music); function room. ½-acre garden: patio, croquet. River (sailing) 5 miles; sea (stony beach) 10 miles. No smoking. No children under 8. No dogs in public rooms. MasterCard, Visa accepted. B&B [2006] £50–£75 per person; D,B&B £72–£99. Set dinner £29.50. Christmas package. 1-night bookings sometimes refused. ***V***

Deadlines: nominations for the 2008 edition of this volume should reach us not later than 15 May 2007. Latest date for comments on existing entries: 1 June 2007.

Thatched Cottage Hotel & Restaurant   *Tel* 01590-623090
16 Brookley Road, Brockenhurst   *Fax* 01590-623479
SO42 7RR   *Email* sales@thatchedcottage.co.uk
                                   Website www.thatchedcottage.co.uk

Dating from 1627, this 'pretty as a picture' timber-framed thatched cottage, near the New Forest national park, is now a restaurant-with-rooms owned by Martin Matysik and his wife Michiyo (the chefs), with brother Mathias (front-of-house). Bedrooms are named after blends of tea: Darjeeling and Pouchkin have an open-hearth gas fire, Assam Bop has a canopied double bed. Low oak beams and, 'at every turn, a profusion of dainty lace, flouncy fabrics, stencilled walls, dried flowers and antiques (perhaps a bit twee for some masculine tastes)'. 'Indulgent' afternoon teas are served on a traditional three-tier stand and, in fine weather, may be taken in the peaceful garden. The three- or five-course dinner menu includes elaborate dishes like roasted poussin with foie gras velouté. 'Cooking is refined, with great emphasis on presentation.' Breakfast, served until 11 am, has freshly baked pastries and a choice of six cooked dishes. Some light sleepers might hear traffic at night. Cookery courses are held.

5 bedrooms. Some on ground floor. Near village centre. Restaurant closed Mon. Lounge, restaurant (classical background music). Small tea garden. No smoking. No children under 12. Amex, MasterCard, Visa accepted. B&B £40–£100 per person. Set dinner £15–£65; full alc £60. 2 nights min. at weekends. Christmas/New Year packages. 1-night bookings refused Sat.

BROMSGROVE Worcestershire   Map 3:C5
See SHORTLIST

BROXTON Cheshire   Map 3:A5

Frogg Manor   *Tel* 01829-782629
Nantwich Road   *Fax* 01829-782459
Broxton, Chester CH3 9JH   *Email* info@froggmanorhotel.co.uk
                                  Website www.froggmanorhotel.co.uk

♕ *César award in 1997*

'Classic bourgeois country house hotel? Not exactly,' says owner John Sykes, about his Georgian manor house dedicated to 1930s/40s music and to frogs, of which there are hundreds (ceramic, straw, brass, etc). 'When I was shown to our bedroom,' confirms a visitor this year, 'I realised I was in for something special.' Bedrooms are themed (Wellington, Nelson, Nightingale, etc), and 'equipped with everything a guest could need, from spare tights to hair conditioner'. Some rooms are vast, and perhaps a little over the top. Public rooms are 'welcoming, with a hint of an Agatha Christie whodunnit', says another report. One dissenter this year wasn't amused and questioned the housekeeping. Dinner, cooked by new chef Sion Newton, is served between 7 and 10 pm in the pretty conservatory dining room: 'Excellent, beautifully presented,' was one verdict in 2006. A light supper can be arranged for latecomers. After-dinner coffee comes with chocolate frogs. Meals are accompanied by jazz classics; there is a small dance floor. Continental breakfast is included in the price; other breakfast dishes are *à la carte*. The large grounds, floodlit at night, have views across Cheshire to the Welsh mountains. (*Joy Harvey, Brenda Darlington, Janet McDonnell, and others*)

7 bedrooms. 1 suitable for &. 12 miles SE of Chester. Ramp. Lounge, bar lounge, restaurant (1930s/40s background music); private dining room; conference/function facilities. 10-acre grounds: tennis. Civil wedding licence. No smoking: restaurant, 2 bedrooms. Dogs in 1 bedroom only; not in public rooms. All major credit cards accepted. B&B £40–£120 per person. Alc breakfast from £5. Set menus £28.35–£39.90. *V*

BRYHER Isles of Scilly   Map 1:C1

Hell Bay Hotel	*Tel* 01720-422947
Bryher, Isles of Scilly	*Fax* 01720-423004
Cornwall TR23 0PR	*Email* contactus@hellbay.co.uk
	Website www.hellbay.co.uk

Good for a family holiday, this conversion of cottages and cowsheds is the only hotel on Bryher (one mile by half a mile, the smallest of the inhabited Scilly Isles). *Hell Bay* is owned by Robert Dorrien-Smith, who also owns the neighbouring island of Tresco, a five-minute boat ride away. Philip Callan manages. Recent visitors 'were well looked after from the moment we were collected from the quay in a Land-Rover'. Inside a 'low-key exterior', said another reporter, is 'a haven of modern art and design'. Accommodation is in suites, most with two bedrooms and a lounge, in buildings around a courtyard and in the garden. The spacious Emperor has 'splendid views, huge bed with baldachin, large private terrace'. Some other suites are 'a bit cramped'. Ten have just been redecorated. In the panoramic dining room (with 'magnificent large semi-abstract paintings'), Graham Shone serves a daily-changing *table d'hôte* menu. Breakfast 'can be as leisurely as you wish'; bar meals are available much of the day; high teas are provided for small children. The hotel has facilities for disabled visitors but points out: 'Bryher has no made-up roads and no dedicated transport system.' (*RC*)

25 bedrooms. In 5 buildings. Some on ground floor. 1 suitable for &. On W coast of island. Boat from Tresco (reached by boat/helicopter from Penzance) or St Mary's. Hotel will make travel arrangements. Open mid-Feb–early Jan. Lounge, TV/games room, bar, restaurant; gym, sauna. No background music. Large grounds: heated swimming pool, giant chess, *boules*, croquet, children's playground, par 3 golf course. Beach 75 yds: bathing; boating, fishing, etc. Civil wedding licence. No smoking: restaurant, bedrooms. No dogs in public rooms. MasterCard, Visa accepted. D,B&B £60–£125 per person. Short breaks. Christmas/New Year packages.

BUCKDEN Cambridgeshire   Map 2:B4

The George   NEW   *Tel* 01480-812300
High Street   *Fax* 01480-813920
Buckden PE19 5XA   *Email* mail@thegeorgebuckden.com
                                  Website www.thegeorgebuckden.com

All the bedrooms are themed to Georges (Orwell, Eliot, etc) at this 'discreetly enlarged' inn on the high street of a village near Huntingdon. Annie, Richard and Becky Furbank have created a 'fashionably stylish' decor of neutral colour, say inspectors, who found much to like, apart from some carelessness at Reception. 'Furnishings are well chosen, comfortable and eye-catching. Public spaces flow into one another. The restaurant has display shelving, chic nightlight holders, quirky prints and polished wooden tables; dining chairs a bit low.' A standard bedroom (Mallory) was 'smartly, if rather sternly decorated' and had double-glazed windows, and a 'slightly cramped, not very well-designed bathroom'. In the busy brasserie, 'cooking was competent if not wildly memorable' and the wine list 'by no means overpriced, with plenty at the £15–£16 range'. Breakfast consisted of 'a tasteful spread of croissants, pastries, fruit, cheese, etc, and any variation of a standard fry-up. Good coffee and plenty of free newspapers.' The manager is Cynthia Schaeffer. Annie Furbank runs a smart clothing boutique next door.

12 bedrooms. Off A1, between Huntingdon and St Neots. Lift. Lounge, bar, brasserie. No background music. Patios. No smoking. No dogs in public rooms. Amex, MasterCard, Visa accepted. B&B £50–£130 per person; D,B&B £80–£160. Full alc £41. Christmas/New Year packages. ***V***

For details of the Voucher scheme see page 60.

BURFORD Oxfordshire   Map 2:C2

Burford House   *Tel* 01993-823151
99 High Street   *Fax* 01993-823240
Burford OX18 4QA   *Email* stay@burfordhouse.co.uk
                                     Website www.burfordhouse.co.uk

The high street of this attractive Cotswold town, filled with antique, craft
and specialist shops, slopes steeply down from the busy A40 to the River
Windrush and a 12th-century church. Here, this half-timbered early 17th-
century listed building is owned by Jane and Simon Henty. Family photos
and souvenirs of foreign travel fill the house. It has a 'cosy' sitting room,
with 'crackling fire, antiques, fresh flowers and expensive pieces of china',
which faces the courtyard garden. Three of the bedrooms have a four-
poster bed, and bathrooms have a 'huge tub and power shower'. The dining
room, where light lunches are served from Monday to Saturday, has been
refurbished this year. Picnic lunches can be supplied. There is a 'short but
interesting' wine list, and an honour bar. 'Breakfast was good,' says one
guest (it includes a variety of fresh and cooked fruits, as well as the usual
'full English'), 'and the staff were very nice.' More reports, please.

8 bedrooms. Central (2 rooms might hear traffic). Free car park nearby. Closed
Christmas. Reception (background music), 2 lounges (1 with honour bar), dining
room. Courtyard. Unsuitable for &. Bicycles available. Smoking in sitting rooms
only. No dogs. Amex, MasterCard, Visa accepted. B&B £80–£130 per person.
1-night bookings refused weekends. ***V***

Jonathan's at the Angel   *Tel* 01993-822714
14 Witney Street   *Fax* 01993-822069
Burford OX18 4SN   *Email* jo@theangel-uk.com
                                     Website www.theangel-uk.com

Originally the *Masons' Arms*, this 16th-century coaching inn, a short walk
from Burford's High Street, has been transformed by owner/chef Jonathan
Lewis and his wife, Josephine, into an informal brasserie-with-bedrooms.
'They are down-to-earth hosts, who really know how to look after their
guests. Attention to detail was top class,' said one report. 'He helped us
park. Drinks and nibbles were sent up to our room.' The restaurant, spread
over two dining areas, has old beams, flagstone floors, sturdy furniture,
large wooden platters on tables. The eclectic cooking uses 'extraordinarily
good ingredients, properly presented', and there are 'plentiful vegetable
side dishes'. Of the themed bedrooms, Camargue has 'interesting drapes,
corner cupboard with TV, video, tea- and coffee-making kit; spotless,

spacious bathroom.' Madras, 'compact, well designed', and done in rich reds, has a window seat overlooking the courtyard (sometimes used for dining). Sirmione is more modern, with a feel of the Italian lakes. A small residents' lounge on the landing has books and guides. At breakfast 'our large round table was laid with fruit, juice; home-made jams and marmalades in jars. A basket of hot croissants and breads came, as well as thick toast. I got stuck into a cholesterol-raising plate of eggs, bacon and black pudding.' (*JH, and others*)

3 bedrooms. Central. Closed 18 Jan–11 Feb, Sun night/Mon. Residents' lounge area, bar, restaurant (background jazz). Walled garden. Unsuitable for &. Smoking in bar only. No dogs. MasterCard, Visa accepted. B&B £46.50–£82.50 per person. Set lunch menus £14.50–£18.50; full alc £35. 1-night bookings refused weekends. *V*

BURNSALL North Yorkshire   Map 4:D3

Devonshire Fell	*Tel* 01756-729000
Burnsall, nr Skipton	*Fax* 01756-729009
BD23 6BT	*Email* res@devonshirehotels.co.uk
	Website www.devonshirefell.co.uk

Stone-built rectangular building, originally club for gentlemen mill-owners, owned by Duke and Duchess of Devonshire (she designed the interior), managed by Richard Palmer. 'A corner of Fulham in the fells.' Contemporary paintings, background music and light lunches in bar; bold, fresh colours, high chairs, sofas, polished floors in lounge. Restaurant, dining terrace; conference facilities. Guests have access to health club at sister Devonshire Arms Hotel, *Bolton Abbey. 'Contemporary English/ Mediterranean cooking' by Medhi Boukemar. ½-acre garden, adjacent to 30,000-acre estate; river (2 mins' walk), beach, fishing. Only restaurant, bar and function room suitable for &. No smoking: restaurant, bedrooms. No dogs in restaurant. All major credit cards accepted. 12 bedrooms (all redecorated this year; front ones may hear traffic). B&B £62.50–£130 per person; D,B&B (min. 2 nights) £85–£125. Full alc £35. More reports, please.* *V*

* *

Traveller's tale This could have been a premier league hotel, but it lacked attention to detail. We were greeted by a gum-chewing girl, not a good first impression. There were plastic flowers in the rooms, in June. The plastic loo seat came off its hinges when lifted. 'Oh, that's always happening,' said a staff member, cheerfully. (*Hotel in Cornwall*)

* *

BURY ST EDMUNDS Suffolk   Map 2:B5

Ounce House   *Tel* 01284-761779
Northgate Street   *Fax* 01284-768315
Bury St Edmunds IP33 1HP   *Email* pott@globalnet.co.uk
                                    Website www.ouncehouse.co.uk

At the high point of one of the finest residential streets in this attractive
town, Simon and Jenny Pott's Victorian merchant's house 'feels very much
like stepping into someone's home'. The drawing room, filled with family
photographs and knick-knacks, is 'nicely furnished, if a little chintzy and
cluttered'. A small library has old games, videos and DVDs, and a small
honesty bar. The individually decorated bedrooms are well-equipped,
'perhaps a bit dated, but impeccably clean', say inspectors. 'Our room overlooked the garden, which has trees that successfully block out surrounding
buildings. We slept with the windows open; the dawn chorus was impressive.' A front bedroom faces the busy road. Breakfast, served communally
around a large table, is 'traditional English, with good ingredients'. A three-
course dinner can be similarly served, for four people or more. Mrs Pott is
'a mine of information on local history'.

3 bedrooms. Central. Off-road parking. Drawing room, snug, bar/library, dining
room. No background music. ¼-acre walled garden. Unsuitable for &. No smoking.
No dogs. All major credit cards accepted. B&B £45–£85 per person. Set dinner (by
arrangement) £30–£40. Weekend rates; reductions for 3 or more nights.

See also SHORTLIST

BUXTON Derbyshire *See SHORTLIST*   Map 3:A6

How to contact the *Guide*
By mail: From anywhere in the UK, write to Freepost PAM 2931,
London W11 4BR (no stamp is needed)
From outside the UK: Good Hotel Guide, 50 Addison Avenue,
London W11 4QP, England
By telephone or fax: 020-7602 4182
By email: Goodhotel@aol.com
Via our website: www.goodhotelguide.com

CALNE Wiltshire

Chilvester Hill House
Calne SN11 0LP

Tel 01249-813981
Fax 01249-814217
Email gill.dilley@talk21.com
Website www.chilvesterhillhouse.co.uk

🏆 *César award in 1992*

In their Victorian home surrounded by fields of grazing sheep, Gill and John Dilley welcome visitors 'to the private country house of a professional family'. 'They are thoroughly charming, and did everything possible to help us enjoy our stay,' says a *Guide* inspector in 2006. 'Dr Dilley gave us a tour of the public rooms: a large drawing room with comfortable seating, magazines, books; a sitting room with a big TV. This and the pleasant dining room are papered with dramatic William Morris designs.' In the large, 'well-furnished' bedroom, 'the floral paper was impressive or startling, depending on taste; there were windows on two sides, TV; fresh fruit, milk, flowers, a royal blue suite in the bathroom, rather 1970s'. Shower addicts can use the large cabinet on the ground floor. Mrs Dilley serves a no-choice menu, by arrangement (no compulsion to dine in), around a long table, in dinner-party style. 'We enjoyed smoked trout, pork casserole, apple crêpes; an exceptional, well-priced wine list.' Breakfast, 'a moveable feast, although most guests settle for something between 8 and 9 am', 'was good; fresh fruit, cereals, cooked English, home-made jams, strong coffee'. No brochure: Mrs Dilley sends a letter 'directed towards specific inquiries'.

3 bedrooms. ½ mile from Calne. Closed 7–10 days in autumn or spring. Drawing room, sitting room with TV, dining room. No background music. 2½-acre grounds (also 5 acres for sheep). Golf, riding locally. Unsuitable for ♿. Smoking banned in dining room, discouraged in bedrooms. No children under 12. No dogs. All major credit cards accepted. B&B [2006] £42.50–£65 per person. Packed/snack lunches. Set dinner £20–£25. 1-night bookings 'very occasionally' refused.

CAMBER East Sussex

The Place
New Lydd Road, Camber Sands
Camber, nr Rye
TN31 7RB

Tel 01797-225057
Fax 01797-227003
Email enquiries@theplacecambersands.co.uk
Website www.theplacecambersands.co.uk

The exterior of this single-storey, white-fronted and red-tiled building is unexciting but 'inside, things are classier', said our inspector of Matthew Wolfman and Mike Ashton's smart restaurant-with-rooms, a conversion of a former motel. Twelve new bedrooms will be added during the winter of 2006/7. The atmosphere is 'cheerful, think Scandinavia or New England. Blue-and-cream striped curtains and cushions; cream carpets and walls. Superb lighting. White cotton bedlinen.' The 'amazingly quiet' bedrooms vary from 'compact' to 'sizeable' and have 'thoughtful details', eg, a digital radio, and 'wonderful, huge pillows'. The much-admired glass-fronted brasserie, popular with locals, has a bare wooden floor ('on the noisy side'), wooden tables (no cloths, paper napkins), plain white china. The monthly-changing menu uses local and organic produce where possible: the fish comes from Hastings, following Marine Stewardship Council standards for sustainable management. 'We care passionately about the ingredients,' says Mr Wolfman. Main courses include bouillabaisse, and wild rabbit stew. At breakfast there are organic free-range eggs cooked to order, home-made preserves, local yogurts and much more. *The Place* is family-friendly: 'We charge by room, not by age of child.' Art exhibitions are held. Camber's famous beach is near. The *Bell Hotel* at Sandwich is now under the same ownership.

18 bedrooms. 12 more by summer 2007. All on ground floor. 1 suitable for ♿. 3 miles SE of Rye. Train: Rye; taxi. Brasserie (background music); conference/meeting room; private dining room. Garden (outside dining). Beach 100 yds: water sports, windsurfing, kite surfing. Smoking banned in bedrooms, 'discretionary' in restaurant. No dogs. Amex, MasterCard, Visa accepted. B&B [2006]: double £80–£110, triple £90–£110, family £99–£130. Full alc £28. Discounts for 2 or more nights off-season. 1-night bookings generally refused weekends. ***V***

CAMBRIDGE Cambridgeshire   Map 2:B4
See SHORTLIST

CANNINGTON Somerset   Map 1:B5

Blackmore Farm BUDGET	*Tel* 01278-653442
Blackmore Lane	*Fax* 01278-653427
Cannington	*Email* dyerfarm@aol.com
nr Bridgwater TA5 2NE	*Website* www.dyerfarm.co.uk

'Ideal for a holiday with children': Ann and Ian Dyer offer traditional farmhouse B&B in their home (a 14th-century Grade I listed building). It retains many period features, including oak beams, stone archways, mullioned windows, medieval garderobes and a 'lovely little chapel'. Scattered about are old pewter pots, hay forks and 'nasty-looking man-traps'. Tea and 'delicious home-made cake' are served free to arriving guests; 'endless goodies' (fruit, biscuits, chocolates) are in the bedrooms. The West room has views to the Quantock hills, while the Gallery looks over the garden and has original oak panelling and beams. Breakfast, in the Great Hall, is a convivial affair: guests eat together at a long refectory table by a massive sandstone fireplace. 'Varied and delicious', it includes fruit, yogurt, scrambled egg with smoked haddock, and a vegetarian option. 'A good pub for dinner is five minutes' walk away', and there are plenty of restaurants nearby. A convenient base for exploring the Quantocks, the west Somerset coast and Exmoor. More reports, please.

6 bedrooms. 3 suitable for &. 4 miles NW of Bridgwater. Lounge/TV room, hall/ breakfast room. No background music. 1-acre garden. Stream (coarse fishing). No smoking. No dogs. All major credit cards accepted. B&B £32.50–£45 per person. 1-night bookings refused bank holiday weekends.

CANTERBURY Kent *See SHORTLIST*   Map 2:D5

CARLISLE Cumbria *See SHORTLIST*   Map 4:B2

CARTMEL Cumbria   Map 4: inset C2

Aynsome Manor	*Tel* 01539-536653
Cartmel	*Fax* 01539-536016
nr Grange-over-Sands	*Email* info@aynsomemanorhotel.co.uk
LA11 6HH	*Website* www.aynsomemanorhotel.co.uk

Ω *César award in 1998*

'We have visited for over 20 years and continue to marvel at the high standard of food, hospitality and friendship.' High praise this year for this traditional Lakeland hotel run for 25 years by the Varley family, Christopher, his wife Andrea, and his parents, Tony and Margaret. Standing between fells and the sea, in the Vale of Cartmel, it has views towards the Norman priory, meadowlands and woods. The bedrooms vary in size; some are suitable for a family. 'Our nicely decorated four-poster room had views over the fields. No traffic sounds. Good fabrics and lighting, masses of storage.' Two rooms are in a cottage with a lounge, across the cobbled courtyard. Christopher Varley tells us that refurbishment of the bedrooms and bathrooms has been completed, and the dining room has had 'its biennial face-lift'. Dinner, in the oak-panelled restaurant, is at 7 pm (except on Saturdays when there are two sittings); men are asked to wear jacket and tie. Gordon Topp offers a daily-changing five-course dinner menu. On Sunday there is a traditional lunch, and a lavish buffet supper. Breakfasts are 'outstandingly good'. (*Ian and Susan Duckworth, and others*)

12 bedrooms. 2 in cottage (with lounge) across courtyard. ½ mile outside village. Open Feb–Dec, except 25/26 Dec. Lunch served Sun only. Dinner for residents only Sun evening. 2 lounges, bar, dining room. No background music. ½-acre garden. Unsuitable for &. No smoking: restaurant, bedrooms, residents' lounge. No children under 5 at dinner. No dogs in public rooms. Amex, MasterCard, Visa accepted. D,B&B £68.50–£97 per person. Set Sun lunch £16, dinner £23–£30. New Year breaks. 1-night bookings sometimes refused Sat, bank holidays. ***V***

CASTLE COMBE Wiltshire   Map 2:D1

The Castle Inn   NEW   *Tel* 01249-783030
Castle Combe   *Fax* 01249-782315
Chippenham SN14 7HN   *Email* enquiries@castle-inn.info
                                    Website www.castle-inn.info

By the ancient market cross in 'one of the most photographed villages in England', this 'very pretty' inn has been 'cobbled together from several dwellings, some of them 12th-century'. 'Inside,' writes an inspector, 'are fireside nooks and cosy corners; upstairs is something of a rabbit warren: rambling corridors, different levels, low beams.' The 'friendly, hardworking' Lisa Bullock and her husband, Charles, bought the inn in early 2006, and have filled it with antiques. 'Our room (No. 5) had a doorway of hobbit-like proportions, but with its soaring beamed ceiling, it was spacious enough.' Another room, 'richly draped in red and gold', has a spa bath. In the 'elegant', green dining room, 'service is unpretentious', and dinner, cooked by Jamie Gemmel, 'was well balanced: plenty of choice; delicious warm bread. Enjoyable sea bass on mashed potato; braised lamb shank. Home-made chocolate torte with orange sorbet too good to miss.' There is less formal dining, with a range of dishes, eg, pork au poivre, in the bar. 'Breakfast, in the conservatory, was let down by poor coffee. Buffet nothing special; ordinary toast. But smoked salmon with scrambled eggs and traditional breakfast (delicious mushrooms) were excellent.' There are good walks from the door.

11 bedrooms. Village centre. 7 miles NW of Chippenham. Closed 25 Dec. 2 lounges, bar, 2 dining rooms; background music at night. Courtyard. No smoking: restaurant, bedrooms. Amex, MasterCard, Visa accepted. B&B £50–£69.50 per person; D,B&B £45 added per couple. Full alc £25. ***V***

Goulters Mill   BUDGET   *Tel/Fax* 01249-782555
Nettleton, nr Castle Combe   *Email* alison@harvey3512.freeserve.co.uk
Chippenham SN14 7LL

Converted 17th-century mill cottage, ¾ mile W of village. In 25-acre organically farmed grounds in wooded valley ('idyllic in summer') with stream, chickens, sheep, owls, Jack Russells; ¾-acre garden (member of National Gardens Scheme). Difficult to find: owners Mike and Alison Harvey provide map. 'Full of charm and interest': lots of books, paintings by owners. Guests' lounge with fire. 3 simple bedrooms, twin has 'amazing Gothic headboards'. 'Excellent' breakfast, in room with fireplace, includes 'chunky white toast, home-made jams'. Evening meal by arrangement (£25): could be watercress soup; chicken & mushroom pie; chocolate tart and cream. No background music. No smoking in bedrooms. 'Well-behaved' dogs by arrangement. Unsuitable for &. No credit cards. B&B £31–£40 per person. **°V°**

CHADDESLEY CORBETT Worcestershire   Map 3:C5

Brockencote Hall   *Tel* 01562-777876
Chaddesley Corbett   *Fax* 01562-777872
nr Kidderminster DY10 4PY   *Email* info@brockencotehall.com
                                   Website www.brockencotehall.com

'Exceptionally good for food, service and atmosphere.' New praise this year from a trusted correspondent for Alison and Joseph Petitjean's late Victorian mansion in large landscaped grounds, part of a 17th-century estate. Apart from one dissenting note, other visitors were equally enthusiastic: 'We have never before experienced service such as we received here; the Petitjeans are proper hosts, who talk to all their guests.' Visitors admire the 'glorious grounds', with their fine specimen trees, half-timbered Tudor dovecote, gatehouse and ornamental lake. Bedrooms are 'spacious and comfortable'. 'Our superior room had a double-aspect view over the lawns. The four-poster bed was huge, and the bathroom had both a shower cabinet and a good-sized bath.' 'Staff in the restaurant could not have been more attentive, and mercifully did not interrupt our meal to ask if "everything is all right".' Tables in the three-part restaurant are 'well spaced, each with nice fresh flower arrangements'. This year there is a new chef, Colin Layfield. One couple thought the food 'over-fussy'. A six-course *dégustation* menu suggests a wine for each course, and there are separate menus for vegetarians and children. (*Gordon Hands, Mr and Mrs I Goldrein, and others*)

17 bedrooms. Some on ground floor. 1 adapted for &. 3 miles SE of Kidderminster. Closed 1st week Jan. Lift, ramp. Hall, 3 lounges, conservatory, restaurant (3 rooms); background CDs; function facilities. 70-acre grounds: gardens, lake (fishing), croquet, tennis. Civil wedding licence. No smoking: restaurant, some bedrooms. No dogs. All major credit cards accepted. B&B £58–£93 per person; D,B&B £90.50–£125. Set dinner £34; full alc £54.50. Christmas/New Year packages. *V*

CHAGFORD Devon   Map 1:C4

Easton Court   **BUDGET**   *Tel* 01647-433469
Easton Cross   *Fax* 01647-433654
Chagford TQ13 8JL   *Email* stay@easton.co.uk
                                       Website www.easton.co.uk

Set beside the River Teign, Debra and Paul Witting's B&B is a Devon hideaway with impeccable literary credentials. In this 15th-century thatched house Evelyn Waugh wrote *Brideshead Revisited*, Alec Waugh *Thirteen Such Years* and Patrick Leigh Fermor *The Traveller's Tree*. Guest accommodation is in a creeper-covered Edwardian wing. The flowery garden, with a huge chestnut tree, has magnificent views in a peaceful setting. The 'welcoming hosts' have been busy this year, redecorating and laying new carpets throughout; one bedroom has been restyled; all have been given a CD-player. The dining and sitting area is a large room with sofas, books, games and a fridge for guests. Breakfast has 'plenty of choice at every stage', and home-made preserves and organic breads. 'I had a delicious soufflé omelette,' one guest wrote. 'When I asked the housekeeper for a bottle of water (on sale with other snacks), she offered me a free bottle of tap water.' The whole place is sometimes let on a self-catering basis. There are several good eating places in Chagford. More reports, please.

5 bedrooms. 1½ miles E of Chagford. Ramp. Breakfast/sitting room. No background music. 4-acre garden, courtyard. Fishing nearby. No smoking. No children under 10. No dogs in public rooms. MasterCard, Visa accepted. B&B £29–£60 per person. 1-night bookings sometimes refused weekends in season.

Mill End Hotel   *Tel* 01647-432282
Sandy Park   *Fax* 01647-433106
nr Chagford TQ13 8JN   *Email* info@millendhotel.com
                                  Website www.millendhotel.com

In the Dartmoor national park, with the River Teign at the bottom of its garden, this white-walled former mill has been sympathetically modernised by owner Keith Green. 'We wanted peace and quiet, and we found it here,' say visitors this year. There are large grounds to explore and the park of Castle Drogo is adjacent. The lounges 'have a homely feel rather than a smart country house look, so the atmosphere is genuinely relaxing', was another comment. There are log fires on cold days. Service is universally praised. The bedrooms vary from a 'superb first-floor suite with large living room' to standard ones that face the road (there may be noise). Each of the three south-facing ground-floor rooms has a private patio. 'Our room was especially good, with masses of space and comfortable chairs.' But one visitor wrote that his ground-floor room had 'narrow beds and soft mattresses'. Non-residents and walkers frequent the bar, and the restaurant whose 'sophisticated decor' (green walls and candlelight) 'complements the cooking' of chef Barney Mason. 'Dinner was something to look forward to; the lobster ravioli was outstanding.' (*Brian and Eve Webb, Andrew Wiltshire, Barbara Rogers, and others*)

15 bedrooms. 3 on ground floor. On A382 2¼ miles NE of Chagford. 3 lounges, bar, restaurant. No background music. 15-acre grounds: river (fishing, bathing). No smoking. No children under 12 in restaurant at night. No dogs in public rooms. MasterCard, Visa accepted. B&B £75–£110 per person; D,B&B £110–£140. Set dinner £38; full alc £38. Christmas/New Year packages. 1-night bookings refused peak weekends. *V*

See also SHORTLIST

CHELTENHAM Gloucestershire   Map 3:D5

Hotel Kandinsky	*Tel* 01242-527788
Bayshill Road, Montpellier	*Fax* 01242-226412
Cheltenham GL50 3AS	*Email* kandinsky@aliashotels.com
	Website www.aliashotels.com

Behind its white exterior, this listed Regency mansion, in Cheltenham's fashionable Montpellier area, is an informal hotel, its quirky decor blending traditional and modern. It belongs to the Alias Hotels group – see also *Hotel Barcelona*, Exeter (*qv*), *Hotel Seattle*, Brighton (Shortlist) – which sold the *Hotel Rossetti*, Manchester, in 2006. Carolyn Lloyd is the manager. Readers were impressed this year: 'Friendly staff, business-like reception; a large, comfortable bedroom.' 'Our spacious room had a sparkling bathroom. First-class breakfast.' 'Value for money.' Some rooms are small. No air conditioning, but in a heatwave a large fan was provided. The 'attractive' bar has wooden floors, big sofas facing each other, lots of private areas. The *Café Paradiso* (open to non-residents; booking advised), long and light, has

Spanish chairs, polished wood tables close together, old wooden high stools, and a wood-fired pizza oven. Lunch was thought 'excellent value' in 2006: 'Tasty tiger prawns on black linguini, perfect starter size; generous portions of beef brisket with kale. Unhurried but prompt service.' Breakfast, which costs extra ('irritating as items mount up'), is buffet-led: 'Good yogurt, fruit, cheese, ham, bread and pastries.' The 1950s-style basement nightclub, *U-bahn*, attracts the local young. (*John Holland, Mrs G Smith, and others*)

48 bedrooms. Some on ground floor. ½ mile from centre. Lift, ramps. Lounge, bar, restaurant, nightclub, cocktail bar; background music in public areas all day. No smoking: restaurant, some bedrooms. No dogs in public rooms. All major credit cards accepted. Room [2006]: single £75, double £105, suite £120–£125. Breakfast £7.75–£10.95. Full alc £36. Weekend D,B&B rates. Christmas/New Year packages. 1-night bookings refused weekends.

Hotel on the Park   *Tel* 01242-518898
38 Evesham Road   *Fax* 01242-511526
Cheltenham GL52 2AH   *Email* stay@hotelonthepark.com
                             Website www.hotelonthepark.com

Visitors celebrating a 'special birthday' at this elegant town house hotel thought that it 'could not have been better'. It stands opposite Pittville Park, near the centre of this well-preserved Regency town. 'It was comfortable, spotlessly clean and carefully decorated. Mr and Mrs Gregory and their staff made us very welcome.' The public rooms, which have antiques, tasselled curtains, mirrors and ticking clocks, have 'clear spaces for smokers and non-smokers, and plenty of magazines'. The library and drawing room look through French windows over the garden. The bar is 'particularly cosy'. This year all bedrooms have had a new, contemporary bathroom fitted, eight of them with a spa bath. The road outside is busy, but front rooms are double glazed. The brasserie, *Parkers*, serves international dishes (eg, roasted sea bass with coriander couscous). There is a new chef, Wayne Sullivan; we would welcome reports on his cooking. Mr Gregory keeps a motor cruiser, available to guests, on the River Severn, six miles away. (*Christopher Smith, NF and CB, and others*)

12 bedrooms. On A435, 5 mins' walk from centre. Brasserie (background music), bar, library. Small courtyard garden. Unsuitable for &. Smoking in bar only. No children under 8. No dogs. All major credit cards accepted. Room: single £99–£126, double £126–£186. Breakfast £6.95–£10.50. Full alc £30. 1-night bookings sometimes refused.

See also SHORTLIST

CHESTER Cheshire   Map 3:A4

Green Bough   *Tel* 01244-326241
60 Hoole Road   *Fax* 01244-326265
Chester CH2 3NL   *Email* luxury@greenbough.co.uk
                                   Website www.greenbough.co.uk

On a tree-lined street of red brick, late Victorian town houses, Janice and
Philip Martin's hotel is a mile from Chester's historic centre. 'Unexpectedly
sumptuous when you enter,' say visitors this year. 'All quite grand, but
everyone was friendly.' The 'plush' lounge/bar, where cream teas are
served, has 'tasteful paintings of Italian antiquity scenes'. Bedrooms vary. A
deluxe room was 'large, light, with antique brass bed, two armchairs, large
squashy sofa, luxurious fabrics'. In the annexe, one room was 'small, but
quiet; no views, but a comfy bed', another, at the front, was 'noisy' and had
'windows we couldn't open, shower not a bath'. The rooftop garden has a
water feature. We'd welcome reports on the *Olive Tree* restaurant ('smart
casual dress' required), where Tim Seddon, the new chef, serves dishes like
sea bream with tartlet of crab, mash, red wine and tarragon butter.
Inspectors in 2006 thought his cooking 'outstanding'. Several visitors
complained that jugs of tap water are not provided in the dining room;
'only bottled water [£3.50] from Hampshire' is served. And one reporter,
while liking the 'relaxed comfort', wrote that many penalties were
threatened (for smoking, smuggling takeaway meals into the bedroom, etc).
(*Stephen and Jane Savery, Prudence Cooper, and others*)

15 bedrooms. 8 in lodge linked by 'feature bridge'. 1 mile from centre. Closed
Christmas/New Year. Ramp. Lounge, champagne bar, 2 dining rooms; evening background music; banqueting room; theatre/conference room. Rooftop garden; small
front garden. No smoking. No children under 13. Guide dogs only. All major credit
cards accepted. B&B £75–£150 per person; D,B&B £95–£170. Set dinner £42.50.
1-night bookings refused during Chester races.

∗∗

Traveller's tale I made a booking for friends to stay at this hotel
and went in person to ensure that payment had been received (a
deposit was required four months before the date of the visit).
When my friends paid the bill on leaving they were charged too
much. I contacted the hotel about this. The woman who
answered the phone was extremely rude. I said that I would
report her appalling manners to the management. She replied:
'Complain as much as you want, it won't do any good. I am the
owner.' (*Hotel in Birmingham*)

∗∗

CHESTERFIELD Derbyshire   Map 4:E4
See SHORTLIST

CHIDDINGFOLD Surrey   Map 2:D3

The Swan Inn & Restaurant   [BUDGET]   *Tel* 01428-682073
Petworth Road   *Fax* 01428-683259
Chiddingfold   *Email* enquiries@theswaninn.biz
GU8 4TY   *Website* www.theswaninn.biz

Old inn, now 'gastropub', on main road of leafy village N of Petworth on A283. Owned by Daniel Hall and Darren Tidd; winner of Les Routiers Inn of the Year 2005. 'Fresh and clean; reasonably priced. Contemporary design; immaculate rooms with fantastic attention to detail. Meals [ranging from ham, egg and chips to duck leg confit with wild mushroom cream sauce] served in bar or restaurant [background music] by extremely friendly staff, in relaxed manner.' Garden. No smoking: restaurant, bedrooms. Unsuitable for &. No dogs in bedrooms. Amex, MasterCard, Visa accepted. 11 bedrooms. B&B £35–£60 per person. Cooked breakfast £5 added. Full alc £35. More reports, please. ***V***

****

Traveller's tale Our bedroom was supposed to be the best in the hotel – a sort of micro-suite. But maintenance was not a strong point. The room was freezing cold and the single radiator was turned to zero; we turned it up but it took for ever to get warm. The loo was in a cubicle within the bathroom but its door had been removed; for privacy you needed to shut the bathroom door. This was so distorted that its handle and bolt could not be used and it therefore swung open. We wanted to wash our hands but there was no hot water. I called Reception and eventually a man came up. He turned on the bath tap and was greeted by streams of air. (*Hotel in Scotland*)

****

CHILGROVE West Sussex   Map 2:E3

The Chilgrove White Horse
Chilgrove, nr Chichester
PO18 9HX

Tel 01243-535219
Fax 01243-535301
Email info@whitehorsechilgrove.co.uk
Website www.whitehorsechilgrove.co.uk

Found 'excellent' in 2006, Charles and Carin Burton's wisteria-clad 18th-century coaching inn (a member of the Green Tourism Business Scheme) has a prominent position on a winding country road across the South Downs between Chichester and Petersfield. All around is heavily wooded countryside. Footpaths lead to the South Downs Way. 'Accommodation, service and quality of everything was first class,' one visitor wrote. The unpretentious bedrooms are in a modern extension at the rear. Each has its own entrance, allocated parking, and use of the secluded walled garden. The large bar has an open log fire, a short menu, and many wines by the glass (600 wines are stocked). The lounge area in the restaurant, decorated in neutral colours, has a 'welcoming log fire on chilly evenings'. The chef, Juan Otero, describes his dishes as 'English/Mediterranean' (perhaps grilled turbot or lemon sole, or baked crab thermidor). Cooked breakfasts are available only for groups that book all the rooms and eat together. Other guests get a 'very good' continental breakfast, brought to the room in a hamper at a chosen time between 8 and 10 am. In summer you can break-fast alfresco. (*Prof. Geoff Southworth, NF, and others*)

8 bedrooms. 1 suitable for &. 5 miles NW of Chichester. Closed Mon. Restaurant closed Sun night/Mon. Lounge area, bar area, restaurant (all only accessible during opening hours); background music; live piano Sat night. 1-acre grounds. Unsuitable for &. Civil wedding licence applied for. No smoking. No dogs in restaurant/lounge area. MasterCard, Visa accepted. B&B £37.50–£95 per person. 2-night min. stay summer weekends. Christmas/New Year/Easter packages.

CHILLATON Devon   Map 1:D3

Tor Cottage
Chillaton, nr Lifton
PL16 0JE

Tel 01822-860248
Fax 01822-860126
Email info@torcottage.co.uk
Website www.torcottage.co.uk

'In its own private valley', Maureen Rowlatt's upmarket B&B has a tranquil, secluded setting. One reader wrote: 'The beauty of the place is that you feel totally away from it all.' Guests are welcomed with a trug containing sparkling wine, home-made truffles and fresh fruit. Ms Rowlatt 'regards all her visitors as friends, and is a joy to be with', says another guest; and a fellow B&B owner reported that 'she made our stay so special'. Each of the garden rooms has a log fire, private terrace, fridge and CD-player; a kitchen has been added to Laughing Waters, a bed-sitting room with Shaker furniture, in a corner of the garden. It has its own gypsy caravan, a hammock, and a barbecue area with decking and a patio heater and may also be available on a self-catering basis. Breakfast, ordered the evening before, is taken in the conservatory, on the terrace in summer, or in the bedrooms. 'It was excellent: enough smoked salmon with the scrambled eggs to warrant on the first day requesting a doggy bag, and on subsequent days to be offered one without asking.' (*EM, SH*)

5 bedrooms. 3 in garden. ½ mile S of Chillaton. Open mid-Jan–mid-Dec. Sitting room, large conservatory, breakfast room (background music). 18-acre grounds: 2-acre garden: heated swimming pool (40 x 15 ft), barbecue, stream, bridleway, walks. River, fishing ½ mile. Unsuitable for &. No smoking. No children under 14. No dogs. MasterCard, Visa accepted. B&B £70–£94 per person (min. 2 nights).

CHIPPING CAMPDEN Gloucestershire   Map 3:D6

Cotswold House   *Tel* 01386-840330
The Square   *Fax* 01386-840310
Chipping Campden   *Email* reception@cotswoldhouse.com
GL55 6AN   *Website* www.cotswoldhouse.com

'Beautifully maintained. Excellent service.' Dominating the main square of this attractive Cotswold town, Ian and Christa Taylor's grand Regency house has a traditional exterior that belies the interior with its striking modern design and furnishings. A magnificent central staircase spirals up to the roof. Arched doors open on to the paved rear garden, which has a fountain, roses, lavender and herbs. The bedrooms have been transformed into 'ultra-chic, Italian-style dens, with deep dark colours, huge, very comfortable bed, many stylish touches'. Guests are offered a choice of duvet or blankets and several kinds of pillow. This year, there are eight new bedrooms in *Montrose House*: two have an outside hot tub, one an enormous stone bath. One suite is across the square. There are two restaurants ('a boon when you stay more than a day or two'). The cooking of chef Jamie Forman is praised. The formal *Juliana's* restaurant has arched windows, modern paintings and a sophisticated menu. In the recently enlarged *Hicks' Brasserie* (which also serves breakfast, morning coffee, afternoon teas and a children's menu), a 'memorable' halibut crème de Paris was consumed. 'Good breakfasts', too: they include porridge with whisky and cream, and scrambled egg with smoked salmon. (*Michael and Eithne Dandy*)

29 bedrooms. Town centre. Some in nearby buildings. Lounge, bar, brasserie, restaurant, garden restaurant; background music; conference/function facilities. 2-acre garden: terrace. Civil wedding licence. No smoking. Amex, MasterCard, Visa accepted. B&B £140–£247.50 per person; D,B&B £187.50–£292.50. Set dinner £49.50. Christmas/New Year packages. 1-night bookings refused Sat. **'V'**

CHITTLEHAMHOLT Devon Map 1:C4

Highbullen Hotel
Chittlehamholt
Umberleigh EX37 9HD

Tel 01769-540561
Fax 01769-540492
Email info@highbullen.co.uk
Website www.highbullen.co.uk

On a huge estate with views towards Exmoor and Dartmoor, the Neil family's 'hotel, golf and country club' offers a wide range of sporting pursuits, indoors and out (see below). An 18-hole par 68 golf course winds its way round the grounds; four grass tennis courts and indoor bowls have been added this year to a list that also includes fishing and swimming. 'Many of our fellow guests had been several times before,' said one couple. Plus points: 'unspoilt views', 'friendly people', 'sheets and blankets not duvets'. Staff are thought 'so pleasant', and prices remain reasonable. Colette Potter (née Neil) is 'very much in charge of the kitchen', and in the large restaurant the daily-changing three-course menu might include quail's eggs in Parmesan tartlets; sautéed guineafowl. The best bedrooms (some 'reached along numerous corridors and stairways') are in the original 19th-century Gothic mansion; many have good views. Most rooms are in cottages in the grounds: 'Basic but immaculate, and the comforts are there.' Breakfast, mainly self-service, has a large buffet (fruit, cereals, etc); cooked dishes cost extra. (*B and EW, and others*)

40 bedrooms. 28 in cottages/converted farm buildings. Some on ground floor. ½ mile from village. Ramps. Lounge, library, bar/brasserie (background music), restaurant; billiard room; indoor swimming pool, indoor bowls, steam room, sunbed, exercise room, table tennis, squash. 200-acre estate: woodland, garden, croquet, putting, 2 swimming pools, 18-hole golf course, indoor/outdoor tennis; golf/tennis tuition; *Pavilion* sports complex: 65-ft swimming pool, beauty treatments, conference suite, dance suite. 10 miles river fishing (ghillie available). Civil wedding licence. No smoking: restaurant, bedrooms. No children under 7. No dogs. MasterCard, Visa accepted. B&B [2006] £48–£100 per person; D,B&B £68–£120. Bar lunches. Set dinner from £27.50. Christmas/New Year breaks. **'V'**

CIRENCESTER Gloucestershire Map 3:E5
See SHORTLIST

CLIMPING West Sussex   Map 2:E3

Bailiffscourt   *Tel* 01903-723511
Climping Street   *Fax* 01903-723107
Climping BN17 5RW   *Email* bailiffscourt@hshotels.co.uk
                                          Website www.hshotels.co.uk

Built in the 1930s for Lord Moyne of the Guinness family, this set of
mock medieval buildings is a short walk across fields from a pebble beach.
Bricks from 12th- and 13th-century buildings on the site were used to
create an 'authentic' effect; there are mullioned windows, rough-hewn
wood, stone doorways, tapestries and flagstones. Most bedrooms are in
buildings in the large grounds. A hotel since 1948, *Bailiffscourt* is part of
Sandy Goodman's small Historic Sussex Hotels group, and is managed
by Chris Alger. One visitor said: 'Most of the receptionists were efficient
and friendly, but it was difficult to get a smile from the waiters. I wouldn't
call the atmosphere convivial.' Another guest enjoyed her stay, with some
reservations: 'We were in the master suite, large, with log fire, two sofas,
Elizabethan-style four-poster bed and separate eating area. The cooked
breakfasts were excellent. The evening meals were good but could have
been better.' There is a spa with indoor and outdoor pools and a gym.
(*VT, and others*)

40 bedrooms. Most in cottages. Some on ground floor. 1 adapted for &. 2 miles W
of Littlehampton. 4 small lounge areas, restaurant; 4 conference/function rooms. No
background music. Spa: swimming pool (36 by 16 ft). 30-acre grounds: garden,
croquet, tennis, heated outdoor swimming pool (43 by 16 ft). Civil wedding licence.
No smoking. No dogs in restaurant and spa. All major credit cards accepted. B&B
£97.50–£230 per person; D,B&B £137.50–£270. Full alc £43.50. Christmas/New
Year packages. 1-night bookings sometimes refused weekends.

COLWALL Worcestershire   Map 3:D5

Colwall Park Hotel   *Tel* 01684-540000
Colwall, nr Malvern   *Fax* 01684-540847
WR13 6QG   *Email* hotel@colwall.com
                                          Website www.colwall.com

In the middle of a quiet village, Iain and Sarah Nesbitt's traditional hotel,
a 1905 mock-Tudor building, stands below the western slopes of the
Malvern Hills in Elgar country. Our inspector found much to like,
especially the food, and most visitors this year enjoyed their stay. The
bedrooms vary in size: their decor may be 'nothing special'. Visitors on a
gourmet break ('good value at £79 per person per night') were upgraded

to a 'huge room, with vast bed, sofa, chair and table, up-to-date glossy magazines; good-sized bathroom (shower over bath)'. Smaller bedrooms face the garden; single rooms may have only a shower; some attic rooms have limited head room. A standard double 'had repro Edwardian furniture, large bed, lovely soft pillows'. Simple meals are served in the *Lantern* bar. In the oak-panelled *Seasons* restaurant, James Garth serves a modern menu. 'Faultless evening meals; breads sliced for you by a white-gloved waiter; suppliers shown on the menus. All ingredients beautifully cooked, crisp and well presented.' Breakfast has a wide choice of continental options, and good cooked dishes, but 'they really should offer fresh juice'. The hotel requests a non-refundable deposit (£40 per room) at the time of booking. (*Christine and Colin Gillott, and others*)

22 bedrooms. Halfway between Malvern and Ledbury on B4218. Train: Colwall. Ramp (bar and restaurant). 2 lounges (1 with TV), library, bar, restaurant (soft background blues/jazz at lunch and dinner). 1½-acre garden: croquet, *boules*. Unsuitable for &. Smoking in bar only. No dogs: public rooms, some bedrooms. MasterCard, Visa accepted. B&B [2006] £60–£79 per person; D,B&B (min. 2 nights) £79–£105. Set dinner £24.95; full alc £25–£40. Christmas/New Year packages. ***V***

CONSTANTINE BAY Cornwall   Map 1:D2

Treglos Hotel   NEW   *Tel* 01841-520727
Constantine Bay   *Fax* 01841-521163
Padstow PL28 8JH   *Email* stay@tregloshotel.com
                                 Website www.tregloshotel.com

Above Constantine Bay, with easy access to the coastal footpath, this traditional hotel has been run by the Barlow family for four decades: Jim and Rose Barlow preside. Its fans love the old-fashioned values: log fires, early morning tea brought to the room (at a charge), nocturnal shoe-cleaning. 'General high standards. Long-serving staff, plus very good Polish waiters. You leave the restaurant satisfied.' 'Excellent value. One of the ever-decreasing band of hotels that change the menu every night; ample choice' (eg, tenderloin of beef with artichokes; grilled local sole). 'Substantial bar snacks' at lunchtime. 'Wonderful, creamy afternoon teas.' The breakfast buffet has a wide choice. Families are welcomed, but children under seven are banned from the restaurant after 6.30 pm; parents with young children have a breakfast service between 8 and 8.30 am. Except during summer school holidays, men must wear jacket and tie in public areas after 7 pm. Bedrooms have light colour schemes. The garden has secluded sitting places and a children's play area. There is a small indoor swimming pool. A wide sandy beach, popular with surfers, is ten minutes' walk away. The Barlows also own Merlin Golf and Country Club, ten minutes' drive. (*Ian Dewey; also Juliet Sebag-Montefiore*)

42 bedrooms. 3 miles W of Padstow. Train: Bodmin. Open 1 Mar–end Nov. Some on ground floor. 2 adapted for &. Lift, ramps. 2 lounges (pianist Mon and Thurs), bar, restaurant; children's den, snooker room; beauty treatments; indoor swimming pool (30 by 15 ft), whirlpool. 2½-acre grounds: croquet, badminton, children's play area. Sand beach 5 mins' walk. Golf club nearby. Smoking in bar only. No children under 7 in dining room after 6.30 pm. No dogs in public rooms. MasterCard, Visa accepted. B&B [2006] £55–£116 per person; D,B&B £70–£131. Set menu £27. Bridge, golf packages. *V*

CORSE LAWN Gloucestershire   Map 3:D5

Corse Lawn House	*Tel* 01452-780771
Corse Lawn GL19 4LZ	*Fax* 01452-780840
	Email enquiries@corselawn.com
	Website www.corselawn.com

Q *César award in 2005*

Set back from the village green and road, this red brick Queen Anne Grade II listed building is fronted by an ornamental pond (originally a coach wash) with ducks. 'Two glorious nights. Welcome just right,' one couple wrote. Other visitors this year had 'an excellent stay. Our quiet suite, at the back, was spacious and well equipped. It had a whirlpool bath big enough for two.' Denis Hine died last year: his widow, Baba ('*Corse Lawn* is my life,' she writes), has taken over front-of-house duties and 'handed the reins in the kitchen to Andrew Poole, who worked beside me for nine years'. 'Superb food, always piping hot. The extensive *carte* menu had many tempting dishes', eg, truffled guineafowl breast with wild mushroom and Madeira sauce. Mrs Hine's son, Giles, who has moved to New Zealand, is responsible for the wine list, which has 'a good non-French selection'. Light meals are available in the brightly decorated bistro. The 'excellent' breakfast, served at the table, has fresh juice, muesli with fresh fruit, 'delicious marmalade' (on sale at Reception). Dogs are welcomed. 'A path is mowed in adjacent fields to make it easier for owners to exercise their dogs.' (*Joanna and Paul Lindsell, John Jenkins and Mark Riches, Joanna Russell*)

19 bedrooms. 5 on ground floor. 5 miles SW of Tewkesbury on B4211. Closed 24–26 Dec. Lounge, bar lounge, bistro/bar, restaurants; 2 conference/private dining rooms. No background music. 12-acre grounds: croquet, tennis, covered swimming pool (41 by 16 ft). Civil wedding licence. No smoking: restaurant, some bedrooms.

All major credit cards accepted. B&B £70–£90 per person; D,B&B £95–£112.50. Set lunch £22.50, dinner £29.50; full alc £35. New Year package. 1-night B&B bookings refused Sat. *V*

COVENTRY Warwickshire *See SHORTLIST*   Map 2:B2

CRANBROOK Kent   Map 2:E4

Cloth Hall Oast   *Tel/Fax* 01580-712220
Coursehorn Lane   *Email* clothhalloast@aol.com
Cranbrook TN17 3NR

'A well-converted oast house, tastefully finished and furnished, in a lovely part of the Kentish Weald', Katherine Morgan's home is just outside an attractive village (which has a windmill and a main street of timber-fronted shops). She is 'a most attentive hostess, maintaining exceptionally high standards', says a visitor this year. There are Persian rugs, beautiful porcelain and silverware and delicate paintings; sofas and armchairs face a deep carved stone fireplace in the elegant lounge where 'expanses of glass look over the garden'. Two bedrooms are in the oast house, the third off a galleried landing. Beds are turned down at night. Bathrooms are 'state-of-the-art'. Mrs Morgan serves tea and cake to arriving visitors, and presides at the communal dinner. 'Relaxed evenings with imaginative, good cooking.' No licence: bring your own wine. 'Fine china, home-made jams and good coffee made breakfast a pleasure.' In the grounds are swimming pool ('heated – great!'), pergola and lily pond. Mrs Morgan is 'informative about local attractions' (Sissinghurst, Chartwell, Bodiam Castle, etc). (*Jonathan Martin, Mrs MJ Tanner, Julia Jary*)

3 bedrooms. 1 mile SE of Cranbrook. Closed Christmas. Sitting room, dining room. No background music. 5-acre garden: croquet, fishpond, heated swimming pool. Unsuitable for &. No smoking in bedrooms. No dogs. No credit cards. B&B (*Not VAT-rated*) £42.50–£80 per person. Evening meal £24. 1-night bookings sometimes refused Sat.

****

Traveller's tale At breakfast I successfully explained to the non-English-speaking help what 'tomato' is. I failed to explain that toast is not warm bread. The fried egg required decent burial. (*Hotel in Suffolk*)

****

CRICKET MALHERBIE Somerset   Map 1:C6

The Old Rectory	*Tel* 01460-54364
Cricket Malherbie, nr Ilminster	*Fax* 01460-57374
TA19 0PW	*Email* info@malherbie.co.uk
	Website www.malherbie.co.uk

On a quiet lane in a conservation hamlet on the edge of an area of outstanding natural beauty, this Grade II listed house has been sensitively restored, say visitors this year. There are flagstones, panelling, Tudor oak beams and 'nice old furniture in the public rooms'. The owners, Michael and Patricia Fry-Foley, cultivate a house-party atmosphere, and serve a no-choice dinner communally, by arrangement, in a room with deep blue walls, Georgian shuttered windows, a wooden floor, and original paintings. The main course could be chicken breast with mushroom sauce and spinach. There is 'a range of interesting drinks based on the local cider apple'. The bedrooms overlook the garden. 'Ours was cottagey and cosy, with a small, well-equipped bathroom and a comfortable bed. We were pleased to find *Fawlty Towers* among the videos by the TV.' Breakfast was 'very well cooked'. Including 'exceptional' fruit compote, it was served by the host, 'very friendly and chatty'. The house is not wheelchair-friendly, but 'every effort is made to accommodate the needs of sight- and hearing-impaired guests'. (*Simon and Alison Routh, and others*)

5 bedrooms. 2 miles SW of Ilminster. Closed Christmas. Dining room closed midday. Sitting room, dining room. No background music. 1¼-acre garden. Civil wedding licence. Unsuitable for &. No smoking. No children under 16. No dogs. MasterCard, Visa accepted. B&B £47.50–£75 per person. Set dinner £30. 1-night bookings refused bank holidays.

CROFT-ON-TEES Co. Durham   Map 4:C4

Clow Beck House	*Tel* 01325-721075
Monk End Farm	*Fax* 01325-720419
Croft-on-Tees	*Email* david@clowbeckhouse.co.uk
nr Darlington DL2 2SW	*Website* www.clowbeckhouse.co.uk

César award: For utterly enjoyable mild eccentricity

Named after the stream which runs through the working farm on which it stands, this 'fascinating and unusual' hotel has 'exceptional hosts', owner/ managers David and Heather Armstrong. The decor is 'unexpected and certainly different', says one report. 'Immaculate bedrooms', in stone-built outbuildings, sit around a 'beautifully landscaped garden', with 'stunning views towards the village and River Tees'. They are large (some more flamboyant than others) and equipped 'to satisfy the hedonist' (digital TV, CD-player, Internet socket, bathrobes, etc). Some have a small garden. 'Ours had sparkly chandeliers, carved wooden ceiling roses and a theatrical effect: bay window area like a proscenium arch.' The 'most attractive', large restaurant on two levels, with beams, arched windows and tiled floor, leads to a terrace. David Armstrong, who greeted inspectors 'resplendent in bright chequered chef's trousers and top', cooks in 'farmhouse' style (eg, rack of lamb with apricots, honey and mustard). There is a vegetarian menu. Portions are generous. Many wines cost under £20. Breakfast includes 'David's special porridge', home-made breads and preserves, 'eggs whichever way'. In the grounds are 'interesting artefacts and ornaments, eg, a miniature cricket team' and a castle for children (they also have special menus, etc). Disabled guests are catered for. George the dog helps with the welcome. (*CL Hodgkin; also Mike Widdall*)

13 bedrooms. 12 in garden buildings. 1 suitable for &. 3 miles SE of Darlington, via unmade road (follow brown signs). Closed Christmas/New Year. Restaurant closed midday. Ramps. Lounge, restaurant (classical background music); small conference facilities. 2-acre grounds in 100-acre farm. No smoking: restaurant, some bedrooms. Guide dogs only. Amex, MasterCard, Visa accepted. B&B £60–£80 per person. Full alc £32–£38.

CROOKHAM Northumberland   Map 4:A3

The Coach House at Crookham   BUDGET   *Tel* 01890-820293
Crookham   *Fax* 01890-820284
Cornhill-on-Tweed   *Email* stay@coachhousecrookham.com
TD12 4TD   *Website* www.coachhousecrookham.com

Noted for its welcome to wheelchair-users, this listed 17th-century dower house stands back from the road near Flodden Field. The 'very friendly' owners, Toby and Leona Rutter, 'run their quiet little establishment with great dedication', say guests this year. Most bedrooms (some suitable for disabled guests) are in single-storey buildings linked by paved paths around a courtyard, and there are adjoining rooms good for a family (children are welcomed, and so are dogs). The vaulted residents' lounge has a large open fire and views over the terrace to the orchard. 'My spacious room had fresh flowers, candles, and views of fields and the Cheviot Hills.' Large-screen TV and DVD/CD-player are provided in the bigger bedrooms. Dinner at 7.30, after 'honesty' drinks in the lounge, 'is fresh, wholesome, tasty' (eg, poached salmon with butter and lemon sauce), and served in generous portions. 'You have to ration how much you eat.' Breakfast 'is another happy experience' (a large selection of fruits, yogurt and cereals; 'the poached eggs easily passed my test'). Teas (free on the day of arrival) and drinks are taken in the former coach house, with its beamed ceiling and huge arched windows. (*Val and Alan Green, TL*)

11 bedrooms. 7 round courtyard. Some suitable for &. On A697, 3 miles N of Milfield. Closed Christmas. Lounge, 2 dining rooms; terrace. No background music. Orchard. No smoking: dining rooms, lounge, some bedrooms. No dogs in public rooms. MasterCard, Visa accepted. B&B £32–£55 per person; D,B&B £51.50–£64.50. Set dinner £19.50.

CROSBY-ON-EDEN Cumbria   Map 4:B2

Crosby Lodge   *Tel* 01228-573618
High Crosby, Crosby-on-Eden   *Fax* 01228-573428
CA6 4QZ   *Email* enquiries@crosbylodge.co.uk
                                       Website www.crosbylodge.co.uk

A castellated and creeper-covered Grade II listed country house (1805), just five minutes from the M6 and close to the Scottish border. Owned by Michael and Patricia Sedgwick, it stands in partly wooded grounds overlooking parkland and the River Eden beyond (fishing can be arranged). 'A lovely building in a beautiful area,' writes a visitor this year. 'Very much owner-run; the staff were charming.' All the bedrooms are individually designed; some face the park. 'Ours was comfortable, with stunning view; a bit old-fashioned (not unhappy with that).' The chintzy decor is thought 'entirely appropriate to the feel of the place'. In the 'lovely' dining room, a four-course dinner ('traditional with a continental touch') is served from a daily-changing menu. Some readers have called the food 'excellent'. One was disappointed by it, but thought breakfast 'fabulous': it has home-baked bread, home-made yogurt, silver teapots and bone china. (*Suzanne MacWhannell, AG, and others*)

11 bedrooms. 2 in stables (ramp). 4½ miles NE of Carlisle, off A689. Open 13 Jan–24 Dec. Lounge/bar, restaurant; function facilities. Background music on request. 4½-acre grounds: walled garden with gazebo. Civil wedding licence. No smoking: restaurant, bedrooms. Dogs in stables rooms only, not in public rooms. Amex, MasterCard, Visa accepted. B&B £70–£95 per person; D,B&B £105–£135. Set dinner £38; full alc £55.

Most hotels have reduced rates out of season, and offer breaks throughout the year. It is always worth checking for special deals on the hotel's website or phoning to ask.

CROSTHWAITE Cumbria   Map 4: inset C2

The Punch Bowl   **NEW**   *Tel* 01539-568237
Crosthwaite, Lyth Valley   *Fax* 01539-568875
LA8 8HR   *Email* info@the-punchbowl.co.uk
                                    Website www.the-punchbowl.co.uk

In 2005, Stephanie Barton of *The Drunken Duck Inn*, Barngates (*qv*), took
over and renovated this 300-year-old inn in the Lyth valley. Stephen
Carruthers is the 'friendly, chatty' manager, Matt Waddington the chef.
Inspectors were impressed: 'Smartly informal. A seriously good selection of
wines and specialist beers.' A 'good choice of brasserie dishes' is served in
the bar; the low-ceilinged restaurant has a modern *carte*. 'Occasional
timidity of flavouring produced some bland dishes, but loin of lamb on
creamed cabbage with a shepherd's pie of neck meat had bags of flavour;
crab ravioli was elaborate but tasty. Desserts well handled and complex.
Home-made rolls.' There are two terraces for alfresco eating and drinking,
and meals are served by a 'cheerful, hard-working young team'. 'Our
spacious, superior double room had high ceiling, vast bed, comfortable,
oversized sofa, huge, low wooden beams, flat-screen TV. Subdued lighting
from table lamps, adequate when supplemented by overhead spots. Big
bathroom with under-floor heating and crab-claw bath.' Unusual breakfast
dishes include potato and dill pancakes with quail's eggs and hollandaise
sauce. 'Juice freshly squeezed, tea-leaf tea.' Complimentary tea and coffee
can be delivered to the bedroom throughout the day. The small lounge has
deep leather sofas.

9 bedrooms. 5 miles W of Kendal, via A591. Lounge, 2 bar rooms, restaurant. No
background music. 2 terraces. Unsuitable for &. No smoking. Dogs by negotiation.
Amex, MasterCard, Visa accepted. B&B: double £100–£180, suite £210–£250. Full
alc £50. Christmas/New Year packages.

DARLINGTON Co. Durham *See SHORTLIST* Map 4:C4

****

Traveller's tale There were dirty carpets throughout, and
decaying furniture in our bedroom. It was reached up narrow,
twisting stairs which made carrying suitcases hazardous; there
was no porter service. At breakfast, served on paper tablecloths,
there were cheap cereals and plastic bottles of sauces.
(*Hotel in Dorset*)

****

DARTMOUTH Devon   Map 1:D4

Knocklayd   NEW   *Tel/Fax* 01803-752873
Redoubt Hill, Kingswear   *Email* stay@knocklayd.com
Dartmouth TQ6 0DA   *Website* www.knocklayd.com

At the highest point of Kingswear village, looking across the estuary
(crossed by a ferry) to Dartmouth, this 'large rambling' house is 'strongly
recommended for dog lovers'. It has been turned into this small guest house
by the 'extremely hospitable' Susan and Jonathan Cardale. 'It is very much
a home, not for those who prefer a sanitised atmosphere,' writes the
nominator. 'Our pretty and thoughtfully appointed room had wonderful
views. Everything was stylish and of quality. The large double bed,
extremely comfortable, was dressed with beautiful fabrics. Fluffy towels
and hot water were abundant. Breakfast was five-star: delicious fruit,
excellent coffee, full English, Vermont or continental, or a combination of
the three. Table laid with beautiful white linen and silverware. A bargain.'
The Cardales own two elderly Labradors, Jack and Jessie, and Molly, a
'woolly little hearing dog for the deaf (retired)'. Visiting dogs sleep in the
utility room or the kitchen. The hostess, a Cordon Bleu cook, will provide
an evening meal based on local fresh fish and meat. There is broadband
Internet access. (*Wendy Ashworth*)

3 bedrooms. 5 mins' walk from ferry to Dartmouth. Closed Christmas. Lounge,
dining room. No background music. Garden. Rock beach 300 yds; sailing
nearby. Unsuitable for &. No smoking. Children 'must be supervised'.
MasterCard, Visa accepted. B&B [2006] £37.50–£50 per person. Set dinner
£25–£30. 3-day off-season rates.

Nonsuch House   *Tel* 01803-752829
Church Hill, Kingswear   *Fax* 01803-752357
Dartmouth TQ6 0BX   *Email* enquiries@nonsuch-house.co.uk
                                     Website www.nonsuch-house.co.uk

Ω *César award in 2000*

On a south-facing hill, with views across the estuary to Dartmouth
(crossed by a ferry), this Edwardian villa is an upmarket guest house,
run by Kit Noble and his wife, Penny, 'lovely hosts'. 'It is a treasure,'
was one comment. This year the Nobles have created a new sitting
room, and added a fourth bedroom. Canary yellow walls, royal blue
carpets, interesting ornaments and books enliven what could have been
a staid building, and on fine days, afternoon tea, with home-made cakes,
is served under a parasol on the terrace, as boats go by. The warm

welcome is regularly praised, and so is 'Kit's tasty cooking'. An evening meal is available four nights a week: the menus, on a blackboard, depend on local produce, eg, Dartmouth crab salad; Devon lamb. Special needs are taken into account. No liquor licence – bring your own wine. Breakfast has 'proper bread', fresh orange juice, home-made muesli. The booking procedure is liked: 'No deposit required; a hand-written letter of confirmation. No reception desk, just an airy hallway.' When the dining room is closed, you could take a ferry ride across the water to 'fabulous restaurants', eg, *The New Angel* (*Michelin* star). (*Janet and Don Wille, and others*)

4 bedrooms. 5 mins' walk from ferry to Dartmouth. Dining room closed midday, and evenings of Tues, Wed and Sat. No telephone. Ramps. Lounge, dining room/conservatory. No background music. ¼-acre garden: sun terrace. Rock beach 300 yds; sailing nearby. No smoking. No children under 10. No dogs. Diners, MasterCard, Visa accepted. B&B [2006] £47.50–£95 per person. Set dinner £27.50. 3-day off-season rates. Christmas/New Year packages. 1-night bookings sometimes refused weekends.

See also SHORTLIST

DEDHAM Essex   Map 2:C5

Dedham Hall & Fountain House Restaurant   *Tel* 01206-323027
Brook Street, Dedham   *Fax* 01206-323293
nr Colchester CO7 6AD   *Email* sarton@dedhamhall.demon.co.uk
                               Website www.dedhamhall.demon.co.uk

In Constable country (Flatford Mill is two miles away), this cluster of old buildings (15th-century cottage, 18th-century house, Dutch barn, now a studio) is informally run by Wendy and Jim Sarton as a guest house/restaurant/art school. There are geese on the pond, daffodils in spring, and views of Dedham's church tower. Visitors attending the painting courses stay in large rooms around the barn; the other guests are in bedrooms in the house (no keys given). One wrote: 'Our room was large, pleasant and comfortable.' Some rooms have a big bathroom with a power shower. Some are approached through the kitchen. The family room is 'palatial'. The lounges (where afternoon tea with cake can be served) have oak beams, books, and paintings. The beamed restaurant, with its red tablecloths, candles and flowers, faces pond and garden. The 'above-average' cooking on the weekly-changing menu might include coq au vin; lemon sole with tartare sauce. Reserve a table when booking. Breakfast has 'toast made from real bread', fresh fruit, 'wonderful bacon', 'delicious scrambled eggs'. 'The owner collected us at Manningtree station and took us back the next day – very nice, and not necessary.' (*WB, KJ*)

18 bedrooms. 13 in annexe (for painting holidays). Some on ground floor. At end of Dedham High St, towards Manningtree, set back from the road. Open 2 Jan–24 Dec. Restaurant closed Sun/Mon. Ramps. 2 lounges, 2 bars, dining room, restaurant; studio. No background music. 6-acre grounds: pond, gardens. No smoking: restaurant, some bedrooms. No dogs. MasterCard, Visa accepted. B&B £47.50–£55 per person; D,B&B £75–£80. Set dinner £28.50. Painting holidays Feb–Nov.

Maison Talbooth   NEW

Stratford Road, Dedham
nr Colchester CO7 6HN

Tel 01206-322367
Fax 01206-322752
Email maison@milsomhotels.com
Website www.milsomhotels.com

In a 'glorious, tranquil location', this pink-washed Victorian mansion (Pride of Britain) stands on a bluff overlooking the Vale of Dedham. Paul Milsom runs it to provide accommodation alongside his restaurant (*Le Talbooth*, by the River Stour) and his busy hotel/brasserie, *milsom's* (extensively refurbished this year), nearby. For dinner, guests can walk or take a courtesy car to the former, or be driven to the latter or to the other sister hotel, *The Pier at Harwich* (*qv*). In the 'very attractive' large drawing room, snacks and drinks are served during the day. An 'excellent' continental breakfast is brought to the bedrooms. Porridge, fruit salad and 'a good range of cooked dishes' are also available. The rooms, each named after a poet, have a sitting area; the best three have a hot tub on a private terrace. Milton looks over the vale, Brooke faces a high bank, Tennyson and Kipling are smaller and cheaper. 'Well-stocked bookshelves include classic authors and lighter fare. Staff were without exception efficient and unobtrusive,' says a visitor this year, 'but our room was not well soundproofed.' *Le Talbooth* is often used for house parties. Bridget Stanley is its manager. In the grounds there is a pond with fountain.

10 bedrooms. 5 on ground floor. 5 miles NE of Colchester, E of A12, exit Stratford St Mary. Drawing room; function facilities. 3-acre grounds: croquet; swimming pool planned for late 2007. *Le Talbooth* restaurant, bar and garden (closed Sun evening Sept–May) on River Stour, 10 mins' walk/courtesy car. Civil wedding licence. Smoking discouraged in restaurant. Guide dogs only. All major credit cards accepted. B&B [2006] £85–£250 per person. *Le Talbooth*: set lunch £25; full alc £48; *milsom's* full alc £35. 2-night breaks. Christmas package. 1-night weekend bookings discouraged.

The Sun Inn   *Tel* 01206-323351
High Street, Dedham   *Email* info@thesuninndedham.com
nr Colchester CO7 6DF   *Website* www.thesuninndedham.com

On the high street, opposite the church, this 15th-century building was refurbished by owner/chef Piers Baker when he bought it in 2003. He describes the decor as 'coaching inn meets small boutique hotel'. Painted yellow outside, it has old oak floorboards and beams, window seats, a huge inglenook fireplace, sofas, club chairs, board games, hardback books, lots of local information. There are large beds, neutral fabrics, 'great showers'. 'Quirky touches', eg, old packing cases for bedside tables, are liked. A fifth bedroom (the largest) is new this year. The daily-changing menu has modern dishes 'with Mediterranean overtones', eg, linguini with clams, tomatoes, garlic; Gloucester Old Spot pork and bean stew. Most ingredients are local. Breakfast (8.30 to 10.30 am) was 'a treat: big jug of fresh orange juice, melon, glass dishes of delicious raspberry jam, marmalade and honey, basket of rolls, toast, etc'. Children are welcomed: 'We adapt the menu for them; there are games and books, and slide, swing, etc, in the large walled garden.' There is a covered terrace with heaters, and a garden barbecue is planned. Background music plays all day, but at night, 'only church bells might disturb the peace'. More reports, please.

5 bedrooms. Central. 5 miles NE of Colchester. Closed 25–27 Dec. Lounge, bar, dining room; background jazz/salsa throughout, all day. ½-acre garden: covered terrace, children's play area. No smoking. No dogs in bedrooms. MasterCard, Visa accepted. B&B £40–£105 per person; D,B&B £57.50–£130. Full alc £31.

DERBY Derbyshire *See SHORTLIST*   Map 3:B6

DODDISCOMBSLEIGH Devon   Map 1:C4

The Nobody Inn   *Tel* 01647-252394
Doddiscombsleigh   *Fax* 01647-252978
nr Exeter EX6 7PS   *Email* info@nobodyinn.co.uk
                                  Website www.nobodyinn.co.uk

Recommended 'for anyone who relishes the understated courtesy of the old West Country', Nick Borst-Smith's 16th-century inn, in a remote Devon hamlet, is a haven for wine- and whisky-lovers (over 600 wines and 240 whiskies in stock). Its lounge has inglenook fireplaces, antique settles, carriage lanterns (no piped music or fruit machines). 'Food and wine were excellent, good value,' say visitors this year. 'When we mentioned the difficulty of finding good New Zealand sweet wines in the UK, two free glasses were presented. The locally sourced ingredients, from cheese board to marmalade, were delicious.' A couple who arrived at 11 pm, due to heavy traffic, found that a meal had been kept for them. The bedrooms above the bar may be 'fairly basic', but housekeeping is 'immaculate'. 'A flask of sherry was very welcome.' The rooms in the annexe, *Town Barton*, reached via a paddock or 'a narrow, raised track', were thought to be 'in need of TLC: peeling paintwork and some rotting woodwork'. 'A continental breakfast is left in a fridge in *Town Barton*; an 'outstanding' cooked breakfast (£4 extra for *Town Barton* guests) is served at the inn. (*Michael Lewis, Jane and Kevin O'Mahoney, and others*)

7 bedrooms. 3 (1 on ground floor) in *Town Barton* 150 yds. 6 miles SW of Exeter. Closed 25 Dec, 31 Dec/1 Jan. Restaurant closed Sun night, Mon night. 2 bars, restaurant. No background music. 7-acre grounds: small garden, patio. Unsuitable for ♿. No smoking: restaurant, bedrooms. No children under 14. No dogs. Amex, MasterCard, Visa accepted. B&B [2006] £25–£50 per person. Full alc £25.

DORCHESTER Dorset   Map 1:C6

The Casterbridge
49 High East Street
Dorchester DT1 1HU

Tel 01305-264043
Fax 01305-260884
Email reception@casterbridgehotel.co.uk
Website www.casterbridgehotel.co.uk

Stuart and Rita Turner, with son-in-law David Thomas, run this modest B&B hotel on the steep high street of Dorset's county town (model for Thomas Hardy's Casterbridge). The family also owns *The Priory*, Wareham (*qv*). Readers write of the friendly welcome, and the 'spotlessly clean, comfortable lounge area'. This year, three bedrooms have been refurbished and their bathrooms upgraded. Street noise may be heard in four front bedrooms, which have no double glazing. There is good family accommodation, but some single rooms are tiny. Breakfast has a large buffet (cereals, muffins, fresh fruit of all descriptions, yogurt, etc), and 'top-quality bacon and sausages, good, yellow-yolked eggs'. No restaurant, but tea and coffee are available all day; guests may picnic in the conservatory next to the breakfast room; and there are plenty of eating places nearby. Outings, guided walks and chauffeur-driven tours of local sights can be arranged. (*JL, and others*)

15 bedrooms. 6 in annexe across courtyard. 3 on ground floor. On main street. 2 garages. On-street parking in front of hotel. Public car park nearby. Closed

24–26 Dec. Ramps. Lounge, bar/library, breakfast room, conservatory. No background music. Small patio garden. No smoking: restaurant, lounge, 13 bedrooms. Guide dogs only. Amex, MasterCard, Visa accepted. B&B £47.50–£77.50 per person. 1-night bookings occasionally refused summer Sat. ***V***

DOVER Kent *See SHORTLIST*   Map 2:D5

DUNSTER Somerset *See SHORTLIST*   Map 1:B5

DUXFORD Cambridgeshire *See SHORTLIST*   Map 2:C4

EARLS COLNE Essex   Map 2:C5

The de Vere Arms	*Tel* 01787-223353
53 High Street	*Fax* 01787-223365
Earls Colne, nr Colchester	*Email* info@deverearms.com
CO6 2PB	*Website* www.deverearms.com

'An excellent stay. We were well looked after.' The nominators of this smart, contemporary hotel in a small village on the Essex/Sussex borders were equally delighted on a return visit. 'The receptionist came out to greet us and carry our bags, closely followed by Martin Hucker, the general manager.' The owners, Michael and Melissa Deckers, who also own the *Carved Angel* pub/brasserie at the other end of the village, have created a 'decidedly different' decor: public areas have antiques, hand-painted murals and striking contemporary paintings. Some of the bedrooms, heavily beamed, are in the old part: 'Ours, at the front, was beautifully designed and fitted out. At the foot of the large bed was an antique *chaise longue*. Plenty of storage. Up three stairs was a stunning bathroom with orange red and yellow tiles.' The lounge has deep sofas and modern artwork. Chef Chris Standhaven has worked at *Hambleton Hall* and *Chewton Glen* (*qqv*). 'Dinner was excellent. Succulent asparagus from a local farm; pan-fried salmon. Vegetarian menu also interesting. Friendly, professional service from two smart Polish girls. Extremely good value.' There is a good choice of continental and cooked dishes at breakfast. 'Any traffic noise disappears at night.' (*Pat and Jeremy Temple*)

9 bedrooms. 1 on ground floor. 3 in annexe. Village centre. Car park. Train: Kelvedon/Colchester. Restaurant closed Sat midday, and a few days after New Year. Ramps. Lounge, bar, restaurant; background music all day. Golf club with swimming pool nearby. No smoking: restaurant, bedrooms. No children under 12 at dinner. No dogs. MasterCard, Visa accepted. B&B [2006] £65–£85 per person; D,B&B £75–£110. Set dinner (midweek) £25; full alc £35. Christmas/New Year packages.

EAST ASHLING West Sussex   Map 2:E3

The Horse and Groom BUDGET	*Tel* 01243-575339
East Ashling, nr Chichester	*Fax* 01243-575560
PO18 9AX	*Email* horseandgroomea@aol.com
	Website www.thehorseandgroomchichester.com

Michael and Michelle Martell's old inn, 3 miles NW of Chichester, on B2178 to Funtington, at foot of South Downs. 'No piped music, no traffic noise. Attractive beamed bedroom.' Characterful bar (flagstone floors, wooden tables, inglenook fireplace). Beer garden. Wide range of food (hearty portions) in restaurant (closed Sun night). 'Good service. Good value.' No smoking: restaurant, bedrooms. No dogs in restaurant. Amex, MasterCard, Visa accepted. 11 bedrooms (5 in converted barn, all on ground floor, 1 suitable for ප්). B&B £32.50–£100 per person. Full alc £15–£25. More reports, please.

EAST GRINSTEAD West Sussex   Map 2:D4

Gravetye Manor	*Tel* 01342-810567
Vowels Lane	*Fax* 01342-810080
East Grinstead RH19 4LJ	*Email* info@gravetyemanor.co.uk
	Website www.gravetyemanor.co.uk

A classic country house hotel (Relais & Châteaux), this creeper-clad Elizabethan manor stands peacefully in grounds designed by William Robinson, pioneer of the English natural garden. It is run by Andrew Russell and Mark Raffan (the chef), who took over from Peter and Sue Herbert in 2004. 'It has blossomed under the enthusiastic young brigade,' says a returning Australian visitor, 'the personal touches, kindness and courtesy are even more in evidence'. Other praise: 'Wonderful, very good food; our children were well looked after.' 'Genuine care and attention to detail.' A discordant note came from a couple who enjoyed a 'delicious' dinner, but found the dining room 'chilly – the promised blazing fire was hardly a glow', and breakfast 'poor, with overcooked scrambled eggs and slow service'. Mark Raffan has a *Michelin* star for his traditional dishes, eg, fillet of beef with aubergine, red pepper and plum tomatoes. The building has an oak-panelled hall and staircase; 'full of antique furniture, the aroma of polish and pot-pourri'. Bedrooms have fruit, books and magazines. The absence of background music is appreciated. (*Dr BW Daniels, Keith Sayfritz, and others*)

18 bedrooms. 4 miles SW of East Grinstead. Restaurant closed to non-residents Christmas night. 3 lounges, bar, restaurant; private dining room. No background music. 30-acre grounds: gardens, croquet, trout lake (fishing). Only restaurant suitable for ♿. Civil wedding licence. No smoking in restaurant. No children under 7, except babies. No dogs. Amex, MasterCard, Visa accepted. Room [2006]: single £100–£155, double £170–£250, suite £260–£325. Breakfast: continental £14, English alc. Set lunch £20–£27, dinner £29–£38; full alc £68. Off-season rates. New Year package. 1-night bookings refused Sat. ***V***

EAST LAVANT West Sussex   Map 2:E3

The Royal Oak   *Tel* 01243-527434
Pook Lane   *Email* ro@thesussexpub.co.uk
East Lavant PO18 0AX   *Website* www.thesussexpub.co.uk

Nick and Lisa Sutherland's listed Georgian flint-stone inn, on the edge of the South Downs, has six modern bedrooms in a converted barn and cottage behind the restaurant; two 'serviced' two-bedroom cottages were due to open as we went to press. Readers like the rooms: 'Welcoming and warm on a winter evening. Pretty soft furnishings and nice touches: fresh flowers, flat-screen TV; CD- and DVD-player, discs and films. A soft but comfortable bed with big, soft, pillows; excellent bathroom with under-floor heating and a strong shower.' The restaurant, which has an *à la carte* menu supplemented by daily blackboard specials, is open seven days a week and is popular with locals. 'It was full of non-residents on a Monday, which says something about the quality.' 'Excellent food, good value.' Breakfast was in keeping, with fresh melon, blueberries, banana and other fruit. 'Cooked dishes well up to standard. Staff both efficient and friendly.' In summer, there are 'pleasant sitting-out spots; views of countryside at the back, or the small front garden'. (*ML, and others*)

10 bedrooms. In adjacent barn/cottages. 2 miles N of Chichester. Closed Christmas/ New Year. Bar/restaurant (background music). Terrace (outside meals), small garden. Unsuitable for ♿. Smoking in bar only. No dogs. Amex, MasterCard, Visa accepted. B&B £45–£70 per person. 1-night bookings refused summer weekends.

EASTBOURNE East Sussex *See SHORTLIST*   Map 2:E4

EMSWORTH Hampshire   Map 2:E3

Restaurant 36 on the Quay   *Tel* 01243-375592
47 South Street   *Fax* 01243-375593
Emsworth PO10 7EG   *Email* 36@onthequay.plus.com
                                       Website www.36onthequay.co.uk

'Everything excellent: staff warm, helpful; high standards.' An endorsement
this year for Ramon (the chef) and Karen Farthing's restaurant-with-rooms.
An attractive 17th-century building on the quayside of this 'interesting little
town', it has 'stunning views'. The cooking ('modern British with a French
influence') has a *Michelin* star (eg, veal fillet with calf's liver and spinach
lasagne). 'All food was excellent. We stayed three nights and were asked if
we wanted anything in addition to the menu. We got it.' A dissenter
thought the cooking 'stuck in a time warp, old-fashioned and heavy', served
in a room 'suffering from an overdose of ruffles and lace'. Four bedrooms
are above the restaurant. Vanilla, pale yellow and cream, with low central
beams, has a large sofa, 'comfortable, if narrow' bed, and view of the
harbour: 'Endless entertainment watching people messing around in boats.'
Clove looks over the boatyard of a nearby sailing club, to the millpond
beyond. A 'superb' continental breakfast is served in the rooms or the
reception area on the landing. 'Segments of pink grapefruit, peeled and
sliced peaches; good coffee, hot brioche toast and croissants.' (*Mr and Mrs
K Robinson, and others*)

6 bedrooms. 1 in cottage (with lounge) across road (can be let weekly). On
harbour. Open late Jan–end Dec, except Christmas, Boxing Day, 1 week Oct.
Restaurant closed Sun/Mon. Lounge area, bar area, restaurant (background music).
Small patio. Only restaurant suitable for &. No smoking in restaurant. Dogs by
arrangement, in cottage only. All major credit cards accepted. B&B £45–£90 per
person. Set dinner £42.95.

EVERSHOT Dorset   Map 1:C6

Summer Lodge   NEW   *Tel* 01935-482000
9 Fore Street   *Fax* 01935-482040
Evershot DT2 0JR   *Email* summerlodge@relaischateaux.com
                                     Website www.summerlodgehotel.com

Designed in part by Thomas Hardy for the Earls of Ilchester, this former
dower house is now a luxury hotel (Relais & Châteaux). Its new owners
(since 2003), the Red Carnation group, have completely renovated.
Charles Lotter is manager. A *Guide* correspondent aged 92, who has known
Summer Lodge for 30 years, wrote of an 'unforgettable' Christmas visit:

'Outstanding staff from all over the world. Welcome efficient. Log fires in the sitting rooms. Everything of high quality. In our bedroom (No. 3) a fire had been lit. Good bathroom. Good coat-hangers. Excellent cooking by Steven Titman.' In the 'elegant dining room', which faces a walled garden, the 'signature' dish is roast loin of Dorset lamb with braised shoulder shepherd's pie. Other visitors wrote: 'Beautiful room, exceptional service, all meals superb, fantastic afternoon tea.' 'Standards as high as ever. Names remembered.' There are fine fabrics and CD/DVD-player in bedrooms, an 'excellent' swimming pool, aromatherapy and reflexology in the new spa. Red Carnation also owns the less expensive *Acorn Inn* in the village, and the little local shop. A large deer park is nearby. (*Eve Webb, Jane Woolcott, and others*)

24 bedrooms. 9 in coach house and courtyard house. 4 in lane. Some on ground floor. 10 miles NW of Dorchester. Train: Yeovil/Dorchester (they will fetch). Ramps. Drawing room, lounge/bar (background music 11 am–12 pm), restaurant. Indoor swimming pool (25 by 13 ft). 4-acre grounds: garden; croquet, tennis. Civil wedding licence. No smoking: restaurant, drawing room. No dogs: some bedrooms, drawing room, restaurant. All major credit cards accepted. B&B £92.50–£185 per person; D,B&B £135–£245. Set menu £42; full alc £68. Christmas/New Year packages. 1-night bookings refused weekends June–Sept. *V*

EVESHAM Worcestershire   Map 3:D6

The Evesham Hotel
Cooper's Lane, off Waterside
Evesham WR11 1DA

Tel 01386-765566
Fax 01386-765443
Freephone 0800-716969 (reservations only)
Email reception@eveshamhotel.com
Website www.eveshamhotel.com

♛ *César award in 1990*

'It was a wrench to leave; our children were doleful, their grandparents keen to book again as soon as possible,' writes a regular visitor to this quirky, child-friendly hotel, which offers 'wonderful, individual' service. 'Favourite rooms need to be reserved well ahead.' Other praise this year: 'The high levels of comfort, efficiency and ambience have no equal.' There are 'fun things in the garden [slides, trampoline, etc], a lovely indoor swimming pool, friendly [all British] staff. Teddy bears everywhere.' The 'eccentric and helpful' owner, John Jenkinson, entertains guests with his 'ridiculous ties' and jokey menus, and recommends 'superb, good-value' wines (from a long list devoid of French vintages). His wife, Sue, designs the bedrooms: many are themed. Alice in Wonderland (a family suite) is among the beams at the top of the main house; South Pacific has a small aquarium under its basin. This year, foreign cheeses have been removed from the eclectic menu, which, says one visitor, 'is pitched at middle England (rich sauces and trimmings); the excellent breakfast is properly English though'. Another guest called the food 'unshowy and delicious'. Lunch has a 50-dish buffet. Children are charged according to age and amount eaten. (*Felicity Chadwick-Histed, Martyn Dormer, and others*)

40 bedrooms. 11 on ground floor. 2 suitable for &. 5 mins' walk from centre, across river. Parking. Closed 25–26 Dec. Lounges, bar, restaurant; function facilities; indoor swimming pool (16 by 39 ft). No background music. 2½-acre grounds: croquet, putting, swings, trampoline. No smoking: restaurant, 1 lounge, 28 bedrooms, pool area. Only guide dogs in public rooms. All major credit cards accepted. B&B: single £76–£92, double £124–£128, suite £168–£172; D,B&B (min. 2 nights) £72–£90 per person. Full alc £33–£36. New Year package. 1-night bookings sometimes refused weekends.

EXETER Devon   Map 1:C5

Hotel Barcelona   *Tel* 01392-281000
Magdalen Street   *Fax* 01392-281001
Exeter EX2 4HY   *Email* barcelona@aliashotels.com
                                        Website www.aliashotels.com

Near the cathedral green, this former Victorian eye hospital (a 'formidable building') was cleverly converted by the Alias Hotels group (see also the *Kandinsky*, Cheltenham (*qv*), and the *Seattle*, Brighton (Shortlist). Details from the hospital have been retained; a huge marble fireplace, parquet flooring throughout, surface pipework left intact. One bedroom still bears the word 'Theatre'. Insulation is not always perfect. There are large floral arrangements in public rooms. The style is youthful: *Kino*, the basement nightclub, open to residents and members, may be busy at weekends, although 'the sound did not permeate to the rest of the hotel'. Some rooms have huge windows and 'marvellous views'; all have CD-player, etc. Front rooms face a main road. 'Mine was spacious, with a wonderfully comfy bed; smart, clean, well-equipped bathroom.' The large, conservatory-style *Café Paradiso* faces a walled garden with a huge red bird sculpture. A chef rolls dough, and cooks 'excellent' pizzas in a Neapolitan wood-burning oven. Service, by girls in T-shirt and jeans, can be 'incredibly slow'. Breakfast ('exceptional') has 'excellent crispy toast, fine coffee; a plate of dried cured ham and cheeses'. (*David Sulkin, and others*)

46 bedrooms. Some on ground floor. 5 mins' walk from centre (front rooms hear traffic). Parking. Lift, ramp. Lounge, bar, restaurant; background jazz; private dining room; nightclub; meeting facilities; large terrace. ½-acre garden. No smoking:

restaurant, some bedrooms. Only guide dogs in public rooms. All major credit cards accepted. Room [2006]: single £90, double £105, suite £115–£125. Breakfast £6.50–£11.50. Full alc £36. Weekend rates (no 1-night bookings). Christmas/New Year packages.

The Galley
41 Fore Street, Topsham
Exeter EX3 0HU

Tel 01392-876078
Fax 01392-876331
Email fish@galleyrestaurant.co.uk
Website www.galleyrestaurant.co.uk

'Homely, friendly, personal', this quirky restaurant is near river and quay in Topsham, the historic port of Exeter, with its 17th-century Dutch gabled merchant houses. Co-owner Paul Da-Costa-Greaves, a Master Chef of Great Britain, says he is 'a spiritual healer and alternative therapist, running his kitchen under the guidance of Zen'. He and his partner, Mark Wright, offer jokey dinner menus: courses called 'Teasing the palate' (eg, duo of mussels and clams); 'Feeding the desire' (eg, sea bass on pesto and lavender-crushed potatoes); 'Keeping the passion alive' (lush puddings with names like 'Take me', 'Seductress'). To drink, you can order local champagne by the glass. For lunch there is a *tapas* menu. The restaurant is decorated with ceramic fish, a huge blue octopus, fake seaweed, etc. The 'nautical accommodation' consists of four 'luxury cabins', some with river views, some with exposed beams, slate floor and open log fire; all have minibar, CD-player, etc. Three rooms are in an old cottage; the suite is up steep stairs above the restaurant. Breakfast (including fruit, smoked salmon, yogurts) is left in the fridge in the room: 'Guests like to eat in their dressing gowns, or in the garden by the jacuzzi.' (*RA, and others*)

4 bedrooms. 3 in separate building. Unsuitable for &. 2 miles from centre. Parking. Train: Exeter St Davids; bus. Closed New Year. TV room, bar, restaurant ('easy listening' background music). 200-ft garden: hot tub. No smoking. No children under 12. Guide dogs only. Diners, MasterCard, Visa accepted. B&B £75–£125 per person. Full alc £45. ***V***

St Olaves Hotel
Mary Arches Street
Exeter EX4 3AZ

Tel 01392-217736
Fax 01392-413054
Email info@olaves.co.uk
Website www.olaves.co.uk

Near cathedral: Grade I listed Georgian merchant's house in small street opposite Mary Arches car park. Owner (since 2005) Carole Livingston has redecorated, Sandra Murrin manages. Chef Simeon Baber serves good food in bar and restaurant ('meals less good in his absence'). 'Lovely, quiet space. Friendly, efficient staff.

Comfortable room. Copious full breakfast,' say inspectors. Closed 26–30 Dec. No background music. ½-acre garden. Unsuitable for &. Civil wedding licence. No smoking: restaurant, bedrooms. No dogs. MasterCard, Visa accepted. 15 bedrooms (1 on ground floor): sound insulation may not always be perfect. B&B [2006] £62.50–£105 per person; D,B&B £77.50–£130. Set dinner £32.50. New Year package. ***V***

See also SHORTLIST

EXFORD Somerset   Map 1:B4

The Crown	*Tel* 01643-831554
Exford	*Fax* 01643-831665
Exmoor National Park	*Email* info@crownhotelexmoor.co.uk
TA24 7PP	*Website* www.crownhotelexmoor.co.uk

Sporting hotel (meeting place of local hunt) on green of picturesque village in Exmoor national park. 'Warm feel; traditional atmosphere.' New owners since September 2005, Chris Kirkbride, Sara and Dan Whittaker, have redecorated. 'Welcoming' public rooms have pictures of country pursuits. Large, rustic bar, popular with locals; cosy residents' bar. 'Expensive menu but competent cooking in restaurant; omnipresent muzak.' Tables and parasols in grounds; water garden; summer dining. 17 bedrooms: 'impressive, traditionally furnished; modern bathrooms.' Unsuitable for &. No smoking: restaurant, bedrooms. MasterCard, Visa accepted. B&B £49.50–£65 per person; D,B&B £59.50–£92.50. Set menu £32.50. Christmas/New Year packages.

FALMOUTH Cornwall *See SHORTLIST*   Map 1:E2

****

Traveller's tale In our suite at this luxury hotel the 'double' was two single beds: they were not joined together, and fell apart during the night. I ended up on the floor. When I asked next morning if the beds could be secured together, the receptionist was clearly not interested. As I walked round the corner, I heard her tell another member of staff and the pair giggled. Needless to say, the beds were not fixed and we had another near miss the following night. (*Hotel in Oxfordshire*)

****

FARNHAM Dorset   Map 2:E1

The Museum Inn   *Tel* 01725-516261
Farnham, nr Blandford Forum   *Fax* 01725-516988
DT11 8DE   *Email* enquiries@museuminn.co.uk
                                Website www.museuminn.co.uk

♀ *César award in 2005*

In a quiet village on the Dorset/Wiltshire border, this thatched 17th-century inn has been given a bright modern look by owners Mark Stephenson and Vicky Elliot, while retaining original features (a bread oven, flagstone floors). This year, the inn has been redecorated. Meals are served at wooden tables in the bar (in three rooms) and, at weekends, in the pretty *Shed* restaurant (once the village hall). The menu is the same in both. 'The place buzzed on Saturday night.' 'Cheery Antipodean waitresses.' The bistro-style cooking of the new chef (former *sous-chef*), Daniel Turner, was liked in 2006: 'Good goat's cheese starter; spicy crab cakes; excellent rhubarb crumble tart.' 'The reasonably priced wine list has a good wine of the week.' The best bedrooms are in the main house: the General's Room has a four-poster, two balconies, a large model boat on a chest of drawers, big bathroom with two windows. Smaller (and cheaper) rooms are in the stables at the back. 'It was wonderfully quiet at night.' Breakfast, with waitress service, has home-made preserves and good granary toast. Dogs are welcomed. Shooting parties are catered for in winter. (*EM, GF, and others*)

8 bedrooms. Some on ground floor. 4 in stable block. 7½ miles NE of Blandford Forum. Closed 25 Dec, evening of 31 Dec. Bar meals daily. Restaurant open Fri night/Sat/Sun midday. Sitting room, bar (3 rooms; occasional jazz), restaurant. No background music. Rear terrace, front garden. Smoking in bar only. No children under 8 as residents ('all ages welcome at lunch'). MasterCard, Visa accepted. B&B £47.50–£85 per person. Full alc £31–£38. 1-night bookings sometimes refused weekends. *V*

****

Traveller's tale Our bedroom was fab, but the owners were not natural hoteliers. She was far too chatty; he told us that all the dinner dishes came from Waitrose. We had to choose our meal the moment we arrived, and then had to wait 15 minutes to be called to table when the food arrived. Breakfast was poor; kipper had to be ordered 24 hours before. Flowers everywhere were fake, huge, blowsy arrangements in horrible colour combinations. (*Hotel in Devon*)

****

FAVERSHAM Kent   Map 2:D5

Read's Restaurant   *Tel* 01795-535344
Macknade Manor   *Fax* 01795-591200
Canterbury Road   *Email* rona@reads.com
Faversham ME13 8XE   *Website* www.reads.com

✿ *César award in 2005*

A handsome Georgian manor house, run as a restaurant-with-rooms by
Rona and David Pitchford. They are 'charming and visible owners', and his
cooking has a *Michelin* star (eg, fillet of sea bass with celeriac purée and
herb gnocchi), and is thought 'excellent' by *Guide* correspondents, though
one would have liked more vegetarian options. The bedrooms are 'old-
fashioned by design rather than default, with rich, thick fabrics'. 'Faultless.
One of the largest, most comfortable beds I've ever slept in.' Guests have
access to the Pantry, which has a fridge 'full of decent half bottles of wine',
and tea- and coffee-making kit (an honesty pad system operates). In the
dining room are 'marvellous, soft upholstered chairs', and candles on the
tables. The walled kitchen garden provides most of the herbs and vegetables for seasonal dishes. The 'fantastic' wine list includes 'some rare and
some very expensive' bottles; but a 'Best Buys' section has many reasonably
priced wines. 'Breakfast excellent too: you can have what you want. Service
from mainly young staff, efficient and knowledgeable.' (*HS, and others*)

6 bedrooms. ½ mile SE of Faversham. Open Tues–Sat, except 25/26 Dec, 2 weeks
Sept. Sitting room/bar, restaurant; private dining room. No background music.
4-acre garden; terrace (outdoor dining). Unsuitable for ♿. Civil wedding licence. No
smoking: restaurant, bedrooms. No dogs. All major credit cards accepted. B&B
£77.50–£155 per person; D,B&B £125–£200. Set dinner £48; full alc £57.

FAWSLEY Northamptonshire   Map 2:B3

Fawsley Hall   *Tel* 01327-892000
Fawsley, nr Daventry   *Fax* 01327-892001
NN11 3BA   *Email* info@fawsleyhall.com
                                    Website www.fawsleyhall.com

Set amid hills and parkland, this Tudor manor house with Georgian and
Victorian extensions is not a typical *Guide* hotel: it is large and has extensive
conference/function facilities. Its general manager is Jeffrey Crockett. 'An
impressive structure with some beautiful rooms if little architectural
coherence,' said one visitor. 'A discreet background smell of apple wood or
pot-pourri is one of its charms.' Drinks and tea are taken in the 'stunning'

Great Hall. There is a conservatory-style bar; also two pretty, low-ceilinged dining rooms and an enclosed stone courtyard. 'Our large bedroom had a floor-to-ceiling bay window that faced a meadow, a small church and a river. All was quiet apart from ducks and geese.' Some rooms are smaller and more basic. In the *Knightley* restaurant, Philip Dixon is head chef (main courses like red mullet with langoustines and saffron potatoes). 'Food and service generally good. Room-service breakfast unspectacular, but fine.' The Great Hall and restaurant are wheelchair-accessible; the spa and gym are well equipped; babysitters can be arranged. In the park are three lakes run by a syndicate: a ghillie and fishing can be arranged. (*JH*)

43 bedrooms. Some on ground floor. 6 miles S of Daventry, midway between Charwelton and Badby. Ramps. Great Hall; bar, restaurant; background music at mealtimes; 5 conference/function rooms; spa, fitness studio, beauty treatment rooms. 10-acre gardens in 2,000-acre park: croquet, tennis, 3 lakes (fishing). Civil wedding licence. No smoking: restaurant, some bedrooms. All major credit cards accepted. B&B £72.50–£212 per person. Set dinner £37.50; full alc £50 (*12½% 'discretionary' service charge added*). Christmas/New Year packages.

FLEET Dorset   Map 1:D6

Moonfleet Manor   *Tel* 01305-786948
Fleet Road, Fleet   *Fax* 01305-774395
nr Weymouth DT3 4ED   *Email* info@moonfleetmanorhotel.co.uk
                             Website www.moonfleetmanorhotel.co.uk

A sprawling Georgian manor house behind the Fleet lagoon and the Chesil Bank on the Dorset coast, at the end of a winding two-mile lane. Part of the Luxury Family Hotels group, it is now owned by von Essen Hotels (see also Bradford-on-Avon and Fowey). Manager Neil Carter and chef Tony Smith have stayed on. 'As good as before,' say repeat visitors in 2006. 'Distinctive, a little moth-eaten in places, but completely unpretentious. The promise to provide a relaxing break for harassed (but relatively well-heeled) parents is completely fulfilled.' The facilities for children of all ages are 'excellent': swimming pool, computer games, ping-pong, indoor tennis, supervised nursery, etc (see below). 'We don't use the crèche, but our two-year-old had so much fun, that we just had a great time with him. The only quibble was the quality of the children's high tea; we don't serve him nursery food, but hotels always play safe on this.' Comments on the meals vary: 'The adult food is still good to very good. Better than one expects at a family hotel.' 'Too much salt.' Breakfast is a big buffet. Strong currents rule out sea bathing, but there are good walks in either direction along the coast path. (*Chris Tennant, Gilbert Hall*)

36 bedrooms. 6 in 2 annexes. 3 on ground floor. 7 miles W of Weymouth. Lift. 2 lounges with dispense bar, restaurant; meeting room; games room/nursery; disco; indoor 33-ft swimming pool, sauna, solarium, sunbed, aromatherapy; snooker. No background music. 5-acre grounds: children's play areas, tennis, bowls, squash, badminton, lagoon. Riding, golf, sailing nearby. No smoking in restaurant. No dogs in public rooms. All major credit cards accepted. B&B [2006]: single £130–£180, double £170–£260, suite £260–£380; D,B&B £90–£225 per person. Bar meals. Set meals £30–£35. Christmas/New Year packages. Weekend bookings generally 2 nights.

FLETCHING East Sussex   Map 2:E4

The Griffin Inn	*Tel* 01825-722890
Fletching, nr Uckfield	*Fax* 01825-722810
TN22 3SS	*Email* info@thegriffininn.co.uk
	Website www.thegriffininn.co.uk

Overlooking the Ouse Valley, this pretty Sussex village is home to the Pullan family's 'cosy' 16th-century Grade II listed inn, liked for its 'oak-panelled warmth'. Its bedrooms, described by visitors as 'charming', have some interesting shapes; some are in the main building, others in a renovated coach house. Many have old beams and a four-poster bed. The efficient bathrooms have a monsoon shower or a Victorian-style roll-top bath. As we went to press, five further bedrooms were due to open in the Victorian house next door. Bar meals are generous, and Andrew Billings's cooking (modern British with Mediterranean influences) in the no-smoking restaurant is inventive. The terrace has a wood-fired oven, where barbecues may be served. There is an 'unconventional but thoughtful' wine list. Home-made croissants appear at breakfast. Children are welcomed: they can play in the large garden, and there is a 'healthy' children's menu. Four golf courses are nearby. More reports, please.

13 bedrooms. 4 in coach house. 5 in next-door house. 4 on ground floor. 3 miles NW of Uckfield. Closed 25 Dec, 31 Dec–2 Jan. Restaurant closed Sun night (bar menu 7 pm–9 pm). 2 lounge bars (1 with TV), restaurant; live music Fri night, Sun midday. No background music. Terrace. 1½-acre garden. No smoking: restaurant, bedrooms. Dogs in bar only. All major credit cards accepted. B&B £40–£80 per person. Full alc £30–£35. 1-night bookings refused bank holidays.

'Set lunch/dinner' indicates fixed-price meals, with ample, limited or no choice on the menu. 'Full alc' is the hotel's estimated price per person of a three-course *à la carte* meal, with a half bottle of house wine. 'Alc' is the price of an *à la carte* meal excluding the cost of wine.

FOLKESTONE Kent   Map 2:E5

Hotel Relish   *Tel* 01303-850952
4 Augusta Gardens   *Fax* 01303-850958
Folkestone CT20 2RR   *Email* reservations@hotelrelish.co.uk
                            Website www.hotelrelish.co.uk

On a clear day you can see France from this 'gorgeous, welcoming', small
B&B hotel in Folkestone's 'West End'. The owner, Michael Begley (his
manager is Svenja Summers), has preserved its Victorian architecture,
while creating a contemporary interior of 'understated elegance' (leather
settees, strong colours). There is free broadband access throughout, and a
wireless Internet network. Most bedrooms have a DVD-player. One guest
wrote: 'My room was perfect. Fabulous bathroom and toiletries, luscious
thick towels and robe, lights bright enough to read by.' But one couple
found their 'tiny' third-floor room poorly equipped and 'suitable for small
people only'. Another comment: 'Excellent service. Quiet position. Very
good breakfast': consisting of a generous buffet followed by cooked dishes,
it can be served alfresco in summer, on a terrace
leading to the garden. Arriving guests are
offered complimentary wine or beer, and they
can help themselves to coffee or tea with cake
whenever they wish. The lounge has newspapers and magazines. Wheelchair access is
limited, but Mr Begley says the *Relish* is 'ideal
for the deaf or arthritic'. Families are welcomed,
and dogs are allowed in the public rooms. 'Lots
of great eating places nearby.' (*VH, RJ Kenber,
and others*)

10 bedrooms. In centre (junction of Sandgate Rd/Trinity Gdns/Augusta Gdns).
Parking. Open 2 Jan–23 Dec. Lounge, hospitality area, breakfast room (Classic FM
all day); terrace. 4-acre garden. Beach 5 mins' walk. Unsuitable for &. No smoking.
Diners, MasterCard, Visa accepted. B&B: single £55–£69, double £79–£89, suite
£115–£130. 1-night bookings may be refused Sat in summer.

See also SHORTLIST

FORDINGBRIDGE Hampshire   Map 2:E2
See SHORTLIST

FOWEY Cornwall   Map 1:D3

Fowey Hall   *Tel* 01726-833866
Hanson Drive   *Fax* 01726-834100
Fowey PL23 1ET   *Email* info@foweyhall.com
                                            Website www.luxuryfamilyhotels.com

The Cornish outpost of the Luxury Family Hotels group, now owned by
the von Essen group, stands high above the sailing and fishing port. The
Victorian mansion has 'nicely furnished' bedrooms named after characters
in *The Wind in the Willows* (the house may have been a model for Kenneth
Grahame's Toad Hall). Twelve new garden rooms were built in 2005.
Parents may pack as many offspring as they can tolerate into their bedroom
at no extra cost. There is a crèche for children under seven; also baby-
listening devices and a babysitting service. Older children have a games
room and lots of activities; adults can retreat to a child-free drawing room
and library. The chef, Glynn Wellington, presides over the restaurants: the
Palm Court (home-made soups, salads, seafood), *Hansons* (where children can
eat with their parents), and the main dining room (no young children). In
the latter two, the menu changes monthly but has daily specials. As we
went to press, we heard that the long-serving manager, Tim Brocklebank,
was leaving: his successor was due to be appointed in September 2006.
More reports, please.

36 bedrooms. 8 in court annexe. Some on ground floor. 2 suitable for &. Top of
town. Parking. Drawing room, library, billiard/meeting room, 3 restaurants (background music); crèche (supervised 10 am–6 pm), children's games room. 5-acre
grounds: garden: covered heated swimming pool (42 by 16 ft), croquet, badminton,
play area. Sea 10 mins' walk. Civil wedding licence. Smoking in library only. No
children under 12 in main restaurant. Dogs in court rooms only, on lead in public
rooms. Amex, MasterCard, Visa accepted. B&B [2006] £75–£215 per person. Set
dinner £35. Christmas/New Year packages. Off-season/last-minute offers (see
website). 1-night bookings sometimes refused weekends.

Old Quay House   *Tel* 01726-833302
28 Fore Street   *Fax* 01726-833668
Fowey PL23 1AQ   *Email* info@theoldquayhouse.com
                                            Website www.theoldquayhouse.com

Part of the charm of Jane and Roy Carson's 'beautifully converted' former
seamen's mission, says one visitor, is 'that like Dr Who's Tardis, it is
deceptively bigger than one might guess. After the bustle of the street, all
is calm.' From the rear terrace, where drinks, snacks and summer dinners
are served, there are 'glorious views of harbour and estuary'. Seagulls can

be a menace – 'each table has a water pistol to ward them off'. Bedrooms are 'simply but comfortably furnished in pale pastel shades; our full-length corner window, leading to a small balcony, overlooked the water'. 'Our small room had a side sea view and a tiny balcony; its small well-equipped bathroom was down a flight of stairs.' There is a 'bistro atmosphere of relaxed formality' in Q, the large restaurant with wooden floor, and white cloths and black napkins on dark brown tables. Ben Bass serves cooking 'of a very high standard'. 'A starter of poached duck egg with asparagus was so good we had it twice. The full English breakfast was excellent.' Thanks to Fowey's narrow streets, the nearest car park is at the top of the hill. (*Richard Barrett, Mr and Mrs KA Winslow*)

12 bedrooms. Central, on waterfront. Help given with parking. Restaurant closed Mon off-season. Open-plan lounge, restaurant with seating area (background music during meals). Waterside terrace. Unsuitable for &. Civil wedding licence. No smoking. No children under 12. Guide dogs only. Amex, MasterCard, Visa accepted. B&B £50–£210 per person; D,B&B £80–£240. Full alc from £32. 1-night bookings refused weekends. *V*

FRITTON Norfolk   Map 2:B6

Fritton House NEW	*Tel* 01493-484008
Church Lane	*Fax* 01493-488355
Fritton NR31 9HA	*Email* frittonhouse@somerleyton.co.uk
	Website www.somerleyton.co.uk

There are two Frittons in Norfolk: this one is on the Norfolk/Suffolk border. On his family's Somerleyton estate, the Hon. Hugh Crossley has turned a 16th-century Grade II* listed old inn, near a lake, into a contemporary hotel/restaurant. It opened in May 2006. Inspectors, visiting soon after, were impressed. 'Comfortable, relaxing, retaining old features, it faces open farmland, mature trees, fields with sheep. We were warmly welcomed by the young manageress [Sarah Winterton]. There were fresh flowers everywhere, interesting artwork. In the lounge, a large fireplace, comfy sofas, plentiful magazines and newspapers. Our bedroom had a mix of antique and modern furniture, a large bay window with sofa. Excellent, large, bright bathroom.' Alan Leech is chef. 'Dinner, using estate produce, was good, prices reasonable but some portions too large. Service was efficient. We enjoyed sea bass with asparagus and wild mushrooms. We thought the background music unnecessary as there was a bustling atmosphere. Breakfast had delicious coffee, a choice of cooked dishes, but orange juice was not freshly squeezed.' 'There is plenty for children to do on the estate,' writes Hugh Crossley. Somerleyton Hall and Gardens are open to the public.

9 bedrooms. 7 miles SW of Great Yarmouth, off A143. Train: Somerleyton. Lounge, bar, restaurant; private dining room; background music throughout, all day. Unsuitable for &. Civil wedding licence. 250-acre estate: formal gardens, lake, golf, walks. No smoking. MasterCard, Visa accepted. B&B double £110–£170. Full alc £30. Christmas/New Year packages. **•V•**

FROGGATT EDGE Derbyshire   Map 3:A6

The Chequers Inn BUDGET	*Tel* 01433-630231
Froggatt Edge	*Fax* 01433-631072
Hope Valley S32 3ZJ	*Email* info@chequers-froggatt.com
	Website www.chequers-froggatt.com

Below the 'spectacular, rugged' Froggatt Edge, this 16th-century traditional country inn in the Peak District is owned by Jonathan and Joanne Tindall. 'A winner,' is a 2006 comment. The white-painted, slate-roofed building has 'no frills', but makes 'a charming base to explore the area', according to inspectors, who wrote of the 'warm welcome, innovative cooking', and 'simple but thoughtfully furnished' bedrooms. 'Our cosy room, of reasonable size, was dominated by a pine four-poster bed whose drapes matched those at the window. Its smallish window looked across road and car park to rolling hills and woodland beyond.' The adjacent road 'suffers severe lorry traffic', at its worst during the day; double glazing cuts out much of the noise at night. Behind the inn, the small elevated garden has panoramic views to the west. The 'very attractive bar/restaurant', where Marcus Jefford serves 'English and European' cooking, has the original heavy lintels, dark beams, etc; also library chairs, high-backed settees, countless knick-knacks. Wines and dishes of the day are listed on a blackboard, and 'portion control is unknown here'. Breakfast has a buffet followed by cooked dishes (including sausages for vegetarians). 'Everything was spotless. Good value.' (*Philip Pettifor, and others*)

5 bedrooms. A625, near Calver Village. Closed 25 Dec. Bar, 2 eating areas; piped music everywhere all the time. Large garden, with seating. Unsuitable for &. No smoking. No dogs. Amex, MasterCard, Visa accepted. B&B £35–£47.50 per person. Full alc £35. 1-night bookings refused weekends.

****

Traveller's tale The decor was fading, and so were the clientele. Nibbles but no drinks were served as we gathered in the lounge before dinner. Conversation was awkward; it felt like the sitting room of an upmarket nursing home. (*Hotel in the Cotswolds*)

****

GATESHEAD Tyne and Wear   Map 4:B4

Eslington Villa Hotel   *Tel* 0191-487 6017
8 Station Road   *Fax* 0191-420 0667
Gateshead NE9 6DR   *Email* eslingtonvilla@freeuk.com
                             Website www.eslingtonvilla.co.uk

'We loved the ambience and style,' say visitors this year to Nick and
Melanie Tulip's 19th-century villa (motto 'heritage with attitude'). It stands
in a big garden ('with rabbits'), in a residential area. Bedroom decor ranges
from traditional, in the older part of the house (one room has a four-poster
bed), to lighter, 'contemporary designer' in the extension. Other comments:
'A good experience.' 'They treat their regulars like family.' But some
drawbacks are reported. One couple 'had a spacious room, but the bed was
rather small and not very comfortable'. Another visitor found the bedroom
lighting 'barely enough to read by. We tried to read in the lounge but were
driven out by appalling loud music.' But the dinners were thought 'first
class'. In the airy restaurant, with its conservatory extension, chef Andy
Moore serves a modern menu, eg, tomato risotto with mussels and
pancetta; marinated loin of venison. Wines are good value. 'Breakfast was
good, as was the service.' Seminars, private meetings and functions are
often held. (*MC and GR Bradshaw, Kelvin Juba, and others*)

18 bedrooms. 3, with separate entrance, on ground floor. 2 miles from centre. Closed
Christmas. Restaurant closed Sun night, bank holidays at midday. Ramp. Lounge/
bar, conservatory, restaurant; background jazz; conference/function facilities. 2-acre
garden, patio. No smoking: restaurant, bedrooms. No dogs in public rooms. All major
credit cards accepted. B&B £42.25–£74.50 per person. Set dinner £22; full alc £29.
New Year package. ***V***

GATWICK West Sussex *See SHORTLIST*   Map 2:D4

GILLINGHAM Dorset   Map 2:D1

Stock Hill House   *Tel* 01747-823626
Stock Hill   *Fax* 01747-825628
Gillingham SP8 5NR   *Email* reception@stockhillhouse.co.uk
                             Website www.stockhillhouse.co.uk

On the borders of three counties, Peter and Nita Hauser's small luxury
hotel (Relais & Châteaux) was much liked by readers this year: 'Our
welcome was warm and genuine. A relaxing four days.' 'We have

consistently enjoyed impeccable service by the well-trained young staff.' The Victorian building sits in landscaped, tree-lined grounds with terraced lawns, herbaceous borders, and a small lake fed by a stream. Public rooms include 'a splendid formal lounge' and 'a cosy "snug" with log fire'. The spacious bedrooms have a mix of antiques and curios. 'Rooms differ tremendously in size and facilities, but the rates reflect fairly this variety.' 'Ours was spotless; excellent bed, plenty of room, two comfortable chairs.' 'Mrs Hauser's eagle eye keeps everything under control' in the dining room where 'tables are spaced to permit conversations with neighbours but far apart enough if you choose to be unsociable'. Mr Hauser's cooking reflects his origins, 'especially the desserts' (eg, Malakoff Torte auf Beerensaft). 'Delicious: the Austrian influence was a bonus.' Men are asked to wear a tie at dinner. The 'outstanding' breakfast has porridge with cream and cinnamon. 'Well-behaved children are welcome.' (*Diana Blackburn, David Ward, GH, and others*)

8 bedrooms. 3 in coach house. On B3081, 1½ miles W of Gillingham. Ramp. 2 lounges, restaurant, breakfast room; private dining room. No background music. 11-acre grounds: tennis, croquet; small lake. Unsuitable for &. No smoking. No dogs (kennels nearby). MasterCard, Visa accepted. D,B&B £100–£165 per person. Set lunch from £26, dinner £36. Christmas/New Year packages. 1-night bookings sometimes refused.

GITTISHAM Devon   Map 1:C5

Combe House
Gittisham
nr Honiton EX14 3AD

Tel 01404-540400
Fax 01404-46004
Email stay@thishotel.com
Website www.thishotel.com

César award: Country hotel of the year

'The well-trained young staff suit the surroundings,' says a visitor this year to Ruth and Ken Hunt's extended Grade I listed Elizabethan manor house, 'gloriously set' up a mile-long drive, in a vast estate with woodland, pheasants, and pastures with Arab horses. Grand public rooms have carved oak panelling, antiques, fresh flowers, 18th-century portraits. 'A lovely place,' says an inspector. Other comments: 'Beautiful, peaceful grounds.' 'Service excellent. Expensive but worth it.' 'Good welcome. Bags carried to our comfortable room. Exceedingly good food.' Philip Leach (a Master Chef of Great Britain) serves contemporary dishes, eg, red mullet with lobster ravioli. 'Jugs of tap water on the table (no attempt to push bottled water). A good wine list.' The menu lists suppliers, all local; many vegetables are home grown. Bedrooms, priced according to size and aspect, have antiques and rich fabrics, and are serviced at night. One is 'oddly shaped, walls and ceiling painted to represent sky, birds, grass and flowers. Bathroom down a short passage. Great fun.' Another has four-poster bed, big chairs and sofas, a panoramic view through mullioned windows. Breakfast, served until 10 am, has freshly squeezed juices, porridge, a wide choice of cooked dishes. Children are welcomed. (*Humphrey Norrington, and others*)

15 bedrooms. 2 miles SW of Honiton. Take A375 towards Sidmouth. Closed last week of Jan. Ramp. Sitting room, Great Hall, bar (classical background music), restaurant; private dining rooms. 10-acre garden in 3,500-acre estate. Helipad. Fishing on River Otter; coast 9 miles. Only public rooms suitable for ♿. Civil wedding licence. Smoking in sitting room only. No dogs in restaurant, some bedrooms. MasterCard, Visa accepted. B&B [2006] £82–£164 per person; D,B&B £115–£204. Set menus £39.50–£41. Midweek and seasonal breaks. Christmas/New Year packages. Fri, Sat min. 2-night bookings.

GLASTONBURY Somerset *See SHORTLIST*   Map 1:B6

GOLCAR West Yorkshire   Map 4:E3

The Weavers Shed   *Tel* 01484-654284
Knowl Road, Golcar   *Fax* 01484-650980
nr Huddersfield HD7 4AN   *Email* info@weaversshed.co.uk
                               Website www.weaversshed.co.uk

'A long, steep climb from Huddersfield, but the journey is most definitely worthwhile. Excellent food in stylish surroundings.' Visitors this year were impressed with this restaurant-with-rooms, a converted 18th-century cloth-finishing mill in a 'deep Pennine valley'. It is run by chef/*patron* Stephen Jackson with his wife, Tracy. 'Its slightly sombre stone exterior fails to convey the warmth and style to be found inside.' The bedrooms, each named after a local textile mill, are in the former mill-owner's house next door, above the restaurant's lounge (there is direct access from the main building). 'Ours was comfortable and spacious, and had a four-poster canopied bed.' Original features (old fireplaces, moulded ceilings, etc) have been retained. Stephen Jackson grows fruit, vegetables and herbs ('as organically as possible') in a kitchen garden in a neighbouring village. Eggs are supplied by the Jacksons' chickens, ducks and quail. The dining room retains the mill's wooden beams and stone arches, with bouquets of wild flowers on the tables in summer. 'The food was extremely tasty; scallops on a bed of lentils, followed by fillet steak.' 'Bargains can be found in the extensive wine list.' Breakfast included 'fresh juice, delicious scrambled egg and black pudding'. (*Robert Gower, JH; also Eric G Hinds*)

5 bedrooms. 2 on ground floor. 4 miles W of Huddersfield. Closed 2 weeks from Christmas. Restaurant closed Sat midday, Sun/Mon. Lounge/bar, restaurant; background jazz/light classical music; function/conference room. Garden. Unsuitable for &. No smoking: restaurant, bedrooms. No dogs. All major credit cards accepted. B&B [2006] £45–£70 per person. Set lunch £13.95–£16.95; full alc £45.

GRANTHAM Lincolnshire *See SHORTLIST*   Map 2:A3

GRASMERE Cumbria   Map 4: inset C2

White Moss House   **BUDGET**   *Tel* 015394-35295
Rydal Water   *Fax* 015394-35516
Grasmere LA22 9SE   *Email* sue@whitemoss.com
                                Website www.whitemoss.com

Close to Rydal Water, Peter and Sue Dixon's restaurant-with-rooms 'has been a favourite or ours for many years', says one reader. The grey-stone creeper-covered house was once bought by William Wordsworth for his son, Willie; the poet's two homes, Dove Cottage and Rydal Mount, are within a mile. 'Very professional and personal,' is another comment. 'The consistency of the cooking, the superb and fairly priced wine list, and Susan Dixon's unobtrusive welcome' are praised. Peter Dixon and co-chef Ian Armstrong serve a daily-changing five-course dinner at 7.30 for 8 pm (except Sundays) with no choice until dessert. The 'unshowy interpretation of English country house cooking' is admired, eg, White Moss trio of salmon; Vale of Lune braised guineafowl. After-dinner coffee is served in a small lounge. A busy road is near but windows are double glazed, and there is little traffic at night. There is a peaceful two-room suite in Brockstone, the cottage up the hill. In the main house, the small bedrooms have a tiny bathroom and many extras (herbal bathsalts, fresh flowers, books, etc). Breakfast includes kippers and Cumberland sausage. A popular venue for house parties and celebrations. Excellent walking all around. (*Mrs CM Moore, Stephen and Pauline Glover*)

6 bedrooms. 1 in cottage (10 mins' drive or footpath). 1 mile S of Grasmere on A591. Open mid-Feb–mid-Nov. Restaurant closed midday all week, Sun night. Lounge, restaurant; terrace. 1-acre garden/woodland. Unsuitable for &. No smoking:

restaurant, bedrooms. Dogs in cottage only. MasterCard, Visa accepted. B&B
£35–£75 per person; D,B&B £65–£109. Set dinner £39.50. Off-season breaks. 1-
night bookings refused Sat at busy times. ***V***

GREAT BIRCHAM Norfolk *See SHORTLIST* Map 2:A5

GREAT CHESTERFORD Essex   Map 2:C4
See SHORTLIST

GREAT DUNMOW Essex   Map 2:C4

The Starr	*Tel* 01371-874321
Market Place	*Fax* 01371-876337
Great Dunmow	*Email* starrrestaurant@btinternet.com
CM6 1AX	*Website* www.the-starr.co.uk

On the marketplace of this busy little town, Terence and Louise George's
restaurant-with-rooms is a timber-framed 15th-century former inn. Inside
all is 'smart and colourful'. The yellow-painted restaurant is in two parts,
one with old beams stripped blond, the other in a conservatory extension.
Bedrooms are in a converted stable block in the rear courtyard: 'Ours was
OK, and had a very smart bathroom.' The best room has a four-poster bed
and a freestanding Victorian bath. The Pine Room has 'his and hers hand
basins set in marble – ideal for honeymooners or a romantic evening'.
'Service was professional, from the black-and-white-suited French girl at
reception to the French waiter.' The head chef, Mark Pearson, offers
'traditional/modern English food with a French accent', eg, confit chicken
risotto with truffle and Parmesan cream. The good breakfast includes
freshly squeezed orange juice, fruit, a fry-up, 'lots of toast and croissants'.
Stansted airport is 15 minutes' drive away. More reports, please.

8 bedrooms. In stable block. 2 on ground floor, suitable for &. Central (some traffic
noise). Open 6 Jan–26 Dec. Restaurant closed Sun night. Reception/bar, restaurant;
2 private dining rooms. No background music. No smoking: restaurant, bedrooms.
No dogs in public rooms. All major credit cards accepted. B&B £60–£95 per person;
D,B&B £102.50–£137.50. Set dinner £42.50.

Make sure the hotel has included VAT in the prices it quotes.

GREAT LANGDALE Cumbria   Map 4: inset C2

Old Dungeon Ghyll   *Tel/Fax* 015394 37272
Great Langdale   *Email* office@oldhotel.fsnet.co.uk
nr Ambleside LA22 9JY   *Website* www.odg.co.uk

At the head of the Great Langdale valley, on the approach to Scafell Pike,
this old mountain hotel has welcomed fell walkers and serious climbers for
over 300 years. Owned since 1928 by the National Trust, it has been run
since 1984 by Neil and Jane Walmsley. 'It must be in one of the remotest
spots in England,' is one recent comment. 'Good value, a friendly welcome.'
The bedrooms have been modernised, but retain 19th-century features and
decor. 'Our family room had a grand view through two windows, but rather
old furniture. Down the corridor were the shower and loo. Good dinner
(plentiful portions) and wine list.' The food is traditional English (steaks,
etc). Children are welcomed (they have their own menu, and games are
provided). The 'shippon' (cowshed) has been converted into a hikers' bar,
and can be lively on Saturday nights (a National Trust campsite is half a
mile away). Popular with climbing and fell-walking clubs, it serves 'a great
range of beers', soups, sandwiches, sausages, etc; guests sit in old cattle
stalls, or at tables in a courtyard. More reports, please.

13 bedrooms. NW of Ambleside by B5343. Closed 21–27 Dec. Residents'
lounge, residents' bar, public bar (folk music 1st Wed of month, and 'when it
happens'), dining room; drying room. No background music. Small garden.
Unsuitable for &. No smoking in dining room. Amex, MasterCard, Visa
accepted. B&B [2006] £42–£50 per person; D,B&B £62–£66. Set dinner £23.
1-night bookings refused weekends.

GREAT MILTON Oxfordshire   Map 2:C3

Le Manoir aux Quat'Saisons   *Tel* 01844-278881
Church Road   *Fax* 01844-278847
Great Milton OX44 7PD   *Email* lemanoir@blanc.co.uk
                          Website www.manoir.com

Q *César award in 1985*

'Hugely expensive, but as an occasional treat well worth while.' Trusted
Guide readers report on Raymond Blanc's famous *domaine* (Relais &
Châteaux, co-owned with Orient Express Hotels). The 'superb' service
begins on arrival: 'A porter takes your car and brings your luggage to the
room.' Bedroom decor varies. 'Our spacious room in the main building was
beautifully furnished in the style of the house; two easy chairs and a settee,

but poor lighting for reading.' A more modern courtyard room 'had grey walls, ceiling spotlights; excellent wardrobe but little drawer space. Good bed: lovely light blankets, pristine cotton sheets. Large shower; masses of towels; lots of mirrors.' Some rooms have an open fireplace. The famous conservatory restaurant (two *Michelin* stars) has a seasonally changing *à la carte* menu, a lunchtime *menu du jour* ('most enjoyable'), and a seven-course *menu gourmand* ('portions not too large, service just the right pace'). 'This was fabulous. We were guided to reasonably priced options by the glass when we asked for appropriate wines. Breakfast also first rate, the default being French continental.' Children are 'welcomed, not just tolerated' at the *Manoir*. 'Beautiful grounds.' (*Tony and Marlene Hall, Nicola Bennett, and others*)

32 bedrooms. 23 in garden buildings. Some on ground floor. 8 miles SE of Oxford. 2 lounges, champagne bar; 'relaxing' background music all day; restaurant; private dining room; cookery school. 27-acre grounds: gardens, croquet, lake. Civil wedding licence. No smoking in restaurant. No dogs in house (free kennels). All major credit cards accepted. B&B [2006]: double £360–£495, suite £530–£1,250; D,B&B (midweek): double £595, suite £665–£895. Cooked breakfast £12. Set lunch £45, *menu gourmand* £95; full alc £125. Midweek breaks; residential cookery courses. Christmas/New Year packages.

GUILDFORD Surrey *See SHORTLIST*   Map 2:D3

GULWORTHY Devon   Map 1:D3

The Horn of Plenty   `NEW`   *Tel* 01822-832528
Gulworthy   *Fax* 01822-834390
nr Tavistock PL19 8JD   *Email* enquiries@thehornofplenty.co.uk
                              Website www.thehornofplenty.co.uk

Chef Peter Gorton earns a star and three red crossed spoon-and-forks from *Michelin* for his 'sharp, confident' cooking and the agreeable ambience of the restaurant-with-rooms near Tavistock that he owns with Paul and Andie Roston. The wisteria-covered stone Georgian house stands up a long drive amid gardens and orchards, and has stunning views of the Tamar valley (the river is a mile away). The most expensive bedrooms are in the main house. Others, each with a balcony (where breakfast can be served) and a small bathroom, are in a converted coach house: these were refurbished in 2006. 'Staff are pleasant. A beautiful area,' say regular *Guide* correspondents. Dinner, served in the L-shaped restaurant, might include steamed lemon sole with king prawn fritters and a white wine and saffron sauce. On Monday evening there is a shorter, reduced-price menu (£25). The cooked breakfast has eggs from resident hens and black pudding made by a local butcher. One couple found the kitchen 'a bit slow'. Another report calls this a 'lovely, friendly' place. There are lots of fresh flowers, and a log fire in the drawing room. Cookery courses are held. (*Anne and Denis Tate*)

10 bedrooms. 6 in stables (20 yds). 4 on ground floor. 3 miles SW of Tavistock. Closed 24–26 Dec. Restaurant closed Mon midday. Drawing room, lounge/ restaurant (occasional classical background music); library/private dining/meeting room. 5-acre grounds. Civil wedding licence. Smoking in drawing room only. No children under 7 at dinner. No dogs in public rooms. Amex, MasterCard, Visa accepted. B&B [2006] £70–£220 per person. Set lunch £26, dinner £42.50. New Year package. •V•

HALIFAX West Yorkshire *See SHORTLIST*   Map 4:D3

HALNAKER West Sussex   Map 2:E3

The Old Store BUDGET	*Tel* 01243-531977
Stane Street, Halnaker, nr Chichester	*Email* theoldstore4@aol.com
PO18 0QL	*Website* www.theoldstoreguesthouse.com

Adjoining the Goodwood estate, this unpretentious guest house is an 18th-century Grade II listed red brick and flint house, once the village store and bakery. Inside are beamed ceilings, and a small lounge and breakfast room downstairs. Some rooms look across fields to Chichester cathedral, some are suitable for a family. 'Mine, attractive, spotless, had mineral water, tea-maker, fresh milk in Thermos flask, biscuits and chocolate. Not only the ubiquitous duvet, but, on a stifling summer's day, a light blanket and cool cotton sheets.' A 'perfect' breakfast had 'hot toast served in folded linen', free-range eggs, local sausages, etc. The owner/managers, Patrick and

Heather Birchenough, are 'helpful about places to eat and details of walks'; they offer a laundry service and will make a packed lunch. 'I left pondering my modest bill. I have often paid double for less.' A half-hourly bus service to Chichester passes the door.

'Traffic begins early on the busy road.' Plenty of interesting sightseeing: Arundel, Petworth, Uppark, Fishbourne Roman palace, etc, and a footpath leads to walks through woods to the South Downs. The village name is pronounced 'Hannaka'. (*JF, JH, and others*)

7 bedrooms. 1 on ground floor. 4 miles NE of Chichester. Closed Christmas/New Year. Lounge, breakfast room. No background music. ¼-acre garden, with seating. Unsuitable for &. No smoking. Guide dogs only. MasterCard, Visa accepted. B&B £33–£45 per person. 1-night bookings sometimes refused weekends.

HAMBLETON Rutland   Map 2:B3

Hambleton Hall	*Tel* 01572-756991
Hambleton	*Fax* 01572-724721
Oakham LE15 8TH	*Email* hotel@hambletonhall.com
	Website www.hambletonhall.com

♟ *César award in 1985*

In 2005, this luxurious country house hotel (Relais & Châteaux) turned 25. Its owner, Tim Hart, writes that 'just as much energy and money' as before goes into running the Victorian mansion, 'memorably set' on a peninsula jutting into Rutland Water. His wife, Stefa, designed the classic interiors (fine fabrics, antiques, good paintings, open fires) with Nina Campbell. The welcome is praised this year: 'Three staff members who knew our names met us, whisked bags to the room, parked our car.' Regulars like the 'approachable' service, the food: 'worth saving up for'. Chef Aaron Patterson (*Michelin* star) serves modern dishes (eg, roast breast of pigeon with foie gras ravioli and Madeira sauce). There is a daily set three-course dinner, and a 'very good' 'lunch for less'. The best bedrooms face Rutland Water (seen through a screen of mature trees); the Croquet Pavilion suite is good for a family – children are welcomed. Some rooms are smaller. There is a swimming pool, but no spa: 'As the craze for spas intensifies,' Mr Hart writes, 'I encourage my clients to balance the joys of gastronomy with a little health-giving exercise in "God's Gym"' (horse-riding and cycling excursions are organised). Tim Hart also owns *Hart's Hotel*, Nottingham (*qv*). (*Sara Stewart, and others*)

17 bedrooms. 3 miles SE of Oakham. Train: Peterborough/Kettering/Oakham (branch line); helipad. Lift, ramps. Hall, drawing room, 2 bars, restaurant; 2 private dining rooms; small conference facilities. No background music. 17-acre grounds: swimming pool (heated May–Oct), tennis, cycling; lake: fishing, windsurfing, sailing. Civil wedding licence. No smoking: restaurant, some bedrooms. No babies in restaurant, except at breakfast. No dogs in public rooms, or unattended in bedrooms.

All major credit cards accepted. B&B [2006] £95–£325 per person. English breakfast £14.50. Set menus £40–£50; full alc £75. Winter rates. Christmas/New Year packages. 1-night bookings refused Sat.

HAROME North Yorkshire   Map 4:D4

Cross House Lodge at the Star Inn
Harome, nr Helmsley
YO62 5JE

Tel 01439-770397
Fax 01439-771833
Website www.thestaratharome.co.uk

Ω *César award in 2004*

Originally a medieval cruck-framed longhouse, Andrew and Jacquie Pern's Yorkshire inn has been known for good food since the early 1970s. Now it has a *Michelin* star for 'original modern cooking' (inspired, writes Andrew Pern, by 'a certain northern rootedness'). This is served in the low-ceilinged, 'atmospheric', if dark, bar and the 'elegant' small dining room (tables close together). Guests this year enjoyed duck liver pâté accompanied by sloe gin and soda; monkfish on mash and mussels. Coffee is taken in the beamed loft. In warm weather, meals are served in the garden, fragrant with herbs and lavender. The bedrooms are in *Cross House Lodge*, opposite, a converted stone farm building. All have TV, CD- and DVD-player, home-made biscuits, fruit, fudge; some have a spa bath; some face the car park. Decor is 'a mix of rustic and modern'. 'Our large beamed room had a big bed and a full-size pool table.' Continental breakfast is served in the bedroom or round a huge table in the Wheelhouse, an arrangement that does not please everyone: 'Our party of four had to sit separately because "people were reluctant to sit next to strangers".' (*Paul and Louise Barron, WK Wood, and others*)

11 bedrooms. 2 in annexe. Village centre. Closed Christmas, 19–27 Feb. 2 lounges, coffee loft, bar, breakfast room, restaurant; private dining room; varied background music. 2-acre garden: small heated swimming pool. Civil wedding licence. Smoking in bar only. Guide dogs only. MasterCard, Visa accepted. B&B £60–£120 per person. Full alc £40–£45. New Year package.

HARROGATE North Yorkshire   Map 4:D4
See SHORTLIST

Report forms (Freepost in UK) are at the end of the *Guide*.

HARWICH Essex   Map 2:C5

The Pier at Harwich	*Tel* 01255-241212
The Quay	*Fax* 01255-551922
Harwich CO12 3HH	*Email* pier@milsomhotels.com
	Website www.milsomhotels.com

On the quay in old Harwich ('an area becoming more gentrified'), these two buildings owned by Paul Milsom (the manager is Nick Chambers) face the harbour ('lots of interest'). The popular restaurants, and most bedrooms, are in the larger building; other rooms and the beamed lounge are in a former pub. The first-floor *Harbourside* restaurant was recently given a 'minimalist' makeover: it has a polished pewter champagne bar. Chef Chris Oakley specialises in local seafood: 'Very fresh ingredients, well cooked,' reports a returning visitor (eg, monkfish medallions with fennel and thyme marmalade). On the ground floor, the informal *Ha'Penny Bistro* (now extended to take in the adjacent bar) serves brasserie-type food ('excellent fish and chips'). Many dishes can be ordered in an 'ample' or a 'generous' portion. The bedrooms vary: 'Ours, smart and comfortable, had a fine view. A good stay in every way.' But a small annexe room had a 'view of the container depot – noisy lorries at night'. Breakfast includes freshly squeezed juice, 'wonderful thick slices of ham and cheese'. 'Management much in evidence. Service both competent and friendly.' In summer, tables and chairs stand on the front terrace (surrounded by potted plants). (*Lynn Wildgoose, Thomas H Blackburn, and others*)

14 bedrooms. 7 in annexe. Some on ground floor, suitable for &. On quay. Ramps. Lounge (in annexe), restaurant, bistro; background music all day. Small front terrace. Civil wedding licence. No smoking in restaurants. Guide dogs only. All major credit cards accepted. B&B [2006] £47.50–£85 per person. Set lunch £20; full alc £40. Christmas/New Year packages.

HATHERLEIGH Devon   Map 1:C4

Pressland Country House	**BUDGET**	*Tel* 01837-810871
Hatherleigh, nr Okehampton		*Fax* 01837-810303
EX20 3LW		*Email* accom@presslandhouse.co.uk
		Website www.presslandhouse.co.uk

'A delight, superb value; we were made to feel like favourite guests even though it was our first visit.' Praise from regular *Guide* correspondents for Graham and Gill Giles's large Victorian manor house, in a landscaped garden with views across fields to Dartmoor. It is 'very comfortable, absolutely everything thought of'; fresh fruit, flowers, good magazines and 'nice toiletries' are in the 'spotless' bedrooms. Mr Giles 'is front man, who greets and advises, serves meals; she is a superb cook', said an earlier visitor. There are three choices per course on her daily-changing dinner menu (available by arrangement): 'Excellent; local produce, beautifully cooked and presented' (eg, duck breast with lime and coriander). Vegetarian meals are a speciality. Breakfast has a wide choice of cooked dishes, including devilled kidneys, poached smoked haddock. Many local attractions, including RHS Rosemoor, Castle Drogo and the Lydford Gorge. (*G and LJ, and others*)

6 bedrooms. 2, on ground floor, in garden annexe. 2 miles S of Hatherleigh. Open Mar–Nov. Lounge, bar, dining room; background music at mealtimes. 1¾-acre garden. Walking, riding, fishing nearby. Unsuitable for &. No smoking. No children under 12. Guide dogs only. MasterCard, Visa accepted. B&B [2006] £30–£78 per person; D,B&B (min. 2 nights) £55–£103. Set dinner £26. Reductions for longer stays. 1-night bookings refused weekends in season, bank holidays.

HATHERSAGE Derbyshire   Map 3:A6

The George Hotel	*Tel* 01433-650436
Main Road	*Fax* 01433-650099
Hathersage S32 1BB	*Email* info@george-hotel.net
	Website www.george-hotel.net

Originally an alehouse serving the packhorse trains trudging between quarries and foundries, this 600-year-old grey stone Peak District inn is now a comfortable hotel (Best Western), owned by Eric Marsh of *The Cavendish* at nearby Baslow (*qv*). Charlotte Brontë is thought to have stayed here while writing *Jane Eyre* and to have based some characters on village residents. There are original stone walls, oak beams, open fires, much antique furniture and original paintings. Bedrooms are 'thoughtfully equipped'; all have been refurbished and there is one more room this year. Front rooms (the least expensive) are double glazed but get some road noise. 'Always ask for a back room,' says one experienced guest. In the restaurant (with contemporary decor), Ben Handley serves modern dishes with a Mediterranean influence, eg, Spanish seafood soup, with Manchego cheese; char-grilled calf's liver with pancetta. A good range of wines by the glass. Breakfast, served until 11 am, includes 'a large selection of fruits, cereals, etc, and a massive grill'. Snacks and 'generous' sandwiches are served at lunchtime in the lounge. More reports, please.

22 **bedrooms.** In village centre. Lounge/bar, restaurant (background music); 2 function rooms. Courtyard. Only restaurant accessible for &. Civil wedding licence. No smoking. No dogs. All major credit cards accepted. B&B [2006] £57–£146 per person. Full alc £42.50. Christmas/New Year packages. 1-night bookings occasionally refused weekends.

HAWORTH West Yorkshire   Map 4:D3

Hill Top Farmhouse   BUDGET   *Tel* 01535-643524
Haworth Moor, Haworth BD22 0EL

In an excellent position for walkers and Brontë enthusiasts, Brenda and Alan Fox's 17th-century farm guest house is much liked for its value and homeliness. On Haworth Moor, the farm is a short distance from the Parsonage Museum, and a longer 'lovely' walk to the Brontë Falls. The sitting room is cosy; a larger lounge/dining room has 18th-century carved wooden furniture, antique crockery and ornaments. Bedrooms have antique bric-a-brac, TV, fresh flowers, a small shower room. Mrs Fox bakes her own bread for breakfast. She will provide a packed lunch, and an evening meal ('straightforward country cooking'), by arrangement (bring your own wine). More reports, please.

3 **bedrooms.** On Haworth Moor. Lounge, lounge/dining room (soft background music). Large grounds. Unsuitable for &. No smoking. No dogs in house. No credit cards. B&B £30–£50 per person. Set dinner £18.

Weaver's   *Tel* 01535-643822
13–17 West Lane   *Fax* 01535-644832
Haworth BD22 8DU   *Email* weaversinhaworth@aol.com
                             Website www.weaversmallhotel.co.uk

In a row of former weavers' cottages, on a cobbled street by the Brontë Parsonage Museum, this bar and restaurant-with-rooms is run by two generations of one family. First and foremost it is a place to eat ('with a large and loyal following'): Colin and Jane Rushworth cook with son Tim; daughters Sally and Lucy are front-of-house. Readers like the 'hospitality and high standards', the 'cosy atmosphere', and the 'good northern regional food'. The Rushworths use local small suppliers, and organic home-grown ingredients in dishes like grilled Filey crab with cucumber and radish salad; skewer of minted Dales-bred lamb, with onion and red pepper. The menu changes seasonally, and extra dishes are shown on a weekly-changing blackboard menu. The cluttered lounge, 'full of character', has old photographs, modern paintings, antiques, bric-a-brac and mementos of the spinners' craft. The three 'stylish and idiosyncratic' bedrooms are on the second and third floors, up a narrow staircase. One looks over the cobbled street, others towards the museum, church, and car park. There are lace-trimmed pillowcases, TV, fresh milk, a cafetière with ground coffee. Breakfast includes smoked haddock omelette; Yorkshire 'fry-up'; vegetarian choices; wholewheat toast. (*KJ*)

3 bedrooms. By Brontë Parsonage Museum (use its car park). Closed 26 Dec–4 Jan, and Mon. Restaurant closed Sun night/Mon; midday Tues, Sat. Lounge, bar (jazz/blues/nostalgia background music), dining room. Unsuitable for &. No smoking. No dogs. All major credit cards accepted. B&B £44.75–£59.50 per person. Set lunch £16.95; full alc £27.50. *V*

HELMSLEY North Yorkshire   Map 4:C4

The Feversham Arms
1 High Street
Helmsley YO62 5AG

Tel 01439-770766
Fax 01439-770346
Email info@fevershamarmshotel.com
Website www.fevershamarmshotel.com

'We're not a country house hotel, nostalgic and backward-looking, neither are we a designer hotel where looks come before comfort,' writes Simon Rhatigan, owner of this former coaching inn on the main street of 'an attractive town with interesting shops'. 'Super hotel. Stunning decor, vibrant colours, well-trained staff,' was one comment. But there were also criticisms of welcome and service. Bedrooms vary. 'Ours was tricked out in pale blue and burgundy. Wonderful bed, excellent pillows, cloud-like duvet.' Fittings include 'cutting-edge' TV, DVD and PlayStation. For families, some rooms have a sofa bed and some are interconnecting. Three suites are new this year. There are 'relaxing' sitting areas and a high-roofed conservatory restaurant; doors lead to the terraced garden and swimming pool, and sloping grounds with a tennis court, and a little garden, facing the church, where tea and drinks are served. 'A very enjoyable dinner (portions not over-large for once). Good choice of reasonably priced wines.' Chef Charlie Lakin's dishes include bresaola of venison; loin of rabbit with black pudding stuffing ('it feels like the south of France, but we make sure you know you're in Yorkshire when you read the menu'). But not everyone liked the background music. More reports, please.

20 bedrooms. 1 in garden. Some on ground floor. Central. Parking. Ramp. 2 lounges, bar, conservatory restaurant (classical background music); private dining room; gym. Terrace (outside dining). 1-acre garden: heated swimming pool, tennis. Civil wedding licence. No smoking: restaurant, bedrooms. Amex, MasterCard, Visa accepted. B&B [2006] £70–£130 per person; D,B&B £100–£160. Set dinner £32; full alc £45. Christmas/New Year packages. 1-night bookings sometimes refused. *V*

HENLEY-ON-THAMES Oxfordshire   Map 2:D3

Hotel du Vin & Bistro
New Street
Henley-on-Thames
RG9 2BP

Tel 01491-848400
Fax 01491-848401
Email info@henley.hotelduvin.com
Website www.hotelduvin.com

The former Brakspear's Brewery, close to the town centre and the river, has been 'brilliantly converted with many of the Hotel du Vin trademarks: airy interiors, white walls, exposed beams and sisal flooring'. Soon after the opening in 2005, *Guide* inspectors praised the service and atmosphere, a view endorsed by readers this year, 'firm fans' of the chain: 'Everything as it should be and so rarely is: friendly, efficient staff; valet car parking, a boon in a crowded town; and in the room a powerful shower, comfortable bed, fresh milk in a fridge. The takeover by the Malmaison group hasn't harmed the concept.' In the bedrooms, each sponsored by a wine house, are plasma-screen TV, huge bed, deluxe bedding, good lighting. 'One strange omission: no radio. The morning is not the same without John Humphrys.' In Dom Perignon, the wet room is in the old brewing copper. Sound insulation may not always be perfect. The bistro and bar are 'full of atmosphere'. Most visitors find the food and wine excellent; 'and the "whatever" dress code works because guests tend to dress in the smart casual style that reflects the ambience'. (*David and Anna Sefton, Wendy and Michael Dods, and others*)

43 bedrooms. Central (front rooms might hear traffic). 50 yds from river. Trains from London/Reading. Parking. Valet parking. Bar (background music all day), bistro; billiard room; 2 private dining rooms; conference/function facilities. No smoking: restaurant, bedrooms. No dogs in bistro. All credit cards accepted. Room: double £115–£170, suite £275–£450. Breakfast £9.95–£13.50. Full alc £35.

The Red Lion
Hart Street
Henley-on-Thames
RG9 2AR

Tel 01491-572161
Fax 01491-410039
Email reservations@redlionhenley.co.uk
Website www.redlionhenley.co.uk

A creeper-clad 16th-century red brick inn of character (where King Charles I once stayed). Some bedrooms overlook the Royal Regatta course on the Thames. It is independently owned, by the Miller family of *Durrants*, London (*qv*). Richard Vowell is the long-serving manager. The public areas have antique panelling and furniture, paintings and prints; there are flagstones, an open fire, leather chairs and rowing memorabilia in the small bar, where light meals can be served. Some of the traditional bedrooms (flowery fabrics, prints on walls) overlook the river; others a pretty church and its graveyard; double glazing mitigates the sound of traffic from a busy bridge close by. Stephane Pasquale has joined as head chef; he serves traditional dishes with a French twist, eg, sea bream, braised orange fennel, bouillabaisse sauce. More reports, please.

26 bedrooms. By Henley bridge (windows double glazed). Trains from London/Reading. Large car park. Ramp. Bar, restaurant; 'easy listening' background music; conference/function facilities. On river: boat hire (picnics arranged). Unsuitable for &. No smoking in restaurant. No dogs. Amex, MasterCard, Visa accepted. Room: single £110, double £130–£155; D,B&B £97.50 per person. Breakfast £9.50–£13.50. Set lunch £17.50; full alc £35. Special offers on website.

HEREFORD Herefordshire   Map 3:D4

Castle House   *Tel* 01432-356321
Castle Street   *Fax* 01432-365909
Hereford HR1 2NW   *Email* info@castlehse.co.uk
                                      Website www.castlehse.co.uk

Two Grade II listed town houses, in gardens beside the old castle moat, have been sensitively converted into a luxury hotel by the Dutch owners, Dr Albert and Mrs Monique Heijn. 'A super hotel with cheerful staff,' one couple wrote. Others told of quiet 'by day and night'. 'Lovely to sit by the moat and hear ducks quacking.' As to the music in public areas: 'Mozart's Requiem Mass contrasted sharply with lovely chocolate soufflé: it reminded us that in the middle of life...' Other comments on the dinners: 'Little choice, small helpings.' 'Good food, but the menu didn't change in three days.' Chef Claire Nicholls serves elaborate dishes like fillet of beef, beetroot fondant; braised beef and horseradish faggot, truffle jus. There are polished wooden floors, bright rugs, lavish fabrics, massive flower arrangements, a wide staircase, artworks everywhere. The bedrooms (most are suites, one is fully equipped for disabled guests) illustrate the joint history of Great Britain and the Netherlands (names like Cavalier and Orange). They are well equipped: there is sherry, and chocolates at turndown. But a single room disappointed: 'Very small, only two coat hangers, peculiar taps, no hot water in the morning.' (*GES, DT, and others*)

15 bedrooms. 1 on ground floor equipped for &. In centre, near cathedral. Parking. Lift, ramps. Lounge, bar, restaurant; classical/light jazz background music. Garden. No smoking: restaurant, lounge. Amex, MasterCard, Visa accepted. B&B [2006] £105–£129 per person; D,B&B (min. 2 nights) £137–£144.50. Full alc £55. Spring breaks. Christmas/New Year packages.

HETTON North Yorkshire   Map 4:D3

The Angel Inn   *Tel* 01756-730263
Hetton, nr Skipton   *Fax* 01756-730363
BD23 6LT   *Email* info@angelhetton.co.uk
                                             Website www.angelhetton.co.uk

An old coaching inn that has for more than 20 years been an institution in
the Yorkshire Dales as a dining pub; guests can stay in five bedrooms in a
converted barn across the road. Mrs Juliet Watkins is the owner, Bruce
Elsworth the long-standing chef. A series of panelled and beamed rooms
leads off the bar, which has nooks and crannies and cosy alcoves. In the
restaurant, modern English dishes are served off a *carte*, eg, poached haunch
of venison, wild mushroom and horseradish mousse. A recent comment:
'Service was efficient without being rushed. Plenty of staff and a *sommelier*
who knew his stuff.' The bar/brasserie has its own menu with blackboard
specials. In summer, meals may be taken on a flagged forecourt overlooking
Cracoe Fell. Bedrooms, with minibar, are liked: 'Our good-sized room had
a large comfortable bed. Breakfast, served until 10 am, has fresh juices,
big bowls of cereals and fresh fruit, and an 'immense' Yorkshire platter.
(*LMM-J, WKW*)

5 bedrooms. In barn across road. 1 suitable for &. Off B6265, 5 miles N of Skipton.
Car park. Closed Christmas Day, New Year's Day, 2nd week in Jan. Bar (3 rooms),
bar/brasserie, restaurant (2 rooms); wine shop. No background music. Terrace
(outside dining). Civil wedding licence. No smoking. No dogs in public rooms.
MasterCard, Visa accepted. B&B [2006] £65–£90 per person; D,B&B (min. 2
nights) £190–£215. Set lunch (Sun) £23.95, dinner (Sat) £34.50; full alc £45. New
Year package.

HEXHAM Northumberland *See SHORTLIST*   Map 4:B3

HINDRINGHAM Norfolk   Map 2:A5

Field House   *Tel* 01328-878726
Moorgate Road   *Email* stay@fieldhousehindringham.co.uk
Hindringham nr Fakenham   *Website* www.fieldhousehindringham.co.uk
NR21 0PT

With wide views over the countryside near the north Norfolk coast, this
modern brick and flint cottage is run as a small guest house by its 'very
hospitable' owners, Wendy and Graham Dolton, who 'have the knack of

being friendly but not intrusive'. 'The ambience is a delight,' wrote a visitor this year. 'Great welcome, an excellent stay.' An earlier report: 'Our room was large, spotless, and full of anything one could want (DVD-player with discs, CD-player, comfortable, large beds, plenty of wardrobe space, etc).' Downstairs are a 'delightful lounge' and a dining room with three tables, which faces the garden 'where pheasants roam'. A four-course, candlelit dinner, cooked by Wendy Dolton and served by her husband, was thought 'delicious'. A typical main course: roast fillet of local beef with parsnip crisps, buttered cabbage and a Madeira jus. Many vegetables are home grown. Unlicensed: bring your own wine. The extensive breakfast menu includes fresh juices, organic cereals, fresh fruit, home-made bread, jams and marmalade, local bacon, fair-trade tea and coffee. 'The peace and quiet, birdsong and fresh air, delighted us Londoners.' (*Patricia Walker, T and PM; also Nigel Honey*)

3 bedrooms. 1, in garden annexe, suitable for &. 6 miles NE of Fakenham. Closed Christmas/New Year. Lunch not served. Lounge, dining room (background music at night). Garden: summerhouse, patio. No smoking. No children under 8. Guide dogs only. No credit cards. B&B £45–£75 per person; D,B&B £77.50–£107.50. Set dinner £32.50. 1-night bookings refused weekends and usually in July/Aug. ***V***

HINTON ST GEORGE Somerset   Map 1:C6
See SHORTLIST

HOARWITHY Herefordshire   Map 3:D4

The Old Mill   BUDGET   *Tel/Fax* 01432-840602
Hoarwithy, nr Hereford   *Email* carol.probert@virgin.net
HR2 6QH   *Website* www.theoldmillhoarwithy.co.uk

This old mill once harnessed the flow of the delightfully named Wrigglebrook Stream, in an unspoilt village on the River Wye. Now, Carol Probert ('such a charming person,' writes a visitor in 2006) runs it as an inexpensive guest house. In its garden are many birds and plenty of secluded areas; but there may be some traffic noise. Recent visitors were given 'an exemplary welcome, warm and friendly', and 'departed to cheery waves'. In cold weather, a log fire burns in the large stone fireplace in the lounge. The best bedrooms are thought 'very nice; ours was good-sized and spotless, with adequate lighting'. But one bathroom was found very cramped. A simple set dinner menu is served at 7 pm by arrangement; local produce is used where possible. No licence: bring your own wine. The *New*

Harp pub, opposite, is also recommended. 'Breakfast was wonderful: fresh fruit; yogurt, home-made marmalade, delicious toast; cooked dishes with excellent ingredients, served piping hot; fresh-ground, seriously strong coffee.' (*R and AL*)

6 bedrooms. 1 on ground floor. In village 4 miles NW of Ross-on-Wye. Parking. Lounge, dining room. No background music. ½-acre garden. No smoking. Guide dogs only. No credit cards. B&B [2006] £26 per person; D,B&B £42. 10% discount for 5 or more days. Christmas/New Year packages. *V*

HOCKLEY HEATH Warwickshire   Map 3:C6

Nuthurst Grange   *Tel* 01564-783972
Nuthurst Grange Lane   *Fax* 01564-783919
Hockley Heath B94 5NL   *Email* info@nuthurst-grange.com
                                         Website www.nuthurst-grange.com

'We knew we were on to a winner when a porter was immediately available to take us to our room on a winter's afternoon.' A visitor this year enjoyed Stephen and Linda Pike's 'well-run, well-maintained' red brick Edwardian house. 'Nicely proportioned and cosy looking,' she adds; 'it has an excellent, relaxing atmosphere.' It overlooks rolling farmland bisected by the M40, which can be heard in the well-tended garden and on the terrace, but is barely audible inside. 'Our corner room, facing the garden, was large, comfortable; lots of extras (fruit, sherry, port, water) and thoughtful touches like fresh milk for the tea tray. There was full turn-down service. No skimping on heating. Dinner was good: plenty of staff in the lounge to bring drinks, take orders. Home-made canapés, bread and petits fours; good rump of lamb, cooked to order.' 'Breakfast was freshly prepared and good, apart from thin toast.' Another guest in 2006 thought the decor 'needed updating'. Earlier visitors disliked the background music, but enjoyed walking along the nearby Stratford Canal. Close to the National Exhibition Centre, *Nuthurst Grange* attracts business visitors during the week; small meetings, functions and weddings are held. (*Lynn Wildgoose, and others*)

15 bedrooms. Off A3400, ½ mile S of Hockley Heath. Ramp. 2 lounges, restaurant; background music; 3 function/private dining rooms. 7½-acre grounds: herb garden, croquet, ponds, woodland; helipad. Riding, tennis, golf, clay-pigeon shooting, canal boating nearby. Civil wedding licence. No smoking in public rooms. No dogs. Amex, MasterCard, Visa accepted. B&B: single £139, double £165–£185, suite £195. Set dinner £30; full alc £35. Special breaks. Christmas/New Year breaks.

Hotels do not pay to be included in the *Guide*.

HOLFORD Somerset   Map 1:B5

Combe House   **NEW**   *Tel* 01278-741382
Holford   *Fax* 01278-741322
Holford Combe   *Email* enquiries@combehouse.co.uk
nr Bridgwater TA5 1RZ   *Website* www.combehouse.co.uk

In a beautiful, peaceful setting, this converted 17th-century tannery,
long and low, still with its large waterwheel, is at the end of a narrow
lane in a valley that leads to the Quantock hills. It was bought in 2004
by Andrew Ryan and Ray Fox-Cumming. They have revamped it both
in and out. 'Good-quality carpets, furniture, art work and pottery
abound,' says a guest who knew the previous regime. 'Lovely handmade
furniture in the restaurant. Food was a highlight: beautifully cooked,
well presented.' Chef Laurence Pratt uses home-grown organic ingredients for his seasonally changing menu (with daily chef's specials), eg,
breast of duckling with ginger, orange and honey glaze and shrimp won
ton. 'Very nice table settings, spring flowers, lovely home-made bread.
Good breakfasts: plenty of choice, excellent toast. Lunch menus unusual
and tasty. Delicious afternoon cream teas served until 5.30 pm. Dinner
is served in the garden in warm weather. All staff, including the head
waiter, were East European, polite, helpful and well groomed. Overall a
most pleasant stay.' At night you hear 'just the ripple of the stream
through the gardens, the sound of wind in the trees, the song of birds'.
A rock beach is nearby. (*Janice Carrera*)

18 bedrooms. 1 on ground floor. 1 in drying house. Off A39 Bridgwater–Minehead.
Train: Taunton. Lounge, bar, restaurant (background music at dinner when it is
quiet), library/private dining room. 5-acre grounds: tennis, croquet, covered 25-ft
swimming pool, sauna, stream. Golf, riding, walking, rock beach nearby. Civil
wedding licence. Smoking in garden only. No dogs in public rooms except bar.
MasterCard, Visa accepted. B&B £60–£67.50 per person; D,B&B £80–£90. Light
lunch from £5; full alc £35. Christmas/New Year packages. 1-night bookings
sometimes refused summer weekends. *V*

HOLKHAM Norfolk   Map 2:A5

The Victoria at Holkham   *Tel* 01328-711008
Park Road   *Fax* 01328-711009
Holkham NR23 1RG   *Email* victoria@holkham.co.uk
                                     Website www.victoriaatholkham.co.uk

On Earl of Leicester's Holkham estate, on main coast road (A149), 2 miles W of
Wells-next-the-Sea: former pub refurbished in Victorian colonial style, managed by

Paul Brown. Darkish decor: stone-flagged, wood or seagrass floors, olive-green walls, carved furniture from Rajasthan; dim lighting. 'Welcome efficient. Service friendly, if sometimes amateurish.' Lounge area, 3 bar rooms; background music; attractive restaurant (good modern English cooking; local fish; game and beef from the estate). Good breakfast. Children welcomed (special menus, etc). Receptions, weddings held off-season (civil wedding licence). 3-acre grounds: courtyard with barbecue; children's play area. Holkham's famous beach 10 mins' walk. No smoking: restaurant, bedrooms. No dogs: bedrooms, eating areas. MasterCard, Visa accepted. 14 bedrooms: some spacious, some small; 1 with access for &. B&B [2006] £57.50–£210 per person. Full alc £30. Christmas/New Year packages. More reports, please.

HOLT Norfolk   Map 2:A5

Byfords	*Tel* 01263-711400
1–3 Shirehall Plain	*Fax* 01263-714815
Holt NR25 6BG	*Email* queries@byfords.org.uk
	Website www.byfords.org.uk

Described with tongue in cheek by its owners as a 'posh B&B', Iain and Clair Wilson's operation on the main square of this enchanting Norfolk town combines a hugely popular café/bistro, a restaurant and a busy deli with some 'brilliantly designed' bedrooms. 'Highly innovative,' said our inspector, whose room, facing a flower-filled courtyard, had 'the largest high-tech TV/DVD/radio I have come across in any hotel, movable, so viewable from sofa or bed; dimmers on all lights; seven pillows/cushions; tea-making equipment with fresh milk, delicious home-made shortbread'. The café serves breakfasts, but residents have their own breakfast room where the meal was 'as generous and posh as the accommodation: jugs of freshly made fruit juices, excellent coffee, home-baked bread and pastries, cooked dishes including kedgeree and kippers'. The Wilsons tell us that the 'eating experience' has changed since our inspection, and a new team in an open kitchen serves traditional dishes 'with a twist' in a new conservatory restaurant, eg, smoked haddock with Welsh rarebit; roasted Gressingham duck with caramelised swede. We would welcome reports on the cooking. Visitors are given a handbook with extensive information on the area.

9 bedrooms. Some on ground floor. Central. Private, secure car park. Ramps. 5 internal eating areas, 1 external; conservatory; background jazz; deli. Beach 4 miles. No smoking. No dogs. Diners, MasterCard, Visa accepted. B&B [2006] £60–£105 per person; D,B&B £87.50–£110. Full alc £25. Christmas/New Year packages. 1-night bookings refused Sat.

HOPE Derbyshire   Map 3:A6

Underleigh House   `BUDGET`   *Tel* 01433-621372
off Edale Road   *Fax* 01433-621324
Hope S33 6RF   *Email* info@underleighhouse.co.uk
                               Website www.underleighhouse.co.uk

'Brilliant, and all for £70.' Our inspectors found much to praise at Philip
and Vivienne Taylor's 'excellent' B&B, a long, low, creeper-covered conversion of a 19th-century barn and cottages in the Hope valley. 'Vivienne
Taylor greeted us by name and offered us tea with delicious lemon cake.
She is delightful, warm, with a giggle.' Earlier visitors from the United
States of America named this 'by far our favourite place in Britain'. A
small bedroom had 'lots of patterns, and views on both sides of fields with
sheep; everything one could want, even bathrobes (nice lightweight ones);
small bathroom with a bath; a comprehensive information pack'; two
bedrooms have been redecorated in 2006. Breakfast, served round a large
oak table in the flagstoned hall, has won awards. The menu is huge; jugs
of orange juice, eight types of home-made jam, own-recipe muesli, fresh
and dried fruits from the buffet; porridge and croissants from the Aga;
huge platters of cooked items. The Taylors serve drinks in a large lounge
(no muzak) with a log fire, or on a terrace. Maps and packed lunches are
provided for walks in the Peak District national park from the door.
(*J and DW, and others*)

6 bedrooms. 2 on ground floor. 1 mile N of Hope. Train: Hope; bus from Sheffield.
Open Feb–Dec. Lounge, breakfast room. No background music. ½-acre garden.
Unsuitable for &. No smoking. No children under 12. Dogs by arrangement.
MasterCard, Visa accepted (*both 3% surcharge*). B&B £35–£55 per person. 3-night
rates. 1-night bookings refused Sat.

HORDLE Hampshire   Map 2:E2

The Mill at Gordleton   *Tel* 01590-682219
Silver Street   *Fax* 01590-683073
Hordle, nr Lymington   *Email* info@themillatgordleton.co.uk
SO41 6DJ   *Website* www.themillatgordleton.co.uk

Recently refurbished by its owner, Liz Cottingham, this 17th-century mill,
with terraces and gardens overlooking a stream, is on the edge of the New
Forest. Terri Seabright is the manager. *Guide* inspectors enjoyed their stay:
'Service was professional and very pleasant.' The 'beautifully sculpted'
gardens have terraces where ducks and geese sometimes wander. 'Although

close to a busy road, our mini-suite (we were upgraded) was well positioned and insulated so there was no trace of noise. It had a small, bright sitting room, pictures, a Victorian birdcage and a fabulous bathroom with beautiful black tiles and a huge double shower (no bath). Good local information but furniture lacked individuality.' In the busy restaurant, which faces the stream, 'all the diners seemed to be enjoying themselves'. The cooking of chefs Karl Wiggins and David Baker is 'English with a contemporary twist', eg, pan-fried scallops marinated in lemon grass oil; rump of Dorset lamb with potato and spinach beignets. 'Starters very good; main courses competent.' There is a vegetarian dish of the day. The good wine list has a wide price range. A good base for visiting Beaulieu, Buckler's Hard, the Isle of Wight, etc.

8 bedrooms. 4 miles W of Lymington. Closed 25 Dec. Restaurant closed Sun night. Lounge, 2 bars, restaurant; background music. 2½-acre grounds on river (fishing rights). Only restaurant suitable for ♿. Smoking in small bar, conservatory only. Dogs in small bar only. Amex, MasterCard, Visa accepted. B&B £45–£120 per person. Set lunch £12.50–£15.50; full alc £35. 1-night bookings sometimes refused Sat.

HOVE East Sussex *See SHORTLIST* Map 2:E4

HUDDERSFIELD West Yorkshire Map 4:E3
See SHORTLIST

HULL East Yorkshire *See SHORTLIST* Map 4:D5

HUNTINGDON Cambridgeshire Map 2:B4

The Old Bridge	*Tel* 01480-424300
1 High Street	*Fax* 01480-411017
Huntingdon PE29 3TQ	*Email* oldbridge@huntsbridge.co.uk
	Website www.huntsbridge.com

A handsome, creeper-clad, 18th-century building, once a private bank, overlooking the River Ouse. It is the only town house hotel in John Hoskins's small Huntsbridge group of inns. In August 2005, Nina Beamond returned as manager (she was once service manager here); Chris

Tabbitt, who has worked at *Bibendum* in London, is the new chef. He serves modern dishes like rabbit and chorizo; roast rump of lamb with sweetbreads. The building is hedged in by a busy traffic system, but bedrooms have triple glazing, most have air conditioning, and the small riverside garden provides a relatively peaceful retreat. The bedrooms (three have been renovated this year) are themed: there are colourful mosaic tiles, *chaises longues*, up-to-date music systems, and smart bathrooms (some have a claw-foot bath). Early morning tea and a free newspaper are brought to the room. Breakfast includes scrambled eggs with smoked salmon. The function area is now self-contained 'so that parties and weddings will not impact on normal guests'. Conferences are also catered for. We would welcome more reports.

24 bedrooms. 2 on ground floor. 500 yds from centre. Car park. Station 10 mins' walk. Ramps. Lounge, bar, 2 restaurants; business centre. No background music. 1-acre grounds: terrace, garden; on river: fishing, jetty (boat trips). Unsuitable for &. Civil wedding licence. Smoking in bar only. All major credit cards accepted. B&B [2006] £67.50–£120 per person; D,B&B £70–£100. Set lunch from £13.50; full alc £28.

HURLEY Berkshire   Map 2:D3

Black Boys Inn   NEW   *Tel* 01628-824212
Henley Road, Hurley   *Email* info@blackboysinn.co.uk
nr Maidenhead   *Website* www.blackboysinn.co.uk
S16 6NQ

The River Thames is a short walk from this old inn. Long reputed for the cooking of Simon Bonwick (*Michelin Bib Gourmand*), it was bought and refurbished in 2004 by the 'warmly welcoming' Adrian Bannister and his wife, Helen. The pale green building faces a busy road: traffic noise is inevitable, but the bedrooms are at the back in converted stables. 'Our decent-sized room,' say inspectors in 2006, 'was well designed. Soft colours, vaulted ceiling with original heavy beams, smallish windows with blinds, fairly disciplinarian antique chairs (we would have liked something more comfortable), free high-speed Internet connection, very pretty bathroom with green walls (water from the inn's own well).' The 'lively but fairly small' bar is separated from the dining room by a wood-burning stove. Both have a polished oak floor. 'Tables well spaced, simply laid (plain white china, good glassware), comfortable Gothic-style chairs, paintings and ornaments representing ducks. The cooking, demonstrating precise technical skills, used the best possible ingredients in generous portions', eg, crayfish with watercress purée; halibut with tomato, herb and shallot compote. 'Good wines by the glass. Staff young, well informed, smartly turned out. At breakfast, the commercial orange juice was out of keeping with the perfectly cooked hot dishes.'

8 bedrooms. 1 suitable for &. 2½ miles E of Henley on A4130 to Maidenhead. Parking. Closed 25 Dec–9 Jan. Small bar area, restaurant; background music; meeting room. 1½-acre grounds. No smoking. No children under 12. No dogs. MasterCard, Visa accepted. B&B double £65–£95. Full alc £31.

HURSTBOURNE TARRANT Hampshire   Map 2:D2

Esseborne Manor	*Tel* 01264-736444
Hurstbourne Tarrant, nr Andover	*Fax* 01264-736725
SP11 0ER	*Email* esseborne@aol.com
	Website www.esseborne-manor.co.uk

In the North Wessex downs, this 'stylish, unstuffy' hotel provides a 'family-run atmosphere and efficient service'. Eleven bedrooms are in the main house (some with spa bath, some with four-poster). Owners Lucilla and Mark Hamilton have added six rooms (good for a family: children are welcomed, though there are no special facilities for them) in a 'sympathetic' extension round a courtyard. Three small rooms are in cottages. Inspectors returned in 2006: 'Attractive house. Lovely grounds (neglected tennis court; beautiful herb garden). Pity about the busy road, but indoors, traffic is not audible; there are inviting lounges. Friendly greeting. Help with luggage. Some Chinese members of staff, very pleasant. We were upgraded to a massive suite with canopy bed and private patio. Good technology. Good lighting (apart from bedside lights). We weren't keen on the opaque glass loo door in the huge bathroom.' In the dining room (red-patterned wallpaper, blue carpet, big windows), Bosnian chef Steven Ratic serves a 'rather conventional' menu ('what our clients prefer'). 'Good-value Menu du Vin: corn-fed chicken with garden vegetables; tasty stuffed aubergine; nice home-baked rolls. Ice cream with chocolate brownie. Uninspiring breakfast buffet, boring toast, but good cooked dishes.' Weddings (marquee on the lawn) and meetings are catered for.

20 bedrooms. Some on ground floor. Midway between Andover and Newbury. Closed New Year. 2 lounges, bar, restaurant; function room. No background music. 3-acre grounds: formal gardens, tennis, croquet. Arrangements with nearby golf club and fitness centre. Civil wedding licence. No smoking: restaurant, bedrooms. No dogs in public rooms. All major credit cards accepted. B&B: single £95–£130, double £125–£180, suite £240; D,B&B £92.50–£160 per person.

ILMINGTON Warwickshire   Map 3:D6

The Howard Arms   *Tel/Fax* 01608-682226
Lower Green, Ilmington   *Email* info@howardarms.com
nr Stratford-upon-Avon CV36 4LT   *Website* www.howardarms.com

'Sophisticated and quintessentially English', Robert and Gill Greenstock's
expanded 400-year-old stone pub stands on the green of a quiet village
south of Stratford-upon-Avon. 'Inside,' writes a recent visitor, 'are a fine
bar, log fireplace, flagged floor, and nooks for eating; a larger room on a
higher level provides more formal dining, and is a lovely, light place for
breakfast.' The three bedrooms upstairs, uncluttered and simple, are 'cosy,
with oak beams, antique furniture and prints, and comfy chairs, but modern
lighting'. 'Spotless bathrooms have all the usual pampering goodies.' The
menu combines 'modern and traditional' dishes, eg, beef, ale and mustard
pie; roast cod, spinach, potato and chorizo; 'copious and interesting. A great
selection of wines and whiskies by the glass.' Breakfast, served by 'pleasant
ladies' (no buffet), must be ordered the night before: it has 'lovely home-
made bread toast, ample strong cafetière coffee'. Summer meals can be
taken in the pretty garden. Residents should not arrive between 3 and
6 pm (they are given a key). Hidcote and Kiftsgate gardens, and Compton
Verney Gallery, are nearby. The Greenstocks' sons, Will and Tom, have
left to embark on their own venture, the *Horse and Groom* at Bourton-on-
the-Hill, nearby. (*IW*)

3 bedrooms. Green of village 4 miles NW of Shipston on Stour. Closed 25/31 Dec.
Snug, 2 bars, dining bar. No background music. ½-acre garden. Unsuitable for &. No
smoking. No children under 8 overnight. Guide dogs only. MasterCard, Visa
accepted. B&B [2006]: single £80, double £105–£120. Set Sun lunch £20.50; full alc
£33.50. 2-night D,B&B breaks. 1-night bookings refused weekends.

****

Traveller's tale This palace of sandstone and marble oozes
ostentation. It has an impressive galaxy of young, smart,
uniformed staff who are most pleasant, and fresh from the
hospitality line, but show no real purpose. The owner, who lives
abroad, turns up once a month and revamps certain areas
according to his whim, throwing another million pounds at
builders and decorators with instructions to change things
immediately. The service in the rooms is poor. They have a lot
to learn in all directions. (*Hotel in Gloucestershire*)

****

IPSWICH Suffolk   Map 2:C5

Salthouse Harbour Hotel   *Tel* 01473-226789
1 Neptune Quay   *Fax* 01473-226927
Ipswich IP4 1AS   *Email* staying@salthouseharbour.co.uk
                          Website www.salthouseharbour.co.uk

On the waterfront, facing the vibrant marina, this seven-storey Victorian
warehouse has been given a stylish makeover by Robert Gough. A
minimalist contemporary decor sits with retained traditional features,
arched windows and high beamed ceilings; modern paintings and prints
are displayed throughout. The staff are young, the service is 'friendly,
courteous'. 'The noisy brasserie has a modern menu (lamb shanks with
leek chestnut mash), served on wooden tables; breakfast is served at table.
The bedrooms have TV with DVD, "tasteful" lighting. Two penthouse
suites have stunning views. Disabled visitors are well provided for.' More
reports, please.

43 bedrooms. 2 suitable for &. 2 mins' walk from centre. Parking. Lounge, bar,
brasserie; background music all day; conference facilities. Civil wedding licence. No
smoking: brasserie, 8 bedrooms. All major credit cards accepted. B&B [2006]
£65–£100 per person. Full alc £38. 2-day breaks. Sun-night rates. Christmas/New
Year packages. 1-night bookings sometimes refused in season.

IREBY Cumbria   Map 4: inset B2

Overwater Hall   *Tel* 017687-76566
Overwater, nr Ireby   *Fax* 017687-76921
CA7 1HH   *Email* welcome@overwaterhall.co.uk
                          Website www.overwaterhall.co.uk

'A little expensive, but it has style.' 'Delightful, elegant.' This castellated
Grade II listed Georgian mansion, owned and run by Stephen Bore (the
'graceful front-of-house') and Adrian and Angela Hyde, stands in large
grounds flanked by Skiddaw and its surrounding fells in the Lake District
national park. The public rooms have a bold decor: 'audacious' wallpaper,
contrasting panelling and lights. Our inspectors found their bedroom
'delightful'. Done in blue and cream; small separate sitting area, 'immaculate white bathroom, spectacular and beautifully lit'. Three new 'superior'
rooms will open in 2007. Dogs are welcomed: no charge; they may sit with
their owners in the lounge, and run about unleashed in the garden.
Children are welcomed too. Adrian Hyde's 'smart menus' offer plenty of
choice of modern dishes: much game, eg, ballottine of guineafowl; wild

rabbit, pheasant and mallard. 'Soups the best I have tasted.' 'A well-balanced, well-proportioned meal. Tables elegantly laid.' But one couple were dissatisfied with the vegetarian dishes. 'Smart casual' dress is expected of diners. Breakfast (served at table) is a 'full Cumbrian' affair. Good walking from the door; red squirrels, deer and woodpeckers can be seen, and ospreys nest nearby. (*Susan Chait, and others*)

12 Bedrooms. 1 on ground floor. 2 miles NE of Bassenthwaite Lake. Closed 1st 2 weeks Jan. Drawing room, lounge, bar area, restaurant; classical background music at night. 18-acre grounds. Overwater tarn 1 mile. No smoking in restaurant. No children under 5 in restaurant at night (high tea at 5.30 pm). Dogs allowed: bedrooms, bar. MasterCard, Visa accepted. B&B £70–£100 per person; D,B&B £90–£120. Set dinner £40. 4-night breaks all year. Christmas/New Year packages. 1-night bookings refused Sat.

IRONBRIDGE Shropshire *See SHORTLIST*   Map 3:C5

KESWICK Cumbria *See SHORTLIST*   Map 4: inset C2

KINGSBRIDGE Devon *See SHORTLIST*   Map 1:D4

KIRTLINGTON Oxfordshire   Map 2:C2

The Dashwood NEW	*Tel* 01869-352707
South Green, Heyford Road	*Fax* 01869-351432
Kirtlington OX5 3HJ	*Email* info@thedashwood.co.uk
	Website www.thedashwood.co.uk

An old pub in this Oxfordshire village (full of mellow stone cottages) has been rescued by Martin and Ros Lewis and turned into a restaurant-with-rooms. When our inspectors called, it had been open just nine months. They reported: 'It is neat and well ordered, both outside and in. Splashes of colour from fabrics and paintings contrast well with the natural look of wood, leather, plain carpeting and stone. Bathrooms are modern. Ours had a shower only.' The rooms have broadband Internet access, slimline TV and hand-made oak furniture. Some are on a courtyard. In the informal bistro-style split-level restaurant, Marcel Taylor is the chef. 'It is staffed by attractive young people wearing black waistcoats. Service was attentive.

Starters more tempting than main courses. We chose devilled kidneys; scallops with saffron rice and spinach. Desserts were not remarkable, especially at their prices. Breakfast until 10 am was limited: nice fresh fruit salad but no muesli or yogurt. Cooked food was fine, but no vegetarian dishes. Very nice croissants, but boring toast.' The main drawback: no guests' sitting room. 'But we had a pleasant stay, smart and unpretentious if not a spoiling experience.'

12 bedrooms. 7 in barn. 1 on ground floor, suitable for &. In village on A4095. 12 miles N of Oxford. Car park. Closed New Year. Small bar area, restaurant; mixed background music all day. Small outside seating area. No smoking. No dogs. Amex, MasterCard, Visa accepted. B&B £55–£85 per person. Full alc £32. Christmas package.

KNIGHTWICK Worcestershire   Map 3:D5

The Talbot **NEW**	*Tel* 01886-821235
Knightwick	*Fax* 01886-821060
WR6 5PH	*Email* info@the-talbot.co.uk
	Website www.the-talbot.co.uk

'If you want to enjoy a traditional inn with a strong huntin', shootin' and fishin' theme, this is the place to be. No smart country house hotel pretensions here.' So writes the nominator of the Clift family's old coaching inn which stands peacefully on the banks of the River Teme in lovely Herefordshire/Worcestershire border countryside. 'On a Friday in February it was heaving with a large shooting party.' The 'lively bar', which leads to a terrace, serves home-brewed ales. In the oak-panelled dining room, the chef, Jamie Tarbox, serves 'really excellent food' (eg, guineafowl breast wrapped in bacon with creamed parsnips and puy lentils). 'Our large bedroom had an ultra-modern power shower. Breakfast with some of the tastiest black pudding and bacon I have had. Special mention for the fire-places: one had almost half a tree blazing in the hearth.' Fishing can be arranged. (*Jon Hughes*)

11 bedrooms. From A44 Worcester–Leominster, turn on to B4197. Parking. Closed 25 Dec evening. Ramp. Lounge bar, restaurant. No background music. Patio; riverside picnic area. Only restaurant suitable for &. No smoking: restaurant, bedrooms. Dogs by arrangement. MasterCard, Visa accepted. B&B £41–£48 per person; D,B&B (in Feb) £65. Set menu £30; full alc £38.50. New Year package.

The 'New' label indicates hotels which are appearing in the *Guide* for the first time or which have been readmitted after an absence.

KNUTSFORD Cheshire   Map 4:E3

Longview   *Tel* 01565-632119
51 and 55 Manchester Road   *Fax* 01565-652402
Knutsford WA16 0LX   *Email* enquiries@longviewhotel.com
                                  Website www.longviewhotel.com

In a pleasant town 18 miles from Manchester (easily reached by train), this popular small hotel is owned and managed by Mrs Lulu Ahooie. Composed of two old houses separated by a children's dancing school, and a new annexe, it looks across a busy commuter road to a large common. Quietest rooms are at the rear (all windows are double glazed). The bedrooms vary from 'cosy' to 'premier'; most have Victorian-style furniture, and extras include nail brush, pincushion, clothes brush, ceiling fan, video- or DVD-player – videotapes and DVDs can be rented. Some walls are thin, and steps are steep. The suites face a private garden; one has its own terrace. Light meals can be taken in the bedrooms or the small, low-ceilinged cellar bar, which is hung with *Punch* prints. In the restaurant, frequented by locals, Ian Evans serves traditional dishes: both the food and service are enjoyed by regular visitors. There is Wi-Fi Internet access throughout the building. (*JG*)

32 bedrooms. 19 in annexes. On road to Manchester. 8 mins' walk from station. Parking. Restaurant closed midday and Sun. Reception, bar, restaurant; 'easy listening' background music 7 am–11 pm. Small grounds. Unsuitable for &. No smoking: restaurant, some bedrooms. No dogs in public rooms. Amex, MasterCard, Visa accepted. B&B: single £59–£83, double £79–£110, suite £136–£145. Full alc £28.

See also SHORTLIST

LACOCK Wiltshire   Map 2:D1

At the Sign of the Angel   *Tel* 01249-730230
6 Church Street   *Fax* 01249-730527
Lacock, nr Chippenham SN15 2LB   *Email* angel@lacock.co.uk
                                      Website www.lacock.co.uk

In an ancient and picturesque National Trust village (a popular setting for period film and TV productions), this half-timbered inn has been run for many years by Lorna and George Hardy (chef and *sous-chef*). It is restored to a full *Guide* entry this year after an endorsement by a discriminating visitor: 'I stayed two nights, and have no complaints. The staff were friendly and efficient.' The inn has low doorways and beams, oak panelling, antique furniture, old, uneven floors with creaky floorboards. Five new rooms have been added in an annexe (converted farm workers' cottages), reached through 'an enchanting garden with a stream'. 'Mine was nicely furnished, and quiet; the four-poster bed was comfy.' Rooms in the main building have been upgraded; they are full of character, but in some of them noise may be heard early and late from the bar and kitchen. 'The food was good, though some might find it on the heavy side' ('resolutely English' dishes like steak and kidney pie; honey-roasted ham hock). There is a log fire in the quiet, oak-panelled residents' lounge. (*Charles Grant*)

11 bedrooms. 4 on ground floor. 5 in annexe. Village centre. Closed Christmas. Ramps. Lounge, bar, restaurant. Civil wedding licence. No smoking: restaurant, bedrooms. No dogs in public rooms. All major credit cards accepted. B&B [2006] £52.50–£85 per person. Set meals £10–£15.

LANGAR Nottinghamshire   Map 2:A3

Langar Hall   *Tel* 01949-860559
Langar NG13 9HG   *Fax* 01949-861045
                                  Email info@langarhall.co.uk
                                  Website www.langarhall.com

♕ *César award in 2000*

Hidden in the Vale of Belvoir, this honey-coloured Georgian house is run in informal style by Imogen Skirving. This year's comments: 'I loved it.' 'Gorgeous, the embodiment of the country house fantasy.' 'Exquisite room, comfortable with nice touches; superb food.' (Mrs Skirving has said that *Langar Hall* is better described as a restaurant-with-rooms to stop complaints from those who find it too crowded at weekends.) 'Excellent welcome in the bar.' The 'lovely' grounds, 'wonderful flowers', 'attention to detail', and the 'eager young staff' were all praised this year. Caveats included a slow response to requests from an annexe room, delivery charges for newspapers (in addition to a 12½% service charge). The drawing room, with its club fender, cheerful pictures, has a 'family feel'; light meals are served all day in a new garden conservatory. The bedrooms are themed: Bohemia has rich fabrics and poetry on the bathroom walls; Agnews is a chalet on the croquet lawn. The daily-changing menu uses local ingredients, and fish from Scotland (eg, pan-roasted cod, chive mash). The grounds have gardens, canals, medieval fishponds and an adventure play area for children. (*Freddie Stockdale, Anne Helme, and others*)

12 bedrooms. 1 on ground floor. Also 1 garden chalet. 12 miles SE of Nottingham. Train: Grantham/Nottingham; link to Bingham, 3 miles. Sitting room, study, library, bar, garden room, restaurant; private dining room; small conference/function facilities. Classical background music 'on request only'. 20-acre grounds: gardens, children's play area, croquet, ponds; fishing. Unsuitable for &. Civil wedding licence. Smoking in bar only. Dogs by arrangement. Amex (by arrangement), MasterCard, Visa accepted. B&B [2006] £75–£110 per person. Set lunch £15, dinner £25; full alc £40. (*Excluding discretionary service charge*) Mid-week offers. 1-night bookings refused for some bedrooms at weekends. *V*

LANGFORD BUDVILLE Somerset   Map 1:C5

Bindon Country House   *Tel* 01823-400070
Langford Budville   *Fax* 01823-400071
nr Wellington TA21 0RU   *Email* stay@bindon.com
                                        Website www.bindon.com

'A delight. We felt like members of the squirearchy.' 'Friendly, unpretentious, well organised.' Praise again for Lynn and Mark Jaffa's hotel (Pride of Britain), set peacefully amid formal and woodland gardens in rural Somerset. The 17th-century building was given a makeover in Victorian times, creating the look of a baroque Bavarian hunting lodge. Its central hall, with 'stunning' floor tiles and a panelled staircase, is 'particularly beautiful'. The lounge and bar, which face the gardens, have 'comfortable sofas and armchairs in small groups, good for intimate conversation'. Public rooms have Wellington memorabilia (the nearby town took its name from the Duke), and each bedroom is named after one of his victories. They vary in size, but all are well equipped and 'most comfortable'; best ones face the grounds. 'Our standard room with four-poster was fine, if a little boring,' said inspectors. Chef Mike Davis is thought 'very good; one got a sense that there was real pride in the cooking. Lamb perfectly done. Portions just right. A generous smattering of little extra courses. Well-spaced tables of various sizes.' This is a child-friendly place (high teas, games, videos, etc, provided). 'A particularly fine breakfast with personal service.' (*JH, and others*)

12 bedrooms. 1 on ground floor. 4 miles NW of Wellington. Only party bookings at Christmas/New Year. Hall (pianist on Sat), lounge, study, bar, restaurant (occasional classical background music); 2 conference rooms. 7-acre grounds: kitchen garden, rose garden, heated 30-ft swimming pool, tennis, croquet, *boules*; chapel; woodland. Coarse fishing 500 yds. Civil wedding licence. Smoking in bar only. Dogs in public rooms 'by discretion'. All major credit cards accepted. B&B [2006] £57.50–£95 per person; D,B&B (min. 2 nights) £85–£130. Set dinner £35; full alc £48. Christmas/New Year packages. 1-night bookings sometimes refused. *V*

LANGTHWAITE North Yorkshire   Map 4:C3

The Charles Bathurst Inn   `NEW/BUDGET`   *Tel* 01748-884567
Langthwaite, Arkengarthdale   *Fax* 01748-884599
DL11 6EN   *Email* info@cbinn.co.uk
                                     Website www.cbinn.co.uk

In 'beautiful, remote' Arkengarthdale, west of Richmond, on the edge of
the Pennine Way, Charles and Stacy Cody's 18th-century inn ('*CB*' to
locals) stands on a narrow road near Reeth. Around is 'wonderful walking
country', says the nominator. 'Our pleasant room had good views, but only
one bedside table and we disliked the soap dispenser. The cooking was
excellent at breakfast and dinner but the coffee was not.' Meal orders are
taken at the bar (the menu, written on a large mirror, includes local game
and fish from Hartlepool), and 'on busy days some meals are served in an
annexe with uncomfortable bench seating. Our favourite table was by the
window. The staff, many of them young and local, were superb. We loved
this lively place, warts and all.' There are open fires and antique pine
furniture. Eleven bedrooms are in a new wing (built 1999): many have an
open truss ceiling. For children there are special menus and a toy box.
(*Kay Hickman*)

19 bedrooms. 5 miles NW of Reeth. Closed Christmas. Ramps. Lounge, 2 bars,
restaurant, pool room. Background music all day. Small garden: children's play area.
No smoking. No dogs in public rooms. MasterCard, Visa accepted. B&B double
£85–£110; D,B&B £50–£72.50 per person. Alc dinner £20. 1-night bookings
refused weekends.

LASTINGHAM North Yorkshire   Map 4:C4

Lastingham Grange   *Tel* 01751-417345/402
Lastingham YO62 6TH   *Fax* 01751-417358
                          Email reservations@lastinghamgrange.com
                          Website www.lastinghamgrange.com

Ϙ *César award in 1991*

A *Guide* favourite since the first edition, the Wood family's converted 17th-
century farmhouse stands in extensive grounds in a historic village on the
edge of the North Yorkshire Moors national park. Dennis Wood died in
October 2005; Mrs Jane Wood, and her sons, Bertie, the manager, and
Tom, continue to run the hotel, 'very well', say returning devotees. 'All
remains the same.' Other praise: 'Our favourite country hotel.' 'Idyllic, quiet
surroundings.' 'Our second home.' 'Staff are good, watchful and attentive.'

Stone-walled, and built around a courtyard, the house is 'not at all grand'. The decor is traditional: 'Floral carpet, floral tiles, floral shower curtain, floral wallpaper, "sitting Thai girl" prints.' So is the cooking of Paul Cattaneo and Sandra Thurlow: 'not fancy or pretentious'. 'My fillet steak was magnificent.' The 'equally good' breakfast has 'delicious sausages; lots of cereals'. Rates include newspapers, morning coffee, afternoon tea. 'Good staff, watchful and efficient.' Children are welcomed: there is an adventure playground. From the garden you can walk straight out on to the moors. (*Anne and Denis Tate, Grant and Nancy Buck, Richard Lamb, Carol Jackson*)

11 bedrooms. 5 miles NE of Kirkbymoorside. Open Mar–end Nov. Ramps. Hall, lounge, dining room; laundry facilities. No background music. 12-acre grounds: terrace, garden, adventure playground, croquet, *boules*. Limited assistance for &. No smoking. No dogs in public rooms. Diners, MasterCard, Visa accepted. B&B [2006] £55–£105 per person; D,B&B £80–£140. Picnic lunches/bar meals available. Set lunch £25, dinner £37.50. **ᵛ**

LAVENHAM Suffolk   Map 2:C5

The Great House
Market Place
Lavenham CO10 9QZ

Tel 01787-247431
Fax 01787-248007
Email info@greathouse.co.uk
Website www.greathouse.co.uk

On the marketplace of an attractive Suffolk wool town, this imposing part-Tudor, part-Georgian house is run as a restaurant-with-rooms by long-time owner/chef Régis Crépy and his wife, Martine. 'It is very "correct" in the French sense,' says a visitor this year. 'The welcome is cool in a professional rather than a glacial way; excellent quality and very good value.' Four of the five bedrooms are suites, with king-size bed, antiques, old beams, a modern bathroom. 'We liked the flask of sherry, fresh ground coffee and leaf tea on the tray, and the fresh flowers. Dinner in the quiet enclosed courtyard on a warm evening was a real pleasure; unobtrusive service.' The candlelit dining room is oak-beamed with wooden floors. M. Crépy's menus have classic French dishes (eg, filet d'agneau au thym); 'not grand, but well conceived and properly prepared; the wine list is not greedily priced and is sourced from many countries'. Light lunches are available from Tuesday to Saturday. There is a small sitting room/bar and a walled garden. 'Very peaceful until the thunderous bells of St Peter and St Paul start for early matins. An excellent relaxed breakfast, again in the courtyard, with fresh orange juice, good croissanterie.' (*Michael Lewis*)

5 bedrooms. By Market Cross, near Guildhall. Public car park. Open Feb–Dec. Lounge/bar, restaurant (French background music). ½-acre garden: patio, swings.

Unsuitable for ♿. No smoking. No dogs in public rooms. MasterCard, Visa accepted. Room [2006]: single £65–£150, double £76–£160, suite £96–£160. Breakfast: continental £6.50, English £9.50. Set lunch £17.95, dinner £24.95; full alc £38. Midweek breaks. 1-night bookings refused Sat.

Lavenham Priory

Water Street
Lavenham CO10 9RW

Tel 01787-247404
Fax 01787-248472
Email mail@lavenhampriory.co.uk
Website www.lavenhampriory.co.uk

Once a priory, later an Elizabethan merchant's home, this white-painted, half-timbered, Grade I listed house has been sympathetically restored by Tim and Gilli Pitt. They are 'friendly, relaxed' hosts. Visitors write of 'a lovely mixture of old-fashioned charm and modern comfort'. The suite has a separate sitting room; the other five 'bedchambers' are spacious, with sloping, beamed ceilings, oak floor. There are unusual beds (four-poster, 'sleigh' or polonaise), slipper baths and power showers. Guests have use of a 'snug' (with TV, videos and books), or the Great Hall (with huge inglenook fireplace, antique furniture and oak Jacobean staircase). A communal breakfast is served around a large table in the 'stunning' Merchants Room. 'You squeeze your own orange juice, and make your own toast', and there are kippers, smoked haddock, scrambled eggs, three types of bread, etc. Breakfast and drinks are served in the herb garden in summer. No dinners, but help is given in booking at the good restaurants nearby, including *The Great House* (see previous entry).

6 bedrooms. Central (rear rooms quietest). Parking. Closed Christmas/New Year. Great Hall/sitting room, snug, breakfast room. No background music. 3-acre garden: medieval courtyard, herb garden. Unsuitable for ♿. No smoking. No children under 10. No dogs. MasterCard, Visa accepted. B&B [2006] £47.50–£85 per person. Discount for 2 nights or more. 1-night bookings refused Sat, some holidays.

LEEDS West Yorkshire   Map 4:D4

42 The Calls

42 The Calls
Leeds LS2 7EW

Tel 0113-244 0099
Fax 0113-234 4100
Email hotel@42thecalls.co.uk
Website www.42thecalls.co.uk

One of Britain's earliest design hotels, this conversion of an old corn mill overlooking the River Aire was bought in February 2006 by MBI International, which has 42 luxury hotels in Europe and the Middle East (see also *The Scotsman*, Edinburgh). But manager Belinda Dawson remains, and for regular *Guide* reporters visiting after the sale, it remains a favourite choice because of the 'pleasant staff, central location and attractive weekend rates'. The 'flair is still there for design and decor'; there are 'hundreds of original paintings and drawings', bold fabrics, stylish public rooms. Bedrooms are 'fully kitted out for the business traveller', (Internet access, Wi-Fi, ironing board, etc). Beds are 'supremely comfortable'; new duvets have a 'high-quality cotton cover'. Rooms overlooking the canal are the quietest; those on the main road may be noisy. A wheelchair-user was pleased with the accessibility of his bedroom. A good continental breakfast can be brought to the room, or taken in a 'lovely room overlooking the river'. The more formal of the two independently run restaurants, *Pool Court at 42*, has closed; it now forms the no-smoking section of *Brasserie 44* (*Michelin Bib Gourmand* for 'superior brasserie fare'). (*David and Kate Wooff, CW*)

41 bedrooms. 1 suitable for &. Central, near Corn Exchange. Closed Christmas. Restaurant closed Sun, bank holidays. Lift. Lounge/bar, breakfast room (background radio), restaurant (independently run; background music); conference facilities. No dogs in public rooms. All major credit cards accepted. B&B [2006] £74–£212 per person. Full breakfast £14. Set lunch (2 courses) £12.50, set dinner (early bird) £19.95; full alc £38. (*10% service charge added to meal price*) Weekend breaks; special packages. **ʼVʼ**

See also SHORTLIST

LEEK Staffordshire *See SHORTLIST*   Map 3:A5

LEOMINSTER Herefordshire   Map 3:C4
See SHORTLIST

How to contact the *Guide*
By mail: From anywhere in the UK, write to Freepost PAM 2931, London W11 4BR (no stamp is needed)
From outside the UK: Good Hotel Guide, 50 Addison Avenue, London W11 4QP, England
By telephone or fax: 020-7602 4182
By email: Goodhotel@aol.com
Via our website: www.goodhotelguide.com

LEONARD STANLEY Gloucestershire   Map 3:E5

The Grey Cottage   `BUDGET`   *Tel/Fax* 01453-822515
Bath Road, Leonard Stanley   *Website* www.greycottage.ik.com
Stonehouse GL10 3LU

💠 *César award in 1999*

'We cannot envisage a better place to stay,' write visitors in 2006 to
Rosemary Reeves's home (since 1979). Nearly 180 years old, the little
stone Cotswolds guest house has been restored while retaining original
features. Arriving guests are greeted with biscuits and a choice of leaf
teas: 'We felt really cosseted.' The 'immaculate', spacious bedrooms have
'wonderful touches', and a wide range of 'goodies' (flowers, fruit, fresh
milk in a Thermos flask, etc). One room has its bathroom down a short
hall. Dinner is by arrangement: no choice; preferences discussed at the
time of booking. 'The food was sumptuous. We had to ask Rosy to reduce
our portions. Baked local poussin with garlic, lemon and parsnip purée;
panna cotta with mixed berries.' There is an honesty bar, and guests can
bring their own wine (no corkage charge). Breakfast includes freshly
squeezed orange juice, smoked salmon with scrambled eggs, home-made
jams, loaves of white and granary bread for DIY toasting. 'A main road
passes the front of the house, but there was no significant noise at night.'
Mrs Reeves writes: 'Many of my guests are over 50; perhaps younger
couples require leisure/pampering facilities.' (*Sue and Colin Raymond, Peter
Townend, and many others*)

3 bedrooms. 3 miles SW of Stroud. Closed Christmas, 'occasional holidays'. Advance
booking essential. Sitting room with TV, conservatory, dining room. No background
music. ¼-acre garden. Unsuitable for ♿. No smoking: dining room, bedrooms. No
children under 10. No dogs. No credit cards. B&B £30–£55 per person; D,B&B
£55–£80. Set dinner £25. 1-night bookings refused bank holidays.

LEWDOWN Devon   Map 1:C3

Lewtrenchard Manor   *Tel* 01566-783222
Lewdown   *Fax* 01566-783332
nr Okehampton EX20 4PN   *Email* info@lewtrenchard.co.uk
                                    Website www.lewtrenchard.co.uk

Once the ancestral home of the Revd Sabine Baring Gould who wrote
'Onward, Christian Soldiers', this romantic old stone house is owned by
the von Essen group. It stands 'idyllically' in large grounds with an avenue
of copper beech and elm trees, dovecote, sunken garden and lake with

swans. Inside is a 'Victorian/Elizabethan fantasy': ornate plaster ceilings, oak panelling, stained glass, huge fireplaces, family portraits and antiques. The bedrooms are off a long music gallery, reached by a fine wooden staircase. Best ones overlook the garden. The long-serving chef, Jason Hornbuckle, known for his 'imaginative' modern cooking, is now also manager. He hopes to create a 'gastronomic destination', using local suppliers and home-grown ingredients. Main courses in the dining room include venison with quince purée, mushroom duxelle and red cabbage. The small, separate *Library* restaurant has a seven-course menu at £90. There is an all-day snack menu (soups, sandwiches, etc). A visitor in 2006 wrote: 'Extremely nice. Very cheerful staff. Excellent food. Good bedrooms except for gloomy lighting.' Earlier guests liked the 'smell of a wood fire on a cold, wet day'. Dogs are generally allowed throughout. Conferences and weddings are held. Falconry packages are available. (*David Fisher, K and ME*)

14 bedrooms. 1 suitable for &. S of A30 Okehampton–Launceston. Nearest station Exeter St Davids (45 mins' drive). 2 lounges, bar, restaurant, 2 dining rooms (classical background music at lunch and dinner sometimes); function facilities. 12-acre garden. Civil wedding licence. No smoking: restaurant, bedrooms. No children under 8 in restaurant after 7 pm. Amex, MasterCard, Visa accepted. B&B £85–£125 per person; D,B&B £122–£162. Set menus £39.50–£90; full alc £47.50. Christmas/New Year packages. 2-night bookings preferred at weekends. *V*

LEWES East Sussex   Map 2:E4

Berkeley House   *Tel/Fax* 01273-476057
2 Albion Street   *Email* enquiries@berkeleyhouselewes.co.uk
Lewes BN7 2ND   *Website* www.berkeleyhouselewes.co.uk

Roy Patten and Steve Johnson's small B&B in attractive old town, handy for Glyndebourne. Late Georgian town house, in good position, with bedrooms on 2nd and 3rd floors (no lift). 'Cordial reception from genial hosts; thoughtful extras' (electric fan, bottled water, alarm clock, etc). Copious breakfast in 'charming room overlooking small courtyard'. Drinks, tea and coffee available 'at all reasonable times'. No background music. Roof terrace with wide view. Restricted street parking 9 am to 6 pm Mon–Sat (1-day vouchers for guests); also 1 parking space; public car park nearby. Closed Christmas/New Year. No smoking: breakfast room, bedrooms. No children under 8. No dogs. All major credit cards accepted. 3 bedrooms. B&B £30–£60 per person. *V*

See also SHORTLIST

LICHFIELD Staffordshire *See SHORTLIST*   Map 2:A2

LIFTON Devon   Map 1:C3

The Arundell Arms   *Tel* 01566-784666
Lifton PL16 0AA   *Fax* 01566-784494
                    Email reservations@arundellarms.com
                    Website www.arundellarms.com

♀ *César award in 2006*

In a small town just off the A30, this creeper-covered sporting hotel has been run for 45 years by Anne Voss-Bark, an experienced fly-fisher. She has 20 miles of fishing on the Tamar and its four tributaries, and a three-acre stocked lake. 'It is not held against one if one doesn't fish,' says a returning visitor who praised the 'good value' and the welcome. All bedrooms have now been refurbished. 'My comfortable room overlooked the garden; classy toiletries, sheets changed every two nights; a bit noisy one night when a private party adjourned to the room below, but not an issue.' Many of the staff are long-serving; Sally Hill has been manager for over 25 years. In the kitchen, Steven Pidgeon, *sous-chef* for a decade, is now in charge. His cooking is thought 'excellent, clever but not fussy: first-class canapés; soup in a little cup; tasty beef, cooked medium rare as requested; trio of apple puddings. Excellent wine list, both by glass and bottle. Attentive waiters, mostly French.' The local suppliers are named on the menu. 'Good bar meals.' But breakfast was 'patchy: no tomatoes one morning; a reassembled kipper'. The terraced rear garden has seating for alfresco meals. (*Richard Parish*)

21 bedrooms. 4 on ground floor. Closed 2 nights over Christmas. ½ mile off A30, 3 miles E of Launceston (road-facing rooms double glazed). Ramp. Lounge, cocktail bar, public bar, 2 dining rooms; classical background music; conference/meeting rooms; games room, skittle alley. ½-acre garden. 20 miles fishing rights on River Tamar and tributaries; 3-acre stocked lake, fishing school. No smoking in restaurant. All major credit cards accepted. B&B [2006] £77.50–£99 per person; D,B&B (min. 2 nights) £97.50–£120. Set lunch £22–£26, dinner £36–£40; full alc £52. 2- to 6-night breaks all year. Off-season breaks: sporting, gourmet, etc. New Year package. *V*

We ask hotels to quote their 2007 tariffs. Many have yet to fix these rates as we go to press. Prices should always be checked on booking.

LINCOLN Lincolnshire *See SHORTLIST*   Map 4:E5

LITTLE SHELFORD Cambridgeshire   Map 2:C4

Purlins   BUDGET   *Tel/Fax* 01223-842643
12 High Street   *Email* dgallh@ndirect.co.uk
Little Shelford CB2 5ES

The architecture of Olga and David Hindley's family home 'reflects something of the design of a medieval manor house'. Set in mature woodland and lawns, it is a 'very nice' B&B, say fans. The host is a musician who does research on birdsong; the hostess was a music librarian. The only background music, they tell us, is 'when he plays the piano'. The village, beside the River Cam, is small and picturesque. The Hindleys willingly lend books and maps, and advise about local restaurants. The bedrooms are 'immaculate, if not large'; some lead off a gallery, some face the garden; so does the conservatory where guests may sit and watch the local wildlife 'from muntjac deer to pheasants, squirrels and foxes'. The 'excellent' breakfast (vegetarian, traditional or continental), ordered the evening before and served between 7.30 and 9 am, includes preserves made from fruit in the garden. Slight noise sometimes, from the M11, nearby, but 'sometimes the pheasants can be noisier'; windows are double or triple glazed. More reports, please.

4 bedrooms. 1 single for occasional use. 2 on ground floor. 4½ miles S of Cambridge. Open 1 Apr–1 Nov. Sometimes closed for owners' breaks. Conservatory lounge, breakfast room, gallery. No background music. 2-acre garden. No smoking. No children under 8. No dogs. No credit cards. B&B [2006] £32.50–£50 per person. 1-night bookings sometimes refused.

* *

Traveller's tale We were greeted by a charming young man who was wearing a suit at least two sizes too large for him and shoes that flopped off as he walked. The bedroom was fine, but the loo had not been flushed. At dinner, the food was only fair. In the bar we watched the new owners trying to manage the place. The wife was trying to train a barman while her husband sat pretending to read a book. If something happened that he did not like, he would look up, make a comment, or get up to speak to a member of staff. It was like watching a *Fawlty Towers* episode. (*Hotel in Devon*)

* *

LITTLEBURY GREEN Essex   Map 2:C4

The Chaff House   BUDGET   *Tel/Fax* 01763-836278
Ash Grove Barns   *Mobile* 07817-724448
Littlebury Green   *Email* dianaduke@btopenworld.com
nr Saffron Walden CB11 4XB

'Standards well maintained,' says a returning visitor to this picturesque barn conversion on a large estate in a quiet rural village not far from the M11. Earlier he wrote of the 'quality of craftsmanship and materials' used, and the 'outstanding' cooking of the owner, Diana Duke. One bedroom is in the *Chaff House*, where Mrs Duke lives; the other two are in the *Log Shed* ('extremely comfortable, though there is some traffic noise by day') and the *Dairy*. 'No baths, but super power showers.' An evening meal (by prior arrangement, weekdays only) might be: goat's cheese and leek tart in walnut and Parmesan crust; lamb chops with couscous; caramel oranges. Good local pubs include *Cricketers* at Clavering, run by Jamie Oliver's parents: Stansted airport and Cambridge are both about 30 minutes' drive away. (*Chris Kay*)

3 bedrooms. 2 adjacent to main house, on ground floor. 4 miles W of Saffron Walden. Closed 25 Dec. Dining room closed midday, and Sat/Sun. Lounge, dining room. Kitchen for guests' use in annexe. No background music. Small courtyard garden. In 900-acre estate. Unsuitable for &. No smoking in dining room. No children under 5. No dogs. Diners, MasterCard, Visa accepted. B&B £35–£40 per person; D,B&B £60–£65. Set dinner £25. (*Not VAT-rated*)

LIVERPOOL Merseyside   Map 4:E2

Hope Street Hotel   *Tel* 0151-709 3000
40 Hope Street   *Fax* 0151-709 2454
Liverpool L1 9DA   *Email* sleep@hopestreethotel.co.uk
                                Website www.hopestreethotel.co.uk

Liverpool's first boutique hotel is in the cultural quarter opposite the Philharmonic Hall, on the road linking the two cathedrals. A sympathetically converted 19th-century carriage works in the style of a Venetian *palazzo*, it has original iron columns, beams and exposed brickwork. Many visitors like it ('outstanding young staff; warm welcome'; 'delicious food'), but things can go wrong. The first impressions of an architect were good: 'Our room looked great, the bed was comfortable, the bathroom tricky but attractive; decor chintz-free throughout. But hope turned to despair when a wedding party started to change for the evening. Corridors lined with wood, floors covered in timber or sea-grass matting, walls with little soundproofing, meant that every noise was amplified. We heard every word said and shared intimate moments with the occupants of the next-door bathroom.' The trendy bar, *The Residents' Lounge*, has leather sofas and pop music. The 'fine dining' restaurant, *The London Carriage Works*, has 'dramatic floor-to-ceiling shards of glass, etched with a water effect'. There is also a brasserie. Breakfast can be *à la carte*, continental or a 'super' cooked affair. More bedrooms and conference facilities are planned for summer 2007. (*DH*)

48 bedrooms. Opposite Philharmonic Hall. Lift. Ramps. Lobby, reading room, bar (live music Fri/Sat), restaurant, brasserie; background music (jazz/soul) 7 am–midnight. No smoking: restaurant, some bedrooms. No dogs in public rooms. Amex, MasterCard, Visa accepted. Room [2006]: single/double £140–£200, suite £225–£350. Breakfast £14.50 (full English). Set dinner (*London Carriage Works*) £50; full alc £65. New Year package. 1-night bookings sometimes refused.

See also SHORTLIST

LIVERSEDGE West Yorkshire   Map 4:D3

Healds Hall   BUDGET   *Tel* 01924-409112
Leeds Road   *Fax* 01924-401895
Liversedge WF15 6JA   *Email* enquire@healdshall.co.uk
                                  Website www.healdshall.co.uk

'Quality of service was hard to fault,' say visitors to Tom and Nora Harrington's inexpensive hotel in the Spen Valley. Built in 1764, it stands up a hill, surrounded by a 'tightly packed housing estate', near an old industrial town. Refurbishment of the bedrooms continues. 'Ours, in the modern extension, was quiet and perfectly adequate.' Inspectors and others agree about the quality of the food. 'The popular restaurant is sober-chic, and very pleasant, atmosphere upbeat and cheerful' (its long *à la carte* menu includes pan-fried breast of pigeon; grilled cutlet of venison). 'One evening we ate in the restaurant, another in colourful bistro [pasta; fish cakes, etc]. Both meals were excellent. But traffic through the bistro area is constant, and tobacco smoke drifts in from the bar.' 'Breakfast very satisfactory. Well-stocked buffet, good cooked platter. The lady of the house was much in evidence.' 'Staff very friendly.' Private functions are often held, as are theme nights (eg, tapas evening, Mexican evening, paella night). And conferences of up to 100 delegates can be accommodated. The Revd

Hammond Roberson, who once lived here, was immortalised as the Revd Matthew Helston in Charlotte Brontë's *Shirley*. (*Brian and Elisabeth Hoyle, Val and Alan Green, and others*)

24 bedrooms. 2 on ground floor, suitable for &. On A62 Leeds–Huddersfield, 3 miles from M62. Parking. Restaurant closed 1 Jan. Bar with conservatory area, restaurant, bistro; background music; conference/function suite. 2-acre grounds: lawns, garden. Civil wedding licence. Smoking in bar only. No dogs: some bedrooms, public rooms. All major credit cards accepted. B&B £25–£65 per person; D,B&B £45–£85. Set lunch £7.50, Sun lunch £15.50; full alc £33. Christmas/New Year packages. **'V'**

LLANFAIR WATERDINE Shropshire   Map 3:C4

The Waterdine	*Tel* 01547-528214
Llanfair Waterdine	*Fax* 01547-529992
nr Knighton LD7 1TU	*Email* info@waterdine.com
	Website www.waterdine.com

In an idyllic setting, with the River Teme (the border between England and Wales) flowing at the bottom of the garden, this old drovers' inn is run as a restaurant-with-rooms by Ken and Isabel Adams. They are said to be 'charming hosts'. He produces 'delicious food' in the restaurant which has two sections: the *Garden Room* with views over hills, and the *Taproom* with beamed ceiling, ancient stone floor, pottery, knick-knacks, fresh flowers and plants. 'Dainty nibbles with pre-dinner drinks set the standard; fresh ingredients were presented with flair,' said one fan. Other praise for the cooking: 'A meaty, gamey menu; chicken and foie gras boudin so good I had it both evenings.' The unpretentious bedrooms are supplied with flowers and fresh fruit. 'No. 3 has the best view and the biggest bathroom (also with view).' One room is divided from its bathroom by a low screen (loo in a separate compartment). Breakfast has freshly squeezed juice, yogurt, home-baked bread, 'delicious local honey'; 'superb eggs Benedict, Bennett, etc'. (*P and MS, SP*)

3 bedrooms. NW of Knighton. Train: Knucklas, 2 miles. Closed 1 week spring, 1 week autumn. Lounge, lounge bar, 2 dining rooms. No background music. ½-acre grounds. Unsuitable for &. Smoking in lounge bar only. No children under 12 ('negotiable'). No dogs. MasterCard, Visa accepted. D,B&B £80 per person. Special offers. 1-night bookings sometimes refused weekends.

If you are recommending a B&B and know of a good restaurant nearby, please mention it in your report.

LODDISWELL Devon   Map 1:D4

Hazelwood House   `BUDGET`   *Tel* 01548-821232
Loddiswell   *Fax* 01548-821318
nr Kingsbridge TQ7 4EB   *Email* info@hazelwoodhouse.com
                                   Website www.hazelwoodhouse.com

In a 'wonderfully tranquil' setting in a Devon valley, this 'lovely, crumbling'
Victorian house is owned by Jane Bowman, Gillian Kean and Anabel
Farnel-Watson. Not at all smart, it is not really a hotel. It won't suit
everyone, but its devotees love the 'spiritual quality', the 'informal but
professional' hospitality, the 'very good' meals, largely based on local
organic produce, and the 'comfort without frills'. Filled with simple
furniture, antiques and paintings, the house stands in meadows and woods
that slope down to the River Avon. Not all bedrooms have facilities *en suite*;
carpeting may be shabby; heating is by electric fires (no central heating, but
log fires in the public rooms). The best bedroom is spacious, but some
rooms are small. The atmosphere is convivial (guests on their own feel at
ease). Cultural courses, concerts and weekends with entertainments (jazz,
painting, story-telling, etc) are held. Water comes from the house's own
spring. Children are welcomed. A cat and a small terrier are in attendance.
There are no ground-floor bedrooms and no lift but, writes Ms Bowman,
'we are supportive if the disability is not too severe'. The sea is about six
miles away. (*Simon Rodway, and others*)

15 bedrooms. 6 with facilities *en suite.* 6 self-catering cottages. 2 miles N of
Loddiswell. Train: Totnes, 10 miles. Hall with piano, drawing room, study/TV
room, dining room; music 'when appropriate'; function/conference facilities. 67-acre
grounds: river, boathouse; former chapel. Civil wedding licence. No smoking in
bedrooms; 'we ask people to be considerate of others when smoking in the house'.
Dogs by arrangement. MasterCard, Visa accepted. B&B £41–£94 per person; D,B&B
£53–£119. Set menus £28.85–£35.25; full alc £45. Negotiable rates for groups.
Christmas/New Year packages. ***V***

****

> **Traveller's tale** The constant background music in the restaur-
> ant was irritating and intrusive, and did not sit well with the
> general ambience of this stylish small hotel. Other guests also
> commented unfavourably. We told several members of staff, but
> the best we could achieve was a slight lowering of the volume,
> never a complete turning off. At one leisurely breakfast we
> had to contend with most of Frank Sinatra's early repertoire.
> (*Hotel in Cheshire*)

****

LOOE Cornwall   Map 1:D3

Barclay House   *Tel* 01503-262929
St Martins Road   *Fax* 01503-262632
East Looe PL13 1LP   *Email* info@barclayhouse.co.uk
                                      Website www.barclayhouse.co.uk

On a hillside above this historic fishing town, this white-painted former
Victorian merchant's house stands amid gardens and woodlands. No longer
a hotel, it is now a B&B with a restaurant open for lunch (served alfresco
when possible, on a panoramic terrace) from Monday to Friday. Chef/
proprietor Nick Barclay and his American wife, Kelli, have made the
change 'to be able to spend more time with our three young children'.
They 'believe there is a massive demand for really good lunches with time
to linger', so last orders will be taken at 3.30 pm. *Barclay House* won the
Cornwall Tourism 'Restaurant of the Year 2005' award, and the 'modern
coastal cuisine' includes Fowey River mussels, with Cornish cider; char-
grilled local mackerel with fresh ginger, coriander and chilli butter. No set
menu: 'Order as much or as little as you like.' The wine list has local Camel
Valley wines and a page of half bottles. Visitors before the transformation
liked the 'friendly atmosphere' and the 'excellent breakfasts'. 'Our large,
bright room had a fine view over the river. Furnishings were modern.'
Public rooms are 'very comfortable in more traditional style'. Some self-
catering cottages share the facilities. More reports, please.

10 bedrooms. 8 self-catering cottages. ½ mile from centre. Closed 22 Dec–14 Jan.
Restaurant closed evenings, and midday Sat and Sun. Sitting room, bar lounge,
restaurant; 'easy listening' music all day; terrace. 3-acre gardens: 'smallish' heated
swimming pool, children's playground; 3-acre woodland. Unsuitable for &. No
smoking. Guide dogs only. MasterCard, Visa accepted. B&B £40–£75 per person.
Alc from £20. 1-night bookings refused bank holiday weekends. ***V***

The Beach House   **NEW**   *Tel* 01503-262598
Marine Drive, Hannafore   *Fax* 01503-262298
Looe PL13 2DH   *Email* enquiries@thebeachhouselooe.com
                          Website www.thebeachhouselooe.com

New owners (since 2005) Rosie and David Reeve are 'working hard to
maintain the high standards this lovely house is known for', say
enthusiastic visitors. White-walled and gabled, it has uninterrupted views
of Looe Bay and the coastline beyond. An easy walk from the town centre,
it stands by the Coastal Path, and it has direct access to the beach. Four
bedrooms face the sea. Rear rooms are 'decent sized' too. 'Our room,

Fistral, the most expensive, was worth it for the view: its huge patio windows opened on to a balcony. The decor was subtle, in cream and gold, and the extras made it more like a five-star hotel than a B&B.' The 'superb' breakfast room faces the sea. One reader would have liked breakfast times to be more flexible. 'Guests were expected to make their choice the evening before and then select a time which did not clash with other guests. Mild panic ensued when we turned up 15 minutes early by

mistake. But the breakfast was excellent: a buffet table with yogurt and juices; generous servings of full English; proper butter in glass dishes.' For meals, *Mawgans* is recommended. A non-refundable deposit of one night's tariff is required to confirm a booking. (*Karen Parker*)

6 bedrooms. ¼ mile from Looe centre. Parking. Closed Christmas. Garden room, breakfast room; classical background music in public areas during the day. Terrace; small garden. Beach opposite. No smoking. No children under 12. No pets. MasterCard, Visa accepted. B&B [2006] £40–£55 per person. Min. 3-night booking July/Aug, public holidays.

See also SHORTLIST

LORTON Cumbria   Map 4: inset C2

New House Farm	*Tel* 01900-85404
Lorton	*Fax* 01900-85478
nr Cockermouth CA13 9UU	*Email* hazel@newhouse-farm.co.uk
	Website www.newhouse-farm.co.uk

'Good atmosphere, accommodation just what we needed, friendly atmosphere,' says a visitor to this 'well-organised country guest house'. Its owner, Hazel Thompson, 'runs it almost single-handed'. The whitewashed farmhouse, 17th-century Grade II listed, was part of Lord Egremont's Cumberland estate in this lovely valley in the north-west corner of the Lake District national park. Period features include oak beams and rafters, flagged floors and stone open fireplaces. The small lounges have bright colours, comfortable seating, silver and antiques. This year, the bedrooms have been refurbished and some have been given a new bathroom. There are 'marvellous views' in all directions. The traditional food is enjoyed: 'After the dinners, we needed to go on a diet.' The no-choice meal might include local shrimps; pheasant cooked in cider. The short wine list has 'sensible, uninflated prices'. Breakfast includes fresh grapefruit, prunes, eggs and bacon, home-made marmalade. Lunches and teas are served in the café, in a converted barn. Pets are allowed the run of the grounds but not the public rooms. Traffic passes on the country road in front of the house, but the two rear bedrooms are 'perfectly quiet'. (*AL Sayers, AW*)

5 bedrooms. 1 in stable, 1 in old dairy. On B5289, 2 miles S of Lorton. 3 lounges, dining room. No background music. 17-acre grounds: garden, hot tub, streams, woods, field. Lake and river (safe bathing) 2 miles. Unsuitable for &. No smoking. No children under 6. No dogs in public rooms. MasterCard, Visa accepted. B&B £69 per person; D,B&B £91–£94. Packed lunch £7. Set dinner £25. Christmas/New Year packages. 1-night bookings sometimes refused.

See also SHORTLIST

LOWESTOFT Suffolk *See SHORTLIST*   Map 2:B6

LUDLOW Shropshire   Map 3:C4

Bromley Court   *Tel* 01584-876996
Broadgate Mews   *Reservations* 0845-065 6192
73–74 Lower Broad Street   *Email* phil@ludlowhotels.com
Ludlow SY8 1PH   *Website* www.ludlowhotels.com

The 'exceptional hospitality', 'generous welcome' and 'atmosphere of a private house, plus freedom and privacy' are much enjoyed at Patricia and Philip Ross's unusual B&B in a quiet street between the old, walled town gate and the river. It consists of three tiny beamed Tudor cottages around a peaceful courtyard garden. Each has a kitchen stocked with croissants, tea cakes, fresh bread, home-made jam and much more, a 'comfortable' bedroom, a 'generously equipped' bathroom and a sitting room with books, maps, etc. You can prepare your own breakfast or cross the road in the morning to *Mews Cottage* where Mrs Ross will cook an 'outstanding' full breakfast. 'Our small suite was a lesson in how a bijou space can be made comfortable,' wrote one couple. 'The country cottage-style bedroom upstairs had thick curtains across low windowsills deep enough to sit on. The well-equipped bathroom was also charming.' Dogs are 'welcomed, provided their owners are well behaved'. The list of suggested restaurants which guests can telephone free of charge, includes *Mr Underhill's* (*qv*, *Michelin* star). (*Susan and John Wilson, and others*)

3 cottage suites. All with DIY breakfast bar. Central. Unrestricted street parking. No smoking. Dogs by arrangement. MasterCard, Visa accepted. B&B £47.50–£57.50 per person. 1-night bookings refused weekends. ***V***

Dinham Hall
Dinham, by the castle
Ludlow SY8 1EJ

Tel 01584-876464
Fax 01584-876019
Email info@dinhamhall.co.uk
Website www.dinhamhall.co.uk

Built in 1792, this was once a boarding house of Ludlow grammar school: some rooms have initials carved by the boys, and school photographs are displayed in the lounge. James Garnett, manager for the Mifsuds of *The Lake*, Llangammarch Wells, Wales (*qv*), 'has the gift of making one feel welcome'. 'Small and intimate. It has everything I look for in a hotel,' one visitor wrote. 'Tremendous welcome' (complimentary tea with biscuits on arrival, 'while your luggage is portered to your room'). Another comment: 'On each visit, we have had nothing but kindness. Downstairs can hardly be faulted. Room service is sketchy, but the general ambience is exactly in keeping with the beautiful old house. Friendly conversation between guests gives ample evidence of this.' The walled garden and some bedrooms (three were refurbished this year) face the Teme valley and 'some lovely houses and gardens'. One suite ('comfortable, spacious') has a private terrace with fountain. The new chef, Dean Banner, serves food that is 'inspired without being pretentious, beautifully presented, cooked to perfection' (eg, sea bass with shrimp bisque). Breakfasts include 'fresh fruit, kippers, lashings of good toast'. Well placed for exploring the town; long country walks are close by. (*Gordon Hands, and others*)

13 bedrooms. 2 in cottage (30 yds). 1 on ground floor. Near castle. Parking. Restaurant closed Mon midday. Ramp. 2 lounges, bar, restaurant; 2 private dining rooms. No background music. 1-acre walled garden. Unsuitable for ♿. Civil wedding licence. Smoking in 1 designated area only. No children under 8 at dinner. No dogs in public rooms. All major credit cards accepted. B&B £70–£120 per person; D,B&B £87.50–£137.50. Set dinner £38.50. Christmas/New Year packages. ***V***

Please always send a report if you stay at a *Guide* hotel, even if it's only to endorse the existing entry.

Mr Underhill's   *Tel* 01584-874431
Dinham Weir   *Website* www.mr-underhills.co.uk
Ludlow SY8 1EH

♛ *César award in 2000*

'An impressive visit.' 'We are delighted to join the fan club.' So say new
visitors to Christopher and Judy Bradley's restaurant-with-rooms on the
River Teme, below Ludlow Castle. 'Our welcome was professional and
warm, with complimentary coffee. Our heroic refusal of chocolate cake was
vindicated by a sublime dinner.' Another guest praised the 'very high
standards', and rebutted a comment in last year's *Guide* about 'frostiness in
the bar'. Mrs Bradley runs front-of-house with 'approachable formality'.
Her husband's cooking, 'excellent, well presented', has a *Michelin* star.
Guests are told the proposed set menu, and are offered alternatives. 'A
doll's-house portion of butternut squash soup; baby pots of foie gras
custard; fillets of well-hung Marches beef; desserts worth getting fat for.'
The two suites in *Miller's House*, across the lane, face Dinham Bridge;
the lower one, by the road, is quite dark. Another suite, *The Shed*, is in the
garden. The double rooms in the house are smaller. 'Fresh milk in
the fridge; wonderful extras in the bathroom.' Breakfast has a 'dinky
amuse-bouche of apple compote with cinnamon crisp'; a choice of fresh fruit
and yogurt, or a cooked dish; 'toast in relays'. (*Catherine Paxton, Anne
Thornthwaite, Padi and John Howard, Christopher McCall*)

9 bedrooms. 3 in annexes. Below castle, on River Teme. Station ½ mile. Parking.
Closed Christmas, 1 week in summer, 1 week in autumn. Restaurant closed
Mon/Tues. Small lounge, restaurant; function facilities. No background music.
½-acre courtyard, riverside garden: fishing, swimming. Unsuitable for ☯. No smoking.
No children 2 to 8. No dogs. MasterCard, Visa accepted. B&B: single £110–£160,
double £135–£170, suite £195–£250. Set dinner £45. New Year package. 1-night
bookings often refused Sat.

LYDFORD Devon   Map 1:C4

 The Dartmoor Inn   NEW   *Tel* 01822-820221
Moorside   *Fax* 01822-820494
Lydford, nr Okehampton   *Email* info@dartmoorinn.co.uk
EX20 4AY   *Website* www.dartmoorinn.com

César award: Newcomer of the year

'Some of the nicest hoteliers we have come across, fantastic staff, very good
cooking and wine list.' Inspectors enthuse in 2006. This ancient inn on the
main road on the west side of Dartmoor was bought, and furnished in

'charismatic style', three years ago by Karen and Philip Burgess (he cooks with Andrew Honey). 'Our bedroom, in minimalist style (no pictures), had a large Louis XVI green upholstered bed and a big sofa. Its large, immaculate bathroom (with window) had a giant power shower over a two-ended bath.' The 'ravishingly pretty' hostess runs a boutique in two of the ground-floor rooms; the others are dining areas, some formal, with wood-burning stove, others more casual. Dinner is much admired: 'Pan-fried sweetbreads in a glorious sauce; delicious bouillabaisse; perfect vegetables; a well-priced St-Émilion. Coffee and florentines by gently flaming logs in the bar. Service impeccable. Breakfast, taken really seriously, must be one of the best anywhere: an artistic array of fresh fruits; fresh juices; crab risotto with smoked salmon; corned beef hash; fine home-made breads and much more. Pristine damask cloths, real table napkins. This place shows care, flair, dedication and talent. The road goes quiet at night, and windows are double glazed.'

3 bedrooms. 6 miles from Tavistock on A386 to Okehampton. Train: Exeter/ Plymouth. Parking. Closed 25 Dec. Bars, restaurant. No background music. Jazz concerts, exhibitions. Small sunken garden. Unsuitable for &. No smoking. Not really suitable for small children. No dogs in bedrooms. Amex, MasterCard, Visa accepted. B&B: single £75–£85, double £90–£125. Set menu £17.50; full alc £39. 1-night bookings sometimes refused bank holiday weekends.

LYME REGIS Dorset *See SHORTLIST*　　　Map 1:C6

LYMINGTON Hampshire *See SHORTLIST*　　Map 2:E2

LYNMOUTH Devon *See SHORTLIST*　　　Map 1:B4

LYTHAM Lancashire *See SHORTLIST*　　　Map 4:D2

****

Traveller's tale I asked for a room with a sea view. On arriving I found this was technically possible by aligning face with window. (*Hotel in Cornwall*)

****

MAIDENCOMBE Devon   Map 1:D5

Orestone Manor   *Tel* 01803-328098
Rockhouse Lane, Maidencombe   *Fax* 01803-328336
nr Torquay TQ1 4SX   *Email* enquiries@orestone.co.uk
                          Website www.orestonemanor.com

On a wooded hillside overlooking Lyme Bay, this large Edwardian house
stands in well-tended grounds, just off the 'hair-bending' coastal road
between Torquay and Teignmouth. It is owned by a group of local business people. They have created a 'contemporary/colonial' decor, with cane
chairs and wooden floors in the 'charming' conservatory and restaurant;
open fires, flowers and plants in the lounge, and an elephant motif
throughout (the *Elephant* restaurant by the harbour has the same owners).
Chef Darron 'Bunny' Bonn won a *Michelin* star in 2006 for, eg, tian of crab
and avocado; stuffed saddle of wild rabbit. 'Good food, excellent service,
comfortable bedroom with very nice views,' runs an endorsement this year.
The rooms vary from 'cosy' on the second floor (no lift) to spacious, lower
down. There are four-poster beds, pale carpets, Art Nouveau-type fabrics.
The Garden Room has an open fireplace and private terrace with 'a fantastic view of distant sea'. One problem: 'Lighting was dim in our bedroom
(excellent in the bathroom); downstairs it was variable, unless you were
near a table lamp in the drawing room. Good walking on the coastal
footpath.' Rose and Mark Ashton, the 'hands-on' managers, left as we went
to press. More reports, please.

12 bedrooms. 1 on ground floor. 3½ miles N of Torquay. Lounge, conservatory,
snooker room, bar, restaurant (with ramps); background music; meeting room. 2-acre
garden: heated 6-ft swimming pool. Unsuitable for &. Civil wedding licence. No
smoking: restaurant, bedrooms. No children under 7 in restaurant at night. No dogs
in restaurant. Amex, MasterCard, Visa accepted. B&B £67.50–£112.50 per person.
Set lunch £14.75–£17.95; full alc £45. Christmas package. **'V'**

MAIDENHEAD Berkshire *See SHORTLIST*   Map 2:D3

The **'V'** sign at the end of an entry indicates a hotel that has
agreed to take part in our Voucher scheme and to give *Guide*
readers a 25% discount on their room rates for a one-night stay,
subject to the conditions explained on page 60 and listed on the
back of the vouchers.

MALVERN WELLS Worcestershire   Map 3:D5

The Cottage in the Wood   *Tel* 01684-575859
Holywell Road   *Fax* 01684-560662
Malvern Wells   *Email* reception@cottageinthewood.co.uk
WR14 4LG   *Website* www.cottageinthewood.co.uk

'We notch up 20 years in 2007, and we still don't argue (much) as a family,'
writes John Pattin, who runs this traditional hotel with his wife, Sue. Their
son, Dominic, is chef; son-in-law, Nick Webb, is manager. It has a splendid
position, high on the wooded eastern slopes of the Malvern Hills, with
views over 30 miles of the Severn vale. Readers have long admired the
family's 'commitment to the comforts of their guests'. The 'happy atmosphere', the comprehensive information guide and the 'stunning walks from
the door' are also mentioned. *The Pinnacles* annexe ran into 'snagging
problems' (shrinking floorboards and insufficient hot water) when it opened
in 2005: these were being addressed as we went to press. Rooms in the main
house are thought 'nice, if not special'. A 'very good meal' was enjoyed this
year. 'Fantastic, with a sense of occasion,' was an earlier comment. Half-
board rates include three courses from the *à la carte* menu of modern dishes,
using local ingredients where possible, eg, trio of pork, pan-roasted
tenderloin, boudin noir, braised belly with anise carrots, sage potatoes.
'Please ask if you would rather have something plain,' says the menu.
(*S and TF, R and CF*)

31 bedrooms. 4 in *Beech Cottage*, 70 yards. 19, 1 suitable for &, in *The Pinnacles*,
100 yards. Off A449 to Ledbury, 3 miles S of Malvern. Train: Great Malvern.
Lounge, bar, restaurant; function facilities. No background music. 7-acre grounds;
terrace. Golf, squash nearby. No smoking: restaurant, lounge, bedrooms. Dogs in
ground-floor bedrooms only; not in public rooms. Amex, MasterCard, Visa accepted.
B&B [2006] £49.50–£110 per person; D,B&B (min. 2 nights) £74–£133. Full alc £45.
Bargain breaks. Christmas/New Year packages. 1-night bookings sometimes
refused. **'V'**

MANCHESTER   Map 4:E3

Eleven Didsbury Park   *Tel* 0161-448 7711
11 Didsbury Park   *Fax* 0161-448 8282
Didsbury Village   *Email* enquiries@elevendidsburypark.com
Manchester M20 5LH   *Website* www.elevendidsburypark.com

This Victorian town house, 'in a convenient, yet peaceful location' (a
conservation area), was converted by Eamonn and Sally O'Loughlin into
Manchester's first design hotel. It is an easy walk from Didsbury green,

20 minutes' bus ride from the city centre, ten minutes' drive from the airport. It is liked by readers for its 'simple stylishness', 'lovely garden' and 'relaxed but efficient' staff. The public rooms have white walls, large steel-framed mirrors, a huge stone fireplace, and coffee tables made of old trunks. The bedrooms (all have been redecorated this year) range from 'Classic', with queen-size bed, and 'Villa', with king-size bed, to large suites with fireplace, balcony and lounge. All have CD-player, DVD-player, modem point, etc, and a modern bathroom. Breakfast is served in a 'nice, friendly' half-basement room, and a reporter was pleased that 'it was available until 3 pm; excellent for a leisurely Sunday'. No restaurant, but light meals can be ordered from a 'Deli Menu'. Oscar the resident cat presides. Sister hotels are the nearby *Didsbury House*, and *The Great John Street Hotel*, in the former Old School House in central Manchester. (*JL, DG*)

19 bedrooms. 1, on ground floor, suitable for &. 43 miles from centre. 2 lounge/bars (background music all day), veranda. Large walled garden. No smoking. Guide dogs only. All major credit cards accepted. Room [2006]: single £108–£145, double £115–£155, suite £155–£250. Breakfast £14.50. Christmas/New Year packages.

See also SHORTLIST

MARAZION Cornwall   Map 1:E1

Mount Haven Hotel & Restaurant	*Tel* 01736-710249
Turnpike Road	*Fax* 01736-711658
Marazion TR17 0DQ	*Email* reception@mounthaven.co.uk
	Website www.mounthaven.co.uk

'Run in a hands-on way' and with 'very nice staff', 'this 'bright and airy, contemporary hotel' is owned by Mike and Orange Trevillion and Tom Johnstone (front-of-house). 'Nothing corporate here,' they promise. In a village opposite St Michael's Mount ('fabulous views'), the former coach house, much altered in 1970, has been refurbished to create a 'tranquil atmosphere'. There are fresh flowers, silks from Mumbai, tapestries from Jaipur, modern paintings and pastel shades; incense burns. The terrace has decking, 'smart steel and slatted furniture'. Many bedrooms face Mount's Bay from a private balcony. Each of the two garden rooms has a patio. 'The food is first class and generous,' says a recent report. The chef, Julie Manley, 'places the emphasis on simplicity and taste', using fresh fish from Newlyn, and local organic ingredients. An earlier comment: 'The welcome is warm (complimentary tea on arrival). Our room was small (others are larger), and quiet at night.' A team of holistic therapists comes to give treatment to guests (Indian head massage, etc). (*Moonyeen Fletcher, J and HW*)

18 bedrooms. Some on ground floor. 4 miles E of Penzance. Car park. Closed 22 Dec–early Feb. Lounge/bar, restaurant; 'chill-out' music all day; healing room (holistic treatments). Sun terrace. Small garden. Rock/sand beaches 100 yds. Unsuitable for &. Smoking in bar only. Dogs in bar and on terrace only. MasterCard, Visa accepted. B&B £42–£80 per person; D,B&B £64–£102. Full alc £33. 3-night breaks Nov–Easter. Min. 2 nights on bank holidays. ***V***

MARKET DRAYTON Shropshire   Map 3:B5
See SHORTLIST

MARKINGTON North Yorkshire   Map 4:D4

Hob Green   *Tel* 01423-770031
Markington   *Fax* 01423-771589
nr Harrogate HG3 3PJ   *Email* info@hobgreen.com
                                   Website www.hobgreen.com

Set in huge grounds with farm, woodlands and award-winning gardens, this 18th-century house was transformed by Mr and Mrs Hutchinson from their family home to a traditional hotel more than 20 years ago. The manager is Christopher Ashby. Readers on a return visit 'were made very welcome. We enjoyed the walks in the grounds and around the village. The secluded setting ensured a total absence of noise and disturbance.' Others said: 'The food was interesting, without being too *nouvelle*.' 'Service willing and competent.' There is original panelling and moulding, antiques and curios, and wide views across the valley from the terrace. The bedrooms, all different 'and characterful', have flowery fabrics and patterned wallpaper. 'Ours was comfortable and had a charming outlook.' In the restaurant (with a green colour scheme), chef Chris Taylor uses local produce where possible, much of it from the kitchen garden. The menu might include galantine of pork, prunes and pistachio; whole roast partridge. There is a 'Fish on Friday' dinner menu. 'Wines sensibly priced. Good breakfast' (in summer it can be alfresco). Light lunches and teas are served. Conferences and functions are catered for. Fountains Abbey is three miles away. (*H and MA, Priscilla Khan*)

12 bedrooms. 1 mile SW of Markington, 5 miles SW of Ripon. Ramp. Hall, dining room, lounge, sun lounge. No background music. 800-acre grounds: 2½-acre garden, children's play area. Unsuitable for &. Civil wedding licence. No smoking:

restaurant, bedrooms. No dogs in public rooms. All major credit cards accepted. B&B £55–£95 per person. Set lunch £15.95, dinner £26.50; full alc £29. Christmas/New Year packages. 1-night bookings refused weekends.

MARTINHOE Devon   Map 1:B4

Heddon's Gate Hotel **NEW**   *Tel* 01598-763481
Martinhoe, Parracombe   *Email* hotel@heddonsgate.co.uk
EX31 4PZ   *Website* www.heddonsgate.co.uk

In steeply sloping grounds on the edge of Exmoor, this Swiss/Victorian lodge has a beautiful, remote setting. 'No noise other than birdsong,' write Anne and Eddie Eyles, who bought it in February 2005. Former guests, they loved it so much that they have changed little, retaining the old-fashioned, 'mildly eccentric' decor, 'more comfortable than plush'. The bar has stags' antlers and black leather furniture; the lounge has tapestries on green walls, and cases of china ornaments. 'We were delighted,' say reporters in 2006, who regularly visited over 20 years under the earlier regime. 'Format much as before. Warm welcome. Excellent food.' The price includes afternoon tea (home-made savouries, scones, cakes), and after-dinner coffee. Guests are expected to take dinner (limited choice, served promptly at 8 pm). The daily-changing menu ('modern and traditional') includes pot-roasted pork loin with cider sauce; roast beef with Yorkshire pudding. Breakfast, not self-service, has freshly squeezed orange juice, eggs of all kinds, wholemeal toast. Packed lunches are provided. The bedrooms vary greatly (some are large). Some are named after their original use: Grandmama's (Victorian bathroom); Nannie's (antique stained-glass windows); The Servants' Quarters (private sitting room). Beds are turned down at night. Good walks start from the door. (*TJ and JE Mallinson*)

11 bedrooms. 6 miles W of Lynton. Train/coach: Barnstaple, 12 miles, taxi. Open mid-Mar–end Oct (or later, subject to demand), Christmas/New Year. 2 reception halls, 2 lounges, library, bar, dining room. No background music. 2½-acre grounds. River, fishing, riding, pony-trekking nearby. Sea ¼ mile. Unsuitable for &. Smoking in bar only. Children 'must be old enough to dine with parents at 8 pm'. MasterCard, Visa accepted. B&B [2006] £50.50–£58.50 per person; D,B&B £78–£86. Set dinner £30. 1-night bookings occasionally refused. Christmas/New Year packages. ***V***

The 'New' label indicates hotels which are appearing in the *Guide* for the first time or which have been readmitted after an absence.

MASHAM North Yorkshire

Map 4:D4

Swinton Park
Masham, nr Ripon
HG4 4JH

Tel 01765-680900
Fax 01765-680901
Email enquiries@swintonpark.com
Website www.swintonpark.com

In huge landscaped grounds with many activities (see below), this creeper-clad, 17th-century castle (Grade II* listed) was extended and castellated in Georgian and Victorian days. It is now a luxury hotel, owned by Mark ('a welcoming host') and Felicity Cunliffe-Lister, and managed by Andrew McPherson. It has large reception rooms (antique furniture, family portraits, mirrors, rugs on polished floors), and a spa (upgraded this year). Reports are mixed: 'A joy. Our stay was something special.' 'Offers much but does not deliver. Food was not hot. Poor breakfasts. We felt the wedding/function trade took precedence over individual guest care.' The spacious bedrooms, all different, have Wi-Fi access. There are 'stunning views' from many, including the shower room in the circular Turret Suite (on three floors). 'We loved the night cream on the bed, and the complimentary gin and tonic.' The restaurant, *Samuel's*, has a gold-leaf ceiling, sumptuous decor, mahogany panelling and an open fire. Guests choose between a daily-changing no-choice dinner, a three-course menu with ample choice, and an eight-course tasting menu. Chef Andy Burton uses estate produce in dishes like haunch of venison with shallot Tatin. (*Guy Macpherson-Grant, and others*)

30 bedrooms. 4 suitable for &. 1 mile SW of Masham. Lift, ramps. 3 lounges, library, bar (background jazz), restaurant, banqueting hall; private dining room (background music); spa; games room, snooker room, cinema; conference facilities. 200-acre grounds: grotto, orangery; 5 lakes: fishing (ghillies available), model boat racing; swings, play castle, bowls, croquet, cricket, 9-hole golf course, clay-pigeon shooting, riding, falconry, kite flying, etc. Civil wedding licence. No smoking: restaurant, bedrooms, some public rooms. No dogs in public rooms. All major credit cards accepted. B&B £75–£175 per person. Set dinner £43–£50. Christmas/New Year. Cookery school. 1-night bookings refused some weekends. ***V***

MATLOCK Derbyshire *See SHORTLIST*

Map 3:B6

If you dislike piped music, why not join Pipedown, the campaign for freedom from piped music? They can be reached at 1 The Row, Berwick St James, Salisbury SP3 4TP. *Tel*: 01722-790622, www.pipedown.info.

MAULDS MEABURN Cumbria   Map 4: inset C2

Meaburn Hill Farmhouse   **NEW/BUDGET**   *Tel* 01951-715168
Maulds Meaburn, Penrith   *Email* kindleysides@btinternet.com
CA10 3HN   *Website* www.cumbria-bed-and-breakfast.co.uk

In their guest house in a 'peaceful and beautiful' village, Annie Kindleysides and Brian Morris are 'excellent hosts, friendly, chatty, but never intrusive', say the nominators of this 'perfect place to stay'. She was an AA Landlady of the Year 2004. 'If you want entertainment, don't go; if you hate dogs, don't go. Otherwise, this is the most blissfully relaxing place in the world. Even our dog was welcome to chill out in front of the fire.' The old farmhouse (16th-century) is a 'comfortable home with knick-knacks everywhere', and oak beams. 'Our room had a cast iron bath in a corner. Bedside lighting might be a problem but the bi-focal-wearing member of our party managed fine.' The Aga-cooked food is 'fabulous (Cumbrian with a fresh twist)': dinner is served six nights a week. 'Excellent beef with home-produced vegetables; salmon and lovage pie for the non-meat-eater.' Vegetarian, Muslim, Hindu and other diets are 'happily catered for'; packed lunches can be supplied. No wine licence: bring your own. At breakfast, eggs cooked to order are supplemented by 'delights like potato cakes, fish cakes, gorgeous vegetarian haggis'. The only disturbance might be 'sound of stream and sheep on village green'. (*Mark and Patricia Jacques*)

5 bedrooms. 2, in adjacent cottage, suitable for &/families. 1 mile N of Crosby Ravensworth. Open 1 Feb–2 Jan. Dining room closed Mon. Library/private dining room, dining room with TV/lounge area; background music during meals on request. 2-acre garden: tea/picnic area, dog-walking area. No smoking. Dogs allowed in public rooms 'if acceptable to other guests'. No credit cards. B&B £40–£45 per person; D,B&B £57.50–£65. Set dinner £20. Christmas/New Year packages for groups, by negotiation. 1-night bookings sometimes refused.

MAWGAN PORTH Cornwall   Map 1:D2

Bedruthan Steps Hotel   *Tel* 01637-860555
Mawgan Porth   *Fax* 01637-860714
TR8 4BU   *Email* office@bedruthan.com
          Website www.bedruthan.com

'Great facilities for parents who want a luxurious rest' are found at this large, modern hotel by a wide sandy beach in north Cornwall. Owned by sisters Emma Stratton, Deborah Wakefield and Rebecca Whittington, it has 'fantastic play areas', swimming pools indoors and out, children's clubs,

234 ENGLAND

activities ('water fun sessions', snorkelling courses, etc), and evening entertainments. Designated 'Hotel of the Year 2005' by the Cornish Tourist Board, and also winner of its Sustainable Tourism award, it is 'turning into a reasonably glamorous place with slate flooring, neutral browns and creams, lots of oak', says a regular visitor. There are babysitters and nannies, 'amazing sea views', coastal walks and spa treatments. Accommodation ranges from 'villa suites', ideal for a family, to 'value rooms' (no view, let at a discount). This year there is a new chef, Adam Clark, so we would welcome reports on the food. He runs two *table d'hôte* restaurants, and *Indigo Bay* for *à la carte* meals. Children under six have high tea, and the brochure promises 'peaceful dining' for guests without children: 'We watched the sun setting over the bay without a small child pulling on our sleeves.' 'Not cheap, but so worth it.' (*RL*)

99 bedrooms. 9 adjacent. 4 miles NE of Newquay. Closed 22–27 Dec. Lift. 3 lounges, 2 bars, 3 restaurants (occasional background music); ballroom (live music 2/3 times a week); 4 children's clubs; spa: indoor swimming pool. 5-acre grounds: swimming pools, tennis, playing field. Civil wedding licence. Smoking in smoking lounge and on terraces only. Guide dogs only. MasterCard, Visa accepted. B&B £70–£153 per person; D,B&B £82–£165. Set dinner £28.50; full alc £45. New Year package. 1-night bookings refused New Year.

MAWNAN SMITH Cornwall   Map 1:E2

Budock Vean   *Tel* 01326-252100
Helford Passage, Mawnan Smith   *Fax* 01326-250892
nr Falmouth TR11 5LG   *Email* relax@budockvean.co.uk
                            Website www.budockvean.co.uk

'Nobody does it better. I cannot spice up my report with minor criticisms,' writes a devotee of this traditional hotel run by 'delightful owners' Martin and Amanda Barlow. It has a nine-hole golf course, and a swimming pool in a building that opens on to a patio in summer and has a log fire in winter. An outdoor hot tub is new this year. Well-equipped bedrooms (all windows are double glazed) lead off corridors enlivened by colourful prints. 'Our superior room contained everything we could need. Its gleaming bathroom had an efficient new shower over the bath.' 'Our large room, well maintained, faced golf course and grounds.' The valley garden leads past terraced ponds and waterfalls to a secluded creek on the Helford river; a 32-foot Sunseeker takes guests on sea trips. 'Public rooms are warm, elegant, comfortable.' Men must wear jacket and tie after 7 pm in the bar and main restaurant. Darren Kelly's cooking is liked: 'Oscar-worthy roast venison; vegetables abundant and tasty.' 'Good if not memorable.' A happy, courteous multinational waiting force. Live music during dinner, but thankfully no background music.' The sister hotel, *Treglos*, Constantine Bay, returns to the *Guide* this year. (*Mary Woods, Kathleen Craddock, J Rudd*)

57 bedrooms. Some self-catering suites. 6 miles SW of Falmouth. Closed 2–23 Jan. Lift. 3 lounges, conservatory, 2 bars, restaurant (pianist/guitarist at night); snooker room. 65-acre grounds: covered swimming pool (45 by 27 ft), hot tub; health spa; country club: bar, restaurant, 9-hole golf course, tennis, croquet, archery, river frontage, water sports, boat trips. Unsuitable for &. Civil wedding licence. No smoking: restaurant, lounges, bedrooms. No children under 7 on ground floor after 9 pm. No dogs in public rooms. Diners (*2% surcharge*), MasterCard, Visa accepted. B&B [2006] £58–£104 per person. Bar lunches. Set Sunday lunch £16.50, set dinner £31; full alc £47. Christmas/New Year/Easter tariffs. 1-night bookings refused weekends.

Meudon
Mawnan Smith
nr Falmouth TR11 5HT

Tel 01326-250541
Fax 01326-250543
Email wecare@meudon.co.uk
Website www.meudon.co.uk

'Old-fashioned values' prevail at the Pilgrim family's traditional hotel in wooded countryside on the south Cornish coast. It stands in a subtropical 'hanging garden' at the head of a valley that leads down to a beach. 'We don't know how many times we have stayed in the last 25 years,' one couple wrote. Other returning visitors add: 'Our room was immaculate, serviced morning and evening. Shoes properly cleaned.' Other comments: 'Staff are professional, friendly, but not obtrusive. They left a tea/coffee tray in our room, having remembered that we don't like early morning tea brought by a maid.' 'A pleasant stay in a well-run hotel.' 'A bright, clean room. Thankfully no chintz.' 'Relaxed and friendly; lovely garden, good position.' All the bedrooms now have double-glazed windows; four have been refurbished. The Pilgrims (father Harry and son Mark) 'encourage a dress code of jacket and tie' in the restaurant where the chef, Alan Webb, uses local produce, including fresh fish from Newlyn, for his English dishes on a daily-changing menu. 'British cooking at its best.' 'More than adequate portions, a wide choice.' (*Ken and Mildred Edwards, AJW and HM Harvey, LM Mayer-Jones, Bob and Barbara Edwards*)

29 bedrooms. 16 on ground floor. 2 suitable for &. Self-catering cottage. 4 miles SW of Falmouth. Car park. Train: Truro. Open 1 Feb–31 Dec. Lift, ramps. 3 lounges, bar, restaurant. No background music. 8½-acre grounds: gardens, private beach. Yacht. Golf, riding, windsurfing nearby. No smoking in restaurant. No dogs in public rooms. All major credit cards accepted. B&B [2006] £66–£135 per person; D,B&B £90–£165. Set dinner £33; full alc £51.50. 3-day winter breaks. Christmas package.

MELTON MOWBRAY Leicestershire   Map 2:A3

Sysonby Knoll   *Tel* 01664-563563
Asfordby Road   *Fax* 01664-410364
Melton Mowbray LE13 0HP   *Email* reception@sysonby.com
                                           Website www.sysonby.com

Run as a hotel by the Howling family since 1965, this red brick Edwardian house is on the edge of the old market town. Its 'magic' garden, with a manicured lawn in front and trees to either side, leads down to the River Eye where guests may fish. The bedrooms vary greatly in size and shape: most face a central courtyard; the two best rooms look over garden and river to cattle in fields. Recent visitors were impressed by the hospitality and food provided by Jenny and Gavin Howling, and liked their 'very good' superior bedroom, facing the inner courtyard. But another guest thought her bedroom decor 'rather dated' and breakfast 'basic'. The daily-changing *table d'hôte* menu has a choice of three dishes for the first two courses (eg, broccoli and Stilton soup; beef Wellington) and there is an 'unusually large' dessert menu. 'When we asked for sandwiches on a Sunday evening (the restaurant was closed), the response was excellent.' Blaze, a German pointer, and Stalky (miniature dachshund) are in attendance, and guests' dogs are welcomed, except in the restaurant. The hotel does not specifically cater for children, says the website, 'but well-behaved children are welcome'; there is a family room, and 'plenty of space in the gardens to let off steam'. (*J and JJ, and others*)

30 bedrooms. 6 in annexe (30 yds). Some on ground floor. On A6006, ¼ mile from town centre. Closed 24 Dec–3 Jan. Restaurant closed Sun nights. Unsuitable for &. Ramps. Reception/lounge, upstairs lounge, coffee lounge, bar, restaurant; function room; background music 'as appropriate'. 5-acre grounds on river: fishing. Smoking allowed: in bar, some bedrooms. No dogs in restaurant. All major credit cards accepted. B&B [2006] £37.50–£82 per person. Set lunch from £8, dinner from £18; full alc £30. ***V***

MIDDLEHAM North Yorkshire   Map 4:C3

Waterford House   *Tel* 01969-622090
19 Kirkgate   *Fax* 01969-624020
Middleham DL8 4PG   *Email* info@waterfordhousehotel.co.uk
                                   Website www.waterfordhousehotel.co.uk

In an unspoilt little town noted for its ruined 12th-century castle and its racehorses, Martin and Anne Cade run this attractive hotel in a Grade II listed Georgian stone house overlooking the main square. Inspectors wrote of 'genuine hospitality and immaculate housekeeping'. You enter through a paved garden filled with flowers in tubs. Inside there are antiques of all kinds, walls crammed with pictures, prints, old photographs and much racing memorabilia. The residents' lounge has a baby grand piano, log fire and huge pine dresser. 'Our bedroom was small but comfortable. Everything in tones of blue: blue-patterned china; blue pencil boxes on the old stove in the original fireplace, blue tassels on the stems of the bedside lamps; blue books, blue shawl draped on a large antique wardrobe.' Canapés are served in the drawing room before dinner, where Anne Cade's menu might include spiced parsnip and apple soup; pheasant, grouse, duck and cherry pie with shortcrust pastry. 'Everything beautifully cooked and presented.' The wine list is 'interesting and keenly priced'. The 'impressive' breakfast includes fresh orange juice, good toast and croissants, huge choice of cooked dishes. 'The best scrambled eggs we've had in years.' Visits to the stables can be arranged. More reports, please.

5 bedrooms. Centre of village. Closed Christmas/New Year. Restaurant closed Sun nights. Drawing room, TV room, restaurant. No background music. Walled garden, patio. Unsuitable for &. No smoking. No children under 12. No pets. MasterCard, Visa accepted. B&B [2006] £42.50–£80 per person; D,B&B £74–£96. Set dinner £31.

MIDHURST Sussex *See SHORTLIST*   Map 2:E3

MIDSOMER NORTON Somerset   Map 2:D1

The Moody Goose   NEW   *Tel* 01761-416784
at The Old Priory   *Fax* 01761-417851
Church Square   *Email* info@theoldpriory.co.uk
Midsomer Norton   *Website* www.moody-goose.com
nr Bath BA3 2HX

Stephen and Victoria Shore have moved their *Michelin*-starred *Moody Goose* restaurant from Bath to this beautiful Grade II listed building, which dates in part to 1152. It stands by the church, in a peaceful garden where our inspectors enjoyed a coffee, brought by the 'very nice manageress', on arrival. 'Our room,' they write, 'not large, was nicely furnished with antiques; its bathroom, by contrast, was very modern.' Other rooms, including the family one, are bigger; some have a four-poster. Some bathrooms have hand-held shower only. Pre-dinner drinks are taken in the lounge with its huge old fireplace, stone-flagged floor, 'comfortable old sofas and chairs'. As to the modern English cooking: 'They offer a very reasonably priced *table d'hôte* menu as well as a *carte*, and all dishes are interchangeable. Paupiette of lemon sole, with mushroom duxelle and a grape sauce was light and tasty; a vegetarian dish of spring vegetables and beetroot vinaigrette was also good. Three types of delicious bread; desserts excellent, not too rich. Service very friendly, if sometimes a little disorganised. The wine list, not over large, was mostly from France. Breakfast in the cheerful rear dining room had freshly baked croissants and brioches; good scrambled eggs. A most relaxing, enjoyable stay.'

7 bedrooms. Closed 2 weeks Jan. 9 miles SW of Bath. 2 lounges, 2 dining rooms (classical background music at lunch and dinner); private dining/function room. 1-acre garden. Unsuitable for &. No smoking. No dogs. All major credit cards accepted. B&B [2006] £50–£90 per person. Set menu £23.50; full alc £57. **'V'**

MILDEN Suffolk   Map 2:C5

Milden Hall   NEW/BUDGET   *Tel/Fax* 01787-247235
Milden, nr Lavenham   *Email* hawkins@thehall-milden.co.uk
CO10 9NY   *Website* www.thehall-milden.co.uk

'What a place,' writes the nominator of Juliet and Christopher Hawkins's 'memorably good', eco-friendly B&B. A listed 16th-century hall farmhouse, 'rejigged in Georgian times', it is 'very, very beautiful'. The 'sympathetic and cultured owners' pride themselves on the 'relaxed family atmosphere'. 'They gave a warm welcome on a cold autumn night. Huge bedroom with amazing array of antique prints and maps of Suffolk. Superb breakfast' (it includes free-range eggs and compote of home-grown fruit). The three bedrooms share one spacious bathroom, and there is a second bathroom downstairs for peak times. Bicycles are available for guests' use. There are books, maps, lots of local information. Wedding receptions and humanist weddings are sometimes held, groups can be catered for, 'well-behaved' children are welcomed (toys, nature trails, etc). The Hawkinses hold a Gold Award for Green Tourism in Suffolk, and on their farm are 'happy pigs and bantams', wildlife habitats and archaeological sites. (*Mark Purcell*)

3 bedrooms. 3 miles SE of Lavenham. Front drive off B1115 between Little Waldingfield and Monks Eleigh. Closed Christmas/New Year. Hall/sitting/dining room. No background music. 3-acre garden; 500-acre farm. Tennis. Unsuitable for &. No smoking. No dogs. No credit cards. B&B £30–£40 per person.

The *Guide* welcomes recommendations from readers for new entries. Please write or send us an email about any hotel, inn or B&B that you feel should be included.

MILFORD ON SEA Hampshire   Map 2:E2

Westover Hall	*Tel* 01590-643044
Park Lane	*Fax* 01590-644490
Milford on Sea	*Email* info@westoverhallhotel.com
nr Lymington SO41 0PT	*Website* www.westoverhallhotel.com

With views across Christchurch Bay to the Needles Rocks and the Isle of Wight, this imposing Grade II listed seafront mansion, built in 1897, has 'a wonderful ambience', say admirers. Owned by brother and sister Stewart Mechem and Nicola Musetti, it has a spectacular galleried hall, with Arts and Crafts stained glass showing Pre-Raphaelite scenes, by the Scottish artist Oscar Paterson. It has been restored to its original form, with family antiques, fashion photographs and contemporary paintings adding interest. This year, there is a new manager, Oliver Richards. The bedrooms have linen sheets ('lovely and crisp'), and a power shower; many have a plasma flat-screen TV, and six have sea views. Jimmy Desrivières, from the *Hôtel Meurice* in Paris, is head chef: his modern, 'skilfully prepared and presented' French dishes might include roasted scallops in the shell; saddle of venison with cassoulet of winter vegetables. One visitor thought the food 'a little OTT', and would have liked some plainer dishes. Another wrote: 'The cooking is excellent.' Most ingredients are local and organic. 'Expensive, but good value.' Functions and weddings are catered for. (*BA Orman, GHP, CJ, and others*)

12 bedrooms. 3 miles SW of Lymington. Ramps. 2 lounges (1 on 1st floor), bar, restaurant; background music; private dining room; conference facilities; terrace. 3-acre gardens. Sea 200 yds (private beach hut). Unsuitable for &. Civil wedding licence. No smoking: restaurant, some bedrooms. No mobile phones in dining room and bar. Dogs on lead in bar and lounge. Amex, MasterCard, Visa accepted. B&B [2006] £100–£180 per person; D,B&B £135–£215. Set dinner £38.50; full alc £53.50. Christmas/New Year packages.

MILTON ABBOT Devon   Map 1:D3

Hotel Endsleigh NEW	*Tel* 01822-870000
Milton Abbot	*Fax* 01822-870578
nr Tavistock PL19 0PQ	*Email* mail@hotelendsleigh.com
	Website www.hotelendsleigh.com

Outside the village, this luxury hotel was opened in 2005 by Olga Polizzi of *Tresanton Hotel,* St Mawes (*qv*); her 'charming' daughter, Alex, manages. Set in huge, 'glorious' grounds, this former fishing/shooting lodge of the dukes of Bedford, 'is a triumph of design, and an obvious labour of love', says this year's nominator. 'I cannot think of another hotel that I have enjoyed as much.' He enthuses about the welcome, the 'magnificent entrance hall', the atmosphere of 'a modern, comfortable country house', and the bedroom. 'Everything exuded quality. At night we heard owls.' A dissenting reporter disliked the decor. Shay Cooper's Italian-influenced cooking, based on local organic ingredients, is served in two 'stunning wood-panelled rooms'. 'Quality good, portion sizes not daunting. Excellent risotto starter; delicious vegetarian dish; best-ever sticky toffee pudding. Well-chosen wine list. First-rate staff, a mixture of locals and Poles.' At night, candles provide much of the lighting. Breakfast has 'everything you could ask for'. Georgina, a miniature pig, 'walks around the courtyard'. The hotel owns seven rods on the River Tamar which flows through the grounds, and there are 'fantastic walks in the gardens with their streams and waterfalls (waterproofs and wellies provided)'. (*Allan Kelly, and others*)

15 bedrooms. 1 on ground floor. 6 miles NW of Tavistock. Train/plane: Plymouth. Lounge, smoking lounge, quiet room, library, 2 dining rooms. Terraces. No background music. 108-acre estate: fishing (ghillie available). Civil wedding licence. No dogs: in bedrooms, restaurant. All major credit cards accepted. B&B double £200–£360. Set lunch £35, dinner £50. 1-night bookings refused weekends. Christmas/New Year packages. **'V'**

MILTON KEYNES Buckinghamshire   Map 2:C3
See SHORTLIST

MINCHINHAMPTON Gloucestershire   Map 3:E5

Burleigh Court   *Tel* 01453-883804
Minchinhampton, nr Stroud   *Fax* 01453-886870
GL5 2PF   *Email* info@burleighcourthotel.co.uk
                           Website www.burleighcourthotel.co.uk

On a steep hillside overlooking Golden Valley, this creeper-covered 18th-century Cotswold stone manor house stands in large gardens (with hidden pathways, stone walls, terraces, ponds and pools) designed by Clough Williams-Ellis. The owner, Louise Noble, aims 'to create the atmosphere of a luxurious but relaxed country house'. 'A blazing fire and fresh flowers in the hall were typical of the welcoming atmosphere,' says a visitor on a three-day bridge break. 'Our bedroom was magnificent. The staff were kindness itself.' An earlier comment: 'Our room was decent sized, well appointed, with views on both sides, fruit, sherry and magazines supplied;

the small bathroom had a modern shower fitting.' There is a 'large, attractive' panelled bar lounge with comfortable chairs and sofas: it serves light meals. In the formal dining room, painted in warm cream and with chandeliers, flowers, white linen, good cutlery and glass, chef Steve Woodcock serves a 'blend of modern and traditional dishes' (eg, duo of lamb with plum tomatoes and basil). 'Delicious. Very good ingredients.' Breakfast has fresh orange juice, fresh fruit and pastries, 'nicely cooked dishes'. Children sharing their parents' room are charged for meals only. (*Juliet Sebag-Montefiore*)

18 bedrooms. 7 in coach house. Some on ground floor. SE of Stroud, via A419 towards Cirencester. Closed 25/26 Dec. Ramps. Lounges, bar lounge, 2 dining rooms; classical background music at mealtimes. 4½-acre grounds: plunge pool, croquet. Civil wedding licence. No smoking: restaurants, bedrooms. Dogs in coach house bedrooms only, not in public rooms. Diners, MasterCard, Visa accepted. B&B £62.50–£85 per person; D,B&B £60–£110. Set lunch £22.95, dinner £29.50. Short breaks. New Year package. **'V'**

MISTLEY Essex   Map 2:C5

The Mistley Thorn **NEW/BUDGET**	*Tel* 01206-392821
High Street	*Fax* 01206-390122
Mistley, nr Manningtree	*Email* info@mistleythorn.co.uk
CO11 1HE	*Website* www.mistleythorn.com

In 2004, Sherri Singleton, from California, and her husband, David McKay, opened this restaurant-with-rooms: she was the first chef in Essex to win a *Michelin Bib Gourmand.* Yellow-painted outside, the Georgian inn has panoramic views from some rooms down the Stour estuary. 'Inside,' writes a *Guide* inspector, 'it has a seasidey freshness. Sage green panelling through-out. Uncluttered bedrooms (No. 4, though not huge, felt spacious) have a decor of taupe and cream, large bed, two chairs, plenty of cupboard space, organic tea and coffee. Bathrooms are well designed. Wooden tables, basket-weave chairs and modern artwork enhance the busy restaurant.' Menus place an emphasis on seafood (mussels, lobster, etc) and seasonal, local produce. 'Hard to choose from the enticing selection of starters (eg, seared scallops with beans, cherry tomatoes and organic leaves), and main courses like local plaice with samphire; chicken with tomato, mozzarella and breadcrumb stuffing and wild mushroom sauce.' A continental breakfast (fresh fruit, yogurt and sourdough toast) is offered; a generous cooked breakfast (£6.95) uses free-range eggs and local bacon. Families are welcomed. 'No sitting area for guests, but there is plenty to do outdoors in this interesting and attractive area.'

5 bedrooms. 9 miles W of Harwich. Bar, restaurant; occasional background jazz. Unsuitable for &. No smoking. MasterCard, Visa accepted. B&B double £70–£85; D,B&B double £110–£135. Full alc £27.95. 1-night bookings refused summer weekends.

MOCCAS Herefordshire   Map 3:D4

Moccas Court   *Tel* 01981-500019
Moccas, nr Hereford   *Fax* 01981-500095
HR2 9LH   *Email* info@moccas-court.co.uk
                              Website www.moccas-court.co.uk

'Excellent in all aspects,' says a report this year. This is one of Herefordshire's finest buildings. A stately home in a park designed by Capability Brown, it stands above the River Wye, on which it has half a mile of fishing rights. Filled with antiques and family portraits, 'it would appeal to anyone who appreciates everything that goes with comfort and the experience of life in a Grade I listed Georgian house'. Grand features – Robert Adam created the round room (with hand-painted wallpaper) where guests eat, and the oval staircase – combine with 'the feel of a home'. The owners, Ben (the chef) and Mimi Chester-Master, serve dinner by arrangement, around a circular table. The choices are limited, they say, because the ingredients are 'as fresh as humanly possible'. Pre-dinner drinks are taken in the library. 'The cooking is superb, and the service is good but informal.' The spacious bedrooms have 'beautiful curtains and wallpapers', a traditional decor, and 'completely up-to-date plumbing'. Four bathrooms are *en suite*; one is adjacent. Views are of the gardens, the Wye, the Malverns or the deer park. Wedding parties are catered for. The 12th-century church in the park has its original stained-glass windows. Zulu, the Labrador, 'gives an enthusiastic welcome'. (*Philip Plant, Annie Maud, JE*)

5 bedrooms. 11 miles W of Hereford. Train: Hereford. 2 lounges, music room, TV room, restaurant. No background music. 100-acre grounds: river, fishing. Unsuitable for &. Civil wedding licence applied for. No smoking. Children by arrangement. No dogs. Amex, MasterCard, Visa accepted. B&B: single £116–£156, double £140–£195. Set dinner £35. Christmas/New Year packages. 1-night bookings occasionally refused.

When you make a booking you enter into a contract with a hotel. Most hotels explain their cancellation policies, which vary widely, in a letter of confirmation. You may lose your deposit or be charged at the full rate for the room if you cancel at short notice. A travel insurance policy can provide protection.

MORETON-IN-MARSH Gloucestershire   Map 3:D6

The Redesdale Arms
High Street
Moreton-in-Marsh
GL56 0AW

Tel 01608-650308
Fax 01608-651843
Email info@redesdalearms.com
Website www.redesdalearms.com

'The staff were without exception courteous, cheerful and hard working,' writes a visitor in 2006 to this centuries-old coaching inn ('which welcomed travellers on the Fosse Way in the reign of Charles II'). It stands on the wide main street of an attractive Cotswold market town. It has 'a pleasant, informal atmosphere', say other guests, and a friendly manager, Robert Smith. Six new luxury rooms are planned for the winter of 2006/7. 'We enjoyed our country-style room, with lots of nice touches, fresh flowers, a complimentary decanter of sherry; the bed was not the most comfortable.' Lighting may not always be adequate. Three bedrooms are in converted stables around a decked terrace at the rear; they are quieter than those in the main building. Front rooms have double-glazed windows, but there may be noise from the street in hot weather, and from the bar (popular with locals) below. A 'long, narrow' single room was thought poor value. The cooking of chef Craig Malins was thought 'excellent', but 'over two nights the menu didn't change'. Breakfast 'was excellent, the best part of the stay'. (*JPH, Ian Malone, and others*)

18 bedrooms. 10 in annexe. 8 on ground floor, suitable for &. High Street by Redesdale Hall and intersection with Bourton Rd. Ramps. Lounge bar/reading room, public bar, 2 restaurants; background music from 10 am. Heated open dining area. Smoking allowed only in bars. No dogs in bedrooms. MasterCard, Visa accepted. B&B £42.50–£72.50 per person. Full alc £29.50. Christmas/New Year packages. 1-night Sat bookings refused 1 Apr–1 Oct.

MORSTON Norfolk   Map 2:A5

Morston Hall
Morston, Holt
NR25 7AA

Tel 01263-741041
Fax 01263-740419
Email reception@morstonhall.com
Website www.morstonhall.com

'A genuinely warm welcome.' 'Our room was homely, good to relax in. Outstanding food.' Visitors again praise this flint and brick Jacobean house in a designated area of outstanding natural beauty on the north Norfolk coast. Tracy and Galton Blackiston run it as a restaurant-with-rooms: he is the *Michelin*-starred chef. 'Samantha Pegg, who cooks with him, is just as good,' say regulars. 'We are saving up the pension for the next trip.' Earlier praise: 'Lovely atmosphere. Not a jot of pretension. Our room in the eaves looked over the garden, and on to marshes and Morston Quay. Little touches made it special – bathsalts, fluffy bathrobes, checkers game, etc.' Six spacious new suites (with fireplace, under-floor heating and plasma TV) are due to open in November 2006. The four-course dinner (7.30 for 8; no choice until pudding or cheese; menus discussed when you book) might include asparagus with bacon in puff pastry; roast breast and confit leg of squab on fondant potato. Vegetarians are catered for. Breakfasts ('a highlight') have freshly squeezed orange juice, toasted home-made bread, local sausages. For children there are high teas, toys, cots, etc. (*ND, TB Collins, Anne and Denis Tate*)

7 bedrooms. 1 on ground floor. 2 miles W of Blakeney. Open 1 Feb–1 Jan, except 25 Dec. Hall, lounge, conservatory, restaurant. No background music. 3½-acre garden: pond, croquet. Only restaurant suitable for &. No smoking: restaurant, conservatory. No dogs in public rooms (free kennels/£5 in room). All major credit cards accepted. D,B&B £120–£145 per person. Set dinner £45. New Year package. 1-night bookings refused Sat.

MORTEHOE Devon   Map 1:B4

The Cleeve House   NEW/BUDGET   *Tel* 01271-870719
North Morte Road   *Email* info@cleevehouse.co.uk
Mortehoe, nr Woolacombe   *Website* www.cleevehouse.co.uk
EX34 7ED

On the South West Coastal Path, this 'good-value, unpretentious', small hotel stands off the main road of a pretty village on a hill above Woolacombe. The owners, David and Anne Strobel, are 'charming people who immediately make you feel at home', says a reporter on her fourth visit. The bedrooms, with their pine furniture, 'are fairly small, but have everything you might need'. Rear rooms have country views. Dinner, in a room hung with local artwork, is 'home cooking of a high standard' (main courses like supreme of chicken with a garlic, lime and Parmesan crust; smoked haddock with mustard sauce). There is a 'comfortable lounge'. Good walks start from the door. A flight of steps leads down to a pebbly cove. (*Mrs CM Moore*)

6 bedrooms. 1, on ground floor, with & access. 4 miles W of Ilfracombe. Train/ coach: Barnstaple. Open 1 Mar–31 Oct. Restaurant closed Wed, and evenings 21 July–31 Aug. Ramp. Lounge, bar area, dining room. No background music. Patio; garden. Golf nearby. Woolacombe beach 1½ miles. No smoking. No children under 12. No dogs. MasterCard, Visa accepted. B&B £39–£56 per person; D,B&B £58–£75.

MUCH WENLOCK Shropshire   Map 3:C5

The Raven   *Tel* 01952-727251
Much Wenlock   *Fax* 01952-728416
TF13 6EN   *Email* enquiry@ravenhotel.com
                              Website www.ravenhotel.com

In a 'lovely little' Shropshire market town, this white-fronted hotel is
'a pleasant place to stay; great value for money', say visitors this year. A
17th-century coaching inn has been combined with 15th-century almshouses and a medieval hall in a quiet street just off the centre. There is safe
off-street parking. The staff, mainly local and young, were found 'uniformly
helpful and attentive'. The bedrooms are all different; one has a four-poster;
the galleried suite is on two levels. 'Three large windows made our room
wonderfully light.' Some rooms are reached from the plant-filled inner
courtyard. In the 'charming, rustic' restaurant, which faces almshouses,
guests can choose from two to four courses on the *table d'hôte* menu, four to
five dishes per course. Local produce is used, and herbs come from the
Raven's garden. 'The cooking is simple, using good ingredients, no fancy
sauces; portions are large.' 'A wonderful place to stay for one night,' says a
visitor, disappointed that the menu didn't alter over three nights. 'Without
a change, good food well cooked still becomes a disappointment.' A bar
menu is also available. (*Jean and Richard Green, Joanna Russell, JP, and others*)

14 bedrooms. 7 across courtyard. 100 yds from centre. Closed 25 Dec. Bar,
2 lounges, 2 dining rooms; classical background music at mealtimes. Courtyard: small
herb garden. Unsuitable for &. No smoking: dining rooms, bedrooms, conservatory.
Guide dogs only. Amex, MasterCard, Visa accepted. B&B [2006] £55–£75 per
person. Set lunch/dinner £20–£30.

MUNGRISDALE Cumbria   Map 4: inset C2

The Mill Hotel   *Tel* 017687-79659
Mungrisdale   *Fax* 017687-79155
Penrith CA11 0XR   *Email* quinlan@themillhotel.demon.co.uk
                              Website www.themillhotel.com

Ü *César award in 1993*

In the Lake District national park, this former mill cottage, built in 1651,
retains millrace, waterfall and trout stream. The 'affable owner', Richard
Quinlan, describes it as 'a comfortable family home', and regular guests
appreciate the 'homely' style. 'We enjoyed our stay,' one visitor wrote this
year, but another thought the hotel 'quite ramshackle, tucked away behind

a pub' (confusingly, it shares an entrance with the larger *Mill Inn*). Some bedrooms are small, but they have 'thoughtful touches' (fruit, current magazines, etc). 'Mine, pleasant and sunny, had a good bathroom.' Two rooms in the old mill share a sitting room. There is a log fire in the beamed lounge, which has old furniture, pictures, fresh flowers, books and magazines. Here, guests take a drink before being called to dinner in succession. In a low-ceilinged, candlelit room ('with high-up windows'), they sit at separate tables, but Mr Quinlan 'likes fostering rapport among diners' while waiting at table. His wife, Eleanor, is the chef: her daily-changing three-course menu has limited choice (the main course could be sea bass with roasted Mediterranean vegetables). 'Delicious bacon at break-fast.' An 'excellent stop-over on the way north'. (*Stephen and Jane Savery, Alan Moulds, and others*)

7 bedrooms. In village 2 miles N of A66 Penrith–Keswick. Open 1 Mar–31 Oct. 2 lounges, sun lounge, dining room (classical background music during dinner); drying room. Small cottage garden: millrace, waterfall, trout stream. No smoking in public rooms. Dogs by arrangement in bedrooms; not in public rooms. No credit cards. D,B&B £69–£85 per person. ***V***

NAYLAND Suffolk   Map 2:C5

The White Hart	*Tel* 01206-263382
11 High Street	*Fax* 01206-263638
Nayland CO6 4JF	*Email* nayhart@aol.com
	Website www.whitehart-nayland.co.uk

A new manager, Gianluca Rizzo, has come from owner Michel Roux's *Waterside Inn*, Bray (*qv*), to run this restaurant-with-rooms in a Suffolk village of old colour-washed houses. The chef, Christophe Lemarchand, is also new. 'All the staff are helpful and friendly,' say visitors who stayed shortly after the changes. 'Our room was a good size, warm, comfortable, full of character.' The food is 'delicious', all agree: 'unfussy French cooking', eg, honey-roast pork belly with green cabbage and lentils. Breakfast is thought 'superb'. Built in the 15th century, and altered in the 18th to give a tunnel entrance for carriages, the old building has 'challenging' sloping floors. The beamed bedrooms vary in size, but all have a king-size bed, bright checked fabrics, toiletries in a blue enamel bucket. Drinks can be taken on the large terrace by the River Stour. Children are welcomed (cots and high chairs provided). Arrival time is 4 pm. Functions are held (a marquee is sometimes erected). (*Neil and Claire Butter, and others*)

6 bedrooms. Village on A134. 6 miles N of Colchester. Car park. Buses from Sudbury, Ipswich, Colchester. Closed 2 weeks after Christmas. Restaurant closed

Mon. Lounge, bar, restaurant; background music all day; private dining/function room; terrace. Riverside garden. Unsuitable for &. Civil wedding licence. Smoking in lounge only. No dogs. All major credit cards accepted. B&B £42.50–£69 per person; D,B&B (midweek) £65–£80. Set lunch £11.50–£15.50; full alc £40. Christmas package. 1-night bookings sometimes refused. *V*

NEAR SAWREY Cumbria   Map 4: inset C2

Ees Wyke Country House   *Tel* 015394-36393
Near Sawrey   *Email* mail@eeswyke.co.uk
Ambleside LA22 0JZ   *Website* www.eeswyke.co.uk

Once the holiday home of Beatrix Potter, Richard and Margaret Lee's 'impressive' Georgian house has panoramic views of Esthwaite Water and the fells beyond. With a 'cosy English decor', it has a 'pleasant, unpretentious atmosphere', said inspectors. Some bedrooms, including the twin with the best view, have their shower room across the landing: 'bring a dressing gown' for the communal bathroom. Water, sherry, biscuits and tea/coffee-making facilities are provided. Mr Lee, the 'affable' chef, serves a five-course dinner in 'English with French influences' style, eg, terrine of pork with prunes in Armagnac; noisettes of lamb, with wine jus and a hint of garlic. The breakfast buffet of cereals, yogurts, freshly squeezed orange juice and fresh fruits can be augmented by local Cumberland sausages, bacon and eggs. More reports, please.

8 bedrooms. 1 on ground floor. Edge of village 1½ miles SE of Hawkshead. 2 lounges, restaurant, veranda. No background music. 1-acre garden. Access to Esthwaite Water (exc. May–Aug). Unsuitable for &. No smoking. No children under 12. No dogs in public rooms. MasterCard, Visa accepted. B&B £51–£72 per person; D,B&B £79–£107. Set dinner £31. Christmas/New Year packages.

NEW MILTON Hampshire   Map 2:E2

Chewton Glen   *Tel* 01425-275341
Christchurch Road   *Fax* 01425-272310
New Milton BH25 6QS   *Email* reservations@chewtonglen.com
                                    Website www.chewtonglen.com

After 40 years, this upmarket hotel/country club/spa was sold to 'a private buyer' in early 2006. Martin Skan remains as non-executive president; his wife, Brigitte, will 'keep an eye' on interior design. Andrew Stembridge stays as managing director. There was some subsequent praise: 'A very pleasant weekend.' 'The international staff [many are Polish] showed an impressive balance of friendliness without familiarity.' But this was tempered by criticism of 'a series of small things that showed a lack of attention to detail'. One couple described the 'curious effect' of a business conference ('it made the hotel seem very empty, as they were meeting away from the main public rooms'). As to the cooking, which has been described as 'classic English seasonal menus designed to soothe rather than set the pulse racing', *Michelin* has removed its star, and a reader wrote: 'Could do better.' The 'plush' red brick mansion stands in large grounds with many outdoors activities (see below). The hydrotherapy spa wins awards. Lounges have antiques, fabrics, paintings and flowers. Suites and bedrooms, some vast, are lavish. Children under five are now welcomed at Easter and in August, and the dress code has been relaxed. More reports, please.

58 bedrooms. Some on ground floor. On S edge of New Forest national park. Ramps. 3 lounges, bar, restaurant; function rooms; snooker room; health club: indoor tennis, swimming pool, gym, beauty salon. 130-acre grounds: swimming pool, tennis, croquet, 9-hole par 3 golf course, lake, jogging course; helipad; bicycle hire. Beach, fishing, sailing, riding nearby. Chauffeur service. Civil wedding licence. Smoking in bar only. Children under 5 accepted Easter and August. All major credit cards accepted. Room [2006]: single/double £290–£445, suite £445–£545. Breakfast £20–£25. Set lunch from £24.50; full alc £75. Min. 2-night bookings at weekends. Various breaks. Christmas/New Year house parties.

NEW ROMNEY Kent   Map 2:E5

Romney Bay House   *Tel* 01797-364747
Coast Road, Littlestone   *Fax* 01797-367156
New Romney TN28 8QY

Built in the late 1920s for the American actress and journalist Hedda Hopper, and designed by Sir Clough Williams-Ellis of Portmeirion fame, this red-roofed, white-fronted house is found 'extremely restful'. 'Well run' (say returning visitors) by owners Clinton and Lisa Lovell, it stands on a private road in a 'strangely lonely position on a wild stretch of coast. The vast skyscapes and seascapes make one feel miles from the hurly-burly of everyday life.' Antiques, pictures and knick-knacks fill the house. The drawing room has 'charm and character'. At night, white candles burn in the public rooms, and there is a log fire in the lounge. Mr Lovell serves an 'excellent' no-choice dinner, eg, fillet of turbot with ginger and orange; duo of lamb, leek and celeriac gratin; tarte Tatin with honey and nutmeg ice cream. 'First-rate coffee' is included in the price. The bedrooms have nearly floor-length windows with views of sea or golf course, plain carpet, light colours, four-poster or half-tester bed, armchairs, etc. Almost all bathrooms have been refitted. Breakfast is full English, or continental with cold meats, cheese, fruits, croissants and toast. The Channel Tunnel is 20 minutes' drive away. (*B and P Orman, SH*)

10 bedrooms. 1½ miles from New Romney. Closed 1 week Christmas. Dining room closed midday, Sun/Mon evenings. 2 lounges, bar, conservatory, dining room; small function facilities. No background music. 1-acre garden: croquet, *boules*. Opposite sea sand/pebble beach (safe bathing), fishing. Unsuitable for &. Smoking in bar only. No children under 14. No dogs. Amex, MasterCard, Visa accepted. B&B £42.50–£95 per person. Set dinner £37.50. New Year package. 1-night advance bookings refused weekends. *V*

NEWBURY Berkshire *See SHORTLIST*   Map 2:D2

NEWCASTLE UPON TYNE Tyne and Wear Map 4:B4

Jesmond Dene House NEW	*Tel* 0191-212 3000
Jesmond Dene Road	*Fax* 0191-212 3001
Newcastle upon Tyne	*Email* info@jesmonddenehouse.co.uk
NE2 2EY	*Website* www.jesmonddenehouse.co.uk

In a 'charming location', at the head of a wooded valley (with waterfalls) within the city limits, this rambling stone building was the home of a Victorian industrialist. Later it became a school. 'Impressive Arts and Crafts interiors' combine with modern decor, say inspectors. The *Michelin*-starred chef Terry Laybourne, with Peter Candler, opened it as a luxury hotel in September 2005. Eric Kortenbach manages. 'Our spacious, restful bedroom, in fashionable "greige" colours, had all the comforts (Internet access, plasma-screen TV, specialist reading lights, etc).' Bathrooms have under-floor heating. 'The welcome was warm. Things didn't always function with precision (no newspaper one morning), but restaurant staff were efficient and friendly. At breakfast, "fresh" orange juice came from a package and tea was made from bags – unacceptable at these prices.' The popular restaurant, in the former music room (with delicate plasterwork) and a light, oak-floored garden room, has menus 'inspired by local traditions'. Some critics found the food 'wonderful', with

'unfussy presentation'; our inspectors thought it 'unexciting' though 'raw materials are first class' (eg, 'tasty, plainly roasted duck'). The wine list 'is an interesting global selection'. Best bedrooms face the Dene; some others are in a new annexe. Conferences are catered for.

40 bedrooms. 8 in adjacent annexe. Some suitable for &. 5 mins' drive from centre via A167; Ilford Rd metro 10 mins' walk. Lift. Lounge, cocktail bar, restaurant (background music 24 hrs); conference/function facilities; personal trainer. Civil wedding licence. 2-acre garden. No smoking: restaurant, lounge, bedrooms. Guide dogs only. All major credit cards accepted. Room [2006]: single £115, double £145–£195, suite £225–£270. Breakfast £15. Set lunch £21.50–£22.50; full alc £50. Christmas/New Year packages. *V*

Malmaison
The Quayside
Newcastle upon Tyne
NE1 3DX

Tel 0191-245 5000
Fax 0191-245 4545
Email newcastle@malmaison.com
Website www.malmaison.com

Not an obvious *Guide* entry, this large hotel, part of a chain (managed by Seamus Coen), is thought to be 'one of the best examples of the group'. In a 'buzzy area, full of bars and restaurants', opposite the Millennium Bridge, the large, square, former warehouse has been converted 'with flair' in contemporary style. It has an Art Deco-style canopy over the entrance, a ground-floor lobby with mirrors and wall-to-wall carpeting. There are strong colours, bold prints, modern furniture. The busy bar has wooden Venetian blinds, tables with blue lamps. Most bedrooms are liked: the open-plan suites on the 'Château' floor, all named after ships built locally, have 'fantastic' views. 'Our large, light room had handmade furniture, heavy window drapes, huge bathroom.' 'Very good room service. Attention to detail. Good minibar.' The brasserie, like many bedrooms, faces the River Tyne. Chef Gareth Marks serves 'well-executed' dishes (eg, venison loin with a shallot and thyme tart; coq au vin with garlic mash). Breakfast includes freshly squeezed orange juice, fruit and cheese, as well as hot dishes. There is non-stop modern music in all public areas. A gym and a spa (holistic and beauty treatments, etc) are in the basement. More reports, please.

120 bedrooms. 5 adapted for &. On quayside, by law courts. Lifts, ramp. 2 lounges, café, bar, brasserie; modern background music 24 hrs; gym, spa; function facilities. No smoking: brasserie, bedrooms. No dogs in public rooms. All major credit cards accepted. Room [2006]: single/double £140, suite £225–£350. Breakfast £12.95. Full alc £30.

See also SHORTLIST

NEWLANDS Cumbria   Map 4: inset C2

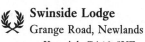 **Swinside Lodge**   *Tel* 017687-72948
Grange Road, Newlands   *Fax* 017687-73312
nr Keswick CA12 5UE   *Email* info@swinsidelodge-hotel.co.uk
                         Website www.swinsidelodge-hotel.co.uk

César award: Lakeland hotel of the year

'Four fabulous nights. Artistic meals.' 'Excellent.' Comments on Eric and
Irene Fell's traditional Regency house. At the foot of Cat Bells, it is
'surrounded by lovely Lakeland countryside', report inspectors in 2006.
'The view is of romantic landscape and sheep in adjoining fields. We have
rarely seen such an immaculate place. Tastefully decorated and furnished,
it has pleasing ornaments and pictures. Mrs Fell is charming; she brought
complimentary tea with gorgeous home-made shortbread.' There are
'lovely flower arrangements', and 'candlelight added to the ambience in the
evening'. Bedrooms, five of which have been redecorated, come in three
sizes: 'Ours, with king-size bed, was large, airy, newly decorated. Textiles
were tasteful, and there were all sorts of thoughtful extras. The immaculate
bathroom was well appointed.' On a winter's night, a north-facing room felt
chilly, despite the central heating. Pre-dinner drinks come with 'delicious'
canapés. In the dark red dining room, dinner is a no-choice menu,
preferences discussed on arrival. Clive Imber's cooking was thought
'exceptional: brilliant goat's cheese soufflé, perfect beef with foie gras pâté
and pine nuts; scrumptious yet light desserts'. One visitor felt 'they could
reduce portions a bit'. Breakfast has 'sensational' marmalade. (*Yvette Hales,
Anne Thornthwaite, and others*)

8 bedrooms. 3 miles S of Keswick. Closed Christmas, 8–22 Jan. Dining room closed
midday. 2 sitting rooms, dining room. No background music. 1-acre garden.
Unsuitable for &. No smoking. No children under 12. No dogs. MasterCard, Visa
accepted. B&B £53–£73 per person; D,B&B £78–£98. Set dinner £35. Breaks.
Christmas/New Year packages.

NEWMARKET Suffolk *See SHORTLIST*   Map 2:B4

'Set lunch/dinner' indicates fixed-price meals, with ample,
limited or no choice on the menu. 'Full alc' is the hotel's estimated price per person of a three-course *à la carte* meal, with a
half bottle of house wine. 'Alc' is the price of an *à la carte* meal
excluding the cost of wine.

NORTH BOVEY Devon   Map 1:D4

Gate House   `BUDGET`   *Tel/Fax* 01647-440479
North Bovey   *Email* gatehouseondartmoor@talk21.com
nr Moretonhampstead   *Website* www.gatehouseondartmoor.com
TQ13 8RB

Built in 1460, and still retaining its 'tough granite walls', this Grade II listed
thatched Devon hall house is in a beautiful Dartmoor conservation village
(with old granite packhorse bridges). It is 'heartily recommended for setting
and ambience' by readers. 'They welcome guests with tea, by a huge fireplace in an oak-beamed sitting room in winter, or by the pool in the garden
in summer.' Each of the 'country style' bedrooms, approached up a winding
staircase, has a view of the garden or the moors beyond. Supper trays can
be served by arrangement, and the 'extremely helpful' hosts, John and
Sheila Williams, will advise about local eating places, eg, the 'excellent'
Ring of Bells pub nearby. Breakfast is a hearty affair. In the garden are seats
with views, and a swimming pool.

3 bedrooms. 2 miles SW of Moretonhampstead. Closed 24–26 Dec. Dining room
closed for lunch. Lounge, dining room. No background music. ¾-acre garden: sitting
areas, swimming pool (33 by 15 ft). Unsuitable for &. No smoking. No children
under 14. No dogs in public rooms. No credit cards. B&B £34–£35 per person.
Supper tray £10. **·V·**

NORTH KILWORTH Leicestershire   Map 2:B3

Kilworth House   *Tel* 01858-880058
Lutterworth Road   *Fax* 01858-880349
North Kilworth LE17 6JE   *Email* info@kilworthhouse.co.uk
                                     Website www.kilworthhouse.co.uk

A log fire burns on cold days in the hall of this magnificent Victorian
country house which has been restored as a luxury hotel by Celia and
Richard Mackay. Set in a large wooded park, it has a fine carved staircase,
mosaic floors and massive stained-glass windows; the carpets are a 'work of
art'. Crystal chandeliers hang in the drawing room, which has 'a plethora
of silks, vibrant fabrics, massive mirrors, leather sofas, deep cushioned
settees, flowers in abundance'. Furniture in the bedrooms is a mix of old
and repro. 'Our room had high ceilings, a tester bed, and a teddy bear,' said
inspectors. Its lavish bathroom had armchairs and deep window seats.
There are two sections in the formal *Wordsworth* restaurant; one with an
ornate ceiling, the other facing a courtyard with water features. The less

formal *Orangery* faces lawns and parkland. Carl Dovey, the chef, serves traditional/modern dishes, eg, confit of belly pork; Dover sole roulade. Conferences, weddings and functions are held. Children are welcomed, and wheelchair-users are well looked after. The M1 motorway is four miles away; Birmingham is 40 minutes' drive. More reports, please.

44 bedrooms. 2 suitable for ♿. S of Leicester, E of Coventry. 4 miles from M1 exit 20. Lift, ramps. 2 lounge areas, library, 2 restaurants; background music all day; private dining rooms; function facilities. 38-acre grounds: gardens, croquet, coarse fishing lake. Civil wedding licence. No smoking. No dogs. All major credit cards accepted. B&B £90–£160 per person. English breakfast £13.50. Full alc from £50. Weekend/midweek rates. Christmas/New Year packages.

NORTH MOLTON Devon   Map 1:B4

Heasley House	*Tel* 01598-740213
Heasley Mill	*Fax* 01598-740677
North Molton EX36 3LE	*Email* enquiries@heasley-house.co.uk
	Website www.heasley-house.co.uk

In a hamlet on the southern edge of Exmoor national park, above the River Mole, this 'unassuming' Grade II listed Georgian dower house has been extensively renovated by Jan and Paul Gambrill ('an enthusiastic couple') since they came here two years ago. 'They made clear that our wishes were paramount,' wrote inspectors in 2006. 'We arrived on a rainy day. They gave us tea with cake by a roaring log fire. His passion is cooking, which he does almost single-handed. She makes the very good bread.' Bedroom upgrading continues: the rooms are freshly painted in pastel colours; all will have *en suite* facilities with power shower. 'Decor like a friend's house. All rooms are spacious, ours had a sitting room. Egyptian cotton bedlinen. Bathroom with a minimum of freebies.' Downstairs are deep leather chairs, stripped wooden floors. The restaurant is open to non-residents. 'Dinner was a treat. Excellent rack of lamb with purée of flageolets; steak in sticky red wine sauce. Breakfast similarly good: freshly squeezed orange juice; porridge with clotted cream.' Other comments: 'Interesting wine list (good medium-priced bottles).' 'The chintz is fast disappearing.' Shooting parties come in winter. Dogs are 'positively welcomed'. (*Jennie Brown, and others*)

8 bedrooms. Some family. 1 on ground floor. Closed Feb. N of North Molton. 2 lounges, bar (background music), restaurant. ¼-acre garden. Unsuitable for ♿. Smoking in bar only. No dogs: lounges, restaurant. MasterCard, Visa accepted. B&B [2006] £48–£55 per person; D,B&B £69.50–£76.50. Set dinner £17.50– £21.50. New Year package. ***V***

NORTH WALSHAM Norfolk   Map 2:A6

Beechwood   *Tel* 01692-403231
Cromer Road   *Fax* 01692-407284
North Walsham   *Email* enquiries@beechwood-hotel.co.uk
NR28 0HD   *Website* www.beechwood-hotel.co.uk

A creeper-clad house, Georgian but 'with Victorian character', once Agatha Christie's Norfolk hideaway, is now this small hotel. It has many devotees: 'We have become addicted to staying here,' one writes. Other comments: 'A delightful escape to gracious living.' 'One of our all-time favourite hotels.' The newer garden suites are liked: 'Huge four-poster bed, leather settee and armchair, large enclosed power shower.' In the dimly lit dining room, the cooking of Steven Norgate ('modern British with a Mediterranean influence', eg, loin of lamb on dauphinoise potatoes with rosemary and wild mushroom jus) is generally admired: 'First class.' 'Impressive quality and presentation.' Breakfast has freshly squeezed juice, cereals galore and an artistic buffet of sliced fruits. The 'hands-on' owners/ managers, Lindsay Spalding and Don Birch, write: 'We guarantee a restful stay, because we don't take large groups, wedding parties or conferences. We have a philosophy to be a friendly hotel and we always try to entertain our guests.' The 'lovely garden' has shrubs, a long lawn and sunken area. Two Airedale terriers, Harry and Emily, appear at night, after their walk. A good base for exploring the Norfolk broads. (*John Albutt, Reg and Jo Newbury, and many others*)

17 bedrooms. Some on ground floor. 1 suitable for &. Near town centre. Closed Christmas. Restaurant closed midday Mon–Sat. 2 lounges, bar, restaurant; classical background music in evening. 1-acre garden: croquet. No smoking. No children under 10. Dogs allowed in some bedrooms. MasterCard, Visa accepted. B&B £45–£80 per person; D,B&B £50–£120. Set lunch (Sun) £19, dinner £34. Winter breaks (3 nights for the price of 2). New Year package. 1-night bookings sometimes refused. ***V***

NORTHAM Devon   Map 1:B4

Yeoldon House   *Tel* 01237-474400
Durrant Lane   *Fax* 01237-476618
Northam, nr Bideford   *Email* yeoldonhouse@aol.com
EX39 2RL   *Website* www.yeoldonhousehotel.co.uk

With lawns sloping down towards the River Torridge, this 'gentleman's residence' is an imposing 19th-century gabled house. The Union flag flies from a staff on its roof. The owners, Jennifer and Brian Steele (he is the chef), have filled it with Victorian bric-a-brac. One guest thought it 'like a setting for an Agatha Christie novel'. There are suitcases and teddy bears on stairs, stained glass, a large lounge and bar. Bedrooms 'each have their own charm': one has a four-poster, another is split-level with its own balcony and lounge area. 'Ours (Crow's Nest) was a bit small, but it overlooked the estuary and had a battlemented balcony. Morning sunshine and the sound of curlews.' The restaurant, which also faces the river, is named after the famous chef, Alexis Soyer; 'a source of inspiration', says Brian Steele. 'We take pride in cooking and presenting good food in a relaxing atmosphere.' Here, 'you will feel comfortable in any attire'. Main courses include tenderloin of pork in bacon with a wholegrain mustard sauce. Books and games are provided; donkeys graze in a meadow up the drive. Nearby are Rosemoor Garden and the delightful fishing town of Appledore. More reports, please.

10 bedrooms. ½ mile N of Bideford. Closed Christmas. Restaurant closed midday and Sun. Lounge/bar, restaurant; classical background music at night. 2-acre grounds. Beach 5 mins' drive. Civil wedding licence. Unsuitable for &. No smoking: restaurant, bedrooms. Amex, MasterCard, Visa accepted. B&B £52.50–£75 per person; D,B&B £75–£105. Set dinner £27.50. New Year package. **'V'**

NORTHLEACH Gloucestershire   Map 3:D6

Yew Tree Cottage	*Tel* 01451-860222
Turkdean, Northleach	*Email* vivien@bestcotswold.com
GL54 3NT	*Website* www.bestcotswold.com

In a peaceful Cotswold hamlet near the wool town, this old stone building 'captivated' visitors from Massachusetts with its 'real cottage feel, lovely rooms and great food'. 'Sheep baa-ing is the noisiest interruption,' says Vivien Burford, the owner. She was 'incredibly helpful with itinerary planning, transporting us to and from local pubs'. One bedroom has an *en suite* bathroom; the other two share a bathroom. For visiting children, there is a stock of board games and a nominal charge of £10. And guests' dogs are 'positively encouraged' (though not in the house); they have 'a real canine B&B treat' with accommodation in a 'super-deluxe kennel suite'. (The Burfords own two black Labradors.) Cream teas with home baking are served in the garden on warm days, or in the kitchen, where 'farmhouse plus' meals can be provided, by arrangement. No wine licence: no corkage charge. (*J and LH*)

3 bedrooms. 3 miles N of Northleach. Train: Kingham or Kemble; bus: Cirencester. Sitting room, study/dining room, kitchen. No background music. 2-acre garden. Unsuitable for &. No smoking. Dogs in kennels only. Amex, MasterCard, Visa accepted. B&B £40–£60 per person Set dinner £20.

NORWICH Norfolk

Map 2:B5

By Appointment
25–29 St George's Street
Norwich NR3 1AB

Tel/Fax 01603-630730

Q *César award in 1999*

'Lovely quirky place. Warm welcome and excellent food.' More acclaim this year for Timothy Brown and Robert Culyer's restaurant-with-rooms in the historic centre of Norwich. 'It's like being a guest in a welcoming home,' said an earlier visitor. The 15th-century merchant's house has a labyrinthine layout: you enter under an arch at the back of the street, through a tiny courtyard with a Della Robbia relief on the wall, and straight into the kitchen. Inside are antiques and 'interesting/unusual pieces'. 'The Victorian clutter might not be to everyone's taste, but we could not fault the place.' One word of warning: 'Not for the disabled or very tall.' Dinner ('delicious and beautifully served') is taken in four rooms dotted around the house. The menu, displayed on gilt-framed blackboards, is read aloud with aplomb by Robert Culyer. Typical dishes: lobster bisque; baked halibut with herb crust and champagne sauce. There is a separate vegetarian menu. Breakfast, 'a treat', has freshly squeezed juice, croissants, and scrambled eggs with smoked salmon and wild mushrooms. (*P and JL, and others*)

5 bedrooms. Central; corner of St George's St and Colegate. Closed Christmas. Restaurant closed midday, Sun/Mon evenings. 2 lounges, restaurant (jazz/classical background music at night; occasional live music). Unsuitable for &. No smoking: restaurant, bedrooms. No children under 12. No dogs. MasterCard, Visa accepted. B&B £55–£70 per person. Full alc £41.

See also SHORTLIST

NOTTINGHAM Nottinghamshire

Map 2:A3

 Hart's Hotel
Standard Hill, Park Row
Nottingham NG1 6FN

Tel 0115-988 1900
Fax 0115-947 7600
Email ask@hartsnottingham.co.uk
Website www.hartshotel.co.uk

César award: City hotel of the year

'First-class service, comfortable bedroom, efficient bathroom.' 'Impeccable reception.' 'All is well thought out.' This year's praise for Tim Hart's purpose-built designer hotel (curved buttresses, lots of glass, limestone floors) in a traffic-free cul-de-sac on the site of Nottingham's medieval castle. Paul Fearon is manager. Five minutes' walk from the city centre, it has a small terrace and private car park on one side, and a secluded garden (residents only) on the other. There are 'breathtaking views' over ramparts to the university and rolling hills beyond. The 'crisp, bright' *Park Bar*, that faces the car park, serves wines and champagne by the glass, 'interesting snacks' all day, and breakfast: 'Good orange juice; buffet with cereals, cooked eggs, etc; boring toast. Attentive young Eastern European waitresses.' Twenty-four bedrooms have a view; the six garden rooms have a private terrace. All rooms have Internet access, voicemail, large TV, etc. 'Our superior double was medium-sized. Duvet promptly replaced by conventional bedding at our request. Excellent information pack.' Booking is necessary for the adjacent 'glamorous' restaurant, *Hart's*, in the former radiology department of Nottingham's general hospital. 'Very good indeed; gazpacho; turbot; passion fruit sorbet.' 'Wonderful bread. A happy atmosphere.' A pre-theatre supper is offered from 6 pm. (*ML Legg, and others*)

32 bedrooms. 2 suitable for &. City centre. Restaurant closed 26 Dec and 1 Jan. Lift, ramps. Reception/lobby, bar (background music), restaurant (30 yds); conference/banqueting facilities; small exercise room. Small garden. Civil wedding licence. No smoking: restaurant, bedrooms. No dogs in public rooms, or unaccompanied in bedrooms. Amex, MasterCard, Visa accepted. Room: £120–£250. Breakfast £8.50–£13.50. Set lunch £15.95, dinner (Sun–Thurs) £21; full alc £40. ***V***

Lace Market Hotel
29–31 High Pavement
Nottingham NG1 1HE

Tel 0115-852 3232
Fax 0115-852 3223
Email stay@lacemarkethotel.co.uk
Website www.lacemarkethotel.co.uk

Facing the former Georgian law courts and the 14th-century church of St Mary the Virgin, four Georgian and Victorian town houses (one a former lace factory) have been turned into this modern, 'relatively reasonably priced' hotel. Its manager is Mark Cox. The bedrooms have a smart, minimalist decor: strong colours and contemporary furniture. All have air conditioning, DVD-player and wireless broadband. 'Superior' rooms are spacious. One couple was pleased to be upgraded to a spit-level studio suite with fine views through huge sash windows. But one reader wrote: 'There is too great an emphasis on show rather than substance, and no amount of clever mirrors can disguise how tiny some of the single rooms are.' The 'classic bistro', *Merchants* (booking recommended), serves brunch all day on Sunday, and on weekdays a good brasserie menu. The hotel's 'gastropub', the *Cock and Hoop*, serves a short menu of salads, burgers, steak, etc. At breakfast the buffet has fresh orange juice, good pastries, 'delicious, treacly compotes'; 'mercifully no sign of butter in foil or sugar in paper wrapping'. Room service is 'prompt and accurate'. A warning: 'The discount arrangement with the local car park becomes invalid after 24 hours.' More reports, please.

42 bedrooms. City centre, opposite Galleries of Justice. Lift. Bar, brasserie, gastropub; background music; lounge; private dining room; boardroom. Free use of nearby health club. Civil wedding licence. Unsuitable for &. No smoking. No dogs in public rooms except gastropub (£15 a night in bedroom). All major credit cards accepted. Room [2006]: single £79–£90, double £99–£139, suite £150–£239. Breakfast £12.95. Set lunch £14.95, dinner £29.50; full alc from £35. 1-night bookings sometimes refused.

ORFORD Suffolk   Map 2:C6

The Crown and Castle   *Tel* 01394-450205
Orford, nr Woodbridge   *Email* info@crownandcastle.co.uk
IP12 2LJ   *Website* www.crownandcastle.co.uk

16th-century in origin, but much altered in 1896, this red brick inn is 'exquisitely set' in a peaceful Suffolk village. Its owners, Ruth and David Watson, say they 'try to maintain the balance between modern facilities and good old-fashioned hospitality'. Praise this year: 'A very good welcome.' 'Staff kind and attentive.' 'Food well prepared and pleasant; rich but they will cook dishes more simply.' The large bar lounge has a big chrome bar and designer tables and chairs. In the *Trinity* restaurant, Ruth Watson, a well-known cookery writer, and Max Dougal have a *Michelin Bib Gourmand* for dishes based on seasonal produce. The wine list is 'informative and unstuffy'. Light meals are available, taken on the terrace in summer. Packed lunches can be provided. Bedrooms, 'stylish, well equipped', are in the main house and the garden. The latter are spacious, decorated in cool stone and beige; each has its own small terrace. 'Ours had good lighting and a first-class bathroom.' Breakfast was 'very good; lovely home-made jam'. Dogs, allowed in some garden rooms, get 'a welcoming bag of organic biscuits'. Children are welcomed, 'but in limited numbers, and not in *Trinity* at dinner'. (*Jennifer Davis, Kathleen Craddock, and others*)

18 bedrooms. 10 (all on ground floor) in garden. 1 in courtyard. Market square. Closed 19–26 Dec. Lounge/bar, restaurant; private dining room. No background music. ½-acre garden. Unsuitable for &. Smoking in bar only. No children under 9 in restaurant at night. No dogs in restaurant. MasterCard, Visa accepted. B&B [2006] £45–£145 per person; D,B&B £60–£180. Full alc £35–£45. New Year package. 1-night bookings refused Sat.

OXFORD Oxfordshire   Map 2:C2

Old Bank   *Tel* 01865-799599
92–94 High Street   *Fax* 01865-799598
Oxford OX1 4BN   *Email* info@oldbank-hotel.co.uk
                                            Website www.oldbank-hotel.co.uk

In a 'marvellous' central position opposite All Souls and St Mary's church,
this elegant conversion of three buildings, one a former bank, is owned by
Jeremy Mogford (see also *Old Parsonage*, next entry). The manager and
chef, Jenny McKeever and Mark Foreman, are new this year. 'Dinner was
good, apart from the cheese. Very friendly service,' say visitors in 2006.
The bedrooms are 'stylish', modern, 'with many extras and nice bathroom'.
An earlier comment: 'Our first-floor room (the cheapest) faced St Mary's.
Efficient double glazing.' A rear room was 'quiet, tasteful, comfortable'. A
collection of contemporary art is displayed throughout: original Stanley
Spencer prints in some bedrooms, large oil paintings in public areas. The
old banking hall houses *Quod*, a lively bar/restaurant, busy from 7 am until
11.30 pm. It serves an 'express lunch', and a new, modern evening menu.
With stone floors, wooden tables (close together), and a zinc-topped bar,
it is a youthful place, popular with students and their parents, but some
guests find the background music intrusive. The 'excellent breakfast' has
fresh fruit salad, freshly squeezed orange juice, cereals, 'great coffee; loads
of bacon and big sausages in the unhealthy version'. (*Michael and Eithne
Dandy, and others*)

42 bedrooms. 1 equipped for &. Air conditioning. Central (windows facing High St
double glazed). Access to rear car park. Closed 24–26 Dec. Lift. Residents' lounge/
bar, bar/grill; 'easy listening' music; dining terrace; 2 meeting/private dining rooms;
conference centre planned. Small garden. No smoking in bedrooms. Guide dogs
only. All major credit cards accepted. Room: single £155–£225, double £170–£245,
suite £255–£330. Breakfast £10–£14. Full alc £30.

Old Parsonage   *Tel* 01865-310210
1 Banbury Road   *Fax* 01865-311262
Oxford OX2 6NN   *Email* info@oldparsonage-hotel.co.uk
                                         Website www.oldparsonage-hotel.co.uk

'Delightful building and ambience. Wonderful location.' Jeremy
Mogford's wisteria-covered 17th-century hotel beside St Giles church is
a popular meeting place for town and gown. The massive front door
opens into a bar/restaurant (redecorated this year) where a log fire burns,
even in summer. Two endorsements came in 2006, with minor

reservations. 'Very friendly staff. My spacious, light and well-appointed room in the old building was above the bar; we could hear the music from below.' A ground-floor room was 'characterful and comfortable, more spacious than some of the rooms on the first floor', says a returning visitor. Earlier an inspector reported that a room off the corridor around the roof terrace was 'small, dark, but well furnished with a sublimely comfortable bed; excellent compact bathroom'. Mark Bristow is the new chef, serving an all-day menu: 'Excellent. Delicious cheese soufflé with walnut salad; perfectly cooked scallops. Service was attentive, efficient.' 'Beautifully cooked and presented, though lack of choice might be a problem on longer stays.' (Mr Mogford's restaurant in a Victorian conservatory, *Gee's*, is a five-minute walk away.) Breakfast is no longer a buffet: a continental basket disappointed, but the cooked breakfast was 'full and satisfying'. In fine weather you can take tea in the walled garden. (*Sue Hamilton, Dr Margaret Mallett*)

30 bedrooms. Some on ground floor. NE end of St Giles. Some traffic noise; windows double glazed. Small car park. Lounge, bar/restaurant (background music). Terrace (live jazz Fri). Roof garden, small walled garden. Unsuitable for &. Civil wedding licence. No smoking: restaurant, bedrooms. No dogs in restaurant. All major credit cards accepted. Room [2006]: single £135–£150, double £165–£205, suite £225–£250. Breakfast £8.50–£12.50. Full alc £30. Christmas/New Year packages.

See also SHORTLIST

PADSTOW Cornwall   Map 1:D2

The Seafood Restaurant
Riverside
Padstow PL28 8BY

Tel 01841-532700
Fax 01841-532942
Email reservations@rickstein.com
Website www.rickstein.com

♛ *César award in 1995*

Celebrity chef Rick Stein and his wife, Jill, offer a multiplicity of places for eating and sleeping in this north Cornish port. Meals are served in their waterfront flagship *Seafood Restaurant* (main courses like monkfish vindaloo; casserole of brill with caramelised shallots, ham, garlic and wild mushrooms); *St Petroc's Bistro* (steak-frites; cod and spring onion mash with a soy butter sauce); a café and a fish-and-chip shop. In January 2006, David Sharland joined as the new executive chef. There are four places to stay: above the restaurant (some 'first-class' bedrooms; two have a balcony); *St Edmund's House*, with its showcase rooms; *St Petroc's House*, one of Padstow's oldest buildings (it has a 'pleasant sitting room and library'); the *Middle Street Café* (the cheapest). Mrs Stein has designed the bedrooms: priced according to size and view. They vary greatly. 'Ours, light and airy, had wide-screen TV, well-designed bathroom, magnificent view if you ignored the municipal car park.' Breakfast has freshly squeezed grapefruit juice, home-made yogurts and jams; 'very good full English, also fish'. Rick Stein may not be around all the time, but manager Rupert Wilson leads a 'friendly, efficient' staff. 'Our little dog was made welcome.' (*JH, CP*)

34 bedrooms. In 4 buildings. *Seafood Restaurant* on harbour; other buildings nearby. Closed 24–26 Dec, 1 May. *Seafood*: conservatory bar, restaurant. *St Petroc's*: lounge, reading room, bar, bistro. Café. Background music at lunch: bistro and café. Unsuitable for &. No smoking: bedrooms, café and bistro. No dogs in *St Edmund's House*. MasterCard, Visa accepted. B&B £45–£125 per person; D,B&B (min. 2 nights, off-season) £70–£150. *Restaurant* tasting menu £65; full alc £60; *St Petroc's Bistro* full alc £40; café full alc £30. 1-night bookings refused Sat.

See also SHORTLIST

PENRITH Cumbria *See SHORTLIST*   Map 4: inset C2

****

Traveller's tale This hotel was musty, shabby and grossly over-priced. Other guests were Japanese or American, ie transient and unlikely to be repeat business. The dinner menu was unchanged over two nights and portions were minute. On two occasions the tea was undrinkable: it seemed to be made from tea dust rather than leaves. The rooms were grubby, with filthy grouting in the bathrooms and cracked panes of glass. The water was warm rather than hot. Reception was staffed by an incompetent member of staff who could not operate the printer so we got a half-legible bill, which he seemed to think perfectly acceptable. (*Hotel in Oxfordshire*)

****

PENZANCE Cornwall   Map 1:E1

The Abbey Hotel   *Tel* 01736-366906
Abbey Street   *Fax* 01736-351163
Penzance TR18 4AR   *Email* hotel@theabbeyonline.com
                               Website www.theabbeyonline.com

High above the harbour, in a narrow street overlooking Mount's Bay,
Michael and Jean Cox's small hotel, now managed by Letitia Hughes, is a
listed mid-17th century building: 'Its contents are fascinating and the
architecture is entrancing,' one visitor wrote (but for the price, he would
have liked a key to his bedroom, and a phone). 'Our bedroom was
charming, with a spectacular view,' was another comment. There are
'gorgeous fabrics and colour schemes, chintz sofas and chairs, elegant Greek
statues, magnificent antiques, curios, fresh flower arrangements, etc'. The
lounge faces the pretty Victorian garden, as do some bedrooms (others face
the harbour). Attic rooms may be 'cramped'. The Coxes no longer own the
Abbey Restaurant next door, and at the time of writing the hotel has no chef,
so only breakfast is served. More reports, please.

6 bedrooms. 300 yds from centre. Parking. Closed Christmas. Drawing room, dining
room. No background music. Small garden. Unsuitable for &. No smoking: dining
room, bedrooms. No dogs in public rooms. Amex, MasterCard, Visa accepted. B&B
[2006] £50–£95 per person. 1-night bookings refused bank holidays. ***V***

Mount Prospect Hotel   *Tel* 01736-363117
Britons Hill   *Fax* 01736-350970
Penzance TR18 3AE   *Email* enquiries@hotelpenzance.com
                             Website www.hotelpenzance.com

In a quiet residential area near the harbour, Yvonne and Stephen Hill's
'very pleasant small hotel' looks over Mount's Bay to St Michael's Mount.
Eighteen of its bedrooms enjoy this view, so does the attractive
Bay Restaurant (with modern decor, sliding glass doors, well-spaced tables,
local artwork and a bar), which is popular with outside diners. The cooking
of Ben Reeve is thought 'excellent' (dishes like grilled sea bass with oyster
mushrooms and a crabmeat, mango and chilli salsa), and 'there is a good
atmosphere throughout', says a recent visitor. Others wrote: 'Our excellent
bedroom had beautiful views. The furnishings were very good, the
bathroom was well fitted.' 'Attractive curtains and bedspreads in bright
modern colours.' 'Staff are friendly' (the manager is Andrew Griffiths). In
the small subtropical garden there is a heated swimming pool. The heliport
to the Isles of Scilly is five minutes' drive away. (*RC, and others*)

24 bedrooms. 2 on ground floor. 10 mins' walk from train/bus station, off Cnyandour Cliff. Ramps. 2 lounges, conservatory, bar/restaurant ('easy listening' music morning and evening). ½-acre garden: terrace, heated swimming pool (30 by 15 ft). Rock beach, safe bathing nearby. Smoking in lounge and conservatory only. No dogs in restaurant. All major credit cards accepted (*2.5% surcharge on Amex*). B&B £53–£74 per person; D,B&B £61–£94. Full alc £40. Christmas/New Year packages. **ᵛᵛ·**

PERRANUTHNOE Cornwall   Map 1:E1

Ednovean Farm   *Tel* 01736-711883
Perranuthnoe, nr Penzance   *Email* info@ednoveanfarm.co.uk
TR20 9LZ   *Website* www.ednoveanfarm.co.uk

'Very civilised', Christine and Charles Taylor's B&B is a converted barn below the brow of a hill in a quiet village above Mount's Bay. Reached along a bumpy track, it has a slate-flagged hall and ancient granite walls. The 'romantic' Pink Bedroom, with four-poster and large *en suite* bathroom (roll-top bath in the middle), was recently liked: 'Candles everywhere, bathrobes and aromatherapy oils. Great views of St Michael's Mount.' The two other rooms are in a separate wing; each has a private sea-facing terrace. Each room has a DVD-player, and there is a collection of DVDs for guests to choose from. Breakfast, at an oak refectory table in the beamed open-plan kitchen/dining room, includes muesli, stewed fruits, local breads, full English 'cooked in front of you'. Classical music plays, and husband and wife 'are supervised by a cat'. Guests are given tea on arrival, and are offered complimentary sherry at night, in the lounge, which has squashy sofas and embroidered silk wall hangings. In summer, you can sit in the Garden Room (its terrace has sea views). In the grounds are secluded corners, statues, an Italian garden, horses and chickens. A sandy beach is nearby. (*EM*)

3 bedrooms. 6 miles E of Penzance. Local bus 5 times a day. Closed Christmas/New Year, occasional other times. Lounge, garden room, breakfast room (background music). 1-acre garden. Unsuitable for ♿. No smoking. No children under 16. No dogs. Amex, MasterCard, Visa accepted. B&B £37.50–£100 per person. 1-night bookings sometimes refused.

We drop a hotel if there has been a change of owner, if this year's reports are negative or in rare cases where there has been no feedback. About 80 hotels fall by the wayside every year, and a similar number are introduced.

PETWORTH West Sussex   Map 2:E3

The Old Railway Station   *Tel* 01798-342346
Petworth GU28 0JF   *Fax* 01798-343066
                                           Email info@old-station.co.uk
                                           Website www.old-station.co.uk

Gudmund Olafsson (Icelandic) and Kate Stormont took over this unusual
B&B in October 2005. The old cream-and-white, Grade II* listed former
Victorian railway station has been restored with flair. The former waiting
room has a 20-foot vaulted ceiling, the original ticket office windows,
cream-and-gold-striped settees and an open fire in winter. Large windows
create 'a colonial feel'. The 'excellent' breakfast ('fresh fruit salad, scrambled
eggs, delicious bacon') is taken here, in the bedroom or, in summer, on the
station platform (where drinks are also served). Waitresses wear modified
railway steward's uniform. The biggest rooms (one up a spiral staircase) are
in the station building. Most rooms are in Pullman cars: narrow and small,
but, said inspectors, 'beautifully restored, well designed, with a particularly
comfortable bed and a surprising amount of furniture'. Menus of local
eating places are in the information folders: the *Lickfold Arms*, a gastropub
at Lickfold, was liked this year. The pretty garden has ancient trees, a
sunken lawn where the railtracks were, and steep banks covered with
shrubs. The main road to Chichester is close, 'but in our carriage we
weren't too bothered by traffic noise; in the morning we heard birdsong'.

8 bedrooms. 6 in Pullman carriages. 1 equipped for &. 1½ miles S of Petworth. Car
park. Train: Pulborough. Closed 3 days Christmas, possibly New Year. Lounge/bar/
breakfast room (background music). 2-acre garden: platform/terrace, tunnel.
Smoking on platform only. No children under 10. No dogs. Amex, MasterCard, Visa
accepted. B&B double £66–£148. 1-night bookings refused weekends, holidays.

* *

> **Traveller's tale** On being shown to our room, we discovered
> that the heating was not working. Reception told us: 'Oh yes, we
> were aware of that. The engineer came this morning and told us
> it was fixed.' Two hours later, on one of the coldest days of the
> year, the receptionist gave us an electric heater. On the morning
> of our departure, the heating was not working again, and we were
> told that the thermostat had been turned down. The manager was
> not available when we checked out, so I emailed him when we
> arrived home. He apologised and said he hoped we had enjoyed
> our stay. (*Hotel in Gloucestershire*)

* *

PICKERING North Yorkshire   Map 4:D4

The White Swan Inn   *Tel* 01751-472288
Market Place   *Fax* 01751-475554
Pickering YO18 7AA   *Email* welcome@white-swan.co.uk
                                  Website www.white-swan.co.uk

Owned by Victor Buchanan, this former coaching inn is halfway up the hill
in this 'characterful' market town in the North Yorkshire moors. Jim Fisher
is manager. 'We do like this place,' say visitors this year who, despite a
booking muddle, 'will definitely return'. The lack of background music is
a plus point. 'The staff are genuine and friendly. A decent room and
bathroom.' The bedrooms, mostly smallish, are done in white, ochre and
beige; all have TV and DVD-player. 'Interesting pieces of furniture' (a
walnut four-poster in one room, a George III mahogany side table in
another). 'The new rooms are very good, and free of traffic noise.' 'An
excellent pint and an inexpensive dinner.' In the candlelit restaurant
(flagstones, open fire, low ceiling, Gothic screens), Darren Clemmit's
'country cooking' uses meat from the nearby Ginger Pig, national food
producer of the year. Main courses include Toulouse sausage casserole;
belly pork with red cabbage. A note on the menu reads: 'If you are not fully
satisfied with your dish, let us know immediately. We will replace it or
refund your money.' The cooked breakfast was 'fine, served promptly, with
a smile'. (*Roger Down, Conrad Barnard, and others*)

21 bedrooms. 9 in annexe. Central. Ramps to ground-floor facilities. Lounge, snug,
2 bars (1 residents), restaurant; private dining room. No background music. 1½-acre
grounds. Small terrace (alfresco meals). Civil wedding licence. Smoking in bar
only. No dogs in restaurant. Amex, MasterCard, Visa accepted. B&B [2006]
£69.50–£129 per person; D,B&B £89.50–£159. Weekend single night supplement
£25. Full alc £35. Christmas/New Year packages. 1-night bookings sometimes
refused weekends. *V*

PICKHILL North Yorkshire   Map 4:C4

The Nag's Head   BUDGET   *Tel* 01845-567391
Pickhill, nr Thirsk   *Fax* 01845-567212
YO7 4JG   *Email* enquiries@nagsheadpickhill.co.uk
                       Website www.nagsheadpickhill.co.uk

The Boynton family have for 30 years owned this busy country inn,
popular with the racing fraternity, in this Domesday-old village in Herriot
country. Edward and Janet Boynton, 'welcoming owners', are now in
charge; the service is 'helpful'. 'Remarkable value for money; a very quiet

place – the village is a dead end,' says a returning visitor this year. 'Small and relatively basic, but very adequate for a short stay.' The bedrooms are comfortable and 'sensibly equipped'. 'We enjoyed a delicious dinner from a menu with a wide choice. For breakfast my large fillet of haddock with poached egg was truly memorable.' (*Sir John Hall*)

14 bedrooms. 7 in annexe. Some on ground floor. 5 miles SE of Leeming, 1 mile E of A1. Closed Christmas Day. Ramps. 2 bars, restaurant (background music). Lawn: croquet, putting. No smoking: restaurant, bedrooms. No dogs in public rooms. MasterCard, Visa accepted. B&B £37.50–£55 per person. Full alc £30. New Year package.

PLYMOUTH Devon *See SHORTLIST*   Map 1:D4

POOLE Dorset *See SHORTLIST*   Map 2:E1

PORLOCK Somerset   Map 1:B5

The Oaks   *Tel* 01643-862265
Porlock TA24 8ES   *Fax* 01643-863131
Email info@oakshotel.co.uk
Website www.oakshotel.co.uk

In an elevated position on the northern edge of Exmoor, with 'great views of the Bristol Channel', this gabled Edwardian country house stands in pretty gardens with wide lawns and oak trees. It is now a small hotel managed by its owners, Tim (a classic car enthusiast) and Anne Riley. Guests returning for their fourth visit in three years write: 'We were welcomed by Anne like long-lost friends. Coffee and shortcake were brought to our room.' Other visitors add: 'An exceptionally quiet hotel. An excellent dinner.' 'There were young guests while we were there. It's reassuring that the hotel is not just for older people.' The bedrooms are 'spotless'. 'Bedlinen is smooth and fresh, towels are thick and huge.' The main lounge has an open fire, oil paintings and prints. The spacious dining room has panoramic views of the village and Exmoor (sunsets are spectacular). The hostess's cooking is admired: 'She has the lightest touch and uses the freshest ingredients.' 'Cornish lemon sole was outstanding. Breakfast also outstanding.' 'The atmosphere is unhurried.' One warning: 'The hotel's entrance is at a sharp angle of the main road.' (*David Sulkin, Ken and Mildred Edwards, DT*)

8 bedrooms. ¼ mile from village. Open Apr–Nov, Christmas/New Year. 2 lounges, bar, restaurant (classical background music at night). 1-acre garden. Sea, pebble beach 1 mile. Unsuitable for &. No smoking. No children under 8. No dogs. Diners, MasterCard, Visa accepted. **Terms** B&B £60–£85 per person; D,B&B (min. 2 nights) £90–£115. Set dinner £32.50. Christmas/New Year packages. **ᵛVᵛ**

PORLOCK WEIR Somerset   Map 1:B4

The Anchor Hotel & Ship Inn
Porlock Weir, nr Minehead
TA24 8PB

Tel 01643-862753
Fax 01643-862843
Email info@theanchorhotelandshipinn.co.uk
Website www.theanchorhotelandshipinn.co.uk

In a lovely seaside village, Harvey and Lynette Allen's hotel and adjacent 16th-century inn have 'fantastic views' over the harbour and the Bristol Channel. 'The welcome was warm, the headwaiter's service was impeccable and the food was good,' said recent visitors. Premier rooms (one has a four-poster) are on the hotel's first floor, with views across the harbour, and also over the Mariners' Bar. The blue-walled lounge has subdued lighting and comfortable chairs. In the *à la carte Harbourside Restaurant*, head chef Kevin Webber cooks in 'traditional English style': main courses might include roast topside of beef or grilled whole trout. The inn, with its open fire, provides pub food and locally brewed ales, and the tea room serves home-made scones and cakes. Functions of all sorts are held, so if you need peace and quiet, you should check the position when booking. (*M and JC*)

17 bedrooms. 4 in *Ship Inn*. Opposite harbour. 2 lounges, 2 restaurants, cocktail bar, tea room, pub; function/conference facilities; varied background music all day. Unsuitable for &. Civil wedding licence. No smoking: restaurant, bedrooms, most public rooms. No dogs in public rooms. Amex, MasterCard, Visa accepted. B&B £39–£78 per person; D,B&B £63–£108. Set menu £22.75–£29.75; full alc £50. Christmas/New Year packages. 1-night bookings refused weekends in season, bank holidays.

Porlock Vale House
Porlock Weir TA24 8NY

Tel/Fax 01643-862338
Email info@porlockvale.co.uk
Website www.porlockvale.co.uk

Q *César award in 2006*

A visitor this year 'enjoyed everything about this hotel' so much that she stayed two extra days. It is well known in equestrian circles, and offers instruction and escorted riding, but non-horsy visitors come for 'relaxation and comfort'. In a fold of ancient oak woodland on the lower slopes of

Exmoor, it stands in large grounds that stretch down to the sea. The owners, Helen and Kim Youd, are 'hospitality personified', but when they were away 'the hotel ran like clockwork, with helpful, charming staff; the atmosphere was friendly yet very professional'. The public rooms have a 'hunting-lodge atmosphere': dark wood panelling and floors, open fires. 'Generous lounges: lots of comfortable seating.' Most public rooms, and some bedrooms, look over the Bristol Channel to South Wales. The Youds tell us that they have updated several old-fashioned rooms in a lighter style: while avoiding 'minimalist modernity', they 'don't want to be left in a chintz time warp'. 'Our room, spacious, spotless, had a magnificent outlook.' Dinner choices are made by 6 pm (two or three courses), and the cooking is thought 'homely', 'excellent and varied' (eg, roast lamb with herb crust; braised belly of pork). 'First-class breakfasts.' (*Jennifer Davis, and others*)

15 bedrooms. 1 mile from Porlock Weir. Closed Christmas, midweek sometimes in winter. Restaurant closed Mon. 3 lounges, bar, dining room; meeting room. No background music. 25-acre grounds leading to sea: gardens, riding stables. Only public rooms accessible for &. Smoking in 1 lounge only. No children under 10. No dogs in house (kennels available). Amex, MasterCard, Visa accepted. B&B £42.50–£85 per person. Set dinner £28.50. New Year package. 1-night bookings sometimes refused weekends.

PORT ISAAC Cornwall   Map 1:D2

Port Gaverne Hotel
Port Gaverne
nr Port Isaac
PL29 3SQ

Tel 01208-880244
Freephone 0500 657867
Fax 01208-880151
Website www.portgaverne.co.uk

Dogs and children are welcomed by Graham and Annabelle Sylvester at their 'classic inn' on a quiet cove north of the busy fishing village of Port Isaac. An unpretentious place, it has 'bags of character' and a lovely setting, looking across the tiny port to the sea. The bar, with its slate floors, wooden beams, local art work (for sale) and log fire, is popular with locals, and serves good food off a blackboard menu. Steep staircases lead to the bedrooms. 'Ours had corn-coloured walls, floral curtains, large leather bedhead; good lighting and lots of storage; a modern bathroom with plenty of hot water, good towels.' But sound insulation may not always be perfect. A visitor this year praised chef Ian Brodey's daily-changing three-course dinner menu (plenty of choice). 'Sublime grilled lobster, haddock; vegetables varied and delicious'; 'good choice of house wines, a jug of water on the table'. Breakfast has a buffet for cereals, packaged juices; good cooked dishes brought to the table; good marmalade, pats of butter. (*Jonathan Mirsky, Kathleen Craddock, and others*)

15 bedrooms. ½ mile N of Port Isaac. Closed Christmas. Restaurant closed 3–31 Jan. Lounge, 2 bars, restaurant. No background music. Beer garden. Rock cove 60 yds; golf, fishing, surfing, sailing, riding nearby. Unsuitable for ♿. No smoking: restaurant, bedrooms. No children under 10 in restaurant at night (room service available). No dogs in eating areas. MasterCard, Visa accepted. B&B £40–£60 per person. Set dinner £27. New Year package.

PORTSCATHO Cornwall   Map 1:E2

driftwood hotel	*Tel* 01872-580644
Rosevine	*Fax* 01872-580801
nr Portscatho TR2 5EW	*Email* info@driftwoodhotel.co.uk
	Website www.driftwoodhotel.co.uk

Sea views, a private beach, and a 'marvellous position' above a quiet cove in the beautiful Roseland peninsula are among the attractions of this 'delightful' hotel. Owners Paul and Fiona Robinson 'were both so nice', say visitors this year, and 'we were relaxed, happy and very well cared for by the pleasant staff'. The contemporary design and interior decoration, with 'simple white background and various shades of blue', were admired by a long-standing *Guide* reporter. There are rugs on bare floorboards, driftwood table lamps and mirrors. Public rooms are 'well thought-out and pleasant', and there was 'always a log fire in the drawing room'. Blue-cushioned sunbeds stand on a panoramic terrace. Steep steps through woodland lead down to the beach. The view is enjoyed from most of the bedrooms. The two-roomed Cabin on the hillside (with sitting room and kitchenette) is thought 'tremendous fun'. In the 'lovely' dining room, chef Rory Duncan serves 'very good' modern European dishes, on a rolling menu (eg, venison loin with confit beetroot and savoy cabbage). 'Breakfasts were lavish and of high quality.' The Eden Project and the Heligan Gardens are within a half-hour drive. (*Eve Webb, M and BH, Tessa Spanton*)

15 bedrooms. 4 in courtyard. Also 2 in beach cabin (2 mins' walk). N side of Portscatho. Closed Christmas, Jan. 2 lounges, bar, restaurant (background jazz/classical music at night); children's games room. 7-acre grounds: terraced gardens, private beach, safe bathing. Unsuitable for ♿. No smoking. No dogs. Amex, MasterCard, Visa accepted. B&B £105–£157.50 per person; D,B&B (Nov–Mar) £85–£127.50. Set menu £38. 1-night bookings refused weekends.

The more reports we receive, the more accurate the *Guide* becomes. Please don't hesitate to write again about an old favourite. New reports help us keep the *Guide* up to date and bring our entries to life.

Rosevine Hotel
Porthcurnick Beach, Rosevine
nr Portscatho TR2 5EW

Tel 01872-580206
Fax 01872-580230
Email info@rosevine.co.uk
Website www.rosevine.co.uk

'Why go abroad when there's a spot like this?' asks a fan of this traditional child-friendly hotel down a narrow road above a cove on the Roseland peninsula. Caroline Davidson (*née* Makepeace), whose brother owns the *Soar Mill Cove Hotel, S*oar Mill Cove (*qv*), near Salcombe, is now owner with her husband, Chris. Other praise this year: 'The staff were friendly, the service was good, as was the food.' 'We were warmly welcomed by receptionist Linda, who took us to our room and offered a complimentary cream tea.' This year, superior bedrooms have been refurbished: some have a balcony overlooking the south-facing semi-tropical garden. 'Ours was pleasantly furnished, and had a good-sized bathroom. Everything worked fine, although the TV was rather old.' In the high-ceilinged former ballroom, a team of chefs, headed by Didier Bienaimé, serves food with a 'strong West Country influence', eg, rack of Cornish lamb with rosemary and garlic. 'The vegetarian menu was outstanding.' Meals are served on a patio in fine weather. Menus are left in bedrooms in the afternoon; guests order by telephone. There is an 'adequate' swimming pool, a new spa bath and a children's paddling pool. Close by is flat, safe Porthcurnick beach. (*Brian Moate, Judy Waller, and others*)

17 bedrooms. 6 in annexe across courtyard. Some on ground floor. Off A3078, N side of Portscatho. Open 26 Jan–27 Dec. Lounge, sun lounge, bar, restaurant (pianist 2 nights a week); games room, children's playroom; indoor swimming pool; laundry, drying room. 3-acre gardens: alfresco dining. Unsuitable for &. Smoking in bar only. No dogs in public rooms. Amex, MasterCard, Visa accepted. B&B [2006] £86–£145 per person; D,B&B £124–£183. Set dinner £38; full alc £49. Christmas package. **•V•**

POSTBRIDGE Devon   Map 1:D4

Lydgate House
Postbridge, Dartmoor
PL20 6TJ

Tel 01822-880209
Fax 01822-880202
Email lydgatehouse@email.com
Website www.lydgatehouse.co.uk

'In the middle of nowhere', Peter and Cindy Farrington's unassuming Victorian country house is near the village's famous clapper bridge over the River Dart. 'The most relaxing place I know other than my sailing boat and that's saying something,' writes this year's reporter. 'We go often and always make friends with the other guests.' An earlier visitor said: 'At last, I have found that long-sought-after bolthole.' The Farringtons are 'civilised owners', who give a 'warm welcome'; they have five 'charming' cats, five dogs (not indoors) and four elderly sheep. There are superb views from the sitting room, the conservatory dining room, and most bedrooms. Two rooms have a small sitting room, and two have a sitting area; they are 'quiet, comfortable, spotless, with excellent beds and bedding; charming unpretentious furnishings'. Meals and cream teas are served to residents only. Guests choose, by about 6.30 pm, from a daily-changing menu of 'simple modern dishes': 'Excellent, unfussy food.' Breakfast has a wide choice of fruits and cereals from a central table; tasty cooked dishes. There is good walking from the door. 'Well-behaved' dogs are welcomed, but not children. (*Hugh Read, AH*)

7 bedrooms. 500 yds off B3212. In winter, open weekends only. Dining room closed to non-residents. Lounge with bar, snug, dining room; classical background music at breakfast. Terrace. 36-acre grounds: moorland, paddock, river (private access for guests; fishing, swimming). Unsuitable for &. No smoking. No children under 16. MasterCard, Visa accepted. B&B £50–£60 per person. Set dinner £28.50; full alc £32. 3-night rates. Christmas package.

PRESTBURY Cheshire   Map 3:A5

White House Manor	*Tel* 01625-829376
New Road	*Fax* 01625-828627
Prestbury SK10 4HP	*Email* info@thewhitehouse.uk.com
	Website www.thewhitehouse.uk.com

Noted for its unusual themed bedrooms, Ryland and Judith Wakeham's renovated manor house is on the edge of this affluent commuter village near Manchester. The recently redecorated Crystal Room 'is the one to ask for', say visitors in 2006. It has a chandelier, a locally crafted four-poster bed, a window seat, and a hydrotherapy bath. The Millennium suite has a bed mounted on glass bricks, with lights underneath; 'there were home-made chocolates, fruit, a hidden TV and CD-player; lots of CDs. Silver lacquer was everywhere. The bathroom had stainless steel floor, loo and basin, and there was a refreshing Turkish steam shower.' Earl Grey has dressers 'laden with fine English bone china'; Trafalgar has burgundy drapes, gold braid and a collection of naval artefacts. 'Continental breakfast, served in the room, was good croissants and muffins wrapped in a napkin.' Cooked breakfasts, including a 'full Cheshire', may be taken in the bedroom, a conservatory, or on a patio. Details are provided of the five eating places in the village, including the *White House* restaurant, though this is no longer owned by the Wakehams. (*Elspeth Jervie and John Gibbon, EM*)

11 bedrooms. 1 in coach house annexe. Edge of village on A538. Closed Christmas. Lounge, conservatory with honesty bar, breakfast room; function facilities. No background music. ½-acre garden. Patio. Unsuitable for &. Smoking in lounge only. No children under 10. No dogs. Amex, MasterCard, Visa accepted. Room: single £45–£75, double £100–£140. Breakfast £6.50–£9.50.

PURTON Wiltshire   Map 3:E5

The Pear Tree at Purton	*Tel* 01793-772100
Church End	*Fax* 01793-772369
Purton, nr Swindon SN5 4ED	*Email* stay@peartreepurton.co.uk
	Website www.peartreepurton.co.uk

'The buildings, garden with pleasant walks and quiet location are the highlights of Francis and Anne Young's Cotswold stone hotel (Pride of Britain),' say visitors this year. Once a vicarage, it is on the edge of a Saxon village in the Vale of the White Horse. The fireplace in the library dates back to 1430. Public rooms are 'open and rather busy, probably aimed at business people', but 'the receptionists were very friendly'. In the bedrooms (each named after a village character), fresh flowers match the colour scheme, and fruit, sweets and biscuits are provided (and replenished). Bathrooms are 'impeccable'; many have a spa bath. 'Our lovely room had a view of the gardens.' One spacious ground-floor room has a private courtyard. Comments on the dinners, served in the candlelit green-and-white conservatory restaurant, vary: 'Beautifully presented; tasted great.' 'Rather fussy.' 'Our request for a small pudding was turned down because "they are all the same size". But we would be happy to stay there again.' 'Breakfast (no buffet, hurrah) was one of the best we've had.' Purton's old church is worth a visit. (*Robin and Heather Harrison, Rachel Ruchpaul, Becky Goldsmith, and others*)

17 bedrooms. Some on ground floor. 5 miles NW of Swindon. Closed 26–30 Dec. Restaurant closed Sat midday. Ramps. Lounge/bar, library, restaurant; function/ conference facilities. No background music. 7½-acre grounds: croquet, pond, jogging route. Civil wedding licence. No smoking in restaurant. No dogs unattended in bedrooms (sometimes allowed in public rooms, if quiet). All major credit cards accepted. B&B £55–£140 per person. Set dinner £33.50. ***V***

The ***V*** sign at the end of an entry indicates a hotel that has agreed to take part in our Voucher scheme and to give *Guide* readers a 25% discount on their room rates for a one-night stay, subject to the conditions explained on page 60 and listed on the back of the vouchers.

QUITHER Devon   Map 1:D4

Quither Mill   NEW   Tel/Fax 01822-860160
Quither, nr Chillaton   Email quither.mill@virgin.net
PL16 0PZ   Website www.quithermill.co.uk

The large original mill wheel still stands outside this Wolsey Lodge, a Grade II listed stonebuilt building in a hamlet on the edge of Dartmoor. 'A gem,' says its nominator. 'The picturesque building has been lovingly restored. The first impression on arriving is a profound silence, broken only by a distant stream and nearby cattle. Inside is a world of flagstone floors, exposed beams, a legion of pictures, and tasteful furnishings.' An evening meal is available by arrangement, served communally with fine china and silver. 'This is the sort of place that seems to encourage lively chat between total strangers. The food is unfussy, piping fresh and quite delicious [main courses like braised lamb shank or beef-steak]. With their warm humour, David and Jill Wright have created a home from home ambience: it is a delight to savour their excellent food and comfort.' There is a 'large, comfortable sitting room with a wood-burning stove'. (*WG Watkins*)

3 bedrooms. 1 in cottage. 4 miles SE of Chillaton. Closed Christmas/New Year. Sitting room, breakfast room, dining room. No background music. 10-acre grounds. Unsuitable for &. No smoking. No children under 12. No dogs. MasterCard, Visa accepted. B&B £40–£55 per person; D,B&B £65–£80. Full alc £25.

RAMSEY Isle of Man   Map 4:D1

Hillcrest House   BUDGET   Tel 01624-817215
May Hill, Ramsey IM8 2HG   Email admin@hillcresthouse.co.uk
                                Website www.hillcresthouse.co.uk

The beautiful Isle of Man does not belong to the UK, so this small guest house is a maverick *Guide* entry. A bay-windowed Victorian building in an old town on the north-east coast, it has marble fireplaces, wood panelling, moulded ceilings, period furniture, patchwork quilts, and an eclectic selection of pictures and books. 'Charming', 'sunny and spacious', it has many fans. Only three bedrooms; all have *en suite* facilities and a CD-player. The owners, Aurea and Anthony Greenhalgh, who 'maintain high standards', are thought 'great fun'. They use organic ingredients for the 'fabulous' breakfasts which include freshly squeezed juices, home-made bread, leaf teas, Manx kippers, kedgeree, home-made breads and yogurts. Vegetarians are catered for. A simple evening meal is sometimes available in winter. The host runs a traditional Chinese medicine clinic from the house. There are country walks in the area, along uncrowded lanes and footpaths; sandy beaches, an 18-hole golf course and ancient Celtic sites are nearby. (*Major and Mrs Magnay, Juliet Millard*)

3 bedrooms. ¼-mile walk from centre. Parking. Bus or tram from Douglas (10 miles) in summer. Lounge, dining room. No background music. Small front garden. Unsuitable for &. No smoking. No children under 10. No dogs. No credit cards. B&B [2006] £30–£37.

RAMSGILL-IN-NIDDERDALE   Map 4:D3
North Yorkshire

The Yorke Arms	*Tel* 01423-755243
Ramsgill-in-Nidderdale	*Fax* 01423-755330
nr Harrogate HG3 5RL	*Email* enquiries@yorke-arms.co.uk
	Website www.yorke-arms.co.uk

Q *César award in 2000*

The 'superb' cooking of Frances Atkins (*Michelin* star) draws visitors to this creeper-clad old inn beside the green of a village in Nidderdale (a designated area of outstanding natural beauty). 'We were prepared to suggest that the prices were a tad high for such a remote location, but found it was real value; it is rare to experience such quality in everything,' say visitors this year. Another comment: 'Stunning food, the best I have had for a long time. A main course of belly pork and pork loin with borlotti beans and tomatoes was a delight.' The wine list is 'strong, but pricey'. All the bedrooms have now been refurbished. 'We were upgraded to a large suite, which had a four-poster bed. Heating not quite adequate for a cold winter's night.' Another couple complained of a small, overpriced room. Breakfast, between 8 and 9 am, includes strong-cured bacon and fresh juices. The sitting areas have flagged floors, settles and wooden tables where walkers take a drink or a snack (bar lunches include home-made soup; fish and chips). 'Staff were friendly and well trained – they actually looked you in the eye and smiled.' (*Mr and Mrs K Robinson, Paul and Louise Barron, and others*)

14 bedrooms. Centre of village. Train: Harrogate. Ramp. Lounge, 2 bars, 2 restaurants (classical background music); function facilities. 2-acre grounds. Unsuitable for ♿. No smoking: restaurant, 1 lounge, bedrooms. No children under 12. Dogs in bar only. All major credit cards accepted. B&B [2006] £75–£120 per person; D,B&B £150–£190. Full alc £70. Christmas/New Year packages.

READING Berkshire *See SHORTLIST* Map 2:D3

REETH North Yorkshire Map 4:C3

The Burgoyne Hotel
On the Green
Reeth, nr Richmond
DL11 6SN

Tel/Fax 01748-884292
Email enquiries@theburgoyne.co.uk
Website www.theburgoyne.co.uk

♀ *César award in 2002*

'Every bit as good as you say.' A reader this year endorses this Grade II listed Regency house in the heart of the Yorkshire Dales national park. Other visitors agree: 'Hospitality, comfort and food could not be faulted.' Named after former residents, the Burgoyne Johnson family, the creeper-covered building is traditionally furnished. There are antiques, an inglenook log fire, books and magazines in the spacious lounge. 'The long-serving staff are discreet, efficient.' In the green-walled restaurant, chef Paul Salonga offers a daily-changing four-course dinner (with choice) of 'traditional dishes with a modern touch' (eg, grilled fillets of sea bass on a bed of spinach with sautéed fennel). There is a selection of wines at reasonable prices. Each bedroom (most are large) is named after a local hamlet, and many rooms face south over Swaledale; those at the back face the car park. The breakfast menu has fresh fruit, Whitby kippers, eggs Benedict, as well as 'a huge mixed grill'. Maps and compasses are provided for walkers. As we went to press, we were sorry to hear of the death of co-owner Peter Carwardine. His partner, Derek Hickson, will be running *The Burgoyne* as usual. (*JP Humphery, Graham and Peta Snowdon, and others*)

8 bedrooms. 1 adapted for ♿. Village centre. Parking. Open 9 Feb–2 Jan. Restaurant closed midday. 2 lounges, dining room (jazz/classical background music 'when needed'). ½-acre garden. Trout fishing on River Swale. Smoking in 1 lounge only. No children under 10. No dogs in dining room or unattended in bedrooms. MasterCard, Visa accepted. B&B [2006] £51.25–£117 per person. Set dinner £29.50. Christmas/New Year packages. 1-night bookings refused Sat in season.

RHYDYCROESAU Shropshire   Map 3:B4

Pen-y-Dyffryn   **NEW**   *Tel* 01691-653700
Rhydycroesau   *Fax* 01691-650066
Oswestry SY10 7JD   *Email* stay@peny.co.uk
                                               Website www.peny.co.uk

ℚ *César award in 2003*

Despite its name, this listed Georgian rectory is on the English side of the
border: it faces Welsh mountains. A 'peaceful place in a beautiful rural
setting', it was sold by Miles and Audrey Hunter in 2004, but they love it
so much they bought it back ten months later and are again running it
'with warmth and friendliness'. They have done some refurbishing, and
revamped the menus (chef David Morris returned with them). Inspectors
wrote of 'a happy atmosphere', and a good welcome (luggage carried,
complimentary tea with cake in the 'cosy lounge'). Bedrooms in the main
house vary in size; the double-aspect Rector's Room is particularly liked.
An 'airy, well-lit' coach house room, reached up steep steps, 'had small
terrace, stone walls covered in clematis, lovely views, intelligent information folder'. In the large dining room, 'there was a happy buzz of conversation; substantial main courses were well executed; excellent vegetables'.
But one visitor thought the room 'overcrowded with tables'. 'Breakfast has
DIY fresh juice, organic porridge', 'excellent full English', 'nothing
packaged'. 'The owners are hands on. Efficient staff, all local.' Dogs are
welcomed. Guests may fish for trout in pools in front of the house. Good
walking from the door, including the Offa's Dyke circular path. (*Christine
Moore, and others*)

12 bedrooms. 4, each with patio, in coach house. 1 on ground floor. 3 miles W of
Oswestry off B4580. Train: Oswestry. Open all year, except Christmas, 2–18 Jan.
2 lounges, bar, restaurant; background music at night. 5-acre grounds: dog-walking
area. Fishing, golf nearby. Smoking in 1 lounge only. No children under 3. No dogs
in public rooms after 6 pm. MasterCard, Visa accepted. B&B £53–£84 per person;
D,B&B £74–£110. Set dinner £33. New Year package. 1-night bookings sometimes
refused weekends. ***V***

****

> **Traveller's tale** First impressions were of a shabby hotel that was
> past its best. Our room, which was approached through a badly
> decorated area, looked drab and suffered from the noise of
> machinery which made sleeping difficult. It was also very hot.
> (*Hotel in Suffolk*)

****

RIPLEY North Yorkshire   Map 4:D4

The Boar's Head   *Tel* 01423-771888
Ripley Castle Estate, Ripley   *Fax* 01423-771509
nr Harrogate HG3 3AY   *Email* reservations@boarsheadripley.co.uk
                                   Website www.boarsheadripley.co.uk

♙ *César award in 1999*

In a model village, this old inn has been given a new lease of life by
Sir Thomas and Lady Ingilby (his family have lived on the castle estate for
650 years). Visitors in 2006 'could not praise this hotel enough; the service,
food and cleanliness of the staff all contributed to an enjoyable stay'. An
earlier view: 'A combination of pub and country hotel, with the elegance
of country house establishments, but without the stuffiness.' The manager,
Steve Chesnutt, 'has eyes everywhere and an easy manner; every guest is
spoken to by name'. The 'superior' bedrooms in *Birchwood House*, across a
courtyard, have 'flowers, fresh fruit, bottled water, sherry; gigantic bed'.
The courtyard rooms, where dog-owners stay (basket, feeding bowl, etc,
provided), are smallish. Lounges have antique and period furniture,
portraits and pictures from the castle's attics. 'The dinner and dining room
were the best feature' for guests whose arrival was 'coloured' by arriving
wedding guests. The breakfast buffet disappointed one guest ('well-cooked
eggs indeed'). Hotel guests have access to the castle's grounds; 'even an
electric scooter is provided'. (*Dave Jackson, JL Derry, and others*)

25 bedrooms. 10 in courtyard. 6 in *Birchwood House* adjacent. Some on ground floor.
3 miles N of Harrogate. 2 lounges, bar/bistro, restaurant. No background music.
150-acre estate (deer park, lake, fishing); 20-acre garden. Civil wedding licence. No
smoking. Dogs allowed in 2 courtyard bedrooms, not in public rooms. All major
credit cards accepted. B&B [2006] £62.50–£125 per person. Full alc £40 restaurant,
£20 bistro. Christmas/New Year packages. ***V***

ROCK Cornwall   Map 1:D2

St Enodoc   *Tel* 01208-863394
Rock, nr Wadebridge   *Fax* 01208-863970
PL27 6LA   *Email* info@enodoc-hotel.co.uk
                                     Website www.enodoc-hotel.co.uk

On the rugged north Cornish coast, this family-friendly hotel has a
'super setting', in a cluster of houses on a hill overlooking the Camel
estuary. Inside, the decor is light, bright and colourful; public rooms
have contemporary paintings and comfortable chairs, and there is a

large, modern wood burner in one of the lounges. There are many facilities for children: baby-listening, a room with toys and videos, etc, and tea at 5.30 pm. 'Our room on the top floor was well furnished and had an outstanding view of the estuary,' says a visitor this year. The general manager is Victoria Hutton; the 'fantastic' head chef is Rupert Brown. Meals are served at wooden tables in the large, split-level restaurant: it has panoramic views and a terrace for summer eating. 'Our dinner was excellent, with Oriental touches.' Bread is home made. There is a gym, and a heated swimming pool in the small garden. The St Enodoc Golf Club is adjacent, and the church in the sand where John Betjeman is buried is nearby. (*Walter Cottingham; endorsed by Kelvin Juba*)

20 Bedrooms. NW of Wadebridge. Open mid-Feb–mid-Dec, 3 nights New Year. Ramps. 2 lounges, library, bar/restaurant (modern background music); playroom, gym, sauna, billiards. ½-acre grounds: heated swimming pool (May–Sept). Sandy beach, water sports, 3 mins' walk. Only restaurant suitable for &. Smoking in bar and billiard room only. No dogs. Amex, MasterCard, Visa accepted. B&B: single £85–£165, double £115–£220, suite £140–£360. Full alc £40–£45. New Year package. 1-night bookings sometimes refused weekends. *V*

ROMALDKIRK Co. Durham   Map 4:C3

The Rose and Crown
Romaldkirk
nr Barnard Castle
DL12 9EB

Tel 01833-650213
Fax 01833-650828
Email hotel@rose-and-crown.co.uk
Website www.rose-and-crown.co.uk

Q *César award in 2003*

Opposite the green (with stocks, a pump and a Norman church) in a lovely Teesside village, Christopher and Alison Davy's 18th-century coaching inn has log fires, panelling, old farming implements, gleaming brasses and fresh flowers. This year Emma Atkinson has been promoted to manager. 'Still a terrific place to stay,' said returning visitors this year, although in the owners' absence 'service was efficient, but a bit remote'. Opinions on rooms vary: 'Ours was large and comfortable, with a good bathroom.' 'Comfortable beds, good sound system [a new one has been installed in each room this year]. You couldn't swing a cat in the small bathroom, but the shower was good.' Some courtyard bedrooms, good for dog owners and walkers, open on to the car park. In the restaurant Christopher Davy and Andrew Lee offer an imaginative four-course dinner menu of 'regional dishes with a modern influence', eg, Lunesdale Farm duckling with apple and sultana compote. Breakfast was thought 'the best I ever get in a hotel'; bread, marmalade, jams and chutneys are home made. The Davys have written a guidebook to local attractions. (*Stephen Edwards, Valerie Bowman; also EM Anderson*)

12 bedrooms. 5 in rear courtyard. Some on ground floor. Village centre. Closed Christmas. Residents' lounge, lounge bar, Crown Room (bar meals), restaurant. No background music. Fishing, grouse shooting, birdwatching nearby. No smoking: restaurant, brasserie, bedrooms. No children under 6 in restaurant. No dogs in public rooms or unattended in bedrooms. MasterCard, Visa accepted. B&B [2006] £63–£90 per person; D,B&B £89–£116. Bar lunches. Set lunch £16.75, dinner £28. New Year package. 1-night bookings refused Sat 'except quiet periods'.   ***V***   (Nov–March)

ROSS-ON-WYE Herefordshire   Map 3:D5

Wilton Court
Wilton Lane, Ross-on-Wye
HR9 6AQ

Tel 01989-562569
Fax 01989-768460
Email info@wiltoncourthotel.com
Website www.wiltoncourthotel.com

'Comfortable, elegantly furnished, in a beautiful position on the River Wye', Helen and Roger Wynn's 'perfect retreat' is on a small country lane near the centre of this small Herefordshire town. They say it has been 'refurbished to reflect its 16th-century origins wherever possible', but modern touches include Wi-Fi broadband throughout. One couple 'were so happy with the relaxed, generous atmosphere that we booked for our return journey'. Bedrooms 'of odd sizes' (one is 'tiny') have mostly been 'well refurbished'. 'Ours was gorgeous, spacious, overlooking the river and with very comfortable beds. A spotless bathroom, plenty of large bottles of toiletries, but towels were rather small.' Public rooms are 'excellent': 'a comfortable sitting room, interestingly furnished, and a good conservatory area'. There are ancient beams, leaded windows, uneven floors, and a huge fireplace with its original iron grate. Lloyd Loom tables and chairs are in the conservatory-style *Mulberry* restaurant (named after the 300-year-old tree in the garden which it faces). 'The food was excellent. Lamb shanks especially good' (there is a new chef, Alistair Forster). Breakfasts were 'really good, with delicious fruit salad and excellent cooked dishes'. One visitor writes of an 'attractive, but neglected' garden. (*Mary Woods, John Borron, Mary Milne-Day*)

10 bedrooms. ¼ mile from centre. Restaurant closed Sun night, and weekdays off-season (bar meals available). Sitting room, bar, restaurant; background music at mealtimes; private dining room. 2-acre grounds: riverside garden, fishing. Unsuitable for &. No smoking: most public rooms, bedrooms. No dogs in restaurant. Amex, MasterCard, Visa accepted. B&B £45–£110 per person; D,B&B (min. 2 nights) £57.50–£135. Full alc £35. Special breaks. Christmas/New Year packages. 1-night bookings occasionally refused Fri/Sat in season. *V* (subject to availability at weekends)

See also SHORTLIST

ROWSLEY Derbyshire   Map 3:A6

East Lodge	*Tel* 01629-734474
Rowsley DE4 2EF	*Fax* 01629-733949
	Email info@eastlodge.com
	Website www.eastlodge.com

An elegant 17th-century country house owned by the Hardman family: it stands up a long tree-lined drive in large grounds, well back from the busy A6 which passes through this Derbyshire village. 'A very pleasant hotel in a beautiful location,' said our inspectors, 'the public rooms and bedrooms are user-friendly, and the staff are charming.' All rooms have been refurbished this year, and there are new bathrooms; three executive suites have been added. The best rooms face the garden (with pond); some lack a view and might feel 'claustrophobic'. The conservatory bar, where light meals are served, has 'plants galore'. In the restaurant, where 'service is by friendly young girls in long, narrow skirts', Marcus Hall leads the kitchen brigade, serving main courses like trio of local lamb with basil dauphinoise potato. Vegetarians have a good choice of dishes. Breakfast is liked: 'Generous selection of cereals, juices, etc; well-cooked, ample "country house breakfast"; toast and tea promptly brought.' Reduced-rate tickets to nearby Chatsworth House can be provided.

12 bedrooms. Some on ground floor. Village centre. Reception/lounge, Garden Room bar, 2 dining rooms, 2 private dining rooms; conference/function facilities; background music in public areas 8 am–11 pm. 10-acre grounds. Civil wedding licence. No smoking. No children under 12. No dogs. Amex, MasterCard, Visa accepted. B&B £80–£130 per person; D,B&B £110–£160. Set dinner £32; full alc £45. Christmas/New Year packages. 1-night bookings refused Sat. *V*

Don't trust out-of-date editions of the *Guide*. Hotels change hands, deteriorate or go out of business. Every year, we add 80 or more entries and drop an equal number.

The Peacock at Rowsley

Bakewell Road
Rowsley DE4 2EB

Tel 01629-733518
Fax 01629-732671
Email reception@thepeacockatrowsley.com
Website www.thepeacockatrowsley.com

Once the dower house for Haddon Hall, this roadside hotel belongs to the Haddon estate of the dukes of Rutland. Its grounds run down to the River Derwent. The 'very attractive' building has a Derbyshire stone exterior, with mullioned windows and leaded lights, giving it the look of a traditional inn. Owned by Lord Edward Manners, it is managed by Ian and Jenni MacKenzie. The interior is 'modern simplicity combined with country antiques and original features such as beams and stone fireplaces'. Upstairs, bedrooms are arranged around a series of corridors, with short flights of steps between different levels. 'We had an excellent stay,' report guests this year. 'Our pleasant room overlooking the garden was quiet, but the bathroom was on the "compact" side.' Road-facing rooms hear traffic. Most guests describe the dining room as 'beautiful, with an impressive fireplace', but one couple thought its 'tables were too close together and the seats too far apart'; another thought it 'gloomy'. But Matthew Rushton's cooking was found 'excellent' ('delicious tian of crab and avocado'). The bar serves lunches and suppers. 'Breakfast was a routine buffet.' Guests can shoot on the estate, and visit Haddon Hall (50% discount). (*Robin and Heather Harrison, Carol Jackson, and others*)

17 bedrooms. Village centre. Lounge (live guitar music Sat), bar, dining room; conference rooms. Garden on river: fishing Apr–Oct. Civil wedding licence. Unsuitable for &. No smoking in restaurant. No children under 12. No dogs in public rooms. Amex, MasterCard, Visa accepted. B&B £72.50–£95 per person; D,B&B £102.50–£130. Full alc £54. Christmas/New Year packages. 1-night bookings sometimes refused Sat.

RUSHLAKE GREEN East Sussex   Map 2:E4

Stone House

Rushlake Green
Heathfield TN21 9QJ

Tel 01435-830553
Fax 01435-830726
Website www.stonehousesussex.co.uk

Part Tudor, part Georgian, this manor house has been owned by the Dunn family since 1495. It is run on house party lines by Jane and Peter Dunn with 'great courtesy and efficiency'. They offer 'a quintessentially English country experience', says one of their many fans. Plenty of sporting activities are available in its huge grounds (see below), and it is popular with opera-goers, being only 20 minutes' drive from Glyndebourne for which a wicker picnic hamper ('a real treat') can be provided, as well as table and chairs (delivery and collection arranged). The largest bedrooms are in the Georgian section: two grand rooms, up a sweeping staircase, have a four-poster and lavish furnishings. The rooms in the Tudor wing have less space but 'lots of character' (beams, sloping ceilings, antiques, old china). The walled garden has an ornamental lake, gazebos, and a 100-foot herbaceous border. Jane Dunn has a *Michelin Bib Gourmand* for her 'French-and Thai-influenced cooking'. Dinner, served in the panelled dining room, has five choices for each course, and the menu changes daily. There is a vegetarian menu and an extensive wine list. Continental breakfast can be taken in the bedroom; a traditional one comes with a 'superb buffet'. (*AG, and others*)

6 bedrooms. 4 miles SE of Heathfield. 2 Jan–23 Dec. Hall, drawing room, library, dining room; billiard room. No background music. 1,000-acre estate: 5½-acre garden, farm, woodland, croquet, shooting, pheasant/clay-pigeon shooting, 2 lakes, rowing, fishing. Unsuitable for &. No children under 9. No dogs in public rooms. MasterCard, Visa accepted. B&B [2006] £62.50–£125 per person. Set meals (advance booking for lunch necessary) £24.95; Glyndebourne hamper (*no VAT*) £32. Weekend house parties, winter breaks. Cookery courses. 1-night bookings sometimes refused Sat. **'V'** (1 Nov–31 Mar; not Fri/Sat)

RYE East Sussex   Map 2:E5

Durrant House   *Tel* 01797-223182
2 Market Street   *Fax* 01797-226940
Rye TN31 7LA   *Email* info@durranthouse.com
                                        Website www.durranthouse.com

Almost surrounded by the sea, Rye is the most complete medieval town in Britain. In its centre, Ron and Jo Kingsland's B&B hotel is a 14th-century Grade II listed building. Pots and hanging baskets filled with flowers add colour in summer to the white Georgian facade, and on fine days the owners serve breakfast, which ranges from 'great English' to vegetarian (with home-made muffins and lentil patties), on the small rear lawn with its 'exhilarating views over the Romney Marsh towards the sea'. From the lounge (well supplied with books) guests can look down East Street and watch the world go by. The breakfast room flanks the entrance hall, and the bedrooms, of varying sizes, are 'fresh, light and clean'; one has a bath; the others a 'good modern shower'. The River Room has a four-poster and wide views. The Kingslands have a drinks licence, and they welcome children and babies (there is a family room where a cot or a child's bed can be provided). More reports, please.

6 bedrooms. Town centre. Lounge with bar, breakfast room (background CDs/radio). Small rear lawn. Unsuitable for &. No smoking. No dogs. MasterCard, Visa accepted. B&B £42.50–£78 per person. 1-night bookings refused weekends.

Jeake's House
Mermaid Street
Rye TN31 7ET

Tel 01797-222828
Fax 01797-222623
Email stay@jeakeshouse.com
Website www.jeakeshouse.com

♥ *César award in 1992*

Built as a wool store in 1689, Jenny Hadfield's ever-popular B&B stands on one of Rye's ancient cobbled streets. The American novelist Conrad Aiken lived here in the 1920s, and was visited by TS Eliot, Malcolm Lowry and others. 'It is like a proper hotel,' says one enthusiastic report in 2006. 'Nice lounge, nice bar. Lovely bedroom, tastefully decorated, with state-of-the-art bathroom. Breakfast was excellent.' The 'attentive hostess' has filled the building with antiques, pictures and samplers; the parlour has an upright piano (*c.* 1860) and a fireplace; the galleried, red-walled breakfast room (with high windows, good china, and plants) was once a Quaker meeting house. In the book-lined bar, furnished with old chapel pews, evening drinks are served and there is a folder of sample menus from nearby restaurants. Each of the 'spotless' bedrooms has a brass or mahogany bed and linen sheets; the Lowry suite has 'a smart four-poster, a walk-in shower and a roll-top bath'. This year, three rooms have been refurbished and there is a new one with a half-tester bed. Breakfast has a buffet with fresh fruit; full English or vegetarian options are cooked to order. (*Wolfgang Stroebe; also Elizabeth Roberts*)

11 bedrooms. Central. Car park (£3 per 24 hours; advance booking needed). Parlour, bar/library, breakfast room (classical background music). Unsuitable for &. No smoking: breakfast room, parlour. No children under 8. No dogs in breakfast room. MasterCard, Visa accepted. B&B £49–£61 per person. Christmas/New Year packages. 1-night bookings sometimes refused weekends. •V•

The Old Vicarage
66 Church Square
Rye TN31 7HF

Tel 01797-222119
Fax 01797-227466
Email info@oldvicaragerye.co.uk
Website www.oldvicaragerye.co.uk

'A delightful place in a wonderful position,' write visitors this year to this B&B on a pretty, traffic-free square, near the church. The pink Georgian house, surrounded by pink roses, has views of medieval houses and cobbled streets. Free decanters of sherry are provided for guests in the evening, and arriving guests get a free pot of (loose-leaf) tea on arrival. The cheerful bedrooms have Laura Ashley prints and fabrics, hot-drinks tray, a small, silent fridge, TV, lots of local information, including a list of restaurants. One room has a four-poster bed, another a new hand-crafted bed made from local oak. 'Our suite, at the top of the house, was charming. The bed was small, but the little sitting room was a real bonus.' The 'excellent hosts', Paul and Julia Masters, provide 'enormous breakfasts', with home-made breads, jams, mustards and muesli. A basket containing packets of cereals stands on each table; warm scones and soda bread are brought as you study the menu: this includes freshly squeezed orange juice, leaf tea, freshly ground coffee, porridge with local honey, fruit compote, free-range eggs, Kentish pork sausages. (*A and M Beard*)

4 bedrooms. By St Mary's church. Closed Christmas. Lounge, lounge/library, dining room. No background music. Small walled garden. Unsuitable for &. No smoking. No children under 8. No dogs. No credit cards. B&B £45–£85 per person. 1-night bookings refused weekends.

See also SHORTLIST

ST ALBANS Hertfordshire   Map 2:C3

St Michael's Manor   *Tel* 01727-864444
Fishpool Street   *Fax* 01727-848909
St Albans AL3 4RY   *Email* reservations@stmichaelsmanor.com
                        Website www.stmichaelsmanor.com

In a large and beautiful garden with a lake, this old manor house, 16th-century in origin, is run by Richard Newling Ward, the third generation of the family in charge. The bedrooms in the main building, named after trees in the grounds which many overlook, are decorated in period style and are 'remarkably quiet'. Those in a new garden wing have a more modern feel. Children are welcomed: they have a special menu, snacks all day, cots and babysitting (but there are no interconnecting or family rooms). Weddings, conferences and functions are often held. To avoid them you could visit one of the 'five attractive pubs down the road at Verulamium', or the family's restaurant, *Darcy's*, 15 minutes' walk away. More reports, please.

30 bedrooms. 8 in garden wing. In old St Albans, near abbey. Ramps. 2 lounges, bar, restaurant, conservatory; classical background music; private dining room. 5-acre gardens: croquet, lake. Civil wedding licence. No smoking: restaurant, 7 bedrooms. Guide dogs only. All major credit cards accepted. B&B [2006]: single £145–£280, double £145–£280, suite £250–£310. Full alc lunch £34, dinner £42. Weekend breaks. Christmas/New Year packages.

ST ERVAN Cornwall   Map 1:D2

St Ervan Manor
St Ervan, nr Padstow
PL27 7TA

Tel 01841-540255
Email info@stervanmanor.co.uk
Website www.stervanmanor.co.uk

There is a *Michelin* star this year for Allan and Lorraine Clarke's Grade II listed former rectory (1856). They offer 'luxury B&B' combined with fine dining. Nathan Outlaw is the chef: 'Avoidance of gimmickry', he writes, is his philosophy. Anjou pigeon with foie gras and lentils, and roast scallops with butternut squash and salsify might feature on his 'tasting menus', served in the blue-walled dining rooms, or, in fine weather, in the peaceful garden. The decor is in country house style, with paintings by local artists. 'All is of the highest quality,' was one comment. At breakfast, both the fresh fruit on the buffet and the cooked dishes were enjoyed. The bedrooms have bright colours, widescreen TV, fresh flowers, etc. Beds are luxurious. The suite is in the garden. John Betjeman mentions the building in *Summoned by Bells*. As we went to press, we heard that *St Ervan Manor* had been put up for sale. Prospective visitors should check the position before booking. More reports, please.

6 bedrooms. 4 miles SW of Padstow. Open 19 Jan–19 Dec. Restaurant closed midday. Ramp. Drawing room/bar, 2 dining rooms; background jazz. 5-acre grounds. Unsuitable for &. No smoking. No children under 14. Guide dogs only. MasterCard, Visa accepted. B&B [2006] £70–£215 per person. Set menus £55 and £75. 1-night bookings refused weekends Easter–end Oct.

If you dislike piped music, why not join Pipedown, the campaign for freedom from piped music? They can be reached at 1 The Row, Berwick St James, Salisbury SP3 4TP. *Tel*: 01722-790622, www.pipedown.info.

ST HILARY Cornwall   Map 1:E1

Ennys   *Tel* 01736-740262
Trewhella Lane, St Hilary   *Fax* 01736-740055
nr Penzance TR20 9BZ   *Email* ennys@ennys.co.uk
                                Website www.ennys.co.uk

'At night it is truly dark here. The only sound you will hear is the hooting
of owls in the woods,' says Gill Charlton, owner of this B&B in a Grade II
listed 17th-century manor house. Creeper-clad and imposing, it stands at
the end of a long, narrow drive, surrounded by fields that lead down to the
River Hayle. Exotic plants grow in the pretty garden, where there is a
swimming pool (not available to residents between 12.30 and 4 pm). There
are 'nice, bright reception rooms with interesting art work': some of the
pieces are souvenirs of Ms Charlton's wanderings (she is a travel columnist
for the *Daily Telegraph*). There are three bedrooms in the house; each has
antiques and a window seat overlooking the garden or countryside. Two
'tastefully furnished' family suites and three self-catering apartments are in
converted barns that open on to a courtyard. Afternoon tea with home-
baked scones and cake is included in the tariff, and broadband Internet
access, including wireless connections, is free. The 'very good cooked
breakfast' is served by 'friendly ladies'. Four pages of recommendations for
local pubs and restaurants are provided. (*NM*)

5 bedrooms. 2 in barn. 3 self-catering apartments (can be B&B off-season). 5 miles
E of Penzance. Open 15 Mar–31 Oct. Sitting room, breakfast room. No background
music. 3-acre grounds: 40-ft heated swimming pool (not available 12.30–4 pm),
tennis. Unsuitable for &. No smoking. No children under 3 (except in self-catering
accommodation). No dogs. MasterCard, Visa accepted. B&B [2006] £50–£80 per
person. 1-night bookings refused high season.

ST IVES Cornwall   Map 1:D1

Blue Hayes   *Tel* 01736-797129
Trelyon Avenue   *Fax* 01736-799098
St Ives TR26 2AD   *Email* bluehayes@btconnect.com
                              Website www.bluehayes.co.uk

'We catch the first of the day's sun,' says Malcolm Herring, owner of this
small luxury hotel overlooking St Ives Bay and harbour, which 'basks
among tropical plants and pines'. Standing in its own grounds on
Porthminster Point, it commands 'wonderful views of coast and sea'. Built
in the 1920s as a private house, it is on a slope: reception is on top; you
work your way down, passing the bedrooms, to the lounges, dining room

and terrace. 'The whole place has a tranquil feel,' wrote recent guests. 'Our comfortable master suite had lovely fabrics, good lighting, the biggest bathroom you could wish for (state-of-the-art shower with body jets, loads of hot water, large, fluffy towels), and a balcony reached through French windows.' On fine days, breakfasts and suppers are served on the wide panoramic terrace. Roger Richards joined as chef in 2005: his supper menu includes 16 dishes (eg, whole Dover sole with citrus butter sauce; navarin of lamb with broccoli florets) plus cheese. The long breakfast menu offers yogurts, smoked salmon and scrambled eggs, traditional British breakfast and much else. 'Hi-tech' facilities include broadband Internet access. A gate leads to the South West Coastal Path. More reports, please.

6 bedrooms. On A3074 outside St Ives. Open Feb–Nov. TV lounge, lounge/bar with terrace, dining room. No background music. ¼-acre garden. Porthminster Beach 4 mins' walk. Unsuitable for &. Civil wedding licence. No smoking. No children under 10. No dogs. Amex, MasterCard, Visa accepted. B&B [2006] £70–£145 per person. Supper £22–£30.

Pedn-Olva
West Porthminster Beach
St Ives TR26 2EA

Tel 01736-796222
Fax 01736-797710
Email pednolva@smallandfriendly.co.uk
Website www.smallandfriendly.co.uk

'Worth an entry for its position alone (seascapes in all directions)', this informal hotel, owned by St Austell Brewery, is built on rocks overlooking the harbour and bay; all bedrooms and public areas have the views. The public areas have been redecorated and given contemporary furnishings. Families are welcomed. From the poolside terrace there is access to safe, sandy Porthminster beach. 'The staff are young, professional and oh so cheerful,' say visitors this year. 'We could have done without the muzak but it was fairly quiet.' Other guests had 'mixed feelings' about their small bedroom ('with a £12 supplement for a shared balcony'); the 'very small toilet/shower room had poor ventilation'. And one room was said to have poor housekeeping and to suffer noise from the bar overhead. 'Not for those with mobility problems; there are stairs everywhere. Our room was four floors down; it was rather overlooked but this was a small price to pay for the wonderful position.' Daniel Chapman's dinner menus change daily, 'to reflect the catch of the day'. 'Fish was excellent; meat was variable. We loved the puddings menu, which included bread and butter pudding and fruit crumble.' 'Portions were large, but beautifully presented.' Bar meals are also served. (*Jan and Alan Codd, and others*)

31 bedrooms. 4 by swimming pool. 2 mins' walk from centre, near train and bus stations. Private parking; also station car park. Sometimes closed Oct/Nov for weddings. Lounge/bar, restaurant; background music all day. Terrace areas: small heated swimming pool. Beach below (5 mins' walk). Unsuitable for &. Civil wedding licence. No smoking: restaurant, lounge area, bedrooms. No dogs. Amex, MasterCard, Visa accepted. B&B [2006] £30–£100 per person; D,B&B £50–£120. Supplement for some balcony rooms. Full alc £45. Off-season breaks.

Primrose Valley Hotel   **NEW**   *Tel/Fax* 01736-794939
Primrose Valley, Porthminster Beach   *Email* info@primroseonline.co.uk
St Ives TR26 2ED   *Website* www.primroseonline.co.uk

Just above the Blue Flag Porthminster Beach, this Edwardian villa has an 'excellent setting'. The eco-friendly owners, Andrew and Sue Biss, have given it a modern make-over: polished wooden floors, leather sofas, specially made walnut and oak tables in the public areas; bright, modern staircase carpets. The bedrooms are on the first and second floors: two have a balcony. Inspectors wrote: 'We loved our sea view though our room, smartly decorated in white, was very small. The host was a friendly presence, bringing us tea with cake on arrival and presiding over the excellent breakfast: good buffet with fresh fruit salad, fresh juices, yogurts, loose-leaf teas and an interesting range of cooked dishes.' Ingredients are local, including Tregothnan English Estate tea. The bar is open all day for drinks, teas and light lunches. An early supper is available by arrangement, and many good eating places are near. An optional £1 charge is added to the bill to go towards marine conservation initiatives. The town is an easy walk away. A little scenic railway runs by the beach, 'but the single-carriage train trundles in and out with very little noise'. For children there are toys and DVDs.

10 bedrooms. Private road 2 mins from station. Parking (£3). Open early Feb–end Nov, New Year. Evening meal available June–Sept. Lounge, bar, dining room (contemporary background music sometimes); patio. Porthminster Beach 4 mins' walk. Unsuitable for &. No smoking. No dogs. MasterCard, Visa accepted. B&B £65–£100 per person.

See also SHORTLIST

Always discuss accommodation in detail when making a booking, and don't hesitate to ask for an upgrade on arrival if a hotel is clearly not full.

THE GOOD HOTEL GUIDE 2007

Use this voucher to claim a 25% discount off the normal price for bed and breakfast at hotels with a ***V*** sign at the end of their entry. **You must request a voucher discount at the time of booking and present this voucher on arrival. Further details and conditions overleaf.** Valid to 2nd October 2007.

THE GOOD HOTEL GUIDE 2007

Use this voucher to claim a 25% discount off the normal price for bed and breakfast at hotels with a ***V*** sign at the end of their entry. **You must request a voucher discount at the time of booking and present this voucher on arrival. Further details and conditions overleaf.** Valid to 2nd October 2007.

THE GOOD HOTEL GUIDE 2007

Use this voucher to claim a 25% discount off the normal price for bed and breakfast at hotels with a ***V*** sign at the end of their entry. **You must request a voucher discount at the time of booking and present this voucher on arrival. Further details and conditions overleaf.** Valid to 2nd October 2007.

THE GOOD HOTEL GUIDE 2007

Use this voucher to claim a 25% discount off the normal price for bed and breakfast at hotels with a ***V*** sign at the end of their entry. **You must request a voucher discount at the time of booking and present this voucher on arrival. Further details and conditions overleaf.** Valid to 2nd October 2007.

THE GOOD HOTEL GUIDE 2007

Use this voucher to claim a 25% discount off the normal price for bed and breakfast at hotels with a ***V*** sign at the end of their entry. **You must request a voucher discount at the time of booking and present this voucher on arrival. Further details and conditions overleaf.** Valid to 2nd October 2007.

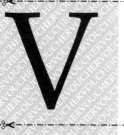

THE GOOD HOTEL GUIDE 2007

Use this voucher to claim a 25% discount off the normal price for bed and breakfast at hotels with a ***V*** sign at the end of their entry. **You must request a voucher discount at the time of booking and present this voucher on arrival. Further details and conditions overleaf.** Valid to 2nd October 2007.

CONDITIONS

1. Hotels with a *v* have agreed to give readers a discount of 25% off their normal bed-and-breakfast rate.
2. One voucher is good for a single-night stay only, at the discounted rate for yourself alone or for you and a partner sharing a double room.
3. Hotels may decline to accept a voucher reservation if they expect to be fully booked at the full room price.

✂ -

CONDITIONS

1. Hotels with a *v* have agreed to give readers a discount of 25% off their normal bed-and-breakfast rate.
2. One voucher is good for a single-night stay only, at the discounted rate for yourself alone or for you and a partner sharing a double room.
3. Hotels may decline to accept a voucher reservation if they expect to be fully booked at the full room price.

✂ -

CONDITIONS

1. Hotels with a *v* have agreed to give readers a discount of 25% off their normal bed-and-breakfast rate.
2. One voucher is good for a single-night stay only, at the discounted rate for yourself alone or for you and a partner sharing a double room.
3. Hotels may decline to accept a voucher reservation if they expect to be fully booked at the full room price.

✂ -

CONDITIONS

1. Hotels with a *v* have agreed to give readers a discount of 25% off their normal bed-and-breakfast rate.
2. One voucher is good for a single-night stay only, at the discounted rate for yourself alone or for you and a partner sharing a double room.
3. Hotels may decline to accept a voucher reservation if they expect to be fully booked at the full room price.

✂ -

CONDITIONS

1. Hotels with a *v* have agreed to give readers a discount of 25% off their normal bed-and-breakfast rate.
2. One voucher is good for a single-night stay only, at the discounted rate for yourself alone or for you and a partner sharing a double room.
3. Hotels may decline to accept a voucher reservation if they expect to be fully booked at the full room price.

✂ -

CONDITIONS

1. Hotels with a *v* have agreed to give readers a discount of 25% off their normal bed-and-breakfast rate.
2. One voucher is good for a single-night stay only, at the discounted rate for yourself alone or for you and a partner sharing a double room.
3. Hotels may decline to accept a voucher reservation if they expect to be fully booked at the full room price.

ST LEONARDS-ON-SEA East Sussex   Map 2:E4

Zanzibar Hotel   **NEW**   *Tel/Fax* 01424-460109
9 Eversfield Place   *Email* info@zanzibarhotel.co.uk
St Leonards-on-Sea   *Website* www.zanzibarhotel.co.uk
TN37 6BY

In June 2005, Max O'Rourke, 'a charming and helpful young man', opened
this exotic small hotel in a 'somewhat run-down seaside resort on the edge
of Hastings'. He has given the Victorian town house themed bedrooms:
Morocco, India, etc. Antarctica, on the second floor, has floor-to-ceiling
bay windows facing the sea. Done in white, cream and chrome, with
varnished wooden floors, it is 'very relaxing', said our inspector. 'We asked
for the duvet to be replaced with blankets and sheets. "First time I've been
asked," said Max, "I don't have any but I'll go and buy some." He did, and
they were perfect. The large bathroom had a sauna and shower unit with
every combination of jets and sprinklers imaginable. "Power on," it said, a
bit alarmingly as you stood there naked. Good lighting.' Breakfast is
ordered by 9 pm the night before. 'Everything from fruit to cereals or full
English. Butter and jams in pots. Excellent coffee and tea.' It is served in
the bedroom or in the Grand Salon, which has sofas, newspapers and
'extravagant flowers'. An informal fish restaurant was due to open in the
hotel in mid-2006.

8 bedrooms. 1 on ground floor, suitable for partially &. Seafront. 600 metres W of
Hastings pier. Free parking vouchers issued. Lounge (non-stop background
Radio 2), bar/restaurant. Garden. Beach across road. No smoking. Dogs must never
be left unattended. MasterCard, Visa accepted. Room with breakfast £80–£240.
£20 supplement for 1-night weekend booking July/Aug, bank holidays. *V*

ST MARTIN'S Isles of Scilly   Map 1:C1

St Martin's on the Isle   *Tel* 01720-422092
Lower Town, St Martin's   *Fax* 01720-422298
Isles of Scilly, Cornwall   *Email* stay@stmartinshotel.co.uk
TR25 0QW   *Website* www.stmartinshotel.co.uk

The only hotel on St Martin's, a 'charming island of heathland and small
bulb fields with high hedges', this Pride of Britain member was built in the
1980s to look like a row of traditional fishermen's cottages. Visitors arrive
by boat, to be met at the quay by the manager, Keith Bradford, and
escorted the short distance to the hotel. 'Delightful in every way,' says a
visitor in 2006. 'Every care for our well-being. No pretentiousness. Good

value.' Staff are 'friendly, they remember your name'. Bedrooms vary in style; many have sea views. A suite was 'grand, with spacious sitting room'. The split-level public rooms have stone walls, 'extravagant flowers'. The *Teän* dining room, on the first floor, has the best views, across the water to Tresco. Chef John Mijatovic serves a classic menu 'with Mediterranean touches', eg, rack of lamb with confit lamb potato cake; Cornish brill with a crab and pea risotto. 'Best ingredients, perfectly cooked. Presentation was fun. Restaurant service just right. Never fussy. Superb breakfast buffet; delicious cooked dishes.' This is a family-friendly place; seekers after peace might want to avoid the school holidays. Birdwatching trips are organised. (*Pam Service, N and JJ*)

30 bedrooms. Some on ground floor. N end of island. Boat/helicopter from Penzance or fixed-wing aircraft from several local airports in SW England. All flights land at St Mary's; then boat to St Martin's. Open Mar–Oct. Ramps. Lounge, lounge bar, restaurant; 33-ft indoor swimming pool. No background music. 2½-acre grounds: garden on beach, jetty, boating, diving, water sports. Civil wedding licence. Unsuitable for ৬ (because of transport). No smoking: restaurant, lower bar. No children under 9 in restaurant. All major credit cards accepted. D,B&B [2006] £130–£208 per person.

ST MARY'S Isles of Scilly   Map 1:C1

Star Castle	*Tel* 01720-422317
The Garrison, St Mary's	*Fax* 01720-422343
Isles of Scilly	*Email* info@star-castle.co.uk
Cornwall TR21 0JA	*Website* www.star-castle.co.uk

Above the town, this Tudor fortress, shaped like an eight-pointed star, was built as a defence against the Spanish Armada. The owner, Robert Francis, manages it with his son, James. They continue to refurbish, while retaining the child-friendly, dog-friendly ambience. Comments in 2006: 'They amalgamate a number of values: friendliness, humour, quality, excellent food and wine.' 'Well run. Professionally trained staff. A taxi from the airport for guests; bags transported direct to the room; a warm welcome.' But one visitor was less keen, complaining about welcome and house-keeping. Two modern blocks in the grounds contain large bedrooms (some with private garden or veranda). More characterful rooms are in the main house. 'Views very good: all islands could be seen. Little room to sit under the eaves. Water and fresh milk provided, bed turned down. Good power shower. Furniture dated, lighting poor.' Chef Simon Shaw serves 'interesting dishes' on a daily-changing menu, eg, roast beef with walnut and blue cheese crust. 'David, the helpful barman, suggested soup and an excellent curry for lunch. Good fish and organic juice at breakfast; full English overcooked.' There are suntrap lawns, enclosed by high hedges, in the subtropical gardens. (*Mr DR Ellis, Roger and Mary Hancock, and others*)

38 bedrooms. 29 in wings. ¼ mile from town centre. Boat (2¾ hours)/helicopter (20 mins) from Penzance. Air links from Newquay, Exeter, Bristol. Open 10 Feb– 30 Nov, Christmas/New Year. Lounge, games room, bar, 2 restaurants. No background music. 4-acre grounds: covered 30-ft swimming pool, tennis. Beach nearby. Golf, bicycle hire, riding, sailing, diving, fishing available. Unsuitable for &. No smoking: restaurant, lounge. No dogs in restaurant. D,B&B [2006] £65–£148 per person. Set meals £30–£32.50. Special breaks, gourmet/wine events. Christmas/ New Year packages.

ST MAWES Cornwall   Map 1:E2

Idle Rocks   NEW
Harbourside
St Mawes TR2 5AN

Tel 01326-270771
Fax 01326-270062
Email reception@idlerocks.co.uk
Website www.richardsonhotels.co.uk

Part of Keith Richardson's small group of hotels, this one has a 'splendid waterfront setting'. Its long terrace forms part of the harbour wall of this attractive village on the south Cornish coast. Here, the nominators took a 'very good' Cornish cream tea ('proper leaf tea'); 'Staff are pleasant.' They add: 'The evening meal was surprisingly good.' Inspectors, visiting shortly after the arrival, in February 2006, of manager Chris Swire, amplify: 'The welcome was exemplary: the receptionist insisted on carrying our bags. The decor is dated: the lounge with its red sofas and patterned carpets reminded us of an old railway hotel. Paintwork on corridors was faded, and our small second-floor room was old-fashioned (frilled pelmets, tasselled lampshades, textured wallpaper). It had a fine sea view, and a more modern bathroom (with window).' The restaurant is on three levels, allowing everyone to enjoy the view. 'Any doubts we had were blown away by the quality of the food [Damian Broom is chef]: delicious *amuse-bouche*; good home-baked breads; oysters and scallops came with caviar and a light sauce; superb sea bass with spider-crab ravioli and shrimps; exceptional desserts. Breakfast kept up the pace: home-made muesli, fresh crois- sants, good cooked dishes, excellent toast, but packaged juice.' (*Susan and John Snoxall, and others*)

33 bedrooms. 10 in 2 annexes. Some on ground floor. Village centre (harbour wall). Parking for 6 cars. Lounge, restaurant; background music at night. Terrace. Sandy beach adjacent. No smoking. No dogs in restaurant. Amex, MasterCard, Visa accepted. B&B £54–£129 per person; D,B&B £84–£159. Full alc £42. Christmas/ New Year packages. ***V***

The Rising Sun

The Square
St Mawes TR2 5DJ

Tel 01326-270233
Fax 01326-270198
Email info@risingsunstmawes.co.uk
Website www.risingsunstmawes.com

Overlooking the harbour, this old inn is part of the group Inns of Cornwall, and licensed to John Milan. 'The distinctive, slightly old-fashioned style' was appreciated by visitors in 2006. Others wrote: 'The decor gives a relaxed feel.' A 'pleasant room with harbour views' was liked; some bedrooms may be dark, but the doubles have basket-weave furniture, ample storage and power shower. The restaurant, with a lounge alongside, is 'elegant' and its menu changes daily. 'The cooking is excellent, and the service professional.' Fish is a speciality of the 'solicitous chef', Anne Long, eg, hot, smoked salmon kedgeree cake with a quail's egg centre; monkfish wrapped in Parma ham. The wine list, which last year was described as 'bizarre', is now more traditionally set out. Good breakfasts include freshly squeezed orange and grapefruit juice, and scrambled eggs with smoked salmon. 'The bar and its simple meals are well patronised and do not detract from the calm. Staff are efficient and cheerful.' On fine days, says the brochure, you can take a cappuccino or a drink on the terrace 'while watching the world sail by'. (*Sir William and Lady Reid, Jane and Christopher Couchman, SP*)

8 bedrooms. Village centre, by harbour. Lounge, bar, restaurant. No background music. Terrace. Only restaurant suitable for &. No smoking and no dogs in restaurant. MasterCard, Visa accepted. B&B £50–£80 per person; D,B&B £80–£110. Set dinner £35.

Hotel Tresanton

27 Lower Castle Road
St Mawes TR2 5DR

Tel 01326-270055
Fax 01326-270053
Email info@tresanton.com
Website www.tresanton.com

'Setting and housekeeping have always been good; service is professional,' write regular visitors to Olga Polizzi's 'casually elegant' hotel on the edge of the village. A cluster of old houses in terraced subtropical gardens, it looks across the Fal estuary. 'This time, the cooking was better than ever, and management of the dining room was excellent.' Other comments: 'High prices, high standards.' 'No piped music!' 'Lots of places to catch the sun.' Federica Bertolini, the 'lively manager', supervises a 'capable young staff', mainly Eastern European. Children have games room, buckets and spades and a special menu. All bedrooms have sea views; the best ones are big; one above the bar can be noisy. In the restaurant ('wonderful white mosaic floor', white-clothed tables close together, large white plates), Paul Wadham serves a daily-changing menu. 'Plump John Dory fillets on perfectly cooked spinach; flavoursome steak.' 'Good breakfast: fruit, croissants, a range of cooked dishes.' *Tresanton* has a cinema, a film library, and a 48-foot racing yacht. '195 steps down to the car park, but staff will collect and deliver.' Mrs Polizzi's new hotel, *The Endsleigh*, Milton Abbot, makes its *Guide* debut this year. (*Margaret and David Mallett, and others*)

29 bedrooms. On seafront. Train: Truro; plane: Newquay. Open Feb–Dec. 2 lounges, bar, restaurant; cinema; conference facilities. No background music. Terrace. ¼-acre garden. By sea: shingle beach, safe bathing, 48-ft yacht. Unsuitable for &. Civil wedding licence. No children under 6 at dinner. Dogs in 2 bedrooms only. Amex, MasterCard, Visa accepted. B&B double £165–£425. Set lunch £21–£28, dinner £38–£45. Bridge/yoga weeks, poker weekends. Christmas/New Year packages. 1-night bookings refused weekends.

SALCOMBE Devon   Map 1:E4

The Tides Reach	*Tel* 01548-843466
South Sands	*Fax* 01548-843954
Salcombe TQ8 8LJ	*Email* enquire@tidesreach.com
	Website www.tidesreach.com

Owned by the Edwards family for two generations, this seaside hotel is in a commanding position above 'a small, but not overcrowded beach'. The 'functional' 1960s white building has angular balconies, bright blue awnings, and south-facing views across Salcombe estuary. 'A nice feel; comfortable; good-value rooms,' say recent visitors. Most bedrooms face the sheltered garden with its large carp and duck pond beside which summer visitors take snack lunches (soups, sandwiches, kedgeree, etc). The best rooms have a balcony. There is a large sea-water aquarium in the bar. In the dining room (sea views from some tables) the chef, Finn Ibsen, serves modern and traditional dishes, eg, tian of Salcombe crab with avocado and tomato; roast pheasant on a pink peppercorn sauce. 'Men were asked to wear jacket and tie, but smart casual was accepted.' The lack of piped music is appreciated. The swimming pool is in an 'exotic conservatory' which opens to the outside on fine days. The centre of Salcombe is reached by a winding road, but pedestrians may prefer the South Sands ferry. There is easy access to the Coastal Path. (*HM, and others*)

32 bedrooms. On Salcombe estuary, 1 mile from town. Feb–Nov. Lift, ramps. 3 lounges, 2 bars, restaurant; leisure centre: indoor swimming pool, gym, games room; beauty treatments. No background music. ½-acre grounds: pond. Sandy beach 10 yds. Unsuitable for &. No smoking: restaurant, 2 lounges, bedrooms. No children under 8. No dogs in 1 lounge. All major credit cards accepted. B&B £55–£130 per person; D,B&B £70–£160. Set dinner £36. 1-night bookings sometimes refused. **'V'**

SALISBURY Wiltshire *See SHORTLIST*   Map 2:D2

SANDWICH Kent *See SHORTLIST*   Map 2:D5

SAXMUNDHAM Suffolk   Map 2:B6

The Bell Hotel   BUDGET   *Tel/Fax* 01728-602331
31 High Street   *Email* thebell@saxhighstreet.fsnet.co.uk
Saxmundham IP17 1AF   *Website* www.bellhotel-saxmundham.co.uk

'Highly recommended' by a reader this year, this old coaching inn is on the high street of this old market town. It is owned by Andrew Blackburn (the chef) and his French wife, Catherine. 'We were checked in by the proprietor, who broke off preparing dinner to do so, and shown to a lovely spacious room with a vast bathroom. It was above the bar, popular with jolly locals, but there was little noise.' Mr Blackburn tells us that the exterior and almost all public areas have now been restored; new water-colours and some old prints have been hung. 'All the bedrooms have been completely and individually redecorated, and have new, modern facilities.' The conservatory-style residents' lounge has cane sofas and chairs and a log fire. The public bar, open all day, serves real ale. In the smartly wallpapered, candlelit dining room, the 'modern/traditional English' cooking (eg, baked cod with cassoulet beans) has a *Michelin Bib Gourmand*. 'An excellent dinner with very good service.' The price includes a contin-ental breakfast ('good juice, pastries and coffee'), served in the room. Cooked dishes cost extra. Summer meals can be served in the small back courtyard. 'Great value.' (*John Albutt, and others*)

10 bedrooms. 5 miles NW of Aldeburgh. Restaurant open Tues–Sat, except spring and autumn half-term weeks; also open on 'special' Sundays, Christmas lunch, New Year's Eve. Lounge, public bar (monthly quiz night), restaurant. No background music. Small back courtyard. Unsuitable for &. Smoking in bar only. No children under 8 in restaurant after 7.30 pm. Guide dogs only. MasterCard, Visa accepted. B&B £35–£42.50 per person. English breakfast £5.95. Set lunch £11.95–£14.50, dinner £17.50; full alc £32.

SCARBOROUGH North Yorkshire   Map 4:C5
See SHORTLIST

SEAHAM Co. Durham   Map 4:B4

Seaham Hall   **NEW**

Lord Byron's Walk
Seaham SR7 7AG

Tel 0191-516 1400
Fax 0191-516 1410
Email reservations@seaham-hall.com
Website www.seaham-hall.com

Lord Byron married Lady Annabella Milbanke in 1815 in this impressive 17th/19th-century building. It stands on a headland above the North Sea. 'Beautifully restored' as a spa hotel by owners Tom and Jocelyn Maxfield, and managed by Matthew Bell, it combines luxury, style and character, says a visitor this year. 'The spa is world class, large, airy, atmospheric; lovely pool; relaxing pool area. Eastern statues and fountains give the feel of a fairy-tale world.' Chef Stephen Smith presides over *The White Room* ('flavoursome steak, luscious turbot; each pudding like a poem on a plate; expensive, but we felt unhurried; staff seemed to care about making our evening memorable') and the less formal *Ozone* ('a wonderful menu of Asian tapas; Thai curries; home-made ice creams and sorbets'). The bedrooms range from 'classic' to 'penthouse'. 'Spacious, harmoniously decorated', they are 'generously supplied with anything you could want', and have 'the latest technology'. 'Ours was in delicious shades of cream and light brown.' The 'most enjoyable' breakfast can be brought to the room. It includes 'scrambled eggs with smoked salmon in an elegant pyramid'. 'The welcome is warm. Service is helpful.' Popular for weddings and conferences. (*Margaret Mallett*)

19 bedrooms. 1 adapted for guests with limited mobility. 1½ miles N of Seaham, which is 5 miles S of Sunderland, by B1287. Lift. Lounge, bar, 2 restaurants; ballroom; meeting/conference facilities; spa: 65-ft swimming pool; constant soft background jazz in public areas. 37-acre grounds: pebble beach 5 mins' walk. Civil wedding licence. No smoking. Children under 12 have limited access to spa. Guide dogs only. All major credit cards accepted. Room with breakfast £195–£575 (includes use of spa, apart from cost of treatments). Set lunch £22; full alc £60. Christmas/New Year packages. 1-night bookings refused weekends.

SEAHOUSES Northumberland   Map 4:A4
See SHORTLIST

SEAVIEW Isle of Wight   Map 2:E3

Seaview Hotel & Restaurant   *Tel* 01983-612711
High Street   *Fax* 01983-613729
Seaview PO34 5EX   *Email* reception@seaviewhotel.co.uk
                           Website www.seaviewhotel.co.uk

'All very comfortable, cheerful and popular', this small hotel/restaurant in
a seaside village on the Isle of Wight has been through major redevelopment under new owner Brian Gardener, a local; his general manager is
Andrew Morgan. Last year saw the creation of a new brasserie and the
refurbishment of the drawing room and four guest rooms; seven new
bedrooms and two suites are to be added during the winter of 2006/7. One
visitor on a three-day package deal in high summer thought her small room
under the eaves 'was like an oven', but fans were provided. Other guests
liked their 'small, modernised non-smoking room with Solent views over
rooftops'. 'The absence of piped music was much appreciated.' Cooking, by
chef Michael Green, was 'good, but the menu was the same for three
nights'. Children are 'welcomed, not merely tolerated' (young ones have
tea at 5 pm), and 'the staff take a pride in their work'. The 'excellent'
breakfast has freshly squeezed orange juice, porridge and kippers. (*Minda
Alexander, and others*)

17 bedrooms. 2, with balcony, in annexe. 1 on ground floor. 2 self-catering cottages.
Village centre. Closed 24–26 Dec. Ramps. Lounge, 2 bars, brasserie, 2 restaurants;
function room; patio. No background music (occasional light jazz in pump bar).
Access to local sports club (swimming pool, gym, tennis, etc). No smoking: restaurants, lounge, 12 bedrooms. All major credit cards accepted. B&B [2006] £50–£137.50
per person; D,B&B £63–£167.50. Set Sun lunch £16.95; full alc from £35. 1-night
bookings refused weekends April–Oct.

SHANKLIN Isle of Wight   Map 2:E2

Rylstone Manor   *Tel/Fax* 01983-862806
Rylstone Gardens, Popham Road *Email* rylstonemanor@btinternet.com
Shanklin PO37 6RG   *Website* www.rylstone-manor.co.uk

Set in lovely parkland gardens, this Victorian country house, owned by
Neil Graham and Alan Priddle, is built in a blend of Gothic, Tudor and
Georgian styles. Nearby is the Chine, a ravine with woodland walks, a
waterfall and rare plants; the view from the house is of lawns and well-
tended flowerbeds, with glimpses of the sea. 'Everything was in pristine
order and ran like clockwork,' said one visitor. The green-walled lounge
has books and ornaments; there is a 'nice Victorian-style covered patio',

with basket chairs and country magazines. 'Our hosts were charming, the staff completely natural, but professional.' The food, served in the pink-walled, candlelit dining room, was thought 'superb'. Typical dishes on the three-course dinner menu: kiln-roasted salmon with sour cream dressing; breast of duckling with a gin and cream sauce. The simple wine list is 'fairly priced'. The bedrooms, named after English trees, vary in size. 'We loved our four-poster, with its beautiful lacy linen and attractive bedding.' From the garden, guests have direct access to beaches via steep cliff steps. (*RW, and others*)

9 bedrooms. ½ mile SE of village. Closed Nov and Jan. Drawing room, bar lounge, dining room; 'easy listening' background music all day. Terrace. 1-acre garden in 4-acre public gardens. Direct access to sand/shingle beach. Unsuitable for &. No smoking. No children under 16. No dogs. All major credit cards accepted. B&B [2006] £50 per person; D,B&B £66. Set dinner £18. Christmas/New Year packages. ***V***

SHIPTON GORGE Dorset   Map 1:C6

Innsacre Farmhouse   *Tel* 01308-456137
Shipton Gorge   *Email* innsacre.farmhouse@btinternet.com
nr Bridport DT6 4LJ   *Website* www.innsacre.com

'Full of charm', this 17th-century farmhouse, with beamed ceilings and antiques, is 'very personally' run by Sydney and Jayne Davies, who say they 'are trying to encourage guests to our modern way of thinking'. They are committed to local produce, organic where possible, 'but hair shirts are entirely absent; injunctions in the rooms about waste and recycling are authentic rather than formulaic,' say visitors. 'He is an interesting and interested host with a wry sense of humour.' 'She is welcoming without being intrusive, and a sound cook.' This year the sitting and dining rooms have been extended and redecorated. Bedrooms are small, furnished in French country style (new soft furnishings this year); there are duvets on oak beds, and simple bathrooms. A three-course no-choice dinner menu is served, by arrangement, at 8 pm. Enjoyed this year: ham hock and sausage casserole; prune flan. Breakfast, at 8.45 am, has 'a daily goody, eg courgettes or mustardy mushrooms'; 'superb fruit compote'. 'The cooing and billing of white doves in the dovecote outside our room was extraordinarily restful.' Dogs are welcomed (£5 per stay). In the grounds there is a nature trail round a hill. (*Alice and John Sennett, Simon Willbourn, and others*)

4 bedrooms. 1 mile SE of Bridport. Closed Christmas/New Year, mid-Sept–mid-Oct. Dining room closed midday, and Sat Apr–Oct. Lounge/bar, dining area. No background music. 24-acre grounds. Fishing, shingle/sand beach nearby.

Unsuitable for &. No smoking. No children under 9. MasterCard, Visa accepted. B&B [2006] £42.50–£95 per person. Evening meal (by arrangement) £21. 1-night bookings refused weekends/bank holidays.

SHREWSBURY Shropshire *See SHORTLIST*   Map 3:B4

SIDMOUTH Devon   Map 1:C5

Hotel Riviera	*Tel* 01395-515201
The Esplanade	*Fax* 01395-577775
Sidmouth EX10 8AY	*Email* enquiries@hotelriviera.co.uk
	Website www.hotelriviera.co.uk

On the seafront, opposite a pebble/sand beach (safe bathing), the Wharton family's long-established, white, bay-windowed hotel has many fans. They write of 'a warm welcome', 'faultless service', good breakfasts ('real orange juice, excellent porridge, no self-service'), good bedroom lighting, 'food of a high quality', 'reasonable choice, portions not excessive', 'excellent bar lunch'. 'Mrs Wharton has the dedication that marks a good hotel, and her staff respond accordingly.' 'Lovely sea view. We heard the waves from our bed.' The chef, Matthew Weaver, serves main courses like roast rack of lamb; turbot with pak choi; always a vegetarian dish. In summer, alfresco meals are taken under blue-and-white parasols on the large terrace which faces Lyme Bay. There are flowers in the bedrooms, afternoon cream teas, and 'good-value breaks'. The *Riviera* has arrangements with Sidmouth Golf Club, and can arrange pheasant and duck shooting on seven nearby estates. There could be traffic noise in summer. (*Elizabeth Pratt, Richard Creed, and others*)

26 bedrooms. 3 mins' walk from centre. Parking. Lift, ramp. Lounge, bar (pianist at weekends), restaurant; background music; function facilities; terrace. No smoking: restaurant, some bedrooms. No dogs in public rooms, some bedrooms. All major credit cards accepted. B&B [2006] £90–£153; D,B&B £104–£167. Set lunch £23, dinner £35; full alc £42.50. 3-day/weekend breaks. Christmas/New Year packages.

See also SHORTLIST

Smaller hotels, especially those in remote areas, may close at short notice off-season. Check before travelling that a hotel is open.

SINNINGTON North Yorkshire   Map 4:C4

Fox & Hounds   *Tel* 01751-431577
Sinnington YO62 6SQ   *Fax* 01751-432791
                      Email foxhoundsinn@easynet.co.uk
                      Website www.thefoxandhoundsinn.co.uk

Midway between Pickering and Kirkbymoorside, in quiet, 'lovely' village by-passed by
busy A170: Andrew and Catherine Stephens's 18th-century coaching inn, starting
point for walks on moors. 'Very good welcome. Small room, good for short stay. Very
good food.' Residents' lounge, 'olde-worlde' beamed lounge bar, public bar, restaurant;
open fires; background music 'during food service'; 2-acre grounds. No smoking:
restaurant, lounge bar, bedrooms. No dogs in lounge, restaurant. Closed 25/26 Dec.
Amex, MasterCard, Visa accepted. 10 bedrooms (all no-smoking; some on ground floor;
1 is small); 5 with new bathroom. B&B £40–£69 per person. Full alc £35 [2006].
New Year package. 1-night bookings refused Sat. More reports, please.

SNETTISHAM Norfolk   Map 2:A4

The Rose & Crown   *Tel* 01485-541382
Old Church Road, Snettisham   *Fax* 01485-543172
nr King's Lynn PE31 7LX   *Email* info@roseandcrownsnettisham.co.uk
                      Website www.roseandcrownsnettisham.co.uk

'We loved this relaxing place to stay. Very much a pub first (a good one),
and a hotel second. It attracts many locals, covering the whole social scene.'
'The staff, all local young people, are well trained, not at all pretentious.
Reception second to none.' Reports this year on Jeannette and Anthony
Goodrich's 14th-century village inn, complete with twisting passages, hidden corners, low ceilings and old beams. Five new bedrooms (two suitable
for guests with mobility problems) have now been completed. A guest who
occupied one of these found it 'well appointed, smaller than some of the
other rooms, but very comfortable. First-class bed and linen.' Former *sous-
chef* Andy Bruce is now head chef: his menu changes every six to eight
weeks, and is supplemented by daily specials. The cooking was liked, but
one guest found meal service 'patchy' at busy times. No separate residents'
lounge, but there is an area of sofas and armchairs around the fire in the
Garden Room (which is being redecorated to give a 'more sophisticated
feel'). The walled garden, once the village bowling green, has herbaceous
borders and two large willow trees. (*Bill Hawkins, Jennifer Davis, and others*)

16 bedrooms. 2 on ground floor. 2 suitable for &. 4 miles S of Hunstanton. Garden
Room with guests' seating area, 3 bars, 3 dining areas. No background music. Large

walled garden: play fort, barbecue, heat lamps. Beaches 5 and 10 mins' drive. Golf, birdwatching nearby. Eating areas suitable for ♿. No smoking: 1 bar, dining areas, bedrooms. MasterCard, Visa accepted. B&B £42.50–£70 per person; D,B&B (not available in high season) £55–£85. Full alc £30. Christmas/New Year package. *V*

SOAR MILL COVE Devon   Map 1:E4

Soar Mill Cove Hotel   *Tel* 01548-561566
Soar Mill Cove   *Fax* 01548-561223
nr Salcombe TQ7 3DS   *Email* info@soarmillcove.co.uk
                                           Website www.soarmillcove.co.uk

In grounds that slope down to a beautiful beach, and surrounded by National Trust land, Keith Makepeace's single-storey stone and slate hotel stands 'idyllically' above an isolated cove. The building 'is functional', its decor 'comfortable rather than chic', but, says one reader, 'there can't be many English hotels where you can look out of a window while changing for dinner, and see a young stag challenging an older one'. Visitors tell of the 'helpful, friendly staff', although one adds: 'If you can find them.' Children are genuinely welcomed (high teas, high chairs, etc). 'Plenty of fresh flowers, in a rather bleak lounge.' 'Our superior room, with four-poster bed and sea view, was comfortable though the furniture was a little shabby.' Some rooms are small. The restaurant has a big window with 'glorious views'. Comments on the food range from 'as good as ever: fish, local lamb and beef all excellent' to 'variable'. *Castaways*, a coffee bar, is 'for muddy paws and boots, and younger guests'. Breakfast has plenty of choice, including fruit salad and 'beautiful' marmalade. A complimentary cream tea is offered on arrival. There is a sister hotel, the *Rosevine*, Portscatho (*qv*). (*Brian Wicks, Ian Sanders, Margaret Box, Eve and Brian Webb, Mr and Mrs KA Winslow, and others*)

24 bedrooms. All on ground floor. Some suitable for ♿. 3 miles W of Salcombe. Open 9 Feb–1 Jan. Lounge, bar, restaurant (background/live music), coffee shop. Indoor swimming pool (30 by 18 ft); treatment room (hairdressing, reflexology, aromatherapy, etc), free Internet access. 10-acre grounds: swimming pool (30 by 21 ft), tennis, putting, donkey, miniature pony, children's play area, jogging trail. Sea, sandy beach, 600 yds. Smoking in bar only to Dec 2006; thereafter, no smoking. No dogs in public rooms. MasterCard, Visa accepted. B&B £80–£170 per person. Set lunch £16.95, dinner £29–£39. Christmas/New Year packages. 1-night bookings sometimes refused Sat.

Report forms (Freepost in UK) are at the end of the *Guide.*

SOMERTON Somerset   Map 1:C6

The Lynch Country House   **BUDGET**   *Tel* 01458-272316
4 Behind Berry   *Fax* 01458-272590
Somerton TA11 7PD   *Email* the_lynch@talk21.com
                    Website www.thelynchcountryhouse.co.uk

On a crest in a small Somerset town above the Cary valley, this 'smart and friendly' B&B in a Grade II listed Regency house is run by Roy Copeland, 'an interesting and interested' host and former jazz musician. This year he has acquired an 18th-century cottage with three bedrooms, next door, which can also be used for self-catering guests (it has a range of domestic appliances). The handsome main house has a large hall and high-ceilinged public rooms, which have been 'sympathetically decorated'. Wildlife is encouraged in the large grounds, where there is a lake with black swans, exotic ducks and a variety of fish. 'We were delighted with our good-sized four-poster room,' says a visitor in 2006. 'Splendid views. Our little pug dog was made most welcome.' Some rooms, under the eaves, are smaller. Four rooms are in the single-storey coach house. There is a small sitting area for visitors, in a room with an orangery extension where breakfast is served: its tall windows overlook the lake. At the top of the house, a small observatory (with telescope) gives wide views. No dinners, but advice is given, with menus, on where to eat. Somerton's church is worth visiting. (*Nigel Mackintosh*)

12 bedrooms. 4 in coach house. 3 in cottage (may also be self-catering). 5 on ground floor. N edge of village. Closed 31 Dec. Breakfast room, small sitting area. No background music. 2½-acre grounds: lake. Unsuitable for &. No smoking. No dogs in public rooms; in bedrooms by arrangement. All major credit cards accepted. B&B £30–£60 per person. 2-night stays preferred at weekends in high season.

SOUTHWOLD Suffolk *See SHORTLIST*   Map 2:B6

How to contact the *Guide*
By mail: From anywhere in the UK, write to Freepost PAM 2931, London W11 4BR (no stamp is needed)
From outside the UK: Good Hotel Guide, 50 Addison Avenue, London W11 4QP, England
By telephone or fax: 020-7602 4182
By email: Goodhotel@aol.com
Via our website: www.goodhotelguide.com

STADDLEBRIDGE North Yorkshire   Map 4:C4

McCoy's at the Tontine	*Tel* 01609-882671
The Cleveland Tontine	*Fax* 01609-882660
Staddlebridge	*Email* enquiries@mccoysatthetontine.co.uk
Northallerton DL6 3JB	*Website* www.mccoysatthetontine.co.uk

♧ *César award in 1989*

'Our 30th anniversary in 2006,' say the McCoy brothers (Peter, Tom and Eugene), owners of this shamelessly eccentric restaurant-with-rooms, a northern institution. 'It feels like we've been here for ever.' A reader found it 'good fun; comfortable rather than smart', adding: 'They care about good food, drink and service.' The bistro ('slightly subterranean, look out of the window and your nose hits the grass') has a blackboard menu and closely packed tables. Stuart Hawkins, the head chef, presents an eclectic menu which might include moules marinière; roast duck with caramelised apple, calvados sauce. The bedrooms have vibrant colours, bright soft furnishings. 'Bathrooms play host to cavernous baths of Edwardian pretension,' say the McCoys. Wallpapers may be dramatic: 'Ours was navy, heavily patterned with sprigs of flowers.' At breakfast there is fresh juice, leaf tea, 'a great plate of exotic fruit, impeccable cooked dishes: excellent scrambled eggs'. The stone Victorian house occupies a triangular site between the A19 and a slip road on the edge of the North Yorkshire moors (windows are double glazed). The brothers also run a restaurant in the Baltic Centre at Gateshead, and a café/bistro in Yarm, near Teesside airport. (*NB*)

6 bedrooms. 6 miles NE of Northallerton, at junction of A19/A172. Closed 25/26 Dec, 1 Jan. 2 lounges (residents only), breakfast room, bar, bistro; background music ('French, Hawaiian, Irish, whatever'). Unsuitable for &. No smoking in some bedrooms. No dogs in public rooms. All major credit cards accepted. B&B £60–£85 per person. Set lunch from £13.95; full alc £45.

STAMFORD Lincolnshire   Map 2:B3

The George	*Tel* 01780-750750
71 St Martins	*Fax* 01780-750701
Stamford PE9 2LB	*Email* reservations@georgehotelofstamford.com
	Website www.georgehotelofstamford.com

With mullioned windows, flagstoned entrance hall, antique panelling, creaking floorboards, a cobbled courtyard, Lawrence Hoskins's 16th-century coaching inn has 'plenty of history and atmosphere' and is generally liked by *Guide* readers. 'Excellent in every department,' was one comment. Chris Pitman is the 'charming' manager (and executive chef). The attractive public rooms 'have the best flower arrangements I have seen anywhere', says a visitor in 2006. No background music, but a dissenter was unhappy about the lack of a non-smoking sitting area, a complaint which he felt was unsympathetically dealt with. The *London Room* and the *York Bar* were once waiting rooms for the 40 coaches ('20 up and 20 down') that called each day. There is a 'good pubby feel – and good beers'. 'It was easy to strike up conversations with locals.' 'Food was good; service enthusiastic.' In the formal dining room, men must wear jacket and tie while consuming traditional dishes, eg, chicken liver terrine; roast sirloin of beef. Meals are also served in the less formal *Garden Lounge*. The bedrooms vary greatly. Some have antiques. Dividing walls can be thin. Roadside rooms get traffic noise, and courtyard-facing rooms might be noisy too. The breakfast buffet 'offered good choice; scrambled eggs on wholemeal toast cooked to order'. (*Joanna Russell, and others*)

47 bedrooms. ½ mile from centre (front windows double glazed). Large car park. Railway station 500 yds. Ramps. 2 lounges, 2 bars, 2 restaurants; 4 private dining rooms; business centre. No background music. 2-acre grounds: courtyard, herb garden, monastery garden, croquet. Unsuitable for &. Civil wedding licence. No smoking: main restaurant until after 10 pm, *Garden Lounge* at breakfast, bedrooms. No dogs unattended in bedrooms, only guide dogs in restaurant. All major credit cards accepted. B&B [2006]: single £78–£125, double £115–£225, suite £155–£225. Set lunch £17.50; full alc £55. Sunday night rates. Special breaks.

See also SHORTLIST

STANSTED Essex *See SHORTLIST*   Map 2:C4

STOCKBRIDGE Hampshire *See SHORTLIST* Map 2:D2

STOKE CANON Devon *See SHORTLIST*   Map 1:C5

If you are recommending a B&B and know of a good restaurant nearby, please mention it in your report.

STOURTON Wiltshire   Map 2:D1

Spread Eagle Inn	*Tel* 01747-840587
Stourton, nr Warminster	*Fax* 01747-840954
BA12 6QE	*Email* enquiries@spreadeagleinn.com
	Website www.spreadeagleinn.com

A traditional British inn, in the middle of Stourhead, one of the great gardens of England. It is owned by Stephen Ross, formerly of the *Queensberry Hotel*, Bath (*qv*), who has renovated bedrooms, bar and restaurant since coming here in 2005. The manager/chef is Tom Bridgeman. 'A bonus of staying here,' said our inspectors, 'is that you get free entry to the gardens and can continue to enjoy them after closing time.' They had a warm welcome from 'helpful young staff' (the Rosses are not resident owners). 'Our room was spacious, well proportioned, with large sash windows, big, comfortable bed, and some nice antiques (some rather worn).' There is a smallish, red-walled sitting room. The large dining room has chandeliers, ornate mirrors and Victorian paintings 'in keeping with the house style'. The cooking places emphasis on English traditional dishes using local produce, much of it from the estate, eg, crab, leek and Cheddar tart; breast of duck with champ and plum chutney. The bar, with simple wooden tables and chairs, has a blackboard menu (soups, salads, 'robust pies and stews') and serves local beers. 'Breakfast had excellent porridge; piping hot toast but commercial little pots of preserves.'

5 bedrooms. 3 miles NW of Mere. Closed Christmas. Lounge, bar, restaurant (background music at night). On 2,650-acre National Trust estate which has civil wedding licence. Unsuitable for ♿. Smoking in bar only. No dogs. MasterCard, Visa accepted. B&B [2006] £49–£75 per person. Set dinner £24; full alc £30. ***V***

STRATFORD-UPON-AVON Warwickshire   Map 3:D6
See SHORTLIST

STUDLAND Dorset *See SHORTLIST*   Map 2:E1

We drop a hotel if there has been a change of owner, if this year's reports are negative or in rare cases where there has been no feedback. About 80 hotels fall by the wayside every year, and a similar number are introduced.

STURMINSTER NEWTON Dorset   Map 2:E1

Plumber Manor   *Tel* 01258-472507
Sturminster Newton DT10 2AF   *Fax* 01258-473370
                                        Email book@plumbermanor.com
                                        Website www.plumbermanor.com

♛ *César award in 1987*

The family home of the Prideaux-Brune family since the early 17th
century, this Jacobean manor house (Pride of Britain) is run as a restaurant-
with-rooms ('homely and comfortable') by Richard Prideaux-Brune, his
wife, Alison, and brother, Brian (the chef). A tributary of the River Stour
runs through the grounds, which have manicured lawns and herbaceous
borders. Fans enjoy the 'efficient yet relaxed service'. One says: 'They
undersell themselves; it is a very well-run hotel.' One couple wrote of 'the
feel of a house party: most other guests had been before, and were engaged
in friendly conversation with the owners.' Bedrooms in the main house lead
off a gallery hung with family portraits. The best rooms are in a converted
barn: 'Plenty of space, comfortable window seat, well-equipped bathroom;
immaculate housekeeping.' 'Delicious food, portion control just right for us
"oldies" who dislike overloaded plates.' 'The menu didn't change, but
choice was adequate.' Some guests were disappointed that afternoon tea
was not available in the lounge: 'We had to make our own, with UHT, in
the bedroom.' At breakfast, 'top-class ingredients are used'. 'Two Labradors
greet every arriving car.' (*Janet Austin, Walter Cottingham, and others*)

16 bedrooms. 10 on ground floor, in courtyard. 2 miles SW of Sturminster Newton.
Closed Feb. Restaurant closed midday, except Sun. Lounge, bar, 3 dining rooms,
gallery. No background music. 2-acre grounds: garden, tennis, croquet, stream.
Smoking in conference room only. No dogs in public rooms; allowed in 2 bedrooms
only. All major credit cards accepted. B&B £55–£110 per person. Set dinner
£23–£26; full alc £36. Christmas package.

Stourcastle Lodge   *Tel* 01258-472320
Gough's Close, Sturminster Newton   *Fax* 01258-473381
DT10 1BU   *Email* enquiries@stourcastle-lodge.co.uk
                                Website www.stourcastle-lodge.co.uk

A family home since the early 18th century, Jill and Ken Hookham-
Bassett's 300-year-old white-painted former farmhouse is 'very relaxing,
with excellent housekeeping and food of a high standard', write guests after
their third visit. In a quaint stone-walled close, just off the main street of
this medieval market town, it has 'a wonderful welcoming atmosphere'. Jill

and Ken are unobtrusive but attentive hosts.' The bedrooms, which look over the village, all have an antique brass bedstead; two have a whirlpool bath. 'Our bright and airy room, Charlotte, had a comfortable bed and a shower room.' On chilly evenings, an open log fire burns in the pink-walled lounge. In the dining room, decorated with antique kitchen equipment, the hostess serves three-course Aga-cooked dinners: 'We enjoyed duck salad; chicken with leeks.' No choice of main course, but 'imaginative vegetarian dishes' are offered. No licence; bring your own wine, no corkage charged. At breakfast, 'the muesli is packed with fruit and nuts'. A south-facing terrace has summer seating. The River Stour is at the end of the garden, in which you might spot the sculptures of Henrietta and her piglets. (*Richard and Jean Green, and others*)

5 bedrooms. Central. Lounge, restaurant. No background music. ⅓-acre garden. 300 yds from River Stour (coarse fishing). Parking. Unsuitable for ♿. No smoking. No children. Guide dogs only. MasterCard, Visa accepted. B&B £41–£57 per person; D,B&B £50–£79. Set dinner £22. Christmas package. 1-night bookings sometimes refused.

SUTTON COLDFIELD Warwickshire   Map 3:C6
See SHORTLIST

SWAFFHAM Norfolk   Map 2:B5

Strattons	*Tel* 01760-723845
4 Ash Close	*Fax* 01760-720458
Swaffham PE37 7NH	*Email* enquiries@strattonshotel.com
	Website www.strattonshotel.com

♥ *César award in 2003*

'We feel passionately about our environmental footprint,' write Vanessa and Les Scott who run their Grade II listed Palladian-style villa along strictly sustainable lines. They have won awards for their control of 'waste streams' and their support of local suppliers. This might not be to all tastes: you should not expect 'extras' such as a dressing gown or fancy toiletries in the bedroom, and one visitor was 'irritated by the homilies about not filling a bath or using a power shower'. But fans remain happy. 'We felt welcome from the moment we arrived.' 'Wonderful surroundings, food and personal service.' A birthday celebration was 'like a lovely family house party'. *Strattons* is filled with original paintings, sculptures and ornaments, and noted for its exotic themed bedrooms: Opium, in the old groom's cottage, has a freestanding bath at the end of the bed; the Red Room has a raised four-poster, and a Moroccan-style bathroom. Mrs Scott, with Maggie Cooper, cooks modern English dishes on a short daily-changing menu (eg, spicy monkfish stew). Breakfast has freshly squeezed juices, free-range eggs and home-made breads. The Scotts' daughter, Hannah, shares the manager's role with Dominic Hughes. (*Mr and Mrs P Brittan, Martine Flavell, and others*)

8 bedrooms. 2 in annexe. 2 on ground floor. Central. Parking. Closed 1 week Christmas. Drawing room, TV room, restaurant. No background music. Terrace. 1-acre garden. Unsuitable for ⅙. No smoking. No dogs in restaurant or unaccompanied in bedrooms (£5.50 per day). MasterCard, Visa accepted. B&B [2006] £65–£150 per person. Set dinner £40. Special breaks. 1-night bookings sometimes refused weekends. New Year package.

SWAY Hampshire   Map 2:E2

The Nurse's Cottage
Station Road
Sway, nr Lymington
SO41 6BA

Tel/Fax 01590-683402
Email nurses.cottage@lineone.net
Website www.nursescottage.co.uk

Once the home of successive district nurses, this cottage is run in very personal style by Tony Barnfield, 'a man of strong views'. The bedrooms, all on the ground floor, are small, but 'a lot is fitted into a small space'. Most visitors enjoyed their stay. 'Our room was genteel, immaculate, well thought out,' wrote an inspector. 'Unusual items included a blank video cassette in case we wanted to record a programme while dining. There were shoe-cleaning kit; fresh milk and juice in a fridge; fruit and flowers; wall-mounted reading lights; sheets and blankets on the bed; a good bathroom. The comprehensive information pack included dire warnings about the consequences of being caught smoking a cigarette.' Residents are expected to dine in, in the attractive blue-and-white conservatory restaurant. The menu changes four or five times a year (but there are normally daily dishes). House specialities include mushroom millefeuille; baked chicken breast stuffed with pork, plum and ginger. The cooking is thought 'very good', but one couple were 'embarrassed to be reprimanded for being ten minutes early for dinner'. The 'enjoyable' breakfast has a buffet, and the usual cooked dishes. (*William Cullen, and others*)

5 bedrooms. All on ground floor. 1 accessible for ⅙, but not suitable for independent wheelchair-user. Village centre. 4 miles NW of Lymington. Train: Sway. Small sitting area, restaurant (background music). Small garden. No smoking.

No children under 10. No dogs in public rooms. Amex, MasterCard, Visa accepted. D,B&B £75–£85 per person. Set dinner £20–£23. Bargain breaks. Christmas/New Year packages.

SWINBURNE Northumberland   Map 4:B3

The Hermitage   BUDGET

Swinburne
nr Hexham NE48 4DG

Tel 01434-681248
Fax 01434-681610
Email katie.stewart@themeet.co.uk

Approached through a grand arch and up a long drive bordered in spring by daffodils, Katie and Simon Stewart's family home has ancestral portraits and antiques. It is not run as a hotel (guests are expected to be out between 10.30 am and 5 pm), but readers enjoy 'the true country house atmosphere', the 'superb public rooms', and the owners' 'warm-hearted, no-nonsense' approach. The bedrooms have period furnishings. 'Ours was large and comfortable, with views over the garden and woodland beyond from one window, and the large vegetable patch from the other.' Three rooms have a bathroom *en suite*, the other's bathroom is down three short flights of steps and round a corner. Breakfast is 'hearty, with lots of thick toast'. In fine weather it is served on a terrace. Several good pubs are within 15 minutes' drive. Swinburne has a large reservoir and a 17th-century house on the site of an old castle. Hadrian's Wall is three miles away. More reports, please.

3 bedrooms. 7 miles NW of Corbridge; turn left on to A6079. Lodge gates 1 mile on right. Open Mar–Sept inclusive. No telephone/TV. Drawing room with TV, breakfast room. No background music. 2-acre garden: tennis. Unsuitable for &. No smoking. No children under 8 except babies. No dogs. No credit cards. B&B £35–£45 per person.

SWINDON Wiltshire *See SHORTLIST*   Map 2:C2

SYMONDS YAT EAST Herefordshire   Map 3:D5

The Saracens Head Inn   NEW

Symonds Yat East
Ross-on-Wye HR9 6JL

Tel 01600-890435
Fax 01600-890034
Email contact@saracensheadinn.co.uk
Website www.saracensheadinn.co.uk

'Jolly, relaxed, unpretentious': in wooded valley in area of outstanding natural beauty, often busy with tourists, 'very helpful' Rollinson family's old inn, part of a

string of white buildings on E bank of River Wye near Welsh border. 'Lively bar with red telephone box, fruit machines and billiard table.' Restaurant, with rustic decor, 'very friendly young staff'. Food on long menu: generous portions. Inspectors thought it over-ambitious: 'Go for the simplest dishes.' Car park. Closed Christmas/New Year. Lounge, TV room. Background music most of the time. Most public areas have wheelchair access. 2 riverside terraces: free fishing. No smoking: dining room, bedrooms. Dogs in bar only. MasterCard, Visa accepted. 10 bedrooms (best ones in Boathouse annexe; 1 on ground floor). B&B [2006] £39–£70 per person. Full alc £30. ***V***

TAUNTON Somerset   Map 1:C5

The Castle at Taunton
Castle Green
Taunton TA1 1NF

Tel 01823-272671
Fax 01823-336066
Email reception@the-castle-hotel.com
Website www.the-castle-hotel.com

Q *César award in 1987*

Once a Norman fortress, this wisteria-covered, castellated hotel is liked for its 'great accommodation and dinners'. Owners Kit and Louise Chapman have led four chefs to a *Michelin* star. The 'elegant' public rooms have old oak furniture, tapestries and paintings, 'lovely flowers'. A fine wrought iron staircase leads to bedrooms of varying size and style: 'Our suite was a delight: bright and colourful, with comfortable furniture and a lovely bathroom.' 'My pleasant single room was well equipped, with good cupboard space and spotless bathroom.' A visitor in 2006 was less impressed by a 'small, shabby double with walls so thin we could hear snoring and ablutions from next door'. In the restaurant, chef Richard Guest serves modern British cooking, eg, baked organic egg with white truffle cream; crispy duck with roast cranberry compote; British cheeses 'chosen with care'. 'The food and wine were delicious, but the kindness, skill and care shown by the staff impressed us most.' Light meals, salads, grills, omelettes, etc, are served in *Brazz*, the lively café/bistro adjacent. The buffet breakfast continues to be criticised: it now has fresh bread and fresh fruit salad, and sausages, etc, are locally sourced, 'but bacon and egg needs to be freshly cooked'. (*Ian Dewey, Christopher Evans, and others*)

44 bedrooms. Central. Main restaurant closed Sun night. Lift, ramps. Lounge, bar, restaurant, brasserie (background music); private dining/meeting rooms. 1-acre garden: shop. No smoking in restaurant. Small dogs only; not in public rooms. All major credit cards accepted. B&B £90–£127.50 per person. Set lunch/dinner from £20. Christmas/New Year packages. ***V***

TAVISTOCK Devon   Map 1:D4

Browns Hotel   *Tel* 01822-618686
80 West Street   *Fax* 01822-618646
Tavistock PL19 8AQ   *Email* enquiries@brownsdevon.co.uk
                            Website www.brownsdevon.co.uk

Q *César award in 2006*

Once an 18th-century coaching inn (built by the seventh Duke of Bedford), this town house, near the fine church in the centre of this handsome old market town, is run by Peter Brown as a hotel/wine bar/brasserie. Martin Ball is manager. 'Delightful. A warm welcome. Excellent food,' says one visitor in 2006. The decor is smart and modern: fawn, terracotta, chocolate-brown carpets, 'interesting art work' in public areas. The 'charm of the lively, supportive staff' is mentioned. The bedrooms are 'immaculate', but some are small. 'Ours was compact to within an inch of its life, the bathroom was minuscule,' was a comment from a reader who was also troubled 'by the mating calls of the local youths in the street at the front'. 'Thoughtful touches' include a video player (there is a library of films). The mews rooms are particularly commended. The music in the restaurant ('exposed bricks, stone floors, big, comfortable armchairs') was thought 'an awful, intrusive noise', but the cooking of David Jenkins was 'a treat' (eg, pan-fried halibut with ragout of mussels). Breakfast, in the conservatory, had 'superb smoked salmon and scrambled eggs'. But the 'light' breakfast was thought 'meagre'. There is a 'state-of-the-art' gym. (*Paul Robinson, Graham Davies, and others*)

20 bedrooms. 4 in mews. Some suitable for &. Town centre. Lift. Conservatory, 2 bar areas, restaurant; background music all day; gym, small indoor swimming pool. Courtyard garden (dining). No smoking: restaurant, 3 bedrooms. Guide dogs only. Amex, MasterCard, Visa accepted. B&B £55–£90 per person. Set dinner £17.50; full alc £27.50. *V*

TEFFONT EVIAS Wiltshire   Map 2:D1

Howard's House   *Tel* 01722-716392
Teffont Evias   *Fax* 01722-716820
nr Salisbury SP3 5RJ   *Email* enq@howardshousehotel.co.uk
                         Website www.howardshousehotel.co.uk

In a tranquil village near Salisbury, this 'fascinating' 17th-century dower house has a 19th-century Swiss-style extension with broad-eaved roofs. Now a small country hotel, managed by Noële Thompson, it is much liked.

Recent comments: 'Well-nigh perfect.' 'Not cheap, but you pay for the unique location and the exceptionally friendly service.' The decor is 'what one might find in a non-designer home'. The lounge has an old stone fireplace (with a fire in winter), yellow walls, bright fabrics and exposed beams. Tea and home-made biscuits are served here and on the terrace. The bedrooms, with their pastel colours and floral prints, are 'characterful and pretty'. 'Ours was spacious, with an idyllic view of the hillside garden and church.' But most rooms are smallish, and beds may be on the small side too. The modern cooking of the 'splendid' chef, Nick Wentworth, is admired (eg, fillet of sea bass, saffron broth, pancetta beignet). 'Good wine by the glass.' 'Breakfast could not be faulted: lovely stewed fruit; huge portion of scrambled egg with smoked salmon; ever-so-light croissants.' In the gardens are ancient box hedges, 'romantic corners', a pond with a fountain, and a herb and vegetable garden. Children and dogs are welcomed (£30 and £7 respectively). (*Anthony Fisher, JF*)

9 bedrooms. On B3089, 10 miles W of Salisbury. Car park. Closed 1 week at Christmas. Lounge, restaurant. No background music. 2-acre grounds: croquet. River, fishing nearby. Unsuitable for &. No smoking in restaurant. Amex, MasterCard, Visa accepted. B&B [2006]: single £100, double £155. Set lunch £25, dinner £26.50; full alc £60. 2-night breaks. New Year package. ***V***

TEIGNMOUTH Devon   Map 1:D5

Thomas Luny House **BUDGET**	*Tel* 01626-772976
Teign Street	*Email* alisonandjohn@thomas-luny-house.co.uk
Teignmouth TQ14 8EG	*Website* www.thomas-luny-house.co.uk

'Like an oasis in the centre of Teignmouth', this 'beautiful house' was built by Thomas Luny, a renowned marine artist, in 1808, when the town was favoured by admirals and captains. It is reached via an archway ('which needs a bit of thought before you drive through') in a high whitewashed wall. Owners John and Alison Allan are 'extremely friendly'. The double drawing room and breakfast room, each with an open fire, lead through French windows on to the 'pretty patio suntrap garden'. 'It is very pleasant to sit outside in summer and drink John's excellent tea and eat Alison's delicious cake,' say their fans. Three bedrooms are spacious, the fourth is small. All have flowers, Malvern water, books and magazines, tea-making facilities and bathrobes. The 'excellent' breakfast, taken at separate tables, includes 'freshly baked bread, fresh fruits, perfect scrambled eggs'. Teignmouth 'seems to be smartening its appearance, and there are some new restaurants with interesting menus', according to one of this year's reporters. (*MC and GR Bradshaw, Marilyn Frampton, and others*)

4 bedrooms. Central. Sometimes closed Christmas. 2 lounges, breakfast room. No background music. Small walled garden. Sea, sandy beach 5 mins' walk. Unsuitable for &. No smoking. No children under 12. No dogs. MasterCard, Visa accepted. B&B [2006] (*Not VAT-rated*) £35–£62 per person.

See also SHORTLIST

TEMPLE SOWERBY Cumbria   Map 4: inset C3

Temple Sowerby House   **NEW**   *Tel* 017683-61578
Temple Sowerby   *Fax* 017683-61958
nr Penrith CA10 1RZ   *Email* stay@temple-sowerby.com
                                 Website www. temple-sowerby.com

With its thick walls and Georgian wing, this old farmhouse, part 16th-century and Grade II listed, has views of Cross Fell, the highest peak in the Pennines. It looks across the busy A66 to the green of this village in the Eden valley, but traffic noise will reduce with the completion of a bypass which is being built. The quietest bedrooms are at the rear. 'It makes a welcome stop-over between south and north,' say visitors this year. The 'welcoming' owner/ managers, Paul and Julie Evans, 'who seem to be on hand to meet visitors' needs at all times', recently opened a new conservatory-style restaurant which faces the walled garden with its terrace which 'in the late afternoon sun is the perfect spot for a glass of local beer'. Chef Ashley Whittaker serves modern British dishes like butter-roasted chicken breast with olive oil and chervil mash. 'The food is very good; wine list good too, and reasonable value.' 'The lounges are cosy,' says another report. 'Bedrooms excellent.' Breakfast has 'delicious bread and rolls', 'nice jam and butter, unwrapped'. Meetings, seminars and 'discreet gatherings' are catered for. Ullswater is 15 mins' drive away. (*Conrad Barnard, Elizabeth Russell, and others*)

12 bedrooms. 2 on ground floor in coach house (20 yds). Centre of village on A66, 6 miles NW of Appleby (front windows double glazed). Closed 1 week at Christmas. 2 lounges, bar, restaurant (varied background music); conference/function facilities. 2-acre garden: croquet. Civil wedding licence. No smoking. No children under 12. Dogs by arrangement, not in public rooms. MasterCard, Visa accepted. B&B £57.50–£105 per person; D,B&B £80–£130. Full alc £43. 2-night breaks. New Year package. 1-night bookings occasionally refused. ***V***

For details of the Voucher scheme see page 60.

TETBURY Gloucestershire   Map 3:E5

Calcot Manor   *Tel* 01666-890391
nr Tetbury GL8 8YJ   *Fax* 01666-890394
                                     Email reception@calcotmanor.co.uk
                                     Website www.calcotmanor.co.uk

♥ *César award in 2001*

A returning visitor 'could not fault anything' about this conversion of a
14th-century Cotswold farmhouse, cottages and outbuildings (Pride of
Britain). Richard Ball is the long-serving managing director. His wife,
Cathy, runs the spa: 'a real bonus in winter', it provides a retreat for adults
(children may use the swimming pool at specified times). 'The best
holiday I have had as a parent,' was another comment. For small children
there is an Ofsted-registered crèche, and a Playzone in a converted tithe
barn. The suites, in the courtyard, have a double bedroom for parents and
a sitting room, with bunks or sofa bed for the young, video, TV, a small
fridge, and baby-listening. 'All staff (many foreign) are polite and cheerful,
creating a good atmosphere.' Tea, coffee and biscuits are supplied in the
bedrooms, where 'pillows are high quality, coat hangers free-range and
many'. The food is thought 'superb', in the conservatory restaurant
(booking advised). Michael Croft serves a modern menu, eg, seared red
mullet with tomato gazpacho. The informal *Gumstool* pub, 'equally good',
'has a great buzz'. Children take high tea here. Breakfasts have fresh orange
juice, local Duchy sausages. Conferences and weddings are held. (*Zara
Elliott, and others*)

35 bedrooms. 10 (family) in cottage. 11 around courtyard, on ground floor. 3 miles
W of Tetbury. Train: Kemble, 10 miles; taxi. Ramps. Lounge, 2 restaurants, 2 bars;
background music at mealtimes; private dining room; cinema; conference facilities;
children's playroom with nanny (4 hrs daily). 220-acre grounds: tennis, heated
outdoor 24-ft swimming pool, children's play area, croquet; bicycles; spa: 48-ft
swimming pool, sauna, treatments, etc. Golf, fishing, riding nearby. Civil wedding
licence. No smoking in main restaurant. Guide dogs only, by arrangement. All major
credit cards accepted. B&B [2006]: single £170, double £195–£235, suite £270;
D,B&B £127–£205 per person. Full alc from £44. 2-day breaks. Christmas/New
Year packages. 1-night bookings refused Sat in season.

* *

Traveller's tale Our room was lovely but dinner, despite its
pseudo-sophistication, was awful. We will never forget the pre-
formed portion of polenta and canteen-style giant head of
yellowing broccoli, dripping with water. (*Hotel in Scotland*)

* *

The Priory Inn   *Tel* 01666-502251
London Road   *Fax* 01666-503534
Tetbury GL8 8JJ   *Email* info@theprioryinn.co.uk
                        Website www.theprioryinn.co.uk

'Parents will never feel uncomfortable here because they have children,'
promise David and Tanya Kelly, owners of this hotel/gastropub/coffee
bar/pizza takeaway in a charming market town on the River Avon.
Parents of young children themselves, they welcome families, providing
high chairs, baby monitors, changing facilities, special menus. Yet, 'the
presence of other people's children was never an issue, it was incredibly
quiet', said visitors without children this year. Staff are 'professional, and
chatty without being intrusive'. The bedrooms have an uncluttered design,
and in each is an original painting. 'Our small room faced the car park,
but it had a bed big enough for a family of four, and crisp white linen.'
There are leather sofas, cappuccinos, newspapers and children's toys in
the coffee bar. A 'beauty and well-being salon' is new this year. The pub,
formerly the stable block, has exposed brick walls, beams, bare floorboards,
oak tables, and a huge walk-around fire. Food ranges from an all-day
English breakfast, home-made soups, sandwiches and wood-fired pizzas, to
dinner dishes like butternut squash and sage risotto; roasted partridge;
baked apple tart; warm chocolate torte. There is live music on Sunday
night. (*Liz and Glen Balmer, and others*)

14 bedrooms. 4 on ground floor. 1 suitable for &. 2 mins' walk from centre.
Gastropub/bar/restaurant (background music; live music Sun night), coffee bar;
conference room; beauty salon. Small garden at front. No smoking: bedrooms,
restaurant, public rooms. Dogs in bar only. Diners, MasterCard, Visa accepted. B&B
£49.50–£89 per person. Full alc £29. Christmas/New Year packages. 1-night
bookings refused high season weekends.

See also SHORTLIST

THIRSK North Yorkshire *See SHORTLIST*   Map 4:C4

When you make a booking you enter into a contract with a hotel.
Most hotels explain their cancellation policies, which vary
widely, in a letter of confirmation. You may lose your deposit or
be charged at the full rate for the room if you cancel at short
notice. A travel insurance policy can provide protection.

THORPE ST ANDREW Norfolk   Map 2:B5

The Old Rectory   *Tel* 01603-700772
103 Yarmouth Road   *Fax* 01603-300772
Thorpe St Andrew   *Email* enquiries@oldrectorynorwich.com
nr Norwich NR7 0HF   *Website* www.oldrectorynorwich.com

In a conservation area, surrounded by mature gardens and overlooking the
River Yare, this creeper-clad Georgian rectory is the family home of Chris
and Sally Entwistle, their son, James, and their Birman cats, Rolo and Milli.
A visitor reports: 'Thoroughly recommended; small but with all the
necessary facilities. My bedroom and bathroom were spacious.' Pre-dinner
drinks are taken in the drawing room, where a log fire, big mirrors,
decorative plates and family photographs create a 'pleasant atmosphere'.
James Perry is the chef: his dishes might include smoked haddock, basil and
Parmesan tart; slow-roasted Barbary duck leg with marinated chickpeas
and baked red peppers. The conservatory overlooks a terrace with a small
kidney-shaped swimming pool. The house stands well back from the road
(the entrance through green gates is quite narrow), and buses to Norwich
stop outside. 'There were several lone female guests (conference folk
escaping the city), all comfortable and at ease.' The small village ('suburbia
really') is just two miles from Norwich city centre.

8 bedrooms. 3 in coach house (20 yds). 2 miles E of Norwich. Closed 22 Dec–3 Jan.
Restaurant closed Sun/Mon. Drawing room, conservatory, dining room; background
music evenings; meeting/function facilities. 1-acre garden: heated swimming pool
(40 by 12 ft). River Yare 450 yds. Unsuitable for &. Smoking allowed only in conservatory. No dogs in public rooms; allowed in 1 bedroom only. Amex, MasterCard,
Visa accepted. B&B £55–£95 per person. Set dinner £25. 1-night bookings refused
weekends Easter–Sept.

TITCHWELL Norfolk   Map 2:A5

Titchwell Manor   *Tel* 01485-210221
Titchwell, nr Brancaster   *Fax* 01485-210104
PE31 8BB   *Email* margaret@titchwellmanor.com
                                      Website www.titchwellmanor.com

Built as a farmhouse in 1890, and facing dunes and salt marshes, this small
hotel/restaurant/bar is owned by Margaret and Ian Snaith who have now
completed the refurbishment of all existing bedrooms, and added 12 new
rooms in the old herb garden. Public rooms have mosaic tiled floors and
dark woodwork, Lloyd Loom furniture, potted plants: 'a fusion of modernity and the traditional values of a Victorian house', says the brochure. 'A

bit Chelsea on sea,' wrote one couple, 'but it's a lovely, comfortable hotel, and they make "well-behaved" children welcome.' Other guests 'had one of the newly refurbished rooms, which was very comfortable'. But some rooms may be small. The food served in the 'nice, light, conservatory dining room with well-spaced wooden tables', found favour: the Snaiths' son, Eric, is the chef. Seafood is a speciality, and the menu might also include local venison. The bar, with its 'feel of a gastropub', serves light meals all day. Children under 12 can mix and match from a 'kids' menu'. Breakfast includes 'outstanding local kippers', smoked salmon and scrambled eggs. The Titchwell nature reserve is close by. (*Celia and Peter Gregory, MC and GR Bradshaw, Philip and Eileen Hall*)

25 bedrooms. 16 on ground floor, in barn annexe. 2 suitable for &. 5 miles E of Hunstanton. 2 lounges, bar, restaurant; background music at night. ½-acre garden. Beaches, golf nearby. No smoking: restaurant, bedrooms. No children over Christmas/New Year. All major credit cards accepted. B&B £45–£85 per person; D,B&B £15 added. Full alc £35. Christmas/New Year packages. 1-night bookings sometimes refused Sat.

TITLEY Herefordshire   Map 3:C4

The Stagg Inn   NEW   *Tel* 01544-230221
Titley, nr Kington   *Fax* 01544-231390
HR5 3RL   *Email* reservations@thestagg.co.uk
                                      Website www.thestagg.co.uk

'This must be the most unpretentious and laid-back *Michelin*-starred establishment in Europe,' say inspectors in 2006. 'The atmosphere is relaxing; the food is superb; the rooms are excellent.' The ancient pub stands on the road in a small, straggling village in the rolling countryside of north-west Herefordshire. Owners Steve and Nicola Reynolds pride themselves on sourcing virtually all their ingredients locally. The restaurant areas are spread around, 'all higgledy-piggledy', some up a few steps, some down. They have 'country-style plain wooden tables and simple upholstered chairs'. Dinner at a candlelit table included 'excellent home-made bread; exquisite seared scallops on cauliflower purée; really fresh red mullet, redolent of the south of France; an amazing cheese trolley'. Three bedrooms are above the pub: 'We were impressed by ours: bright, tastefully decorated, reasonably sized, heavily beamed. Good lighting and storage, not a lot of furniture, interesting photos and pictures. Bright, clean bathroom. A garden-facing window: some passing traffic.' Three other rooms, also found 'charming', are in a listed Georgian vicarage down the road, backed by a garden with stream and chickens. Breakfast includes fresh fruit, 'excellent scrambled eggs, toast made from lovely bread, a really large chunk of butter'. Service by young girls was 'friendly and very efficient'.

6 bedrooms. 3 at *Old Vicarage* (300 yds). On B4355 between Kington (3½ miles) and Presteigne. Closed Sun night/Mon and 1st 2 weeks Nov. Sitting room and garden at *Old Vicarage* (no smoking, no dogs). Pub has bar, restaurant areas and small garden. No background music. Unsuitable for &. MasterCard, Visa accepted. B&B £40–£90 per person. Full alc £35.

TORQUAY Devon *See SHORTLIST*   Map 1:D5

TORVER Cumbria   Map 4: inset C2

The Old Rectory	**BUDGET**	*Tel* 015394-41353

Torver, nr Coniston   *Fax* 015394-41156
LA21 8AX   *Email* enquiries@theoldrectoryhotel.com
                            Website www.theoldrectoryhotel.com

Standing in gardens and woods in farmland beneath the peaks of Coniston Old Man, Paul and Elizabeth Mitchell's unpretentious 19th-century white-painted house was liked again this year. 'Excellent hospitality, outstanding home-made food and beautiful decor. Warm and comfortable. Offers relaxation and nourishment after a long day walking or sailing.' Earlier visitors reported: 'All rooms were well furnished, and spotlessly clean. Our superior bedroom was bright and had a modern bathroom.' In the conservatory dining room, an 'adventurous traditional' four-course dinner, no choice until dessert (preferences discussed), is served. Main courses could include slow-roasted lamb with a mustard and mint marinade, or breast of chicken with a caramelised shallot sauce. Vegetarians are catered for, given notice. 'Breakfasts were consistently good.' In the lounge are books and guidebooks. Coniston Water is reached by a 20-minute stroll along a tarmac lane. Good walking and climbing. (*Peter Knight, DP*)

9 bedrooms. 1 in annexe. 1 on ground floor. 2½ miles SW of Coniston on A593. Open Feb–Nov. Dining room closed to non-residents. Lounge, dining room. No background music. ½-acre garden plus 2-acre woodland. ¾ mile from Coniston

Water. No smoking. No dogs in public rooms. MasterCard, Visa accepted. B&B £32–£38 per person; D,B&B £55–£61. Set menus £23. 1-night bookings refused bank holidays, half-term.

TOTLAND BAY Isle of Wight   Map 2:E2

Latton House   *Tel/Fax* 01983-754868
Madeira Road   *Email* lattonhouse@aol.com
Totland Bay PO39 0BJ   *Website* www.lattonhouse.co.uk

'Friendly and knowledgeable' Malcolm and Avril Turner run this modest guest house in their red brick Victorian home in a quiet residential area on the west of the Isle of Wight. The sea is not far away. The bedrooms are 'spotless': another one has been given a Victorian decor this year. Mr Turner is the cook, serving 'excellent, plentiful' three-course meals by arrangement; options are discussed with guests before 'custom-made' menus are printed. 'Bring your own wine (no corkage charge). No packaged butter, etc. We make our jams and marmalades.' Seats on the veranda face the road and the hotel's car park, but allow guests to enjoy the evening sun. In cold weather, a log fire burns in the lounge. (*Ron E Adams, D Bumby*)

3 bedrooms. Off A3054 Yarmouth–Totland. Large car park. Open Easter–Sept. Dining room closed midday. Lounge, dining room. No background music. Veranda. Small garden. Beach 200 yds. Unsuitable for &. No smoking. No children under 12. No dogs. No credit cards. B&B £30–£40 per person. Set dinner £30. Reductions for 2 or more nights. 1-night bookings refused peak weekends.

TOTNES Devon *See SHORTLIST*   Map 1:D4

TRESCO Isles of Scilly   Map 1:C1

The Island Hotel   *Tel* 01720-422883
Tresco, Isles of Scilly   *Fax* 01720-423008
Cornwall TR24 0PU   *Email* islandhotel@tresco.co.uk
                                      Website www.tresco.co.uk

On Robert Dorrien-Smith's tiny private island, famed for its subtropical Abbey Gardens, this sprawling one-storey hotel 'has a wonderful location'. Arriving guests are welcomed by the manager, Euan Rodger: 'You bump to the door in tractor and trailer.' Praise came again this year, but also brickbats. 'Everything excellent. We would certainly return, but hotel prices seem increasingly unreal on the out islands.' 'Ambience of peace and comfort. Mercifully no muzak. Helpful reception. Other staff varied in efficiency, but all were cheerful.' Idyllic setting; superb collection of original artwork. Tables are rotated in the restaurant so everyone can enjoy the view. In good weather dinner may be alfresco. A visitor in 2005 found the food good, but in 2006 it came in for criticism. 'Dinner patchy. Delicious fish, ice creams and other desserts, but steak flabby and tasteless; a chicken dish was inedible. At breakfast, fruit, juices and pastries were fine, but cooked dishes were not always very hot; toast was poor.' Families, welcomed with buckets, spades, pushchairs, etc, are attracted by the large sandy beach. 'Fine modern paintings' hang in public rooms and bedrooms: 'A wonderful room facing the sea; comfortable bed, lovely bathroom.' Rooms in the Flower wing have been redecorated. (*Diana Goodey, RW, Tessa and Graham Spanton, and others*)

48 bedrooms. 8 in 2 annexes. 3 on ground floor. NE side of island. Boat/helicopter from Penzance. Hotel will make travel arrangements and meet guests. Open Mar–Nov. Lounge, TV room, games room, bar, 2 dining rooms. No background music. 2-acre grounds: terrace, tennis, croquet, bowls, heated 75-ft swimming pool (May–30 Sept); beach: safe bathing, diving, snorkelling. Bicycle hire (book in advance). Golf buggies and wheelchairs for &. No smoking: restaurant, bedrooms. No dogs allowed on Tresco. MasterCard, Visa accepted. D,B&B £125–£300 per person. Set dinner £40. Snacks/packed lunches £5–£15. 5% discount for 5 or more days. **'V'**

TROUTBECK Cumbria   Map 4: inset C2
See SHORTLIST

TRURO Cornwall   Map 1:D2

Royal Hotel   *Tel* 01872-270345
Lemon Street   *Fax* 01872-242453
Truro TR1 2QB   *Email* reception@royalhotelcornwall.co.uk
                                Website www.royalhotelcornwall.co.uk

'Very good value', Lynn Manning's 200-year-old Grade II listed inn (where Prince Albert stayed in 1846) is in the centre of the cathedral city. Recently modernised, it has a 'pleasant, light decor with abstract prints, and a relaxed atmosphere'. The young staff 'have a good attitude, all eager to please' and, said an inspector, 'my reception was efficient and informative'. Modern brasserie-style food ('eclectic, with a Thai or American twist') is served from 11 am to 10 pm in the restaurant, where wooden tables are 'reasonably far apart' (some on a platform). Starters include bruschetta 'to dip and share'; main courses include satay fish sizzler. 'Service was very good and helpings were generous. Because I was eating alone, I was offered a selection of newspapers and magazines to read, which was nice. At breakfast there were newspapers, a buffet with a large choice, and the food was good, though butters and jams were packaged. My bedroom at the rear was quiet, with good-quality fittings; housekeeping was good and the bed was comfortable.' The lounges are 'stylish'. The bar, open until midnight, serves 'funky cocktails'.

44 bedrooms. 9 apartments (1 adapted for &). Central. Closed Christmas. Lounge, bar, restaurant; 'mellow' background music; boardroom. No smoking. Guide dogs only. All major credit cards accepted. B&B [2006] £45–£69 per person. Full alc £50.

TUNBRIDGE WELLS Kent   Map 2:D4

Hotel du Vin & Bistro

Crescent Road	*Tel* 01892-526455
	Fax 01892-512044
Tunbridge Wells	*Email* info@tunbridgewells.hotelduvin.com
TN1 2LY	*Website* www.hotelduvin.com

'Delightful.' 'In a class of its own'. Praise again for this member of the small Hotel du Vin group. Tom Ross is the manager. 'Service was superb. Rooms excellent, very opulent.' The 18th-century Grade II listed sandstone building was extended in the 1830s by Decimus Burton (known for the Palm House at Kew Gardens). Bedrooms vary considerably in size. Our inspector's room, though 'cupboard-size', 'had all the latest gadgets: large flat-screen TV, DVD-player, smart tea-making gizmos'. Other guests were 'upgraded for no known reason to a suite, one of the nicest hotel rooms we have stayed in, large, well equipped, with lovely views. The enormous bed could have accommodated four (we did not put this to the test).' Each bedroom is sponsored by a wine or champagne company. The quietest ones, at the back, overlook Calverley Park (at the front is a busy road on a steep hill). Reservations are necessary for the 'lively' bistro where a light lunch was 'impeccable', and dinner 'very good indeed'. 'Excellent' breakfasts have 'wonderful breads and cereals'. 'Staff were attentive, courteous, well trained.' Wedding receptions and other functions are held. (*Christopher Ackroyd, Peter Mueller, P and JL*)

34 bedrooms. 4 in adjacent cottage. Central, opposite Assembly Hall. Lift. 2 lounges, bar, snooker room, bistro; private dining/meeting rooms. No background music. 1-acre grounds: *boules*, small vineyard. Civil wedding licence. No smoking: restaurant, 1 lounge, some bedrooms. No dogs in bistro. All major credit cards accepted. Room £105–£295. Breakfast from £9.95. Set Sun lunch £25; full alc £40. New Year package.

See also SHORTLIST

TWO BRIDGES Devon   Map 1:D4

Prince Hall Hotel	*Tel* 01822-890403
Two Bridges PL20 6SA	*Fax* 01822-890676
	Email info@princehall.co.uk
	Website www.princehall.co.uk

In the middle of Dartmoor, near a packhorse bridge, this 18th-century house has panoramic views over the West Dart valley. 'The ambience is professional,' say fans, and the owners, John and Anne Grove (she is the chef, he is 'very attentive in the bar'), are 'welcoming hosts'. This year they have introduced freshly squeezed orange juice at breakfast, and an *à la carte* menu instead of a set dinner (main courses like mélange of fish with Cajun spices and prawn cream sauce). 'Our meal was faultless,' was one comment. Other reports told of 'a wonderful setting', 'excellent service', 'a quite elaborate meal', 'a large, comfortable, spotless bedroom'. 'The house is well maintained, nicely proportioned, decor in keeping, not over-fancy.' 'Breakfast had warm toast and good cooked dishes (excellent sausages).' The best bedrooms, like the public areas, face the moors; standard ones are above a courtyard (you might hear a water pump). Cream teas are served, in the garden in summer. You can walk from the grounds straight on to the moor. This is a genuinely dog-friendly hotel, say the Groves. (*FEB Critchley, Trevor Lockwood, and others*)

9 bedrooms. 1 mile E of Two Bridges, on B3357 towards Ashburton. Train: Plymouth/Newton Abbot. Open early Feb–1 Jan. Sitting room, bar, restaurant; jazz/classical background music at night. 5-acre grounds. River Dart, fishing, 5 mins' walk; riding, shooting, golf nearby. Only restaurant and bar suitable for &. Smoking in bar only. No children under 10. No dogs in restaurant. Amex, MasterCard, Visa accepted. B&B [2006] £60–£90 per person; D,B&B £95–£125. Full alc £37.50. 3-day breaks. Christmas/New Year packages. 1-night bookings occasionally refused Fri/Sat in season. **˙V˙**

All our inspections are paid for, and carried out anonymously.

ULLSWATER Cumbria   Map 4: inset C2

Howtown Hotel   *Tel* 01768-486514
Ullswater, nr Penrith CA10 2ND

♔ *César award in 1991*

'Still a rock-solid *Guide* entry', this simple guest house has been run for many years by Jacquie Baldry with her son, David. It has 'a lovely quiet setting' up a narrow lane leading to the end of the valley. 'You need to drive the last three miles with care, but it is worth the effort.' Popular with walkers, *Howtown* is often fully booked. Mrs Baldry 'keeps a watchful eye, with humour'. Her young staff are 'easy-going and efficient'. 'Tea in the garden after a day's walking is most enjoyable,' says a returning visitor. 'All bedrooms now have a private bathroom, some across the corridor. They are nicely completed.' In the main building, early morning tea is brought to the room, and there is an evening turn-down service. In the dining room (tables close together), the four-course dinner (three choices of main course and dessert) is at 7 pm. 'Traditional food; no surprises; generally good.' 'Good wine list', too. On Sunday, there is a set lunch and a cold supper. 'Eggs as you wish' appear at the generous breakfasts. A substantial picnic can be provided. 'Very good value, considering the thought and care put into the hospitality.' (*David Reed, Brian Pullee*)

13 bedrooms. 4 in annexe. 4 self-catering cottages for weekly rent. E shore of lake, 4 miles S of Pooley Bridge. Bus from Penrith station, 9 miles. Open 30 Mar–1 Nov. 3 lounges, TV room, 2 bars, dining room. No background music. 2-acre grounds. 200 yds from lake: private foreshore, fishing. Walking, sailing, climbing, riding, golf nearby. Unsuitable for &. 'We ask guests not to smoke in the dining room.' No children under 7. Dogs by arrangement; not in public rooms. No credit cards. D,B&B [2006] £65 per person (reductions for 4 or more nights). Set lunch: weekdays from £10, dinner from £19; cold Sun supper from £13. 1-night bookings sometimes refused.

Sharrow Bay   *Tel* 01768-486301
Ullswater   *Fax* 01768-486349
nr Penrith CA10 2LZ   *Email* info@sharrowbay.co.uk
                              Website www.sharrowbay.co.uk

Spectacularly set on Lake Ullswater, this famous hotel (Relais & Châteaux) is owned by von Essen hotels. Another new manager, Andrew King, arrived in October 2005. Shortly after, a regular guest wrote, telling of continuing high standards. Other comments: 'Rooms exceptionally comfortable; thoughtful provision of books and games.' 'Bedrooms cosy if dated.

Fantastic view.' 'Lovely sheets, masses of storage space, two small glasses of sherry.' 'Lacks a true mine host, but staff were friendly. We enjoyed our stay, but the lady is showing her age. Food perhaps the best feature.' Chef Colin Akrigg's *Michelin*-starred six-course menu is left in the bedrooms each day. Served in two dining rooms, one above the water, it includes elaborate dishes like noisette of venison with casserole of the leg, braised red cabbage, juniper berry and rosemary sauce. 'Dinner [at 8, preceded by drinks at 7.30] was good, if short on vegetables and fruit. Service excellent, from young French waiting staff.' 'Breakfast [between 9 and 9.45] is wonderful. Staff (many long-serving) attentive to the last detail.' The bedrooms in the main building are small, but there are spacious rooms in the garden and in *Bank House*, up the hill (transport provided). (*G Brooks, MH, SI*)

24 bedrooms. 6 in garden. 4 in lodge, 6 at *Bank House* (1¼ miles). 1 on ground floor (ramp, wide doors). E shore of Ullswater, 2 miles S of Pooley Bridge. 3 lounges, 2 dining rooms in main house; 2 lounges, breakfast room in *Bank House*. No background music. 12-acre grounds: gardens, woodland; ½-mile lake shore, safe (cold) bathing, pier. Civil wedding licence. No smoking: bedrooms, restaurant, some public rooms. No children under 13. No dogs. Amex, MasterCard, Visa accepted. B&B [2006] from £135 per person; D,B&B £175–£220. Set lunch £39.50, dinner £52.50. Christmas/New Year packages. 1-night bookings refused weekends.

See also SHORTLIST

ULVERSTON Cumbria   Map 4: inset C2

The Bay Horse	*Tel* 01229-583972
Canal Foot	*Fax* 01229-580502
Ulverston LA12 9EL	*Email* reservations@thebayhorsehotel.co.uk
	Website www.thebayhorsehotel.co.uk

'A civilised place to stay', this whitewashed 18th-century house, once a staging post for coaches crossing the sands of Morecambe Bay, stands at the water's edge of the Leven estuary. 'Excellent for food, comfort and atmosphere,' says a regular visitor, 'such a glorious and peaceful location' (though the approach is past an unappealing pharmaceutical plant). Owned by Robert Lyons (also the chef), it is managed by Lesley Wheeler, who came here with him 19 years ago. It's 'more of an inn/pub than a hotel' (no residents' lounge), but 'the staff's helpfulness is unmatched in my experience'. Bedrooms are 'small but well equipped', though decor may sometimes be 'in a seventies time warp'. Three have just been refurbished.

Front rooms have a balcony, binoculars and a bird-watching guide. In the conservatory restaurant overlooking the estuary, dinner is at 7.30 for 8. Robert Lyons 'delivers sound cooking with the accent on flavour'. 'Excellent pork fillet, just as good guineafowl; perfectly cooked vegetables; starters and sweets good too (ingredients are locally sourced).' 'Impressive' breakfasts have fresh orange juice, 'proper tea'; 'an excellent fried platter with white and black pudding, eggs with good yellowy yolks'; 'superb home-made raspberry jam'. (*Lynn Wildgoose, Elizabeth Roberts, David and Kate Wooff*)

9 bedrooms. 8 miles NE of Barrow-in-Furness. Closed 3–5 Jan. Bar lounge, restaurant; mixed/classical background music. Unsuitable for &. No smoking: restaurant, bedrooms. No children under 10. Only guide dogs in restaurant. All major credit cards accepted. B&B [2006] £40–£80 per person. Bar meals. Set dinner £31.50; full alc £52. Christmas/New Year packages. 1-night bookings refused bank holidays.

VENTNOR Isle of Wight   Map 2:E2

The Hambrough NEW		*Tel* 01983-856333
Hambrough Road		*Fax* 01983-857260
Ventnor PO38 1SQ		*Email* info@thehambrough.com
		Website www.thehambrough.com

Opened July 2005, in 'fantastic position' on quiet road overlooking Ventnor's cascade gardens: small hotel owned by Kevin Sussmilch, managed by Frédéric Sol. Contemporary decor. 'Spacious, quiet, well-appointed bedrooms' (but some housekeeping lapses). 'Cheerful service, excellent restaurant, superb breakfast,' say visitors in 2006. Bar lounge, terrace; background music all day. Parking. Unsuitable for &. Smoking in bar lounge only. No dogs. MasterCard, Visa accepted. 7 bedrooms. B&B double [2006] £130–£200. Set menu £35. Christmas/New Year packages.

The Wellington Hotel	*Tel* 01983-856600
Belgrave Road	*Fax* 01983-856611
Ventnor PO38 1JH	*Email* enquiries@thewellingtonhotel.net
	Website www.thewellingtonhotel.net

'Beautifully situated', built into cliffs and a minute's walk down to a 'safe and friendly' sandy beach, this 'smart, stylish' hotel has 'grandstand views of waves' from its balconies, terraces and large sun deck. It 'is not run like an army camp', writes Marios Porfiropoullos, the Greek-Cypriot managing director. 'Guests are the bosses. If someone wants a lie-in, late breakfast is arranged.' All but two bedrooms (the best have a private balcony) face the sea. 'The only noise at night is the sound of waves.' 'The rooms are pleasantly furnished,' said a guest who liked the 'contemporary minimalism' (bare floorboards in public areas). In the spacious dining room (two floors below the bedrooms; no lift), guests eat from a 'straightforward' *table d'hôte* menu or *à la carte* (eg, roast rump of lamb; magret de canard with port and wild mushrooms). There is a 'decent breakfast' (full English) and 24-hour room service. Ferry-inclusive packages can be arranged. (*AF*)

28 bedrooms. Some on ground floor. Some no-smoking. 5 mins' walk from centre. Limited off-street parking. Lounge, bar, restaurant (background music). Sun deck: steps to beach. Unsuitable for &. No pets. Amex, MasterCard, Visa accepted. Double room [2006] B&B £90–£118; D,B&B £110–£158. Full alc £25. Christmas/New Year packages. 1-night bookings refused Sat in high season.

See also SHORTLIST

VERYAN-IN-ROSELAND Cornwall   Map 1:D2

The Nare   *Tel* 01872-501111
Carne Beach   *Fax* 01872-501856
Veryan   *Email* office@narehotel.co.uk
nr Truro TR2 5PF   *Website* www.narehotel.co.uk

♀ *César award in 2003*

'Perfect, as usual.' 'I still say that this is the best hotel in England.' 'Such a good atmosphere throughout.' 'Stunning location. Lovely gardens.' Praise continues for Toby Ashworth's unashamedly old-fashioned hotel above a beautiful bay in the Roseland peninsula. He hosts a weekly drinks party for guests. Trim lawns and flowerbeds lead down to a large, safe, sandy beach. Although it appeals to a mature clientele, there are no age restrictions on the young: 'It was nice to see children of all ages, and family parties.' Bedrooms vary in the rambling building: 'Our deluxe double had big windows, patio with wonderful views, all comforts and a decanter of sherry.' Dinner in the dining room is an 'event'; jacket and tie 'preferred' for men. 'We like to watch the hors d'oeuvre and sweet trolleys come round.' Suppers and light lunches are served (alfresco in summer) in the less formal *Quarterdeck* restaurant. Wines are thought 'a bit pricey', but the house wine is 'good value'. The half-board rate includes 'unmissable' afternoon tea, with home-made cakes, scones, jams and biscuits. A 22-foot boat, the *Maggie O'Nare*, is available for charter. (*Rodney Bourne, Zara Elliott, Carol Jackson, HJM Tucker, Ann H Edwards*)

39 bedrooms. Some on ground floor. 1 suitable for ♿. S of Veryan, on coast. Lift, ramps. Lounge, drawing room, sun lounge, bar, billiard room, light lunch/supper room, 2 restaurants, conservatory; indoor swimming pool, spa bath, sauna, gym. No background music. 5-acre grounds: garden, heated swimming pool, tennis, croquet, children's play area, safe sandy beach, fishing. Concessionary golf at Truro golf club. No smoking: restaurant, drawing room. No dogs in public rooms. MasterCard, Visa accepted. B&B [2006] £95–£277 per person; D,B&B (min. 3 nights) £110–£292. Set dinner £39.50; full alc £60. Christmas/New Year packages.

WAREHAM Dorset   Map 2:E1

The Priory	*Tel* 01929-551666
Church Green	*Fax* 01929-554519
Wareham BH20 4ND	*Email* reservations@theprioryhotel.co.uk
	Website www.theprioryhotel.co.uk

♧ *César award in 1996*

Owned by Anne Turner with her brother-in-law, Stuart, and managed by her son, Jeremy Merchant, the former Priory of Lady St Mary (16th-century) stands by the River Frome. It is approached across a green ('a coloured oasis of Georgian houses') and a flagstoned courtyard. 'It meets all my criteria for a really good hotel: real orange juice; staff address you by name; good lighting for reading in bed; no muzak; beds turned down while you dine,' says a visitor this year. Other praise: 'We loved the surroundings; the staff were particularly friendly.' The bedrooms vary greatly in size and aspect; some have a four-poster. 'We were delighted with our room in the Boathouse. It was prettily furnished and had a small balcony overlooking the garden. There was a huge circular bath – bliss!' 'Very comfortable' public rooms are in 'country house style'. An upstairs lounge faces garden, river and meadows. Drinks in the beamed drawing room precede dinner in the 'elegant' stone-vaulted Abbots' Cellar. Christopher Lee's cooking was enjoyed but not 'the supplementary charge to several items on the menu'. The Turner family also own *The Casterbridge*, Dorchester (*qv*). (*Nigel and Jennifer Jee, Anne Ramsbottom, Kay Hickman, and others*)

18 bedrooms. 5 in Boathouse. Some on ground floor (in courtyard). Central. Ramps. 2 lounges (1 with pianist Sat night), bar, 2 dining rooms. 4-acre gardens: croquet; river frontage: moorings, fishing; bicycle hire. Unsuitable for ♿. No smoking. No children under 14. Guide dogs only. Diners, MasterCard, Visa accepted. B&B [to 31 March 2007] £105–£170 per person; D,B&B £130–£195. Set dinner £35. Off-season breaks. Christmas/New Year packages. 1-night bookings refused weekends.

Make sure the hotel has included VAT in the prices it quotes.

WARMINSTER Wiltshire *See SHORTLIST*   Map 2:D1

WARTLING East Sussex   Map 2:E4

Wartling Place   *Tel* 01323-832590
Wartling, Herstmonceux   *Email* accom@wartlingplace.prestel.co.uk
nr Eastbourne   *Website* countryhouseaccommodation.co.uk
BN27 1RY

Built in 1728, this white-walled Grade II listed ex-rectory is run as an upmarket B&B by its owners, Barry and Rowena Gittoes. On a hill near the 13th-century church, it overlooks Pevensey Levels and has views to the South Downs. 'Our room was beautifully finished,' says a visitor this year. All the spacious bedrooms have cream carpet, Egyptian cotton bedlinen, large fluffy towels. The two best rooms have an antique four-poster bed, flat-screen TV and DVD-player. There is 'amazingly generous' storage space. Some visitors have noticed slight road noise, but there are padded blinds and thick curtains. Staircases in this former rest home have short, wide flights. In the elegant lounge are comfortable settees and chairs, antiques, an honesty bar, and a long, polished breakfast table in front of the windows. The 'exceptional' breakfast, served between 8.30 and 9 am (9.30 at weekends), includes fruit, kedgeree, omelettes, waffles with maple syrup, full English, fresh-baked rolls. The attractive garden has paths and a patio with fountain. An evening meal is available by arrangement. For dining out, *The Lamb*, almost opposite, was liked: 'Good food. Rowena helped to book.' A list of other eating places is available. (*Mike Inglis, MD*)

4 bedrooms. Also self-catering cottage. 3 miles N of Pevensey. Lounge/dining room with honesty bar and CD-player (classical background music all day). 3-acre garden. Unsuitable for &, except ground floor of cottage. No smoking. No dogs. Amex, MasterCard, Visa accepted. B&B £50–£120 per person. Evening meal by advance arrangement £35. Golf, Christmas/New Year packages. 1-night bookings occasionally refused weekends in season.

WARWICK Warwickshire *See SHORTLIST*   Map 3:C6

The *Guide* has hotels to meet most tastes and budgets. We are as pleased to hear about simple, cheaper hotels as we are about the better-known expensive ones.

WASDALE HEAD Cumbria   Map 4: inset C2

Wasdale Head Inn   *Tel* 019467-26229
Wasdale Head   *Fax* 019467-26334
nr Gosforth CA20 1EX   *Email* wasdaleheadinn@msn.com
                                   Website www.wasdale.com

Remote, unspoiled Wasdale has 'England's deepest lake, highest mountain
and smallest church', says the website for this informal three-gabled inn,
popular with climbers and hikers. Owned by Nigel Burton and managed
by Howard and Kate Christie, it stands in a garden with stream and
woodpeckers, seven miles up a dead-end road. The decor is traditional:
solid old furniture, wood panelling, climbing photographs; books and games
in the residents' lounge. Bedrooms are 'comfortable, basic, well equipped':
in one, 'the low central beam (ouch) added to the character'. This year a
new single bedroom has been added; other rooms have been redecorated,
as has the main bar. The inn's own micro-brewery produces some of the
beers. In the restaurant, Will Weightman ('Cumbria's Young Chef of the
Year 2005') serves traditional dishes 'with lighter touches' (eg, poussin with
sweet potato purée and bacon sauce). Breakfast was 'outstanding: buffet of
cereals; everything that could be present in an enormous fry-up'. Packed
lunches and cream teas are available. At Christmas there is a 'Bah Humbug'
package: 'No crackers, no silly hats, no Santas', but instead a picnic lunch
(sandwiches, Mars bars, crisps) to be eaten in the hills. More reports, please.

15 bedrooms. 2 on ground floor. 6 self-catering apartments. 10 miles NE of
Gosforth. Restaurant closed midweek Oct–Mar. No TV (poor reception). Ramps.
Lounge, residents' bar, public bar, restaurant; drying room. No background music.
3-acre grounds: beer garden, stream, pond, fitness trail. Unsuitable for &. No
smoking. No dogs: some bedrooms, some public rooms. Amex, MasterCard, Visa
accepted. B&B £54 per person. Bar/picnic lunches. Set dinner £29. Christmas/New
Year packages. 1-night bookings sometimes refused weekends.

WATERMILLOCK Cumbria   Map 4: inset C2

Rampsbeck   *Tel* 01768-486442
Watermillock on Ullswater   *Fax* 01768-486688
nr Penrith CA11 0LP   *Email* enquiries@rampsbeck.fsnet.co.uk
                                Website www.rampsbeck.fsnet.co.uk

A white-fronted 18th-century house in splendid gardens on the shores of
Lake Ullswater, with splendid views of lake and fells. Run by its owners,
Tom and Marion Gibb, with her mother, Mrs MacDowall, it was liked
again this year: 'Wonderful setting, good food, friendly service.' 'A lovely

place. We arrived late, and were served a delicious omelette in a palatial lounge overlooking the lake.' An imposing entrance opens to a sweeping staircase. Elegant lounges have large bay windows, high ceilings and elaborate mouldings. One has its original marble fireplace and lake views; another, smaller, faces the garden. The best bedrooms have lake views and a balcony where a continental breakfast can be taken. 'Our room was excellent in every respect.' Three rooms have just been refurbished. Guests have the option of tea-making facilities or early morning tea brought to the room. In the dining room ('very comfortable, but the decor is a peculiar mix of lurid styles'), Andrew McGeorge's dinner menu offers a wide choice of 'modern British and French dishes' (eg, halibut with baked croustade of wild mushrooms; roast beef with Yorkshire pudding). One visitor wasn't too keen on the puddings. But all agree: 'The staff are as welcoming and efficient as ever.' (*BJ Hanbury, Wendy and Michael Dods, and others*)

19 bedrooms. 5½ miles SW of Penrith. Open 9 Feb–2 Jan. 2 lounges, bar, restaurant. No background music. 18-acre grounds: croquet; lake frontage: fishing, sailing, windsurfing, etc. Unsuitable for &. Civil wedding licence. No smoking: restaurant, 1 lounge, 6 bedrooms. No young children in restaurant at night. Dogs in 3 rooms only; not in public rooms, except hall. MasterCard, Visa accepted. B&B [2006] £60–£125 per person; D,B&B £99.50–£165. Set lunch £29, dinner £40–£47. Christmas/New Year packages. 1-night bookings occasionally refused.

WATFORD Hertfordshire *See SHORTLIST*   Map 2:C3

WATH-IN-NIDDERDALE North Yorkshire   Map 4:D3

The Sportsman's Arms   *Tel* 01423-711306
Wath-in-Nidderdale, Pateley Bridge   *Fax* 01423-712524
nr Harrogate HG3 5PP   *Email* info@sportsmansarms.fsnet.co.uk
                              Website www.sportsmans-arms.co.uk

Reached across an old packhorse bridge over the River Nidd, Ray and Jane Carter's unpretentious but smart Dales pub is popular with sporting visitors. Locally, there is good shooting, walking, birdwatching and fishing (it has rights on the Nidd). 'An excellent small hotel; good food, good service in a lovely spot,' says a visitor this year. Mr Carter works in the kitchen with his head chef, Seth Marsland, and his son, Jamie. They serve an English menu 'with a French flavour' in both bar and restaurant, eg, fillet of turbot on spinach, with an artichoke sauce. Lamb, pork and game are local; fish comes from Whitby. The traditional Sunday lunch is a 'superior version of the genre'. Breakfast has 'proper butter, blackberry jam, honey and marmalade, decent coffee and excellent cooked dishes – spicy sausages, fresh eggs'. Some of the bedrooms are in a converted barn and stables around the courtyard; some have an antique four-poster, others more modern furniture. 'Our room, their best, was large, with large bathroom; both had pine fittings, fabrics to match the red toile de Jouy wallpaper. Plenty of storage, lots of surfaces for bathroom clutter.' (*Roger Down, and others*)

11 bedrooms. 6 in barns and stables (25 yds). 1 on ground floor. 2¼ miles NW of Pateley Bridge. Closed 25 Dec. 2 lounges, public bar (background music 'when quiet'), restaurant; private dining/meeting room. 1-acre garden. River 150 yds (fishing). Unsuitable for &. No smoking: restaurant, bedrooms. No dogs: restaurant, bedrooms. MasterCard, Visa accepted. B&B £60–£65 per person. Full alc £28–£38. Midweek breaks.

WELLS Somerset   Map 1:B6

Canon Grange NEW/BUDGET		*Tel* 01749-671800
Cathedral Green		*Email* canongrange@email.com
BA5 2UB		*Website* www.canongrange.co.uk

Annette Sowden's friendly no-smoking B&B: 15th-century listed house on green, facing cathedral's magnificent west front (floodlit at night). Ask for a room with that view. Exposed beams, walnut furniture. Cathedral wall runs through the 5-acre garden. Dining room (church music). Breakfast English, vegetarian or 'lighter' (for dieters); evening meal by arrangement (£18). No dogs. MasterCard, Visa accepted. 5 bedrooms with period decor (1 family, 1 on ground floor). B&B: single £45, double £63; D,B&B £40.50–£63 per person.

WEST HADDON Northamptonshire   Map 2:B3

Pear Trees Country House BUDGET		*Tel* 01788-510389
Station Road		*Email* info@pear-trees.co.uk
West Haddon NN6 7AU		*Website* www.pear-trees.co.uk

In a picturesque Northamptonshire village, Carolyn and Brian Hyde run their small guest house in an 18th-century building, full of character. There are original oak beams, ancient flagstones, and a marble fireplace (where logs burn in winter) in the lounge. 'Excellent food and accommodation,' say visitors. Mr Hyde, 'a wonderful host', is the village postman ('though I may hang up my bag soon'). Canadian guests, whose stay was extended because of illness after a long-haul flight, reported: 'We couldn't have been "stuck" in a better place. They went out of their way to look after us.' Two bedrooms overlook the walled garden: 'Ours was decent sized, well furnished and decorated. We were given tea/coffee on arrival with excellent home-made pastries. Breakfast was good and plentiful.' Mrs Hyde, 'a superb cook', will provide an evening meal by arrangement: traditional Aga-cooked dishes, eg, steak casserole; chicken breasts with cheese, leek and bacon. No licence. Bring your own wine. Meals may be served in the garden ('where there are loads of birds singing') in fine weather. There are other eating places in the village. Good for walkers: the village is on the Jurassic Way and near the Grand Union Canal. (*FS, J and MW*)

3 bedrooms. Village centre. Lunch not served. Sitting room with TV, dining room; background music when requested. Walled garden: covered patio (summer meal service). Unsuitable for &. Smoking in garden only. No dogs. No credit cards. B&B £28–£49 per person. Evening meal by arrangement: £17–£25. ***V***

WEST STOKE West Sussex   Map 2:E3

West Stoke House   *Tel* 01243-575226
West Stoke, nr Chichester   *Fax* 01243-574655
PO18 9BN   *Email* info@weststokehouse.co.uk
                                  Website www.weststokehouse.co.uk

'The food at this masterpiece of shabby chic gets better and better,' says a returning visitor to this large, white Georgian mansion. 'Warm, friendly, historically interesting', it stands in large grounds in 'glorious country' on the edge of the Downs. Rowland and Mary Leach run it informally with their 'supremely professional' manager, Richard Macadam. 'The charmingly eccentric owner with out-of-control hair wears shorts all year round.' Antiques stand on polished floorboards in the public rooms. There is 'an interesting collection of mismatched, comfortable chairs', plenty of art on display, most of it by local artists and for sale. 'Our large bedroom had comfortable bed with duvet, good carpet, partial garden view through a large sash window. It was sparsely furnished (some nice antiques). Fittings were trendy. Small bathroom with powerful shower.' In the blue-walled dining room, chef Darren Brown's menu might include prawn and lobster risotto or slow-braised pork cheek with boudin noir. 'Exceptionally good cheeses; well selected wines, mark-ups below average.' The good English breakfast, served until 10 am, includes free-range eggs from the West Stoke hens. Weddings and other celebrations are held in the ballroom. The house is busy when races are on at Goodwood (picnics provided). (*BB*)

5 bedrooms. 3 miles NW of Chichester. Closed Christmas. Restaurant closed Sun evening/Mon/Tues. Lounge, restaurant; background music; ballroom. 5-acre grounds: garden games. Unsuitable for &. Civil wedding licence. Smoking in lounge only. Amex, MasterCard, Visa accepted. B&B [2006] £65–£85 per person; D,B&B £100–£120. Set menus £35–£40; full alc £40. New Year package. 1-night bookings refused weekends.

WESTON-SUPER-MARE Somerset   Map 1:B6
See SHORTLIST

WHITBY North Yorkshire *See SHORTLIST*   Map 4:C5

WHITSTABLE Kent   Map 2:D5

Windy Ridge	**NEW/BUDGET**	*Tel* 01227-263506
Wraik Hill		*Email* scott@windyridgewhitstable.co.uk
Whitstable CT5 3BY		*Website* www.windyridgewhitstable.co.uk

Overlooking the town ('amazing sea views'), about a mile and a half uphill from the seafront, Hugh and Lynda Scott's B&B stands by a small road. It is a characterful conversion of two former farm cottages: there are beamed ceilings, a wood-burning stove in the lounge, and cast iron fireplaces. 'It was wonderful; they could not have been kinder to me and my dog (no extra charge),' says one of this year's reports. 'The lounge is cosy, and the bedrooms have been refurbished to a very high standard. The cheese on toast for breakfast was delicious.' A supporting letter tells of a warm welcome, adding: 'It is indeed windy.' There are vegetarian options for breakfast, and an evening meal by arrangement. 'The dining room, facing the estuary, is lovely.' A 'big dog' is in attendance. There are two family suites. One double room has a four-poster bed. (*Val Hennessy, Jane Northcote*)

10 bedrooms. 1 on ground floor. 1½ miles from centre, off A299. Parking. Possibly closed part of Jan. Lounge, bar, dining room; low background music; meeting facilities. ½-acre garden: gazebo. Civil wedding licence. No smoking indoors. MasterCard, Visa accepted. B&B £35–£60 per person. Christmas/New Year packages. 1-night bookings occasionally refused at weekends. *V*

For details of the Voucher scheme see page 60.

WICKHAM Hampshire   Map 2:E2

The Old House	*Tel* 01329-833049
The Square	*Fax* 01329-833672
Wickham PO17 5JG	*Email* oldhousehotel@aol.com
	Website www.oldhousehotel.co.uk

On huge main square (quiet at night) of delightful old village in Meon valley, 3 miles N of Fareham: red brick, creeper-covered, Grade II listed early Georgian town house owned by Paul and Lesley Scott. 'Warm reception. Characterful rooms': some have sloping beams; 'beautifully designed' ones in garden annexe. 'Marble bathroom like something from a Roman consul's villa.' 'Excellent' cooking by James Fairchild-Dickson. Lounge (large fireplace), bar, restaurant; background music; private dining/conference room, function room. ¼-acre walled garden. Civil wedding licence. Unsuitable for &. Closed 26–30 Dec. No smoking: restaurant, bedrooms. No dogs. Amex, MasterCard, Visa accepted. 15 bedrooms. 4 in annexes. B&B £42.50–£75 per person. English breakfast £7.50. Full alc about £27.50.

WILLINGTON Cheshire *See SHORTLIST*   Map 3:A5

WILMINGTON East Sussex   Map 2:E4

Crossways Hotel	*Tel* 01323-482455
Lewes Road	*Fax* 01323-487811
Wilmington BN26 5SG	*Email* stay@crosswayshotel.co.uk
	Website www.crosswayshotel.co.uk

David Stott (the chef) and Clive James are the hosts at this pretty country house in an affluent village in the Cuckmere valley. Ideally placed for Glyndebourne, it is 'well attuned to the particular requirements of the opera set', says a returning guest this year. 'The welcome gets ever warmer, and nothing troubles them. No heavy weather is made of a two- or three-night single booking. No exorbitant supplement charged.' 'They uncomplainingly chilled wine for a picnic, etc.' Only drawback: the large garden, with a pond, rabbits and a herb garden, runs down to a main road which is 'relentlessly busy' during the night. 'What do people *do* in Eastbourne at 3 am?' But front rooms have double-glazed windows. In the 'intimate' dining room, the four-course menu changes monthly, and local produce is used when possible. Main courses include game pie; calf's liver and bacon with onion sauce. No guest lounge, but bedrooms contain 'every appliance imaginable: fridge, TV, clock, knick-knacks galore'. Some rooms have a sofa; one has a balcony. Breakfast is 'fresh, delicious, copious'. (*Richard Parish, and others*)

7 bedrooms. Self-catering cottage. 6 miles NW of Eastbourne on A27. Open Feb–23 Dec. Restaurant closed midday, and Sun/Mon. Breakfast room, restaurant (light classical background music). 2-acre grounds: duck pond. Unsuitable for &. No smoking: restaurant, bedrooms. No children under 12. No dogs. Amex, MasterCard, Visa accepted. B&B £49.50–£65 per person. Set dinner £35.95.

WINCHCOMBE Gloucestershire   Map 3:D5

Wesley House   *Tel* 01242-602366
High Street   *Fax* 01242-609046
Winchcombe GL54 5LJ   *Email* enquiries@wesleyhouse.co.uk
                            Website www.wesleyhouse.co.uk

Matthew Brown is the 'attentive host' at this 'quirky' restaurant-with-rooms which, say admirers, 'jostles successfully between things medieval and things 21st-century'. The 15th-century half-timbered building is on the main street of this attractive Cotswold wool town. Its lounge has an inglenook fireplace and comfortable seating. Beyond are the striking two-tiered, air-conditioned restaurant and an atrium where drinks and breakfast are served. This year a wine bar/bistro has been added, next to the restaurant. The 'stylish' bedrooms (all but one are small) are up a steep, beamed staircase ('pitons required'). 'Full marks for the lighting. Plenty of space for clothes. The bathroom could not have been smaller, but the shower worked and the water was hot.' Some rooms get street noise, and one faces the kitchen of the pub next door, lively until late. Almsbury has a private terrace overlooking the North Cotswold Edge. There is fresh fruit on a landing, and milk is supplied in a Thermos flask. The modern British dishes of chef Martin Dunn were enjoyed (eg, organic salmon with risotto of forest mushrooms). The 'excellent' breakfast ('we were waited on') has freshly squeezed orange juice, warm rolls, croissants, butter, jams and home-made whisky marmalade in little bowls. (*JH*)

5 bedrooms. Central. Closed 25/26 Dec. Restaurant closed Sun evening, except bank holidays. Lounge/bar ('easy listening' background music in bar area), bar/bistro, restaurant, atrium dining room; function facilities. Unsuitable for &. Civil wedding licence. No smoking: restaurant, bedrooms. No dogs. Amex, MasterCard, Visa accepted. D,B&B [2006] £75–£120 per person. B&B rates negotiable for longer stays. Set dinner £35. New Year package. 1-night bookings sometimes refused bank holidays and race week. ***V*** (not Sat)

WINCHELSEA East Sussex   Map 2:E5

The Strand House   `BUDGET`
Tanyard's Lane
Winchelsea TN36 4JT

Tel 01797-226276
Fax 01797-224806
Email info@thestrandhouse.co.uk
Website www.thestrandhouse.co.uk

'Beautifully renovated', while retaining ancient beams and inglenook fireplaces, this B&B is a half-timbered 15th-century malt house. Backed by a green lawn and old trees, it stands beneath Winchelsea's 13th-century Strand Gate. 'The welcome from the owner/managers, Janet and Peter Clarke, is warm,' says an admirer, 'and the decor is attractive. Our room was comfortable, though low beams must be avoided.' There is a 'nice lounge', with log fire, for residents. The traditional English breakfast, using local produce, is thought 'excellent', and the Clarkes will advise about local eating places (one is opposite). 'Though the house stands on a main road,
it is far enough back for even
our sensitive ears to be
undisturbed.' *Michelin* awards a
blue bib for quality combined
with a reasonable price. Rye,
Battle, Hastings, Hever and
Bodiam castles and many
other attractions are near. (*AS*)

10 bedrooms. 1 on ground floor. 2 miles SW of Rye. 300 yds from centre. Parking. Reception (classical background music), lounge, bar, breakfast room. ¾-acre garden. Unsuitable for &. Sea 1 mile (safe bathing). No smoking. No children under 5. No dogs. Diners, MasterCard, Visa accepted. B&B [2006]: single £50–£85, double £60–£85. Christmas/New Year packages. 1-night bookings refused Fri/Sat in season.

WINCHESTER Hampshire   Map 2:D2

Hotel du Vin & Bistro
14 Southgate Street
Winchester SO23 9EF

Tel 01962-841414
Fax 01962-842458
Email info@winchester.hotelduvin.com
Website www.hotelduvin.com

The first, and the smallest, hotel in this small chain (dedicated to wine) is a conversion of a Grade II listed Queen Anne town house. James Nichols is the general manager. 'Great wine, great atmosphere, great food and wine list,' one couple wrote about the restaurant. 'The whole place had a classy combination of character and style,' said another. 'All the staff had just the right blend of politeness and informality.' In the lively bistro (pale yellow, softly lit and music-free, with wooden floors, small polished mahogany tables), food ranges from 'simple classics' (eg, steak tartare; liver and bacon with mashed potatoes) to dishes like confit of duck leg, pak choi, red wine jus; linguine with courgettes and slow-roast tomatoes. The high-ceilinged sitting room has a large *trompe l'œil* painting, huge sofas, squashy armchairs. Bedrooms are 'nicely kitted out', with glossy magazines, 'a wonderful bed and splendid bathroom'; a garden room 'was quiet, luxurious and spacious' (some other rooms hear traffic). There is an 'interesting continental breakfast'. (*Wendy and Michael Dods, JW, and others*)

24 bedrooms. 4 in garden. 2 in cottage. 1 on ground floor with &. access. Central (rear rooms quietest). Car park. Station 10 mins' walk. Ramp. Lounge, bar, restaurant. No background music. Small walled garden, *boules*. Civil wedding licence. No smoking: restaurant, bedrooms. Guide dogs only. All major credit cards accepted. Room [2006]: single/double £120–£130, suite £175. Breakfast £9.95–£13.50. Full alc £40. Christmas/New Year packages.

See also SHORTLIST

WINDERMERE Cumbria   Map 4: inset C2

Gilpin Lodge   *Tel* 015394-88818
Crook Road   *Fax* 015394-88058
nr Windermere LA23 3NE   *Email* hotel@gilpinlodge.com
                                                    Website www.gilpinlodge.com

♥ *César award in 2000*

'What a lovely place,' says an enthusiastic visitor to this classic country house hotel (Relais & Châteaux). 'One of our all-time favourites.' Set well back from the road, it is surrounded by moors, woodlands and gardens. 'As perfect an experience as always,' said another returning visitor. Owners John and Christine Cunliffe run it informally (no reception area, no bar). They say: 'No weddings or conferences here, just the art of relaxation.' Each bedroom is named after a local beauty spot; some have a four-poster, some a whirlpool bath; many are spacious, with sitting area and good views. This year, six garden suites have been added. There are four dining rooms, 'all lovely in different ways'. The chef, Chris Meredith, earned a *Michelin* star in 2006 for his 'carefully cooked modern British dishes using prime Lakeland ingredients' (eg, turbot with bouillabaisse of mussels and fennel purée; venison with creamed cabbage and a juniper jus). Lunches range from a full meal in the restaurant to a light one in the lounge. Afternoon teas are 'a work of art'. The lengthy breakfast menu includes strawberry sorbet with pink champagne, Buck's Fizz, salad of exotic fruits, and many cooked dishes. (*David Reed, Wolfgang Stroebe, and others*)

20 bedrooms. 6 in separate building. On B5284 2 miles SE of Windermere. Ramps. 2 lounges, 4 dining rooms. No background music. 20-acre grounds: ponds, croquet. Free access to nearby country club: swimming pool, sauna, squash. Golf course opposite. Unsuitable for &. No smoking. No children under 7. No dogs. All major credit cards accepted. D,B&B £120–£175 per person. Christmas/New Year packages. 1-night bookings sometimes refused weekends.

Holbeck Ghyll   NEW
Holbeck Lane
Windermere LA23 1LU

Tel 015394-32375
Fax 015394-34743
Email stay@holbeckghyll.com
Website www.holbeckghyll.com

In a 'wonderful position' (lake and mountain views), David and Patricia Nicholson's luxurious hotel (Pride of Britain) stands in large grounds with streams, wildlife, tennis, etc, that slope down to the lake. Not everyone loved it last year ('pretentious', 'relentlessly *nouvelle* food', were comments), but there is also praise: 'Staff took care to know your name, but weren't unctuous. Wonderful food. Our dog was welcomed.' 'Expensive, but we got what we wanted. If you like a country house feel, this is for you. Service very good.' 'Friendly but never intrusive hosts.' 'Impeccable' public rooms have stained glass, open fires, wood panelling, antiques and free Internet access. There is a small spa. David McLaughlin serves *Michelin*-starred dishes in two dining rooms, one oak-panelled, the other with French windows that lead on to a terrace (with fountain) for alfresco meals. Male diners should wear jacket and tie. 'Good rabbit terrine; tasty pigeon; not many vegetables; a large cheeseboard.' Breakfast has a large buffet, good cooked dishes. Some bedrooms (with balcony or patio) are in a lodge. Children are accepted, but there are few special facilities for them. A new manager, Blanca Gilardo, arrived in 2006. (*Shirley Campbell, Shirley Tennent*)

22 bedrooms. 6 (3 with kitchenette) in lodge. 1 adapted for &. 3 miles N of Windermere off road to Ambleside. Open 19 Jan 2007–2 Jan 2008. Ramp. 2 lounges (1 with background music), bar, restaurant; function facilities; small spa: sauna, steam room, etc. 7-acre grounds: streams, ponds, woods to lake shore (800 yds), tennis, putting, croquet, jogging track. Civil wedding licence. Smoking in 1 lounge only. No children under 8 in restaurant. No dogs in public rooms. All major credit cards accepted. B&B £95–£200 per person; D,B&B £125–£230. Set menu £50. Off-season, Christmas/New Year packages. 1-night bookings sometimes refused Sat. *V*

WINSTER Derbyshire   Map 3:B6

The Dower House   *Tel* 01629-650931
Main Street   *Fax* 01629-650932
Winster, nr Matlock   *Email* fosterbig@aol.com
DE4 2DH   *Website* www.dowerhousewinster.com

Looking down the main street of this conservation village in the Peak
District national park, this 'comfortable B&B' is a 16th-century Grade II
listed building which the Curzon family owned from 1737 to 1861. 'All
rooms are generously proportioned, and beautifully warm,' say visitors this
year. 'The house faces three adjoining roads, but is set back, and quiet.' The
owners, John and Marsha Biggin, are found 'very helpful'. 'They willingly
exchanged the duvet on our bed for sheets and blankets.' One bedroom has
window seats facing the main street, and an *en suite* bathroom; a spacious
twin-bedded room has a stone fireplace, private bathroom, and views
through mullioned windows of the 'lovely walled garden', where 'an
impressively large cat stalked autumn leaves'. The guests' sitting room has
beams, the original sash windows and a log fire. Breakfast was 'delicious,
particularly the local oatcake cushioning nicely yolked eggs'. A private gate
gives access to the village churchyard. The pub in the village 'has solid and
reasonable food'. The 'plague village' of Eyeham, close by, is worth a visit.
(*Patricia and David Elliott, A and DG*)

4 bedrooms. 3 miles W of Matlock. Closed Christmas/New Year. Sitting room,
bar, dining room (classical radio 'as appropriate'). ½-acre walled garden: pond.
Unsuitable for &. No smoking. No children under 10. 'Well-behaved' dogs only,
not in public rooms. No credit cards. B&B £45–£75 per person. 1-night bookings
refused Fri/Sat in season.

WOBURN Bedfordshire *See SHORTLIST*   Map 2:C3

WOLD NEWTON East Yorkshire   Map 4:D5

The Wold Cottage   BUDGET   *Tel/Fax* 01262-470696
Wold Newton, nr Driffield   *Email* katrina@woldcottage.com
YO25 3HL   *Website* www.woldcottage.com

'Grand, and lovingly restored', this spacious red brick Georgian manor
house was once a gentleman's retreat in the Yorkshire countryside. The
owners, Katrina and Derek Gray, manage 300 acres of land and, with a
neighbouring family, the Mellors, they established the Wold Top Brewery,

using pure, chalk-filtered water from the farm to produce Mars Magic, Falling Stone and Wold Top Bitter (available by draught at their pub, *The Falling Stone*, two miles away, or sold in bottles at *The Wold Cottage*). The 'very friendly' Grays welcome guests with tea and cake, and provide 'very good value'. 'My large room in the stable annexe was airy and had fresh flowers, but the hot water ran out when I had a bath.' Extras include dressing gowns, hot-water bottle, fresh milk in a flask. Dinner (arrange when booking) is preceded by complimentary sherry, and served by candlelight, communally or at separate tables: 'Good plain cooking [eg, beef stew and dumplings], and a short wine list.' 'Breakfast was served by one of the Grays' wonderfully helpful sons who was enjoying loud rock music in the next room.' It has 'chunky toast from home-made bread, delicious local preserves and good coffee'. (*David Sulkin, and others*)

5 bedrooms. 2 in converted barn. 1 on ground floor. Just outside village. Lounge, dining room (background music at mealtimes). 3-acre grounds in 300-acre farmland: croquet. No smoking. No dogs. MasterCard, Visa accepted. B&B £35–£55 per person; D,B&B £50–£73. Set dinner £18.50.

WOLTERTON Norfolk   Map 2:A5

The Saracen's Head   NEW   *Tel* 01263-768909
Wolterton, nr Erpingham   *Fax* 01263-768993
NR11 7LX   *Email* saracenshead@wolterton.freeserve.co.uk
                                Website www.saracenshead-norfolk.co.uk

This popular local eating place, set amid fields, calls itself a 'lost inn' (directions are given when you book). The 'hands-on' owner/chef Robert Dawson-Smith ('resplendent in cravat, chinos, checked shirt and denim apron') has presided for 17 years. His daughter, Rachel, runs the Shed, a workshop selling retro furniture, pictures, etc. It won't suit all comers: 'too much of a pub' for some, and bedroom maintenance may not be perfect, but a visitor this year had a 'most enjoyable' three-day stay: 'Excellent welcome and service. Wide choice of first-class food. Well-thought-out wine list. Dogs in our bedroom free of charge.' An earlier comment: 'A genuine family affair. Real bedrooms: iron bedsteads and patchwork quilts. Lovely courtyard.' Three bedrooms, reached up steep steps, are in the roof; they have rounded dormer windows, sloping ceilings. 'Ours was fair-sized, decorated in bold colours.' The public rooms are 'cosy, candlelit, filled with paintings and bric-a-brac (a stuffed fox's head, etc)'. The blackboard menu changes with each meal: it might include baked Cromer crab with apple and sherry; scallops with rosemary and cream. The two-course weekday lunch is 'amazing value' (£8). In summer, meals are served alfresco. Breakfast ('especially good') includes freshly squeezed orange juice, fruit, fresh bread, good kippers. (*Jane Legate, Ralph Kenber, and others*)

6 bedrooms. Closed 25/evening of 26 Dec. 5 miles from Aylsham. Lounge, 3 dining rooms. No background music. Courtyard. 1-acre garden: shop. Accommodation unsuitable for &. No smoking in bedrooms; discouraged elsewhere and banned in eating areas before 10 pm. No dogs in public rooms. Amex, MasterCard, Visa accepted. B&B £40–£50 per person; D,B&B £65–£75. Alc from £20. Off-season rates negotiable. 1-night bookings refused weekends. ***V***

WOODSTOCK Oxfordshire   Map 2:C2

The Kings Arms   **NEW**   *Tel* 01993-813636
19 Market Street   *Fax* 01993-813737
Woodstock OX20 1SV   *Email* stay@kingshotelwoodstock.co.uk
                        Website www.kingshotelwoodstock.co.uk

In this 'nice Oxfordshire village' (famous because Blenheim Palace is there), David and Sara Sykes's small hotel is made up of converted Georgian houses. 'The service was excellent, proprietor much in evidence during the day,' say the nominators. 'A very pleasant dinner (good food and helpful service). Breakfast ditto.' In the 'interestingly decorated' bistro, 'residents get a free bottle of wine if they dine'. Dean Collins goes in for dishes like beef and red wine stew; herb-crusted lamb cutlets with redcurrant sauce. 'The comfortable bedrooms have been recently furbished in contemporary style. Only criticism: bath towels rather small.' There is non-stop 'easy listening' music in the bars and bistro, but not in the upstairs residents' lounge. (*Michael and Eithne Dandy*)

15 bedrooms. Central. 8 miles N of Oxford on A44. Lounge, 2 bars, bistro (non-stop background music). Unsuitable for &. No smoking: 1 bar, restaurant, all bedrooms. No children under 12 in accommodation. No dogs. Amex, MasterCard, Visa accepted. B&B £65–£100 per person; D,B&B £85–£120. Full alc £30.

WORFIELD Shropshire   Map 3:C5

The Old Vicarage   *Tel* 01746-716497
Worfield   *Fax* 01746-716552
nr Bridgnorth WV15 5JZ   *Email* admin@the-old-vicarage.demon.co.uk
                        Website www.oldvicarageworfield.com

'We are a family-run hotel, proud of the relaxed style,' say David and Sarah Blakstad, owners of this gabled, red brick Edwardian former parsonage in rural Shropshire. Visitors arrived to find 'guests sunning themselves on the granite terrace in lush wooded surroundings: a manicured lawn with statues and seats around venerable oaks gave a continental air'. Most bedrooms have antique furniture; one has a Victorian four-poster, another a walnut half-tester bed. Some rooms in the main house may need 'a tidy-up'. Four luxury rooms are in a converted coach house. 'Our spacious suite had large sitting room, bathroom with good thick towels, fresh milk in the fridge.' Pre-dinner drinks are taken on the patio in fine weather. 'Dinner and breakfast both good.' In the *Orangery* restaurant (good views), the dress code is 'smart casual, no jeans please'. Chef Martyn Pearn serves a 'modern European' menu (eg, potted ham hock and foie gras terrine; roasted rack of Shropshire lamb with a mustard, herb and brioche crust). Breakfast had 'very good' sausages, smoked haddock with poached egg, kippers. 'Fruit included passion fruit and figs.' The Blakstads, parents themselves, write: 'While we have limited facilities for children, we actively encourage them to stay.' (*AT, RV, and others*)

14 bedrooms. 4 in coach house. 2 on ground floor. 2 suitable for &. 3 miles NE of Bridgnorth. Ramps. Lounge, bar, restaurant; background music; 2 private dining rooms; small conference facilities. 2-acre grounds: patio, croquet. No smoking. Only guide dogs in public rooms. Diners, MasterCard, Visa accepted. B&B: £49.75–£87.50 per person. English breakfast £10.50. Set lunch £21.50; full alc £45. **•V•**

WYE Kent *See SHORTLIST*   Map 2:D5

YARM North Yorkshire   Map 4:C4

Judges Hotel   *Tel* 01642-789000
Kirklevington Hall   *Fax* 01642-787692
Yarm TS15 9LW   *Email* enquiries@judgeshotel.co.uk
                    Website www.judgeshotel.co.uk

In a prosperous small market town in a loop of the River Tees this Victorian building, owned by Michael Downs, is managed by Tim Howard. It stands in wooded grounds with stream and landscaped gardens (floodlit at night). A visitor this year, who was welcomed in the car park on a blustery day by 'a cheerful porter with a large umbrella', was impressed by the 'attention to detail' and the bedrooms. 'Ours had grand four-poster, large living space, plenty of furniture, satellite TV, scented candles in the bathroom.' Each room has a resident goldfish ('in case guests on their own feel lonely'), which may be fed once a day. 'Ours was called Alfonso.' In the conservatory restaurant, chef John Lyons serves 'French, modern' cooking. 'Dinner was sensational, to look at and to taste. Soup made with superb stock; enjoyable rabbit terrine; a perfect fillet steak. On the extensive wine list there are good buys to be had.' Light meals can be served during the day in the panelled bar or the lounge, with its antiques, fire and flowers. 'Breakfast was good, though not of the quality of dinner: no freshly squeezed juices.' Tickets for York races can be arranged. (*Robert Gower*)

21 bedrooms. Some on ground floor. 1½ miles S of centre. Lounge, bar, restaurant; private dining room; function facilities; business centre. No background music. 31-acre grounds: paths, running routes. Access to local spa and sports club. Civil wedding licence. No smoking in restaurant. Guide dogs only. All major credit cards accepted. B&B [2006] £92–£144 per person; D,B&B £127.50–£177. Set dinner £37.50; full alc £47.50. Christmas/New Year packages. ***V***

YARMOUTH Isle of Wight *See SHORTLIST*   Map 2:E2

YEOVIL Somerset *See SHORTLIST*   Map 1:C6

YORK North Yorkshire   Map 4:D4

The Grange	*Tel* 01904-644744
1 Clifton	*Fax* 01904-612453
York YO30 6AA	*Email* info@grangehotel.co.uk
	Website www.grangehotel.co.uk

'We enjoyed our stay: good food, nice staff, convenient setting.' One of this year's comments on this Grade II listed Regency town house owned by Jeremy Cassel and managed by Annie Postings. Its many original features include a wrought iron filigree staircase and stone-flagged entrance hall. The public rooms have panelling, family portraits, hunting scenes and open fires. 'We were impressed. The bedrooms are pleasantly furnished and well equipped,' says a visitor in 2006. 'Staff are pleasant, but possibly lack training.' Eating arrangements have changed: the *Ivy* restaurant, completely refurbished, now serves brasserie-type food in a 'more relaxed' atmosphere. The bar, in the basement, serves light meals. Bedrooms have antiques, chintzes, good lighting, a smart bathroom; the best rooms are 'very romantic': two have a four-poster, and the suite has two bedrooms and a sitting room. 'Our bed was comfortable. Fresh milk for tea was a nice 'touch.' Front rooms face a busy road, but windows are double glazed. Children are welcomed. Parties and functions are catered for. (*Harry and Annette Medcalf, Richard Parish*)

30 bedrooms. 6 on ground floor. 1 suitable for ♿. 500 yds from city wall. Ramps. Lounge, morning room, 2 bars, restaurant (jazz/modern background music); conference/function facilities. Civil wedding licence. No smoking in restaurant. No dogs in public rooms. All major credit cards accepted. B&B £75–£130 per person; D,B&B (min. 2 nights) £90–£140. Set lunch £17.95; full alc £32–£35. Christmas/ New Year packages. 1-night bookings sometimes refused Sat. **ᵛVᵛ**

Middlethorpe Hall
Bishopthorpe Road
York YO23 2GB

Tel 01904-641241
Fax 01904-620176
Email info@middlethorpe.com
Website www.middlethorpe.com

'Magnificent, in a class of its own,' says a returning visitor to this 'stunning' red brick William III house, once the home of the diarist Lady Mary Wortley Montagu. In a large park near York racecourse, it has walled garden, small lake and venerable trees (but traffic from the busy nearby road is audible). Now a luxury hotel (Relais & Châteaux), managed by Lionel Chatard, it has been restored by Historic House Hotels Ltd (see also *Hartwell House*, Aylesbury, *Bodysgallen Hall*, Llandudno). There are antiques, period fabrics, fine porcelain, and Wi-Fi in the main house. The best bedrooms are enormous; some have a sitting room with a gas coal fire. Cheaper rooms are in converted stables and cottages round a courtyard. All rooms now have a DVD-player. Beds are 'deliciously comfortable'. Lee Heptinstall, the chef, serves 'British modern cuisine with a continental touch', eg, pork loin and belly with pease pudding. Dinner is served by candlelight in interlinked rooms facing the 'delightful' garden. Men must wear jacket and tie in the formal dining room; there is also a simpler grill room. There is a spa in a converted coach house. (*Jane and Martin Bailey*)

29 bedrooms. 3 in garden. 1 suitable for ♿. 16 in courtyard. 1½ miles S of centre, by racecourse. Drawing room, sitting rooms, library, restaurant, grill room; private dining rooms; function facilities. No background music. 20-acre grounds: walled garden, white garden, croquet, lake; spa: health and beauty facilities, swimming pool. Civil wedding licence. No smoking: restaurant, main house bedrooms, most public rooms. No children under 6. Guide dogs only. Amex, MasterCard, Visa accepted. B&B (continental breakfast) £90–£197.50 per person; D,B&B (min. 2 nights) £120–£210. English breakfast £6.95 extra. Set dinner £39–£55. Christmas/ New Year packages.

See also SHORTLIST

SCOTLAND

There are encouraging signs of a revival in Scottish hospitality, which reflects the increase in visitor numbers, thanks, at least in part, to the expansion of low-cost flights within the United Kingdom. Our inspectors and readers have found high standards this year. Two of our *César* award winners are Scottish: the *Isle of Eriska* hotel, a baronial mansion on a private island; and *Ardeonaig Hotel*, a white-painted inn on the shores of Loch Tay.

Isle of Eriska, Eriska

ABERDEEN *See SHORTLIST*   Map 5:C3

ACHILTIBUIE Highland   Map 5:B1

Summer Isles Hotel   *Tel* 01854-622282
Achiltibuie   *Fax* 01854-622251
by Ullapool IV26 2YG   *Email* info@summerisleshotel.co.uk
                              Website www.summerisleshotel.co.uk

Ϙ *César award in 1993*

'Unbridled luxury. Wonderful views. Superb dinner,' write visitors in 2006.
In a remote, unspoilt village reached by a single-track road, this popular
'croft-style' hotel/restaurant has a stunning setting, with 'sublime views'
over the sea to the Summer Isles and the Hebrides. The owners, Mark and
Gerry Irvine, and their staff are thought 'outstandingly friendly'. The
bedrooms are 'smart', comfortable and 'full of personal touches'. Three are
in the main house, others are in an annexe (it has two sea-facing suites).
There are also some 'very comfortable' log cabin-style rooms, and the Boat
House suite in a stone cottage by the road. Chris Firth-Bernard's *Michelin*-
starred cooking is much admired (eg, langoustine in filo pastry; a 'stupendous pudding trolley'); his five substantial courses, served at 8, are no-
choice but accommodate dietary requirements. 'Nearly everything is home
produced or locally caught,' says the brochure. The bar, a friendly local,
serves meals including a 'superb sea platter', until 8.30. Breakfasts have
'fantastic' home-made bread and rolls, muesli, fruit and cooked dishes.
(*Mike and Shirley Stratton, and others*)

13 bedrooms. Some in annexe and cottages. NW of Ullapool. Open 1 Apr–mid-Oct.
Sitting room, sun lounge, cocktail bar, public bar (background music), restaurant.
Small garden. Sea 100 yds. Unsuitable for &. No smoking. No children under 8.
Dogs by arrangement, not in public rooms. MasterCard, Visa accepted. B&B
£61–£155 per person; D,B&B £110–£204. Bar lunches. Set dinner £50.

How to contact the *Guide*
By mail: From anywhere in the UK, write to Freepost PAM 2931,
London W11 4BR (no stamp is needed)
From outside the UK: Good Hotel Guide, 50 Addison Avenue,
London W11 4QP, England
By telephone or fax: 020-7602 4182
By email: Goodhotel@aol.com
Via our website: www.goodhotelguide.com

ANNBANK South Ayrshire   Map 5:E2

Enterkine   **NEW**   *Tel* 01292-520580
Annbank, by Ayr   *Fax* 01292-521582
KA6 5AL   *Email* mail@enterkine.com
                                        Website www.enterkine.com

Approached by a long gravel drive lined by trees, this small country hotel
(a 1930s residence) stands in large grounds near Ayr. Owned by Oswald
St George Browne, it is managed by Louis MacCallum. 'A relaxing place,
unashamedly "country house", and none the worse for that. The staff are
friendly,' says its nominator. 'We were comfortable and well looked after.
Our Labrador was welcomed. In the pretty gardens we enjoyed a scenic
walk along the River Ayr. The lounge has squishy seating, the conservatory
dining room has great views, and the cooking of Paul Moffat is always a
treat.' Saddle of rabbit with smoked shallot ham, and lobster soufflé were
particularly enjoyed. Six bedrooms are in the main house, the others are in
a 'bothy' and two cottages. 'Ours was spacious, with high ceiling, big
windows, good-sized bathroom, large, comfortable bed, good seating.'
Breakfast, served at table, includes 'a good selection of juices, fruit salad,
etc, pastries, croissants; cooked breakfast in many combinations'. Local
sporting pursuits include shooting, fishing and golf. Glasgow Prestwick
airport is ten minutes' drive away. In the 'peaceful, rolling' countryside
around, there is good walking. (*Shirley Tennent*)

13 bedrooms. 6 in 2 cottages. 5 miles E of Ayr. 2 sitting rooms, sun lounge, library
(Internet access), restaurant; private dining room; meeting room. Background
music throughout. Occasional jazz or opera nights. 350-acre grounds: clay-pigeon
shooting, quads, archery. 6 miles from sea. Unsuitable for &. Wedding facilities.
No smoking. Dogs allowed only in bedrooms (depending on size). All major credit
cards accepted. B&B £95–£120 per person. Set meals £32–£45. Christmas/New
Year packages. ***V***

ARDUAINE Argyll and Bute *See SHORTLIST* Map 5:D1

ARISAIG Highland *See SHORTLIST*   Map 5:C1

The 'New' label indicates hotels which are appearing in the *Guide*
for the first time or which have been readmitted after an absence.

AVIEMORE Highland   Map 5:C2

Corrour House   *Tel* 01479-810220
Inverdruie, Rothiemurchus   *Fax* 01479-811500
by Aviemore   *Email* enquiries@corrourhousehotel.co.uk
PH22 1QH   *Website* www.corrourhousehotel.co.uk

'A house of real antique character, scrupulously maintained', this bay-windowed former dower house of the Rothiemurchus estate is beautifully situated amid secluded gardens and woodland, with 'outstanding' views across to the Lairig Ghru pass and the Cairngorms. Visitors this year say that owners Carol and Robert Still 'take immense trouble to make sure their guests have all they need, and to give them information about the neighbourhood'. The lounge and dining room have open fires; bedrooms are 'chintzy'. 'Dinner was excellent': the chef, Sebastien Voisin, serves a substantial, limited-choice, five-course candlelit dinner (eg, turbot with caper butter sauce), and as you dine, you might see deer cross the lawn. (*Prof. Robert and Mrs Pat Cahn*)

8 bedrooms. ¼ mile S of Aviemore. Open New Year–mid-Nov. Lounge, cocktail bar (background music when guest numbers are small), dining room. 4-acre gardens and woodland. Unsuitable for ♿. No smoking. No dogs in public rooms, unsupervised in bedrooms. MasterCard, Visa accepted. B&B £40–£50 per person; D,B&B £65–£75. Set dinner £28.50. Reductions for 3 or more nights. New Year package. ***V***

BALLACHULISH Highland   Map 5:C1

Ballachulish House   *Tel* 01855-811266
Ballachulish   *Fax* 01855-811498
PA49 4JX   *Email* mclaughlins@btconnect.com
                               Website www.ballachulishhouse.com

Full of history, this elegant former laird's house is 'very well managed' as an upmarket country hotel by the owner, Marie McLaughlin, 'outgoing, friendly, energetic'. In serene countryside between Loch Linnhe and the mountains, the house has connections with the Massacre of Glencoe and the Appin murder which inspired RL Stevenson's *Kidnapped*. Our inspectors were 'welcomed with great warmth'; bags were carried to the room. 'It was large, with a nice mix of antique and repro furnishings, fresh fruit and flowers, good lighting, generous dressing table, large wardrobe; a small, well-equipped bathroom.' A piper might play as guests take drinks from an honesty bar in the drawing room, where dinner orders are taken from 7.30 pm by Mrs McLaughlin. The chef, Allan Donald (his wife,

Eileen, is *sous-chef*), has a *Michelin* star for his modern dishes on a five-course menu (mostly no-choice), eg, smoked duck with orange and elder-berry sauce; seared scallops in puff pastry. Dining is a protracted affair, with 'horrid background music'. Breakfast has a 'beautifully displayed buffet' of cereals, etc; freshly squeezed juice, carefully presented cooked dishes, good home-baked granary toast. Check-in time is 4 pm. A scenic 9-hole golf course runs through the grounds.

Note: Not to be confused with the *Ballachulish Hotel* on the main road.

8 bedrooms. Just SW of Ballachulish bridge. Drawing room with honesty bar, library, dining room (background music). Walled garden; 9-hole golf course. Sea loch 5 mins' walk; fishing, skiing nearby. No smoking. Children by arrangement. No dogs. MasterCard, Visa accepted. B&B [2006] (*Excluding VAT*): single £75, double £125–£188, family £195. Set dinner £37.50–£47.50. Off-season breaks.

BALLANTRAE South Ayrshire   Map 5:E1

Cosses Country House
Ballantrae KA26 0LR

Tel 01465-831363
Fax 01465-831598
Email info@cossescountryhouse.com
Website www.cossescountryhouse.com

Outside an old fishing village in south-west Scotland, Susan and Robin Crosthwaite's guest house sits in a secluded wooded valley. A long, low, white 17th-century hunting lodge, it has a 'comfortable and chintzy' interior, filled with antiques and souvenirs from the owners' years in the Middle and Far East. The lounge, where they meet with their guests for pre-dinner drinks, has been refurbished this year. There is a double bedroom in the main house; two large suites, with sitting room/second bedroom, good for a family, are in converted byres and stables across the courtyard. All rooms have king-size bed and large bathroom. Mrs Crosthwaite's four-course dinners, served communally, are no-choice, but preferences are discussed beforehand. Her style is modern, eg, seafood sausage with seared prawns; loin of lamb with garlic and ginger. Generous breakfasts are often served informally in the kitchen. Drying facilities are available. (*WKC*)

3 bedrooms. 2 miles E of Ballantrae. Open 1 Mar–30 Nov. Occasionally closed other times. Lounge, dining room; utility room. No background music. 12-acre grounds: garden, woods. Unsuitable for &. No smoking. No children under 12. No dogs in public rooms; by arrangement in bedrooms. MasterCard, Visa accepted. B&B £40–£62.50 per person. Set dinner £27.50. Reductions for 3 nights or more.

BALLATER Aberdeenshire   Map 5:C3

Balgonie Country House   *Tel* 01339-755482
Braemar Place   *Fax* 01339-755497
Ballater AB35 5NQ   *Email* balgoniech@aol.com
                                    Website www.balgonie-hotel.co.uk

Overlooking Ballater golf course and the hills of Glen Muick, this Edwardian country house stands in lovely grounds. The resident owners, John and Priscilla Finnie (who once worked for the royal household), and their competent staff, including the 'brilliant' manager, Moira McDougall, are thought especially welcoming. The light, comfortable interior is 'tastefully furnished'; the elegant dining room and lounge look on to the tree-lined grounds, and a sun terrace leads off the 'cosy' bar. Bedrooms are named after fishing pools on the River Dee. Chef John Finnie's four-course 'modern British' dinners (eg, halibut with spring onion risotto) are generally praised. Breakfast is found 'excellent'. Local attractions include the Royal Highland Games at Braemar; salmon fishing on the Dee can be arranged. (*AM, RGJT, and others*)

9 bedrooms. W outskirts of Ballater. Open 1 Apr–31 Oct (possibly Christmas/New Year). Lounge, bar, dining room. No background music. 4-acre garden: croquet. Unsuitable for &. No smoking. No dogs. Amex, MasterCard, Visa accepted. B&B £45–£80 per person; D,B&B £75–£115. Set dinner £40. 1-night bookings refused Royal Highland Games, Easter. ***V***

BALLOCH West Dunbartonshire   Map 5:D2
See SHORTLIST

The ***V*** sign at the end of an entry indicates a hotel that has agreed to take part in our Voucher scheme and to give *Guide* readers a 25% discount on their room rates for a one-night stay, subject to the conditions explained on page 60 and listed on the back of the vouchers.

BALLYGRANT Argyll and Bute   Map 5:D1

Kilmeny Country Guest House   *Tel/Fax* 01496-840668
Ballygrant, Isle of Islay   *Email* info@kilmeny.co.uk
PA45 7QW   *Website* www.kilmeny.co.uk

With 'spectacular views' over countryside and moorland, Margaret and
Blair Rozga's elegant guest house is a traditional, white-painted 19th-
century farmhouse in a beautiful garden on a working beef farm. The
guest sitting room and the three bedrooms (Pink, Yellow and Apricot)
are well furnished, with antique furniture and chintzes; *en suite*
bathrooms have quality toiletries; bedrooms have home-made biscuits.
Guests sit together around one large mahogany dining table, and can
bring their own wine (no licence) to accompany Mrs Rozga's 'absolutely
delicious' five-course dinners (after canapés and complimentary whisky
or sherry). Served on weekdays only, they have two choices for each
course and use local ingredients. Breakfasts are generous. Mrs Rozga is
a 'sparkling and friendly' hostess, say admirers, and 'everything is
immaculate'. Islay, though small, is home to a range of wildlife, including
the geese who feed on Kilmeny's grasslands, and eight of the best – and
some of the smokiest – whiskies in the world.

3 bedrooms. 2 on ground floor. ½ mile south of Ballygrant village. Open Mar–Nov.
Restaurant closed midday and Sat/Sun. Sitting room, dining room. No background
music. ½-acre garden in 300-acre farm. Unsuitable for &. No smoking. No children
under 7. No dogs. No credit cards. B&B £55–£75 per person. Set dinner £35.
1-night bookings sometimes refused.

BALQUHIDDER Stirling   Map 5:D2

Monachyle Mhor   *Tel* 01877-384622
Balquhidder   *Fax* 01877-384305
Lochearnhead FK19 8PQ   *Email* info@monachylemhor.com
                                        Website www.monachylemhor.com

'On the road to nowhere (one can amble by the loch and enjoy the
peace)', Tom and Angela Lewis's pale-pink 18th-century farmhouse
with outbuildings is at the end of a single-lane track, by Loch Voil, in
Scotland's first national park. 'So enjoyable, I hope to return ere long,'
says a visitor this year. Public rooms have open fires, antiques and
modern furnishings. 'The tiny sitting room and bar can get very
crowded.' Some bedrooms have a fire, some have a flat-screen TV, and
all have a DVD-player. Smaller rooms were less liked this year: 'Ours
was cramped, and had a blind of such stupendous complexity that we

could not lower it, despite a security light outside.' 'My room was small but the bathroom was super-luxurious.' Housekeeping may not be perfect. No doubts about the food, however. 'Dinner was something else, undoubtedly very good value.' Tom Lewis uses local produce and vegetables and herbs from the organic walled garden (eg, freshly shucked oyster with spiced lemon and shallot; braised belly of pork and loin, roasted fig). There are inventive vegetarian dishes, good bar meals and 'exceptional breakfasts', too. 'Service couldn't be friendlier.' (*Dorothy Brining, Robert and Pat Cahn, and others*)

13 bedrooms. 1 on ground floor. 5 in courtyard. Self-catering cottages. 11 miles NW of Callander. Closed 5 Jan–6 Feb. Sitting room, bar (background music at night), conservatory restaurant. 2,000-acre estate: garden, *pétanque* pitch. Wedding facilities. No smoking. No children under 12. Dogs by arrangement; not in public rooms. MasterCard, Visa accepted. B&B £47.50–£110 per person. Set dinner £44.

BANCHORY Aberdeenshire *See SHORTLIST* Map 5:C3

BLACKFORD Perth and Kinross   Map 5:D2

Blackford Hotel
Moray Street
Blackford PH4 1QF

Tel 01764-682497
Fax 01764-682597
Email info@blackfordhotel.co.uk
Website www.blackfordhotel.co.uk

'Small but beautifully formed.' Our inspectors were impressed by Mark and Claire Stevens's white-painted former 1830s coaching inn, two miles from Gleneagles and its famous golf course. 'They run it as a restaurant-with-rooms cum village pub; it is a tribute to them that these disparate elements coexist so remarkably well. When we wanted to change rooms, Mark arranged this without a blink; he is involved in virtually every activity, accomplishing all with natural charm and unforced efficiency.' There are wood-burning stoves in the bar and restaurant, and 'a good log fire' and tartan carpeting in the lounge/entrance hall. 'Cleverly arranged pine furniture, pale-coloured walls and most attractive fabrics made our small room seem spacious. Everything was spotlessly clean. Bedside lighting was a bit dim.' But a dissenter had a room that was poorly maintained and subject to noise from above. There are two bay-windowed turret rooms (one has a four-poster), and eiderdowns for cold nights. The new chef, Robert Monteith, serves a 'thoroughly enjoyable' two- or three-course menu of 'simple food, well done: generous helpings attractively served, good flavours and textures, particularly good vegetables'. Breakfast had 'excellent scrambled eggs, properly cured local bacon'. Children are welcomed, and provided with paper and crayons. The lively bar has a pool table, jukebox, widescreen TV, etc.

8 bedrooms. Centre of village, 2 miles SW of Gleneagles. Free street parking. Closed 1st week Jan. Public bar (entertainments), reception lounge, lounge bar, dining room; function room; background music. Small beer garden. No smoking. Dogs in public bar only. Amex, MasterCard, Visa accepted. B&B [2006] £37.50–£50 per person. Full alc £25. ***V***

BLAIRGOWRIE Perth and Kinross   Map 5:D2

Kinloch House   *Tel* 01250-884237
Dunkeld Road   *Fax* 01250-884333
by Blairgowrie PH10 6SG   *Email* reception@kinlochhouse.com
                                          Website www.kinlochhouse.com

Three years ago, the Allen family, who ran the much-admired *Airds Hotel*, Port Appin (*qv*) for 25 years, moved to this grand 19th-century Scottish mansion. A Relais & Châteaux member, it stands on a sloping hillside facing a wide valley, in large grounds with a Victorian walled garden. With its oak-panelled hall, *objets d'art*, log fires, portrait gallery and ornate glass ceiling, 'it feels nothing like a hotel', according to visitors this year. 'The impression is of an elegant country house with pastoral views. Graeme Allen presides affably but not intrusively, supported by superbly trained staff. The kitchen team, led by Andrew May, former *sous-chef*, 'has flair and dedication. The Arbroath smokie soufflé was perfection.' The extensive wine list includes some expensive bottles as well as 'a good selection of fairly priced quality house wines'. Most bedrooms are spacious; they are 'tastefully furnished, without being fussy or twee'. Some have a four-poster bed and a large Victorian bath. Most showers are hand-held. 'Those seeking comfort and quality will not be disappointed.' Male guests are asked to wear a jacket at dinner. The health centre (see below) is another attraction. (*Tony and Maryanne Dear*)

18 bedrooms. 4 on ground floor. 3 miles W of Blairgowrie, on A923 Dunkeld Rd. Closed 14–29 Dec. Ramp. Drawing room, lounge, conservatory, bar, dining room; private dining room; health centre (35-ft swimming pool, sauna, etc). No background music. 25-acre grounds: walled garden, field with Highland cattle and horses. No smoking. No children under 7 in dining room at night. Dogs by arrangement (dog units available). Wedding facilities. Amex, MasterCard, Visa accepted. D,B&B £112–£180 per person. Set lunch £24, dinner £44. New Year package.

BOWMORE Argyll and Bute   Map 5:D1

Harbour Inn & Restaurant	*Tel* 01496-810330
The Square, Bowmore	*Fax* 01496-810990
Isle of Islay PA43 7JR	*Email* info@harbour-inn.com
	Website www.harbour-inn.com

Spectacular views across Loch Indaal and surrounding countryside from Neil and Carol Scott's old whitewashed inn by harbour of village on E side of loch. Tasteful contemporary decor. 'Helpful staff, friendly public bar.' Conservatory lounge, lounge bar, restaurant (new chef, Paul Lumby, this year: modern Scottish cooking on long menu); background music. Good breakfasts. Small garden. Guests have free use of local leisure centre (swimming pool, gym). Closed Christmas. Unsuitable for &. No smoking. No children under 10. No pets. MasterCard, Visa accepted. 7 'large, well-furnished' bedrooms (2 family). B&B [2006] £50–£65 per person. Full alc £45. More reports, please.

BRODICK North Ayrshire *See SHORTLIST*   Map 5:E1

CALLANDER Stirling   Map 5:D2

The Roman Camp	*Tel* 01877-330003
off Main Street	*Fax* 01877-331533
Callander FK17 8BG	*Email* mail@romancamphotel.co.uk
	Website www.romancamphotel.co.uk

Just off the main street of this old town east of the Trossachs, Eric and Marion Brown's luxury hotel stands amid gardens in large grounds on the banks of the River Teith. The much-extended, pink, turreted hunting lodge takes its name from earthworks to the east of the walled garden, believed to be the site of a Roman fort. Most recent visitors found it 'excellent', with 'outstanding staff', though one couple encountered some linguistic difficulties. It has a country house atmosphere, with log fires, panelling, oak beams, four-poster beds. Some of the spacious bedrooms in a modern wing have a door leading on to a garden; those in the old house vary in size and style; all bathrooms are being refurbished this year; there will be marble tiles and spa baths. In the oval dining room, with its tapestries, large fireplace and garden views, the long-serving chef, Ian McNaught, serves an 'imaginative' menu, 'skilfully blending ingredients', eg, calf's liver with lemon and black pepper pomme purée; fennel pollen crusted salmon. 'Breakfast equally impressive; excellent afternoon tea (sandwiches, scones and cakes).' Guests have access to the golf course nearby. (*IMcD, and others*)

14 bedrooms. 7 on ground floor, 1 designed for &. E end of Main Street. 3 lounge areas, bar, 2 dining rooms; chapel; conference/function facilities. No background music. 17-acre grounds: ¼-mile river, fishing. Golf nearby. Wedding facilities. No smoking. No dogs in public rooms. All major credit cards accepted. B&B: single £75–£145, double £125–£185, suite £185–£225. Set menus £45; full alc £60. 2-night winter breaks. Christmas/New Year packages. *V*

CAMPTOWN Borders *See SHORTLIST*   Map 5:E3

CHIRNSIDE Borders   Map 5:E3

Chirnside Hall	*Tel* 01890-818219
Chirnside, nr Duns	*Fax* 01890-818231
TD11 3LD	*Email* chirnside_hall@btconnect.com
	Website www.chirnsidehallhotel.com

In lovely Borders countryside, Christian and Tessa Korsten's 1830s brick-built mansion has 'stunning views' over wheat fields to the Cheviot Hills. Beautifully restored and 'elegantly decorated', with bold colours and rich fabrics, it has open fires in marble fireplaces in the spacious comfortable lounges, and in the handsome small dining room with its big tables and upholstered chairs, where chef Gary Imlach serves a short four-course menu. Sample dishes: mackerel recheado; saddle of roe deer over braised baby gems, with a raspberry jus. Bedrooms are well furnished; one has a four-poster bed and a sofa; bathrooms are well equipped, and have lots of hot water. Some top-floor rooms may be 'a little dark'. 'Tessa Korsten and her small staff are charming.' Hunting and fishing parties make the hotel lively in winter; it is often quieter in summer. (*John Edwards, J and MB*)

10 bedrooms. 6 miles NE of Duns. Closed Mar. 2 lounges, dining room ('easy listening' background music); billiard room; fitness room; library/conference room. 6-acre grounds. Unsuitable for &. Wedding facilities. No smoking. No dogs in public rooms. Amex, MasterCard, Visa accepted. B&B [2006] £75–£85 per person; D,B&B £95–£105. Set dinner £30. Christmas/New Year packages.

If you remember a hotel's name but not its location, consult the alphabetical hotel list on page 552.

CLACHAN SEIL Argyll and Bute   Map 5:D1

Willowburn Hotel
Clachan Seil, Isle of Seil
by Oban PA34 4TJ

Tel 01852-300276
Email willowburn.hotel@virgin.net
Website www.willowburn.co.uk

'We rate it very highly,' says one of this year's enthusiastic reports on this small hotel. A long, low, narrow building, it has a lovely setting on the little island of Seil (reached across a short, 18th-century, semi-circular stone bridge over the Atlantic). Inspectors agreed, commending 'the kindness of the owners, Jan and Chris Wolfe, the friendly atmosphere, the good food and the views'. The lounge (with open fire) and the restaurant (both with picture windows), the small bar and all bedrooms but one face the quiet waters of Clachan Sound. Decor is unpretentious and homely. Neat bedrooms, 'small but exceptionally clean', 'like a ship's cabin', have 'good toiletries', 'comfortable bed, excellent reading lights'. 'Everyone was invited into the bar at 7 pm to view the menu.' 'At dinner, we chatted with guests at the other tables.' Local fishermen and the hotel's garden supply Chris Wolfe's four-course dinners. 'A particularly good crab and avocado starter', 'fantastic chocolate and liqueur roulade'. 'After dinner there was lots of laughter over coffee in the lounge.' 'Delicious bread' appears at dinner and breakfast. Prospective canine guests get a letter from the resident dogs and cat. Two 'territorial' swans, Mr and Mrs D52, often visit *Willowburn*, so do many birds. (*Mike Widdall, and others*)

7 bedrooms. 14 miles S of Oban. Bus from Oban. Open mid-Mar–mid-Nov. Lounge, bar, dining room (quiet background music at night). 1½-acre grounds. Shore 100 yds. No smoking. No children under 8. No dogs: lounge, dining room. MasterCard, Visa accepted. D,B&B £85 per person. Set dinner £36. Reductions for 3 or more nights.

COLINTRAIVE Argyll and Bute   Map 5:D1

Colintraive Hotel   BUDGET
Colintraive PA22 3AS

Tel/Fax 01700-841207
Email enquiries@colintraivehotel.com
Website www.colintraivehotel.com

'Welcome to my house,' was the greeting given by Patricia Watt to two rain-soaked cyclists calling at her small white-painted, Victorian former hunting lodge of the Marquis of Bute. 'An amazingly wonderful hotel' was a 2006 comment. On the shore of the Cowal peninsula, it has 'wonderful' views over the Kyles of Bute. The light, pretty bedrooms have white and cream furnishings; there are family rooms. There is a 'comfy' lounge, and a 'buzzy little bar' with a log fire, popular with locals, serving 'proper bar food, like scallops and venison sausages'. Miss Watt (who also owns the adjoining shop and post office) 'is a star, serving in the bar, receiving guests and helping in the small dining room', where chef David Cumming's *à la carte* menus provide 'great food', making use of local produce (eg, salmon fillet poached in port with crayfish sauce; noisette of Bute lamb with crushed baby potatoes). In summer, meals are served alfresco. Children, and pets, are welcomed. (*Wendy Brooks, J and SB*)

4 bedrooms. Centre of village, near ferry pier. Closed 25 Dec. Ramp. Bar, restaurant, coffee lounge. No background music. Moorings, sailors' shower room. Only bar and restaurant suitable for &. No smoking. MasterCard, Visa accepted. B&B [2006] £35–£70 per person. Full alc £32. 3-night packages.

COLONSAY Argyll and Bute — Map 5:D1

Isle of Colonsay Hotel — NEW
Isle of Colonsay
PA61 7YP

Tel 01951-200316
Fax 01951-200353
Email reception@thecolonsay.com
Website www.thecolonsay.com

There is little to do on this 'idyllic' Hebridean island, 'apart from exploring wildlife and archaeological remains, basking on a splendid golden beach', according to a regular *Guide* correspondent in 2006. This 'cool, stylish' hotel 'provides a luxurious nest, where to be pampered is a real treat'. Managed by Jo Crowley, the 'unpretentious old inn' has been transformed, since being taken over in 2005 by the local laird, his wife and two partners. They promise 'simple rooms, luxurious beds, sea views, whisky galore'. 'It keeps its intimate character. Staff show a level of personal commitment unusual in hotels these days. They treat you like a real person.' The bar, in pastel colours, serves 'a healthy and delicious lunch' and has 'a buzz of cheerfulness most of the day'. 'For peace and quiet there is a comfortable library.' The breakfast room 'is all floorboards, vibrant abstract paintings'. There are 'plenty of other public areas, lots of log fires, deep sofas and chairs'. In the contemporary-style dining room, the 'very good food' is 'modern, but not flamboyant, with a strong local accent: oysters, bursting with natural flavour; the freshest of shellfish, venison and scallops'. (*John Rowlands; also JA Fisher*)

9 bedrooms. No telephone. 3 have TV. 400 yds W of harbour. Lounge, library, log room, conservatory, bar, restaurant; background/live music during opening hours. Large gardens. Beach 5 miles. Unsuitable for &. Smoking outside only. MasterCard, Visa accepted. B&B £45–£65 per person. Full alc £25. *V*

CONTIN Highland   Map 5:C2

Coul House Hotel   NEW   *Tel* 01997-421487
Contin   *Fax* 01997-421632
IV14 9ES   *Email* stay@coulhousehotel.com
                                Website www.coulhousehotel.com

*Architecturally striking 19th-century stone mansion ½ mile from Highland village,
run by 'proud owner' (since 2004) Stuart Macpherson, who plans major refurbishment
for winter 2006/7. Good views of Strathconon valley and mountains beyond. 'Comfy'
drawing room (some kitchen noise); ornate plaster ceilings and log fires in lounge bar;
central octagonal dining room with 18-foot ceiling, full-height windows. 'Enjoyable'
3-course dinner by chef Garry Kenley. Background music. 'Friendly staff.' Children
and pets welcomed. 21 bedrooms, individually decorated, 'clean, comfortable, good
pillows'. Ground-floor rooms suitable for ⅗. Stone terrace (drinks served), 8-acre
grounds: 9-hole pitch and putt. Wedding facilities. No smoking. Amex, MasterCard,
Visa accepted. B&B [2006] £49.50–£94.50 per person; D,B&B £72–£117. Full alc
£37.50. Christmas/New Year packages, off-season breaks.* •V•

CRINAN Argyll and Bute   Map 5:D1

Crinan Hotel   NEW   *Tel* 01546-830261
Crinan   *Fax* 01546-830292
by Lochgilphead PA31 8SR   *Email* nryan@crinanhotel.com
                                Website www.crinanhotel.com

The setting is 'sensational', all agree: overlooking the Crinan Canal basin,
this white-painted hotel has been owned for 35 years by Nick and Frances
Ryan (the artist Frances Macdonald). He is 'very much in evidence,
involved and caring'; her large seascapes hang in the public rooms. It
returns to the *Guide* after an endorsement, with reservations, by inspectors
in 2006. 'We were warmly welcomed by a remarkable woman with a
smiling face, who was omnipresent, morning till night. Luggage was carried
to our agreeable room, spacious, with large bed, armchairs from which to
admire the view. Small touches abounded, like fresh flowers and ornaments;
the bathroom was bright, clean, with robes.' But some visitors disliked the
pine furniture. Tea and shortbread in the 'wide, handsome' lounge was
'expensive (£8.30 for two)'. In the 'well-proportioned' *Westward* restaurant,
with candles and linen cloths, the starters (terrine of foie gras and duck;
smoked salmon) and the home-baked rolls were 'excellent'; but the fresh
jumbo prawns were 'overcooked, inedible. Mr Ryan apologised and
deducted the wine from the bill. We will return.' Another visitor thought

the dinner 'jolly good' and the waiting staff 'charming'. 'Impressive breakfast: fresh juice, just-right fruit salad, superb cooked dishes, proper toast, attentive service.' (*AL, and others*)

20 bedrooms. Village centre. Closed Christmas, 8 Jan–7 Feb. Lift, ramp. 3 lounges, cocktail bar, rooftop bar, public bar, restaurant, coffee shop. No background music. ½-acre garden. Safe, sandy beaches nearby; fishing. Boat trips. No smoking. No dogs in restaurant. MasterCard, Visa accepted. B&B £55–£85 per person; D,B&B £85–£145.

DORNOCH Highland   Map 5:B2

2 Quail

Castle Street
Dornoch IV25 3SN

Tel 01862-811811
Email goodhotel@2quail.com
Website www.2quail.com

'An excellent choice,' says a visitor this year to this restaurant-with-rooms in a Victorian town house on the main street (a conservation area) of this attractive, small seaside town. The owners, Michael and Kerensa Carr, run it single-handed, so, they say, 'service is very personal'. He, *Ritz*-trained, is the chef, she ('a strong personality, cheerful, amusing, efficient') is front-of-house, also wine waiter, bartender, housekeeper and bookkeeper. 'Their hospitality is outstanding.' The house has antique furniture, good fabrics, including soft tartans. Bedrooms are 'comfortable' and well proportioned. 'The shower room was spacious, with super-soft towels and quality toiletries.' Housekeeping is 'exemplary'. The lounge, with its large bookcase, is small but comfortably arranged. 'The dining room is delightful: more books, a fireplace, four well-spaced tables.' 'Michael's cooking is superb.' The no-choice, four-course menu changes daily. Typical dishes: potted langoustines with tomato confit; beef fillet with rösti. Residents need to book a table in the popular dining room which has only 12 covers. Breakfasts have 'eggs and bacon cooked to perfection' and toasted home-made bread. 'We are undoubtedly the smallest golf hotel and restaurant in Scotland,' say the Carrs, keen members of Royal Dornoch. (*Richard Lamb, and others*)

3 bedrooms. Central. Street parking. Closed Christmas. Limited opening in winter. Restaurant closed midday, and Sun/Mon. Lounge, restaurant; occasional background music. Unsuitable for &. No smoking. No children under 10. Guide dogs only. Amex, MasterCard, Visa accepted. B&B £37.50–£60 per person. Set dinner £39.

Hotels cannot buy an entry in the *Good Hotel Guide* as they do in most rival guides.

DULNAIN BRIDGE Highland   Map 5:C2

Auchendean Lodge   *Tel* 01479-851347
Dulnain Bridge   *Email* hotel@auchendean.com
Grantown-on-Spey PH26 3LU   *Website* www.auchendean.com

'So much that delighted us; we felt as if we'd stayed with old friends,' report
visitors this year to this Edwardian hunting lodge on a hillside in the Spey
valley. It has spectacular views over the river to the Cairngorm mountains.
The traditional interior has many original Arts and Crafts features,
including two large Art Nouveau stained-glass windows and a fine fireplace
in the entrance hall. It is crammed with 'a feast of books, pictures, clocks,
ceramics and other treasures'. Bedrooms vary in size: 'We found fresh
flowers, crisp bedlinen, comfortably firm beds, a sitting area with a
magnificent view, and an unusually spacious, well-equipped bathroom.'
The 'engaging and opinionated' owners, Ian Kirk and Eric Hart, introduce
guests to each other, producing a 'relaxed house-party atmosphere'. Chef
(and mushroom enthusiast) Eric Hart serves four courses of 'superbly
prepared, delicious food' with 'imaginative use of home-grown produce,
like a wonderfully smooth tomato-and-blue-cheese soup, invented because
of a tomato glut'. The wine list includes 60 from Ian Kirk's native New
Zealand. 'We loved exploring their magical, natural garden.' *Auchendean
Lodge* is proud of its green credentials (line-dried laundry, no bleach, much
recycling, etc). (*Brian Whalley and Veronica Joiner, Eppie Thin*)

5 bedrooms. 1 self-catering flat. On A95, 1 mile S of Dulnain Bridge. Open Easter–
1 Nov. 2 lounges, restaurant. No background music. 1¼-acre garden: 9-hole pitch and
putt. Only restaurant suitable for &. No smoking. 'Not suitable for small children.'
No dogs in 1 lounge. MasterCard, Visa accepted. B&B £53–£55 per person. Set
dinner £34. 1-night bookings sometimes refused if more than 1 week in advance.

DUNDEE *See SHORTLIST*   Map 5:D3

DUNKELD Perth and Kinross   Map 5:D2

Kinnaird   *Tel* 01796-482440
Kinnaird Estate   *Fax* 01796-482289
by Dunkeld PH8 0LB   *Email* enquiry@kinnairdestate.com
                                Website www.kinnairdestate.com

The atmosphere of a grandly welcoming country house pervades this
creeper-covered Grade B listed mansion (Relais & Châteaux). Its owner,

Constance Ward, is American, as are many guests. It stands in woodland in a vast Perthshire estate with the River Tay flowing through. Once the dower house to Blair Castle, it is sumptuously furnished, and has family portraits, grand piano, antiques, flowers, billiards, and perpetually burning fires. Most bedrooms are large, with a view of the valley. 'Each morning the chambermaid brings tea on an immaculate tray, and lights the gas log fire.' Men wear a jacket and tie at dinner in the elegant frescoed restaurant (refurbished this year), where acclaimed chef Trevor Brooks serves a three-course set dinner using home-produced or locally sourced ingredients; *Kinnaird* has its own smokehouse and a walled kitchen garden. The wine list has many half bottles. Good breakfasts have freshly squeezed juice, and porridge which can come laced with whisky. Guests may fish for salmon and trout in the Tay, and for trout in *Kinnaird*'s lochs. Health and beauty treatments are available in *The Retreat*. There is, again, a new manager this year, James Payne, former assistant manager at *Sharrow Bay* (*qv*). We would welcome reports.

9 bedrooms. 1 on ground floor. 6 self-catering cottages in grounds (2 can be let as a suite). 6 miles NW of Dunkeld. Lift, ramp. 2 lounges, billiard room, restaurant, dining room; function facilities; beauty/therapy room. No background music. 9,000-acre estate: gardens, tennis, croquet, shooting, walking, birdwatching, salmon fishing on River Tay, 3 trout lochs. Wedding facilities. No smoking. No children under 12. No dogs in house (heated kennels available). Amex, MasterCard, Visa accepted. B&B [2006] £122.50–£375 per person; D,B&B £147.50–£425. Set lunch from £15, dinner £55. Christmas/New Year packages.

DUNOON Argyll and Bute   Map 5:D1

The Enmore	*Tel* 01369-702230
111 Marine Parade, Kirn	*Fax* 01369-702148
Dunoon PA23 8HH	*Email* enmorehotel@btinternet.com
	Website www.enmorehotel.co.uk

We continue to get good reports of this small seaside hotel, an 18th-century 'gentleman's retreat', on a seafront road. It has lovely views across the Firth of Clyde. Regular visitors consider Robert and Wendy Thomson's new regime 'a huge improvement'. Inspectors thought the Thomsons, new to the hotel trade, 'charming and obliging'. Public rooms are well proportioned, the lounge is 'uncluttered and airy, with a large period fireplace with a log fire'. Bedrooms are smart and comfortable. 'Ours had an enchanting seating area overlooking the firth, and a well-appointed bathroom.' Meals are 'entirely satisfactory', and generous. 'They were very obliging about serving us an early breakfast

to allow us to catch a ferry.' *The Enmore* owns the only squash courts in this part of Argyll, free for guests' use. Thanks to the local car ferries, Dunoon, 'a jewel on the Clyde', provides good access to the West Highlands. (*A Mitchell, and others*)

10 bedrooms. 1 on ground floor. Seafront, 1 mile from centre. Parking. Ramp. Reception lounge, sitting room, restaurant (background music), bar; meeting room; 2 squash courts. 1¼-acre garden. Shingle beach. Wedding facilities. No smoking. Dogs by arrangement. Diners, MasterCard, Visa accepted. B&B £40–£69 per person; D,B&B £22.50 added. Bar lunches. Set dinner £20–£29 (2–5 courses). Special breaks. Christmas/New Year packages. *V*

DUNVEGAN Highland   Map 5:C1

The Three Chimneys	*Tel* 01470-511258
and The House Over-By	*Fax* 01470-511358
Colbost, Dunvegan	*Email* eatandstay@threechimneys.co.uk
Isle of Skye IV55 8ZT	*Website* www.threechimneys.co.uk

Q *César award in 2001*

A white-painted crofter's cottage (the restaurant) and the recently but traditionally built adjoining house 'over-by' comprise Eddie and Shirley Spear's award-winning restaurant-with-rooms in north-west Skye. Standing across a single-track road (some light day traffic, quiet at night) from Loch Dunvegan, it has a beautiful location. Though remote, it attracts food lovers from far and wide, eager to sample dishes like mussel risotto with seared squid and scallops; grilled loin and slow-roasted shoulder of lamb with kidneys and shortbreads. In the two-room restaurant there are candles, dark beams, stone walls, a fire in the adjoining bar. Michael Smith, head chef (Shirley Spear is 'chef/*patron*'), serves three or four courses using fresh local ingredients. At breakfast, as well as croissants, freshly squeezed orange juice, fruit salad, etc, there are cheeses, porridge, smoked salmon and venison. The split-level bedrooms, all facing the sea, have a contemporary, stylish decor, comfortable beds, luxurious bathroom, flat-screen TV and DVD-player. Young children are welcomed: cots are supplied; there is children's tea and baby-listening; also a wide choice of DVDs, CDs, books and maps.

6 bedrooms. All on ground floor in separate building. 1 suitable for &. 5 miles W of Dunvegan. Closed 7–27 Jan. Restaurant closed midday in winter, Sun midday all year. Ramps. Reception/morning room, bar, breakfast room, restaurant. No background music. Garden on lochside. No smoking. No children under 8 at dinner. Guide dogs only. Amex, MasterCard, Visa accepted. B&B [to Apr 2007] £125 per person; D,B&B (off-season) £130. Set lunch (2–3 courses) £21–£27, dinner (3–4 courses) £47.50–£55. Autumn/winter breaks. Christmas/New Year packages. 1-night bookings refused Sat.

DUROR Argyll and Bute   Map 5:D1

Bealach House   BUDGET   *Tel* 01631-740298
Duror, Appin   *Email* info@bealach-house.co.uk
PA38 4BW   *Website* www.bealach-house.co.uk

'Everything superb.' 'Possibly the best guest house we have ever stayed in.' Much praise this year for Jim and Hilary McFadyen's home, originally a shepherd's croft, then a farmhouse, the only dwelling in the Salachan Glen. 'One-and-a-half miles up a forestry track, but well worth the ride', it has lovely views, 'surrounded by woods and mountains' (golden eagles and deer are sometimes seen). It is 'beautifully decorated': muted colours and tasteful furnishings, a fire in the lounge, plenty of books and games. Bedrooms, not large, are 'warmly furnished, immaculately clean and extremely comfortable'. Bathrooms have a power shower (one also has a bath). 'Hilary's cooking is delightful'; her mantra is 'if it can be made on the premises, it is', including the cake with the arrival cup of tea, breads, jams and ice creams. Dinner is three courses, each with three alternatives (eg, pan-fried sea bass on roast tomatoes with pesto) including a vegetarian option. 'The food is outstanding.' A complimentary glass or two of wine is offered with dinner (the McFadyens have no licence and are happy for guests to bring their own). Breakfasts are 'innovative', and include fresh pressed juices of the day. (*JD Hartley, GM, Michael Schofield*)

3 bedrooms. Off A828 midway between Oban and Fort William. Open Feb–mid-Dec. Lounge, conservatory, dining room; occasionally classical background music evenings. 8-acre grounds. No smoking. No children under 14. No dogs. MasterCard, Visa accepted. B&B £30–£55 per person. Set dinner £25.

The 'Budget' label by a hotel's name indicates an establishment where dinner, bed and breakfast cost around £55 per person, or B&B no more than £35 and an evening meal about £20. These are only a rough guide, and do not always apply to single accommodation, nor do they necessarily apply in high season.

EDINBANE Highland   Map 5:C1

Greshornish House   *Tel* 01470-582266
Edinbane, by Portree   *Fax* 01470-582345
Isle of Skye IV51 9PN   *Email* info@greshornishhouse.com
                                   Website www.greshornishhouse.com

'Wonderfully set' by beautiful Loch Greshornish, this handsome white
manor house, 18th-century with Victorian additions, has extensive gardens
and wooded grounds and lovely views across the loch to Trotternish.
Visitors this year thought it 'very comfortable' and praised the 'friendly
management' of owners Neil and Rosemary Colquhoun who bought the
listed building in 2004. They have carried out extensive refurbishment,
with improvements in 2006 to the dining room, a new disabled toilet, and
a south-facing 'midge-free' conservatory. The kitchens have been rebuilt
and a new chef, Graham Stewart, is in charge: his three-course *table d'hôte*
dinner (local seafood may carry a supplement) is served in the candlelit
dining room. Sample dishes: heather-smoked quail; slow-roasted belly pork
with Stornoway black pudding stuffing. There is a 'welcoming log fire' in
both the drawing room and the cocktail bar/reception lounge. Bedrooms
are well furnished: one is the former music room, another was a drawing
room; two have a four-poster; some are spacious, some are under the eaves
with sloping ceilings; some look over the loch, some over the Victorian
walled garden. There is a billiard room and, in the grounds, a tennis court
and a croquet lawn. (*Jill Palmer*)

9 bedrooms. 12 miles NW of Portree. Closed 2 weeks Nov, 2 weeks Feb, occasional
midwinter Mon/Tue. Drawing room, lounge/cocktail bar, billiard room, dining
room (background music 'only if requested'), conservatory. 10-acre grounds: croquet,
tennis; sea loch. No smoking. No dogs in public rooms; only accompanied in
bedrooms. Amex, MasterCard, Visa accepted. B&B £50–£80 per person. Set dinner
from £32.50. Seasonal and 3- or 4-day breaks. New Year package. *V*

****

Traveller's tale The bedroom was huge and lovely, but one of
the radiators needed bleeding, and the staff could not find the key
for this. The bottom sheet was too small for the three-foot bed,
purgatory for an insomniac like me. Perhaps due to the addition
of an electric heater, to compensate for the defective radiator, the
lights fused twice. The first time the night manager came up and
showed me how to reset it; the second time I was able to do it.
Bit of a pain crawling around the fuse compartment in the dark.
(*Hotel in Norfolk*)

****

EDINBURGH   Map 5:D2

The Scotsman	*Tel* 0131-556 5565
20 North Bridge	*Fax* 0131-652 3652
Edinburgh	*Email* reservations@thescotsmanhotelgroup.co.uk
EH1 1YT	*Website* www.thescotsmanhotel.co.uk

Now owned by MBI International, which has 42 hotels in Europe and the Middle East (see also *42 The Calls*, Leeds), this striking ten-storey Edwardian building was once the office of the *Scotsman* newspaper. A smart conversion has retained many original features including a 'wonderful' black-and-white marble staircase and intricate stained-glass windows. Bedrooms are 'attractive, with individual touches. There are big, comfortable beds and great bathrooms with a fabulous selection of toiletries,' says a visitor this year. 'We liked the hatches for room service [so you don't have to open the door] and the Edinburgh Monopoly board.' Another guest was disappointed with his room: 'The high-tech lighting was fiddly to operate, the bedside lights were dim; maintenance was slack.' There are two restaurants: *Vermilion*, with a rich red decor, and the slightly brasher *North Bridge Brasserie*. The 'efficient, chatty, but not intrusive' manager, Jonathan Dawson, has stayed on from the previous regime. His staff are 'helpful and friendly'. More reports, please.

69 bedrooms. Some suitable for &. Central, by Waverly Station. *Vermilion* restaurant closed Mon/Tues. Ramps, lifts. Drawing room, breakfast room, brasserie, restaurant; modern background music; health spa: 48-ft swimming pool, sauna, gym, etc. Wedding facilities. Smoking in a few designated bedrooms only. Dogs by arrangement; not in public rooms. All major credit cards accepted. B&B [2006]: double £200–£350, suite £380–£1,200; D,B&B £122–£620 per person. Breakfast £17.50. Set dinner (between 6–7 pm only) £16; full alc: brasserie £30, restaurant £55. Weekend rates and packages on website. 1-night bookings often refused Fri/Sat, rugby weekends, New Year.

Seven Danube Street	*Tel* 0131-332 2755
7 Danube Street	*Fax* 0131-343 3648
Edinburgh EH4 1NN	*Email* seven.danubestreet@virgin.net
	Website www.aboutedinburgh.com/danube.html

Q *César award in 2002*

'We still love this place,' say returning visitors to Fiona Mitchell-Rose's B&B, a handsome Georgian terrace in a curved, cobbled street. Near the Water of Leith in Stockbridge, it is within walking distance of Princes Street. 'Fiona and her husband, Colin, are welcoming, helpful and treat us as friends rather than clients.' The elegant house has inherited pictures, good furniture, a lovely cupolaed staircase – also George, a sociable black pug, and Doris, a friendly Staffordshire bull terrier. Bedrooms on the lower floor (guests have their own front door and key) are 'beautifully furnished', 'outstandingly comfortable', and well equipped, even the small single. Beds have an electric blanket; 'spick-and-span' bathrooms have a power shower. 'Breakfast is a sumptuous feast': home-made bread, scones, croissants, freshly squeezed juice, fresh fruit salad, fruit compote, good coffee and cooked dishes are served around one big table. There are also two bedrooms in a flat around the corner (usually self-catering). (*Wendy and Dr Michael Dods*)

3 bedrooms. Also 1 self-catering flat for 4–6 people, 50 yds. Stockbridge. Meter parking. Closed Christmas. Breakfast room. No background music. Small rear garden. Unsuitable for &. No smoking. Dogs by arrangement. MasterCard, Visa accepted. B&B [2006] £50–£75 per person. 1-night bookings refused New Year.

---

16 Lynedoch Place   `BUDGET`   *Tel* 0131-225 5507
16 Lynedoch Place   *Fax* 0131-226 4185
Edinburgh EH3 7PY   *Email* susie.lynedoch@btinternet.com
Website www.16lynedochplace.co.uk

'A little gem of a guest house, right in the centre of Edinburgh': Susie and Andrew Hamilton's Grade A listed Georgian terraced house is stylishly decorated. 'Susie is a delightful hostess, most welcoming and charming,' says a visitor this year. There are the personal touches of a family home – 'innumerable ornaments', teddies on the graceful, if narrow, winding staircase, and the Hamiltons' Labrador, Gertie, and cat, Holly, who welcome all guests, including children and pets. Residents have their own sitting room and key. Generous breakfasts are eaten at a large communal table in the elegant, bow-walled dining room with a view of the Dean Bridge. (*Patricia Ann Lonsdale*)

3 bedrooms. West End. Free parking nearby. Closed Christmas. Sitting room, dining room. No background music. Small walled garden. Unsuitable for &. No smoking. MasterCard, Visa accepted. B&B £35–£60 per person.

Windmill House   *Tel/Fax* 0131-346 0024
Coltbridge Gardens   *Email* windmillhouse@btinternet.com
Edinburgh EH12 6AQ   *Website* www.windmillhouse.co.uk

'A delight', Vivien and Michael Scott's imposing Georgian-style house overlooks the Water of Leith. Though only a mile from Princes Street, it has a peaceful, rural setting in a secluded valley, by a waterfall, weir and historic 17th-century windmill. There are lovely views to the Pentlands. Badgers are regular visitors at twilight. The stylish interior has antiques, open fires and flowers. Double doors open on to an entrance hall with staircase, atrium and galleried landing. The elegant drawing room leads on to a wide terrace where breakfast is sometimes served, weather permitting. Bedrooms are 'huge' and tastefully furnished, and have sherry and mineral water, but no tea- or coffee-making equipment, and no door lock. Breakfast in the handsome dining room has a good choice of cereals, 'delicious fruit, generous cooked dishes'. The Scotts are helpful and full of information. The secure parking is appreciated. The Scottish National Gallery of Modern Art is nearby. A visitor this year was disappointed to be billeted in the *Coach House*. (*WK, and others*)

3 bedrooms. 1 mile W of centre. Closed Christmas/New Year. Drawing room, dining room. No background music. Terrace. 2-acre garden, riverside walks. Unsuitable for &. No smoking. No dogs. No credit cards. B&B £52.50–£75 per person. 1-night bookings sometimes refused Aug.

The Witchery by the Castle
Castlehill
The Royal Mile
Edinburgh EH1 2NF

Tel 0131-225 5613
Fax 0131-220 4392
Email mail@thewitchery.com
Website www.thewitchery.com

Two adjacent 16th-century buildings at the top of the Royal Mile, by the castle, contain this dramatically original and romantic 'restaurant-with-suites'. Owned by award-winning restaurateur James Thomson, it is wonderfully theatrical and opulent. The huge suites (Vestry, Library, Guardroom, etc) are decorated in Gothic style, with ornate paintwork, antiques, oak panelling and original fireplaces, enormous four-poster beds draped with tapestries and velvet hangings, French gilded sofas and a huge roll-top Victorian bath in each marble-floored bathroom. There are also 21st-century extras, including CD- and DVD-player, and a complimentary bottle of Pol Roger. Of equal importance, 'the staff are all so friendly, the service is brilliant – and so is the food'. This is served in the original *Witchery*, with its 17th-century oak panelling, tapestries, gilding, red leather upholstery and antique church candlesticks, and the *Secret Garden*, with its painted ceiling. You might dine on sea bass baked in rosemary with broad bean cassoulet, or roast loin of roe deer with braised red cabbage. A two-course light menu is offered at lunch and at pre- and post-theatre times. (*HS*)

7 suites. In 2 buildings. Next to Edinburgh Castle. 2 restaurants (background music). Small terrace. Unsuitable for &. Wedding facilities. No smoking. No dogs. All major credit cards accepted. B&B suite £295. Set lunch/theatre supper £12.50; full alc £45.

See also SHORTLIST

ELGIN Moray *See SHORTLIST*   **Map 5:C2**

ERISKA Argyll and Bute   **Map 5:D1**

Isle of Eriska	*Tel* 01631-720371
Benderloch, Eriska	*Fax* 01631-720531
by Oban PA37 1SD	*Email* office@eriska-hotel.co.uk
	Website www.eriska-hotel.co.uk

César award: Scottish hotel of the year

'Great for a spot of Scottish country house living', this 19th-century Scots baronial mansion (Pride of Britain) sits on a 300-acre private island, reached from the mainland by a wrought iron vehicle bridge. Beppo Buchanan-Smith and his brother, Chay, run it as a hotel and spa, with a 'well-trained, dedicated, young, mainly Polish staff'. There are wellington boots by the entrance, comfortable sofas, a year-round log fire, panelled lounges. 'Beautiful, peaceful location; outstanding service and attention to detail,' says a returning visitor. 'Everything immaculate,' add inspectors. Bedrooms vary: 'All are well appointed.' 'Ours had sofa, decent-sized TV, huge bed (made while we breakfasted).' Each of the spa suites in the grounds has a conservatory and private garden with hot tub. Robert MacPherson's six-course dinner (male guests wear jacket and tie) was found 'reliable as ever: outstanding soups; venison, turkey, beef carved from the trolley; amazing selection of cheeses'. 'Lots of vegetables, offer of a salad with the main course; delicious, fancy puds (savoury alternative, eg, haggis on toast); impeccable, formal waiting.' Light meals are served in the modern veranda. Breakfasts have 'limitless freshly squeezed orange juice'; 'wonderful haddock and kippers'. 'So much to do [see below], you need never leave the island.' (*Roland Cassam, Joanna Russell, and others*)

22 bedrooms. 2 on ground floor. 12 miles N of Oban. Closed 3 Jan–3 Feb. Hall, drawing room, bar/library, dining room; leisure centre: 50-ft swimming pool, gym, sauna; massage, beauty treatments, bar, restaurant. No background music. 350-acre island: tennis, croquet, 6-hole par 22 golf course, market walks, clay-pigeon shooting. Wedding facilities. No children under 5 in swimming pool; under 16s allowed 10 am–5 pm only. No dogs: public rooms, unaccompanied in bedrooms. Amex, MasterCard, Visa accepted. B&B (*min. advance reservation 2 nights*): single £210, double £275–£320, suite £375. Set dinner £38.50. Weekly rates. Off-season breaks. Christmas/New Year packages.

ESKDALEMUIR Dumfries and Galloway   Map 5:E2

Hart Manor   *Tel/Fax* 01387-373217
Eskdalemuir, by Langholm   *Email* visit@hartmanor.co.uk
DG13 0QQ   *Website* www.hartmanor.co.uk

In an 'idyllic and peaceful location', this small, unpretentious hotel is near a picturesque hamlet in the lovely Esk valley. The former shooting lodge is 'most comfortable', and well decorated in a contemporary style. 'We had a beautiful, spotless bedroom and bathroom with lovely views over the countryside,' one guest wrote. Owners Kath and John Leadbeater are 'industrious, friendly, helpful and hospitable'. Mr Leadbeater's 'jovial banter' is appreciated as much as the afternoon tea on arrival and his wife's 'superb' and generous Aga-baked dinners. Her forte is 'traditional British farmhouse' cooking (eg, roast loin of pork with crackling and roast apples with cream and haggis sauce). Portions may be a bit large for some. 'Vegetables taste the way they used to – like Grandma's.' 'A fine choice of wines at reasonable prices.' 'Breakfasts, too, were excellent': they include daily-changing special dishes, such as kedgeree or fish cakes. 'We loved the birdsong and red squirrels in the garden.' (*John M Dinwoodie, John and Ann Finchett, Dr M Tannahill, and others*)

5 bedrooms. 15 miles NE of Lockerbie. Closed Christmas/New Year. Lounge, lounge/bar, 2 dining rooms. No background music. 3-acre garden. No smoking. No children under 10. No dogs. MasterCard, Visa accepted. B&B £48.50–£61.50 per person; D,B&B £72.50–£85.50. Set dinner £30.

****

Traveller's tale My small single room had a very narrow bed and was so hot I had to keep a fan on all night. The food was good, but staff seemed flustered. At breakfast a waitress shouted in the kitchen: 'Toast for the woman sitting by herself.' I found this disconcerting. (*Hotel in Dorset*)

****

FORT WILLIAM Highland   Map 5:C1

The Grange   *Tel* 01397-705516
Grange Road   *Fax* 01397-701595
Fort William PH33 6JF   *Email* joan@thegrange-scotland.co.uk
                               Website www.thegrange-scotland.co.uk

Set on a hill in attractive grounds, this white-painted, turreted Victorian
Gothic B&B has wonderful views over Loch Linnhe and beyond to the
hills above Treslaig. 'Immaculately' and tastefully furnished, and with large
windows, it is light and airy. There are log fires, fresh flowers and crystal.
Tea is served to arriving guests in the lounge. Each bedroom is individually
decorated. Rob Roy, where Jessica Lange stayed while making the
eponymous film, has a colonial-style bed; the Terrace Room has its own
terrace, a king-size antique bed and a Victorian slipper bath; the Turret
Room faces the garden and loch, and has a Louis XV king-size bed. All
rooms have fresh flowers and complimentary sherry. The 'welcoming,
helpful' owners, John and Joan Campbell, show 'superb attention to detail',
say their fans. The good breakfast, ordered the night before, includes fruit
compote, smoked haddock and potato pancakes. It is judged 'excellent
value'. (*TC*)

4 bedrooms. 1 on ground floor. Outskirts of town. Open Mar–Nov. Lounge,
breakfast room (classical background music). 1-acre garden. Unsuitable for &. No
smoking. No children under 12. No dogs. MasterCard, Visa accepted. B&B
£47.50–£100 per person. 1-night bookings sometimes refused.

See also SHORTLIST

FORTROSE Highland *See SHORTLIST*   Map 5:C2

GATEHOUSE OF FLEET   Map 5:E2
Dumfries and Galloway *See SHORTLIST*

The more reports we receive, the more accurate the *Guide*
becomes. Please don't hesitate to write again about an old
favourite. New reports help us keep the *Guide* up to date and
bring our entries to life.

GATESIDE Fife   Map 5:D2

Edenshead Stables   **NEW/BUDGET**   *Tel/Fax* 01337-868500
Gateshead, by Falkland   *Email* info@edensheadstables.com
KY14 7ST   *Website* www.edensheadstables.com

John and Gill Donald, who earlier ran the much-loved *Todhall House* at
Dairsie, have turned a ruined stable on the edge of this village on the River
Eden (which flows past the foot of their garden) into this 'luxury B&B'. It
is a modern one-storey building, quite unlike their earlier Georgian house.
'The interior is immaculate,' says a visitor this year. 'Beautiful furnishings,
lovely paintings, and an air of relaxed comfort throughout. The dining
room is formal and elegant, the sitting room [which leads on to a patio]
large, comfortable, and full of inviting books and local information.' Breakfast, communally served round one large table, in a room with antiques and
Spode china, includes local kippers, Arbroath smokies, oatmeal porridge
and home-made preserves. 'All the good things said about *Todhall* still
apply. The Donalds are charming hosts.' They write: 'As the house is all
on one floor, we can offer
accommodation to physically
disabled, but not wheelchair-
bound, guests.' Dinner may be
available for groups of four to six
guests. Two Hungarian Vizslas,
Rosa and Zeta, complete the
picture. (*Barbara and John Glover*)

3 bedrooms. All on ground floor. Outside village 12 miles SE of Perth. Parking.
Train: Ladybank/Cupar. Open 1 Mar–30 Nov. Lounge, dining room. No background music. 3-acre grounds on River Eden. Unsuitable for &. No smoking. No
children under 12. Guide dogs only. MasterCard, Visa accepted. B&B £35–£50 per
person. 1-night bookings occasionally refused July/Aug. **'V'** (only for 1 night of a
stay of min. 2 nights)

GLAMIS Angus   Map 5:D2

Castleton House   *Tel* 01307-840340
by Glamis   *Fax* 01307-840506
DD8 1SJ   *Email* hotel@castletonglamis.co.uk
                                      Website www.castletonglamis.co.uk

Built on the site of a medieval fortress and surrounded by a dry moat
(grown over with trees and flowers), this Edwardian stone country house
is now a popular small hotel. 'We were impressed by how well run it is,'

was one recent comment. Owner/managers David and Verity Webster are 'warmly welcoming', service is 'friendly and unobtrusive'. In the well-furnished public rooms there are tasteful colour schemes, antiques, large log fires. The 'most attractive' conservatory has under-floor heating for winter. Chef Andrew Wilkie's 'very good' two- or three-course dinners are served here or in the formal dining room. Spacious bedrooms have 'good bedlinen', 'lots of towels', flowers from the garden, mineral water, coffee and tea. For children there are special meals, a climbing frame in the garden, also ducks and chickens (they provide eggs for the 'excellent' breakfasts), Tamworth pigs, croquet, and 'space for golf and throwing frisbees'. Dogs are welcomed. The house is on a busy road, though screened by trees. (*EJ, and others*)

6 bedrooms. On A94 Perth–Forfar, S of Glamis. Drawing room, library/bar, conservatory/dining room, dining room; conference facilities; background jazz afternoon and evening. 10-acre grounds: stream; climbing frame, croquet, putting. Only dining room suitable for &. Wedding facilities. No smoking. Amex, MasterCard, Visa accepted. B&B £95–£150 per person. Set dinner £40; full alc £50. Discounts for 2 or more nights. Gourmet events. Christmas/New Year packages. 1-night bookings occasionally refused.

GLASGOW   Map 5:D2

Malmaison Glasgow   *Tel* 0141-572 1000
278 West George Street   *Fax* 0141-572 1002
Glasgow G2 4LL   *Email* glasgow@malmaison.com
                                      Website www.malmaison.com

Once a Greek Orthodox church, this branch of the Malmaison chain is in the city's financial district. The decor is 'unfussy', contemporary. Staff are 'incredibly helpful', says a 2006 visitor. There is a magnificent Art Nouveau central staircase, and a champagne bar in the atrium, open to the glass roof of the first floor. In the bedrooms, there are bold colours and stripes, prints and black-and-white photographs (also CD-player, minibar, big bed, etc). An earlier comment: 'Our spacious suite had a well-furnished sitting room, all the usual goodies one associates with Malmaison.' The Big Yin suite, named in honour of Glaswegian comedian Billy Connolly, has a scroll-top tartan-painted double bath on a platform of pebbles in the living area. Some street-side rooms hear traffic. Informal meals ('classic French bistro dishes, and locally inspired dishes') are served in the brasserie in the vaulted basement, and the champagne bar serves snacks, light meals, tea and coffee. For keep-fit enthusiasts there is the Gymtonic. The manager is Pauric McGurren. (*Stephen Holman*)

72 bedrooms. Some on ground floor. 4 adapted for ♿. Central (windows double glazed). NCP nearby. Lift. Champagne bar, brasserie/bar; fitness room; meeting room. 'Cool, funky' music in public areas all day. No smoking. All major credit cards accepted. Room: single/double from £145, suite from £195. Breakfast £9.75–£12.75. Set menu (5.30–7 pm) £14.95; full alc £40. 2-day weekend breaks. Christmas/New Year packages.

See also SHORTLIST

GLENFINNAN Highland   Map 5:C1

Glenfinnan House   *Tel/Fax* 01397-722235
Glenfinnan, by Fort William   *Email* availability@glenfinnanhouse.com
PH37 4LT   *Website* www.glenfinnanhouse.com

'A good atmosphere throughout the hotel made for a very pleasant stay.' Spanish visitors, who used the *Guide* on a journey through Scotland this year, endorse Jane MacFarlane-Glasgow's handsome Victorian mansion with 18th-century origins. It has a beautiful position on the shores of Loch Shiel, looking across the water to Ben Nevis and the Glenfinnan Monument (where Bonnie Prince Charlie raised the standard at the start of the 1745 Jacobite Rebellion). Fans of the *Harry Potter* movies will recognise the Glenfinnan Viaduct. The hotel is managed by Duncan and Manja Gibson; the staff are 'helpful and efficient; they kindly lent us a boat and fishing rod'. The hotel is well furnished, with traditional decor and wood panelling. All the front bedrooms have 'superb views'; one has a four-poster. In the 'relaxing dining room', Duncan Gibson serves traditional Scottish and French dishes, eg, nage of West Coast scallops and mussels; roast noisettes of lamb. 'Good meals' are served in the 'pleasant' bar; a popular local, it also has fine views. 'Breakfast was excellent' (including smoked salmon, haddock, venison, kippers). Children are welcomed (under-twelves accommodated free) and have their own short menu. (*Flo Giro and Felipe Parajua*)

13 bedrooms. NW of Fort William. Open beginning Mar–end Oct. Hall, drawing room, TV/playroom, bar, dining room; background music; function/conference facilities. ⅔-acre grounds: children's playground. Unsuitable for ♿. Wedding facilities. No smoking. 'Well-behaved dogs welcome', except in restaurant. All major credit cards accepted. B&B [2006] £37.50–£70 per person; D,B&B £59.50–£96. Full alc £35. Bar meals/packed lunches. **˙V˙**

GLENLIVET Moray   Map 5:C2

Minmore House   *Tel* 01807-590378
Glenlivet   *Fax* 01807-590472
AB37 9DB   *Email* enquiries@minmorehousehotel.com
                       Website www.minmorehousehotel.com

A handsome, white-painted, stone-built country house, this small hotel has
wonderful views of the hills of the surrounding Crown-owned Glenlivet
Estate. Formerly the home of the founder of the famous distillery, it is now
owned by David and Jill Pethick and managed by Victor and Lynne
Janssen. Elegantly furnished, it has open fires in the entrance hall, the
spacious, 'light and airy' drawing room and the wood-panelled bar, which
stocks over 100 malt whiskies. Bedrooms are comfortable (one has a four-
poster), though bathrooms can be small and plumbing elderly. There is a
new suite this year. Mr Janssen is the chef, and his four-course dinner (no-
choice but preferences accommodated) was thought good – if there's room
for it after Mrs Janssen's tea: 'Gorgeous things – little savoury puffs,
sandwich fingers, cake, meringues, home-made jam, sparkling silver teapots,
fine china.' The hotel has one-and-a-half miles of fishing on the River Avon
(pronounced 'aarn'). (*CB, NB*)

9 bedrooms. By Glenlivet distillery. Open 29 Dec–25 Nov. Drawing room, bar,
dining room; background music at mealtimes. 4-acre grounds. Fly-fishing. Unsuitable
for &. No smoking. No children under 7 in dining room at night. Dogs by
arrangement; not in public rooms. Amex, MasterCard, Visa accepted. B&B £48–£92
per person. Set lunch £25, dinner £38. New Year package. 1-night bookings
sometimes refused at high season weekends.

GRANTOWN-ON-SPEY Highland   Map 5:C2
See SHORTLIST

GRULINE Argyll and Bute   Map 5:D1

Gruline Home Farm   *Tel* 01680-300581
Gruline, Isle of Mull   *Fax* 01680-300573
PA71 6HR   *Email* boo@gruline.com
                             Website www.gruline.com

On a remote peninsula of 'exceptional wild beauty', this 'handsomely
converted' Georgian/Victorian farmhouse and outbuildings has lovely
views of the foothills of Ben More and the surrounding countryside. These

can even be enjoyed midge-free from the garden, promise owners Colin and Angela Boocock. Access to their 'warmly welcoming' guest house is along a long, rough drive which also leads to the Macquarie Mausoleum where lies the 'father of Australia'. The house is well decorated, with good antique and modern crafted furniture. Mrs Boocock is 'passionate about quality and service', and her husband's four-course, no-choice dinners are highly praised (eg, pan-fried loin of lamb with a rosemary jus). No licence (bring your own wine; no corkage), but you are offered complimentary sherry and introduced to other guests before eating (a dinner-party atmosphere is encouraged). Breakfast, with lots of cooked dishes to choose from, is 'superb', served, like dinner, on stylish crockery. 'One of the best places to stay on Mull.' (*IK and EH*)

3 bedrooms. 1 in annexe. 14 miles S of Tobermory. Closed Christmas, New Year. Lounge, conservatory, dining room; light classical background music. 1½-acre garden: stream. No smoking. No children under 16. Dogs in annexe only. MasterCard, Visa accepted. D,B&B (min. 2 nights) £87–£142 per person. Set dinner £32.

GULLANE East Lothian   Map 5:D3

Greywalls	*Tel* 01620-842144
Muirfield, Gullane	*Fax* 01620-842241
EH31 2EG	*Email* hotel@greywalls.co.uk
	Website www.greywalls.co.uk

Considered an 'excellent hotel', this elegant building of warm stone in a graceful crescent shape was designed by Sir Edwin Lutyens in 1901 for a keen golfer who wanted to be within a mashie niblick shot of the 18th green at Muirfield. Many guests are American golfers. It has belonged to the family of owners Giles and Ros Weaver since 1924. Managed by Sue Prime, it is 'comfortable and friendly', with the feeling of 'a luxurious private house'. The interior is richly and tastefully furnished. There are two drawing rooms (one with an open fire, one with a decorative Edwardian stove), a conservatory, and a panelled library. Chef David Williams's 'modern British' cooking is served in two airy dining rooms overlooking Muirfield's tenth tee. Bedrooms are light and spacious and furnished with antiques; the best look over the links to the Firth of Forth or over farmland to the Lammermuir Hills. In the garden is another large, comfortable room, called the King's Loo, recalling its purpose when Edward VII was a visitor, and the Colonel's House, suitable for a group of eight. The beautiful walled gardens were designed by Lutyens's regular collaborator, Gertrude Jekyll, and have been sympathetically restored. (*CH*)

23 bedrooms. 6 in lodges. 4 on ground floor. Off A198, near Gullane village. Open Mar–Dec. 2 lounges, conservatory, library, bar, 2 dining rooms. No background music. 6-acre grounds: walled garden, croquet, tennis, putting. No smoking. No dogs in public rooms. All major cards accepted. B&B £120–£135 per person. Set dinner £45. Spring/autumn breaks. *V*

HEITON Borders   Map 5:E3

The Roxburghe Hotel & Golf Course
Heiton, by Kelso
TD5 8JZ

Tel 01573-450331
Fax 01573-450611
Email hotel@roxburghe.net
Website www.roxburghe.net

On a huge estate with mature woodland, rolling parkland and its own golf course (the only championship course in the Scottish Borders), this impressive, castellated Scots baronial country house stands by the River Teviot. Owned by the Duke and Duchess of Roxburghe and managed by William Kirby, it has 'particularly comfortable public rooms' with rich furnishings, ancestral portraits, log fires and fresh flowers. Both the welcome and service are 'warm and relaxed'. Bedrooms (feature, deluxe and standard) are designed by the Duchess. 'Ours was spacious and well equipped, with comfortable beds and a large bathroom.' Some rooms have a four-poster bed and a sofa; two have a log fire. 'Good dinners' – two or three courses – by chef Keith Short, are served in the red-walled, candlelit dining room. A simpler lunch menu is available in the library bar. 'Breakfast a little disappointing: tinned orange juice and flabby pastries.' There is a health and beauty salon. The hotel can arrange fishing on the duke's private beats on the River Tweed or on the stocked trout pond, and many activities are available on the estate (see below). (*Sir John B Hall, and others*)

22 bedrooms. 6 across courtyard. Some on ground floor. 3 miles S of Kelso. Ramps. Drawing room, library bar, dining room, conservatory; function facilities; health and beauty suite. 500-acre grounds: woodland walks, golf course, fishing, clay-pigeon shooting, falconry, archery, horse riding, croquet, mountain bikes. Wedding facilities. No smoking. Amex, MasterCard, Visa accepted. B&B £85–£145 per person. Set dinner £27–£32. Seasonal packages, midweek breaks, golfing breaks. 1-night bookings sometimes refused weekends.

****

Traveller's tale The staff, particularly the waitresses, were very helpful. What upset us was the way in which the proprietor spoke to them in front of guests: very unprofessional, and in a manner that most industries would consider inappropriate. (*Hotel in Wales*)

****

INVERGARRY Highland   Map 5:C2

Tomdoun Sporting Lodge   `NEW/BUDGET`   *Tel* 01809-511218
Invergarry   *Fax* 01809-511300
PH35 4HS   *Email* enquiries@tomdoun-sporting-lodge.com
                                    Website www.tomdoun.com

'An authentic Highland lodge experience' triggered the nomination of
Michael and Sheila Pearson's simple sporting hotel which overlooks the
Upper Garry river on the old road to Skye. 'No TV, phone or fax in the
bedrooms,' they promise. It is 'furnished with old bits and pieces; ancient
leather luggage in the hall. Four or five dogs wandered about. Everything
was clean. There was a welcome buzz in the bar, a cosy fire burning in the
grate.' Front bedrooms have views of Glengarry; simpler, cheaper rooms
share a bathroom. Guests can eat in the bar (popular with locals and
holidaymakers), or around a communal table in the dining room. Jason
Wilson's set three-course dinners, served at 8 pm, use local produce where
possible, including seafood from the Kyle of Lochalsh. Simpler accommodation is available in the *Bunkhouse*, next to the lodge. Sporting pursuits of
all kinds are available, including excellent fishing, and walking from the
door. (*Elizabeth Roberts*)

10 bedrooms. 5 with facilities *en suite.* 10 miles W of Invergarry; 6 miles off A87.
Drawing room, bar, dining room. 100-acre grounds. Fishing, walking, stalking,
shooting, mountain biking. No smoking. MasterCard, Visa accepted. B&B £35–£50
per person. Packed lunch £5.95. Set dinner £22.95.

INVERNESS Highland *See SHORTLIST*   Map 5:C2

IONA Argyll and Bute   Map 5:D1

Argyll Hotel   `BUDGET`   *Tel* 01681-700334
Isle of Iona PA76 6SJ   *Fax* 01681-700510
                 Email reception@argyllhoteliona.co.uk
                 Website www.argyllhoteliona.co.uk

The smaller of the two hotels on this 'spiritual' island, this 19th-century
building in a row of houses in the centre of Iona village is a short walk
from the jetty where the ferry from Mull docks. Trolleys are usually
supplied for guests' luggage (no cars on Iona). There are 'idyllic' views
from some bedrooms and the comfortable public rooms. Lounges are
book-filled, one has an open fire, and the conservatory is 'a haven on

sunny days'. Bedrooms vary: some are small, but with 'good storage, pleasant watercolours, paperback books and a well-planned bathroom'. The owners, Daniel Morgan and Claire Bachellerie, have a strong ecological ethos: most of their produce is organically home grown, local or Fair Trade, and they are committed recyclers and users of environmentally friendly products. They cater for vegetarians and vegans. The food is thought 'extremely good'. Light lunches (soups and pies) are served; picnics are provided. Children are welcomed – and can have an early supper – and so are dogs, 'but local crofters insist they be exercised on a lead'. In Iona's beautiful 11th-century abbey, many early kings of Scotland, and also John Smith, former leader of the Labour Party, are buried. (*MM, and others*)

16 bedrooms. 7 in annexe. Centre of village. Closed Dec–Jan. 2 lounges, conservatory, TV/computer room, restaurant (background music). Large organic garden. Unsuitable for &. No smoking. MasterCard, Visa accepted. B&B [2006] £23–£79 per person; D,B&B £42–£174. Full alc £27. 1-night bookings sometimes refused.

KILCHRENAN Argyll and Bute   Map 5:D1

Ardanaiseig   *Tel* 01866-833333
Kilchrenan   *Fax* 01866-833222
by Taynuilt PA35 1HE   *Email* ardanaiseig@clara.net
                              Website www.ardanaiseig-hotel.com

'Wonderfully set in a beautiful garden on Loch Awe', this grand, grey stone baronial mansion has bold colour schemes, rich furnishings, and many antiques (Bennie Gray, of Gray's Antiques Market in London, is the owner, Peter Webster his manager). Our inspectors report: 'We passed a lovely tapestry on bright blue walls on the way to our beautiful, large bedroom. This had apple-green walls, fine old furniture, a big bed, an attractive bathroom.' Some rooms have a four-poster; one has Chinese-style lacquered furnishings and an open-plan 'bathing room' with central bath, big enough for two. A boat house has been converted into a 'romantic loch-front room'. The long drawing room has panelled walls painted in mottled gold. Open fires burn here and in the 'cosier' library bar. In the candlelit green dining room, Gary Goldie's four-course dinners are no-choice: 'The food was good: tomato and mint soup; monkfish; sliced duck; good house wine; fine service.' Breakfast has brown toast, honey, preserves in jars, tea-bag tea. Guests can watch activities on the loch through a telescope, and go in the hotel's boats to its own island. In a small amphitheatre in the garden, performances of song and dance are held.

17 bedrooms. Some on ground floor. 1 in boat house. 2 self-catering cottages. 3 miles E of Kilchrenan, by Loch Awe. Open 10 Feb–2 Jan. Drawing room, library/bar, restaurant. No background music. 60-acre grounds on loch: gardens, open-air theatre, tennis, croquet, safe bathing, fishing, boating. Wedding facilities. No smoking. No children under 12 at dinner. No dogs in public rooms. All major credit cards accepted. B&B £53–£158 per person. Set dinner £45. 3-night packages. Spring/ autumn reductions. Christmas/New Year packages. **ᵛVᵛ**

KILLIN Perth and Kinross   Map 5:D2

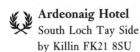 **Ardeonaig Hotel**   *Tel* 01567-820400
South Loch Tay Side   *Fax* 01567-820282
by Killin FK21 8SU   *Email* info@ardeonaighotel.co.uk
                                 Website www.ardeonaighotel.co.uk

César award: Inn of the year

In a 'beautiful, isolated spot', with majestic views of Ben Lawers, South African Pete Gottgens and his wife, Sara, run their popular white-painted old inn. The grounds lead down to Loch Tay: on the pier are tables and chairs where drinks can be served. 'A lovely relaxed atmosphere. Sara much in evidence, very hospitable. The staff (mostly South African) couldn't do more for you.' 'Utterly charming. Delicious food. Being snowed in, we had to spend an extra night. They bent over backwards to make our stay pleasurable.' Public areas are 'luxurious and comfortable': there are open fires, and sitting rooms 'ooze style'. The white lounge has generous sofas, plates of sugared figs; the brown snug is 'cosy'; the library, with books and board games, has the best views. 'Simple but very comfortable' bedrooms (no TV) have fresh milk, good bedlinen and toiletries, flannel bathrobes. 'Beds are vast.' Some bathrooms are small, and some walls thin. At night, candles line the route to the dining room where the host, a renowned chef, offers plenty of options for gourmets, including a tasting menu and a three-course *table d'hôte* menu. Summer meals can be taken in the 'very pretty' courtyard. Breakfast has a 'long and interesting' set of choices and freshly squeezed orange juice. (*Jackie Tunstall-Pedoe, Avril Reynolds, ANR, and others*)

20 bedrooms. 2 in courtyard. S shore of Loch Tay. Lounge, library, snug, bar, restaurant; background music. 13-acre grounds on loch. Wedding facilities. No smoking. Dogs by arrangement, in snug and bar only; not unattended in bedrooms. MasterCard, Visa accepted. B&B from £58.50 per person; D,B&B from £75. Set dinner £26.50. Midweek breaks. Christmas/New Year packages. 1-night weekend bookings accepted only close to date. **ᵛVᵛ**

For details of the Voucher scheme see page 60.

KINCLAVEN Perth and Kinross   Map 5:D2

Ballathie House NEW	*Tel* 01250-883268
Kinclaven	*Fax* 01250-883396
Stanley	*Email* email@ballathiehousehotel.com
nr Perth PH1 4QN	*Website* www.ballathiehousehotel.com

A grand, gabled and turreted 19th-century country house, managed by Christopher Longden: it makes a welcome return to the *Guide* after an endorsement this year. The extensive grounds, with a Victorian garden, 'wonderful trees', and lawns that sweep down to the broad River Tay, also house the new, white-painted *Riverside* building which has bedrooms, suites and meeting rooms. The main house is traditionally furnished, with ornate plasterwork, antiques, deep sofas and open fires. 'Public rooms, apart from the small bar, are spacious, the drawing room is very pleasant, overlooking the grounds, the large and bright dining room has a lovely view down to the river.' Bedrooms vary in size; some have a four-poster. They are well appointed, 'comfortable and well cared for; our suite was an amazing size, and had a large bathroom with gold fittings and a whirlpool bath, but the towels didn't quite live up to this splendour'. Chef Kevin MacGillivray's 'modern Scottish' three- or four-course dinners were of 'excellent quality [main courses like roasted monkfish on creamed soft polenta], as was the service (a good number of waiters)'. (*Evelyn Schaffer*)

41 bedrooms. 1 suitable for &. 16 in *Riverside* building. 8 miles N of Perth. Ramp. Drawing room, morning room, bar, dining room. No background music. 100-acre grounds: walks; river (some fishing rights). Wedding facilities. No smoking. No children under 12 in dining room at night. No dogs in public rooms. All major credit cards accepted. B&B £82.50–£125 per person; D,B&B £112.50–£155.50. Set lunch £19.50, dinner £42.50. 2-day breaks. Christmas/New Year packages.

KINGUSSIE Highland   Map 5:C2

The Cross at Kingussie	*Tel* 01540-661166
Tweed Mill Brae, Ardbroilach Road	*Fax* 01540-661080
Kingussie PH21 1LB	*Email* relax@thecross.co.uk
	Website www.thecross.co.uk

'As good as ever: accommodation and hospitality still of the highest order,' write returning guests of David and Katie Young's restaurant-with-rooms, a handsome stone-built, 19th-century tweed mill in attractive wooded grounds by the River Gynack. 'The millstream and the gardens border a pretty terrace' where drinks are served in summer. 'Katie is a natural front-of-house, charming and hospitable, so eager to help. She really wants you to have a good stay'; the 'warmly welcoming' David, a former AA hotel inspector, shares the cooking with Becca Henderson. He tells us redecoration is almost complete, with 'appropriate Scottish art', and new place settings (Scottish slate mats on wood tables) in the restaurant. Interiors are tastefully decorated, 'light and bright'. 'Our spacious room, thoughtfully prepared, had a selection of books and music, ample lighting, large, comfortable bed and the restful noise of the river running by.' There are 'top-quality toiletries'. The food is 'beautifully cooked and presented, eg, spiced sea bass with tamarind dressing, fillet of venison with red cabbage. Breakfasts are 'high grade, with excellent juice, fruit, croissants, etc' and a daily-changing hot dish of the day. (*Tony Hall, Brenda Melville, Sarah de Lisle*)

8 bedrooms. Tea-making facilities on request. 440 yds from village centre. Open 9 Feb–16 Dec, New Year. 'Mostly' closed Sun/Mon (except Easter, some bank holidays). 2 lounges; restaurant. No background music. 4-acre grounds: woodland, river (no bathing/fishing), *pétanque*. Only restaurant suitable for &. No smoking. 'Not ideal' for children under 9 (accepted on 'case by case' basis). No dogs. Amex, MasterCard, Visa accepted. B&B [2006] £50–£175 per person; D,B&B £80–£210. Set dinner £39. New Year package. Website packages.

KINROSS Perth and Kinross *See SHORTLIST* Map 5:D2

KIRKBEAN Dumfries and Galloway   Map 5:E2

Cavens
Kirkbean, by Dumfries
DG2 8AA

Tel 01387-880234
Fax 01387-880467
Email enquiries@cavens.com
Website www.cavens.com

'We shall certainly return,' say visitors this year to this handsome 18th-century bow-windowed, white-painted country house near the Solway coast. Built by a tobacco baron in 1752, it stands in landscaped grounds. The owner/managers, Jane and Angus Fordyce, are 'visible and friendly', say guests. 'Their staff are all very pleasant.' Interiors are elegant and well furnished; fires burn in the large sitting rooms, which open on to a terrace. 'Our bedroom, large and well decorated, overlooked the large back garden.' In the 'light and pretty' dining room, Mr Fordyce offers a highly praised three-course dinner, 'beautifully prepared and a joy to eat'. No choice, but Mr Fordyce happily cooks special dishes and vegetarian options on request. 'Breakfasts were very good, including gorgeous muesli

– the best I've ever eaten.' Children are welcomed, but not at dinner if under 12 (there is high tea). Free broadband Internet access is new this year. (*Ann Douglas*)

7 bedrooms. 12 miles S of Dumfries. Closed Jan/Feb. 2 sitting rooms, dining room; computer room. No background music. 6-acre grounds. Unsuitable for &. No smoking. No children under 12 in dining room at dinner. No dogs in public rooms. Diners, MasterCard, Visa accepted. B&B £40–£100 per person; D,B&B £65–£130. Set dinner £25. ***V***

KIRKCUDBRIGHT Dumfries and Galloway   Map 5:E2

Gladstone House   BUDGET   *Tel/Fax* 01557-331734
48 High Street   *Email* hilarygladstone@aol.com
Kirkcudbright DG6 4JX   *Website* www.kirkcudbrightgladstone.com

'Endorsed without reservation', Gordon and Hilary Cowan's 'smallish, attractively proportioned Georgian town house', Grade II listed, is in a 'pleasant little town [pronounced 'Kurcoobrie'] which most people rush past on the A75'. We were 'welcomed like old friends with tea and cake on arrival', say visitors this year. The light, elegant building, 'beautifully decorated', has a 'fine drawing room with comfortable seating, which takes up most of the first floor'. Bedrooms are cosy, well furnished, with a good bathroom. The best is a double whose window seats overlook the impressive architecture of the high street and the maze of gardens running to the river. Breakfast and evening meals (the latter by arrangement – no licence; bring your own wine) are served in the pretty dining room. 'We were the only guests eating in, and enjoyed Parma

ham and papaya, pork fillet with a mustard sauce, with wonderful one-to-one service interspersed with anecdotes.' 'It might not be expensive or grand, but it is the sort of place that many independent travellers look for,' says a trusted correspondent. (*David and Joan Marston, EC*)

3 bedrooms. Town centre. Closed Christmas; open New Year by arrangement. Occasional closures for owners' holidays. Lounge, dining room. No background music. ½-acre garden. Unsuitable for &. No smoking. No children under 14. No dogs. B&B [2006] £32–£41 per person. Set dinner £18. 3- or more night breaks. New Year package. ***V***

KIRKTON Dumfries and Galloway   Map 5:E2

Wallamhill House   `BUDGET`   *Tel/Fax* 01387-248249
Kirkton   *Email* wallamhill@aol.com
Dumfries DG1 1SL   *Website* www.wallamhill.co.uk

In peaceful farming village 3 miles N of Dumfries, Gordon and Margaret Hood's single-storey, no-smoking B&B ('better than many 5-star hotels'). Large, well-furnished drawing room with writing desk. Big garden: croquet. Four large bedrooms, all on ground floor: 'magnificent country views – cows grazing in next field'; king-size beds; power showers; lots of extras: TV, video, sherry, biscuits, chocolate, fridge with water and fresh milk. Breakfast (last orders 8.30 am) has choice of fruit and cereals; freshly cooked dishes. Fitness room, sauna, steam room. Safe parking. Walking, cycling, fishing, golf nearby. MasterCard, Visa accepted. B&B £25–£30 per person [2006]. More reports, please.

KYLESKU Highland   Map 5:B2

Kylesku Hotel   `NEW`   *Tel* 01971-502231
Kylesku   *Fax* 01971-502313
by Lairg IV27 4HW   *Email* info@kyleskuhotel.co.uk
                                              Website www.kyleskuhotel.co.uk

White-painted 17th-century former coaching inn with modern extensions in 'most beautiful position' close to (former ferry) slipway where Lochs Glendhu and Glencoul meet. 'Superb views', especially from restaurant where 'first-class chef' Thomas McGovern offers 2 or 3 courses, including 'largest, juiciest langoustines; rich puddings'. Good bar meals. New owners Struan ('excellent hands-on host') and Louise Lothian are beginning 'necessary' refurbishment; 'looks promising,' says nominator. 'Friendly staff, high standard of cooking, but breakfasts could be improved.' Open 1 Mar–mid-Oct. Lounge (wood-burning stove), bar (stove, background music), restaurant. Small garden (tables for outside eating). Unsuitable for &. No smoking. Children welcomed. No dogs: bar, restaurant. MasterCard, Visa accepted. 8 bedrooms, 1 in annexe. B&B [2006] £40–£50 per person. Set dinner £25–£29.

Italicised entries are for hotels on which we need more feedback
– either because we are short of detailed or recent reports, or
because we have had ambivalent or critical comments.

LANARK South Lanarkshire   Map 5:E2

New Lanark Mill   *Tel* 01555-667200
Mill 1, New Lanark Mills   *Fax* 01555-667222
Lanark ML11 9DB   *Email* hotel@newlanark.org
                                       Website www.newlanark.org

An 18th-century cotton mill in a dramatic location – a steep wooded valley
of the River Clyde, just below the Falls of Clyde and the associated
Wildlife Reserve – this hotel is part of the regeneration of the village and
mill complex developed by the philanthropic socialist Robert Owen. A
World Heritage Site, it is owned by New Lanark Conservation Trust,
which has restored the buildings to create a visitor centre, shops, self-
catering accommodation, and a youth hostel as well as this hotel. 'The
conversion and restoration is of a high standard, and staff are helpful and
friendly.' Original features of the cotton mill, such as the Georgian
windows and barrel-vaulted ceilings, have been kept. The decor is light,
simple, modern; the spacious bedrooms have good views of the Clyde or
the surrounding conservation area. 'Ours was in soothing earshot of the
nearby falls.' In the dining room, with its river view, new chef Gregor
Brown serves an 'excellent' 'Scottish traditional' three-course dinner.
Ceilidhs and party nights are held in winter. The Waterhouses – self-
catering cottages – are attached to the hotel. The accessible Clyde walkway
leads to the Falls of Clyde Wildlife Reserve. (*T and JS, JA Fisher*)

40 bedrooms. 5 equipped for &. 1 mile S of Lanark. Lounge, bar, restaurant; varied
background music. Heated swimming pool. Wedding facilities. No smoking. No dogs
in public rooms. All major credit cards accepted. B&B £40–£74.50 per person. Set
dinner £26.50. Christmas/New Year packages. *V*

LOCHCARNAN Western Isles   Map 5: inset A1

Orasay Inn   *Tel* 01870-610298
Lochcarnan   *Fax* 01870-610267
Isle of South Uist HS8 5PD   *Email* orasayinn@btinternet.com

The restaurant is the main attraction of Alan and Isobel Graham's low,
white modern inn, where Mrs Graham's much-admired and creative
dinners use fresh local produce (eg, pan-seared ginger salmon and scallops
on onion mash). But accommodation, too, has been judged 'faultless'. 'Our
room, newly decorated, looked over the loch.' Deluxe rooms have a private
decking area; some rooms have a bathroom equipped for the disabled. A
peat fire burns in the lounge. The restaurant, with its conservatory extension, has 'outstanding views' over the water; summer meals are also served

on the adjacent decked area, which has patio heaters for cool summer evenings. The inn is also the local pub, serving 'high-standard' food all day. Breakfasts are also good, with freshly squeezed orange juice. Alan Graham is a 'very hospitable, tactful and helpful' host. More reports, please.

9 bedrooms. 2 suitable for assisted &. NE corner of South Uist. Group bookings only Christmas/New Year. Ramps. Residents' lounge, lounge bar, dining room, conservatory/dining room; Celtic background music on request. ¾-acre grounds. No smoking. Dogs by arrangement, in some bedrooms; not in public rooms. Amex, MasterCard, Visa accepted. B&B £36–£50 per person. Full alc £28. **°V°**

LOCHINVER Highland   Map 5:B1

The Albannach   *Tel* 01571-844407
Baddidarroch   *Fax* 01571-844285
Lochinver IV27 4LP   *Email* info@thealbannach.co.uk
                                      Website www.thealbannach.co.uk

'Nice rooms, great meals, great staff – owners and non-owners alike – helpful, considerate but unpretentious and easy.' So write delighted visitors to Colin Craig and Lesley Crosfield's handsome, white-painted 19th-century house, sheltered by trees and a surrounding walled garden, on a hill above Lochinver's harbour. Returning visitors concur: 'Still our favourite Scottish hotel.' The public rooms and all but one bedroom have views over the deep sea loch to the darkly romantic, massive dome of Suilven and, beyond, the mountains of Assynt, one of Europe's last wildernesses. 'Our spacious room had a four-poster.' A new penthouse suite up steep steps is 'large and luxurious'. The award-winning owner/chefs serve 'high-quality food' in the wood-panelled, candlelit dining room. Imaginative five-course dinners (no choice; menu discussed in advance; alternatives available) feature local fish, meat and game, and home-grown and organic vegetables from Assynt crofters (eg, pigeon breast and crushed beetroot with wild mushroom ravioli and game chocolate sauce). Drinks and coffee are taken in the panelled 'snug' with its central fireplace, or in the conservatory. Breakfasts are good. 'Expensive but terrific.' (*Ian McBride, GC*)

6 bedrooms. 1 in byre, with private patio. ½ mile from village. Open Mar–Nov, except Mon. Snug, conservatory, dining room. No background music. ½-acre garden; 12 acres croftland. Unsuitable for &. No smoking. No children under 12. No dogs. MasterCard, Visa accepted. D,B&B £110–£150 per person. Set dinner £47.

> Hotels will often try to persuade you to stay for two nights at the weekend. Resist this pressure if you want to stay only one night.

Inver Lodge   *Tel* 01571-844496
Iolaire Road   *Fax* 01571-844395
Lochinver IV27 4LU   *Email* stay@inverlodge.com
                                   Website www.inverlodge.com

'As it is a purpose-built hotel, the bedrooms and bathrooms are predictable, well fitted, with good furnishings but little character. It is the excellent staff who create the atmosphere. The manager, Nicholas Gorton, leads by example, and the mixture of locals and South Africans do him proud.' An award-winning *Guide* hotelier's accolade this year for Edmund and Anne Vestey's modern hotel on a hill above Lochinver's harbour, surrounded by the dramatic beauty of the mountains of Assynt. Other praise: 'One of the best hotels I've stayed in.' 'Nowhere better, a yardstick to measure others by.' The interior is light and well decorated, with comfortable furniture, stags' heads, an open fire in the lounge, and picture windows everywhere. 'The location is stunning, the view from the dining room breathtakingly beautiful'; tables at dinner are re-allocated daily to ensure it is enjoyed by all. Peter Cullen's six-course dinners are thought 'very, very good – excellent local lobster and halibut cooked with flair'. Breakfasts are liked, too. 'A nice touch – the bed is made whilst you're having breakfast, so the room is tidy when you come back; the rest of the servicing is done later.' (*Yvonne Howes, EM Arnold, AP Munro*)

20 bedrooms. ½ mile from village. Open 5 Apr–30 Oct. 2 lounges, bar, restaurant; sauna, solarium; gift shop. No background music. ½-acre garden. Unsuitable for &. No smoking. No children under 10 in restaurant at night. No dogs in public rooms except foyer lounge. All major credit cards accepted. B&B [2006] £80–£100 per person; D,B&B £110–£135. Set dinner £40. **'V'**

LOCHRANZA North Ayrshire   Map 5:D1

Apple Lodge   *Tel/Fax* 01770-830229
Lochranza
Isle of Arran KA27 8HJ

♧ *César award in 2000*

Close to the sea, and a mile from the small ferry to Kintyre, this white-painted guest house, a former manse, has wonderful views. Owned by John and Jeannie Boyd, it has a homelike atmosphere, with many handmade artefacts, family photographs, books and a plethora of teddy bears. Beds are comfortable, bathrooms 'beautifully fitted'. Guests are consulted in the morning about the three-course, no-choice set dinner; no dish is repeated during a stay. 'The cooking is of excellent quality and well presented,' say visitors in 2006. 'Desserts in the "comfort" range (tarts and crumbles).' No licence; bring your own wine. The sun sets romantically over the ruins of Lochranza Castle, and there are good walks from the doorstep. Useful for those without a car: the house is on a bus route. (*Joan and David Marston*)

4 bedrooms. 1 on ground floor. Outside village on N side of island. Closed Christmas/New Year. Dining room closed Tues. No telephone (payphone available). Lounge, dining room. No background music. ¼-acre garden. Unsuitable for &. No smoking. No children. No dogs. No credit cards. B&B £36–£50 per person. Set dinner £23. Usually min. 3-night booking.

LOCKERBIE Dumfries and Galloway   Map 5:E2
See SHORTLIST

LYBSTER Highland *See SHORTLIST*   Map 5:B3

MAYBOLE South Ayrshire   Map 5:E1

Ladyburn   *Tel* 01655-740585
by Maybole KA19 7SG   *Fax* 01655-740580
                                Email jh@ladyburn.co.uk
                                Website www.ladyburn.co.uk

In a lovely Ayrshire valley, surrounded by woods and fields, this white former dower house dates from the 17th century. Owners Jane Hepburn and her daughter, Catriona, run it like a friendly family home. The interior is comfortable and well furnished, with family antiques; the lounge is light and airy, the library has a wood fire. Some bedrooms have a four-poster. There is additional accommodation in the 'Granny Flat', accessible from the main house but also with its own entrance. The three-course dinner menu offers two choices for each course of 'good traditional Scottish home cooking, with French overtones', eg, roast Ayrshire gigot of lamb with home-made mint jelly. In spring, rhododendrons, azaleas and bluebells grow in the large garden, which is part of Scotland's Gardens Scheme (it has a noted rose collection). *Ladyburn*'s guests may walk in the grounds of the magnificent adjacent Kilkerran estate. Shooting parties are catered for. The golf courses of Turnberry are a short drive away, and salmon fishing can be arranged. (*RMW*)

5 bedrooms. 3 more in adjoining apartment. 10 miles S of Ayr. Restricted opening Nov–Mar. Drawing room, library, dining room. No background music. 5-acre garden: croquet. Unsuitable for &. Wedding facilities. No smoking. No children under 16. Guide dogs only. MasterCard, Visa accepted. B&B from £80 per person. Set dinner from £32.50.

MELROSE Borders   Map 5:E3

Burts NEW	*Tel* 01896 822285
Market Square	*Fax* 01896 822870
Melrose TD6 9PL	*Email* burtshotel@aol.com
	Website www.burtshotel.co.uk

On the market square of this ancient burgh, this white-painted hotel in a listed 18th-century building has been owned by the Henderson family for more than 35 years. They are 'very hands-on, always around', says a report in 2006. 'The friendly staff, mainly young South Africans and Australians, were professional.' 'Good food; lovely, homely hotel,' is another comment. The residents' lounges are small, 'but the large bar, with live fire, is friendly and much used by locals'. Bedrooms are 'acceptable, not luxurious'. The restaurant, with its green-striped walls, is 'the star attraction', with an 'excellent daily menu served with style' (main courses like seared king scallops, halibut sausage, chorizo and creamed leeks). The cheaper bar menu is also liked: 'Good value.' 'Breakfast was excellent.' The family also own *The Townhouse*, close by (see Shortlist). A good base for touring the Borders. (*Christopher Beadle, Beau Senior, and others*)

20 bedrooms. Central. Closed 26 Dec. 2 lounges, bar, 2 dining rooms; conference facilities. No background music. ½-acre garden. Unsuitable for &. No smoking. No babies in restaurant. No dogs in restaurant. MasterCard, Visa accepted. B&B [2006] £53–£65 per person; D,B&B £79–£83. Set dinner £31.75. 2-day breaks. New Year package.

See also SHORTLIST

****

Traveller's tale In the dining room, which was below our bedroom, piped music came on at 7 am. During breakfast an awful, moaning tape was being played. We turned it off, to the other guests' satisfaction. The waiters seemed not to notice. (*Hotel in Devon*)

****

MUIR OF ORD Highland   Map 5:C2

The Dower House   *Tel/Fax* 01463-870090
Highfield   *Email* info@thedowerhouse.co.uk
Muir of Ord IV6 7XN   *Website* www.thedowerhouse.co.uk

'I felt totally restored and pampered: beautiful garden, pretty house, comfortable bedroom,' writes a visitor in 2006 to this gabled, one-storey *cottage-orné*, former dower house of a mansion that no longer exists. 'More like a home than a hotel,' say owners Robyn and Mena Aitchison. 'Warmly welcoming', they run it as a guest house. It stands in a large wooded garden bordered by the rivers Beauly and Conon. Inside are antiques, chintzy wallpaper, flowery fabrics. The small lounge has potted plants, open fire, ornaments, books, and a bar cupboard full of malt whiskies. Some bedrooms are small, but all have large bed, well-equipped bathroom, 'central heating that comes up instantly when turned on'. There are three additional rooms in a gatehouse (also let as self-catering). Guests are expected to dine in. The host's cooking 'is a dream: light, beautifully flavoured with fresh herbs, leaves and flowers. Puddings magnificent.' The three-course, no-choice dinners are served at 'gleaming mahogany tables set with lovely cutlery, glass and china'. Main courses include breast of guineafowl with wild mushrooms. Generous breakfasts have local heather honey and home-laid eggs. Children are welcomed: those too young to appreciate a two-hour dinner can have high tea. (*Elizabeth Roberts, RW*)

4 bedrooms. 3 more in lodge (also let as self-catering unit). 14 miles NW of Inverness. Closed Christmas. Lounge, dining room. No background music. 4-acre grounds: small formal garden, swings, tree house. No smoking. No dogs in public rooms. MasterCard, Visa accepted. B&B [2006] £60–£85 per person. Set dinner £38.

NEWTON STEWART   Map 5:E1
Dumfries and Galloway

Kirroughtree House   *Tel* 01671-402141
Newton Stewart DG8 6AN   *Fax* 01671-402425
                                           Email info@kirroughtreehouse.co.uk
                                           Website www.kirroughtreehouse.co.uk

Q *César award in 2003*

'Friendly and personal service' contributed to 'a contented visit in bad autumn weather' this year at this imposing, white, bow-windowed mansion in large grounds by the Galloway Forest Park. Built as a private home in 1719 (later visited by Robert Burns), it is owned by the small McMillan group, and ably managed by Jim Stirling. A devoted regular reports: 'Another excellent stay, everything as good as ever, and two improvements: a lift has been installed, and the access roads have been resurfaced and given new passing places.' There are three oak-panelled lounges, hung with oil paintings, and a wooden 'modesty staircase' (panels prevent glimpses of a lady's ankles). Bedrooms are supplied with sweet sherry and fruit. Upper rooms are large and have good views, and some have a lounge or sitting area; ground-floor rooms are smaller and some might be a bit basic. Men are required to wear a jacket at dinner. 'Charming' chef Rolf Mueller's 'modern British' three courses (with 'pre-starter') are generally liked, and there are vegetarian options. 'Breakfast is really good.' 'Staff some of the nicest we have encountered anywhere.' (*Martin Arnold, Evelyn Schaffer, Adrian Turner*)

17 bedrooms. 1½ miles NE of Newton Stewart. Open mid-Feb–2 Jan (restricted opening Dec, Feb/Mar). Lift. 2 lounges, 2 dining rooms. No background music. 8-acre grounds: gardens, tennis, croquet, pitch and putt. No smoking. No children under 10. Dogs in some bedrooms only; not in public rooms. Amex, MasterCard, Visa accepted. B&B £60–£105 per person. Set dinner £32.50. 2- or more night breaks. Christmas/New Year packages. 1-night bookings sometimes refused.

OBAN Argyll and Bute   Map 5:D1

Lerags House   **NEW**   *Tel* 01631-563381
Lerags, by Oban   *Email* stay@leragshouse.com
PA34 4SE   *Website* www.leragshouse.com

'A really lovely place, and excellent value,' says the nominator of this handsome grey stone house in a mature garden by Loch Feochan. It has been owned and run for five years by Charlie and Bella Miller, who came here from Perth, Australia, 'for a summer', 12 years ago – and kept coming back. 'Our suite was attractive and spacious with lovely views. The bed was one of the best ever, and beautifully made up with crisp white linen.' Public rooms and bedrooms are comfortably furnished and elegantly decorated in

white with a few stylish touches of colour. Mrs Miller's three-course dinners ('Scottish with Australian flair') offer 'delicious food, imaginatively prepared' (eg, broad bean and chorizo salad with Stornoway black pudding). There is no choice, but she is 'very flexible to guests' requests'. The Millers and their Hungarian Vizsla bitch, Libby, offer a warm welcome, and the atmosphere is informal and home-like: 'We are a hybrid, not really a hotel, not really a guest house (horrid word); here it is just Bella and me to look after people,' writes Mr Miller. (*Tessa Mack*)

6 bedrooms. 4½ miles S of Oban, by Loch Feochan. Closed Christmas. Sitting room, dining room; background music. 2-acre grounds. Unsuitable for &. No smoking. No children under 12. Dogs by arrangement; not in house. MasterCard, Visa accepted. D,B&B [2006] £71–£95 per person. 1-night bookings sometimes refused holiday weekends.

The Manor House   *Tel* 01631-562087
Gallanach Road   *Fax* 01631-563053
Oban PA34 4LS   *Email* info@manorhouseoban.com
                  Website www.manorhouseoban.com

'A very comfortable hotel in a quiet location': Leslie and Margaret Crane's Georgian stone house is beautifully situated on a rocky headland half a mile from the centre of town. Built as the principal residence of the Duke of Argyll's estate in 1780, it has spectacular views over Oban's busy harbour and bay to the Morvern hills and the Isle of Mull; binoculars are provided in each 'well-appointed' bedroom. 'Ours was on the small side, but immaculately clean and well decorated.' 'The bar has good views across the water, and so does the little lounge.' In the candlelit dining room, chef Patrick Freytag serves five substantial courses, including soup and sorbet: 'The food on the daily-changing menu was excellent and very well presented.' Staff are 'very friendly and attentive'. The bar, a popular local, has 'good lunches, nicely served', though 'Beethoven's Fifth Symphony seemed an inappropriate accompaniment to the delicious fish soup'. 'First-class' breakfasts have fresh orange juice and 'outstanding' kipper and haddock. (*CH Hay, David and Joan Marston, and others*)

11 bedrooms. ½ mile from centre. Closed Christmas. 2 lounges, bar, restaurant; 'easy listening' background music. ½-acre grounds. Wedding facilities. No smoking. No children under 12. No dogs in public rooms. Amex, MasterCard, Visa accepted. B&B [2006] £74–£140 per person; D,B&B £94–£157. Set dinner £32.50. New Year package.

See also SHORTLIST

Hotels do not pay to be included in the *Guide*.

PEEBLES Borders   Map 5:E2

Castle Venlaw   *Tel* 01721-720384
Edinburgh Road   *Fax* 01721-724066
Peebles EH45 8QG   *Email* stay@venlaw.co.uk
                                  Website www.venlaw.co.uk

Owned by John and Shirley Sloggie, this handsome 18th-century Scots
baronial mansion stands in wooded grounds on the slopes of the Moorfoot
hills, overlooking this pretty Borders town. Bedrooms, each named after a
malt whisky, are comfortable and have good views; two 'romantic' suites
have an antique four-poster and a second bathroom with a double bath,
heated floor tiles, fibre optic lighting, music system and champagne cooler.
The family suite, in a tower, has a children's 'den' with bunk beds, games
and books. Visitors commend the 'high quality of service'. There is a book-

lined lounge bar with a 'club-
like atmosphere', and the light
dining room has a parquet
floor and elegant furnishings.
Diners are offered two or three
courses, including imaginative
vegetarian dishes (eg, pumpkin
risotto with mascarpone). (*DO
and NJC*)

12 bedrooms. 1 mile NE of Peebles. Library/bar (background music at lunch and
dinner), restaurant. 4-acre garden: woodlands. Unsuitable for &. Wedding facilities.
No smoking. No children under 5 in restaurant at night. No dogs in public rooms.
MasterCard, Visa accepted. B&B £63–£120 per person. Set dinner £30. 1-night
bookings occasionally refused. Short breaks. Christmas/New Year packages.

Cringletie House   *Tel* 01721-725750
Edinburgh Road   *Fax* 01721-725751
Peebles EH45 8PL   *Email* enquiries@cringletie.com
                                 Website www.cringletie.com

Turreted and gabled, this pink stone Victorian baronial mansion has
been refurbished as a luxury hotel (Pride of Britain) by Jacob and
Johanna van Houdt. 'Serious money has been well spent. It looks smart,
but retains charm,' say visitors this year. 'All is now of a high standard,'
is another comment. Built in 1861 by the renowned Scottish architect
David Bryce, for the Wolfe Murray family of Quebec, the house stands
in a large wooded estate in 'glorious' Borders countryside. There are

good facilities for disabled visitors, and 'the staff are very helpful'. Public rooms, on the ground and first floors, are 'splendidly spacious'; an 'attractive' standard bedroom on the second floor in one of the turrets 'had a sofa, dressing table and wardrobe; particularly good mirrors'. In the large restaurant, with its painted ceiling depicting the wedding of Elizabeth Wolfe Murray and George Sutherland, the chef, Paul Hart, serves a modern menu with 'finesse'; but background music ('lots of singing') was 'intrusive'. 'The staff, Scottish and Dutch, were friendly; Johanna van Houdt was much in evidence.' (*John Gibbon, Michael Price*)

14 bedrooms. 1, on ground floor, adapted for ♿. 2 miles N of Peebles, off A703. Closed early Jan–early Feb. Lift, ramps. Drawing room, library, conservatory, lounge bar, dining room; background music; private dining room; conference facilities. 28-acre grounds. Wedding facilities. No smoking. No dogs in public rooms. Amex, MasterCard, Visa accepted. B&B [to 30 Apr 2007] £95–£155 per person; D,B&B £125–£185. Set lunch £15–£19.50, dinner £37.50; full alc £50. Christmas/New Year packages.

See also SHORTLIST

PENNYGHAEL Argyll and Bute   Map 5:D1

Pennyghael Hotel   *Tel* 01681-704288
Pennyghael, Isle of Mull   *Fax* 01681-704205
PA70 6HB   *Email* enquiries@pennyghaelhotel.com
                    Website www.pennyghaelhotel.com

'The perfect place to get away from it all.' 'Good in every respect.' This low-roofed, white-painted small hotel, originally a 17th-century farmhouse, is in a tiny village on the foreshore of Loch Scridain, a deep inlet on Mull's west coast. There are 'magnificent views' across the water to Ben More (the island's highest mountain) and down the loch to Iona. 'Welcoming' owners Jane and Norman Latimer continue to make improvements, and the hotel is 'clean, comfortable and extremely well run'. Bedrooms are well equipped, and have plenty of storage space. A complimentary dram of Mull whisky is provided. 'The comfortable lounge, with its squashy sofas and good selection of magazines, has good views. The patio and garden offer a pleasant prelude to dinner.' Mrs Latimer's four-course menu is short, but 'the food was delicious – the best sirloin I have ever tasted, local seafood, all beautifully cooked'. For children there is a play area with climbing frame, ponies they can ride, and high tea for the under-tens. For when the weather is unkind, the hotel has 'a massive library of some 7,000 volumes'. (*Margaret Mason, Janet and Dennis Allom, and others*)

6 bedrooms. 2 on ground floor. 3 self-catering cottages. On A849 to Iona, by Loch Scridain. Ramps. Lounge (occasional background music), dining room. 1-acre grounds on sea loch (shingle beach). No smoking. No dogs in public rooms. MasterCard, Visa accepted. B&B [2006] £45–£65 per person. Set dinner £27.50. Reductions for 3 or more nights. 1-night bookings refused high season. ***V***

PERTH *See SHORTLIST*   Map 5:D2

PITLOCHRY Perth and Kinross   Map 5:D2

Pine Trees **NEW**	*Tel* 01796-472121
Strathview Terrace	*Fax* 01796-472460
Pitlochry PH16 5QR	*Email* info@pinetreeshotel.co.uk
	Website www.pinetreeshotel.co.uk

White Victorian mansion owned and managed by Mr and Mrs Kerr. 5 mins' walk from centre in 7-acre wooded grounds (deer and red squirrels). 'Warm welcome. Helpful staff. Superb accommodation. Good value,' says nominator. Chef Christian Cojocaru cooks 'Scottish traditional dishes with Mediterranean influence' (eg, saddle of venison with red cabbage and juniper berry jus). Lounge, bar lounge, bistro, restaurant; background music at night. Unsuitable for &. Fishing nearby. No smoking. Amex, MasterCard, Visa accepted. 20 bedrooms. B&B £36–£79 per person; D,B&B £56–£99. Full alc £35.50. Christmas/New Year packages. 1-night bookings refused at weekends. ***V***

See also SHORTLIST

****

Traveller's tale We asked if there were tea-making facilities. There were none, so we ordered some tea. When we left, two days later, the tray was still in our room, despite two requests that it be removed. Just one instance of the sloppiness and downright bad value for money in a place we had looked forward to visiting. (*Hotel in Sussex*)

****

PLOCKTON Highland   Map 5:C1

Plockton Hotel	*Tel* 01599-544274
Harbour Street	*Fax* 01599-544475
Plockton IV52 8TN	*Email* info@plocktonhotel.co.uk
	Website www.plocktonhotel.co.uk

'Beautifully situated' on the palm-fringed waterfront of one of the prettiest
villages in Scotland, and with spectacular views over Loch Carron to the
Applecross hills beyond, the Pearson family's award-winning inn offers
'a warm welcome and superb accommodation'. Part of a terrace of mainly
white-painted, stone-built houses, the hotel is in one building, the bar – a
popular local – and small dining room are in an adjoining one, and there
is a cottage annexe a few doors along. Bedrooms are comfortable, stylishly
and individually furnished, with 'Mackintosh-inspired fabrics, lighting and
furniture' and a 'good, large bathroom'. 'The chintzy lounge bar, very
welcoming, and the dining room also have echoes of Mackintosh.' Food,
cooked by Alan Pearson with Cara Cowray, 'was always excellent,
especially the seafood'. The Pearsons lead 'such friendly, helpful staff'.
There are 'lovely grounds': a garden in front across a small road, above the
beach, and a terraced garden with waterfall at the rear. This lively place
has weekly bar entertainments, and the restaurant has a ceilidh dance floor.
(*Brenda Melville, Allan Burton*)

15 bedrooms. 1 suitable for &. 4 in cottage annexe. Village waterfront. Closed
Christmas. Small lounge, lounge bar, public bar, snug, restaurant; Scottish background music. Front and rear gardens. Wedding facilities. No smoking. Dogs in
public bar only. Amex, MasterCard, Visa accepted. B&B £45–£50 per person. Full
alc £30–£35. Off-season discounts.

PORT APPIN Argyll and Bute   Map 5:D1

The Airds Hotel	*Tel* 01631-730236
Port Appin PA38 4DF	*Fax* 01631-730535
	Email airds@airds-hotel.com
	Website www.airds-hotel.com

'Even better than before; the food and accommodation were excellent;
service was faultless,' say visitors returning in 2006 to this white-painted
former ferry inn for the first time since it was taken over by Shaun and
Jenny McKivragan. 'First-class staff,' was another comment. 'They are
tidy and well turned out.' The owners, former guests who loved the
place so much they bought it, have appointed Martin Walls as manager

this year to replace Janette Macdonald (now responsible for marketing). The award-winning chef, Paul Burns, serves 'delicious' modern French dishes ('with a hint of Scottish'), eg, seared tuna with Niçoise salad; best end of lamb, braised shoulder, gratin potatoes. The bedrooms have floral fabrics and antiques; best ones have flat-screen TV and DVD-player; some are small. 'We always try for the suite, which has a wonderful view over Loch Linnhe.' The well-furnished lounges have open fires, flowers and large bowls of apples. Pre-dinner drinks are served in the pretty conservatory. Breakfasts are 'excellent' (freshly squeezed juice, home-made jams, etc; 'very good kippers'), as are packed lunches and afternoon tea. 'Not cheap but excellent value for money.' (*Peter and Audrey Hutchinson, Michael Price, PW*)

14 bedrooms. 25 miles N of Oban. Closed 8–30 Jan. 2 lounges (occasional guitarist), conservatory, restaurant. No background music. 1-acre garden. Wedding facilities. No smoking. No children under 8 in dining room in evening. Dogs by prior agreement; not in public rooms. MasterCard, Visa accepted. D,B&B [2006] £120–£265 per person. Set dinner £49.50. Off-season breaks. Christmas/New Year packages.

PORT CHARLOTTE Argyll and Bute   Map 5:D1

Port Charlotte Hotel
Main Street
Port Charlotte
Isle of Islay PA48 7TU

Tel 01496-850360
Fax 01496-850361
Email info@portcharlottehotel.co.uk
Website www.portcharlottehotel.co.uk

On the water's edge in a pretty conservation village of white-washed cottages (built by an enlightened laird in 1829), Graham and Isabelle Allison's small hotel has lovely views across the water. It is attractively furnished, with polished wood floors, 'nice antique furniture and rugs'. It has 'a very comfortable sitting room and locally popular bar (118 single malts), with good open fires'. You can reach the sandy beach from the small garden that leads out from the conservatory. A visitor who enjoyed his stay despite the worst storms for 20 years wrote of 'helpful, friendly staff who looked after us very well'. But another guest, who arrived on a late ferry, complained of being rushed through dinner and breakfast, and wrote of 'a cacophony of music: live Scottish music in the bar, and different piped music in the restaurant'. Some bedrooms and bathrooms are small. 'Ours was comfortable and warm, with a good-sized, well-fitted bathroom.' Former chef William Broderick is now executive chef and assistant manager; Rangasamy Dhamodharan is the new head chef. (*IGC Farman, and others*)

10 bedrooms. 2 on ground floor. Village centre. Parking. Closed 24–26 Dec. Lounge, conservatory, bar, restaurant; background music. Small garden (bar meal service). No Smoking. No dogs in public rooms. Diners, MasterCard, Visa accepted. B&B [2006] £57.50–£70 per person. Full alc £40. 3 nights for the price of 2, Oct–Mar.

PORTPATRICK Dumfries and Galloway   Map 5:E1

Knockinaam Lodge	*Tel* 01776-810471
Portpatrick	*Fax* 01776-810435
DG9 9AD	*Email* reservations@knockinaamlodge.com
	Website www.knockinaamlodge.com

In a 'wonderful location' on the Irish Sea, at the end of a long drive, this secluded grey stone 19th-century hunting lodge has cliffs and thickly wooded hills on three sides, and its own private beach. Now a luxury hotel (Pride of Britain), owned by David and Sian Ibbotson, it is where Eisenhower and Churchill met secretly during the Second World War. 'We had Churchill's comfortable bedroom, with its enormous bath (stool provided so you can climb in),' say visitors this year. 'We liked the genial but unobtrusive host.' An earlier comment: 'If you want to escape the pressures of day-to-day living and enjoy sheer tranquillity of life, this is the place for you.' The house is 'beautifully decorated': there are rich fabrics, antiques, oak panelling, open fires. The 'sybaritic luxury of the bedrooms' is mentioned. In the formal dining room, chef Tony Pierce's four-course, no-choice (except for dessert or cheese) dinner is 'exquisite'. 'The best lobster bisque I've ever tasted; delicious breast of grouse.' Portions are 'small but satisfying', and 'the full Scottish breakfast more than makes up in quantity'. (*Sarah Curtis, M and JT-E*)

9 bedrooms. 7½ miles SW of Stranraer. Closed Christmas. 2 lounges, bar, restaurant (background music). 30-acre grounds. Sand/rock beach 50 yds; fishing. Only restaurant suitable for &. Wedding facilities. No smoking. No children under 12 in dining room after 7 pm (high tea at 6). No dogs: public rooms, some bedrooms. Amex, MasterCard, Visa accepted. D,B&B £105–£190 per person. Set lunch £25–£37.50, dinner £47.50. Reductions for 3 or more nights and off-season. New Year package. 1-night bookings refused holiday weekends ***V***

The ***V*** sign at the end of an entry indicates a hotel that has agreed to take part in our Voucher scheme and to give *Guide* readers a 25% discount on their room rates for a one-night stay, subject to the conditions explained on page 60 and listed on the back of the vouchers.

PORTREE Highland   Map 5:C1

Cuillin Hills   NEW   *Tel* 01478-612003
Portree   *Fax* 01478-613092
Isle of Skye IV51 9QU   *Email* info@cuillinhills-hotel-skye.co.uk
                             Website www.cuillinhills-hotel-skye.co.uk

A former Victorian hunting lodge, this traditional hotel stands in wooded
grounds just outside Portree and has 'remarkable views across the bay to
the Cuillin Hills'. Owned by the small Wickham Hotel group, it is
managed 'smoothly and efficiently' by Scott MacDonald; 'Many of the
staff are local, and are characteristically friendly and helpful,' says one of
the nominators. 'There is a sense of space in the comfortable rooms;
plenty of storage.' Another visitor had 'a premium room, with a
breathtaking view; spacious, warm and sparklingly clean; serviced twice
daily; fruit and shortbread replenished if necessary'. There is a log fire in
the lounge. The conservatory bar serves informal meals. The daily-
changing dinner menu in the restaurant was enjoyed: 'A good choice and
high standards.' Highland game, and local fish and seafood are served by
chef Robert MacAskill. 'A wedding reception was handled without any
adverse effect on the services provided to residents.' (*John and Theresa
Stewart, CH Hay*)

27 bedrooms. 10 mins' walk from town. Lounge, 2 bars, restaurant; function rooms.
15-acre grounds. No smoking. No dogs. Amex, MasterCard, Visa accepted. B&B
[2006] £60–£115 per person; D,B&B (min. 2 nights) £65–£140.

Viewfield House   *Tel* 01478-612217
Portree   *Fax* 01478-613517
Isle of Skye IV51 9EU   *Email* info@viewfieldhouse.com
                                 Website www.viewfieldhouse.com

♺ *César award in 1993*

'A breathtakingly delightful experience,' say enthusiastic visitors to
'affable proprietor' Hugh Macdonald's 200-year-old ancestral home in
large wooded grounds on the outskirts of Skye's main town. Elegantly
decorated, with family pictures, Persian carpets on polished wood floors,
Indian brass and other souvenirs of Empire, it has 'tremendous, almost
theatrical character', and a 'very pleasant' atmosphere. Wi-Fi Internet
access has been installed throughout. No hotel-style reception or bar,
but drinks are served more or less on request. Bedrooms are 'prettily
furnished and very comfortable'; some face the bay. 'Our huge room, full

of Victorian antiques, had a vast bathroom.' Dinner, announced by a gong and served with heavy old family silver and crystal in the candlelit dining room, is universally praised. 'Food is superb – no choice but often a fish option and alternative dessert, and friendly staff anticipate every need. After dinner you relax with coffee and handmade chocolates in front of the peat fire in the beautiful drawing room.' Breakfasts are 'equally good, with wide choice including haddock and excellent kippers'. Children are welcomed. The first night of a stay is accepted on a half-board basis only. 'Very good value.' (*Judith and Andrew Makoff, Glyn Maddocks, Derek Proud*)

12 bedrooms. 1 on ground floor equipped for &. S side of Portree. Open mid-Apr–mid-Oct. Ramp. Drawing room, morning/TV room, dining room. No background music. 20-acre grounds: croquet, swings. No smoking. No dogs in public rooms. MasterCard, Visa accepted. B&B £40–£60 per person. Set dinner £28. 3- to 5-day rates. 1-night group bookings sometimes refused. ***V***

RODEL Western Isles *See SHORTLIST*   Map 5:B1

ST ANDREWS Fife   Map 5:D3

Rufflets   **NEW**   *Tel* 01334-472594
Strathkinness Low Road   *Fax* 01334-478703
St Andrews   *Email* reservations@rufflets.co.uk
KY16 9TX   *Website* www.rufflets.co.uk

Built in the 1920s in Scots baronial style, this turreted white mansion stands in award-winning gardens just outside St Andrews. Owned by Ann Murray-Smith, it has been in her family for more than 50 years. Its manager is Stephen Owen. It is upgraded from the Shortlist to a full entry after an enthusiastic report this year: 'We loved this hotel. Everything about it was of the highest standard. The welcome was extremely warm.' Interiors are richly and stylishly decorated; the elegant drawing room has an Adam fireplace. Each 'lovely, comfortable bedroom' has a teddy bear and a supply of shortbread; all rooms are individually furnished and have a smart bathroom. One has a four-poster. 'The food was so good': chef, Jeremy Brazelle, uses local ingredients, 'many from the hotel gardens', for modern menus which include, eg, roulade of lemon sole with smoked trout and langoustine sauce. Light lunches are served in the split-level music room, with its antique fireplace and curved, intricately carved bar. 'A wonderful breakfast.' (*Sue Kinder*)

25 bedrooms. 5 in lodges in grounds. Some suitable for ♿. 1 mile W of St Andrews. Drawing room, music room/bar, restaurant; background music. 10-acre grounds. Golf nearby. Wedding facilities. No smoking. No dogs. All major cards accepted. B&B [2006] £80–£199 per person; D,B&B £110–£231.50. Set dinner £38.50. 3-day breaks. New Year package.

See also SHORTLIST

ST BOSWELLS Borders   Map 5:E3

Dryburgh Abbey Hotel   *Tel* 01835-822261
St Boswells   *Fax* 01835-823945
Melrose   *Email* reservations@dryburgh.co.uk
TD6 0RQ   *Website* www.dryburgh.co.uk

Old house in Scottish baronial style, 'beautifully situated' in open countryside by eponymous abbey, on banks of River Tweed, 40 miles S of Edinburgh; 4 miles N of St Boswells on A68. Owned by Grose family of hoteliers. 'Hands-on manager, Kevin Keenan; first-class staff.' 'Pleasing large room, comfortable bed, inadequate storage.' Traditional decor. Lift, ramp. Lounge, lounge bar, 'magnificent' first-floor restaurant overlooking river (background music sometimes); indoor 30-foot swimming pool; wedding facilities. 10-acre grounds: putting, croquet; falconry centre; salmon fishing by arrangement. No smoking. All major credit cards accepted. 40 bedrooms, some on ground floor. B&B £69–£159 per person; D,B&B £88–£178. Set dinner £32.50 [2006].

ST MARGARET'S HOPE Orkney   Map 5:A3

The Creel   *Tel* 01856-831311
Front Road   *Email* alan@thecreel.freeserve.co.uk
St Margaret's Hope   *Website* www.thecreel.co.uk
KW17 2SL

'We wish we'd stayed for a week,' say guests on an all-too-brief visit to this old, pretty, cream-coloured house which stands on the seafront of the tiny, picturesque main village of South Ronaldsay. Alan and Joyce Craigie's restaurant-with-rooms, 'renowned in Orkney', has three simple bedrooms with beautiful views over St Margaret's Hope bay, and one in a nearby annexe. 'Ours was lovely, spacious and well furnished.' Both the restaurant (decorated with local artwork) and the breakfast room (used for dinner on busy evenings) have a window looking over the bay, but not all tables have a view, owing to the narrowness of the rooms. Alan Craigie's award-winning dinners offer from one to three courses (eg, seared scallops and steamed sea witch with basil and red pepper pesto), each offering three or four alternatives. 'We have never had fresher and better fish than here. Everything we tried was superb. Breakfast was also excellent.' Children are welcomed. (*Richard Lamb, and others*)

4 bedrooms. 1 in annexe. Seafront of village. Open Apr–mid-Oct. Small lounge, 2 dining rooms. No background music. Only restaurant suitable for &. No smoking. No dogs. MasterCard, Visa accepted. B&B £45–£75 per person. Set dinner £33.

ST OLA Orkney   Map 5:A3

Foreran	*Tel* 01856-872389
St Ola	*Fax* 01856-876430
Kirkwall KW15 1SF	*Email* foveranhotel@aol.com
	Website www.foveranhotel.co.uk

In attractive countryside on the west Orkney mainland, the Doull family's simple, one-storey, purpose-built hotel is praised by two reporters this year. 'They really care about their guests. Such a warm welcome from Helen Doull, with an instant tray of tea – the beginning of a lovely week.' The 'small but immaculate and comfortable' bedrooms are 'decorated in blond woods, with simple designs', and have 'everything one might need'. The lounge, with open fire, can be crowded when the restaurant is busy, but the latter, 'large, light and airy', has 'well-spaced tables' and a lovely view over Scapa Flow and beyond to Kirkwall. Paul Doull is 'an excellent chef'. The food is 'consistently good, with emphasis on local produce – scallops, monkfish, lamb, all delicious'. 'There is a constant throng of locals coming in to dine, understandably.' 'Breakfast was excellent.' 'Service from a splendid team of youngsters.' 'The place has a relaxed feel but is very professionally run.' A fine base for exploring Orkney, its abundant wildlife and fascinating archaeological sites. (*Maggie Washington, Richard Parish*)

8 bedrooms. All on ground floor. 3 miles SW of Kirkwall. Open mid-April–early Oct; by arrangement at other times. Lounge, restaurant (Scottish background music in evening). 12-acre grounds; private rock beach. Wedding facilities. No smoking. No dogs. MasterCard, Visa accepted. B&B £49.50–£59.50 per person; D,B&B £72–£82. Full alc £30. 1-night bookings sometimes refused.

> Please always send a report if you stay at a *Guide* hotel, even if it's only to endorse the existing entry.

SCARISTA Western Isles   Map 5:B1

Scarista House   *Tel* 01859-550238
Scarista   *Fax* 01859-550277
Isle of Harris HS3 3HX   *Email* timandpatricia@scaristahouse.com
                                        Website www.scaristahouse.com

Framed by the Atlantic, a 'glorious' three-mile-long sandy beach and
heather-covered mountains, this handsome white Georgian manse has a
spectacular setting. Run by Tim and Patricia Martin (co-owners with Neil
King), it is beautifully decorated, and has elegant furniture and fabrics,
antiques, paintings and books in every room. The drawing room (where
pets like Molly, the Martins' spaniel, and Max, the cat, are not allowed)
and the library (which Max likes to occupy) both have an open fire. There
are three moderate-sized bedrooms in the house, two suites in the adjacent
Glebe Building, which is purpose-built in matching vernacular style (it also
houses two self-catering units). All rooms have sea views. Meals are
thought 'marvellous, including breakfast'. Everything is home made, home
grown or locally sourced (eg, braised turbot with courgette timbale). The
three-course dinner is no-choice, but Mr Martin is happy to accommodate
dietary preferences. Children are welcomed: under-eights have an early
evening meal which they can help prepare. (*B and LK*)

5 bedrooms. 2 self-catering units. 15 miles SW of Tarbert. Open Apr–Oct, New
Year; only groups Nov–Mar. Drawing room, library, dining room. No background
music. 1-acre garden; trampoline. Wedding facilities. No smoking. No children
under 8 at dinner. No pets in drawing room. MasterCard, Visa accepted. B&B
£86.50–£100 per person. Set dinner £43.50.

SCOURIE Highland *See SHORTLIST*   Map 5:B2

SHAPINSAY Orkney   Map 5:A3

Balfour Castle   *Tel* 01856-711282
Shapinsay   *Fax* 01856-711283
KW17 2DY   *Email* balfourcastle@btinternet.com
                                        Website www.balfourcastle.co.uk

On a small hill above Shapinsay harbour, this magnificent, turreted 19th-
century castle has been the Zawadski family home for more than 40 years;
it is run by Mrs Catherine Zawadski, and her daughters, Patricia and Mary.
The castle retains echoes of their predecessors, the Balfours. 'Mementos are

everywhere of a family long since gone,' said one visitor; another was 'in heaven' at this 'marvellous time warp; a real Victorian country house, with essential modernising: heating, bathrooms with lashings of hot water'. The handsome drawing room has wide views over the water to St Magnus Cathedral and Kirkwall; French doors lead to a conservatory; you help yourself to a drink in the oak-panelled library. In the lovely dining room, guests sit around a communal table for the no-choice (with vegetarian options) three-course dinners; these are 'simple and fresh', perhaps local hot cure salmon; wild duck breasts with plum sauce. 'Apart from the new-built bathroom, our large bedroom was furnished as if this were 1900; it was wonderful.' The 'beautiful grounds' have a wood, and a walled garden which produces 'particularly good' fruit and vegetables. Shapinsay has a wealth of birds, seals, wild flowers, good walks. (*RF, and others*)

6 bedrooms. 5 mins' walk from harbour. Ferry (20 mins) to Shapinsay from Kirkwall; they will meet. Closed Christmas/New Year/Jan/Feb. Drawing room, library, dining room, breakfast room, conservatory; billiard room. No background music. 70-acre grounds: beaches, fishing, wildlife walks. Unsuitable for &. Wedding facilities. MasterCard, Visa accepted. No smoking. No dogs in house. D,B&B £100–£120 per person. 10% discount for 3 or more nights.

SHIELDAIG Highland   Map 5:C1

Tigh an Eilean   *Tel* 01520-755251
Shieldaig, Loch Torridon   *Fax* 01520-755321
IV54 8XN   *Email* tighaneileanhotel@shieldaig.fsnet.co.uk

Ⓠ *César award in 2005*

'Superbly located', in a pretty village of white cottages on the shores of Loch Torridon, Christopher and Cathryn Field's 'charming small hotel' was praised again this year. Most bedrooms of the old inn have fine views across the sea to Shieldaig Island (a sanctuary for ancient pines), as do the two 'comfortable and friendly' lounges (one with wood-burning stove), and the stylish dining room, with its large windows. 'Our small room was well furnished, immaculately decorated, warm and comfortable.' 'Very clean' bathrooms have fluffy towels and good toiletries. The welcome is 'warm'; staff are 'attentive'. 'The cosy bar is run on an honesty basis' with 'complimentary tea, coffee and shortbreads available all day'. Christopher Field cooks 'fresh local seafood and high-quality meat to perfection': his three-course dinners are found 'delightful, and the wines good value'. 'Breakfasts extremely generous; we loved the smoked haddock. The best home-made yogurt ever tasted.' The Fields also own the adjacent village

pub, where you can be 'inexpensively and well fed'. Children are welcomed, and so are dogs. There is a spacious drying room; guests can use
the owners' kayaks and their ten-inch astronomical telescope. (*Janet and
Dennis Allom, Shirley Tennent, Prof Robert and Mrs Pat Cahn*)

11 bedrooms. Village centre. Open mid-Mar–end Oct. 2 lounges (1 with TV and
wood-burning stove), bar/library, village bar (separate entrance), dining room;
drying room. No background music. Small front courtyard, small rear garden.
Unsuitable for &. Wedding facilities. No smoking. No dogs in public rooms. Amex,
MasterCard, Visa accepted. B&B [2006] £68–£72 per person; D,B&B £106–£110.
Bar meals. Set dinner £41 (non-residents). Reductions for 5 or more nights (3 in
Mar/Apr and Oct). **·V·**

SKIRLING Borders   Map 5:E2

Skirling House   *Tel* 01899-860274
Skirling, by Biggar ML12 6HD   *Fax* 01899-860255
                              Email enquiry@skirlinghouse.com
                              Website www.skirlinghouse.com

Q *César award in 2004*

'The standards remain as high as ever,' say delighted visitors returning to
this fine Arts and Crafts house, a Wolsey Lodge, on the green of a tiny
village surrounded by the lovely countryside of the Borders. 'It is one of
the most comfortable and relaxing places we know, with good food,
congenial company, and the special atmosphere that Bob and Isobel Hunter
have created in their unique home.' Built in 1908 as the summer retreat of
a Scottish art connoisseur, its elegant interior is beautifully decorated and
filled with 'a stunning collection of artworks', books and fresh flowers. The
drawing room has a 16th-century carved wood ceiling, full-height
windows, a log fire and a baby grand piano. The bedrooms, 'large and
charming', have CD-player, 'exquisite toiletries and bathrobes'. Mr Hunter
looks after the guests and the cooking (his wife, who works as an equities
banker in Edinburgh, serves dinner), offering – after discussing guests'
preferences – a four-course (including cheese), no-choice menu. Breakfasts
are 'super', with fresh orange juice, French toast with caramelised apples
and black pudding, and much else. Children are welcomed. 'Three
Labradors: you never lack company on walks.' (*Phillip Gill and Anton van der
Horst, Tom Shaw, Robert Freidus*)

5 bedrooms (plus 1 single available if let with a double). 1 on ground floor, suitable
for &. 2 miles E of Biggar. Open Mar–Dec, except 1 week Nov/Dec. Ramp.
Drawing room, library, conservatory (occasional classical background music), dining
room. 5½-acre garden (tennis, croquet) plus 100-acre estate with mature and new

woodland. No smoking. Dogs by arrangement, not in public rooms or unattended in bedrooms. MasterCard, Visa accepted. B&B [2006] £45–£55 per person; D,B&B £72.50–£82.50. Set dinner £30. *V*

STRATHYRE Stirling   Map 5:D2

Ardoch Lodge   BUDGET   *Tel/Fax* 01877-384666
Strathyre   *Email* ardoch@btinternet.com
FK18 8NF   *Website* www.ardochlodge.co.uk

◊ *César award in 2006*

'A perfect stay. This delightful home is thoroughly worthy of its *César* award,' say visitors this year to this white-painted, early Victorian country house owned by the 'charming and charismatic' John and Yvonne Howes. In the secluded setting of the forest of the Loch Lomond and Trossachs national park, it has 'magnificent' views across wooded hills to the rugged peaks of Ardnadave and Ben Vane. 'Our large, extremely comfortable bed-room had easy chairs, a large table, plenty of space, excellent tea, coffee and shortbread. The bathroom was huge, luxuriously equipped and well heated.' The drawing room and conservatory are 'spacious and comfort-able'. In the attractive yellow dining room, elegantly laid tables are well spaced, 'service was immaculate, with just the right amount of attention, and the cooking is good'. Guests are asked to decide in advance from a choice of two dishes for each of three courses, but alternatives and vegetarian options are willingly supplied. There is also a 'lighter, enticing supper tray you can have in your room, the conservatory or outside'. Unlicensed, but guests can bring their own drinks (no corkage charge). 'Breakfast was a civilised affair; they had thought of everything.' Dogs are welcomed. (*Janet and Dennis Allom, Flo Giro and Felipe Parajua*)

3 bedrooms. No telephone/TV. 3 self-catering cabins/cottages in grounds. W of Strathyre. Open Easter–mid-Nov. Drawing room (with TV), conservatory, dining room (classical background music at night). 12-acre grounds: walled garden, wildflower meadow, riverside walk. Fishing. Unsuitable for &. No smoking. No dogs in dining room. MasterCard, Visa accepted. B&B [2006] £35–£60 per person. Set dinner £26; supper tray £14. Special breaks.

The 'Budget' label by a hotel's name indicates an establishment where dinner, bed and breakfast cost around £55 per person, or B&B no more than £35 and an evening meal about £20. These are only a rough guide, and do not always apply to single accommodation, nor do they necessarily apply in high season.

STROMNESS Orkney   Map 5:A3

Miller's House **BUDGET**	*Tel* 01856-851969
13 and 7 John Street	*Fax* 01856-851967
Stromness	*Email* millershouse@orkney.com
KW16 3AD	*Website* www.orkneyisles.co.uk/millershouse

Near the ferry terminal in this attractive fishing port, Maureen and Magnus Dennison run their B&B in two buildings. The 17th-century *Miller's House* is the earliest dateable house in Stromness, and provides a large breakfast/ sitting room with polished wood floors and an open fire. The six 'clean and adequate' bedrooms are close by, in *Harbourside Guest House*. Good breakfasts have a wide choice, including home-made breads, scones, jams, fresh and smoked fish, and a number of vegetarian cooked dishes. More reports, please.

6 bedrooms. In annexe. Shower only. No telephone. Harbour front. Open Easter– end Oct.. Lounge/breakfast room; background music in lounge at breakfast time. Small garden. Unsuitable for &. No smoking. Guide dogs only. MasterCard, Visa accepted. B&B £25–£40 per person.

STRONTIAN Highland   Map 5:C1

Kilcamb Lodge	*Tel* 01967-402257
Strontian	*Fax* 01967-402041
PH36 4HY	*Email* enquiries@kilcamblodge.co.uk
	Website www.kilcamblodge.co.uk

Reached by a steep, scenic road through Glen Tarbert, this Georgian stone country house (with sympathetic Victorian additions) sits surrounded by woodland and hills on the edge of Loch Sunart. It has lovely views across to 'grand hills towering above the opposite shore'. Owned by David and Sally Ruthven-Fox, 'friendly and helpful', and managed by Cheryl Frith, it is 'beautifully furnished'. There are open fires, fresh flowers, decorative plates and 'spacious, comfortable period lounges'. Bedrooms are 'cosy', with 'excellent linen and towels', and a 'pleasant bathroom'. The best rooms are large and have an 'enormous bed, a window seat and loch view'. A new suite has been created from two small bedrooms this year. The attractive dining room also faces the loch. Neil Mellis serves an enjoyable and 'artistically displayed' four-course dinner (main courses like roasted mint-marinated lamb loin with sweetbread casserole, ratatouille and rosemary jus). Breakfast has freshly squeezed fruit juices, newly baked croissants, a good selection of cereals, free-range eggs. There is much wildlife to be seen in the 'spectacular' surrounding countryside. (*IK and EH*)

10 bedrooms. On edge of village. Open 1 Feb–4 Jan. Drawing room, lounge bar, dining room (background music). 22-acre grounds: Victorian bath house with hot tub. Loch frontage: beach (safe bathing), fishing, boating. Unsuitable for &. Wedding facilities. No smoking. No children under 12. No dogs in public rooms. MasterCard, Visa accepted. B&B £71–£98 per person. Set dinner £42. Christmas/New Year packages. **'V'**

SWINTON Borders *See SHORTLIST*   Map 5:E3

TAYNUILT Argyll and Bute *See SHORTLIST* Map 5:D1

TIGHNABRUAICH Argyll and Bute   Map 5:D1

The Royal at Tighnabruaich	*Tel* 01700-811239
Shore Road	*Fax* 01700-811300
Tighnabruaich PA21 2BE	*Email* info@royalhotel.org.uk
	Website www.royalhotel.org.uk

'The views are superb' at Roger and Bea McKie's white, bay-windowed hotel across a small road from the shore in this unspoilt fishing village on the Kyles of Bute. Most rooms, including both picture-windowed dining rooms, look across the sea to Bute. Bold colours are used in the 'attractive and comfortable' public rooms, which have local paintings and sculptures, books and family memorabilia, and also in the tastefully decorated bedrooms. Visitors who this year had some criticisms of the housekeeping wrote of 'average and expensive' bedrooms, but another guest thought them 'fine, with all mod cons'. Staff are 'friendly, helpful and unpretentious'. Daughter Louise McKie's 'modern Scottish' cooking, specialising in local seafood, is served both in the wooden-floored *Deck* brasserie, and in the 'fine-dining' *Crustacean* restaurant. This was universally praised: 'Dinner was magnificent; we had scallops, oysters, lobsters, and the crème brûlée was the best ever.' The bar is popular with locals. (*MW, and others*)

11 bedrooms. On shore road. Closed Christmas. 2 lounges, bar, 2 restaurants; background music in bar in evening. ½-acre grounds; 100 yards from sea: shingle beach. Only restaurant and bar suitable for &. No smoking. Dogs by arrangement (£3 a night). MasterCard, Visa accepted. B&B £50–£90 per person. Set dinner £35. Special breaks. New Year package. 1-night bookings sometimes refused July/August. **'V'**

TIRORAN Argyll and Bute   Map 5:D1

Tiroran House   *Tel* 01681-705232
Tiroran, Isle of Mull   *Fax* 01681-705240
PA69 6ES   *Email* info@tiroran.freeserve.co.uk
                                          Website www.tiroran.com

'More private house than hotel,' say Laurence Mackay and Katie Munro
of their attractive, white-fronted Victorian house. 'Superbly located' (say
guests), it stands in secluded gardens with woodland, rose gardens, a burn
and waterfalls running down to Loch Scridain. It has 'magnificent views'
across the water to the mountains beyond. Refurbished since the owners
took over in 2004, it is tastefully decorated: one sitting room has a polished
wood floor, and both have log fire and fresh flowers; bedrooms, each with
individual colour-themed decor, are thought 'charming'. In the small dining
room, or the adjacent conservatory (shaded by an indoor vine), Katie
Munro serves three 'superb' courses (each with three options) using fresh
local produce (eg, salmon fillets baked with lemon and bay leaf, with a
creamy watercress sauce). The 'perfect host' turns pre-dinner drinks into 'a
social event'. Children are welcome: under-14s can have an early supper
or, 'by negotiation', dinner. Breakfast, in a conservatory, has home-made
muesli, breads, marmalade and preserves, and free-range eggs. It is normally served at 8.30, but 'should you want a lie-in, we will be happy to
oblige'. Mull's highest mountain, Ben More, is nearby. (*RA, RH*)

7 bedrooms. 1 annexed to self-catering cottage. 1 on ground floor. N side of Loch
Scridain. Drawing room (traditional/'easy listening' background music at night),
sitting room, dining room, conservatory. 17½-acre grounds: river; beach front
(mooring). Wedding facilities. No smoking. Dogs allowed in 1 bedroom; not in
public rooms. Amex, MasterCard, Visa accepted. B&B £58–£80 per person. Set
dinner £30. 1-night bookings sometimes refused.

TORRIDON Highland   Map 5:C1

Loch Torridon Country House   *Tel* 01445-791242
Torridon, by Achnasheen   *Fax* 01445-712253
IV22 2EY   *Email* enquiries@lochtorridonhotel.com
                                      Website www.lochtorridonhotel.com

At the foot of Ben Damph, this turreted former shooting lodge on the
shores of Upper Loch Torridon is owned by Rohaise and Daniel Rose-
Bristow and managed by Robert Ince. In a remote and beautiful setting,
surrounded by a large estate, it has spectacular views across the water to
the Torridon Mountains. Built in 1887 for the first Earl of Lovelace, it

retains a sense of Victorian grandeur and many original features, including decoratively patterned ceilings in the public rooms. 'An outstanding place; excellent service and food,' say visitors this year (although they would have appreciated help with carrying their luggage to their car). There are traditional furnishings, wood panelling, big open fireplaces. Bedrooms are warm and well furnished; some have a king-size bed, and a claw-footed freestanding bath; one has a four-poster. 'We were upgraded to a splendid room with a view over the loch, even from the bathroom.' The chef, Kevin John Broome, serves three-course dinners ('very good, if occasionally over-elaborate') in the panelled dining room. At breakfast there is porridge with whisky, kippers, haggis, highly praised raspberry jam. The bar lunch is 'good if pricey'. A popular wedding venue. (*Flo Giro and Felipe Parajua, Dr Alec Frank*)

19 bedrooms. 1, on ground floor, adapted for &. 1 suite in cottage. On W coast, 10 miles SW of Kinlochewe. Closed Jan, Mon/Tues Nov–Mar. Lift. Drawing room, library, whisky bar, dining room (classical background music at night). 50-acre grounds: croquet, kitchen garden, river, nature walk, loch. Wedding facilities. No smoking. No children under 10 in dining room in evening. Dogs in cottage only. Amex, MasterCard, Visa accepted. B&B £70–£180 per person; D,B&B £105–£220. Set dinner £40. Special breaks. Christmas/New Year packages.

ULLAPOOL Highland   Map 5:B2

The Sheiling   BUDGET   *Tel*/*Fax* 01854-612947
Garve Road   *Website* www.thesheilingullapool.co.uk
Ullapool IV26 2SX

Looking across Loch Broom to the mountains beyond, this popular B&B is a modern white-painted, low-roofed building in vernacular style (a sheiling was a traditional summer shelter for hill-cattle herders). Interiors are light and contemporary, with pine furniture. There are magnificent views, especially from the breakfast room with its picture windows, where 'excellent breakfasts' including home-made venison sausages and freshly caught trout are served. Bedrooms are spacious, with good beds and views. Guests may sit by a log fire in the residents' lounge, or on a patio overlooking the loch (there is direct access to its rocky foreshore from the grounds). The atmosphere is 'relaxed'; the 'generous and attentive hosts', Duncan and Mhairi MacKenzie, offer 'a glass of wine or sherry most evenings, ice cream, home-made sloe gin', and advise on outings and restaurants (Ullapool is well provided with eating places). Fisherfolk are splendidly catered for: they can make use of the MacKenzies' wild brown-trout fishing rights (availability is limited) – a boat is kept for guests to use – and a

'Sportsman's Lodge' in the grounds contains a self-service laundry, drying room, rod room and sauna. More reports, please.

6 bedrooms. S side of village. Closed Christmas/New Year. Lounge with TV, breakfast room. No background music. Log cabin: laundry, drying room, sauna, shower, rod room, motorcycle store. 1-acre grounds: lochside patio. Trout fishing free to guests. Unsuitable for &. No smoking. No dogs. MasterCard, Visa accepted. B&B £28–£40 per person.

WALKERBURN Borders *See SHORTLIST*   Map 5:E2

WHITHORN Dumfries and Galloway   Map 5:E2

The Steam Packet Inn   NEW/BUDGET   *Tel* 01988-500334
Harbour Row   *Fax* 01988-500627
Isle of Whithorn   *Email* steampacketinn@btconnect.com
Newton Stewart DG8 8LL   *Website* www.steampacketinn.com

'Beautifully situated' on the tiny harbour of a pretty village near the southernmost tip of the Machars peninsula (not an island), this inn was recommended (apart from the breakfast) by a regular *Guide* correspondent in 2006. Alasdair Scoular, whose family have owned it for 20 years, is the 'helpful manager'. 'My bedroom had two enormous picture windows (with window seats and cushions) looking over the harbour, large coffee table, two comfortable armchairs, big bed and clean bathroom. Dinner was of a high standard. The restaurant, popular locally, was packed every night. Dishes are designed for hearty appetites (roast boar, cod loin, venison; excellent local langoustines).' There is a 'comfortable, low-ceilinged bar'. White tables and chairs stand in the garden. The area has interesting archaeological remains, 'wonderful coastal walks along springy turf, and some beautiful gardens'. (*Elizabeth Roberts*)

7 bedrooms. Village centre. 9 miles S of Wigtown. Closed Christmas. 2 bars, 2 restaurant areas. No background music. Small garden. Unsuitable for &. No smoking. MasterCard, Visa accepted. B&B [2006] £30–£35 per person. Full alc £20.

✱✱

Traveller's tale The windows did not fit properly, and on a cold night we went to bed in our clothes. Staff were polite and helpful, but the meal service was so slow that on one occasion we waited an hour between our first and second courses. (*Hotel in Ireland*)

✱✱

WALES

A high standard of cooking is a common factor
to many of our Welsh hotels. Again this year,
our Welsh *César* winner is a restaurant-with-rooms,
The Drawing Room, Cwmbach, a beautifully restored
Georgian building in Powys where the service
is professional but relaxed. Welsh place names
may sometimes be difficult to unravel,
but you can unlock our Welsh secrets
with the help of our map.

The Drawing Room, Cwmbach

ABERAERON Ceredigion   Map 3:C2

Harbourmaster Hotel   *Tel* 01545-570755
Pen Cei, Aberaeron   *Email* info@harbour-master.com
SA46 0BA   *Website* www.harbour-master.com

♥ *César award in 2005*

In a prime position on the harbour of this pretty town, Glyn and Menna Heulyn's Georgian hotel is liked by its fans for its 'eye-catching' modernity: 'It has that "look at me" impression, with blue and lilac gleaming paintwork, and it does not disappoint when you stay there.' 'Highly recommended: friendly staff, excellent, imaginative food, comfortable, clean room. Not cheap, but good value,' says a visitor this year. The Heulyns have 'brilliantly updated' the house, creating a nautical decor throughout. The bedrooms, reached by a 'magnificent spiral staircase', are named after historic sailing ships. 'Our first-floor room had exposed stone walls, contemporary Welsh fabrics, a well-equipped bathroom.' Another room, higher up, 'has a comfortable settee where you can sit and enjoy the view'. There is a note of dissent from one reader: 'Bedroom not too well designed. The busy bar, which opens directly on to the dining room, has priority over residents.' Booking is advised for the popular small restaurant. Stephen Evans has been promoted to head chef: the Welsh-inspired menu changes daily, and 'local meats are justly famous'. (*LW, Derek Shepherd, MH Brown, and others*)

9 bedrooms. 2 in cottage. Central, on harbour. Closed 25 Dec–9 Jan. Restaurant closed Mon midday. Bar, restaurant; background music. Pebble beach, safe bathing nearby. Unsuitable for &. No smoking: restaurant, bedrooms. No children under 5. No dogs. MasterCard, Visa accepted. B&B £55–£70 per person. Full alc £30. 1-night bookings refused weekends.

ABERDYFI Gwynedd   Map 3:C3

Penhelig Arms   *Tel* 01654-767215
Terrace Road   *Fax* 01654-767690
Aberdyfi LL35 0LT   *Email* info@penheligarms.com
                                           Website www.penheligarms.com

Owned and managed by Robert and Sally Hughes, this 19th-century former fishermen's inn stands on the harbour on a busy coast road. Filled with flowers, original artwork and family photographs, it has log fires in the public rooms. All but one of the 'comfortable' bedrooms face the Dyfi estuary; some have flat-screen TV and DVD. *Pen House*, suitable for families, is a 'delightful' loft-style apartment with its own terrace. 'Must be one of the best-run small hotels in Wales,' say visitors in 2006 who 'greatly enjoyed' the meals in the 'charming' dining room. 'Helpful young staff.' But there were dissenters: one couple who visited in the owners' absence wrote of a poor welcome, and were less enthusiastic about the food, 'plonked, rather than placed, in front of us'. The menus place an emphasis on seafood (eg, sea bass with couscous and chive oil). The 300-strong wine list (many bottles under £20; 30 available by the glass) has won awards (eg, *Good Pub Guide* UK wine pub of the year 2006). The beamed bar (which also serves meals) has been refurbished; so have some bedrooms. Guests get concessionary fees at a nearby championship golf course. (*KN Symons, and others*)

16 bedrooms. Central, by harbour. Closed 25/26 Dec. Lounge, public bar, small cocktail bar, restaurant. No background music. Unsuitable for &, but 'please telephone for advice'. No smoking: restaurant, part of bars, bedrooms. MasterCard, Visa accepted. B&B [2006] £39–£70 per person; D,B&B £67–£95. Set menu £29. 1-night bookings refused Sat. *'V'*

Trefeddian Hotel   *Tel* 01654-767213
Tywyn Road   *Fax* 01654-767777
Aberdyfi LL35 0SB   *Email* info@trefwales.com
                                          Website www.trefwales.com

'It's a "return again and again" place,' writes one devotee of this much-loved, family-oriented hotel. 'Having brought my children, I'm now back with the grandchildren,' says another. 'Beautifully situated', overlooking Cardigan Bay, the large Edwardian building has been owned and managed by the Cave family for three generations. Staff (many are long serving) are 'very friendly; we were extremely well looked after by the housekeeper'. A visitor during a packed half-term week reports that the hotel 'somehow absorbed all the children and kept cool'. One lounge is reserved for adults; there's another 'large and airy' one for families; dogs are allowed in a third room (one visitor complained of too many of them, 'leaving sand and mud marks'). In off-season, many guests may be elderly: but *Trefeddian* 'doesn't have the sense of an old people's hotel'. Bedrooms, some with balcony, are 'well furnished', bathrooms 'leaned to a high standard'; 'very comfortable beds'. Food, served in generous portions, is 'good, if fairly traditional'. 'A spinach-based soufflé was sheer bliss, as was the grilled cod.' Disabled guests are 'marvellously catered for'. 'Great walking from the door; the four-mile beach is fantastic.' (*Mrs MB Blackburn, Dorothy Brining, and others*)

59 bedrooms. ½ mile N of village. Closed 25 Nov–23 Dec. Lift. 3 lounges, bar lounge, restaurant; fitness centre: indoor swimming pool (40 by 20 ft), beauty salon. No background music. 15-acre grounds: tennis, 9-hole pitch and putt, children's playground. Smoking in bar lounge only. Dogs allowed: 1 lounge, some bedrooms. MasterCard, Visa accepted. B&B [2006] £40–£60 per person; D,B&B £70–£95. Full alc £36–£50. Christmas/New Year packages. 1-night bookings sometimes refused.

ABERGAVENNY Monmouthshire   Map 3:D4
See SHORTLIST

ABERSOCH Gwynedd   Map 3:B2

Porth Tocyn Hotel	*Tel* 01758-713303
Bwlch Tocyn	*Fax* 01758-713538
Abersoch LL53 7BU	*Email* bookings@porthtocyn.fsnet.co.uk
	Website www.porth-tocyn-hotel.co.uk

♺ *César award in 1984*

'Warmly approved' by returning visitors this year, this traditional, family-run hotel stands above Cardigan Bay and has 'breathtaking' views of Snowdonia. Nick and Louise Fletcher-Brewer are 'excellent' hosts, say fans. They combine a 'relaxed attitude with high professionalism'. 'He and his charming staff helped us unpack our car, and gave us tea after a long journey.' Converted from a row of lead miners' cottages, the 'agreeable, rambling' building has 'grown organically'. Bedrooms, most with sea views, are cottagey rather than luxurious. This year, many bathrooms have been modernised and given a power shower. Children are welcomed: several rooms are interconnecting, and bunk beds are available. 'Our children enjoyed their stay, making new friends and exploring the hotel and the grounds.' Parents can relax on sunbeds in the pretty garden, or in the comfortable lounges, with their antiques, books and fresh flowers. The food provided by Louise Fletcher-Brewer and Tony Cowley is praised again this year: 'The family consensus is that the kitchen is better than ever.' 'Well cooked, charmingly served,' says another visitor. The building is not ideal for disabled visitors: prospective guests with a disability should call to discuss their needs. (*Richard Creed, Joy Harvey, Gwyneth Brock, Lloyd Wilkinson*)

17 bedrooms. 2 miles outside village. 2 weeks before Easter–early Nov. Sitting rooms, children's rooms, bar, dining room, conservatory. No background music. 25-acre grounds: swimming pool (heated May–Sept; 32 by 18 ft), tennis. Beach (5 mins' walk), sailing, fishing, golf, riding nearby. No smoking: restaurant, 1 sitting room, bedrooms. No tiny children at dinner (high tea at 5.30 pm). No dogs in public rooms. MasterCard, Visa accepted. B&B: single £65–£85, double £87–£162. Cooked breakfast £5.75. Set dinner £32–£38.50. 1-night bookings sometimes refused.

BEAUMARIS Gwynedd   Map 3:A3

Ye Olde Bulls Head   *Tel* 01248-810329
Castle Street   *Fax* 01248-811294
Beaumaris, Anglesey   *Email* info@bullsheadinn.co.uk
LL58 8AP   *Website* www.bullsheadinn.co.uk

With its beams and creaking staircases, this atmospheric old coaching house not only 'feels like a Dickensian inn', but has actually played host to the author. Other illustrious guests in its 500-year history include Samuel Johnson. Bedrooms, named after Dickens characters, are small and 'smartly cosy'; decor ranges from traditional to 'more contemporary'. Mr Pickwick has a carved four-poster bed. Stairs can be steep. The popular bar, where a visitor this year enjoyed 'meeting locals', has brass knick-knacks, a rare 17th-century brass water clock, antique weapons and the town's oak ducking seat; a huge coal fire burns in winter. There is a 'very comfortable' residents' lounge. Owner/managers, Keith Rothwell and David Robertson, have appointed a new chef, Matthew Leech, to run the *Loft* restaurant upstairs (where main courses include local grey mullet with tagliatelle, broad beans, crisp ham and balsamic glaze). Simon Doyle continues to head the brasserie (dishes like ragout of venison; smoked haddock and chive risotto with poached egg). 'Both were first class,' says a visitor this year. 'Friendly, effective service. A splendid choice.' Breakfast is 'nicely done (freshly squeezed juice, etc)'. The medieval town is 'fun to explore'. (*Thomas H Blackburn, and others*)

13 bedrooms. 2 on ground floor suitable for &. Main street. Closed 25/26 Dec, 1 Jan, *Loft* restaurant closed Sun. Lounge, bar, brasserie (background music), restaurant. Sea 200 yds. Smoking in bar only. No children under 7 in restaurant or bedroom suites. No dogs. Amex, MasterCard, Visa accepted. B&B: single £77–£125, double £98.50–£100, suite £127–£155. Set dinner (Loft restaurant) £37; full alc £48.25.

'Set lunch/dinner' indicates fixed-price meals, with ample, limited or no choice on the menu. 'Full alc' is the hotel's esti-mated price per person of a three-course *à la carte* meal, with a half bottle of house wine. 'Alc' is the price of an *à la carte* meal excluding the cost of wine.

BODUAN Gwynedd   Map 3:B2

The Old Rectory   *Tel/Fax* 01758-721519
Boduan   *Email* thepollards@theoldrectory.net
nr Pwllheli LL53 6DT   *Website* www.theoldrectory.net

Standing in woodland in a village in the Lleyn peninsula, this small, pale
yellow B&B is 'strongly recommended' by its fans. The 'very kind hosts',
Roger and Gabrielle Pollard, have 'beautifully restored' the former
Georgian rectory. Elegant public rooms are full of antique family
furniture, paintings and photographs. Fires are lit in the colder months.
Bedrooms are individually styled: 'Ours, shining clean, had hairdryer, tea-
making facilities, and fine views over fields.' Some bathrooms have a roll-
top bath. Mrs Pollard, 'an excellent cook', serves meals by arrangement on

some nights (main courses like
marinated cod with a roast
leek and fennel-seed sauce).
Otherwise, reservations can be
made for guests at local
restaurants. Nearby are three
golf courses, coastal footpaths,
and splendid sandy beaches.
More reports, please.

3 bedrooms. Also self-catering cottage. 4 miles NW of Pwllheli. Closed Christmas.
Drawing room, dining room. No background music. 3½-acre grounds. Unsuitable for
&. No smoking. No dogs: bedrooms, public rooms. No credit cards. B&B [2006]
£40–£60 per person. Set menus £20–£25. 1-night bookings refused bank holidays.

BRECHFA Carmarthenshire   Map 3:D2

Tŷ Mawr   *Tel* 01267-202332
Brechfa SA32 7RA   *Email* info@wales-country-hotel.co.uk
                           Website www.wales-country-hotel.co.uk

'A remarkable find,' comments a visitor in 2006 to this welcoming 15th-
century farmhouse which stands on a quiet road on the edge of the Brechfa
forest. Owners Annabel Viney ('intelligent, responsive and helpful') and
Stephen Thomas (the chef), who took over in 2004, have 'done an
exemplary job in making the house and grounds attractive', said our
inspector. A micro-brewery and tap room have been added. Many original
features, such as thick stone walls and wooden beams, have been retained,
and bedrooms are 'decorated in cottage style (nice old pine furniture and

painted walls)'; each has a deep claw-footed bath. 'We spent a delightful night; only sounds the hooting of owls and the noise of the stream. The welcome was perfect, cuisine flawless, the room one of the most comfortable we have stayed in.' Another report: 'Our room had everything that mattered except a telephone: large comfortable bed, outsize TV, good lighting, excellent towels, lots of toiletries.' Stephen Thomas 'takes his cooking seriously', using local produce (organic Fferm Tyllwyd Welsh Black fillet steak). Guests are 'invited to be taken for a walk by Portia the dog'. (*Stephen and Miranda Aldhouse-Green, Philip Harris, and others*)

5 bedrooms. Village centre. Sitting room, bar, breakfast room, restaurant (background music). 1-acre grounds by River Marlais. Limited & access. Smoking in bar only. No children under 12. No dogs in restaurant. Amex, MasterCard, Visa accepted. B&B: single £65, double £95; D,B&B £76.50–£94 per person. Set menu £24–£29. Christmas/New Year packages. **'V'**

BRECON Powys *See SHORTLIST*   Map 3:D3

BRIDGEND *See SHORTLIST*   Map 3:E3

BROADHAVEN Pembrokeshire   Map 3:D1

The Druidstone   **BUDGET**   *Tel* 01437-781221
nr Broadhaven   *Fax* 01437-781133
Haverfordwest SA62 3NE   *Email* jane@druidstone.co.uk
                                   Website www.druidstone.co.uk

'The perfect antidote to overpriced designer hotels', this long-running, characterful 'family holiday centre' stands on cliffs above 'one of the best beaches in Britain'. It is owned by Jane and Rod Bell and son Angus. 'We are constantly adding to the team and training young people,' they say. The 19th-century house, with its wooden floors and worn antiques, has a 'relaxed ambience plus real sense of comfort'. Public rooms are 'set up for reading the paper, playing cards, drinking cappuccino or eating delicious food' (the *Druidstone* has had a *Good Food Guide* entry for 32 years). This is served in the 'cosy' bar, used by locals, and the dining room. Both open on to a sea-facing terrace and garden. Angus Bell's cooking, based on local and organic ingredients, is described as 'international fusion', and there is a theme night twice a week. The hotel's own fisherman catches mackerel and sea bass before breakfast. 'The restaurant is excellent, and children's high tea is always interesting.' The two 'rather luxurious' penthouse bedrooms each have a balcony facing the bay; other rooms are less smart: only four have a private bathroom. The cottages in the grounds include the tiny Roundhouse, which derives its energy from the sun. Pets are welcomed. Popular for 'house party-style' gatherings (birthdays, weddings, reunions and away days). (*Matthew Greenfield*)

11 bedrooms. 5 cottages. 2 suitable for &. 7 miles W of Haverfordwest. Sitting room, bar (background music/occasional live music), TV room, restaurant; small conference/function facilities. 22-acre grounds. Sandy beach, safe bathing 200 yds. Civil wedding licence. Smoking in bar only (after 10.15 pm); discouraged in bedrooms. No dogs in restaurant. Amex, MasterCard, Visa accepted. B&B £42–£69 per person. Full alc £31.50. Courses, conferences. Christmas/New Year and mid-week packages. 1-night advance bookings refused for Sat.

CAERNARFON Gwynedd *See SHORTLIST*   Map 3:A2

CAPEL GARMON Conwy   Map 3:A3

Tan-y-Foel Country House   *Tel* 01690-710507
Capel Garmon   *Fax* 01690-710681
nr Betws-y-Coed LL26 0RE   *Email* enquiries@tyfhotel.co.uk
    Website www.tyfhotel.co.uk

'We were full of admiration for the family of three who run this delightful hotel,' writes a visitor this year to this quiet little hideaway. Sitting high on wooded hills in the Snowdonia national park (the name means 'house under the hillside'), it has 'superb' views of the Conwy valley. The Pitmans, who bought it near-derelict 14 years ago, have created a contemporary interior inside the 17th-century stone building. Public rooms are decorated in understated earth tones; colours in bedrooms can be bolder; fabrics are lavish. Some rooms have a 'magnificent view' of the valley; some have a four-poster bed; two have their own entrance. Bathrooms are 'capacious and well equipped'. Flat-screen TV and DVD-players are available. 'Mum does the cooking, dad plays Man Friday and daughter serves drinks and waits at table. They perform magnificently.' Janet Pitman's highly praised 'modern fusion' cooking uses local and organic produce where possible; the menu changes daily. The fresh-cooked breakfast is thought 'excellent'. Fellow guests are likely to be 'serious walkers'. Advance reservations only, both for lodging and dinner. 'Car essential,' the owners warn. (*AJ Ward, TO'K, and others*)

6 bedrooms. 1½ miles off A470 (N), E of Betws-y-Coed. Open Feb–Dec. Lounge, breakfast room, restaurant. No background music. 6-acre grounds. Unsuitable for &. No smoking. No children under 7. Guide dogs only. MasterCard, Visa accepted. B&B £49.50–£150 per person. Set dinner £39. 1-night bookings refused weekends, bank holidays.

CARDIFF   Map 3:E4

Jolyon's NEW   *Tel/Fax* 029-2048 8775
Bute Crescent   *Email* info@jolyons.co.uk
Cardiff CF10 5AN   *Website* www.jolyons.co.uk

In 'gloriously transformed' Cardiff Bay, opposite the new Millennium Centre, home of the Welsh National Opera, this restored Georgian town house, 'a lovely old building', says a visitor this year, is run as a boutique hotel by the 'laid-back' Jolyon Joseph. 'Very personable', he made a good first impression on *Guide* inspectors, as did the 'pale oak fittings'. In the bedroom, 'contemporary touches are enhanced by antiques. A large wardrobe had Art Nouveau designs; a massive Jacobean mirror was hung behind the bed, which was large enough to sleep three. The large chrome-fitted bathroom was a joy, modern yet cosy; a leaf-shaped bath, fluffy towels, lots of hot water. No information pack, so we were clueless about local restaurants, mealtimes, etc.' One room has a whirlpool bath, another a veranda on the roof. Downstairs is the 'friendly' *Bar Cwtch* (Welsh for 'cosy'), popular with non-residents, which has an eclectic wine list. An 'adequate' continental breakfast is served here; cooked dishes cost extra. Light meals, eg, a cheese platter, can be served by arrangement. Jolyon Joseph says: 'It is a Georgian house, but we do everything we can to look after disabled guests.' (*JC, and others*)

6 bedrooms. 1 on ground floor. Cardiff Bay waterfront. Residents' lounge, bar. Terrace. No smoking. No children under 15. No dogs. MasterCard, Visa accepted. Room (with continental breakfast) £85–£195. Cooked breakfast £8.50.

See also SHORTLIST

> When you make a booking you enter into a contract with a hotel. Most hotels explain their cancellation policies, which vary widely, in a letter of confirmation. You may lose your deposit or be charged at the full rate for the room if you cancel at short notice. A travel insurance policy can provide protection.

COLWYN BAY Conwy   Map 3:A3

Rathlin Country House   *Tel* 01492-532173
48 Kings Road, Colwyn Bay   *Fax* 0871 661 9887
LL29 7YH   *Email* enquiries@rathlincountryhouse.co.uk
                    Website www.rathlincountryhouse.co.uk

'Well decorated, very comfortable', this imposing red brick B&B sits in a leafy conservation area a mile from the sea. Marian and Anthony Faragher are the 'friendly yet unobtrusive' owner/managers. All bedrooms are on the first floor (no lift). Room 2 (one of the front ones) was liked by recent guests. 'Super spa bath, excellent variety of fruit infusions as well as complimentary mineral water, tea and filter coffee, and a DVD collection.' All rooms have wireless Internet access and – as of this year – a fridge with fresh milk. Breakfast, in the original oak-panelled lounge (with inglenook fireplace and parquet floor), is 'plentiful, tasty and well presented'. It includes fresh orange juice, fresh fruit, free-range eggs, kippers and toasted wholemeal bread. The hallway, with stained-glass windows, is 'stunning'. In the garden are a swimming pool (available in summer) and a sauna (available all year). More reports, please.

3 bedrooms. ½ mile from centre. Lounge/breakfast room. 1-acre grounds: 25-ft outdoor heated swimming pool (May–Aug), sauna. Unsuitable for ♿. No smoking. No pets, except assistance dogs. MasterCard, Visa accepted. B&B [2006]: single £55, double £78. 1-night bookings refused bank holidays.

CRICKHOWELL Powys   Map 3:D4

Glangrwyney Court   *Tel* 01873-811288
Glangrwyney, Crickhowell   *Fax* 01873-810317
NP8 1ES   *Email* info@glancourt.co.uk
                        Website www.glancourt.co.uk

'We entertain guests in our family home,' say Christina and Warwick Jackson, who provide B&B at their Grade II listed house on the edge of the Brecon Beacons national park. 'Very comfortable. Large bedroom, good bathroom and guest lounge,' says a visitor this year. 'But it is a bit eccentric, wildly over-furnished, every surface cluttered with ornaments, trinkets and paintings. The breakfast is excellent. Good value for money.' Earlier praise: 'Beautifully appointed house, lovely gardens, warm welcome.' The house has a cantilevered staircase of architectural significance, log fires and a 'well-stocked' honesty bar. All rooms face the garden. The master suite has a steam shower; one twin room has a spa bath. Some beds are king-size. A simple evening meal, eg, Thai prawn balls; roast rib of Welsh beef with Yorkshire pudding, can be served by arrangement, and there are plenty of restaurants nearby, including *The Bear* pub. (*Chris Head, MK, and others*)

5 bedrooms. Also 2 in self-catering lodge. 2 miles SE of Crickhowell. Sitting room, library with honesty bar, dining room (background music at dinner if requested). 4-acre garden: croquet, *boules*, tennis. River 500 yds: fishing by arrangement. Unsuitable for &. Civil wedding licence. No smoking. No dogs. MasterCard, Visa accepted. B&B [2006] £32.50–£75 per person. Set dinner (by arrangement) £25–£30. Off-season discounts. 1-night bookings sometimes refused.

Gliffaes
Crickhowell
NP8 1RH

Tel 01874-730371
Fax 01874-730463
Email calls@gliffaeshotel.com
Website www.gliffaeshotel.com

Fishing is the major draw at this smart sporting hotel: the 19th-century Italianate building, owned by one family since 1948, has a private stretch of the trout- and salmon-laden River Usk within its large wooded grounds. Most bedrooms (best ones have a river view and balcony) are large. Inspectors found theirs 'attractive and comfortable', adding: 'The sitting areas are nice, particularly the conservatory. The gardens are lovely and you can go for long walks from the door.' Owners Susie and James Suter are 'helpful'. *Gliffaes* belongs to the 'Slow Food Movement': chef Stephen Tricini sources local produce and only uses 'environmentally responsible' fish. 'Food fantastic, especially Sunday lunch. Cosy afternoon tea in front of log fire.' Another view: 'Quite elaborate with no simple dishes, surprising in view of the traditional clientele; service was a little disorganised.' Breakfasts are copious. Three-day fly-fishing courses for beginners are run in June. 'A beautiful setting and hotel,' say devotees. 'The owners treated our children as if they were their own, and always managed to accommodate their requests. We now go at least once a year.' (*Jackie Pethick, AH and HH, and others*)

23 bedrooms. 1 on ground floor. 3½ miles W of Crickhowell. Closed Jan. Ramp. Sitting rooms, conservatory, bar, dining room. Tennis, croquet, golf practice net, putting, fishing (ghillie available). Civil wedding licence. No smoking: dining room, bedrooms. No dogs in house. Amex, MasterCard, Visa accepted. B&B [2006] £50–£75. Set dinner £31. Website deals. Christmas/New Year packages. 1-night bookings refused weekends.

If you remember a hotel's name but not its location, consult the alphabetical hotel list on page 552.

CWM TAF Powys   Map 3:D3

Nant Ddu Lodge   *Tel* 01685-379111
Cwm Taf, nr Merthyr Tydfil   *Fax* 01685-377088
CF48 2HY   *Email* enquiries@nant-ddu-lodge.co.uk
                                             Website www.nant-ddu-lodge.co.uk

'We shall definitely be back,' say visitors this year to Daniel Ronson's hotel, bistro and spa, a former hunting lodge on the edge of the Brecon Beacons national park. 'Decent value; an enjoyable atmosphere; friendly staff who really want you to be happy.' Bedrooms are 'bland but comfortable'; the best have queen-size bed, sofa and widescreen TV. There are some family rooms. Some other rooms may be 'cramped'. Some rooms hear road noise, in others, 'the sound of the river roaring past was soothing'. Richard Wimmer is chef. The bistro, 'busy with locals', serves 'excellent, interesting food', eg, loin of wild boar on a blueberry and cider ragout. The bar, with its log fire and real ales, is popular too. Breakfast is a generous cold buffet, with a 'very good' cooked breakfast at extra cost. Outside dining is possible. 'Tall conifers and flowerbeds, well-kept lawns with tables, benches and chairs, make this a nice place to sit in the sun.' Spa treatments are reasonably priced and 'strict rules about children's hours in the swimming pool meant that early morning was blissfully quiet for grown-ups'. (*Mike and Sharon Amos, and others*)

31 bedrooms. Ground-floor rooms suitable for ♿. 6 miles N of Merthyr Tydfil. Closed Christmas. 3 lounges, bistro, bar; background music; spa: 60-ft heated swimming pool, gym, saunarium, lounge, bar. 4-acre grounds. No smoking in restaurant. No dogs: some bedrooms, public rooms. Amex, MasterCard, Visa accepted. B&B: single £69.50–£79.50, double £89.50–£99.50, suite £125. Full alc £30. 1-night bookings refused Sat.

CWMBACH Powys   Map 3:C3

 The Drawing Room   *Tel* 01982-552493
Cwmbach   *Email* post@the-drawing-room.co.uk
Newbridge-on-Wye   *Website* www.the-drawing-room.co.uk
Builth Wells LD2 3RT

César award: Welsh restaurant-with-rooms of the year

'Everything was impeccable,' say inspectors this year of Colin and Melanie Dawson's 'very personally run' restaurant-with-rooms. 'From the welcome (she carried our bags) to the offer of hot chocolate as a nightcap.' The Georgian building has been 'beautifully restored and smartly decorated':

bedrooms are '1920s in feel' with 'top-quality modern Laura Ashley fabrics, simple, classic-style furniture, ample storage space, TV/DVD-player, Internet connection'. There are original fireplaces and black glass chandeliers. Bathrooms, with roll-top bath and lots of towels, are thought 'superb'. The lounges are more traditional in feel, with their comfortable sofas and armchairs, log fires and *objets d'art*. Colin Dawson is the chef, his wife is *sous-chef*, responsible for desserts, breads and pastry, and also front-of-house in the small restaurant overlooking the garden. 'Dinner was excellent, my monkfish, with leek and prawn risotto, was delicious and served properly hot.' 'Menu surprisingly large. Everything perfectly cooked and presented; service professional throughout; relaxed atmosphere. Breakfast was a civilised delight: beautifully set tables, long, appetising menu; really fresh orange juice, toast made from super bread.' The only drawback is the building's position on a main road, but there is little traffic at night, and windows are double glazed. (*P and JT, and others*)

3 bedrooms. On A470, 3 miles N of Builth Wells. Closed 2 weeks Jan, 2 weeks Sept. 2 lounges, restaurant; private dining room; background CDs at night. Small garden. Only restaurant suitable for ♿. No smoking. No children under 12. Guide dogs only. MasterCard, Visa accepted. D,B&B £90–£110 per person. Set lunch £19.50; full alc £45. Christmas/New Year packages (min. 6 people).

EGLWYSFACH Powys   Map 3:C3

Ynyshir Hall   *Tel* 01654-781209
Eglwysfach   *Fax* 01654-781366
nr Machynlleth SY20 8TA   *Email* info@ynyshir-hall.co.uk
                                          Website www.ynyshir-hall.co.uk

♥ *César award in 1997*

'Expensive, but a short step from heaven.' 'It remains a favourite hideaway.' Rob and Joan Reen's small luxury hotel (Relais & Châteaux), a former shooting lodge in 'wonderful gardens' on the Dovey estate, wins more accolades this year. 'She welcomed us with natural warmth.' 'They work incredibly hard.' 'They never rest on their laurels, there is constant redecorating.' 'A guest was well cared for after a small accident.' Bedrooms, each named after a famous artist, are done in bold colours. 'A dramatic decor, not to everyone's taste perhaps, but preferable to uniform anonymity.' In the dimly lit dining room, Adam Simmonds's cooking 'is up there with the best in the country'. 'He has imaginative but precise technical skills, creating dishes arranged with panache, full of contrasting texture and flavours.' His savoury ice creams 'bring out the flavours: onion with pork, celery sorbet with cheese'. Some dishes might be 'a bit over-adventurous'. Breakfast 'receives the same attention': freshly squeezed juice, home-made jams, two cooked fish options, 'porridge worthy of the three bears'. The landscaped gardens (a Zen one has been added) on the Dyfi estuary are surrounded by an RSPB reserve. A non-refundable 20% deposit is requested at the time of booking. (*Christopher McCall, John and Jane Holland, David Wooff, Padi Howard*)

9 bedrooms. 6 miles SW of Machynlleth. Closed Jan. Drawing room, bar lounge, breakfast room, restaurant (background classical music occasionally at night), spa treatments. 14-acre gardens in 365-acre bird reserve: croquet, putting. Civil wedding licence. No smoking. No children under 9. Dogs by arrangement. All major credit cards accepted. B&B: single £150–£200, double £180–£285, suite £280–£375. Set menu £62–£72. Christmas/New Year packages. 1-night bookings sometimes refused busy weekends, bank holidays.

FELIN FACH Powys   Map 3:D4

The Felin Fach Griffin
Felin Fach, nr Brecon
LD3 0UB

Tel 01874-620111
Fax 01874-620120
Email enquiries@eatdrinksleep.ltd.uk
Website www.eatdrinksleep.ltd.uk

'The atmosphere is relaxed,' says a visitor this year to this 'civilised' terracotta-coloured inn between the Brecon Beacons and the Black Mountains. It may be on a main road, with a large car park in front, but it is found 'life enhancing and unforgettable'. It comprises a series of interlinked rooms round the bar area. No residents' lounge, but leather sofas round a fireplace, and a big table with newspapers. Owners Charles and Edmund Inkin 'want you to feel it's a private home where your wish is their command'. Julie Bell is the new manager. Chef Ricardo Van Ede, at 21, had his own *Michelin*-starred restaurant in Amsterdam. His 'delicious' dinners, 'piping hot, stylishly presented', are based on local ingredients, many home grown. Bedrooms are simple but comfortable:

'decor a mix of old and new'; 'luxurious bedlinens'. One couple had a room that was 'very small, with a high window', and they thought 'the hotel side of things lacked a personal touch'. The simple breakfast has boiled eggs or a fry-up, and you make your own toast, from 'excellent bread', on the Aga. 'We enjoyed sitting on the lawn after a long car journey.' Excellent walking nearby: 'Go out the front door and up a country road surrounded by sheep farms and you'll be in an earlier century.' (*Deborah Starbuck-Edwards, Robert Lenzner and Katherine Courage, and others*)

7 bedrooms. 4 miles NE of Brecon. Closed Christmas. Bar, dining areas; background music/radio most of the time; private dining rooms. No TV, 'except for very special events'. 2-acre garden: croquet, stream. Unsuitable for &. No smoking: dining rooms, bedrooms. No dogs in public areas, except bar. Diners, MasterCard, Visa accepted. B&B: single £67.50, double £97.50, suite £125. Full alc £36. Longer stays negotiable. Wine, fishing, shooting packages. 1-night bookings occasionally refused.

FISHGUARD Pembrokeshire   Map 3:D1

The Manor Town House   **BUDGET**   *Tel/Fax* 01348-873260
Main Street   *Email* enquiries@manortownhouse.com
Fishguard SA65 9HG   *Website* www.manortownhouse.com

In August 2005, Gail and James Stewart took over this Georgian Grade II listed building in this pretty harbour town. They 'have more than maintained the high standards', writes a returning visitor. Other correspondents agree: 'They were warm, friendly, helpful; Gail's cooking was excellent.' 'They could not have done more to make our stay enjoyable.' Most bedrooms face the sea: 'Ours had a stunning view of the old harbour, one of the most comfortable beds we have ever had, furniture of the "whatever comes to hand" variety. Above all, it was quiet.' 'Ours was a good size, with nice furniture, but its bathroom was small.' Front rooms may get street noise. Antiques 'give character' to the public rooms. There is a sea-facing patio and gazebo for summer meals and drinks. In the 'homely' basement dining room, the food is 'first rate'. 'Only two choices for each course, but each was meticulously prepared, using fresh local ingredients. Memorable dishes included a superb fish pie, a delicious beef stew.' The wine list is 'modest in scope and price, but all that we tried were good'. Only drawback: the nearest public parking lot is 150 yards away. (*Mavis Humphreys, Charles Grant, Charles and Jean Mellows*)

6 bedrooms. Near town square. Closed Christmas, 'occasionally off-season for owners' holidays'. Restaurant closed midday. 2 lounges, bar/restaurant (classical background music at mealtimes). Walled garden: terrace, gazebo. Sea, safe bathing 2 miles. Unsuitable for &. No smoking except in summer house. No dogs (but kennels nearby). MasterCard, Visa accepted. B&B [2006] £30–£35 per person. Set dinner £20. New Year package. 1-night bookings refused weekends in season.

HARLECH Gwynedd *See SHORTLIST*   Map 3:B3

HAVERFORDWEST Pembrokeshire   Map 3:D1
See SHORTLIST

KNIGHTON Powys   Map 3:C4

Milebrook House   *Tel* 01547-528632
Milebrook   *Fax* 01547-520509
nr Knighton   *Email* hotel@milebrook.kc3ltd.co.uk
Powys LD7 1LT   *Website* www.milebrookhouse.co.uk

Much praise again this year for Beryl and Rodney Marsden's small hotel,
a creeper-covered 18th-century house once owned by the explorer
Sir Wilfred Thesiger and visited by Emperor Haile Selassie. A *Guide*
hotelier commends the 'informal country hospitality'. 'Came up to expectations in every single way. As a single guest I was made to feel very
welcome,' said another visitor. Its greatest fan, on his fourth visit, writes:
'The quintessential country hotel run by lovely people in a lovely house.
A relaxing but professional atmosphere.' A dissenter, however, complained
of being treated with 'indifference'. 'Pleasingly informal' public rooms have
a 'delightful country house ambience'. 'The decor is impeccable, with light
pastels, but not boring.' A room at the front is near the road, but most
people find this quiet at night. The quiet rear bedrooms have thick carpets,
a blue-tiled bathroom. The restaurant, popular with locals, has a new chef,
Steven Burnham: his cooking is thought 'excellent' (eg, roast pork filled
with roasted peppers, tomatoes, sage jus). Sunday lunch is a traditional
affair. 'An excellent wine list: particularly good choice by the glass.' From
the pretty garden you can look across the River Teme to England. (*Alastair
Kameen, Ann Zwemmer, Richard Creed, and others*)

10 bedrooms. 2 on ground floor. On A4113, 2 miles E of Knighton. Restaurant
closed Mon midday. Lounge, bar, 2 dining rooms (soft background music in the
evening). 3-acre grounds on river: terraces, pond, croquet, fishing. No smoking. No
children under 8. No dogs. MasterCard, Visa accepted. B&B [2006] £55.50–£65.50
per person. Set menu £31.50. Christmas/New Year packages. 1-night bookings
sometimes refused busy weekends.

All our inspections are paid for, and carried out anonymously.

LLANARMON DYFFRYN CEIRIOG   Map 3:B4
Denbighshire

The Hand at Llanarmon   `BUDGET`   *Tel* 01691-600666
Ceiriog Valley   *Fax* 01691-600262
Llanarmon Dyffryn Ceiriog   *Email* reception@thehandhotel.co.uk
LL20 7LD   *Website* www.thehandhotel.co.uk

In a tiny village above the Ceiriog valley (described by Lloyd George as 'a little bit of heaven on earth'), this 16th-century inn is 'very much the centre of the community': weddings and functions are held, and it is 'well used by the local population', say visitors this year. 'A friendly atmosphere prevails in the bar', and the owners, Gaynor and Martin De Luchi, and their staff are 'happy and welcoming'. Bedrooms have been redecorated this year: 'Ours was spacious (as was the bathroom); we faced a gentle hill where sheep were grazing.' 'Lots of cupboard space, pine furniture, comfortable bed.' There is an 'excellent' residents' lounge, and a room with pool table and darts. Chef Grant Mulholland serves 'well-prepared country food', using local sources; inclusive dinner rates 'present tremendous value for money'. Breakfasts also 'deserve a mention'. Shooting parties come in the season. 'We can arrange for you almost any country pursuit, even white-water rafting,' say the owners. 'You can step out of the front door and walk for miles in any direction and probably not see another soul.' (*Mr and Mrs J Jennings, Françoise Vassie*)

Note Not to be confused with the *Hand Hotel* at Chirk.

13 bedrooms. Some on ground floor. Accommodation closed at Christmas. 10 miles W of Oswestry. Lounge, bar, restaurant, games/TV room. No background music. ¼-acre grounds. Civil wedding licence. No smoking: restaurant, lounge, bedrooms. No dogs in public rooms, except bar and lounge. MasterCard, Visa accepted. B&B [2006] £35–£60 per person; D,B&B £50–£75. Full alc £25. New Year package. ***V***

See also SHORTLIST

The 'Budget' label by a hotel's name indicates an establishment where dinner, bed and breakfast cost around £55 per person, or B&B no more than £35 and an evening meal about £20. These are only a rough guide, and do not always apply to single accommodation, nor do they necessarily apply in high season.

LLANDRILLO Denbighshire   Map 3:B4

Tyddyn Llan   *Tel* 01490-440264
Llandrillo   *Fax* 01490-440414
nr Corwen LL21 0ST   *Email* tyddynllan@compuserve.com
                                             Website www.tyddynllan.co.uk

♀ *César award in 2006*

There is much praise this year for Bryan and Susan Webb's small
restaurant-with-rooms in the peaceful vale of Edeyrnion. 'A really pretty
old house. Very peaceful. Furnishing throughout top quality, plenty of
ornaments and paintings; more like home than hotel.' Public rooms have
antiques, period furniture and clever use of colour. 'Delightful, and hard to
fault,' thought earlier inspectors. 'The welcome was genuine.' Susan Webb
is 'a charming hostess', and 'staff are well trained'. Bedrooms, decorated in
country style, vary in size and are 'thoughtfully equipped' (CD-player,
bathrobe, 'exquisite sheets'). One visitor found the walls in the new wing
'very thin – we suggest staying in the original building'. There are 'lots of
nice seating areas', a covered terrace, and a pond in the 'immaculate'
garden. 'The food is excellent,' all agree. In the 'delightful' dining room,
Bryan Webb offers a *carte* and a seven-course tasting menu (eg, leek risotto
with truffles; wild bass with laverbread). Wines are 'well priced'. 'Service is
leisurely,' says one couple, who otherwise found their experience 'absolutely spot-on'. (*Lynn Wildgoose, John and Jackie Tyzack, and others*)

13 bedrooms. 1 suitable for &. 5 miles SW of Corwen. Closed last 2 weeks Jan.
Restaurant closed midday Mon–Thurs. 3 lounges, bar, 2 dining rooms; occasional
background music at mealtimes. 4-acre grounds. Fishing, riding, golf, sailing, walking
nearby. Civil wedding licence. Smoking in bar only. No dogs in public rooms.
MasterCard, Visa accepted. B&B £65–£120 per person; D,B&B £85–£150. Set meals
£35–£55. Christmas/New Year house parties. **▼V▼**

LLANDUDNO Conwy   Map 3:A3

Bodysgallen Hall and Spa   *Tel* 01492-584466
Llandudno LL30 1RS   *Fax* 01492-582519
                                             Email info@bodysgallen.com
                                             Website www.bodysgallen.com

♀ *César award in 1988*

Providing 'great old-fashioned luxury', this Grade 1 listed, 17th-century
mansion, owned by Historic House Hotels, sits amid parkland with a knot
garden, a Victorian walled garden, follies and views of Snowdonia and

Conwy Castle. There are fine panelled public rooms, ancestral portraits, antiques, splendid fireplaces and stone mullioned windows. Bedrooms are traditionally furnished: some are 'large and elegant', some have a four-poster. But one couple this year found their bathroom 'definitely small'. The cottage suites (Pineapple Lodge, Gingerbread House) suit families (children must be over six). Try for a window table in the restaurant ('fine views'). Chef John Williams prepares 'pricey but excellent' modern British dishes (eg, roast lamb with lentils, aubergine purée and white pudding). At dinner, male guests are asked to dress 'smartly' (the jacket and tie rule is eased in summer). The manager is Matthew Johnson; 'staff are very good, a mix of Welsh, English, Italian, French'. Another comment: 'Well-equipped spa, superb gardens, beautifully decorated bedrooms.' (*HM, and others*)

33 bedrooms. 16 in cottages, 1 suitable for &. On A55 towards Llandudno. Hall, drawing room, library, bar, dining room; conference centre. No background music. 220-acre park: gardens, tennis, croquet; spa: 65-ft swimming pool, gym, sauna, beauty treatments. Riding, shooting, fishing, sandy beaches nearby. Civil wedding licence. No smoking: dining room, drawing room, bedrooms. No children under 6, under 8 in spa. No dogs. Amex, MasterCard, Visa accepted. B&B: single £125, double £165–£375, suite £180–£375. Set menu £40. Special breaks. Christmas/ New Year packages.

St Tudno Hotel
The Promenade
Llandudno LL30 2LP

Tel 01492-874411
Fax 01492-860407
Email sttudnohotel@btinternet.com
Website www.st-tudno.co.uk

♀ *César award in 1987*

On the promenade opposite the town's Victorian pier, garden and beach, this Grade II listed hotel has been owned and run by the Bland family for 32 years. Sadly, Janette Bland died in 2005; her husband, Martin, 'is now back to his best', writes a regular visitor. 'His genial welcome is much appreciated.' His 'young, enthusiastic' staff are also praised. Bedrooms have brightly painted walls, quality linen and toiletries; the ones at the front are best. 'Our small second-floor room had sea view, furniture a bit rickety, but comfortable bed (extra pillows came as soon as we asked), lots of hanging space; delicious shortbread and fresh milk with the tea tray; wonderful use of space in the small bathroom.' Public rooms have patterned wallpaper, swagged drapery, potted plants. *The Terrace* restaurant is Italianate, with murals of Lake Como, tented ceiling, and chandeliers. Andrew Williams is the new head chef: reports on his cooking would be welcome (main courses like chicken breast, wild mushroom and tarragon polenta, mustard cream). There is a 'nice indoor swimming pool'. (*PG Knowles, and others*)

18 bedrooms. Central, opposite pier. Lift. Sitting room, coffee lounge, lounge bar; harpist Sat evening; restaurant; indoor 25-ft swimming pool; 'secret garden'. Secure car park, garaging. No smoking: restaurant, bedrooms. Dogs by arrangement; not in public rooms or unattended in bedrooms. All major credit cards accepted. B&B: single £75–£85, double £94–£220, suite £250–£300. Set lunch £18.50, dinner £38.50; full alc £42.50. Christmas/New Year packages. 1-night bookings very occasionally refused. **˙V˙**

LLANGAMMARCH WELLS Powys   Map 3:D3

The Lake   *Tel* 01591-620202
Llangammarch Wells   *Fax* 01591-620457
LD4 4BS   *Email* info@lakecountryhouse.co.uk
                                  Website www.lakecountryhouse.co.uk

Q *César award in 1992*

A spa overlooking the lake and offering health and beauty treatments is new this year at Jean-Pierre Mifsud's mock Tudor Edwardian hotel which stands in 'magnificent' grounds: its lawns slope down to the River Irfon (some of the best fishing in Wales is nearby). 'English within, Welsh without,' wrote inspectors. 'Walk through the front door and you are in the home counties: hushed afternoon teas, *maitre d'* with watch chain and tail-coat, bedroom TV tuned to London news. Walk outside and you enter Wales. Daffodils dominate in spring', and there are lambs and sightings of red kites and red-breasted mergansers. The large lounge has log fire, paintings, grand piano. 'We were upgraded to the Heron suite: good lighting, large bed, expansive bathroom with gold taps, pure-milk soap, gloriously fluffy white towels.' Twelve more suites have been added this year. The 'modern British' food is thought good, and the young waiting staff are 'responsive'. Breakfast is 'everything you'd expect at a country house hotel'. The owner has a 'well-earned reputation locally as a people-person, and likes to circulate the dining room chatting to guests'. (*JB, and others*)

30 bedrooms. 8 miles SW of Builth Wells. 2 lounges, bar, billiard room, restaurant; spa: 50-ft swimming pool, sauna, gym. No background music. 50-acre grounds: lake (fishing), river, tennis, croquet, 9-hole par 3 golf course, clay-pigeon shooting, archery. Civil wedding licence. No smoking: restaurant, lounges, bedrooms. No children under 8 in dining room after 7 pm (high tea provided). Dogs in some bedrooms (£6 a day); only guide dogs in public rooms. All major cards accepted. B&B [2006] £80–£120 per person. Set menus £39.50. Special breaks (min. 2 nights). Christmas/New Year packages. **˙V˙**

LLANSANFFRAID GLAN CONWY Conwy   Map 3:A3

The Old Rectory Country House	*Tel* 01492-580611
Llanrwst Road	*Fax* 01492-584555
Llansanffraid Glan Conwy	*Email* info@oldrectorycountryhouse.co.uk
nr Conwy LL28 5LF	*Website* www.oldrectorycountryhouse.co.uk

Ψ *César award in 1994*

In a lovely position on a hillside overlooking the Conwy estuary, Edward I's castle and Snowdonia, is Wendy and Michael Vaughan's Georgian house. Until recently, Mrs Vaughan headed a much-admired restaurant on the premises, but as of 2007 they will offer only 'luxury B&B' (they will advise on good local restaurants). Mr Vaughan ('he made us very welcome') greets guests, carries bags. The public rooms are 'well furnished', with antiques, porcelain and pictures, a grand piano and a harp. The bedrooms (some are small) are 'lavishly decorated, lots of cushions, easy chairs or a sofa, masses of goodies: fresh fruit, etc'. Most bathrooms are large: 'Our bath was like a crescent-shaped paddling pool.' Breakfasts are 'good and traditional'. In front of the house, descending in terraces towards the road, are gardens, part formal, part quite wild. More reports, please.

5 bedrooms. 1 suite in coach house (30 yds). 2 miles from Llandudno Junction station. Closed mid-Dec–early Feb. Lounge, dining room. 2½-acre grounds. No background music. Sea, safe bathing 2 miles. No smoking. No children under 5, except babies under 6 months. Dogs in coach house only (not in garden). MasterCard, Visa accepted. B&B: single £79–£129, double £99–£159, suite £139–£189. 1-night bookings refused high-season weekends, bank holidays.

LLANWRTYD WELLS Powys   Map 3:D3

Carlton House **BUDGET**	*Tel* 01591-610248
Dol-y-coed Road	*Email* info@carltonrestaurant.co.uk
Llanwrtyd Wells LD5 4RA	*Website* www.carltonrestaurant.co.uk

Ψ *César award in 1998*

'More like home than hotel', Mary Ann and Alan Gilchrist's 'mildly eccentric', 'unpretentious' restaurant-with-rooms, is a bright pink Victorian villa in this old spa town. 'The decor may not be to everyone's taste,' writes one fan. 'Some of the furniture could have come from your granny, the choice of pictures is bizarre, and ornaments are a mish-mash, but the important things are all there: a genuinely warm welcome, cleanliness, a relaxed atmosphere free of background music, attentive but unobtrusive service, excellent food.' Mrs Gilchrist ('entertaining and forthright') offers a no-choice menu as well as the *carte*: the latter might include seared scallops with buttered leeks, tagliolini and a white wine and wholegrain mustard sauce. The wine list has over 20 half bottles. The panelled restaurant, which seats just 14, is in the bright front room; the lounge is a small, darker room at the back. 'Breakfast had fresh orange juice and the best scrambled eggs ever' (if you want it before 9 am, you must ask). 'Good, plentiful coffee.' Some rooms are interconnecting, ideal for a family. Some are large, but some get traffic noise. Stairs to upper floors are steep. (*AS, GC, and others*)

6 bedrooms. Town centre. No private parking. Closed 6–30 Dec, restaurant closed Sun. Lounge, restaurant. No background music. Small garden. Unsuitable for &. No smoking. No dogs in public rooms. MasterCard, Visa accepted. B&B £30–£45 per person. Set menu £25; full alc £42.50. Special breaks. New Year package. 1-night bookings occasionally refused. **'V'**

LLYSWEN Powys   Map 3:D4

Llangoed Hall
Llyswen
nr Brecon LD3 0YP

Tel 01874-754525
Fax 01874-754545
Email enquiries@llangoedhall.com
Website www.llangoedhall.com

The hotel of choice for literary bigwigs during the Hay-on-Wye book festival, this grand 17th-century mansion sits in glorious countryside beside the River Wye. Redesigned by Clough Williams-Ellis in 1919, it was turned into a hotel by its owner, Sir Bernard Ashley, in 1990. Calum C Milne is manager. There is a Great Hall with log fires, a morning room with piano, a library with snooker table. Everywhere are pictures and 'fascinating antiques'; fabrics are from Sir Bernard's in-house textile printing business. 'Rooms are spacious: ours had a newly upholstered floral bed, plenty of sitting areas, a grand Victorian mirror. The feel is casual, like visiting a family home.' 'Staff, mainly Polish, very polite.' Another comment: 'The lighting everywhere is too dim, and the menu is the same every night, yet the place itself is the draw.' The 'very good' chef, Sean Ballington, describes his cooking as 'modern European with a traditional twist' (eg, supreme of guineafowl with roasted root vegetables and a red wine jus). Men are asked to wear a jacket at dinner. There are fine walks in the grounds, fishing and walking in the Black Mountains and the Brecon Beacons. (*John Tyzack, and others*)

23 bedrooms. 11 miles NE of Brecon. 4 lounges (1 with pianist at weekends), restaurant, billiard room; private dining room; function rooms. 17-acre grounds: tennis, croquet, maze; River Wye (200 yds), fishing. Helipads. Riding, golf, gliding, clay-pigeon shooting, canoeing nearby. Civil wedding licence. Unsuitable for &. No smoking: restaurant, 1 lounge. No children under 8. Only guide dogs in house (heated kennels in grounds). All major cards accepted. B&B: single £150–£345, double £195–£385, suite £350–£385. Set dinner £45. 2-night and Christmas/New Year packages.

MUMBLES Swansea *See SHORTLIST*   Map 3:E3

NANT GWYNANT Gwynedd   Map 3:A3

Pen-y-Gwryd Hotel   BUDGET   *Tel* 01286-870211
Nant Gwynant   *Website* www.pyg.co.uk
LL55 4NT

Ω *César award in 1995*

'For all those who love the mountains': Brian and Jane Pullee's quirky, inexpensive inn, at the foot of Snowdonia, was used in 1953 as a training base for Hillary and the Everest team (their signatures are scrawled on the ceiling of the bar, whose corners are filled with well-worn boots and ice picks). 'The opposite of a chain hotel', it has clean but simple rooms (no telephones or TV). The Pullees ('great characters') have strong views, insisting on 'proper behaviour: no baseball caps indoors, no drinking straight from a bottle, no uncontrolled children running around'. The inn is run on house-party lines, and there is a 'great social mix of guests', who eat at the same time. 'We found it great for the children,' writes a visitor this year. 'We all loved the freezing cold natural pool alternated with the sauna – very invigorating!' The 'most enjoyable' dinners, announced by a gong, are 'hearty, as hikers need'. Bedrooms (five have facilities *en suite*) have old-fashioned furniture and 'masses' of warm bedding. 'Excellent value for money: comfort, cleanliness, good food and wine, charming hosts.' 'We would love to go back. So would our dog.' (*Anne Wright, Kate and Bill Hawes, Mark and Angela Parry*)

16 bedrooms. Between Beddgelert and Capel Curig. Closed Nov–Mar, except New Year and weekends Jan/Feb. Lounge, bar, games room, dining room; chapel. No background music. 2-acre grounds: natural swimming pool, sauna. No smoking. No credit cards. B&B [2006] £35–£40 per person. Set dinner £24. 3-night rates. 1-night bookings sometimes refused weekends.

Report forms (Freepost in UK) are at the end of the *Guide*.

NEWPORT Pembrokeshire

Map 3:D1

Cnapan	*Tel* 01239-820575
East Street, Newport	*Fax* 01239-820878
nr Fishguard SA42 0SY	*Email* cnapan@ukonline.co.uk
	Website www.cnapan.co.uk

'Lovely hotel in attractive little town, good value, very nice food, friendly owners.' Praise for this long-established, pink-painted restaurant-with-rooms. On the fairly quiet main street of a small Pembrokeshire seaside town (the larger Newport is in Gwent), it has been owned and run by John and Eluned Lloyd for 22 years, with daughter and son-in-law, Judith and Michael Cooper (the women are the chefs). 'On arrival one is greeted with a blast of "hellos", there is much hustling and bustling.' Bedrooms are small, 'as with a Georgian house', and have pine furniture and bright colours. One guest wrote of a 'tiny' shower room (there is a large bath along the corridor). Downstairs, a traditional Welsh dresser, crowded with family treasures, stands in the hall; a wood-burning stove warms the guests' sitting room; books, magazines and local information are everywhere. 'We were very well fed, vegetables especially good. Service was brisk and attentive,

everyone showed kindness.' Huge breakfasts include home-made marmalade, free-range eggs and kippers ('I was generously asked, after eating one, if I wanted a second'). In summer, drinks and tea are served in the garden. The sea is five minutes' walk away. (*P and JL, David Sulkin, and others*)

5 bedrooms. Town centre. Closed early Jan–mid-Mar, Christmas. Restaurant closed Tues. Lounge, bar, restaurant (background music). Small garden. Unsuitable for &. No smoking. Guide dogs only. MasterCard, Visa accepted. B&B £40–£47 per person; D,B&B £67–£74. Full alc £35. 1-night bookings occasionally refused peak season, and Sat.

'Set lunch/dinner' indicates fixed-price meals, with ample, limited or no choice on the menu. 'Full alc' is the hotel's estimated price per person of a three-course *à la carte* meal, with a half bottle of house wine. 'Alc' is the price of an *à la carte* meal excluding the cost of wine.

PENMYNYDD Gwynedd   Map 3:A3

Neuadd Lwyd   **NEW**   *Tel/Fax* 01248-715005
Penmynydd, nr Llanfairpwllgwyngyll   *Email* post@neuaddlwyd.co.uk
Anglesey LL61 5BX   *Website* www.neauddlwyd.co.uk

Set amid farmland, and looking over fields towards Bangor and the
Snowdonia mountains, this Victorian rectory was turned into a small,
upmarket guest house by Susannah and Peter Woods. They are proud of
the Welsh atmosphere. Inspectors in 2006 were enchanted: 'Lovely house,
spotlessly clean, beautifully furnished, warm and friendly.' Spacious rooms
and bright interiors combine with Victorian details. 'Lots of pictures;
attractive chandeliers.' From the terrace and the comfortable bay-
windowed lounge (binoculars provided) you can admire the 'wonderful'
views while consuming fruitcake, warm from the oven. 'Our lovely
bedroom had white-painted cast iron bedstead and furniture, pink-and-
white wallpaper, original black slate fireplace. Lots of local information,
free-range coat hangers, a striking bathroom (white floorboards and tiles;
bath recessed behind an arch).' Susannah Woods and Delyth Gwynedd,
who both trained at the Ballymaloe cookery school in Ireland, use local
ingredients for their 'superb' no-choice, four-course dinner, served at
'beautifully laid' tables. 'Very good sea bass with saffron sauce.' 'Lovely
cheeses.' 'First-class breakfast: fresh orange juice, melon, home-made
preserves, creamy scrambled eggs, Welsh rarebit. When we left, everyone
came out to say goodbye.' The Woodses hold a key to the adjacent church.
The village is the birthplace of ancestors of the Tudor monarchs.

4 bedrooms. 3 miles W of Menai Bridge. Train: Bangor. Closed Sun/Mon (except
bank holiday Sun). Drawing room, lounge, dining room; background music at night.
6-acre grounds. Unsuitable for &. No smoking. No children under 12. No dogs.
MasterCard, Visa accepted. B&B: single £80–£100, double £135–£150; D,B&B:
single £115–£135, double £205–£220. Set dinner £35. New Year package.

PORTHKERRY Vale of Glamorgan   Map 3:E3

Egerton Grey   *Tel* 01446-711666
Porthkerry, nr Cardiff CF62 3BZ   *Fax* 01446-711690
                                       Email info@egertongrey.co.uk
                                       Website www.egertongrey.co.uk

In a wooded valley, this former Victorian rectory has a lovely terraced
garden looking towards a magnificent viaduct and the Bristol Channel
beyond. 'A good place,' said inspectors. 'We were impressed by the

welcome; the co-owner, Richard Morgan-Price, was called out of the dining room at a busy lunchtime. He shook hands, carried our bags and led us upstairs to our room.' Guests' names are placed on their bedroom door, house-party style. Most rooms are spacious; they have colourful wallpaper and fabrics, thick carpet, and antique or repro furniture. Some have beams, some a four-poster. Public rooms, some panelled, are filled with antiques and 'interesting old pictures'. Dinner, cooked by Katie Mitchell, is by candlelight in the former billiard room ('nice panelled walls but maddening background music'). The food is generally enjoyed, but one visitor this year was disappointed ('tough beef'). Breakfast has 'a nice choice of well-cooked classics'. The hotel is popular for functions: 'Beware of private parties at weekends taking up the best lounge space.' Small children are 'warmly welcomed'. No main roads are near, but planes at Cardiff airport, close by, bring some noise 'quite early in the morning'. (*SB, and others*)

10 bedrooms. 10 miles SW of Cardiff. 2 lounges, library, restaurant; classical background music; conservatory; private dining room; function facilities. 7-acre garden: croquet. Rock beach 400 yds; golf nearby. Only restaurant suitable for &. Civil wedding licence. Smoking in 1 lounge only. No dogs in public rooms. Amex, MasterCard, Visa accepted. B&B [2006]: single £90, double £130, suite £150. Set menus £10–£30. Christmas/New Year packages. 1-night bookings occasionally refused. **⋆V⋆**

PORTMEIRION Gwynedd   Map 3:B3

Portmeirion Hotel   *Tel* 01766-770000
Portmeirion LL48 6ET   *Fax* 01766-771331
                              Email stay@portmeirion-village.com
                              Website www.portmeirion-village.com

'As lovely as ever,' writes one returning visitor to this 'enchanting' Italianate village, created by Sir Clough Williams-Ellis on a private peninsula above an estuary on the Snowdonia coast: 'a lovely setting'. There are three areas of accommodation: the Victorian hotel on the shore; *Castell Deudraeth* (a turreted 1850s folly overlooking the estuary); and 17 cottages scattered around the village. The first has bright fabrics, furniture and ornaments from Rajasthan and a 'Mughal-style' bar. Its luxurious rooms include the Peacock suite (where Edward VIII once stayed), with 'vast marble fireplace' and 'bed so high that footstools are needed to climb into it'. *Castell Deudraeth* is the 'boutique' option, with 'striking, well-designed interiors'. Rooms in the village, each different, should be chosen carefully, as 'a ground-floor room can leave you vulnerable to curious eyes among the day visitors'. Praise in 2006: 'Service, setting and food all excellent; we loved the magical wood in the grounds with its subtle planting.' 'A blissful winter weekend; excellent; wonderful staff; very clean.' Meals are served in the main hotel dining room (which has 'unequalled views'), or more casually in *Castell Deudraeth*'s brasserie. Weddings can make the village noisy at weekends. (*CM, John and Theresa Stewart, H Brown, and others*)

14 bedrooms in hotel, 26 in village, 11 in *Castell Deudraeth*. Between Penrhyndeudraeth and Porthmadog. Free minibus service from Minffordd station. Hall, 3 lounges, 2 bars, restaurants (harpist sometimes), children's supper room; function room; beauty salon. No background music. 170-acre grounds: garden, heated swimming pool (May–Sept); spa, tennis, lakes, sandy beach. Free golf nearby. Civil wedding licence. Smoking allowed in some bedrooms, bar. Guide dogs only. All major credit cards accepted. B&B [2006]: single £153, double £188, suite £242. Breakfast £13.50. Set dinner £38.50. 2-day breaks. 3 days for the price of 2, 31 Oct– 13 Apr. Christmas/New Year packages.

PWLLHELI Gwynedd

Map 3:B2

Plas Bodegroes	*Tel* 01758-612363
Nefyn Road	*Fax* 01758-701247
Pwllheli LL53 5TH	*Email* gunna@bodegroes.co.uk
	Website www.bodegroes.co.uk

♜ *César award in 1992*

Visitors in 2006 'fell in love with' Chris and Gunna Chown's restaurant-with-rooms, a white Georgian house in wooded grounds on the Lleyn peninsula. Others found it 'restful, civilised and homely'. The Scandinavian-inspired interior is admired: 'The dining room is gorgeous: delightful illuminated display cabinets, polished wood floors, a wealth of serious works of art.' Chris Chown's 'culinary wizardry' (*Michelin* star) was 'mostly superlative' (eg, caramelised lamb breast with braised leeks and artichoke foam). 'The staff are utterly charming.' 'They made a huge fuss of our young Border terrier.' Bedrooms vary: larger ones have a four-poster. 'Ours, elegantly furnished, had comfortable beds and beautiful bedding, no tea tray or bathrobe.' Another room was 'not large enough for comfort'. Two rooms are in a cottage at the rear, facing a tranquil courtyard garden, with 'wonderful, fully blown clusters of roses climbing up the trellises'. Housekeeping may not always be perfect. The 'enjoyable breakfast' includes fresh orange juice, 'perfectly cooked hot dishes, very good toast'. A dissenter found service slow. Another visitor wrote: 'One or two warts, but these have to be forgiven when the overall picture is so pleasing.' (*Gill Trousdale, Mary Woods, and others*)

11 bedrooms. 1 mile W of Pwllheli. Open mid-Mar–mid-Nov. Closed Sun night/ Mon. Lounge, bar, breakfast room, restaurant (occasional background music). 5-acre grounds. Unsuitable for &. No smoking. No dogs in public rooms. MasterCard, Visa accepted. B&B £50–£85 per person. Set lunch (Sun) £17.50, dinner £40. Midweek breaks. 1-night bookings refused bank holidays, summer weekends.

RUTHIN Denbighshire *See SHORTLIST*   Map 3:A4

ST DAVID'S Pembrokeshire *See SHORTLIST* Map 3:D1

SKENFRITH Monmouthshire   Map 3:D4

The Bell at Skenfrith   *Tel* 01600-750235
Skenfrith NP7 8UH   *Fax* 01600-750525
Email enquiries@skenfrith.co.uk
Website www.skenfrith.co.uk

Q *César award in 2004*

'A complete surprise: an unpretentious pub that's also a terrific restaurant. It is cleverly but simply decorated, combining the old with the new.' A visitor this year agrees with previous praise for Janet and William Hutchings's 17th-century inn. In a tiny village in the wooded Monnow valley, it faces ruined Skenfrith Castle. Other reports describe it as 'expensive but likeable'. Regulars wrote: 'Standards kept up. A comfortable and comforting place to be.' Dissenters disliked their bedroom. The building has been 'cleverly modernised', while retaining 'the charm of the old Welsh inn'. Bedrooms, all with views of river or hills, are individually styled and have 'every comfort' (eg, CD- and DVD-player, Internet connection). 'Large bedroom, king-size bed, spacious bathroom well stocked with freebies.' Staff are found 'welcoming'. David Hill, the chef, serves 'well-constructed and presented' modern British dishes, and there is a large wine list, with 'a great choice of half bottles'. Children are welcomed (though under-eights are not allowed in the restaurant at night) and have their own organic menu. Huge breakfasts include freshly baked croissants. (*Richard Barrett, Ken and Mildred Edwards, Stephen and Jane Savery, and others*)

8 bedrooms. 9 miles W of Ross-on-Wye. Closed last week Jan/first week Feb, and Mon Nov–Mar. 2 bars, 2 restaurants. No background music. 1-acre grounds. River opposite. Quad biking; archery, go-karting, clay-pigeon shooting, fishing nearby.

Unsuitable for ♿. No smoking. No children under 8 in restaurant in evening. No dogs in restaurant. Amex, MasterCard, Visa accepted. B&B £50–£110 per person. Set Sun lunch £21.50; full alc £35. Christmas/New Year packages. 1-night bookings refused weekends.

SWANSEA *See SHORTLIST*   Map 3:E3

TALSARNAU Gwynedd   Map 3:B3

Maes-y-Neuadd   *Tel* 01766-780200
Talsarnau LL47 6YA   *Fax* 01766-780211
                    Email maes@neuadd.com
                    Website www.neuadd.com

Q *César award in 2003*

'My favourite hotel in Britain,' writes a fan returning in 2006 to this 'mansion in the meadow' (as the name translates), on a wooded hillside with views of Snowdonia and Cardigan Bay. Another comment: 'Two nights in appalling weather did not detract from its excellence.' The owners, Peter and Lynn Jackson and Peter Payne, are 'cheerful'. 'Staff, largely Polish, were attentive' (but one diner 'grew a little tired of being asked whether I'd enjoyed each course'). Lounges are 'lovely and bright'; the bar is 'rather dark'. There are oak beams, good antique and modern furniture, an ingle-nook fireplace, and 'caged canaries in the seating area'. The bedrooms (four are in a converted coach house) vary in style and size. One was thought to be in need of renovation, and one visitor found the lighting 'barely satisfactory', but views from the front rooms are 'excellent'. Peter Jackson is the chef, using local meat and vegetables organically grown on-site: guests are encouraged to visit the walled garden. 'Breakfasts the best we have enjoyed for many a year. A good selection of dishes both hot and cold. Three stars for serving real tea.' (*Gordon Hands, John Bowes, GC*)

16 bedrooms. 3 miles NE of Harlech. Lift. 2 lounges, bar, conservatory, restaurant; business facilities; terrace. No background music. 80-acre grounds. Civil wedding licence. No smoking: restaurant, lounge, bedrooms. Unsuitable for ♿. Dogs in coach house only. All major credit cards accepted. B&B [2006] £65–£117.50 per person. Set dinner £33–£37. 2/3-night breaks. Christmas/New Year packages.

Make sure the hotel has included VAT in the prices it quotes.

TALYLLYN Gwynedd   Map 3:B3

Tynycornel   *Tel* 01654-782282
Talyllyn, Tywyn   *Fax* 01654-782679
LL36 9AJ   *Email* reception@tynycornel.co.uk
                           Website www.tynycornel.co.uk

On the shore of 222-acre Lake Talyllyn, which it owns, this snug white-
fronted inn stands below Cader Idris, the mountain that marks the end of
the Snowdonia range. It has been a fishing hostelry for two centuries. 'It
deserves an entry for the location alone,' said one visitor. 'It was very
enjoyable, everyone was friendly, service was good.' The bedrooms are
'clean, well presented, though no extras in the bathrooms'. 'Ask for No. 8.'
The 'good, freshly cooked food' is liked: 'superb lamb shank; flavoursome
steak'. Wines are 'well priced and reasonably varied'. There is a gluten-
free/vegan menu. Breakfast has 'a good choice of teas, cereals, fruits, etc;
classic cooked dishes'. The lounge faces the lake and has an open fire and
paintings by the local bird artist Terence Lambert. Esoteric fly-fishing
stories abound in the bar; the lake has one of the few remaining natural

brown trout fisheries south of
Scotland. Tuition, tackle hire
and picnic lunches are offered;
there is a drying room and
freezer facilities. Reception
and the restaurant have been
refurbished this year, and six
new bedrooms were under
construction as we went to
press. More reports, please.

16 bedrooms. (6 more in late 2006.) 9 in annexe. Some on ground floor. 9 miles SW
of Dolgellau. Train: Machynlleth, 10 miles. Only restaurant open Christmas. Ramp.
Lounge, bar, restaurant, conservatory restaurant; background music at night; live
Welsh music sometimes; conference facilities; drying room. ½-acre grounds. Civil
wedding licence. No smoking. Dogs in kennels only. MasterCard, Visa accepted.
B&B [2006] £40–£73.50 per person. Set dinner £30; full alc £30. New Year
package. **⁕V⁕**

TREDUNNOCK Monmouthshire   Map 3:E4

The Newbridge   NEW   *Tel* 01633-451000
Tredunnock, nr Usk   *Fax* 01633 451001
NP15 1LY   *Email* eatandsleep@thenewbridge.co.uk
                                    Website www.thenewbridge.co.uk

By an old bridge on a bend of the River Usk, this country pub has 'been
given a new lease of life' as a restaurant-with-rooms; Iain Sampson is the
executive chef. 'Excellent. The surroundings are peaceful and bucolic,
the atmosphere relaxing,' say trusted *Guide* reporters, who were
impressed to be shown a room before booking, by the 'charming
Romanian front-of-house manager', Alex Pastrav. 'Our first-floor room
in the new, discreet annexe was light and spacious, with beams, solid oak
furniture, polished floors. The bed was large and firm; the huge
bathroom had roll-top bath and separate shower.' The main building has
bar with 'many different seating areas, comfy sofas, wooden chairs and
tables'. There are benches and tables in a riverside garden. 'Our dinner,
at a table overlooking the river, was excellent; an interesting menu with
local ingredients, the fish specials listed on a blackboard came from
Cornwall; the wine list also a winner, reasonably priced. A Welsh oak-
smoked haddock was full of flavour; good lemon sole with baby
vegetables.' Breakfast has a large buffet platter of cheese, meat and fresh
fruit; 'unfortunately orange juice not squeezed, a basket of home-baked
breads, well-made scrambled eggs'. (*Pat and Jeremy Temple*)

6 bedrooms. All in annexe, 30 yds. Some on ground floor. 5 miles S of Usk. Closed
26 Dec, 1 week early Jan. Lounge, bar, restaurant. No smoking. No dogs. All major
credit cards accepted. B&B [2006] £55–£110 per person; D,B&B £80–£130. Full
alc £35. *V*

* *

Traveller's tale We were met by a member of staff who was
polite but was on only her second day and knew little of proce-
dures. Our bedroom was cold. She told us that the system was on
a time clock and could not be advanced. When the heating finally
came on, the bathroom remained cold. The double bed was one
of the worst we have ever slept in. The dining room was sparse
and functional; our waiter was on his first day. Breakfast was
accompanied by loud Radio 2. Toast came with the cereal, so was
cold and tough when we wanted to eat it. (*Hotel in Somerset*)

* *

TREMADOG Gwynedd   Map 3:B3

Plas Tan-Yr-Allt   *Tel* 01766-514545
Tremadog, nr Porthmadog   *Email* info@tanyrallt.co.uk
LL49 9RG   *Website* www.tanyrallt.co.uk

Colloquially known as 'Tanny', this Grade II listed house, overlooking the Glaslyn estuary, was once the home of Shelley, who described it as 'tasty enough for the villa of an Italian prince'. Now it is a boutique hotel run by Michael Bewick and Nick Golding, who aim for an 'informal house-party atmosphere'. Inspectors reported: 'In the striking red-painted hall, Percy, the parrot in a cage, says "Hello", and there are "ghost" plastic chairs by Philippe Starck. The lounge, more traditional, has sofas and comfy armchairs around a blazing fire, interesting pictures and prints, and lots of decorative items.' Each bedroom is different: 'Ours, Madocks, had domed ceiling, stunning views, white paintwork, huge modern chandelier, metal-framed bed (very comfortable), settee, TV/DVD-player. The stunning bathroom had heated slate floor, white-tiled walls, modern chrome fittings.' Guests dine together at a huge refectory table after drinks in the lounge. 'Nick is the chef, and a jolly good one' (main courses like steak poached in Barolo with celeriac purée). Breakfast, 'another social affair', includes 'a local sausage fry-up'. Food is locally sourced and water comes from the house's spring. 'We very much enjoyed our stay.'

6 bedrooms. 1 mile N of Porthmadog. Closed Christmas, 2 weeks Feb. Drawing room, library, dining room. No background music. 47-acre grounds. Unsuitable for &. Smoking in library only. No children under 16. No dogs. Amex, MasterCard, Visa accepted. B&B: single £70–£100, double £95–£130. Set dinner £30. New Year package. 1-night bookings refused weekends Apr–Oct.

WHITEBROOK Monmouthshire   Map 3:D4

The Crown at Whitebrook   *Tel* 01600-860254
Whitebrook, nr Monmouth   *Fax* 01600-860607
NP25 4TX   *Email* info@crownatwhitebrook.co.uk
                                        Website www.crownatwhitebrook.co.uk

'In a wonderful position in the Wye valley', this restaurant-with-rooms stands amid woods near Monmouth. Recent visitors found the food 'outstandingly good'. Another couple wrote: 'We were well treated in a comfortable environment.' The 'light and simple decor' is admired. Chef James Sommerin describes his cooking as 'modern British with French flair', eg, wild mushroom and truffle tortellini with artichoke velouté; duck breast with shallot marmalade and bubblegum panna cotta. The wine list is 250 strong (plenty of half bottles). Public rooms in the 17th-century inn have wood fires; bedrooms, in a 20th-century extension, have 'the latest technological advancements' (Internet facilities, flat-screen TV, etc), as well as extensive views. All bathrooms have under-floor heating; those in the suites have a walk-in power shower and a double-ended bath. Michael Obray recently took over as general manager. 'Tintern Abbey, just three miles down the road, notwithstanding its crowded coach and car parks, still delivers a genuine Wordsworthian experience.' (*DCT, and others*)

8 bedrooms. 6 miles S of Monmouth. Closed Christmas/New Year and Mon. Lounge/bar, restaurant; varied background music; business facilities. 2-acre garden. River Wye 2 miles, fishing. Unsuitable for &. No smoking: restaurant, bedrooms. No dogs. MasterCard, Visa accepted. B&B single £60–£85, double £75–£120, suite £100–£120. Set meals £17.50–£37.50. *V*

CHANNEL ISLANDS

Close to Normandy, these *Îles Anglo-Normandes*, as the French call them, have a distinct French flavour, notably in their cooking of lunch and dinner (breakfast tends to be boldly British). Two of our entries (one a *César* winner) are long-time favourites on car-free Sark; a third is on the tiny island of Herm. The sumptuous *Longueville Manor*, in St Saviour, with its *Michelin*-starred restaurant, returns this year after a time with no reports, and we are grateful to the correspondents who wrote a detailed report on *Fleur du Jardin* on Guernsey, enabling us to promote it from the Shortlist.

Hotel Petit Champ, Sark

CASTEL Guernsey   Map 1:D5

Cobo Bay Hotel   NEW   *Tel* 01481-257102
Cobo Coast Road   *Fax* 01481-254542
Castel   *Email* reservations@cobobayhotel.com
GY5 7HB   *Website* www.cobobayhotel.com

By 'spectacular' Cobo Beach, on Guernsey's west coast, David and Julie
Nussbaumer's modern hotel faces an 'attractive rock-strewn beach'. 'Staff
were welcoming and helpful,' writes the nominator. 'Our room, though not
large, had all one expects nowadays: attractive bathroom, comfortable beds
with duvets, etc.' Pre-dinner drinks are taken in a large lounge with dark
red leather settees. In the 'large, attractive' restaurant that faces the sea
('views of sunsets'), 'dinners were highly enjoyable. Plenty of choice for
each of three courses. Main courses tended towards fussiness in presentation but were of excellent quality. Two or three fish dishes; also steak,
Aylesbury duck, rack of lamb. Unpretentious wine list; house wine at £9.95
a bottle. Breakfast well up to standard. A comprehensive and well-
organised bus service, which stops close by the hotel, enabled us to see
much of this charming island.' Fourteen of the bedrooms have sea views.
Some rooms have a balcony. There are three golf courses within three
miles. (*Donald J Barnes*)

36 bedrooms. 1 suitable for &. 3 miles from St Peters Port, on main coast road on
W coast. Closed 1 Jan–28 Feb. Lift. Lounge with bar, TV room, restaurant; back-
ground CDs/radio 7am–11pm; function room; health suite: whirlpool, sauna, etc.
Front outdoor sitting area. No smoking in restaurant. No dogs. Amex, MasterCard,
Visa accepted. B&B £34–£79 per person; D,B&B £49–£94. Set meals £22. Special
break: 7 nights for the price of 6. Christmas/New Year packages.

HERM   Map 1:D6

The White House   *Tel* 01481-722159
Herm, via Guernsey GY1 3HR   *Fax* 01481-710066
                               Email hotel@herm-island.com
                                 Website www.herm-island.com

� *César award in 1987*

This beautiful, tiny island (about a mile long; fewer than 100 inhabitants)
has neither cars nor TV. 'Extremely peaceful, particularly when the day-
trippers have left', it has birdwatching, shell gathering, bathing, fishing, high
cliffs, a little harbour, pastel-painted cottages, three shops, an inn, a 10th-
century chapel. This low, white building, by a beach, is its only hotel.

Owned by Adrian and Pennie Heyworth, it is managed by Jonathan Watson with an 'efficient young staff from around the world'. Guests are met at the boat: many are regulars. Neighbouring islands are visible from the lounge (which has board games and free self-help tea and coffee). Many bedrooms are suites, with a second room with a bunk bed. Spacious cottage rooms have small garden and balcony. The four-course dinner provided by Neil Southgate is enjoyed: 'Excellent main courses, good choice of puddings.' 'A varied wine list. As you dine, you watch the sun setting over Guernsey.' The light lunch is 'ample and good'. 'Blessedly, no muzak in the main house.' 'Exceptional value.' The bedrooms lack 'upmarket extras' like bathrobes, minibar and telephone, but there is baby-listening, plenty of storage space, and an evening turn-down service. (*N and JJ*)

40 bedrooms. 16 in 3 cottages. Some on ground floor. By harbour. Air/sea to Guernsey; ferry to Guernsey (20 mins). Open 30 Mar–7 Oct. 3 lounges, 2 bars (background music in *Ship Bar*), carvery, restaurant; conference room. 1-acre garden: tennis, croquet, 20-ft solar-heated swimming pool; beach 200 yds. On 300-acre island: boating, fishing, snorkelling. Herm unsuitable for &. No smoking: restaurant, 1 lounge. No children under 9 in restaurant at night (high teas provided). Guide dogs only. Amex, MasterCard, Visa accepted. D,B&B [2006] £73–£110 per person. Set menu £24; full alc £23.50.

KING'S MILLS Guernsey

Map 1:D5

Fleur du Jardin   NEW

King's Mills, nr Castel
Guernsey GY5 7JT

Tel 01481-257996
Fax 01481-256834
Email info@fleurdujardin.net
Website www.fleurdujardin.guernsey.net

'The erudite and charming Keith Read runs an admirable ship,' says an enthusiastic report in 2006, promoting this 'delightful' hotel from the Shortlist. In a 'lovely, peaceful village', the old stone building, once a working farmhouse, has been well updated, retaining low beams (tall visitors should mind their head in the bar, which serves local real ale), granite walls and open fires. Named for a prizewinning Guernsey cow (her portrait can be seen), the hotel stands in a 'lovely flowered garden, well tended even in February' with swimming pool. The food is found 'excellent; very good value: super grilled cheese starter; superb fish, local scallops and shellfish; unforgettable chocolate pudding. Interesting wine selection, 19 available by the glass. A superb, cheerful team of staff. Our well-appointed bedroom had a modern bathroom. If you don't want to hire a car, Reception will find a knowledgeable local taxi driver to take you to places of interest.' A bus stops at the door ('50p gets you round the island'),

and bicycles can be hired. There is a two-bedroom suite with lounge and kitchen. 'Perfect for a "get-away-from-it-all" break at any time of year.' (*Doris and John Anderson; also Stephen Holman*)

17 bedrooms. SW of Castel. Lounge, 2 bars, restaurant; background music throughout. 2-acre garden: heated swimming pool. No smoking: restaurant, bedrooms. Guide dogs only. B&B [2006] £39–£58 per person; D,B&B £21 added.

ST BRELADE Jersey   Map 1:E6

St Brelade's Bay Hotel   *Tel* 01534-746141
St Brelade JE3 8EF   *Fax* 01534-747278
                             Email info@stbreladesbayhotel.com
                             Website www.stbreladesbayhotel.com

A 'wonderful place for a family holiday'. All generations are kept happy, say fans of this 'large, glamorous' hotel. 'Luxurious throughout', it is run by Robert Colley (the fifth-generation owner/managing director) with manager Claire Scott. 'Staff are friendly'; 'we were looked after marvellously,' are recent comments. The long, white, modern building, flower-bedecked in summer, faces the sea on Jersey's loveliest bay: the 'beautiful beach' is across the road. Elegant public rooms have parquet floors, moulded ceilings, chandeliers, oriental rugs and formal flower arrangements. Loungers stand on wide lawns near the freshwater swimming pools. In summer, alfresco lunches are served. Bedrooms are spacious; front ones have a balcony and views over the bay; second-floor ones above the kitchen can be noisy. There are communicating family rooms, cots, high chairs, a children's playroom, etc (see below). Small children have tea at 5.15–6 pm: they must not be in the restaurant after 7. Franz Hacker, the chef, keeps guests happy with his 'fantastic' six-course dinners, and the English breakfast is thought 'superb'. 'Smart casual' clothing is expected in the restaurant, and mobile phones are 'not welcome' in public rooms and gardens. More reports, please.

76 bedrooms. 5 miles W of St Helier. Bus from St Helier. Open end Apr–beginning Oct. Lift, ramp. 2 lounges, cocktail bar (evening entertainment: singers, disco, magician, etc, daily except Sun); restaurant; toddlers' room, games room, snooker room; sun veranda. 7-acre grounds: outdoor restaurant, 2 heated swimming pools (1 for children) with bar and grill; sauna, mini-gym; tennis, croquet, putting, *boules*, children's play area. Beach across road. Golf nearby. Smoking in bar only. No dogs. Amex, MasterCard, Visa accepted. B&B £55–£114 per person; D,B&B £80–£139. Set menu £35; full alc £45.

There is no VAT in the Channel Islands.

ST MARTIN'S Guernsey *See SHORTLIST*   Map 1:E5

ST SAVIOUR Jersey   Map 1:E6

Longueville Manor   NEW   *Tel* 01534-725501
Longueville Road   *Fax* 01534-731613
St Saviour JE2 7WF   *Email* info@longuevillemanor.com
    Website www.longuevillemanor.com

'A pleasant air of confidence', says a report this year, pervades Jersey's most sumptuous hotel (Relais & Châteaux). The 'beautifully kept', extended 13th-century manor house stands inland from St Helier, in wide grounds by a lovely wooded valley. Malcolm Lewis is the 'always attentive' third-generation owner, Andrew Baird the *Michelin*-starred chef. 'Excellent dishes, some with ingredients from the garden (there must have been a glut of artichokes).' Other comments: 'A superb cheese trolley', 'wonderful vegetarian dishes'. There is a 400-strong wine list (mark-ups may be high). Meals are served in a large, light room facing the garden, or a darker panelled one. The decor is smart – swagged curtains, oriental rugs, original paintings, antiques, repro furniture, but the atmosphere is 'unstuffy'. 'Guests share the reception rooms with the house cats and dogs.' 'Obliging staff dealt with everything with military precision but no loss of approachability. Our bedroom was lavishly decorated: comfortable chair in front of fireplace, just like home. Breakfast was a relaxed affair; a wide choice of cooked dishes, proper tea.' Lunches and afternoon teas are served by the swimming pool. The Royal Jersey Golf Club is near. Day-trips to France are arranged. (*Jane White*)

31 bedrooms. 8 on ground floor. 1 mile E of St Helier by A3. Double-glazed windows throughout. Lift. 2 lounges, bar, 2 dining rooms (1 no-smoking); function/conference facilities. No background music. 16-acre grounds: woodland, croquet, tennis, heated swimming pool. Golf, bowls, squash nearby; sea 1 mile. Wedding facilities. All major credit cards accepted. B&B [2006] £115–£400 per person; D,B&B £160–£490. Set menus £55 and £95; full alc £62.50. Winter weekend breaks. Christmas/New Year packages.

SARK   Map 1:E6

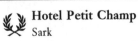

Hotel Petit Champ	*Tel* 01481-832046
Sark	*Fax* 01481-832469
via Guernsey GY9 0SF	*Email* info@hotelpetitchamp.co.uk
	Website www.hotelpetitchamp.co.uk

César award: Island hotel of the year

'Our 11th visit. It gets better and better.' 'The perfect place to relax.'
Enthusiasm again for Caroline and Chris Robins's 'delightful' small hotel
on little Sark's west coast. A late Victorian granite building, 'cosy, bright',
and well modernised, it stands alone on a headland (superb views,
spectacular sunsets). There is regular praise for the 'most welcoming'
owners, the 'old-fashioned values', and the cooking. Chef Tony Atkins
specialises in local lobster and crab. 'Interesting menus, good-quality
ingredients'; 'portions are never too big'. The wine list 'lacks greedy mark-
ups'. Breakfast has ample choice and a weather forecast on each table. 'Our
bedroom with balcony, well decorated, had generous storage and a lovely
view.' 'Good housekeeping: rooms done during breakfast, beds turned down
at night.' There are 'plenty of lounges where one can lose oneself'. Games,
puzzles, etc, are supplied for children. Tips are not expected. A secluded
beach, sandy at low tide, is a steep walk down from the hotel; many other
safe beaches are near. No cars on Sark, but the hotel's visitors can be met
by a horse and carriage, and bicycles can be hired. (*Alan Lyne, HJ Martin
Tucker, and many others*)

10 bedrooms. 15 mins' walk from village. Open Apr–early Oct. 3 sun lounges,
library lounge, TV room, cocktail bar (background CDs), restaurant. 1-acre garden:
solar-heated swimming pool (40 by 15 ft), putting, croquet. Sark unsuitable for &.
No smoking: restaurant, library lounge. 'Children must be old enough to sit with
parents at dinner (approx. 7 yrs).' Guide dogs welcomed, otherwise no dogs in
bedrooms or restaurant. All major credit cards accepted. B&B £42.75–£54.25 per
person; D,B&B £58.75. Sun lunch £12.25, set dinner £20.25; full alc £29.75. **•V•**

La Sablonnerie	*Tel* 01481-832061
Little Sark	*Fax* 01481-832408
Sark, via Guernsey GY9 0SD	

In a quiet southern corner of the island, reached by an isthmus, stands
Elizabeth Perrée's much-loved hotel, 'stylish, idiosyncratic', 'run with
gusto'. Its white walls are festooned with bushes and flowers; indoors are
low ceilings and oak beams, a bar with log fire; the grounds are 'lovely';
cows graze opposite the front door. The 'consistently high standards' are

regularly admired by visitors to this 'place of many delights'. 'The enthusiastic, young, multi-ethnic staff all seemed to want us to have fun.' The food is admired (eg, savarin of red mullet with a chive tapenade sauce; venison with fricassée of oyster mushrooms). There is a separate lobster menu. Many ingredients come from the home farm. Breakfasts can start with champagne, and include continental or 'freshly cooked Sark Breakfast' (porridge with cream; eggs, kippers, etc). The tea room serves 'very good lunches'. The bedrooms are thought 'charming but not luxurious': some are reached through a tiny door in the bar; some spacious ones are in cottages. Weddings are held. You should pack rubber-soled shoes for bathing from rocks or shingle, a torch for caving, a dress or tie for dinner. Nearby are the natural pools of Venus and Adonis, cliffs, coves, sandy beaches. More reports, please.

22 bedrooms. Some no-smoking. Some in cottages. S part of island. Boat from Guernsey; hotel will meet. Open Easter–Oct. 3 lounges, 2 bars (background music), restaurant. 1-acre garden: tea garden/bar, croquet. Sark unsuitable for &. Dogs at hotel's discretion; not in public rooms. Amex, MasterCard, Visa accepted. B&B (*excluding 10% service charge*) £40–£77 per person; D,B&B £51.50–£89.50; full board £61.50–£94.50. Set menu £22.80; full alc £38.50.

IRELAND

Some of the *Guide*'s favourite hotels are in Ireland,
which has always been fruitful ground for travellers
seeking small, individually run establishments.
You might find that, even in the far west,
the staff these days are recruited from all corners
of Europe; but the warmth of the welcome remains
truly Irish. In many of the smaller places,
you will be received as a friend of the family and
given an insight into the Irish way of life.

The Mill, Dunfanaghy

ADARE Co. Limerick   Map 6:D5

Dunraven Arms   *Tel* 00 353 61-396633
Fax 00 353 61-396541
Email reservations@dunravenhotel.com
Website www.dunravenhotel.com

'If you play golf, hunt or fish, this is the place for you,' says a 2006 visitor to this much-expanded, yellow-fronted coaching inn, 'charmingly located' in this pretty village. 'A cracking hotel. Growing in size but it retains a personal touch' (12 bedrooms were added in 2005, making it large for the *Guide*). The owners, Brian and Louis Murphy, 'are very much in charge'. 'Nice atmosphere, pleasant staff,' affirms our inspector. 'Proprietor on hand at breakfast' (this was 'fine, with proper butter and jam, linen serviettes'). Bedrooms are in several wings, along 'long corridors hung with hunting and equestrian prints'. 'Our spacious suite lacked charm but had everything the traveller could need' (lots of storage space, apples, whiskey; slippers provided with the evening turn-down). In the 'well-managed', 'splendidly old-fashioned' *Maigue* restaurant, 'the atmosphere is lively', and 'the food is first rate'. 'A generous helping of roast rib of beef, cooked just as required, from a silver trolley. Hot chocolate pudding, equally pleasing. All the staff (mainly French or Polish) were well trained.' There are small lounges 'for quiet reading', and a leisure centre. Guests can hunt with the famous local packs. Salmon and trout fishing are nearby. (*Mike Hutton, and others*)

76 bedrooms. In village, 10 miles SW of Limerick. Private parking. Lift. Lounge, writing room, TV room, residents' bar (pianist at weekends), public bar, restaurant, conservatory; conference/function facilities; leisure centre: 50-ft swimming pool, steam room, gym. 3-acre gardens. River, fishing, golf, riding, fox-hunting nearby. No smoking. No dogs. All major credit cards accepted. (*Excluding 12½% service charge*) Room [2006]: single €180, double €195, suite €335. Breakfast €20. Full alc €50.

AUGHRIM Co. Wicklow   Map 6:C6

Clone House   *Tel* 00 353 402-36121
Fax 00 353 402-36029
Email stay@clonehouse.com
Website www.clonehouse.com

The personality of the owner, Carla Edigati from Florence, is pervasive at this rambling converted farmhouse, ochre coloured and 200 years old, in the pretty Wicklow hills. She runs it as a guest house with her Californian husband Jeff Watson (they met in America). 'She seems to do everything indoors, helped by two female staff,' said our inspector, 'while Jeff looks after the large garden.' There is a 'good atmosphere' in the house, which has period furnishings, strong colours, wooden floors, a reading room, a small bar, a large 'snug' with old Irish artefacts. Guests are expected to dine in. 'Tasty nibbles' are served in the lounge, before dinner in the green-walled dining room. Using organic ingredients from the garden, the hostess serves Tuscan dishes on a five-course menu, eg, black risotto with squid and chilli; veal, porcini mushrooms, cream sauce. 'Good if expensive,' was one verdict. Most of the bedrooms have a log or peat fire; all have views of the surrounding mountains. There are canopied beds and modern bathrooms (not all are *en suite*). Breakfast has 'better than average fare' (pain au chocolat, etc). In the gardens are a pond, a creek, stone walls, 'thousands of flowers'. More reports, please.

7 bedrooms. 2 miles SW of Aughrim. Train: Rathdrum/Arklow; taxi. Drawing room, library, music room, dining room (background music: classical/soft); function facilities; gym, sauna. 4½-acre grounds. Riding, fishing, golf nearby. Unsuitable for &. No smoking. No dogs. MasterCard, Visa accepted. B&B €70–€100 per person. Set dinner (*10% non-discretionary service charge added*) €55–€66. 1-night advance bookings refused bank holiday Sat.

BAGENALSTOWN Co. Carlow   Map 6:D6

Lorum Old Rectory   *Tel* 00 353 59-977 5282
Kilgreaney   *Fax* 00 353 59-977 5455
                                  Email bobbie@lorum.com
                                  Website www.lorum.com

Bobbie Smith, the owner of this rectory, built of local granite in 1863, 'knows every inch' of the rolling land at the foot of Mount Leinster and, 'it seems, every inhabitant'. She is 'helpful, genuinely interested in her guests, never gushing', said the nominators of this 'uniquely wonderful place'. On a chilly afternoon, 'we were soon in another world, sitting in front of a crackling log fire, taking tea and delicious scones, hot from the kitchen. Each of the bedrooms is perfectly proportioned, and has a spacious *en suite* bathroom cleverly added. Bobbie has an eye for colour, and our four-poster bed was artfully draped without being fussy.' Bobbie Smith is a member of Euro-Toques, a European community of cooks dedicated to using local and organic produce. Dinner, served at a large mahogany table in the red dining room, included 'sublime fennel soup; superb rack of lamb roasted in a pesto coating'. The award-winning breakfast has a 'good full Irish, home-baked breads, much fruit – and the feeling that you have all day to enjoy it'. Nearby are the gardens at Kilfane, Woodstock and Altamont. (*A and JA*)

5 bedrooms. 4 miles S of Bagenalstown on R705 to Borris. Open Mar–Nov. Drawing room, bar, dining room. 1-acre garden: croquet. Unsuitable for &. No smoking. Children by arrangement. No dogs in bedrooms. Amex, MasterCard, Visa accepted. B&B €75–€80 per person. Set dinner €45. 10% discount for stays of more than 3 nights.

BALLYCASTLE Co. Mayo   Map 6:B4

Stella Maris   **NEW**

Tel 00 353 96-43322
Fax 00 353 96-43265
Email info@stellamarisireland.com
Website www.stellamarisireland.com

'I cannot recall staying in a hotel as close to the sea. All you hear is wind and waves,' says the nominator of this converted 19th-century coastguard station at the end of a cul-de-sac in north Mayo. It was bought four years ago as a near ruin by Frances Kelly, a local who has lived in the United States, and her American husband, Terence McSweeney. Their 'most inspired idea' was to build a hundred-foot conservatory along the front of the building: it has 'uninterrupted views to Downpatrick Head'. They are 'convivial hosts'. He 'dispenses drinks and conversation with laid-back ease', she is 'an accomplished cook: first-class beef, lamb and fish, all locally sourced; though the same vegetables were served every night. The wine list is a model of what a short list should be. But the constant background music was irritating.' Bedrooms, each named after a golf course, 'are not large'; there is a suite at one end of the building. 'Our room was plainish but comfortable; lots of hot water in the bathroom.' Breakfast ('very good')

 has fresh orange juice, fruit platter, home-made preserves, 'high-quality' cooked dishes. Mr McSweeney, who works for the US PGA during the winter, can advise on nearby golf courses. The local terrain is 'hauntingly beautiful'. (*Ann Walden, and others*)

12 bedrooms. 1½ miles W of village, 16½ miles NW of Ballina. Open Apr–end Oct. Restaurant closed to non-residents on Mon. Ramps. Lounge, bar, restaurant, conservatory; background music throughout. 3-acre grounds. Golf, sea/freshwater fishing, sandy beach nearby. No smoking. No dogs. MasterCard, Visa accepted. B&B: single €145, double €190, suite €400. Full alc €55.

BALLYCOTTON Co. Cork   Map 6:D5

Bayview Hotel   *Tel* 00 353 21-464 6746
                                          Fax 00 353 21-464 6075
                              Email res@thebayviewhotel.com
                              Website www.thebayviewhotel.com

Long, low and white, Carmel and John O'Brien's holiday hotel stands in
well-tended gardens on the edge of cliffs, above a little fishing harbour; the
manager is Stephen Belton. All bedrooms have sea views (some take in the
picturesque harbour); they are 'clean and modern', if 'unremarkable', with
'nice touches; beds turned down during dinner; bottles of mineral water;
classy toiletries'. The better rooms have full-length windows, a small
balcony; those on the second floor are smaller, 'attic style' with dormer
windows. The hotel has long been liked by readers, though one recent
reporter thought it 'looked unloved' and hated the 'intrusive taped music
in all public areas'. Another wrote of a 'lack of direction'. The modern
cooking of Ciaran Scully in the hotel's *Capricho* restaurant is praised: 'some
of the best I've had in Ireland'; 'very good, if stylised'. Dishes might include
'fishy, fishy, fishy' (brochette of salmon, deep-fried prawns, smoked tuna
with wasabi mayonnaise); loin of lamb with aubergine caviar. The breakfast
menu lists the local suppliers of the ingredients; it has 'good fresh bread,
scones, compote of rhubarb; high-quality bacon, sausages, fish options' but
'poor toast and coffee'.

35 bedrooms. 4 on ground floor. Village centre, near harbour. 20 miles SE of Cork
city. Open Apr–Oct. Lift. 2 lounges, bar, restaurant; Irish and classical background
music; 2 meeting rooms. 1-acre grounds. Access to public (rock) beach. No smoking:
public rooms, some bedrooms. No dogs. All major credit cards accepted. B&B [2006]
€79–€111 per person; D,B&B €110. Set lunch €28; full alc €50. 2- and 3-night rates.

BALLYLICKEY Co. Cork   Map 6:D4

Seaview House   *Tel* 00 353 27-50073
Ballylickey, Bantry Bay   *Fax* 00 353 27-51555
                              Email info@seaviewhousehotel.com
                              Website www.seaviewhousehotel.com

'A very comfortable holiday hotel, with good-sized rooms, nice food, and
attentive service.' Renewed praise this year for Kathleen O'Sullivan's
extended, white, bay-windowed Victorian house in a quiet west Cork village.
She was born in the house and, says another visitor, she 'runs it with loving
care; her dedication shows. Our bedroom in the main house was not

particularly smart; the bathroom was old-fashioned. But it had style and a homely feel, unlike so many hotel rooms.' A large bedroom in the new wing, with under-floor heating in the bathroom, was also enjoyed. Rooms at the top of the house have 'great views of Bantry Bay'. The food, served in an attractive restaurant with a conservatory extension, is a 'highlight'; Eleanor O'Donovan's daily-changing five-course dinner menu, with extensive choice, has 'wonderful fish (especially Dover sole) and lamb'. 'The choice at breakfast was especially good.' There's a library with books in mahogany cases, and a lounge with an open fire, flowers, antiques, paintings and ornaments. 'The gardens, beautifully maintained, are full of colour, a real suntrap.' Children get special meals, games and reduced rates. (*P and JL, and others*)

25 bedrooms. 2 on ground floor suitable for &. 3 miles N of Bantry. Open 15 Mar–15 Nov. Lounge bar, library/TV room, restaurant/conservatory. No background music. 5-acre grounds on waterfront: fishing, boating; riding, golf nearby. Smoking in some bedrooms only. No dogs in public rooms. All major credit cards accepted. B&B €85–€105 per person. Full alc €50. Special breaks. ***V*** (only on bookings at full rack rate)

BALLYVAUGHAN Co. Clare   Map 6:C4

Gregans Castle   *Tel* 00 353 65-707 7005
                                             Fax 00 353 65-707 7111
                                             Email stay@gregans.ie
                                             Website www.gregans.ie

For 30 years, the Haden family have owned this country house hotel on a hill above Galway Bay; Simon Haden, of the second generation, and his wife, Frederieke, are its managers. It is liked for the 'authentically Irish feel': turf fires burning constantly; paintings and photographs of local characters in the hall and drawing room. Wi-Fi Internet access is available, but not television: 'Our guests come for the peace and quiet,' says Mr Haden. Our inspector enjoyed the 'magical rock scenery' of the Burren from her window. 'Comfort was total: good mahogany furniture, bathrooms well fitted.' In the elegant dining room, which has a glorious view of the bay, smart casual dress is required. Adrian O'Farrell's modern Irish cooking has French influences, eg, slow-braised cheek of beef, wild mushroom crépinette; grilled halibut, mango and buttermilk risotto. Vegetarians are catered for. The long wine list includes organic and 'biodynamic' wines. Small children are fed at 7 pm. There is live classical harp or piano music during dinner, and a pianist plays Irish folk and jazz in the *Corkscrew Bar*. Guided walks of the Burren, and day trips to the Aran Islands can be arranged. More reports, please.

21 bedrooms. Some on ground floor. On N67, 3½ miles SW of Ballyvaughan. Open 31 Mar–31 Oct. Radio on request; no TV. Hall, lounge/library, bar, dining room. No background music (live harp 3 nights a week). 13-acre grounds: ornamental pool, croquet. Safe sandy beach 4½ miles; golf, riding, hill walking nearby. No smoking. Dogs in stables only. Amex, MasterCard, Visa accepted. B&B: single €130–€180, double €180–€225, suite €270–€420. Full alc €59. 2- and 3-night breaks.

BELFAST   Map 6:B6

Ash-Rowan   *Tel* 028-9066 1758
12 Windsor Avenue   *Fax* 028-9066 3227
Belfast BT9 6EE

'Minimalists would be horrified' by the 'charming, cluttered decor' of Evelyn and Sam Hazlett's well-known Victorian house in a 'lovely quiet situation' on a leafy avenue near Queen's University. 'It's like living in an upmarket antiques shop,' writes an inspector. Walls are covered with pictures, prints and china. The conservatory/sitting room has newspapers, as well as old copies of the *Picture Post*. The best rooms are the larger doubles on the top floor (one has a bath); one of the smaller bedrooms was not liked this year: 'A cramped, tiny, cold bathroom.' And some redecoration may be needed. But the linen sheets and lace-trimmed pillowcases are liked ('One sleeps so well'). Breakfast, ordered the night before, 'to permit the soaking of the porridge oats in Drambuie', is 'yummy; a delicious lemon-lime drink, home-made wheaten bread, and an individual cafetière'. Cooked dishes include kedgeree; mushrooms sautéed in cream and sherry. The Hazletts, former restaurateurs, will serve a three-course meal by arrangement. 'There is little demand,' they say, 'for we are surrounded by excellent restaurants': menus for some are displayed in the conservatory. Popular with university visitors and musicians.

5 bedrooms. Just off Lisburn road, 1½ miles SW of centre. Car park, buses. Closed Christmas. Lounge, dining room, conservatory. No background music. ⅓-acre garden. Unsuitable for &. No smoking. No children under 12. No dogs. MasterCard, Visa accepted. (*5% service charge added*) B&B: single £56–£66, double £79–£96. Evening meal (by arrangement) £45.

See also SHORTLIST

Inevitably, some hotels change hands or close after we have gone to press. It is prudent to check the ownership when booking, particularly in the case of small establishments.

BLACKLION Co. Cavan   Map 6:B5

MacNean House   **NEW**   *Tel* 00 353 7198 53022
Main Street   *Fax* 00 353 7198 53404

Blacklion may be an unremarkable border village, but this plain town
house, opposite the Garda station, has special status in Irish gastronomic
circles. It is the family home of Neven Maguire, Ireland's best-known
celebrity chef; here he runs a small restaurant with six simple rooms above.
Our inspector was enchanted by the quality of the cooking: 'A plate of
delicious hot herb breads with a herb dip was followed by an *amuse-bouche*
of pumpkin; the waitresses were attentive without being in your face.' Mr
Maguire uses locally sourced produce that he champions in his writing for
his modern dishes, eg, seared scallops with black pudding sausage; assiette
of rare breed pork (caramelised belly, peppered fillet). There is a 'serious'
wine list. Bedrooms are simple, 'warm and homely, perfectly comfortable;
hot water in the bathroom'. At a 'fine' breakfast, 'Neven Maguire came for
a long chat; he is charming and modest'. Children are welcomed. 'No
lounge, so not for an extended stay.'

6 bedrooms. Centre of village on N16 Belfast–Sligo. Closed 2 weeks Christmas,
1 week Oct, Mon–Wed (off-season), Mon/Tues (high season). 2 dining rooms. No
smoking. Pets by arrangement. MasterCard, Visa accepted. D,B&B €95–€120 per
person. Set Sun lunch €27, dinner €55.

BUSHMILLS Co. Antrim   Map 6:A6

Bushmills Inn   **NEW**   *Tel* 028-2073 3000
9 Dunluce Road   *Fax* 028-2073 2048
Bushmills BT57 8QG   *Email* mail@bushmillsinn.com
                               Website www.bushmillsinn.com

In a village which gives its name to the world's oldest distillery (Old
Bushmills was first licensed in 1608), this coaching inn was traditionally the
last stop for visitors to the Giant's Causeway, two miles away. It fell into
disrepair but was renovated, with bedrooms added in the adjoining mill
house on the banks of the River Bush, in the late 1980s. It receives a full
entry after a strong endorsement from a regular *Guide* reader who stayed
for one night, and immediately booked a longer visit. 'The public rooms
would be ideal for hide and seek, a series of small rooms leading into each
other. The mixture of old furniture, pictures, bits and pieces and comfortable sitting areas creates a relaxing atmosphere.' There are four turf fires
and a 'secret library'. 'The staff were consistently welcoming and helpful.
Our standard *Mill House* room was spacious, traditionally furnished, with a

small dressing room; nice extras included bathrobes.' Five rooms in the main building overlook the main street (some noise). 'The dinner menu was interesting; breakfast standard but fine.' Royal Portrush golf course, the only Irish course to host the Open Championship (in 1951), is close by. (*Jean Evans*)

32 bedrooms. 1 ground-floor room designed for &. 200 yards from centre. Car park. Closed 25 Dec. Hall, drawing room, library, loft; 2 bars, restaurant in 3 sections; private dining room; conference room. 3-acre grounds. No smoking: restaurant, bar counters, bedrooms. Dogs by arrangement. Amex, MasterCard, Visa accepted. B&B [2006] £44–£144 per person. Full alc £38. Short breaks. 1-night bookings refused Sat in winter.

CAHERLISTRANE Co. Galway   Map 6:C5

Lisdonagh Manor House

Caherlistrane, nr Headford

Tel 00 353 93-31163
Fax 00 353 93-31528
Email cooke@lisdonagh.com
Website www.lisdonagh.com

In remote country north of Galway city, John and Finola Cooke have lovingly restored this white Georgian manor house, which stands in a large, peaceful estate with ancient trees and a lake. Our inspectors received a 'gracious welcome' in 2006: 'She is charming, interested and interesting. We were offered tea in the drawing room, but went instead for a woodland walk, guided by the family pet, Fibber, a delightful retriever.' There are 'expertly restored' murals in the hall, and 'well-proportioned' public rooms. A splendid spiral staircase runs through the centre of the house. 'No shabby chic here, more like a hotel (very smart, brand-new doors).' Bedrooms on the first floor have views of the lake or the garden. 'Ours, the Yeats suite, had plenty of storage, chairs, dressing table, bright lights; a well-integrated bathroom.' Four rooms at garden level are 'not as dark as you would expect'. Two South African chefs prepare the 'serious' set evening meal (vegetarian option available): 'Portions are generous; a crèpe tower of mushrooms (yum yum), butternut and coriander soup, tender fillet steak. Intrusive background music alas.' Breakfast has an 'excellent fruit platter, catering-style muesli, good croissants, well-presented poached egg'. Children are welcomed. House parties are catered for.

10 bedrooms. 4 at garden level. 2 self-catering apartments in courtyard. Open May–Oct. 20 miles N of Galway city, off R333. Drawing room, library with honesty bar, dining room; background CDs. 200-acre estate: walled garden, kitchen garden; lake (fishing); woodland walks; horses. No smoking. No dogs in house. Amex, MasterCard, Visa accepted. B&B €120–€150 per person. Set dinner €45 (2 courses €28).

CAPPOQUIN Co. Waterford   Map 6:D5

Richmond House

Tel 00 353 58-54278
Fax 00 353 58-54988
Email info@richmondhouse.net
Website www.richmondhouse.net

Built by the Earl of Cork in 1704, this substantial house stands in parkland in the Blackwater valley. Run as a small hotel/restaurant by Paul and Claire Deevy, it has 'a lived-in feel, highly conducive to relaxation', say recent visitors. Mr Deevy is the award-winning chef, his wife the hostess 'who keeps her eye on the ball'. The building retains its Georgian feel: 'Our second-floor bedroom was impressively large, with king-size bed, wardrobe, chest of drawers and other antique furniture; the bathroom was well proportioned and equipped.' Menus are studied over drinks in the drawing room. The cooking is modern, with a French influence, eg, grilled fillet of beef, champ potatoes, red wine jus. 'An arrestingly fresh Dover sole was beyond reproach.' The traditional breakfast includes freshly squeezed juice, crisp hot toast. 'Good value.' (*AW*)

9 bedrooms. ½ mile E of Cappoquin on N72. Open mid-Jan–mid-Dec. Restaurant closed Sun/Mon (except July/Aug). Lounge, restaurant; 'easy listening' background music. 14-acre grounds. Fishing, golf, pony trekking nearby. No smoking. No dogs. All major credit cards accepted. B&B €75–€120 per person. Set dinner €52. **'V'**

CARAGH LAKE Co. Kerry   Map 6:D4

Carrig House   **NEW**
Caragh Lake
Killorglin

Tel 00 353 66-976 9100
Fax 00 353 66-976 9166
Email info@carrighouse.com
Website www.carrighouse.com

'In a sublime location, in a sheltered lakeside dell', Mary and Frank Slattery's bright yellow 1850s house, with a recent extension, stands in large grounds with camellias and azaleas. It returns to the *Guide* after a period without feedback thanks to a positive inspection report. 'Frank Slattery, a large, dapper man, greeted us warmly. Our pleasant ground-floor room had doors leading on to a patio with the most beautiful view of the lake and mountains behind. It had all you could need for a comfortable stay.' Mr and Mrs Slattery look after the dinner orders in the 'handsome drawing room, with an open fire'. Main courses include supreme of chicken stuffed with curry and walnut butter on a tarragon risotto. A meal in the bay-windowed dining room was enjoyed, except for the pianist playing 'very loud "light" music'. In the grounds are 950 species of trees, rare flowers and shrubs; also marked walks, a stream and waterfalls.

16 bedrooms. Some on ground floor. 22 miles W of Killarney. Open Mar–Nov. Lunch not served. 2 lounges, snug, library, TV room, dining room (classical background music or pianist). 4-acre garden on lake: croquet; private jetty, boat, fishing; walks. 10 golf courses locally. Smoking in some bedrooms only. No children under 8. No dogs in house. Diners, MasterCard, Visa accepted. B&B €65–€175 per person. Full alc €55.

CARRICK-ON-SHANNON Co. Leitrim   Map 6:B5

Hollywell Country House   *Tel/Fax* 00 353 71-962 1124
Liberty Hill   *Email* hollywell@esatbiz.com
      Website www.hidden-ireland.com/hollywell

In a 'fine position' just outside this pretty town on the west bank of the Shannon, Tom and Rosaleen Maher's rambling Georgian house is 'no spit-and-polish affair, truly a home from home', said the nominator. Two bedrooms at the back look over the large gardens which run down to the river. 'Our large front bedroom had a lived-in look, comfy and friendly, with books, artefacts, a table and chairs, tea- and coffee-making facilities.' Visitors can sit in front of an open fire in the large drawing room; seating is 'cleverly arranged so that groups of guests do not have to eyeball each other'. Breakfast, served at separate tables, has 'fresh orange juice, cereals, fresh fruit, porridge, and an Irish fry or smoked salmon and scrambled egg'. No dinner, but the Mahers' two sons run an 'excellent' restaurant, *The Oarsman*, a short walk away. Forty lakes are within a six-mile radius of the town, famed for its angling. Or you could sit in the garden 'and watch the leisure cruisers on the river'. (*EC*)

4 bedrooms. 500 yds NW of Carrick-on-Shannon. Open early Feb–early Nov. Drawing room, dining room. No background music. 2½-acre grounds. Fishing. Unsuitable for &. No smoking. 'Not suitable for young children.' No dogs. Amex, MasterCard, Visa accepted. B&B [2006] €50–€70 per person. Midweek breaks.

∗∗∗

Traveller's tale The receptionist treated me as a complete idiot when I couldn't remember our car's registration number. The food was portion controlled; other guests who asked for more vegetables were told they were having a well-balanced meal. Our room was noisy, though we had asked for a quiet one: staff seemed to leave at midnight and mysterious vans arrived in the early hours. (*Hotel in Cumbria*)

∗∗∗

CARRIGBYRNE Co. Wexford   Map 6:D6

Cedar Lodge   NEW   *Tel* 00 353 51-428386
Carrigbyrne, Newbawn   *Fax* 00 353 51-428222
                                       Email cedarlodge@eircom.net
                            Website www.cedarlodgewexford.com

Well placed on the main road to Cork, 20 miles from Rosslare, Tom and
Ailish Martin's modern hotel has long been a popular stopping-off point
for ferry passengers. It returns to the *Guide* after a period without reports.
'We always stay with the Martins on our way in and out of Ireland,' says
a regular visitor. 'There is a happy, homely atmosphere; the bedrooms are
extremely comfortable, quiet and well equipped.' The host is 'amusing,
garrulous and helpful'; staff are 'courteous and well trained'. Mrs Martin's
traditional cooking is 'very good (though the menu doesn't change too
often); the wine list is excellent'. Main courses include guineafowl with
coriander; veal with white wine sauce. The low, white building stands in
award-winning gardens below the slopes of Carrigbyrne forest. 'You don't
notice the main road' (rooms facing it are triple glazed). (*JF Rickett*)

28 bedrooms. On N25, 14 miles W of Wexford. Open 1 Feb–20 Dec. Ramp.
Lounge, lounge bar, restaurant; varied background music; occasional pianist. 1½-acre
garden. No smoking. Dogs by arrangement. Amex, MasterCard, Visa accepted. B&B
€75–€120 per person. Set dinner €50. 3-day D,B&B package.

CASHEL BAY Co. Galway   Map 6:C4

Cashel House   *Tel* 00 353 95-31001
                                            Fax 00 353 95-31077
                              Email res@cashel-house-hotel.com
                            Website www.cashel-house-hotel.com

Run by the McEvilly family, Kay, Dermot, Frank and Lucy, this
civilised place (Relais & Châteaux) is in wild Connemara country. The
19th-century manor house was put on the map in 1969, the year after it
opened, when General de Gaulle stayed for two weeks. *Guide* readers
recently wrote: 'Kay McEvilly was always in evidence, charming and
efficient.' She supervises the dining room, with its conservatory
extension, where 'the service was outstanding'. Her husband oversees the
kitchen with manager Ray Doorley. The Irish/French cooking of Arturo
Amit and Arturo Tillo 'is beautifully prepared and presented', perhaps
Claggan mussels with chilli garlic; sea bream 'deserving a gold star'.
Breakfasts are 'copious'. There is a comfortable lounge, with antiques

and fresh flowers, a library, and a big modern bar. Bedrooms vary in size; not all have a sea view, but the 'lively and interesting' gardens are noteworthy. Developed by Jim O'Mara, a parliamentarian and keen botanist, who lived in the house for 30 years, they run down to a private beach. More reports, please.

32 bedrooms. 42 miles NW of Galway. Open 2 Feb–2 Jan. 2 lounges, bar, library, dining room/conservatory. No background music. 50-acre grounds: tennis, riding; small private beach. Smoking in some bedrooms only. No dogs in public rooms. Amex, MasterCard, Visa accepted. B&B €85–€155 per person; D,B&B €125–€195. Set dinner €50–€52; full alc €65 (12½% service charge added). Winter breaks. Christmas/New Year packages. *V*

CASTLEHILL Co. Mayo   Map 6:B4

Enniscoe House   *Tel* 00 353 96-31112
Castlehill, nr Ballina   *Fax* 00 353 96-31773
                                        Email dj@enniscoe.com
                                    Website www.enniscoe.com

'Strongly recommended' this year, Susan Kellett's mansion is 'one of the most beautiful country houses in Ireland'. She operates a heritage centre on the large estate, helping returning emigrants trace their Irish roots. The house is run as a small private hotel. It has elegant 18th-century plasterwork, and two large sitting rooms with original furniture; polished wood floors with rugs throughout. They are 'packed with books on Irish art and history, not the usual hotel tat', says one visitor, 'ideal for a wet day, or if you are dining alone. The magnificent staircase is one of the great sights in County Mayo.' Renovation has been completed this year: two bedrooms redecorated, and three canopy beds re-draped. Dinner is a five-course affair, cooked by Ms Kellett in Irish country style ('very appetising', eg, pot roast venison in red wine). There's a working farm on the estate, an organic vegetable garden which supplies the kitchen, a Victorian walled garden with a tea room, and a resident fishing manager – brown trout can be caught in the lough. Nearby are the great cliffs of north Mayo, and three golf courses. (*Mark Purcell*)

6 bedrooms. Self-catering units, 1 suitable for ♿, behind house. On R315, 2 miles S of Crossmolina. Open 1 Apr–31 Oct. Groups only at New Year. 2 sitting rooms, dining room. No background music. 150-acre estate: garden, tea room, farm, heritage centre, conference centre, forge, fishing (tuition, ghillie). Golf, riding, cycling, shooting nearby. Unsuitable for ♿. No smoking. Dogs by arrangement. MasterCard, Visa accepted. B&B €88–€115 per person. Set dinner €48. New Year package. 10% discount for 3 nights or more. 1-night bookings refused bank holiday Sat.

CASTLELYONS Co. Cork   Map 6:D5

Ballyvolane House

Tel 00 353 25-36349
Fax 00 353 25-36781
Email info@ballyvolanehouse.ie
Website www.ballyvolanehouse.ie

After an international career in hotel-keeping, Justin Green returned in 2004 to his family home, a Georgian house modified in Italianate style. He runs it ('magnificently', said one reader), with his wife, Jenny, not as a 'B&B, guest house or hotel', but as a 'family heritage home'. 'A delight,' said our inspector. Mr Green's most recent position was as manager of the funky *Babington House* in Somerset, which may explain his plans to build five bedroom 'pods' in the style of Mongolian yurts (tents) within his walled garden. 'We want to appeal to younger professionals while maintaining the integrity of the house,' he says. Due to open in the autumn of 2006, each will have a wood-burning stove, and an antique bath at the foot of the bed. In the original building, bedrooms are large, comfortable, public rooms are elegant: the drawing room has been restored in traditional style. Guests are encouraged to eat communally around the main dining table (country

house cooking, eg, confit of Barbary duck, lentils du puy, red wine jus). Breakfast is served at any time before noon. There are three trout lakes in the grounds, and *Ballyvolane* has six miles of fishing on the River Blackwater. (*CH, and others*)

6 bedrooms. 1 on ground floor. 5 'pod' rooms due to open autumn 2006. 22 miles NE of Cork. Closed 24 Dec–2 Jan. Hall, drawing room, honesty bar, dining room. No background music. 15-acre grounds: garden, croquet; 3 trout lakes. No smoking. No dogs: public rooms, bedrooms. All major credit cards accepted. B&B €80–€135 per person. Set dinner €50.

How to contact the *Guide*
By mail: From anywhere in the UK, write to Freepost PAM 2931, London W11 4BR (no stamp is needed)
From outside the UK: Good Hotel Guide, 50 Addison Avenue, London W11 4QP, England
By telephone or fax: 020-7602 4182
By email: Goodhotel@aol.com
Via our website: www.goodhotelguide.com

CLIFDEN Co. Galway   Map 6:C4

The Quay House   *Tel* 00 353 95-21369
Beach Road   *Fax* 00 353 95-21608
                                        Email thequay@iol.ie
                                        Website www.thequayhouse.com

♥ *César award in 2003*

Once the harbourmaster's house, this cluster of three buildings on the
waterfront is run as a B&B by Paddy and Julia Foyle. 'They are a delight,
as is their home,' was one recent comment. A visitor this year reports: 'A
lovely building, friendly and generally comfortable, though we were
disappointed with housekeeping and did not like the three yapping dogs.'
Perhaps because of these small dogs, visitors' pets are not welcome. The
decor is 'amusingly eccentric', with Irish paintings and antiques, and
Napoleonic mementos. The 'cosy' drawing room has gilt-framed family
portraits, a peat fire at night, large sofas, some draped with animal skins.
'Our bedroom, Napoleon, was large, with good views over the peaceful
harbour; there was a bit too much clutter and the bath filled very slowly.'
There are seven studios; one on the fourth floor at the top was 'full of light,
mirrors, and birds (painted and stuffed), and had a little balcony overlooking the estuary'. Service may be 'a bit chaotic' at breakfast in the
conservatory; it has fresh juice, good coffee. As is the Irish way, guests
returning from dinner in one of the nearby restaurants may find the Foyles
holding open house, serving drinks in party style. (*S and JS, and others*)

14 bedrooms. 1 on ground floor. 7 studios (6 with kitchenette) in annexe. Harbour;
8 mins' walk from centre. Open mid-Mar–end Oct. Ramps. 2 sitting rooms, breakfast
conservatory. No background music. ½-acre garden. Fishing, sailing, golf, riding
nearby. No smoking. No dogs. MasterCard, Visa accepted. B&B €70–€120 per
person. 1-night bookings refused bank holidays.

COLLINSTOWN Co. Westmeath   Map 6:C5

Lough Bishop House   `BUDGET`   *Tel* 00 353 44-61313
Derrynagarra   *Email* chkelly@eircom.net
                                       Website www.derrynagarra.com

On a south-facing hillside overlooking Bishop's Lough, Helen and
Christopher Kelly, 'friendly owners', raise sheep and draught horses, and
take B&B guests at their renovated 19th-century farmhouse. Visitors may
join them as they go about their business on the farm. The nominators
reported: 'The bedrooms are decorated in keeping with the character of the

house.' Some are good for a family. 'They have lovely views; we slept peacefully, with only the sounds of birds and sheep to wake us in the morning.' Mrs Kelly, 'an excellent cook', will serve dinner by arrangement, using lamb, pork and vegetables from the farm. 'The scrumptious breakfast has home-baked bread, jams made from fruit in the orchards.' (*DV and RR*)

3 bedrooms. 8 miles NE of Mullingar. Closed Christmas. Lounge, dining room. No background music. Farmland. Fishing nearby. Unsuitable for &. No smoking. No dogs. No credit cards. B&B €50 per person. Dinner €30.

CONG Co. Mayo   Map 6:C4

Ballywarren House	*Tel/Fax* 00 353 9495-46989
Cross	*Email* ballywarrenhouse@gmail.com
	Website www.ballywarrenhouse.com

A 'welcoming' peat fire burns in the large hall of David and Diane Skelton's creeper-covered replica Georgian family house in farming country between Lough Corrib and Lough Mask (good fishing). 'We were offered tea and home-made cake in the sitting room, which had books, magazines and games,' says a visitor who enjoyed a 'romantic break'. In the pretty pink-and-green candlelit dining room, Mrs Skelton serves French/Irish meals with local (often organic) ingredients ('delicious crab starter and guineafowl'). 'We had after-dinner drinks by the fire with the Skeltons.' There are chocolates and sherry in the bedroom: 'Our four-poster bed had good white linen; the huge bath was deep and double-ended, and there was a pile of lovely thick towels.' Breakfast has a 'brilliant buffet spread', and a choice of six cooked dishes, home-made bread, jams and marmalades; eggs come from the hens which roam the grounds with Rodney, the cockerel. (*TB, and others*)

3 bedrooms. On R346, 2 miles E of Cong. Reception hall, 2 sitting rooms, dining room. No background music. 7-acre grounds: 1-acre garden. Lake, fishing nearby. Unsuitable for &. No smoking. No children under 12. No dogs: bedrooms, public rooms. Amex, MasterCard, Visa accepted. B&B: single €98–€136, double €124–€148. Set dinner €37.50.

DINGLE Co. Kerry *See SHORTLIST*   Map 6:D4

Hotels will often try to persuade you to stay for two nights at the weekend. Resist this pressure if you want to stay only one night.

DONEGAL Co. Donegal   Map 6:B5

St Ernan's House   *Tel* 00 353 74-97 21065
St Ernan's Island   *Fax* 00 353 74-97 22098
                                     Email res@sainternans.com
                                     Website www.sainternans.com

Once a home for retired clergymen, this white two-storey house is 'a serene and elegant place', on a wooded tidal island reached by a single-track causeway. 'We trade as a historic house, not a hotel,' says the owner, Brian O'Dowd. 'Charming, spacious and well run; we felt welcome and pampered,' says a visitor who 'loved everything about it'. Named after a 7th-century saint, it was built in 1826 by a young landowner, John Hamilton, nephew of the Duke of Wellington. There are antiques, period prints and a log fire in the drawing room. The chef, Gabrielle Doyle, serves tradi-  tional country dishes (beef fillet with red wine sauce) in the dining room, which faces the water. No garden, but 'the short walk around the island, full of wild flowers, is pleasant'. Nearby is the fine Donegal golf course. (*JBS*)

8 bedrooms. On R267, 2 miles S of Donegal town. Open mid-Apr–end Oct. Hall, 2 lounges, restaurant. No background music. 8-acre grounds. Unsuitable for &. Smoking in bedrooms only. No children under 6. No dogs. MasterCard, Visa accepted. B&B €125–€185 per person. Set dinner €50.

See also SHORTLIST

DONERAILE Co. Cork   Map 6:D5

Creagh House   *Tel* 00 353 22-24433
Main Street   *Fax* 00 353 22-24715
                                 Email creaghhouse@eircom.net
                                 Website www.creaghhouse.ie

At the end of the only real street in this north County Cork town by the River Awbeg, this listed Regency 'town house with a difference' was bought as a shell eight years ago by Michael O'Sullivan ('larger than life') and his partner, Laura O'Mahony. Their restoration, which continues, was much admired by a *Guide* inspector: 'Those devalued words "fantastic" and "fabulous" are appropriate. Magnificent friezes have been restored. The huge dining room and drawing room have been filled with furniture on the same large scale: 11-foot-high bookcases, imposing sideboard, huge mirrors.' The owners will serve a simple supper (must be booked the day before), which they might take with their guests. 'Hearty rather than fancy fare, but none the worse for that'; perhaps roast lamb, pear sponge pudding. Tea and home-baked cake are served to arriving guests. Children are welcomed. The garden is being restored. Close by are 'the best nine-hole golf course in Ireland', and Doneraile Court in 400 acres of parkland. More reports, please.

3 bedrooms. 7 miles NE of Mallow. Private secure car park. Open Apr–Oct. Lounge, dining room. 2-acre garden. Unsuitable for ♿. No smoking. No dogs: public rooms, bedrooms. Amex, MasterCard, Visa accepted. B&B €80 per person. Supper (book previous day) €25.

DUBLIN   Map 6:C6

Aberdeen Lodge
53 Park Avenue,
Ballsbridge, Dublin 4

Tel 00 353 1-283 8155
Fax 00 353 1-283 7877
Email aberdeen@iol.ie
Website www.halpinsprivatehotels.com

'Standards remain high,' says a visitor returning in 2006 to Pat Halpin's small hotel in a 'quiet, leafy, residential area' of south Dublin. It has good train and bus connections to the centre. 'We wouldn't stay anywhere else in Dublin,' writes another fan. The 'effective but discreet' management, 'exceptional value' and 'excellent attention to detail' are all praised. 'The Slovakian girl who welcomed us on a chilly evening sat us in a warm lounge, spirited our luggage away, and brought tea and biscuits before asking us to register.' Staff are 'unfailingly smart and well motivated'; the babysitting service is a 'real treat'. There is Wi-Fi Internet access throughout the house, as well as antiques, and a garden where guests may take a drink. Bedrooms are 'well equipped, comfortable'. Breakfast, in the 'attractive' dining room, has a good selection of fruits and cereals, and a choice of hot dishes, including a 'delicious Irish fry'. A limited drawing room/room-service menu is available: 'Snacks and wine, beautifully presented.' The Halpin family owns three other hotels in Dublin, and one in Kilkee, County Clare (see website). (*Trevor Lockwood, AW, and others*)

17 bedrooms. S of city, close to DART station. Ramps. Drawing room, dining room; classical background music. ½-acre garden. Beach nearby. No smoking. Guide dogs only. All major credit cards accepted. B&B €64.50–€160 per person. Full alc €35. Christmas/New Year packages. 1-night bookings refused during major events. *V*

Ashbrook House   `BUDGET`   *Tel/Fax* 00 353 1-838 5660
River Road, Ashtown   *Email* evemitchell@hotmail.com
Castleknock, Dublin 15

In 'a relatively peaceful area', ten minutes' drive from the airport and city centre, Eve and Stan Mitchell's lovely Georgian house has a large garden with 'trees as far as you can see'. Though surrounded by housing development, it is 'like a time warp of pre-suburban Dublin'. The hostess is 'helpful and happy to offer advice'. There is an 'agreeable lounge'; 'lovely colours everywhere; lots of books'. 'Our bedroom was comfortable but the shower room was small,' said a visitor this year. Another comment: 'Our pretty room, overlooking the garden, had an enormous bed.' Breakfast, taken at a long dining table, and 'cheerfully served', is much liked: it has 'rhubarb with the cereals, a reasonable fry-up'; 'generous scrambled eggs with smoked salmon'. Frequent buses to the city centre go from a nearby stop (remember to have the correct fare in coins); it is a fairly long journey and readers suggest that a car is useful for reaching nearby pubs, and Phoenix Park ('the parking at *Ashbrook House* is a bonus in Dublin').

4 bedrooms. NW of centre, near Phoenix Park and ring road to airport. Parking. Closed 19 Dec–2 Jan. Lounge, breakfast room. No background music. Large garden: tennis. Golf, fishing, tennis, polo, swimming nearby. Unsuitable for &. No smoking. No dogs. MasterCard, Visa accepted. B&B: single €60, double €90. *V*

Belcamp Hutchinson   *Tel* 00 353 1-846 0843
Carrs Lane, Malahide Road   *Fax* 00 353 1-848 5703
Balgriffin, Dublin 17   *Email* belcamphutchinson@eircom.net
                                  Website www.belcamphutchinson.com

'As good as ever,' says a returning visitor to this 'beautifully restored' Georgian mansion. Near the airport on the outskirts of Dublin, it is a good base for travellers on an early or late flight. It is run as a guest house by co-owners Count Karl Waldburg and Doreen Gleeson: she is 'charming and a good hostess'. Once the home of Francis Hely-Hutchinson, third Earl of Donoughmore, it is 'elegant yet comfortable'. It has two 'large, wonderful' fanlights, high ceilings, smart furnishings, moulded fireplaces; 'comfortable sofas, log fire, guide books and an honesty bar in the drawing room'.

In the 'glorious' garden are wildflower meadows, a privet maze ('great fun'), neat lawns, abundant flowers, herbs, soft fruit. Each bedroom is different, themed to a colour or material. 'This time we stayed in the Blue Room, as beautifully decorated as the others. Standards are extremely high.' Breakfast, served communally around a long table, includes fruit compote, creamy porridge, home-made soda bread, jams, 'excellent coffee'. 'Everyone is very friendly; the dogs are well behaved and adorable. Doreen provides guides for restaurants, timetables and change for the bus fare.' Only drawback: the inevitable aircraft noise. Malahide, an interesting old village, is nearby. (*Jeanette Bloor, DS*)

8 bedrooms. 3 miles NE of centre. Parking. Buses. Closed 20 Dec–1 Feb. Drawing room with TV, breakfast room. No background music. 4-acre garden. Golf, riding, horse racing nearby. Unsuitable for &. No smoking. No dogs in breakfast room. MasterCard, Visa accepted. B&B [2006] €75 per person.

The Clarence	*Tel* 00 353 1-407 0800
6–8 Wellington Quay	*Fax* 00 353 1-407 0820
Dublin 2	*Email* reservations@theclarence.ie
	Website www.theclarence.ie

On Dublin's lively 'left bank' (south of the Liffey), this handsome 19th-century warehouse was restored with 'minimalist designer chic' by Bono and The Edge, of the rock group U2. This is the place to encounter the city's youthful Zeitgeist; the bar is often busy with 'upwardly mobile young Dubliners', though residents can take refuge in *The Study*, a large, 'pleasant' lounge. Bedrooms have Egyptian cotton sheets, huge pillows; good wardrobe space; abundant thick towels and upmarket toiletries in the tiled bathroom. Simple meals are served from 11 am to 5.30 pm in the *Octagon* bar; an 'excellent' dinner was enjoyed at the white-painted, large-windowed *Tea Room*. The cooking is modern French/Irish, eg, sea bass, confit tomatoes santini, cannellini beans; rack of lamb in vandouvan, preserved lemon. A good breakfast, with a 'tasty full Irish', was taken in the same room. There is Wi-Fi Internet access in all public areas. More reports, please.

49 bedrooms. Central: in Temple Bar on S bank of Liffey. Valet parking. Closed Christmas. *Tea Room* closed Sat lunch. Lounge, bar, restaurant (*Tea Room*); varied background music all day. Smoking in some bedrooms only. No dogs. All major credit cards accepted. Room [2006]: single/double €340, suite €700–€2,500. Breakfast €20.50–€27.50. Bar meals. Full alc €80. Special breaks, midweek packages, courses. New Year package. 1-night bookings refused weekends.

See also SHORTLIST

DUNFANAGHY Co. Donegal   Map 6:A5

The Mill   `BUDGET`   *Tel/Fax* 00 353 74-913 6985
Figart   *Email* themillrestaurant@oceanfree.net
                                  Website themillrestaurant.com

César award: Irish restaurant-with-rooms of the year

'A friendly place in a lovely setting': Susan and Derek Alcorn's restaurant-
with-rooms is a white, late 19th-century house on a lake. It was the home
for 40 years of her grandfather, Frank Egginton, a watercolour artist. 'She
is a vivacious hostess, and his cooking is excellent,' says our inspector.
'She welcomed us with pleasing informality, carrying our bags to our room,
offering tea or coffee. Dinner, the main event, is ordered over drinks and
canapés in the cosy lounge; the house was buzzing with visitors, mainly
from Northern Ireland. The imaginative menu, which changes every four
to six weeks, has a bias towards fish. We loved a starter of seared scallops,
smoked salmon and John Dory on mini potato cakes; the house speciality,
upside down fish pie, is magnificent.' Bedrooms vary: an earlier visitor had
a 'spacious, well-lit room facing the lake; large sleigh bed, antiques'. 'Ours,
smallish but light, had a mix of old and new furnishings; good-sized
bathroom.' Breakfast has 'an above-average buffet with treats like rhubarb
compote, carrageen milk mousse; lovely home-made breads and preserves;
super bacon and sausage'. 'Remarkable value.' All rooms are hung with
paintings by Egginton and his nephew, Robert.

6 bedrooms. At Figart, ½ mile W of Dunfanaghy. Open mid-Mar–mid-Dec.
Weekends only Mar, Nov/Dec, except Christmas/New Year. Restaurant closed
Mon. Sitting room, conservatory, restaurant (background music). 1-acre grounds.
Lake. Beach ½ mile. Only restaurant suitable for &. No smoking. No dogs. Amex,
MasterCard, Visa accepted. B&B €45–€60. Set dinner €39.

DUNGARVAN Co. Waterford   Map 6:D5
See SHORTLIST

***

****

Traveller's tale Our bedroom was an expensive disappointment.
The 'tea and coffee facilities' amounted to one tea bag, one herbal
tea bag, one sachet of coffee, two cream sachets (one used) and two
out-of-date biscuits. The radio alarm, which we had not set, went
off early in the morning. The view was over a busy road junction.
Lighting was poor, making the room dingy. (*Hotel in Norfolk*)

****

ENNISCORTHY Co. Wexford   Map 6:D6

Ballinkeele House   *Tel* 00 353 53-38105
Ballymurn   *Fax* 00 353 53-38468
                                          Email john@ballinkeele.com
                                          Website www.ballinkeele.com

The Maher family built this classic manor house in 1840; John and
Margaret Maher, the fifth generation to live here, offer guests 'the
hospitality of a gentler age' in their home. Much of the furniture is original,
as are many of the paintings and prints; the spacious hall has Corinthian
columns and large fireplace. Mr Maher is the 'modest and thoughtful host',
she the 'homely yet sophisticated cook', said one visitor. 'No pretension;
one is made to feel part of the family, but with enough distance for
comfort.' The host serves cocktails in a drawing room before leading guests
into the 'wonderful' dining room whose furnishings were designed by the
architect. The cooking is 'homely yet sophisticated' (eg, beef stroganoff,
creamed potatoes). 'We have always enjoyed the dinners and the great
breakfasts: John appears in the morning with a smile and a plaid apron.'
Guests can play croquet on the lawn, or walk around the farm and estate.
Enniscorthy has a fine cathedral and 13th-century castle. (*PP*)

5 bedrooms. 6 miles N of Enniscorthy. Open Feb–Nov. 2 drawing rooms, 1 dining
room (radio by request). 350-acre estate: garden; lake, pond. Unsuitable for &. No
smoking. No children under 3. No dogs. MasterCard, Visa accepted. B&B €85–€110
per person. Set dinner €40.

Salville House   *Tel/Fax* 00 353 54-35252
Salville   *Email* info@salvillehouse.com
                                          Website www.salvillehouse.com

At their Victorian house, on a hilltop outside the town, Jane and Gordon
Parker 'continue to do an excellent job', says one returning visitor. 'Food
exceptional; outstanding value,' writes another. On the Wexford road, well
placed for visitors to the opera festival, it overlooks the River Slaney and
the Blackstairs mountains. Mr Parker, 'a gracious host', serves a four-course
no-choice dinner menu at 8 pm: it must be booked the night before (likes
and dislikes discussed before arrival). 'The very best cuisine: over four
nights we enjoyed a great selection of dishes, using local meat and poultry
as well as locally caught fish; many ingredients are organic and from the
garden. Desserts were out of this world, and we finished with coffee in front
of an open fire in the lounge.' 'An early "Opera Supper" is no problem.' No
liquor licence; no corkage charge. Bedrooms (Pink, Yellow and Blue in the

main house; two others in a self-contained apartment) are mostly spacious: 'Ours was lovely and bright, with a large bed and plenty of facilities; excellent bathroom.' Breakfast has fresh orange juice, fruit compote, toasted honey and oats; a full Irish or smoked haddock with rösti and poached egg. (*David Ayres-Regan, Simon Willbourn*)

5 bedrooms. 2 in apartment at rear. 2 miles S of town. Closed Christmas. Dining room closed Sun. Drawing room, dining room. No background music. 4-acre grounds: 'rough' tennis, croquet. Golf nearby; beach, bird sanctuary 10 miles. Unsuitable for &. No smoking. Dogs by arrangement; not in public rooms, bedrooms. No credit cards. B&B €55–€65 per person. Dinner €39. Weekend house-party package.

FEENY Co. Londonderry   Map 6:B6

Drumcovitt House   NEW/BUDGET   *Tel/Fax* 028-7778 1224
704 Feeny Road   *Email* drumcovitt.feeny@btinternet.com
Feeny BT47 4SU   *Website* www.drumcovitt.com

In May 2005, on the death of his father, Frank Sloan, Christopher and Sarah Sloan took over the running of the family's listed, creeper-covered farmhouse, set amid parkland facing the Sperrin mountains. They are 'gracious hosts', reports an American visitor in 2006, who came for one night and stayed for two. 'Sarah built a fire for us, prepared tea, and provided plates and utensils for the light supper we had brought with us.' Built around 1670, the 'wonderful big house' was extended and given a Georgian front in 1796. The three bedrooms share a bathroom and a shower room, which have been refurbished this year. 'Our room (the Azalea) was spacious, yet cosy, beautifully appointed.' Other visitors enjoyed the 'very good breakfast' which includes soda bread, and an Ulster Fry as well as vegetarian and vegan options. Meals are now provided only for parties, by arrangement. Belfast is an hour's drive away. (*Dotty Collins, and others*)

3 bedrooms. 2 shared bathrooms. Also 6 in 3 self-catering cottages (1 with & access). On B74, ¼ mile E of Feeny. Closed Christmas/New Year. Drawing room, dining room. No background music. 3-acre grounds. No smoking. No dogs in house. All major credit cards accepted. B&B £25–£29 per person.

The 'Budget' label by a hotel's name indicates an establishment where dinner, bed and breakfast cost around £55 per person, or B&B no more than £35 and an evening meal about £20. These are only a rough guide, and do not always apply to single accommodation, nor do they necessarily apply in high season.

GALWAY Co. Galway   Map 6:C5

Killeen House   *Tel* 00 353 91-524179
Bushypark   *Fax* 00 353 91-528065
                                          Email killeenhouse@ireland.com
                                          Website www.killeenhousegalway.com

On the shores of Lough Corrib, this attractive 1840s building, long, low and
white, has been restored with 'good taste and panache' by Catherine Doyle,
who runs it as an upmarket B&B. 'Just about as perfect as it can be, far
above the standards of most hotels,' said a trusted *Guide* correspondent.
Each of the four front bedrooms is in a different style – Art Nouveau,
Regency, Edwardian, Victorian. A room at the side of the house is 'massive
and magnificent, with a king-size bed, beautiful furnishings, wide-screen
TV, lovely bathroom, and a third single bed in an annexe'. The two
drawing rooms have antique furniture, china in cabinets, a fine octagonal
rug on a parquet floor; all 'a delight to look at'. 'Everything is stylish at
breakfast: tea and coffee in silver pots, tea strainer provided; fresh orange
juice (you can hear the juicer in the kitchen); wonderful porridge, home-
made muesli, free-range eggs.' (*EC*)

6 bedrooms. On N59, 3 miles NW of Galway city. Closed Christmas. 2 drawing
rooms, breakfast room. No background music. 25-acre grounds, by lake. Unsuitable
for &. Smoking in some bedrooms only. No children under 12. No dogs. All major
credit cards accepted. B&B €75–€110 per person. ***V***

GLASLOUGH Co. Monaghan   Map 6:B6

Castle Leslie   *Tel* 00 353 47-88109
                                          Fax 00 353 47-88256
                                          Email info@castleleslie.com
                                          Website www.castleleslie.com

꙰ *César award in 1998*

The charismatic owner, Samantha Leslie, whose family has lived at this
'Gothic pile' since 1661, continues to expand the range of facilities on the
estate. As we went to press in 2006, 12 self-catering cottages were being
completed, 30 bedrooms were being added at the equestrian centre, and
a cookery school was planned. The castle itself is run in high Victorian
style with more than a touch of eccentricity. The huge public rooms have
old tapestries, suits of armour, a painted Della Robbia fireplace from
Florence, a harp given by Wordsworth, an emerald bracelet from the
Empress of China. The decor has been described as 'shabby chic'. Some

bedrooms are intentionally comic, some 'truly beautiful'. In the former nursery, a vast doll's house facade hides the bathroom, and a giant stuffed poodle and seal 'create a nostalgic atmosphere'. 'New Age Irish' is how the chef, Noel McMeel, describes his cooking, eg, seared Finn Brogue venison, casserole of lentils. No children are allowed at the castle, but they are welcomed at the more casual hunting lodge at the equestrian centre. More reports, please.

20 bedrooms. N edge of Glaslough village, 6 miles NE of Monaghan town. Drawing room, dining room, gallery; billiard room; conference/function facilities. No background music. 1,000-acre grounds: 14-acre gardens: church, tennis, equestrian centre, wildlife, lakes, boating, fishing. No smoking. No children. No dogs in house. Amex, MasterCard, Visa accepted. B&B [2006] €145–€195 per person; D,B&B €200–€250. Set dinner €60. 1-night bookings refused weekends. Christmas/New Year packages.

GLIN Co. Limerick   Map 6:D4

Glin Castle

Tel 00 353 68-34173
Fax 00 353 68-34364
Email knight@iol.ie
Website www.glincastle.com

'The most relaxing place in all Ireland,' said recent visitors of this 'fabulous' Georgian Gothic castle, beautifully set on the Shannon estuary. It is the country seat of Desmond and Olda FitzGerald. He is the 29th Knight of Glin, and his forebears have owned the land for 800 years. Visitors might find The Knight, as he is formally titled, in residence: he sometimes dines with guests. A respected collector, he has filled the house with 'the beautiful and the exquisite'. His manager, Bob Duff, 'welcoming and entertaining', runs it with 'great attention to detail'. There are secret doorways, Corinthian pillars, an unusual flying staircase. The drawing room has an Adam-influenced plaster ceiling; huge windows face the garden. The guest bedrooms are lavish: there are four-poster beds, *chaises longues*, porcelain plates and Irish prints on walls, river or garden views. New chefs, Eddie Baguo and Seamus Hogan, came this year: we would welcome reports on their 'modern Irish' cooking (eg, beef Wellington with morel and Armagnac sauce). Breakfast is thought 'outstanding'. The wooded estate has 'wonderful' formal gardens and a dairy farm. Twice a week there is live Irish music in the main hall. (*GCG*)

15 bedrooms. Edge of village, 32 miles W of Limerick. Open 1 Mar–30 Nov. Hall (traditional music twice weekly), drawing room, sitting room, library, dining room (classical background music in evening). 500-acre estate: 5-acre garden, tennis, croquet, shooting, tea/craft shop, parkland, dairy farm, clay-pigeon shooting. On

Shannon estuary: boating, fishing; golf nearby. Unsuitable for &. No smoking. No children under 10. No dogs in house (kennels available). All major credit cards accepted. B&B €140–€220 per person. Set dinner €52. Off-season rates. House parties (max. 20). *V*

HOLYWOOD Co. Down   Map 6:B6

Rayanne Country House	*Tel/Fax* 028-9042 5859
60 Demesne Road	*Email* rayannehouse@hotmail.com
Holywood BT18 9EX	*Website* www.rayannehouse.co.uk

'A ringing endorsement' is given by a *Guide* inspector in 2006 for Conor and Bernadette McClelland's guest house, a lovely old Victorian building in this attractive suburban town on the Belfast Lough. The house has wide landings and sweeping stairs; display cabinets and ornamental bits and pieces everywhere with an Art Deco theme. An extension adding three bedrooms (one equipped for disabled visitors) was being completed as we went to press. Many of the rooms look over the town and across the lough to the Antrim hills. 'Ours, on the top floor, was enormous; pretty blue and primrose yellow decor; an electric blanket had been switched on; the huge bathroom under the eaves had lots of fluffy towels and toiletries.' Conor McClelland, who worked as a chef in New York before returning home, serves meals by arrangement: 'He is your personal chef, cooking to the highest standard; wonderful confit of duck, large scallops and prawns with a sizzling dauphinois gratin. He knows his wines, too.' Highlights of his award-winning breakfast, ordered the evening before, were 'gorgeous prune mousse, and fruit platters'; other interesting dishes include potato bread with melted cheese, bacon and spicy chutney.

11 bedrooms. 1, on ground floor, suitable for &. ¼ mile from town centre, 6 miles E of Belfast. Parking. Train: Holywood. Restaurant closed 23 Dec–2 Jan. 2 lounges, dining room (classical/jazz background music). 1-acre grounds. Smoking in 1 lounge only. No dogs. MasterCard, Visa accepted. B&B: single £67.50, double £87.50. Set menus £38.50.

****

> **Traveller's tale** The welcome was non-existent: 'Sign here; here's your key. Joan will take you to your room.' Joan carried the lightest bag. I took the rest (my wife, following an operation on her foot, was on crutches). Our room, the most expensive, was in need of refurbishment, as was most of the hotel. The resident proprietors, who have run it for years, were not much in evidence. (*Hotel in Cheshire*)

****

KENMARE Co. Kerry   Map 6:D4

Hawthorn House   **BUDGET**   *Tel* 00 353 (0)64-41035
Shelbourne Street   *Fax* 00 353 (0)64-41932
                              Email info@hawthornhousekenmare.com
                              Website www.hawthornhousekenmare.com

'Attractively situated', five minutes' walk from the pier of this pretty, small resort town at the eastern end of the Ring of Kerry, is Noel and Mary O'Brien's B&B. Mrs O'Brien, 'a bubbly personality', is 'superbly welcoming', and provides a 'reasonably priced stay in a very good spot', say fans. Furnished in pine, with 'good reading lights', the bedrooms are spacious, clean and comfortable, and have a power shower in the good bathroom (four also have a bath). Breakfast includes porridge and Irish fries, but 'service can be slow'. There are plenty of good restaurants in Kenmare. (*MR*)

8 bedrooms. S edge of village. Parking. Closed Christmas. Lounge, breakfast room (varied background music). Small garden. Sea ¼ mile; walking, cycling, golf, water sports, fishing nearby. Unsuitable for &. No smoking. No dogs. MasterCard, Visa accepted. B&B €40–€45 per person.

Sallyport House   *Tel* 00 353 64-42066
Shelbourne Street   *Fax* 00 353 64-42067
                                           Email port@iol.ie
                                   Website www.sallyporthouse.com

The Arthur family's 1930s home stands beside lakes and trees by the River Kenmare, just outside the town. It is run as a 'luxury B&B' by Janie Arthur, 'a delightful hostess', her brother John, and his wife, Helen. The house, built from the stone of an old famine workhouse, contains a fine staircase, antique furniture and a large collection of Irish paintings. From the large landing you can watch the sun set over Kenmare Bay. The 'beautifully furnished' bedrooms, all different, have a sleeping area with a king- or queen-size bed, and a 'comfortable, light' sitting area. 'Our bathroom was large and spotless.' Breakfast has fresh orange juice, fresh fruit salad, proper conserves, linen napkins, full Irish breakfast, pancakes and maple syrup. A deposit of £50 (by personal cheque) is required to secure a booking. Reenagross Woodland Park is adjacent, and 'for dinner, it is a two-minute walk into town'. More reports, please.

5 bedrooms. S of village on N71. Open 1 Apr–1 Nov. Drawing room, breakfast room; background music. Garden. Sea ¼ mile; walking, cycling, golf, water sports, fishing nearby. Unsuitable for &. No smoking. No children under 13. No dogs. No credit cards. B&B [2006] €75–€100 per person.

Shelburne Lodge
Cork Road

Tel 00 353 64-41013
Fax 00 353 64-42135
Email shelburnekenmare@eircom.net
Website www.shelburnelodge.com

'Our favourite in Ireland,' one couple wrote of this stylish B&B, a large, half-timbered 1740s farmhouse on the eastern edge of Kenmare. It stands in a large garden with lawns, a herb garden, an orchard and a grass tennis court. The decor is thought 'charming', and Tom and Maura Foley are 'generous and professional hosts'. Returning visitors were 'treated (ie, no charge)' to coffee and home-baked cake on arrival. One wrote: 'Because I had to leave early and had no breakfast, they deducted €15 from the bill.' The house, filled with antiques and modern art, is 'elegant, spacious and extremely comfortable'. One bedroom 'had stripped pine, a cosy alcove, attractive repro furniture, but the bathroom was cramped'. An 'even nicer' room at the front has a large bathroom. There are log fires in the 'charming' drawing room and library. Tom Foley serves an award-winning breakfast in a 'large and airy' room. He explains the interesting menu, which might include a 'wonderful piece of plaice'. The Foleys also own *Packies,* a popular pub/restaurant in the town, which is noted for its fine fish. (*P and JL, EC*)

8 bedrooms. On R569 to Cork, ½ mile E of town centre. Open mid-Mar–30 Nov. Lounge, breakfast room. Garden: tennis. Golf adjacent. Unsuitable for &. No smoking. No dogs. MasterCard, Visa accepted. B&B €60–€95 per person.

Virginia's Guesthouse   BUDGET
36 Henry Street

Tel 00 353 64-41021
Fax 00 353 64-42415
Email virginias@eircom.net
Website www.virginias-kenmare.com

In the centre of this 'busy but charming little town', Neil and Noreen Harrington's small guest house is above *Mulcahy's*, a popular restaurant. 'They are an engaging couple,' writes an inspector in 2006. Mrs Harrington's three-course breakfast menu (ordered the night before) is well regarded: fresh juice, home-made preserves, home-baked bread, poached seasonal fruit, some 'fabulous' cooked dishes (banana pancakes with maple syrup). In the New Year package, it also includes champagne. Guests may sit in the 'pleasant little library' with its wood-burning-effect stove and tea/coffee bar. Cable TV and safes are in the bedrooms; no baths but power showers.

8 bedrooms. Central, near pier. Train: Killarney; bus. Closed 20–25 Dec, 1–7 Nov. Library, breakfast room; background music. Unsuitable for &. No smoking. No children under 12. No dogs. MasterCard, Visa accepted. B&B €40–€80 per person. New Year package. 1-night bookings refused bank holidays. *V*

KILKENNY Co. Kilkenny *See SHORTLIST*   Map 6:D5

KILLARNEY Co. Kerry   Map 6:D4

Aghadoe Heights   *Tel* 00 353 64-31766
Aghadoe   *Fax* 00 353 64-31345
                        Email info@aghadoeheights.com
                        Website www.aghadoeheights.com

With 74 bedrooms, this luxury hotel, with a recently added spa, is on the large size for the *Guide*, but it is family-owned by Jerry and Anne O'Reilly, and the joint general managers are a married couple, Pat and Marie Chawke. 'All doubts vanished' for our inspector once he passed beyond the ugly exterior ('like a food-processing factory'). The interior is 'beautifully conceived', with large marble foyer with open fire, creating a 'feeling of well-being'. 'The staff are professional, cheerful, chatty. We were greeted warmly, and escorted round the important areas, including the lovely swimming pool. Our room had a "hall" with built-in wardrobe, a generous sitting area and, through an archway, a large sleeping area; a beautifully fitted bathroom with bath, separate shower and twin sinks.' The restaurant is on two levels to allow every table to enjoy the 'magnificent' view of Killarney's lakes and fells: 'The food is excellent, with generous helpings; lamb cutlets cooked to perfection; pan-fried chicken with prawns.' Breakfast, sensibly served between 7.30 and 10 am, has a huge array of fruit and fruit juices, cereals, cheese and breads; a mountainous Irish Fry; thoughtful touches like a tea strainer. Quite expensive, but not eye-wateringly so, and good value.'

74 bedrooms. 1 adapted for &. Off N22, 3 miles NW of Killarney. Closed New Year. Lounge, 2 bars, restaurant; function facilities; leisure centre: swimming pool, fitness room, sauna, spa. 8½-acre grounds: river, fishing. Golf, sea/lake fishing, riding nearby. No smoking. No dogs. All major credit cards accepted. B&B: single €210–€290, double €250–€370, suite €350–€2,000. Set dinner €65; full alc €80. Special breaks. Christmas package.

Hotels do not pay to be included in the *Guide*.

Cahernane House   **NEW**
Muckross Road

Tel 00 353 64-31895
Fax 00 353 64-34340
Email info@cahernane.com
Website www.cahernane.com

Facing lakes and mountains, this 19th-century house is approached down a long tree-lined drive through parkland. Owned by Jimmy and Sara Browne, it is one of Killarney's oldest hotels, once the residence of the Earls of Pembroke. The public rooms are in the old part: 'Most are charming, with burnished wooden floors, nice furniture and pictures.' The 'rather gloomy' foyer, with a fine staircase, leads to a 'cosy' lounge with open fire, and a 'splendid' drawing room, but 'the dining room has a slightly dingy feel'. Most bedrooms are in a new wing: 'Our ground-floor room, with little veranda, had huge bed, writing desk, comfortable chairs, good lighting.' Some rooms have a spa bath. A 'magnificent' suite had 'every accessory one could need', a bathroom with under-floor heating, and a balcony with a bucolic view. 'Very satisfactory dinner: scallops with grilled black pudding and asparagus; grilled black sole with toasted almond and lemon butter.

Decent breakfast: proper preserves, butter, a strainer for tea. Service by smartly dressed staff.' One couple's visit coincided with a wedding party which took over the public rooms, so they had to dine in a 'depressing auxiliary room with loud muzak'. But at other times 'all is tranquil'.

38 bedrooms. 27 in new wing. Edge of national park, 1 mile from centre. Open 1 Feb–1 Dec. Lifts. Drawing room, library; cellar bar, restaurant (background music); conservatory; snooker room. 20-acre grounds: croquet. Smoking in some bedrooms only. No dogs. All major credit cards accepted. B&B: single €180–€255, double €224–€299, suite €290–€380. Set dinner €60. 2-night rates. **'V'**

Killarney Royal
College Street

Tel 00 353 64-31853
Fax 00 353 64-34001
Email royalhot@iol.ie
Website www.killarneyroyal.ie

Margaret and Joe Scally are the third generation of her family to run this 'excellent hotel, for business or pleasure' opposite the railway station of this busy resort town. Their staff are thought 'professional and cheerful'. 'Our large bedroom had no view but good lighting, restful colours, even a walking stick and umbrella; and a large bathroom,' said an inspector. 'Generous portions' are served from a 'bill of fayre' in the bar; modern Irish dishes (eg, baked pavé of salmon) in the dining room. 'We took coffee in the lounge (with a real coal fire). It was a most comfortable place for watching the world go by: in this case, a big group of American golfers. At 6 am, the porter was the soul of *bonhomie*. Breakfast was excellent (proper conserves and butter).'

29 bedrooms. Central. Closed 23–27 Dec. Lift. Lobby, lounge (background music), bar/bistro (live music Sat), restaurant; massage room. No smoking. All major credit cards accepted. B&B €75–€205 per person. Set dinner €30; alc €47. New Year package.

See also SHORTLIST

KILLEAGH Co. Cork   Map 6:D5

Ballymakeigh House   *Tel* 00 353 24-95184
Killeagh, nr Youghal   *Fax* 00 353 24-95370
                              Email ballymakeigh@eircom.net
                              Website www.ballymakeighhouse.com

♀ *César award in 2006*

'Do they teach charm in Irish schools?' asked a reporter this year after visiting Margaret Browne's farm guest house in green countryside close to the estuary town of Youghal. He judged the service 'effortlessly excellent'. Earlier visitors found the hostess 'a wonderful presence', 'full of local knowledge'. She is 'very much in evidence', as are her husband, Michael, and daughter, Kate. Mrs Browne is 'something of a star of the Irish culinary scene'; she has published a cookbook and runs courses in winter. 'Each meal was made special by her manner and outstanding cooking,' said American guests. She serves 'farmhouse helpings' of Irish dishes 'with a twist' (eg, baked hake with tomato, herb and pine nut dressing). The house has been redecorated this year, and the bathrooms have been upgraded. An 'excellent' breakfast has fresh juices, grainy porridge, and six cooked choices. Meals are taken in a spacious, south-facing conservatory 'with nice views of the pastures and flowers surrounding the house'. Children are welcomed: Mrs Browne's nearby equestrian centre offers riding courses and treks to sandy beaches. (*THT, and others*)

6 **bedrooms.** 6 miles W of Youghal. Open 1 Mar–1 Nov. Drawing room, conservatory, restaurant. 180-acre farm: 2-acre garden, tennis, play area. Unsuitable for &. No smoking. Guide dogs only. MasterCard, Visa accepted. B&B €65–€70 per person. Set dinner €45. Cookery courses. New Year package. *V*

KILLYBEGS Co. Donegal *See SHORTLIST*   Map 6:B5

KILMALLOCK Co. Limerick   Map 6:D5

Flemingstown House   BUDGET   *Tel* 00 353 63-98093
Kilmallock   *Fax* 00 353 63-98546
                                             Email info@flemingstown.com
                                             Website www.flemingstown.com

Ω *César award in 2005*

In her 18th-century house on a working dairy farm near an important medieval town, Imelda Sheedy-King runs a 'flawless' guest house. Returning visitors this year 'wholeheartedly endorse' previous *Guide* praise: 'She is the heart and soul of the establishment, greeting us with extraordinary warmth, and insisting on helping us with our luggage.' Her 'energy and attention to detail' are commended. The ambience is 'comfortable rather than luxurious'; there is a 'cosy lounge with mostly 19th-century pieces'. Bedrooms are spacious: 'Our well-lit room had a cheerful air, a crystal chandelier, superb views across fields to the Ballyhoura mountains.' Mrs Sheedy-King's five-course dinner, served in a room with big stained-glass windows, is 'the highlight of a stay'. 'Scrumptious and plentiful, I even carved my own lamb.' Her sister's own Cheddar cheese might be on the menu. Breakfast includes fresh juices, muesli, traditional Irish cooked, pancakes with banana and grapes, and scrambled eggs with smoked salmon. Breads, cheeses, jams and cakes are home made. Families are accommodated. They can explore the farm and watch the cows being milked. The local pub has live music at weekends. (*John and Joan McLaughlin, and others*)

5 **bedrooms.** On R512, 2 miles SE of Kilmallock. Closed 2 Nov–31 Jan. Lounge, dining room (classical background music). 2-acre garden in 100-acre farm. Golf, riding, fishing, cycling nearby. Unsuitable for &. No smoking. No children under 3. No dogs. MasterCard, Visa accepted. B&B €60–€75 per person. Set dinner €40–€45.

Hotels cannot buy an entry in the *Good Hotel Guide* as they do in most rival guides.

KINLOUGH Co. Leitrim   Map 6:B5

The Courthouse **NEW/BUDGET**   *Tel* 00 353 71-984 2391
Main Street   *Fax* 00 353 71-984 2824
                                  Email thecourthouserest@eircom.net
                                  Website www.thecourthouserest.com

In the pink-painted old courthouse of this little town outside the resort
town of Bundoran, Sardinian chef/*patron* Piero Melis (his wife, Sandra, is
from Belfast) 'provides fine Italian food at very reasonable prices', reports
a *Guide* inspector in 2006. The 'very busy' restaurant has pine furnishings,
honey-coloured walls, a 'welcome open fire on a cold evening'. 'Excellent
seafood risotto and ravioli; generous portions of the good specials, rabbit
and quail; a creamy tiramisu. A good Sardinian wine; well paced service by
the helpful staff.' Upstairs, the three bedrooms are simple ('the shower was
lukewarm'), but 'a real bargain'. 'The friendly Belfast waitress cooked
breakfast, and made a good job of it; generous fruit salad and decent
cafetière coffee.' 'No residents' lounge, so not suitable for a long stay.'

4 bedrooms. Village centre. Closed Christmas, 10 days Nov, 10 days Feb. Restaurant
(background music). No smoking. No dogs. MasterCard, Visa accepted. B&B €35–
€40 per person; D,B&B €70–€80. Full alc €40.

KINSALE Co. Cork   Map 6:D5

The Old Presbytery **BUDGET**   *Tel* 00 353 21-477 2027
43 Cork Street   *Fax* 00 353 21-477 2166
                                        Email info@oldpres.com
                                        Website www.oldpres.com

Once the home of priests at the nearby church of St John the Baptist, this
red-doored Georgian house is run as a B&B by Philip and Noreen
McEvoy, a 'friendly, chatty couple'. 'They welcomed us as old friends on
our second visit,' says a recent guest, endorsing a favourable report by
inspectors. It is 'a lovely, rambling house, all ups and downs'; the sitting
room is 'Victorian in every detail'. Bedrooms are 'comfortable, well
appointed', with old pine furniture; bedlinen was 'a particular pleasure'.
Some rooms have Victorian light fittings; three have a spa bath. The
penthouse suite has its own kitchen and a 'superb' view over the harbour.
Breakfasts include fresh orange juice, muesli, fresh fruit salad, organic
yogurt. 'The other guests seemed happy: some were eating stuffed pancake
or full Irish with black and white pudding.' Kinsale, a short drive from Cork
airport, has an annual gourmet festival. (*RC*)

6 bedrooms. Also 3 self-catering apartments. Some on ground floor. Central; near parish church. Car park. Open 14 Feb–30 Nov. Lounge with TV, conservatory, breakfast room (classical/Irish background music). Sea/river fishing, water sports, golf nearby. Unsuitable for &. No smoking. No dogs. MasterCard, Visa accepted. B&B €50–€100 per person.

Pier House Guesthouse
Pier Road

Tel/Fax 00 353 21-477 4475
Email pierhouseaccom@eircom.net
Website www.pierhousekinsale.com

Reached from the pier or the main street of this old fishing town, Patrick and Ann Hegarty's family home has been renovated in modern style. There are dark wood floors, white walls and works of art in the public areas. The bedrooms vary in size. Several have a balcony (where breakfast may be served) with harbour views. One has a sitting area and another has a private garden. There are sleigh beds and goose-down duvets. Bathrooms have a slate tile floor with under-floor heating, black granite sink surrounds, 'terrific shower with smart toiletries'. Rooms that face the main street may suffer from noise, especially at weekends. In the grounds are a deck area with a terracotta 'chiminea', lawns, hot tub and sauna. More reports, please.

10 bedrooms. Central, on pier. Closed Christmas. Lounge, hall (background music). Large garden: sauna, hot tub. Unsuitable for &. No smoking. No dogs. MasterCard, Visa accepted. B&B [2006] €60–€120 per person.

LAHINCH Co. Clare   Map 6:C4

Moy House
Tel 00 353 65-708 2800
Fax 00 353 65-708 2500
Email moyhouse@eircom.net
Website www.moyhouse.com

An 'architectural oddity', with two floors on one elevation and one on the other, this flat, white, tower-topped building stands on a headland in a rugged, dramatic landscape. With stunning views over Lahinch Bay, it has a Gothic look, but 'inside, it is warm and welcoming', say visitors. Built in the 18th century for Sir Augustine Fitzgerald, it has been turned 'with panache' into a hotel by the owner, Antoin O'Looney; the 'charming' Brid O'Meara is the new general manager. 'Our bedroom, down a spiral stair-case, was tastefully lavish; a king-size bed with a canopy of gold brocade; excellent reading lights; generous supplies of lotions and potions in the bathroom. When we came up for drinks before dinner, the wind was howling and the rain lashing outside, but the hall was a delight, filled with lighted candles and flowers.' Chef Verry Samudra's country house ('with a hint of French') menu changes daily. Breakfast has fresh orange juice; home-made muesli; the usual Irish cooked dishes. 'Only health warning: the place can be full of golfers': Lahinch has a renowned championship course. More reports, please.

9 bedrooms. 4 on ground floor. 1 mile S of Lahinch. Open Feb–Nov. Ramp. Drawing room with honesty bar, library, dining room (background music during meals). 15-acre grounds; access to beach. No smoking. Unsuitable for young children. Guide dogs only. All major credit cards accepted. B&B [2006]: single €135–€165, double €160–€250. Set dinner €48.

LEENANE Co. Galway   Map 6:C4

Delphi Lodge	*Tel* 00 353 95-42222
Leenane	*Fax* 00 353 95-42296
	Email stay@delphilodge.ie
	Website www.delphilodge.ie

'Delightful, but it doesn't pretend to be a hotel,' is a recent verdict on this lovely old sporting lodge by a lake in glorious upland country north of Connemara. It is run on house-party lines by Peter Mantle: no keys to the bedrooms; drinks from an honesty bar; meals are taken around a communal oak table. The main pursuit is fishing; advance booking is required for Mr Mantle's fishery, famous for its salmon fly-fishing, with courses and ghillies available. Non-fisherfolk enjoy hill walking, open fires, and the peace. Evenings are convivial; Mr Mantle or 'the captor of the day's biggest salmon' presides. The cooking is 'eclectic' (from traditional to oriental), the wine list 'serious'; coffee and home-made chocolates are served in the piano room. Breakfast is 'quietly sociable', too: good porridge, good fry, home-made marmalade. Most bedrooms are large; some have a four-poster, all have lake and mountain views. The lodge can be taken for house parties, small weddings and conferences. 'Due to the remote location, there is little point in making a one-night booking,' writes Mr Mantle. More reports, please.

12 bedrooms. 2 on ground floor. 20 miles SW of Westport. Open 10 Jan–20 Dec. Drawing room, library, dining room; billiard room. No background music. 1,000-acre estate: 15-acre gardens, lake, fishing. Unsuitable for &. No smoking. Children under 12 'not encouraged'. No dogs. MasterCard, Visa accepted. B&B [2006] €77–€155 per person; D,B&B €126–€204. Set menu €49. 3-night rates. Fly-fishing tuition weekends. ***V***

LETTERFRACK Co. Galway   Map 6:C4

Rosleague Manor
Tel 00 353 95-41101
Fax 00 353 95-41168
Email info@rosleague.com
Website www.rosleague.com

'A beautiful house in a glorious place', this Georgian manor on the Connemara coast has 'breathtaking' views across mature gardens to sea and mountains. Owned by Edmund Foyle and his son, Mark, it earns unreserved praise from two visitors this year, for the 'welcoming atmosphere', the 'relaxed and relaxing ambience'. 'It is Mark, an entertaining conversationalist, who is the admirable host'; the staff, local and European, are 'friendly, helpful'. The house is 'charmingly decorated in country house style, comfortable but not too grand'; two elegant lounges have turf and wood fires; pre-dinner drinks are served in the conservatory set in an internal courtyard with trees and shrubs. In the 'truly beautiful' dining room, the French chef, Pascal Marinot, 'resists any temptation to over-elaborate: black sole with nothing more than garlic and parsley butter was as good as we've had; high-quality beef served properly rare'. 'The ice cream was particularly delicious.' Breakfast has freshly squeezed juice, home-made scones; good cooked dishes, including fresh fish. 'Our room, in shades of blue and yellow, was large enough to contain good antiques without feeling cluttered; a freestanding Victorian bath with its original shower was in the spacious bathroom.' (*Ann Walden, Lady Huxtable*)

20 bedrooms. 7 miles NE of Clifden. Open 15 Mar–15 Nov. 2 drawing rooms, conservatory/bar, dining room. No background music. 30-acre grounds; tennis court. Unsuitable for &. No smoking. Only 'well-behaved dogs' in public rooms. Amex, MasterCard, Visa accepted. B&B €80–€145 per person. Set dinner €45. 1-night bookings refused Sat bank hols. ***V***

LISDOONVARNA Co. Clare   Map 6:C4

Sheedy's
Tel 00 353 65-707 4026
Fax 00 353 65-707 4555
Email info@sheedys.com
Website www.sheedys.com

In a spa resort famed for its annual match-matching festival in September, this yellow building, in neat grounds, has been in the family of owner/chef John Sheedy since the 18th century. He is an 'accomplished cook'; his wife, Martina, is the 'hands-on, charming' manager. Our inspector liked 'the personal approach'. Other praise: 'The attention to detail is unremitting; housekeeping is meticulous, and staff are well trained.' The bedrooms are 'faultless, spotless and quiet; restful colours, comfortable beds and chairs'. 'Ours, in the modern extension, was well cared for; the bright, modern bathroom had an enclosed shower cubicle.' Pre-dinner drinks are taken in a bright sun lounge; the cooking, served in a 'pleasant, light' dining room, is modern and 'outstanding'. It might include main courses like baked hake with crab risotto and prawn sauce, or seared scallops with coriander and lentil sauce. Breakfast, served at the table, has real juice, home-made preserves, good teas; 'excellent alternatives to the staple full Irish: pancakes with fresh fruit; a platter of goat's cheese'. Nearby are the Cliffs of Moher. (*AW, and others*)

11 bedrooms. Some on ground floor. 1 suitable for ♿. Village centre, 20 miles SW of Galway. Open Easter–mid-Oct. Restaurant may close 1 night a week Mar–Apr. Ramp. Sitting room/library, sun lounge, bar, restaurant (background jazz). Garden, rose garden. No smoking. Restaurant 'not suitable for children under 10'. No dogs. MasterCard, Visa accepted. B&B [2006] €65–€100 per person. Full alc €65. 1-night bookings refused Sept.

LONGFORD Co. Longford   Map 6:C5

Viewmount House NEW	*Tel* 00 353 43-41919

Dublin Road   *Fax* 00 353 43-42906

Email info@viewmounthouse.com

Website www.viewmounthouse.com

In the geographical centre of Ireland, Longford may be an 'anonymous' county town, but Jim and Beryl Kearney's informal B&B is popular with visitors driving west from Dublin. The 'truly handsome' Georgian house is 'welcoming, comfortable and homely', says a visitor in 2006. Our inspector agreed: 'Jim Kearney greeted us warmly, carrying our bags to a second-floor bedroom. When we asked what time breakfast was served, he answered: "What time would you like it?" Perfect.' The hall has a sweeping staircase ('not for the infirm'); the first-floor library/sitting room has 'period pieces, bookcases, two wonderful chandeliers'. Bedrooms have rugs on polished wooden floors. 'They are well supplied, for the price, with fresh fruit, flowers, bottled water, facecloths in the bathroom'. Breakfast, served by 'the charming Beryl' in a room with a vaulted ceiling, is 'superb: fresh orange juice, home-made muesli and wheaten bread, proper butter and preserves, good coffee (including decaffeinated)'. 'They are developing the house and its wonderful gardens in true Irish style – everything happening at once.' A 50-seat restaurant in a converted stable block was due to open as we went to press. 'The Kearneys' instinctive hospitality is most unlikely to be diminished by their grand plans.' (*EC, and others*)

6 bedrooms. ¼-mile E of Longford. Library/sitting room, breakfast room (background music). Unsuitable for &. No smoking. No dogs. Amex, MasterCard, Visa accepted. B&B €55–€80 per person. *V*

MALIN Co. Donegal   Map 6:A6

Malin Hotel   NEW/BUDGET   *Tel* 00 353 74-937 0606
Fax 00 353 74-937 0770
Email info@malinhotel.ie
Website www.malinhotel.ie

In 'pretty little village' 10 miles from Malin Head, Ireland's most northerly point ('magnificent coastal scenery'), small hotel with 'warm welcome'. 'Small but comfy' lounge. Popular Green's *bar (bar meals; regular live music). 'Atmospherically lit'* Jack Yeats's *restaurant: 'straightforward food, good quality, plenty of it; decent wine list'. Children's supervised play area on Sun, 4–9 pm. No smoking. Weddings and entertainment. Golf packages. 13 bedrooms, ranging from 'quaint and cosy village rooms' to 'tranquil countryside' ones. B&B [2006] €55–€85 per person. Set dinner from €18.*

MAYNOOTH Co. Kildare   Map 6:C6

Moyglare Manor   *Tel* 00 353 1-628 6351
Maynooth   *Fax* 00 353 1-628 5405
Email info@moyglaremanor.ie
Website www.moyglaremanor.ie

In green countryside just outside Maynooth, the home of Ireland's leading Catholic theological college, Nora Devlin's Georgian stone manor house has an 'almost oppressive grandeur'. The interior has an 'extraordinary' decor: 'not an inch of wall space is left uncovered by pictures, mirrors, heavy, dark Victorian plush wallpaper and velvet curtains'. The grandeur continues at dinner, with silver cutlery and a silver-haired pianist. Edward Cullen serves 'huge portions' of 'modern traditional' dishes, eg, slow-roasted goose with savoury nut stuffing, perigourdine sauce. Readers like the bedrooms: 'Ours was vast, with a bathroom bigger than most hotel bedrooms.' Another room 'was comfortable, and its bathroom good, despite the gimcracks and gewgaws like the toilet-roll-holder doll'. Breakfast, in a 'gorgeous, airy' room, has fresh orange juice. Mary Breslin has taken over as manager. Dublin airport is 30 minutes' drive away. More reports, please.

16 bedrooms. 2 miles N of Maynooth. Closed 24–26 Dec. Restaurant closed Good Friday. Ramps. 2 lounges, 2 bars; pianist 3–4 evenings a week; TV room, 3 dining rooms; conference facilities. 17-acre grounds. Golf, shooting, hunting, horse riding, tennis nearby. No smoking. No children under 12. Guide dogs only. Amex, MasterCard, Visa accepted. B&B: single €100–€150, double €180–€250, suite €300–€350. Set dinner €60.

MILLSTREET Co. Waterford   Map 6:D5

The Castle Country House **NEW/BUDGET**   *Tel* 00 353 58-68049
Millstreet   *Fax* 00 353 58-68099
Cappagh   *Email* castlefm@iol.ie
                         Website www.castlecountryhouse.com

A visitor from New Zealand 'stumbled' upon Joan and Emmett Nugent's unusual farmhouse, a restored wing of a 15th-century tower house built to protect livestock. 'We were given the best welcome with tea and scones. Our room had a wonderful view down the valley; the biggest bed and a lovely hot tub. Fresh flowers through the house, not a speck of dust.' Mrs Nugent serves traditional country dishes in the original castle dining room (with five-foot walls); breakfast ('at a time of your convenience') has fresh fruits, porridge, home-baked breads, and an interesting cooked selection (eg, bacon with brie and cranberry sauce). The gardens run down to the River Finisk (good fishing here and on the nearby Blackwater). Guests are encouraged to 'lend a hand' on the family dairy farm. (*Emma O'Brien*)

Note: There are two villages called Millstreet in County Waterford and one in neighbouring County Cork. This is the one closest to the estuary town of Dungarvan.

5 bedrooms. In village, 10 miles NW of Dungarvan. Open Mar–Nov. Drawing room, dining room (classical background music). Unsuitable for &. No smoking. MasterCard, Visa accepted. B&B €45–€65 per person. Set dinner €30.

MILTOWN MALBAY Co. Clare   Map 6:C4

Admiralty Lodge   *Tel* 00 353 65-708 5007
Spanish Point   *Fax* 00 353 65-708 5030
                                       Email info@admiralty.ie
                                       Website www.admiralty.ie

'Hands-on' owner/manager Pat O'Malley has transformed this much extended Georgian country house in an opulent style, 'without transgressing good taste'. It has wood-panelled rooms, marble fireplaces, ornate ceilings, and a flower-filled courtyard. The public rooms 'showed the handiwork of an interior designer of quality; colours blended to complement the neo-Georgian style', said the nominators, who chanced on it 'by happy accident'. They were as impressed with the 'excellent' contemporary cooking of Nadine Le-Gallo (eg, medallions of monkfish in a sesame crust; rack of lamb with sage sauce). 'An adequate wine list had reasonably priced house wines. Our bedroom was sumptuously furnished; it had a large bathroom and separate shower, air conditioning and flat-screen TV.' Good local golfing includes the championship links at nearby Lahinch. (*D and JH*)

11 bedrooms. 1 mile SW of village. Closed Jan/Feb. Ramps. 3 lounges, bar, restaurant; background music. ½-acre grounds. Helipad. Beach 2 mins' walk. Golf, fishing nearby. No smoking. No dogs. Amex, MasterCard, Visa accepted. B&B [2006]: single €100–€165, double €150–€200, suite €256–€295. Set dinner €42.

MOUNTRATH Co. Laois — Map 6:C5

Roundwood House
Mountrath

Tel 00 353 502-32120
Fax 00 353 502-32711
Email roundwood@eircom.net
Website www.roundwoodhouse.com

César award in 1990

In a 'wonderful' setting, 'with shimmering trees and meadows, bluebells and blackberries' below the Slieve Bloom mountains, this 18th-century Palladian villa has a 'slightly shabby Irish charm'. 'The house is warm and comfortable. Good conversation and excellent meals more than compensate for a somewhat battered interior,' said one correspondent. The 'gracious and unaffected' hosts, Rosemarie and Frank Kennan, often join their guests after dinner for whiskey and coffee. They have worked for more than 20 years to restore the house, which they bought from the Irish Georgian Society. It has creaking floorboards and an eclectic collection of books, furniture and ornaments. The Kennans tell us they have added more paintings, more books, and made 'improvements in the gardens' this year. The first-floor Blue bedroom, large and high-ceilinged, is 'very comfortable'. Dinner, served at two communal tables, and separate ones too, is 'based on what is in the market', eg, crispy roast duck with sweet and sour grapefruit. Breakfast includes fresh orange juice; oaty black pudding. Children are welcomed (there is a 'wet day' nursery with toys) and encouraged to feed the donkeys, ducks, horses, etc. A coach house, forge and cottage have been turned into self-catering units. (*ES, and others*)

10 bedrooms. 4 in garden annexe. 3 miles N of village. Closed 25 Dec, 1 Jan–1 Feb. Drawing room, study/library, dining room; playroom, table tennis room. No background music. 20-acre grounds: garden, woodland. Golf, walking, river fishing nearby. Unsuitable for &. Smoking in 4 bedrooms only. No dogs: public rooms, bedrooms. All major credit cards accepted. B&B €75–€105 per person; D,B&B €120–€150. Set dinner €45. 3-night breaks. **°V°**

MULTYFARNHAM Co. Westmeath   Map 6:C5

Mornington House   *Tel* 00 353 44-72191
                                                    Fax 00 353 44-72338
                                          Email stay@mornington.ie
                                          Website www.mornington.ie

'Grand yet homely', Warwick and Anne O'Hara's old Anglo-Irish house stands in large grounds with ancient trees near Lough Derravaragh. 'Absolutely delightful,' says a visitor from the United States this year. 'They are wonderful, welcoming hosts, and great conversationalists.' The house has been in the family since 1858 – much original furniture and many portraits remain. There are bright red walls in the hall. Patterned yellow wallpaper hangs in the lounge, where a turf and log fire burns in cold weather. Guests, who are entertained on house-party lines, help themselves to drinks before dinner in the 'pleasant, light' drawing room. The 'very good' four-course meal (no choice of the first two courses) is taken around a large table in the candlelit dining room. 'Salmon was delicious, as was the steak in Guinness; the cheesecake was sublime, like a soufflé.' Bedrooms are 'a bit idiosyncratic': 'Ours was large, quiet, with plenty of light.' The O'Haras tell us they have 'much improved' two rooms this year. Breakfast is 'very good': linen napkins; fresh orange juice; 'superb home-made muesli and brown bread; a full Irish Fry'. The nearby lake has trout, pike, eel, canoes and boats. (*Michael J Wieloszynski, and others*)

5 bedrooms. 9 miles NW of Mullingar. Open early Apr–end Oct. Drawing room, dining room. No background music. 50-acre grounds: bicycle hire. Unsuitable for &. No smoking. No dogs in house. All major credit cards accepted. B&B €65–€95 per person. Set dinner €42.50.

The **°V°** sign at the end of an entry indicates a hotel that has agreed to take part in our Voucher scheme and to give *Guide* readers a 25% discount on their room rates for a one-night stay, subject to the conditions explained on page 60 and listed on the back of the vouchers.

NEWPORT Co. Mayo   Map 6:B4

Newport House   *Tel* 00 353 98-41222
                                               Fax 00 353 98-41613
                                               Email info@newporthouse.ie
                                               Website www.newporthouse.ie

'Delightful in every way' (this year's accolade), Thelma and Kieran
Thompson's creeper-covered Georgian mansion (Relais & Châteaux) is on
an estuary facing Achill Island, in a village on lovely Clew Bay. They run
it 'like a large private home', with 'friendly, helpful staff' (most are local).
Earlier praise: 'Fabulous people; it feels like every country house hotel
should but rarely does.' There are fine plasterwork, chandeliers, cheerful
fires burning in the public rooms; a grand staircase has a lantern and dome.
Some bedrooms are in self-contained units, good for a family; others are in
two houses near the courtyard. 'We had a most comfortable room in the
old gatehouse.' The chef, John Gavin, describes his style as 'country house/
French', eg, avocado and asparagus salad; escalope of veal with ratatouille.
'Very good indeed,' is this year's view. 'Breakfast was our best in Ireland,
thanks largely to the incomparable eggs Benedict.' 'Not cheap, but very
good value.' (*ADL Melville, and others*)

18 bedrooms. 5 in courtyard. 4 on ground floor. In village, 7 miles N of Westport.
Open 19 Mar–10 Oct. Dining room, sitting room, bar, restaurant; billiard/TV room,
table-tennis room. No background music. 15-acre grounds: walled garden. Private
fishing on Newport river; golf, riding, walking, shooting, hang-gliding nearby.
Unsuitable for &. Smoking in bedrooms only. Dogs in courtyard bedrooms only.
B&B [2006] €108–€188 per person. Set dinner €63.

OUGHTERARD Co. Galway   Map 6:C4

Currarevagh House   *Tel* 00 353 91-552312
Oughterard   *Fax* 00 353 91-552731
                                               Email mail@currarevagh.com
                                               Website www.currarevagh.com

۞ *César award in 1992*

'Even a regular forgets some of the delights of *Currarevagh*: the absence
of room keys, the warmth of the rooms on miserable early autumn days,
the changing light on Lough Corrib. But nothing else changes.' A
devotee explains the charms of Harry and June Hodgson's guest house,
which has had an entry in every edition of the *Guide*. Visitors are
welcomed with free afternoon tea, scones, cakes, good china, in the

drawing room. Bedrooms have fresh flowers, hot-water bottles; many have wonderful views 'over the trees and lake where fishing boats came in'. And 'there is no single-occupancy-of-a-double-room supplement'. Dinner is announced by a gong. June Hodgson is helped in the kitchen by her son, Henry; their cooking is, this year, 'if anything a notch better, more adventurous (is this Henry's influence?)'. The handwritten five-course set menu features traditional dishes, eg, cod with a garlic crust; roast loin and belly of pork with apple sauce. Coffee is taken in the lounge – 'a sociable affair'. The buffet breakfast includes kedgeree; black pudding. *Currarevagh* has its own boats and ghillies for fishing on Lough Corrib ('probably the best wild brown trout lake in Europe'); also good swimming and boating. (*Richard Parish*)

15 bedrooms. 2, on ground floor, in mews. 4 miles NW of Oughterard. Open 31 Mar–mid-Oct. Sitting room/hall, drawing room, library/bar with TV, dining room. No background music. 170-acre grounds: lake, fishing (ghillies available), boating, swimming, tennis, croquet. Golf, riding nearby. Unsuitable for &. Smoking in a few bedrooms only. Not suitable for very young children. Dogs by arrangement; not in dining room. MasterCard, Visa accepted. B&B [2006] €80–€134 per person; D,B&B €122.50–€176.50. Snack/picnic lunch available. Set dinner €45. 3-day/weekly rates. Winter house parties. 1-night bookings sometimes refused 'if too far ahead'.

RAMELTON Co. Donegal   Map 6:B5

Frewin   *Tel/Fax* 00 353 74-915 1246
Rectory Road   *Email* flaxmill@indigo.ie
                                    Website www.frewinhouse.com

'A country house in miniature', this Victorian rectory in mature grounds, outside a 'heritage' Georgian port at the mouth of the River Lennon, has been renovated 'with flair' by Regina and Thomas Coyle. It has an elegant staircase, stained glass and a library; there are wellington boots in the hall, and a croquet lawn in the garden. The largest bedroom, on a corner at the front, has views to both sides, and its own sitting room, 'a lovely little nook'. It has been revamped this year and given a shower *en suite*. Mrs Coyle, 'a charming hostess', serves dinner on request ('on about two nights a week') round a communal table in the 'atmospheric' (darkish) dining room. The three-course meal might include curried parsnip soup; braised beef with peppercorn sauce; apple crumble and cream. 'Simple but satisfactory,' said our inspector. 'Breakfast was good, with home-made muesli, fresh fruit, home-baked bread and freshly squeezed juice; proper butter and conserves; good tea and coffee; also a full fry-up.'

4 bedrooms. Outskirts of town. Closed Christmas. Private parties New Year. Dinner by arrangement. Sitting room, library, dining room. No background music. 2-acre garden. Golf, horse riding, beaches nearby. Unsuitable for &. No smoking. 'Not suitable for children under 8.' No dogs. MasterCard, Visa accepted. B&B €60–€90 per person. Set dinner €45.

RATHMULLAN Co. Donegal   Map 6:B5

Fort Royal   **NEW**   *Tel* 00 353 74-915 8100
                                               Fax 00 353 74-915 8103
                                               Email fortroyal@eircom.net
                                               Website www.fortroyalhotel.com

On the scenic shores of Lough Swilly, this rambling white house stands in the shadow of the neighbouring *Rathmullan House* (see next entry), which is larger and grander. Tim and Tina Fletcher have recently become the third generation of his family to run the hotel. With some reservations, our inspector recommends *Fort Royal* as a less expensive option, with a better view from 'magnificent grounds'. 'The foyer, which like the drawing room and bar has an open fire, is a welcoming place. Our bedroom, in the eaves, was plainly furnished but comfortable.' Mr Fletcher is the chef: 'Dinner on our first evening was disappointing (his night off?); much better the second

evening, with good fish cakes, excellent pork. It was a pity the staff laid tables for breakfast before we had finished.' Breakfast had fresh juice, 'proper conserves and good bacon and sausages'. 'With a bit more polish, this could be a very good hotel.'

15 bedrooms. 4 in annexe. ¼ mile N of village. Open Easter–mid-Oct. 2 lounges, bar (background music). 17-acre grounds: tennis, pitch-and-putt golf. Unsuitable for &. Smoking in bedrooms only. No dogs in public rooms. All major credit cards accepted. B&B [2006] €80–€95 per person; D,B&B €112–€129. Set dinner €46. 1-night bookings refused Sat, bank hols.

'Set lunch/dinner' indicates fixed-price meals, with ample, limited or no choice on the menu. 'Full alc' is the hotel's estimated price per person of a three-course *à la carte* meal, with a half bottle of house wine. 'Alc' is the price of an *à la carte* meal excluding the cost of wine.

Rathmullan House

Tel 00 353 74-915 8188
Fax 00 353 74-915 8200
Email info@rathmullanhouse.com
Website www.rathmullanhouse.com

The Wheeler family's handsome, white 1800s mansion stands in a well-tended garden on a two-mile sandy beach on Lough Swilly (an inlet of the sea). 'Thoroughly well managed', it has long been popular with *Guide* readers for the range of facilities, the cooking, and the staff, 'helpful, with the right balance of discretion'. But a few linguistic problems were encountered in 2006. Spacious public rooms have high ceilings, chandeliers, antiques, marble fireplaces, log fires, oil paintings, lots of books. In the conservatory-style dining room, with its tented ceiling, Peter Cheesman cooks elaborate dishes using home-grown organic fruit and vegetables, locally caught fish and seafood. The cellar bar/bistro serves simpler meals, and lunches on a terrace in fine weather. Bedrooms come in various styles. Ten recently added themed rooms (one with 'a room within the room' for visiting dogs) are spacious, with restful colours, under-floor heating. Some older rooms are 'classic country house', some with a lough view, some with a balcony. Simpler rooms are good for a family. Breakfast has a wide choice. There's a large indoor swimming pool and a pretty ornamental garden. Outside the gates are some ugly holiday bungalows. You can go for walks up the Fanad peninsula, with fine views. (*JMRI, Esler Crawford, and others*)

32 bedrooms. Some on ground floor. 2 suitable for &. ½ mile N of village. Bus: Letterkenny; hotel will meet. Closed 9 Jan–8 Feb. Ramps. 4 lounges, library, TV room, cellar bar/bistro, restaurant; 50-ft indoor swimming pool, steam room; small conference centre. No background music. 10-acre grounds: tennis, croquet; direct access to sandy beach, safe bathing. Golf, boating, riding, hill walking nearby. Smoking in some bedrooms only. 1 dog-friendly room; no dogs in public rooms. Amex, MasterCard, Visa accepted. B&B €85–€185. Set dinner €50; full alc €65. 1-night bookings refused weekends, bank holidays.

RIVERSTOWN Co. Sligo   Map 6:B5

Coopershill

Tel 00 353 71-916 5108
Fax 00 353 71-916 5466
Email ohara@coopershill.com
Website www.coopershill.com

Q *César award in 1987*

In the seventh generation of family ownership, this fine Palladian mansion is, 'unlike some of its Irish peers', in 'pristine condition'. It stands in a large estate traversed by the River Arrow (fishing available), in Yeats country. The owners, Brian and Lindy O'Hara, are an 'engaging couple', says a visitor this year. 'She, along with her three dogs, warmly welcomed us, providing some nice boiled cake.' The 'lovely' bedrooms are 'large, and luxuriously homely'; most have a four-poster or a canopied bed. 'The house was full, and our bathroom was down the corridor; no great inconvenience as bathrobes and slippers were provided. When the immersion heater timer failed, Brian O'Hara offered us the use of his private bathroom.' Dinner, by candlelight, with family silver and glass, starts at 8.30 or so and is leisurely; guests dine at separate tables, and are served each course at the same time. Mrs O'Hara's traditional cooking (eg, smoked trout ramekins; filet of pork with apricots) is 'excellent, nicely balanced'. There is a comprehensive wine list. A 'fine breakfast' has fresh orange juice, leaf tea with a strainer. Children are welcomed. The O'Haras run a sizeable farm; deer and sheep roam the estate. (*Esler Crawford*)

8 bedrooms. 11 miles SE of Sligo. Open Apr–Oct. Off-season house parties by arrangement. 2 halls, drawing room, TV room, dining room; snooker room. No background music. 500-acre estate: garden, tennis, croquet, woods, farmland, river (trout fishing). Unsuitable for &. No smoking. No dogs in house. All major credit cards accepted. B&B €104–€148 per person; D,B&B €159–€203. Set dinner €55–€60. Discounts for 3 or more nights. **'V'**

ROSSLARE Co. Wexford   Map 6:D6

Churchtown House   *Tel* 00 353 53-32555
Tagoat   *Fax* 00 353 53-32577
                    Email info@churchtownhouse.com
                    Website www.churchtownhouse.com

'Comfortable, quiet, and spotless.' This year's endorsement for Austin and Patricia Cody's handsome white Georgian house, 'very convenient' for Rosslare, which has ferries to Wales and France. Meals are geared towards the needs of the guest. Breakfast ('superb') can be provided early for those catching a dawn ferry; an early supper is served to those staying for the October opera festival in nearby Wexford. Set in large grounds, the house is liked for the 'calm atmosphere'; the Codys are 'very professional' hosts, who cater 'kindly and sensibly' for children. There are 'tasteful modern *objets d'art*' in rooms and passages, and Irish paintings hang on the walls. The 'Irish country' cooking is based on 'what is in season in our locality, be it seafood from Kilmore Quay, lamb from the county, and vegetables and fruit from our garden'. Guests meet for sherry before dinner, but sit at separate tables. (*P and JL, and others*)

12 bedrooms. 5 on ground floor. On R736, 2½ miles S of Rosslare. Open Mar–Oct. Restaurant closed Sun and Mon. 2 lounges, 2 dining rooms; private dining room. No background music. 8-acre grounds. Golf, fishing, riding, beaches nearby. No smoking. No dogs in house. Amex, MasterCard, Visa accepted. B&B [2006] €60–€95 per person. Set dinner €39.50.

SCHULL Co. Cork   Map 6:D4

Rock Cottage   *Tel/Fax* 00 353 28-35538
Barnatonicane   *Email* rockcottage@eircom.net
                                      Website www.rockcottage.ie

♔ *César award in 2004*

Standing among grassy hillocks, with mature trees and a well-kept garden, Barbara Klötzer's 'charming' Georgian hunting lodge, run as a small guest house, has 'stunning views' of Dunmanus Bay. Her slate-sided house has fine furnishings, an eclectic collection of paintings and prints, ornaments and flowers ('she is a consummate lover of all things bright and beautiful'). Two of the three bedrooms are 'spacious and airy'; bathrooms are good (one is adjacent). Drinks and *amuse-gueule* are taken by the drawing room fire before dinner, served at 7.30 pm. Ms Klötzer's cooking is 'based on fresh local produce' (warm Ardsallah goat's cheese with aubergine); 'delicious food, enormous quantities', said a visitor. No choice: 'Let me know your preferences, otherwise it is a surprise.' Breakfast, in the dining room with cheery yellow table linen, has fresh orange juice; cooked dishes include Parasher Special (named after a guest who liked fried mushrooms), Gubbeen lardon and tomatoes topped with Parmesan shavings; or a 'healthy continental with an abundance of fruit'. Donkeys, hens, dogs and cats roam on the working farm next door. (*DD, and others*)

3 bedrooms. Also 1 self-catering cottage. 8 miles NW of Schull. Lounge (background music 'when guests want it'), dining room. 17-acre grounds. Unsuitable for &. No smoking. No children under 10. Guide dogs only. MasterCard, Visa accepted. B&B €55–€90 per person. Set dinner €45. 1-night bookings refused bank holidays.

When you make a booking you enter into a contract with a hotel. Most hotels explain their cancellation policies, which vary widely, in a letter of confirmation. You may lose your deposit or be charged at the full rate for the room if you cancel at short notice. A travel insurance policy can provide protection.

SHANAGARRY Co. Cork   Map 6:D5

Ballymaloe House

Tel 00 353 21-465 2531
Fax 00 353 21-465 2021
Email res@ballymaloe.ie
Website www.ballymaloe.com

Q *César award in 1984*

'The epitome of a good hotel', the Allen family's hotel/restaurant and cookery school has been a favourite of *Guide* readers since the first edition. The veteran Myrtle Allen still presides; one daughter-in-law, Hazel, is manager; another daughter-in-law, Darina, the food writer, runs the cookery school. The 'highlight of our holiday' for a visitor attending the school this year was chef Jason Fahy's five-course dinner, served in one of *Ballymaloe*'s five small dining rooms. 'Delicious onion and thyme leaf soup; a plate of locally smoked fish; roast duck the best any of us had tasted.' Other recent praise: 'All the staff are enthused by the mission to make you feel cherished.' 'Like a cultured private home', the ivy-clad Georgian house is filled with paintings and books; it stands in extensive grounds (with sculptures, ponds with duck and geese, and a swimming pool) on a large farm which supplies the kitchen. Some bedrooms are in a Norman keep; those in the main house are largest; some others may be cramped. 'Our comfortable room in a new wing had French doors on to the garden.' Breakfast has 'very good marmalade and kippers'. (*Graham Greetham, and others*)

33 bedrooms. 10 in adjacent building. 4 on ground floor. On L35 Ballycotton road 20 miles E of Cork. Closed 22–26 Dec. Drawing room, 2 small sitting rooms, conservatory, 5 dining rooms; conference facilities. No background music. Irish entertainment weekly in summer. 40-acre grounds: farm; gardens, tennis, swimming pool (heated in summer), 6-hole golf course, croquet, children's play area; craft shop. Cookery school nearby. Sea 3 miles: sand and rock beaches; fishing, riding by arrangement. Unsuitable for &. No smoking. No dogs. All major credit cards accepted. B&B €105–€180 per person; D,B&B €170–€245. Set dinner €65. **'V'**

STRANGFORD Co. Down   Map 6:B6

The Cuan   `NEW/BUDGET`
Strangford BT30 7ND

Tel 028-4488 1222
Email info@thecuan.com
Website www.thecuan.com

Peter and Caroline McErlean's 'licensed guest inn', on main street of conservation village on shores of Strangford Lough (ferries to Portaferry). Jolly local, with roaring fires in winter, decent, comfortable rooms, good beer, 2 bars, good Irish home cooking in restaurant. Friendly proprietors and staff, reasonable prices.' Small function facilities. Closed 25 Dec. Smoking in bar only. Dogs in bar only. 9 bedrooms. Amex, MasterCard, Visa accepted. B&B [2006] £35–£50 per person; D,B&B £49–£64.

THURLES Co. Tipperary   Map 6:C5

Inch House   *Tel* 00 353 504-51348
Inch, Thurles   *Fax* 00 353 504-51754
                                            Email mairin@inchhouse.ie
                                            Website www.inchhouse.ie

'We adored this gem; it was like staying with a family, we were sorry to leave.' This year's praise for John and Nora Egan's fine Georgian mansion which they run as a country house and restaurant. 'We were welcomed by their daughter, Mairin, who runs front-of-house with efficiency. We were invited to relax in the drawing room while a tray of tea was brought with delicious home-made profiteroles and caramel sauce.' For those whose appetite isn't diminished, the chef, Kieran O'Dwyer, serves 'European dishes with an Irish influence', eg, pan-fried goat's cheese, duo of salmon and monkfish with a beurre blanc sauce. 'The food was excellent, the service efficient but not intrusive. A well-stocked wine cellar.' The bedrooms are large and comfortable: 'Ours, the largest, had a sofa by the fireplace.' The Egans tell us that all rooms have been redecorated this year. The 'magnificent public rooms' are decorated in Adam style, with period furniture. The dining room, elegant in red and green, has a log fire; the drawing room has a huge stained-glass window. There may be noise when diners leave the restaurant. Breakfast has fruit, yogurt, home-made jams and soda bread. (*Nikki Wild*)

5 bedrooms. On R498, 4 miles W of Thurles. Closed Christmas/New Year. Dining room closed midday, Sun night, Mon night. Drawing room, bar, restaurant (Irish background music); chapel; conference/function facilities. 2-acre garden in 250-acre farm. Golf, riding, fishing nearby. Unsuitable for &. No smoking. No 'very small' children in the restaurant. Guide dogs only. MasterCard, Visa accepted. B&B €55–€70 per person. Set dinner €47–€49.

How to contact the *Guide*
By mail: From anywhere in the UK, write to Freepost PAM 2931, London W11 4BR (no stamp is needed)
From outside the UK: Good Hotel Guide, 50 Addison Avenue, London W11 4QP, England
By telephone or fax: 020-7602 4182
By email: Goodhotel@aol.com
Via our website: www.goodhotelguide.com

WATERFORD Co. Waterford   Map 6:D5

Foxmount Country House   NEW   *Tel* 00 353 51-874308
Passage East Road   *Fax* 00 353 51-854906
                              Email info@foxmountcountryhouse.com
                              Website www.foxmountcountryhouse.com

Reached by a long tree-lined drive, David and Margaret Kent's lovely
creeper-covered 17th-century house is on a working dairy farm 'though
you would hardly know it'. 'Mrs Kent was friendly without being
imposing,' said the nominator. 'When we phoned to say our ferry was
late, she booked a table for us at a restaurant in Waterford to ensure that
our evening was not spoiled.' Guests can take tea in front of the log fire
in the sitting room, and bring their own pre-dinner drinks. 'Our bedroom
was clean and homely, with fresh fruit; a pretty view; lovely towels

in the huge bathroom.'
Mrs Kent's award-winning
breakfast has home-made
scones, preserves and bread.
'Her scrambled eggs passed
the test, as good as it gets.'
The garden is immaculately
kept; 'a most relaxed place'.
(*Nick Slattery*)

5 bedrooms. 4 miles E of Waterford. Open 10 Mar–1 Nov. Sitting room, dining
room (background music). 4-acre grounds. No smoking. No dogs. No credit cards.
B&B €55–€65 per person.

See also SHORTLIST

WEXFORD Co. Wexford *See SHORTLIST*   Map 6:D6

∗∗

Traveller's tale We asked for tea in the garden. We waited and
waited. I went inside. They said: 'Oh, we weren't sure where you
were' (the garden is not large) and then: 'Oh, and we weren't sure
how many there were of you.' Talk about fumbling for excuses.
Eventually someone shuffled out with a tea tray (no biscuits).
(*Hotel in Wales*)

∗∗

SHORTLIST

Our selection of hotels for main entries in the *Guide* is based on quality and character rather than on location. This means that we may have a limited choice in some towns and cities (or in certain cases no hotels at all). This Shortlist is designed to fill the gaps. We have looked for hotels, guest houses and B&Bs which we believe should provide reasonable accommodation in those areas where our choice is limited. Some are more business-oriented than those we also feature in the main section; some (usually new nominations not yet checked out) may later qualify for a full entry. We would welcome readers' reports on all of the hotels on the Shortlist. Those places which do not also have a full entry in the *Guide* are indicated on the maps by a triangle.

LONDON   Map 2:D4

Apex City of London 1 Seething Lane EC3N 4AX. *Tel* 0845-365 0000, www.apexhotel.co.uk. Near Tower of London, hi-tech, contemporary hotel; panoramic views. *Addendum* restaurant and brasserie, chic bar; business facilities; gym, sauna, steam room. 130 bedrooms. B&B from £59.50 per person. (Underground: Tower Hill)

B+B Belgravia 64–66 Ebury Street SW1W 9QD. *Tel* 020-7259 8570, www.bb-belgravia.com. Sleek accommodation at posh town house address. Welcoming staff. Lounge with open fire, free Internet, complimentary tea/coffee. 17 bedrooms: single £94, double £99–£105. (Underground: Sloane Sq)

City Inn Westminster 30 John Islip Street SW1P 4DD. *Tel* 020-7630 1000, www.cityinn.com. Large, contemporary hotel (City Inn group) by Tate Britain. Modern art, ruby-red decor in *Millbank* cocktail bar; *City* café. Gym. 460 bedrooms. B&B double from £149. Special breaks. (Underground: Pimlico)

The Colonnade 2 Warrington Crescent, Little Venice W9 1ER. *Tel* 020-7286 1052, www.theetoncollection.com. In Little Venice, near Regent's Canal: 2 Victorian town houses converted into lavishly decorated boutique hotel. Wedgwood fireplace; Art Deco lift. 43 bedrooms (some split-level). B&B double from £185. (Underground: Warwick Rd, Paddington)

County Hall Premier Travel Inn Belvedere Road SE1 7PB. *Tel* 0870-238 3300, www.premiertravelinn.com. Budget hotel, newly refurbished, in old County Hall building by London Eye, opposite Houses of Parliament. Bar, restaurant, lift. 314 uniform bedrooms: from £92. Breakfast £7.50. (Underground: Waterloo)

Covent Garden Hotel 10 Monmouth Street WC2H 9HB. *Tel* 020-7806 1000, www.coventgardenhotel.co.uk. Dramatic interior, appropriate for theatreland location (Royal Opera House nearby): part of Firmdale Hotels group, managed by Helle Jensen. Drawing room, library, bar, *Brasserie Max;* screening room; gym; beauty treatments. 58 bedrooms: single from £220, double £265–£495, suite £350–£950. Breakfast from £15. (Underground: Covent Garden)

Dorset Square Hotel 39 Dorset Square NW1 6QN. *Tel* 020-7723 7874, www.dorsetsquare.co.uk. Grand country house style facing garden square, site of Thomas Lord's first cricket ground. Modern English cuisine in *Potting Shed* restaurant. Lounge, bar. Leisure centre nearby. 37 bedrooms: double £220–£260, suite £350. Breakfast £13.22–£15.75. (Underground: Marylebone)

Dukes St James's Place SW1A 1NY. *Tel* 020-7491 4840, www.dukeshotel. com. Behind a small courtyard in side street, discreet hotel with traditional decor, up-to-the-minute features. 'Immaculately clean.' Lounge, restaurant (modern British), bar; 24-hour room service; health club; Zen garden. Sold in July 2006 to a Dubai-based developer. 90 bedrooms: single £145–£235, double £165–£340, suite £315–£850. (Underground: Green Park)

Kensington House 15–16 Prince of Wales Terrace W8 5PQ. *Tel* 020-7937 2345, www.kenhouse.com. In quiet street near Kensington Gardens and High Street: 19th-century stucco-fronted town house. Contemporary decor. Informal dining in *Tiger Bar*; 24-hour room service. 41 bedrooms. B&B (continental): single £150, double £175–£195, suite £215. Breakfast £14.50–£19.75. Weekend offers. (Underground: High St Kensington)

Knightsbridge Hotel 10 Beaufort Gardens SW3 1PT. Tel 020-7584 6300, www.knightsbridgehotel.com. Chic, homely, B&B hotel in quiet tree-lined cul-de-sac near shops. Part of Firmdale Hotels group. Lounge, library, bar; room service meals. 44 bedrooms: single £150–£160, double £180–£260, suite £295–£450. Breakfast alc £14.50. (Underground: Knightsbridge)

The Langorf 18–20 Frognal NW3 6AG. *Tel* 020-7794 4483, www. langorfhotel.com. In quiet residential area near Hampstead: unpretentious B&B in Edwardian red brick building. Bar, breakfast room facing garden; room service. 31 bedrooms, 5 apartments. B&B (continental buffet): single £82, double £98–£110. (Underground: Finchley Rd)

Malmaison Charterhouse Square EC1M 6AH. Tel 0854-365 4247, www.malmaison.com. Former nurses' hostel, in quiet square in trendy Clerkenwell. Informal style; earth tones with splashes of red; oak, chrome, cubist-style furniture. Bar, restaurant; gym. Dogs welcome (£10 charge). 97 bedrooms: from £205. Breakfast £16.95. (Underground: Farringdon, Barbican)

Miller's Residence 111a Westbourne Grove W2 4UW. Tel 020-7243 1024, www.millersuk.com. 18th century-style furnishing, a treasure trove of nymphs, cherubs and candelabras, embellish this house on Westbourne Grove. Owned by Andrew Miller (author of eponymous antiques guide). Large breakfast room/bar/drawing room. 5 bedrooms, 2 suites. B&B (continental; evening cocktails; *excluding VAT*): double £150–£185, suite £230. (Underground: Notting Hill Gate, Bayswater, Queensway)

Pavilion Hotel 34–36 Sussex Gardens W2 1UL. *Tel* 020-7262 0905, www.pavilionhoteluk.com. Danny Karne's funky 'fashion glam and rock 'n' roll' hotel, near Hyde Park. Not for the conventional or faint-hearted; liked by pop stars and models. Steam room; car park. 30 bedrooms (Indian Summer, Casablanca Nights, Chapter & Verse, etc). B&B: single £60–£85, double £100. (Underground: Edgware Rd, Paddington)

Portobello Gold 95–97 Portobello Road W11 2QB. *Tel* 020-7460 4910, www.portobellogold.com. Mike Bell's quirky restaurant-with-rooms on street famed for Saturday market. Work by local and international artists in Gold Gallery. Conservatory restaurant, bar; Internet café, function facilities. 8 bedrooms; 1 roof terrace apartment: double £55–£180, suite £180. Breakfast £6.95. (Underground: Notting Hill Gate)

The Rockwell 181 Cromwell Road SW5 0SF *Tel* 020-7244 2000, www.therockwellhotel.com. Contemporary Earl's Court hotel opened in May 2006. Plain furnishing, flamboyant wallpaper. Restaurant, bar; garden. 40 bedrooms (some with south-facing patio; some split level). B&B: single from £100, double £160–£180. (Underground: Earl's Court, Gloucester Rd)

The Rookery Peter's Lane, Cowcross Street EC1M 6DS. *Tel* 020-7336 0931, www.rookeryhotel.com. Peter McKay's quirky conversion of Georgian buildings in Smithfield: wood panelling, antiques, Victorian bathroom fittings. Library, drawing room, conservatory (honesty bar); conference facilities. Tiny garden. 33 bedrooms: single £175, double £205–£255, suite £395. Continental breakfast £9.75. (Underground: Farringdon)

Royal Park Hotel 3 Westbourne Terrace, Lancaster Gate W2 3UL. *Tel* 020-7479 6600, www.theroyalpark.com. Near Hyde Park: elegant conversion of 3 listed Georgian town houses. Victorian and Georgian antiques; plain-painted walls in Regency colours. Four-poster and half-tester beds. Drawing room. Small room-service menu. 48 bedrooms: single £170, double £195–£225, suite £265–£300. Breakfast £9.95. (Underground: Paddington)

St James's Club & Hotel 7–8 Park Place, St James's SW1A 1LP. *Tel* 020-7629 7688, www.stjamesclubandhotel.co.uk. Smart facade, subdued interior: boutique hotel in former 'gentlemen's chambers for the aristocracy' (1892). Courteous staff. Lounge, bar, restaurant; function facilities; fitness room; sauna. 56 bedrooms (*excluding VAT*): double £145–£245, suite from £350. (Underground: Green Park)

Searcy's Roof Garden Rooms 30 Pavilion Road, Knightsbridge SW1X 0HJ. *Tel* 020-7584 4921, www.30pavilionroad.co.uk. Stylish B&B in Georgian town house off Sloane St, owned by Searcy's catering group, managed by Dimitrios Neofitidis. No public rooms. Large roof garden. 10 bedrooms: single/double from £99, suite from £189. (Underground: Sloane Sq)

Shaftesbury Hotel 65–73 Shaftesbury Avenue W1D 6EX. *Tel* 020-7871 6000, www.shaftesburyhotellondon.co.uk. 'Fantastic location' in theatreland, Best Western member with ultra-modern interior: mood lighting, TV in bathrooms, air conditioning. Lounge, restaurants, *Premier* bar; 'slow' lift; fitness room; conference facilities. 67 bedrooms. B&B: single from £195, double from £250. (Underground: Piccadilly Circus, Leicester Sq)

The Soho Hotel 4 Richmond Mews, off Dean Street W1D 3DH. *Tel* 020-7559 3000, www.sohohotel.com. Chic luxury hotel (the first in Soho), opened in 2004 by Tim and Kit Kemp of Firmdale Hotels. Granite, oak, and glass bathrooms. Drawing room, library, bar/restaurant, 4 private dining rooms; 2 screening rooms. 85 bedrooms (some suitable for &): £240–£295; 29 suites: £350–£2,500. Breakfast from £16. (Underground: Leicester Sq)

The Stafford 16–18 St James's Place SW1A 1NJ. *Tel* 020-7493 0111, www.thestaffordhotel.co.uk. In quiet backwater off St James's St: sedately elegant hotel, 'quiet; good service'. Lounge, American bar (food served), restaurant. Children welcomed. Access to nearby health club. 68 bedrooms. B&B (*excluding VAT*): single £230, double £250–£335, suite £405–£595. (Underground: Green Park)

10 Manchester Street 10 Manchester Street W1U 4DDG. *Tel* 020-7486 6669. Privately owned red brick 'no-frills' B&B hotel near Marylebone High St. Spacious rooms. Lounge, breakfast room. 46 bedrooms (largest overlook square; quietest ones at rear). B&B (continental): single £60–£80, double £80–£120, suite £110–£140. (Underground: Baker St)

Thanet Hotel 8 Bedford Place WC1B 5JA. *Tel* 020-7636 2869, www.thanethotel.co.uk. Grade II listed Georgian terrace B&B, near British Museum, run by owners, Richard and Lynwen Orchard. Reading room, breakfast room. 17 basic bedrooms (some family; rear ones quietest), with shower/WC. B&B: single £76, double £100. (Underground: Holborn, Russell Sq)

Threadneedles 5 Threadneedle Street EC2R 8AY. *Tel* 020-7657 8080, www.theetongroup.com. Near Bank of England: 1856 banking hall strikingly converted into 'luxury boutique hotel'. Original glass dome towers over reception lounge. Bar, restaurant (closed weekends); 3 meeting rooms; health/fitness club; conference facilities. 69 bedrooms: single/double £260–£285, suite £440–£470. Breakfast £20. (Underground: Bank)

Twenty Nevern Square 20 Nevern Square SW5 9PD. *Tel* 020-7565 9555, www.twentynevernsquare.co.uk. Red brick Victorian town house, overlooking garden square. Emphasis on natural materials. Hand-carved furniture. Lounge, *Café Twenty.* 23 bedrooms. B&B: single £79–£140, double £80–£159, suite £159–£199. (Underground: Earl's Court)

ENGLAND

ALDEBURGH Suffolk   Map 2:C6
White Lion Market Cross Place IP15 5BJ. *Tel* 01728-452720, www.whitelion.co.uk. Aldeburgh's oldest hotel (16th-century; Best Western). Central, opposite beach. Oak panelling, beams, inglenook fireplace.

2 lounges, 2 bars, restaurant (emphasis on fish and seafood). 'Most enjoyable; cuisine good, staff helpful.' Parking. 38 bedrooms (no-smoking; some with sea view). B&B £46.50–£126 per person.

ASHFORD Kent   Map 2:D5

Eastwell Manor Eastwell Park, Boughton Lees TN25 4HR. *Tel* 01233-213000, www.eastwellmanor.co.uk. 4 miles N of centre, near Channel Tunnel/Ashford International Railway Station: grand Tudor-style 1920s house in 62-acre grounds on 3,000-acre estate. Original features: moulded ceilings, huge fireplaces. Lounges, bars, restaurant, brasserie; spa, gym, beauty salon, indoor/outdoor swimming pools, tennis; function facilities. 62 bedrooms; family apartments in mews (some suitable for &). B&B double £190–£434; D,B&B double £265–£490.

BATH Somerset   Map 2:D1

Aquae Sulis 174–176 Newbridge Road BA1 3LE. *Tel* 01225-420061, www.aquaesulishotel.co.uk. 'Smashing' family-run hotel in Edwardian house, traditionally furnished: short bus trip from Abbey (Park & Ride close by). Lounge, restaurant bar; patio garden. 'Excellently executed meal, lovely breakfast too.' Parking. 13 bedrooms (some family). B&B: single £49–£59, double £55–£95.

The Ayrlington 24–25 Pulteney Road BA2 4EZ. *Tel* 01225-425495, www.ayrlington.com. Oriental touches (Buddha in hallway, incense, Asian works of art) amid luxury at Simon and Mee-Ling Roper's listed Victorian house. 'Really enjoyed. Close to centre, and I could park my car – a rare thing in Bath.' Lounge/bar, breakfast room. Garden. Parking. No smoking. 14 bedrooms. B&B £75–£175 per person.

Kennard 11 Henrietta Street BA2 6LL. *Tel* 01225-310472, www.kennard.co.uk. Colourful 18th-century town house, well positioned (just across Pulteney Bridge) for exploring Bath. Breakfast room. No background music. No smoking. Patio garden. Parking passes. 14 bedrooms (2 on ground floor). B&B £48–£79 per person.

Number 30 30 Crescent Gardens BA1 2NB. *Tel* 01225-337393, www.numberthirty.com. 5 mins' walk from centre, light, airy (no-smoking) B&B owned by David and Caroline Greenwood. Vegetarian/healthy option breakfast. Parking. 6 bedrooms (1 room designed for allergy sufferers). B&B: single £57–£72, double £75–£99.

BATTLE East Sussex   Map 2:E4

Little Hemingfold Farmhouse Telham, TN33 0TT. *Tel* 01424-774338, www.littlehemingfoldhotel.co.uk. Down ½ mile track, Paul and Allison

Slater's peaceful retreat in 43 acres of woods and farmland, with 2-acre spring-fed trout lake for boating, fishing or swimming. 2 sitting rooms, dining room, bar. Tennis court; dogs welcome. 'Lovely scenery, with long walks from the door.' 12 bedrooms. B&B £58–£99 per person; D,B&B from £74.50.

The PowderMills Powdermill Lane TN33 0SP. *Tel* 01424-775511, www.powdermillshotel.com. Douglas and Julie Cowpland's country house hotel in listed 18th-century building on site of former gunpowder works. Elegant drawing room; library, *Orangery* restaurant, conservatory; function/ wedding facilities. 200-acre grounds: unheated swimming pool, 7-acre fishing lake, woods. 40 bedrooms (5 suites in *Pavilion*). B&B: single from £99, double £110–£155, suite £195.

BEAULIEU Hampshire   Map 2:E2
The Master Builder's House Buckler's Hard SO42 7XB. *Tel* 01590-616253, www.themasterbuilders.co.uk. Rambling building in lovely setting overlooking river; direct sailing to Solent from garden pontoon. Near Maritime Museum. Lounge, *Riverview* restaurant, *Yachtsman's* bar; conference facilities. Garden. Parking. 25 bedrooms. B&B double £134–£242; D,B&B double (min. 2 nights) £226–£283.

Montagu Arms Palace Lane SO42 7ZL. *Tel* 01590-612324, www.montaguarmshotel.co.uk. In New Forest riverside village: sprawling, elegantly restored, 1930s building. 'Lunch was an absolute treat.' 'Excellent breakfast.' Lounge, library/bar, conservatory, *Terrace* restaurant, *Monty's* bar/brasserie; conference/function facilities. Garden. Parking. 23 bedrooms. B&B: single £130, double from £195, suite from £235.

BERWICK-UPON-TWEED Northumberland   Map 4:A3
Marshall Meadows TD15 1UT. *Tel* 01289-331133, www.marshallmeadows.co.uk. England's most northerly hotel, 400 yds from Scottish border. Georgian building in 15-acre gardens and woodland. Lounge, bar, restaurant; conference/function facilities. 19 bedrooms (farmland or garden views). B&B: single £85–£95, double £120–£130, suite £150-£165; D,B&B (min. 2 nights) from £55.50 per person.

BIRMINGHAM West Midlands   Map 2:B2
Malmaison The Mailbox, 1 Wharfside Street B1 1RD. *Tel* 0121-246 5000, www.malmaison.com. In Mailbox complex: converted 1960s Royal Mail sorting office, short walk from station. Funky design. Hi-tech facilities. Bar, brasserie; gym; meeting/function facilities. 184 bedrooms: double from £160. Breakfast £9.95–£12.75.

BLACKBURN Lancashire   Map 4:D3
Millstone Church Lane, Mellor BB2 7JR. *Tel* 01254-813333, www. millstonehotel.co.uk. 3 miles N of centre: stone-built former coaching inn retaining country style, owned by Shire Hotels, and run by chef, Anson Bolton. 2 lounges, bar, *Millers* restaurant (emphasis on Lancashire produce). Parking. 23 bedrooms (some no-smoking; 6 in courtyard; 1 suitable for &). B&B £48–£109 per person; D,B&B from £86.50

BLACKPOOL Lancashire   Map 4:D2
Number One 1 St Lukes Road, South Shore FY4 2EL. *Tel* 01253-343901, www.numberoneblackpool.com. Mark and Claire Smith's stylish B&B in period house on regenerated South Shore. Up-to-the-minute bathrooms; state-of-the-art gadgetry. Generous breakfast in red-walled room. No smoking. Large garden. Ample parking. 3 bedrooms (plasma TV, DVD-player, etc). B&B from £60 per person.

BOSCASTLE Cornwall   Map 1:C3
Trerosewill Farmhouse Paradise PL35 0BL. *Tel* 01840-250545, www. trerosewill.co.uk. On 40 acres of farmland (with badger sett), Steve and Cheryl Nicholls's B&B. Coastline views, northwards to Hartland Point and Lundy Island; south-west to Tintagel and the Rumps. Home-made breakfast using local produce, in conservatory dining room. 1-acre garden. 6 bedrooms. B&B £30–£79 per person.

BOURNEMOUTH Dorset   Map 2:E2
Whitehall Exeter Park Road BH2 5AX. *Tel* 01202-554682, www. thewhitehallhotel.co.uk. Edwardian hotel, 2 mins' walk from centre, run by owners, Sara and Bernard Uzzell, with help from long-serving staff. Traditional decor. Views from terrace over Lower Gardens. Direct access to beach (5 mins). 2 lounges, bar, dining room; conference/function facilities. Parking. 46 bedrooms. B&B from £36 per person.

BRIGHTON East Sussex   Map 2:E4
Fivehotel 5 New Steine BN2 1PB. *Tel* 01273-686547, www.fivehotel.com. Caroline and Simon Heath's period town house in Kemp Town Regency square; crisp, contemporary rooms. Organic breakfasts; sea views. No smoking. 10 bedrooms. B&B from £30 per person.

Nineteen 19 Broad Street BN2 1TJ. *Tel* 01273-675529, www.hotelnineteen. co.uk. Stunning interior in Kemp Town house: white walls, blue lighting, glass beds, slatted silver blinds, contemporary artwork by local artists. Breakfast served in bedroom; kitchen facilities: complimentary drinks and snacks. 8 bedrooms (flat-screen TV, CD, DVD-player). B&B (continental) double £120–£250.

Paskins Town House 18–19 Charlotte Street BN2 1AG. *Tel* 01273-601203, www.paskins.co.uk. 100 yds from sea, Susan and Roger Marlowe's eco-friendly town house. Organic/locally produced ingredients at breakfast; vegetarian/vegan dishes a speciality. Art Nouveau reception; 2 lounges, bar, Art Deco breakfast room. 19 bedrooms (most with shower). B&B double from £70.

Hotel Seattle Brighton Marina BN2 5WA. *Tel* 01273-679799, www.aliashotels.com. In waterfront development, 1 mile E of centre: owned by Alias Hotels, managed by Chris Williams. Contemporary style (nautical undertones), amusing touches, informal ambience. Black-and-white cocktail bar; saloon lounge with decking; sea-facing *Café Paradiso* (Mediterranean food); meeting/function facilities. Large free car park. 71 bedrooms (some suitable for &): double £100–£160.

Square 4 New Steine BN2 1PB. *Tel* 01273-691777, www.squarebrighton.com. Keith Allison's Regency town house in Kemp Town garden square. Glamorous interior: suede sofas, fur throws, deep baths. 'Reverse penthouse' in basement. Bar. No children. 9 bedrooms (some with sea view). B&B: double £160–£210, penthouse £380.

BRISTOL   Map 1:B6
Hotel du Vin & Bistro Narrow Lewins Mead BS1 2NU. *Tel* 0117-925 5577, www.hotelduvin.com. Converted warehouses in city centre; modern style, glassed canopy entrance, 'dark, sombre colours'. Limited secure parking. Busy bistro (booking advised). 40 bedrooms, some loft style on two levels: £130–£350. Breakfast £9.95–£13.50.

BROMSGROVE Worcestershire   Map 3:C5
Ladybird Lodge 2 Finstall Road, Aston Fields B60 2DZ. *Tel* 01527-889900, www.ladybirdlodge.co.uk. Handy for Birmingham and NEC: recently built extension to *Ladybird Inn*. Lounge, pub, *Rosado's* restaurant (Italian); conference facilities. Parking. 43 bedrooms (DVD-player, modem, etc; views of countryside). B&B (continental): single £44–£65, double £54–£75.

BURY ST EDMUNDS Suffolk   Map 2:B5
Ravenwood Hall IP30 9JA. *Tel* 01359-270345, www.ravenwoodhall.co.uk. Historic home (Tudor origins) of Craig Jarvis, in 7-acre garden and woodlands. Child-friendly (toys, games, colouring books, goats). Off A14 (some traffic noise), 3 miles SE of Bury. Lounge (inglenook fireplace), bar,

restaurant; conference/wedding facilities; croquet, heated outdoor pool. 14 bedrooms (7 in mews). B&B: single £85–£115, double £110–£165.

BUXTON Derbyshire   Map 3:A6

Grendon Bishops Lane SK17 6UN. *Tel* 01298-78831, www. grendonguesthouse.co.uk. Hilary and Colin Parker's welcoming, no-smoking guest house, ½ mile from centre on quiet country lane leading to Goyt valley hills. Lounge, dining room (bring your own wine); 'superb breakfast – everything home-made'; terrace, garden. Parking. 5 bedrooms. B&B £30–£45 per person. Set dinner £15.

Old Hall The Square SK17 6BD. *Tel* 01298-22841, www.oldhallhotelbuxton. co.uk. Across square from opera house, reputedly oldest hotel in England. Peaceful setting; traditional decor. 2 lounges, wine bar, *George Potter* bar, restaurant; conference facilities. 38 bedrooms. B&B £55–£75 per person; D,B&B (2-night break) £135–£145.

CAMBRIDGE Cambridgeshire   Map 2:B4

Cambridge Lodge 139 Huntingdon Road CB3 0DQ. *Tel* 01223-352833, *email* cambridge.lodge@bt.connect.com. Darren and Stephanie Chamberlain's mock Tudor house 1 mile from centre. Oak-beamed restaurant; 'very good food, especially Sunday lunch'. Parking. Gardens. 15 bedrooms: single £77.50, double £99.

Hotel Felix Whitehouse Lane, Huntingdon Road CB3 0LX. *Tel* 01223-277977, www.hotelfelix.co.uk. 1½ miles from centre, on edge of city: business people's hotel. Extended, late Victorian yellow brick mansion. 'Clean-cut, style-conscious' decor; king-size beds. Small lounge, bar, *Graffiti* restaurant (modern Mediterranean cooking); function facilities; 3½-acre garden, terrace. Parking. 52 bedrooms (some suitable for &). B&B: single from £136, double from £168, suite from £255.

Wallis Farmhouse 98 Main Street, Hardwick CB3 7QU. *Tel* 01954-210347, www.wallisfarmhouse.co.uk. Late Georgian farmhouse B&B in village 5 miles W of Cambridge. Communal breakfast. Pub nearby for evening meal. Large gardens and meadows adjoining woodland. Parking. 6 bedrooms (all on ground floor, in barn conversion across courtyard). B&B: single £45–£50, double/family £60–£90.

CANTERBURY Kent   Map 2:D5

Ebury Hotel 65–67 New Dover Road CT1 3DX. *Tel* 01227-768433, www.ebury-hotel.co.uk. Near cathedral: Henry Mason's solid Victorian house (*c.* 1840) with many original features (including Charlie the 'labradoodle'). Lounge, restaurant (French cuisine); indoor swimming pool.

Large garden. Parking. 15 bedrooms. B&B £47.50–£75 per person; D,B&B £62.50–£90.

Magnolia House 36 St Dunstan's Terrace CT2 8AX. *Tel* 01227-765121, www.magnoliahousecanterbury.co.uk. Late Georgian no-smoking guest house, in residential street ½ mile from centre. Isobelle Leggett offers complimentary drinks on arrival; dinner by prior arrangement (Nov–Feb). Lounge, dining room. Walled garden. Parking. 7 bedrooms (some cramped; 1 on ground floor). B&B £47.50–£67.50 per person.

CARLISLE Cumbria   Map 4:B2
Willowbeck Lodge Lambley Bank, Scotby CA4 8BX. *Tel* 01228-513607, www.willowbeck-lodge.com. Liz and John McGrillis's bright, modern Scandinavian-style lodge in woodland, 2½ miles from centre. Garden: stream, birdlife. Contemporary lounge (soaring ceiling, gallery, wood-burning stove) faces large pond. Library, dining room (evening meal by arrangement, £20). Parking. 4 bedrooms (1 on ground floor). B&B double £85–£105.

CHAGFORD Devon   Map 1:C4
Parford Well Sandy Park TQ13 8JW. *Tel* 01647-433353, www.parfordwell.co.uk. 'Comfortable and tasteful. Should remain a secret!' Smart, small B&B owned by Tim Daniel, in walled garden within Dartmoor national park. 3 bedrooms. B&B £32.50–£70 per person.

CHELTENHAM Gloucestershire   Map 3:D5
Milton House 12 Bayshill Road, Royal Parade GL50 3AY. *Tel* 01242-582601, www.miltonhousehotel.co.uk. 'Charming' Claude Cittadino's elegant Grade II listed Regency house near Promenade. Lounge, conservatory breakfast room. Parking. 8 bedrooms. B&B: single £65–£75, double £85–£115.

The Townhouse 12–14 Pittville Lawn GL52 2BD. *Tel* 01242-221922, www.cheltenhamtownhouse.com. Adam and Jayne Lillywhite's smart modern B&B, done in creams, caramel and coffee shades, 10-min walk from Pump Rooms. 'Good location; comfortable and quiet.' Lounge, bar, dining room; sun deck. Parking. 22 rooms. No smoking. B&B: single £50–£78, double/family £60–£140.

CHESTERFIELD Derbyshire   Map 4:E4
Buckingham's 85 Newbold Road S41 7PU. *Tel* 01246-201041, www.buckinghams-table.com. In 2 Victorian town houses in residential area 5 mins' walk from centre, 'small hotel with a difference' run by Nick

Buckingham, former chef at *The Cavendish*, Baslow (see main entry) and family. 'You give a list of likes and dislikes, and they suggest a menu', served in restaurant (with one communal table) or *Clowns* conservatory (separate tables, open all day). Bar, lounge ('stunning afternoon teas'). 10 bedrooms. B&B: single £62.50–£90, double £90–£105. Dinner £18–£30.

CIRENCESTER Gloucestershire   Map 3:E5

Dix's Barn Duntisbourne Abbots GL7 7JN. *Tel* 01285-821249, *email* wilcox@dixsbarn.freeserve.co.uk. Rosemary Wilcox's budget B&B: converted barn on working farm in lovely countryside 5 miles NW of Cirencester. Tea and cake by log fire in winter, in garden (30-mile views) in summer. 'Excellent breakfast.' Lounge. Non-smokers preferred. 4 bedrooms. B&B from £20 per person.

COVENTRY Warwickshire   Map 2:B2

The Chace Hotel London Road, Toll Bar End CV3 4EQ. *Tel* 0870-609 6130, www.corushotels.com. Convenient for NEC, 3 miles from centre, off A46: Victorian chain hotel in landscaped gardens. Lounge, restaurant, bar; pool table; function facilities. Parking. 66 bedrooms. B&B from £36 per person.

Coombe Abbey Brinklow Road, Binley CV3 2AB. *Tel* 02476-450450, www.coombeabbey.com. Just outside city, in Coombe Country Park: 16th-century Cistercian Abbey turned into 'out-of-the-ordinary' hotel. 'Eccentric collections': ecclesiastical architecture, bishop's tomb; Gothic reception. Bar, restaurant; banqueting hall; function/wedding facilities. Moat; formal gardens. 83 'bedchambers'. B&B double/suite £145–£345.

DARLINGTON Co. Durham   Map 4:C4

Headlam Hall nr Gainford DL2 3HA. *Tel* 01325-730238, www.headlamhall. co.uk. In lower Teesdale hamlet, in 200-acre farmland: Robinson family's 'pleasantly relaxed' hotel in rambling building, half Jacobean, half 18th-century. Lounge, bar, restaurant; indoor swimming pool, sauna; billiard room; conference/function facilities. 4-acre walled garden: lake, tennis, 9-hole golf course, croquet. 34 bedrooms (6 in mews, 9 in coach house, some on ground floor). B&B £50–£120 per person.

DARTMOUTH Devon   Map 1:D4

Dart Marina Sandquay Road TQ6 9PH. *Tel* 01803-832580, www. dartmarinahotel.com. Stylish hotel on waterfront, overlooking marina. Lift. 2 lounges, 2 bars, *River* restaurant (terrace – alfresco dining), *Wildfire* bistro. Lift. Health spa. Parking. Pebble beach. 49 bedrooms (all with river view, some with balcony or French window). B&B: double from £119, suite from £159.

DERBY Derbyshire   Map 3:B6

Mickleover Court Etwall Road, Mickleover DE3 0XX. *Tel* 01332-521234, www.menzies-hotels.co.uk. Modern hotel (Menzies group), 4 miles from centre. Designed around central atrium. Glass lift, 2 bars, Italian restaurant, brasserie; indoor leisure facilities (gym, swimming pool, etc); extensive conference/function facilities. Good access throughout for &. 99 bedrooms. B&B: double from £150, suite £165–£310.

The Stuart 119 London Road DE1 2QR. *Tel* 01332-340633, www.thestuart. com. Near centre and station: privately owned commercial hotel, renovated in contemporary style: dark wood, designer fabrics. Bar, restaurant; conference/wedding facilities. Parking. 90 bedrooms. B&B from £52.50 per person.

DOVER Kent   Map 2:D5

Loddington House 14 East Cliff CT16 1LX. *Tel* 01304-201947, *email* loddingtonhotel@btconnect.com. Kathy and Robert Cupper's seafront Regency Grade II listed guest house. Harbour views; convenient for terminals; 10 mins' walk from centre. Lounge, dining room (evening meal by arrangement, £25). Small garden. 6 bedrooms (rear ones quietest). B&B: single £45–£55, double £65–£75.

DUNSTER Somerset   Map 1:B5

Luttrell Arms Exmoor National Park TA24 6SG. *Tel* 01643-821555, www.luttrellarms.co.uk. In Exmoor national park: small hotel (former 15th-century guest house for abbots of Cleeve). High ceilings, oak beams, four-poster beds. 2 bars, restaurant. Garden: terrace (alfresco meals). 28 bedrooms. B&B: single from £67, double from £94.

DUXFORD Cambridgeshire   Map 2:C4

Duxford Lodge Ickleton Road CB2 4RT. *Tel* 01223-836444, www. duxfordlodgehotel.co.uk. Off M11, near Imperial War Museum: 1900s red brick house (some motorway noise), traditional decor. Cambridge 20 mins' drive N. Lounge bar (pictures of aeroplanes and fighter pilots), *Le Paradis* restaurant; function/wedding facilities. Garden. 15 bedrooms. B&B: single £76–£93.50, double £116–£131.

EASTBOURNE East Sussex   Map 2:E4

Grand Hotel King Edwards Parade BN21 4EQ. *Tel* 01323-412345, www.grandeastbourne.com. Traditional 5-star 19th-century seafront 'white palace'. Live band at weekend; monthly teatime Palm Court quartet. 'Impeccable service.' Suitable for ♿; children welcomed (playroom, carers, high teas). 3 lounges, bar, 2 restaurants; conference/function facilities; health spa; indoor and outdoor swimming pools; garden: putting, etc. Parking. 152 bedrooms (many with sea view). B&B: single £140–£205, double £170–£235.

EXETER Devon   Map 1:C5

The Royal Clarence Cathedral Yard EX1 1HD. *Tel* 01392-319955, www.abodehotels.co.uk. Boutique hotel in heart of city, owned by Andrew Brownsword and Exeter-born, *Michelin*-starred chef Michael Caines. 2 bars, restaurant (food boutique). Fitness spa. 53 bedrooms. B&B double £125–£225.

FALMOUTH Cornwall   Map 1:E2

Green Lawns Western Terrace TR11 4QJ. *Tel* 01326-312734, www.greenlawnshotel.com. Ivy-clad, privately run hotel in style of small French château, near centre. Views across Falmouth Bay. 3 lounges, 2 bars, *Garras* restaurant; leisure/conference/function facilities (indoor swimming pool). Garden: patio area. 39 bedrooms (11 on ground floor). B&B £50–£110 per person.

Greenbank Harbourside TR11 2SR. *Tel* 01326-312440, www.greenbank-hotel.com. 'Warm welcome' at this white hotel (said to be first in Cornish port) by water's edge: panoramic views. 2 lounges, bar, *Harbourside* restaurant 'excellent'. Private quay, small garden. 59 bedrooms ('tastefully refurbished'); some suitable for ♿. B&B double £105–£260.

Park Grove 58 Kimberley Park Road. *Tel* 01326-313276, www.parkgrovehotel.com. Overlooking park, white-painted, family-run hotel, short walk from harbour, town and beaches. 'Unpretentious but comfortable.' Bar, restaurant. Parking. 17 bedrooms. B&B from £39 per person.

Penmere Manor Mongleath Road TR11 4PN. *Tel* 01326-211411, www.penmere.co.uk. In subtropical gardens and woodland, 1 mile from sandy beaches and port, seaside hotel (Best Western) owned by Terzeon family. Lounge, bar, restaurant; gym, solarium, beauty treatments; indoor and outdoor swimming pool, croquet lawn. 37 bedrooms. B&B £51–£82 per person; DB&B £72–£103.

The Rosemary Gyllyngvase Terrace TR11 4DL. *Tel* 01326-314669, www.therosemary.co.uk. 'One is made to feel special' at Suzanne and Geoff Warring's no-smoking, informal hotel with 'superb service' and 'magnificent' sea views. Near coastal path and beaches; short walk to centre.

Lounge, bar. Garden, terrace. 10 bedrooms (2 family). B&B from £31 per person.

FOLKESTONE Kent   Map 2:E5
Sandgate Hotel 8 Wellington Terrace, The Esplanade CT20 3DY. *Tel* 01303-220444, www.sandgatehotel.com. 'Splendid stopover on way to the Continent' (2 miles from Eurotunnel terminal). Opposite pebble beach ('great sea views'); Victorian facade, smart, modern interior. Bar, restaurant (vegetarian, gluten-free and diabetic dishes available); floodlit terrace. 15 rooms. B&B from £37.30 per person.

FORDINGBRIDGE Hampshire   Map 2:E2
Three Lions Stuckton SP6 2HF. *Tel* 01425-652489, www. thethreelionsrestaurant.co.uk. Mike and Jane Womersley's restaurant-with-rooms in New Forest national park. Conservatory sitting room, bar, restaurant. 2-acre garden: sauna, whirlpool. 7 bedrooms (4 ground floor): single £65–£95, double £75–£115.

GATWICK West Sussex   Map 2:D4
Langshott Manor Langshott RH6 9LN. *Tel* 01293-786680, www. alexanderhotels.co.uk. Classic timber-framed Tudor house, now luxury hotel (Alexander Hotels), in 3-acre garden (ancient moat). 5 mins' drive from airport. Lounge, restaurant. 22 bedrooms (some in mews): single from £170, double £190–£320.
Latchetts Cottage Norwood Hill, nr Horley RH16 0ET. *Tel* 01293-862831, www.latchettscottage.co.uk. David Lees's small B&B: 2 converted 1820s farmworkers' cottages, 3 miles from Gatwick but off flight path. Residents' lounge. Cottage-style garden. Local pub for meals 200 yds. Parking. 3 bedrooms (plain; pine furniture). B&B £25–£35 per person.
Lawn Guest House 30 Massetts Road, Horley RH6 7DF. *Tel* 01293-775751, www.lawnguesthouse.co.uk. Carole and Adrian Grinsted's B&B: imposing Victorian house, 1½ miles from airport, 2 mins' walk from Horley centre. Lounge, breakfast room. Secluded garden. Long-term parking/ transfer service. No smoking. 12 bedrooms (some family). B&B: double £58, family £70–£85.
Wayside Manor Farm Norwood Hill, nr Charlwood, Surrey RH6 0ET. *Tel* 01293-862692, www.wayside-manor.com. 'Comfortable bedroom, splendid bathroom, excellent breakfast' at Viv and Phil Plumb's creeper-covered Edwardian house, 8 mins' drive from airport (transport arranged; long-term parking). Lounge, breakfast room. Garden. Pub opposite. 4 no-smoking bedrooms. B&B: double £65, suite/family £80.

GLASTONBURY Somerset   **Map 1:B6**
Number Three Magdalene Street BA6 9EW. *Tel* 01458-832129,
www.numberthree.co.uk. Patricia Redmond's Georgian town house B&B,
by abbey ruins. Breakfast room. Large walled garden. Parking. No
smoking. 5 bedrooms (1 on ground floor). B&B: single £85–£95, double
£110–£120.

GRANTHAM Lincolnshire   **Map 2:A3**
Allington Manor NG32 2DH. *Tel* 01400-281358, www.allingtonmanor.
co.uk. Grand Jacobean manor house (Grade II listed). Drawing room,
dining/breakfast room, imposing red hall (2 large fireplaces), galleried
landing; display of arms and armour. No smoking. 3 bedrooms. B&B £75–
£125 per person.
Angel & Royal High Street NG31 6PN. *Tel* 01476-565816, www.
angelandroyal.co.uk. Ancient inn (1203); once hostel for Brotherhood of
Knights Templar. Lounge, 2 bars, King's Room restaurant, *Simply Bertie's*
bistro; function facilities. 29 bedrooms (1 on ground floor). B&B: single £75-
£85, double £90–£110, suite from £130.

GREAT BIRCHAM Norfolk   **Map 2:A5**
The King's Head Lynn Road PE31 6RJ. *Tel* 01485-578265, www.
the-kings-head-bircham.co.uk. Handsome Victorian inn, extended and
refurbished with contemporary interior: king-size beds, play station (CD,
DVD), Internet. 8 miles to Brancaster Beach; Sandringham close by.
Lounge, bar, restaurant (brasserie and *à la carte* menu); courtyard; function
facilities. 9 bedrooms. B&B: single £69.50–£150, double £125–£175.

GREAT CHESTERFORD Essex   **Map 2:C4**
The Crown House CB10 1NY. *Tel* 01799-530515, www.
thecrownhousehotel.com. Grade II listed building in large garden, 5 mins'
walk from station of village 3 miles NW of Saffron Walden, 15 mins' drive
from Cambridge. Lounge, bar, restaurant. 22 bedrooms (10 in stable block).
B&B: single £65–£74.50, double £84–£145.

GUILDFORD Surrey   **Map 2:D3**
The Angel Posting House 91 The High Street GU1 3DP. *Tel* 01483-
564555, www.angelpostinghouse.com. Historic black-and-white inn
(member of Small Luxury Hotels of the World) on pedestrianised cobbled
high street. Galleried lounge; panelled dining room, vaulted crypt; tranquil
feel. 24-hour room service; conference facilities. 21 bedrooms
(1 suitable for &). double from £155, suite £190–£200. Breakfast £13.50.

HALIFAX West Yorkshire   Map 4:D3

Holdsworth House Holdsworth HX2 9TG. *Tel* 01422-240024, www.
holdsworthhouse.co.uk. 4 miles N of centre: 17th-century manor house,
owned and run by Pearson family for over 40 years. Beams, log fires;
friendly staff. Lounge, bar, restaurant; function rooms. 2-acre garden with
Grade II listed gazebo. 40 bedrooms (4 split-level suites; four-poster/half-
tester beds). B&B (continental): single from £105, double £120–£150, suite
£175. Full breakfast £10.95.

HARROGATE North Yorkshire   Map 4:D4

Ascot House 53 Kings Road HG1 5HG. *Tel* 01423-531005, www.
ascothouse.com. In red brick Victorian building, traditional, family-run
hotel 'an easy walk into town centre'. 'Requests dealt with promptly, with
a smile.' Lounge, bar, restaurant; function facilities. 19 bedrooms. B&B:
single £61–£105, double £90–£120.

Grants Swan Road HG1 2SS. *Tel* 01423-560666, www.grantshotel-
harrogate.com. Peter and Pam Grant's 'good-value' central, secluded,
terraced hotel. Lift. Lounge, *Harry Grant's* bar, *Chimney Pots* bistro; business/
function facilities. Suitable for ♿. Patio garden. Leisure club affiliation.
Parking. 42 bedrooms. B&B: single £110–£118.50, double £118.50–£174.

HEXHAM Northumberland   Map 4:B3

Langley Castle Langley-on-Tyne NE47 5LU. *Tel* 01434-688888, www.
langleycastle.com. Atmospheric 14th-century fortified castle with 21st-
century comforts, 11 miles W of centre. Lounge, bar, restaurant;
conference/function/wedding facilities; outdoor activities (archery, fishing,
shooting, hot-air ballooning). 10-acre grounds. 18 bedrooms (some in
2 listed buildings in grounds). B&B £59.50–£184.50 per person.

HINTON ST GEORGE Somerset   Map 1:C6

The Lord Poulett Arms High Street TA17 8SE. *Tel* 01460-73149,
www.lordpoulettarms.com. In pretty village 30 mins from Taunton, 17th-
century inn, restored in 2003 by Steve Hill and Michelle Paynton.
Flagstone floors, exposed stone walls, antique furniture. 'Exceptionally
good' locally sourced food (Japanese chef). Aromatic garden; *boules*.
4 bedrooms. B&B from £36 per person.

HOVE East Sussex   Map 2:E4

Claremont House Hotel Second Avenue BN3 2LL. *Tel* 01273-735161,
www.claremonthousehotel.co.uk. Boutique hotel in Victorian villa just off
seafront: bright colours, exhibitions by local artists. Breakfast room;

conference facilities. No smoking. 12 bedrooms. B&B: single £55–£75, double £100–£175.

HUDDERSFIELD West Yorkshire   Map 4:E3
Three Acres Inn & Restaurant Roydhouse, Shelley HD8 8LR. *Tel* 01484-602606, www.3acres.com. In Pennine countryside, 5 miles SE of centre: Neil Truelove and Brian Orme's smart old coaching inn. Regional products/restaurant dishes from on-site *Grocer* delicatessen. Bar, 2 restaurants. Garden: dining terrace. 20 bedrooms (11 in adjacent cottages). B&B £45–£70 per person.

HULL East Yorkshire   Map 4:D5
Willerby Manor Well Lane, Willerby HU10 6ER. *Tel* 01482-652616, www.willerbymanor.co.uk. In rural setting 10 mins' drive NW of centre: Edwardian mansion, family run (Best Western). *Everglades* brasserie, *Icon* restaurant; health club (swimming pool, gym, etc), crèche; extensive business/function facilities. 3-acre gardens. Parking. 51 bedrooms. B&B: single £57–£104, double £90–£130.

IRONBRIDGE Shropshire   Map 3:C5
Severn Lodge New Road TQ7 2DS. *Tel* 01952-432147, www.severnlodge. com. Julia Russell's B&B: Grade II listed house (1842) in secluded position overlooking gorge, 2 mins from river. Walled garden (2 gazebos, elevated walkway). Parking. Pubs, restaurants nearby. 3 bedrooms. B&B double from £72.

KESWICK Cumbria   Map 4: inset C2
The Borrowdale Hotel Borrowdale CA12 5UY. *Tel* 017687-77224, www. theborrowdalehotel.co.uk. Family-run, traditional Lakeland hotel at head of Derwentwater, 3 miles from Keswick. 2 lounges, bar, dining room, restaurant (6-course dinner). Dogs welcome. 36 bedrooms (some family; 2 suitable for &.). B&B £65–£95 per person.

KINGSBRIDGE Devon   Map 1:D4
Buckland Tout Saints Goveton TQ7 2DS. *Tel* 01548-853055, www. tout-saints.co.uk. Queen Anne mansion in 'glorious' rural setting near Kingsbridge. Wood-panelled public rooms, open fires; contemporary bedrooms. 5½-acre grounds. Lounge, bar, restaurant; function facilities. 16 bedrooms. B&B: double £135–£215, suite £245–£295.
Thurlestone Hotel Thurlestone TQ7 3NN. *Tel* 01548-560382, www.thurlestone.co.uk. Family-friendly, coastal hotel in 'unique position in

lovely grounds' (19-acre subtropical gardens), 5 mins' walk from sea. 9-hole golf course adjacent. 'Breakfasts as good as ever.' Lounges, bar, *Margaret Amelia* restaurant; function facilities; leisure complex and beauty spa (indoor and outdoor heated swimming pools, fitness suite, tennis, squash, badminton, etc). Garden: terrace. 64 bedrooms. B&B from £87 per person.

KNUTSFORD Cheshire   Map 4:E3
Belle Epoque Brasserie 60 King Street WA16 6DT. *Tel* 01565-633060, www.thebelleepoque.com. Owned and run by Mooney family for 30 years, restaurant-with-rooms in commuter town near Manchester. Art Nouveau dining room with original Venetian glass floor, marble-pillared alcoves, statuary, lavish drapes, tall glass vases and cosy recesses. Bar, roof terrace. 6 bedrooms. B&B from £44 per person.

LEEDS West Yorkshire   Map 4:D4
Malmaison 1 Swinegate LS1 4AG. *Tel* 0113-398 1000, www.malmaison. com. Former bus/train administration building on River Aire, in Calls district. Now city-centre hotel with 'a buzz, that makes it an exciting place to return to'. Bedrooms in aubergine and plum tones. Bar, brasserie (vaulted ceiling; 'good food'); meeting rooms; wheelchair lift; high-tech gym. 100 bedrooms. B&B from £55 per person.

Quebecs 9 Quebec Street LS1 2HA. *Tel* 0113-244 8989, www. theetoncollection.com. Luxury town house B&B in Victorian red brick building (former Leeds and County Liberal Club), 2 mins' walk from station. Grand oak staircase, stained glass window, panelled lounge, bright breakfast room, library, conservatory; 24-hour room service. 45 bedrooms (some small): from £119.

Woodlands Gelderd Road, Gildersome LS27 7LY. *Tel* 0113-238 1488, www.woodlandsleeds.co.uk. Textile mill owner's residence in landscaped gardens, 3 miles from centre, now modern, 'quality' hotel (Tomahawk group). Lounge, bar, 3 dining rooms; function facilities; gym, swimming pool. 17 bedrooms. 'Everything you could wish for.' B&B: double £160–£230, suite £500.

LEEK Staffordshire   Map 3:A5
Cottage Delight at Number 64 64 St Edward Street ST13 5DL. *Tel* 01538-381900, www.number64.com. In listed Georgian building near High Street. Cellar wine bar/coffee lounge, restaurant; private dining room; gourmet food shop/patisserie; *en suite* accommodation on top floor. Garden. 3 bedrooms. B&B double from £65.

LEOMINSTER Herefordshire   Map 3:C4

Ford Abbey Pudleston HR6 0RZ. *Tel* 01568-760700, www.fordabbey.co.uk. Half-timbered, medieval farmstead, once part of Leominster Abbey, luxuriously converted by Dr Albert Heijn. Lounge, library/TV room, restaurant, courtyard; heated swimming pool, gym; wedding facilities. 320-acre landscaped grounds: large patio areas, duck pond, farm animals, woodland, clay-pigeon shooting. 12 bedrooms (1 on ground floor). B&B double £125–£199.

LEWES East Sussex   Map 2:E4

Shelleys High Street BN7 1XS. *Tel* 01273-472361, www.shelleys-hotel. com. Once owned by poet's family: 16th-century, yellow manor house, in centre. 'Charmingly relaxed.' Lounge, bar, restaurant; function facilities. Terrace ('lovely lunch'). Garden. Parking. 19 bedrooms (rear ones overlook garden). B&B: single £90–£130, double £110–£275.

LICHFIELD Staffordshire   Map 2:A2

Swinfen Hall Swinfen WS14 9RE. *Tel* 01543-481494, www. swinfenhallhotel.co.uk. Helen and Victor Wiser's restored 18th-century manor house, 3 miles S of Lichfield on A38, 20 mins' drive from Birmingham, on 100-acre estate in rolling countryside. 5-acre garden: terrace, croquet, tennis, ornamental ponds; deer park. Period decoration in 1st-floor bedrooms; 2nd-floor rooms more contemporary. Cocktail lounge, 2 bars, restaurant ('limited but good-quality menu'), banqueting hall; conference/wedding facilities. 19 bedrooms. B&B (continental): single £125–£210, double £135–£250.

LINCOLN Lincolnshire   Map 4:E5

Hillcrest Hotel 15 Lindum Terrace LN2 5RT. *Tel* 01522-510182, www. hillcrest-hotel.com. 'Lovely views' over parkland from Jennifer Bennett's Victorian vicarage; cathedral 7 mins' walk. 'Very caring' staff. Lounge/ bar, conservatory, restaurant (Braille menu; closed Sun); conference facilities. Garden. 14 bedrooms. B&B: single £59–£79, double £89–£99; D,B&B £65–£99.

LIVERPOOL Merseyside   Map 4:E2

Racquet Club Hargreaves Buildings, 5 Chapel Street L3 9AA. *Tel* 0151-236 6676, www.racquetclub.org.uk. Crisp, chic style in city-centre Victorian building: spa/sports club/dining establishment/small hotel. Bar, *Ziba* restaurant (all-day menu); gym, sauna; exercise room, 2 squash courts; function facilities. 8 bedrooms: from £110. Breakfast £6–£10.

Thornton Hall Neston Road, Thornton Hough, Wirral CH63 1JF. *Tel* 0151-336 3938, www.thorntonhallhotel.com. In hamlet midway between Liverpool (20 mins) and Chester: owned by Thompson family, former home of 19th-century shipping magnate. Many original features. Lounge, bar, restaurant; function/conference facilities; swimming pool, health club, beauty spa. 7-acre garden. 63 bedrooms (most in modern annexe): double £119–£169, suite £195–£485. Breakfast from £13.

LOOE Cornwall   Map 1:D3
Fieldhead Hotel Portuan Road, Hannafore PL13 2DR. *Tel* 01503-262689, www.fieldheadhotel.co.uk. Built 1896 as private residence, in elevated position 15 mins' walk from centre. Traditional ambience. Lounge with huge bow window (views across Looe Bay), bar, *Horizons* restaurant specialising in seafood. 1½-acre garden: terrace, swimming pool. Trudy, the King Charles spaniel, available for walks. 16 bedrooms. B&B from £36 per person; D,B&B from £60.

LORTON Cumbria   Map 4: inset C2
Winder Hall Low Lorton, Cockermouth CA13 9UP. *Tel* 01900-85107, www.winderhall.co.uk. 15 mins' drive from Keswick: 17th-century manor house, in grounds sloping down to River Cocker. Lounge, restaurant (oak-panelled dining room, mullioned windows); summer house with sauna, spa bath. 7 bedrooms (fell views). B&B double £35–£65, D,B&B £67–£97 per person.

LOWESTOFT Suffolk   Map 2:B6
Ivy House Country Hotel Ivy Lane, off Beccles Road, Oulton Broad NR33 8HY. *Tel* 01502-501353, www.ivyhousecountryhotel.co.uk. Caroline and Paul Coe's converted farm buildings, near Norfolk Broads national park. Lounge, conservatory, courtyard, summer house; 18th-century, thatched *Crooked Barn* restaurant; function/conference facilities. 4-acre garden (2 lily ponds) surrounded by farmland. B&B: single £95, double £125–£162, suite £230.

LYME REGIS Dorset   Map 1:C6
Alexandra Hotel Pound Street DT7 3HZ. *Tel* 01297-442010, www. hotelalexandra.co.uk. Kathryn Richards has taken over the running of this old-fashioned (built 1735), 'homely' hotel with loyal clientele, from her parents. 'Excellent' position (fine sea views) above The Cobb, 'yet good value'. Lounge, conservatory, restaurant. Garden. Town 100 yds; beach 300 yds. Parking. 26 bedrooms. B&B: single £65, double £105–£150.

LYMINGTON Hampshire   Map 2:E2

Britannia House Mill Lane SO41 9AY. *Tel* 01590-672091, www.britannia-house.com. Tobias Feilke's B&B in 2 brick-built houses opposite each other, 5 mins' walk from High Street and quayside. 'Stunning decor', 'immaculate' rooms and 'superb' breakfast. 'He is a perfectionist.' Lounge; courtyard. Parking. No smoking. 6 bedrooms. B&B: single £50, double £75.

Wistaria 32 St Thomas Street SO41 9NE. *Tel* 01590-688090, www.wistaria.org.uk. Wistaria-clad Georgian town house (Grade II listed), transformed, after 62 years as a doctor's surgery, into smart, modern restaurant-with-rooms. 'An excellent all-round service that doesn't break the bank.' Bar, restaurant. Terrace. No smoking. 3 bedrooms. B&B £47.50–£67.50 per person.

LYNMOUTH Devon   Map 1:B4

Shelley's Hotel 8 Watersmeet Road EX35 6EP. *Tel* 01598-753219, www.shelleyshotel.co.uk. Jane Becker and Richard Briden's 18th-century cottage B&B in centre (Percy Bysshe Shelley is said to have honeymooned here): views over Lynmouth Bay. Lounge, bar, conservatory breakfast room. 11 no-smoking bedrooms (1 on ground floor). B&B £34.75–£75 per person.

LYTHAM Lancashire   Map 4:D2

Clifton Arms West Beach FY58 5QJ. *Tel* 01253-739898, www.cliftonarms-lytham.com. Paul Caddy's traditional seafront hotel opposite Lytham Green. Lounge/cocktail bar, library/TV room, *The West Beach* restaurant, *Churchills* brasserie; conference/banqueting facilities. Small garden. Parking. 48 bedrooms (some suitable for &). B&B £65–£100 per person.

MAIDENHEAD Berkshire   Map 2:D3

Fredrick's Shoppenhangers Road SL6 2PZ. *Tel* 01628-581000, www.fredricks-hotel.co.uk. Lösel family's lavish hotel with luxury spa, overlooking Maidenhead golf club. Lounge, bar, restaurant; terrace; conference/function facilities. 2½-acre landscaped gardens: sculptures. Parking. 34 bedrooms. B&B: single from £215, double from £295, suite from £450.

MANCHESTER   Map 4:E3

Bewley's Hotel Outwood Lane, Manchester Airport M90 4HL. *Tel* 0161-498 0333, www.bewleyshotels.com. Large, modern chain hotel with triple glazing. 10 mins' walk to Terminal 1, 20 mins to Terminal 2. Bar, brasserie; business facilities. 226 bright, good-value bedrooms (some suitable for &): single/double £69. Breakfast from £6.95.

The Lowry 50 Dearmans Place, Chapel Wharf M3 5LH. *Tel* 0161-827 4000, www.thelowryhotel.com. Contemporary luxury hotel owned by Rocco Forte Hotels. Central (part of Chapel Wharf development). Bar, restaurant; terrace (alfresco dining); spa/fitness suite. Parking. 165 bedrooms (most are spacious, some overlook River Irwell): single £205–£255, double £230–£290, suite £650–£1,750. Breakfast from £17.50.

The Midland Peter Street M60 2DS. *Tel* 0161-236 3333, www.themidlandhotel.co.uk. Next to G-Mex centre: old-style luxury hotel with terracotta tile work, built for Midland Railway Company (1903). Lavish decoration. Bar, French restaurant, *The Trafford* dining room, *Octagon* terrace; health club (gym, swimming pool, squash). Parking (charge). 303 bedrooms: double from £167. Breakfast from £14.

Hotel Rossetti 107 Piccadilly M1 2DB. *Tel* 0161-247 7744, www.abodehotels.com. Conversion of red stone building, formerly the headquarters of the Horrocks cotton dynasty, to 'very friendly' hotel. Bought by Abode group; will be 're-launched' in early 2007 as *Abode*. 'Innovative, minimalist but interesting and comfortable rooms.' *Café Paradiso* bar and restaurant, basement club. 61 bedrooms: double £110, penthouse £265. Breakfast £12.

MARKET DRAYTON Shropshire   Map 3:B5

Goldstone Hall Goldstone TF9 2NA. *Tel* 01630-661202, www.goldstonehall.com. Cushing family's sprawling house in 5-acre grounds, in hamlet 4½ miles S of Market Drayton. 2 lounges; bar, conservatory, Edwardian panelled restaurant; snooker room; function/wedding facilities. 16 bedrooms (2 on ground floor). B&B £60–£100 per person. Dinner £23.50–£29.

MATLOCK Derbyshire   Map 3:B6

The Red House Old Road, Darley Dale DE4 2ER. *Tel* 01629-734854, www.theredhousecountryhotel.co.uk. Victorian architect's country home, now David and Kate Gardiner's well-run hotel, on quiet road off A6, 2½ miles NW of centre. Views over Derwent valley. Many original features. No smoking. 2 lounges, bar, dining room. ¾-acre garden. Next to carriage museum (horse riding, carriage driving). Parking. 10 bedrooms (3 in coach house). B&B £50–£60 per person. Set dinner £25.

MIDHURST Sussex   Map 2:E3

The Spread Eagle South Street GU29 9NH. *Tel* 01730-816911, www.hshotels.co.uk. 15th-century coaching inn (Historic Sussex Hotels). Residents' lounge (huge fireplaces, Tudor bread oven), lounge bar, conservatory, restaurant (inglenook fireplace), conservatory, terrace (alfresco dining); function facilities; spa: swimming pool, gym. 1-acre garden. 39 bedrooms. B&B: single £80–£180, double £99–£240.

MILTON KEYNES Buckinghamshire   Map 2:C3
Different Drummer 92–94 High Street, Stony Stratford MK11 1AH. *Tel* 01908-564733, www.hoteldifferentdrummer.co.uk. Quirkily restored 15th-century coaching inn in High Street. Lounge, bar, wine bar, *Al Tamborista* Italian restaurant. Courtyard. Limited parking. 19 bedrooms (1 on ground floor, 1 cottage). B&B £44.50–£49 per person.

NEWBURY Berkshire   Map 2:D2
The Vineyard at Stockcross RG20 8JU. *Tel* 01635-528770, www. the-vineyard.co.uk. 3 miles NW of centre, Sir Peter Michael's (founder of Classic FM) 'restaurant with room to stay' (Relais & Châteaux): extravagantly decorated former hunting lodge housing eclectic art collection. *Michelin* star for chef, John Campbell. Bar, lounge, music room, conservatory, restaurant; function facilities; spa: swimming pool, gym. Garden: patio. Parking. 49 bedrooms: single £200, double £317, suite £411–£785. Breakfast £13.50–£18.50.

NEWCASTLE UPON TYNE Tyne and Wear   Map 4:B4
greystreet hotel Grey Street NE1 6EE. *Tel* 0870-412 5100, www. greystreethotel.com. Niche Hotels' conversion of Grade II listed former bank in World Heritage Site street, near quay, theatre, shopping. Neutral tones, mood lighting; minimalist design in *living room* piano bar/restaurant; function facilities. 24-hour room service. 49 bedrooms: single £135, double £135–£170. Breakfast £8.95–£12.95.
The Vermont Castle Garth NE1 1RQ. *Tel* 0191-233 1010, www.vermont-hotel.co.uk. Plush, 12-storey, independently owned luxury hotel by castle, facing River Tyne. Lounges, 2 bars (*The Redwood, Martha's*), *Bridge* restaurant; fitness centre; function facilities. Parking. 101 bedrooms: double from £125.

NEWMARKET Suffolk   Map 2:B4
Bedford Lodge Bury Road CB8 7BX. *Tel* 01638-663175, www.bedfordlodgehotel.co.uk. Georgian hunting lodge in 3-acre secluded gardens near racecourse. Lounge, bar, *Orangery* restaurant; extensive function/wedding/conference facilities; fitness centre: indoor swimming pool, beauty salon. 55 bedrooms (1 on ground floor). B&B: single from £135, double £170–£215, suite £185.

NORWICH Norfolk   Map 2:B5

Annesley House 6 Newmarket Road NR2 2LA. *Tel* 01603-624553, www.bw-annesleyhouse.co.uk. In conservation area, short walk from centre: Best Western member composed of 3 Georgian houses. Bar/lounge, conservatory restaurant (facing water gardens and koi pond); conference/ function facilities. Garden. Parking. 26 bedrooms. B&B £42.50–£118 per person.

Barnham Broom Hotel Honingham Road NR9 4DD. *Tel* 01603-759393, www.barnham-broom.co.uk. In same ownership as *Bedford Lodge*, Newmarket (*qv*), golf hotel in 250 acres, 10 miles W of Norwich. Lounge, 2 bars, *Flints* restaurant; 2 tennis courts; function facilities; health/fitness club (indoor swimming pool). 52 rooms. B&B: single £115–£170, double £140–£195.

Beaufort Lodge 62 Earlham Road NR2 3DF. *Tel* 01603-627928, www. beaufortlodge.com. 5 mins' walk from centre: Julia and Chris Dobbins's hospitable, no-smoking B&B in Victorian villa. No children. Breakfast room. 4 bedrooms. B&B: single £50, double £65.

Catton Old Hall Lodge Lane, Old Catton NR6 7HG. *Tel* 01603-419379, www.catton-hall.co.uk. Roger and Anthea Cawdron's characterful small hotel, built 1632, in village 2½ miles NE of centre. Afternoon tea, dinner. Vegetarian options at breakfast. Lounge, dining room. Garden. 7 bedrooms. B&B: single £70–£90, double £85–£120.

Norfolk Mead Church Loke, Coltishall NR12 7DN. *Tel* 01603-737531, www.norfolkmead.co.uk. Fleming family's Georgian manor house in 8-acre grounds by River Bure, 7 miles NE of Norwich, on edge of Norfolk Broads. Lounge, bar, 2 dining rooms, candlelit restaurant, conference facilities, beauty salon. Walled garden: unheated swimming pool; fishing lake; off-river mooring. 12 bedrooms. B&B: single £75–£95, double/suite £100–£160.

OXFORD Oxfordshire   Map 2:C2

Burlington House 374 Banbury Road OX2 7PP. *Tel* 01865-513513, www.burlington-house.co.uk. Large Victorian merchant's house, now no-smoking B&B. In leafy Summertown, 1½ miles from centre on busy road. Lounge, Japanese courtyard. 12 bedrooms (3 on ground floor). Internet access. B&B £40–£60 per person.

Cotswold House 363 Banbury Road OX2 7PL. *Tel* 01865-310558, www.cotswoldhouse.co.uk. Derek and Hilary Walker's 'good-value, well-decorated' B&B. Cotswold stone house, 2 miles from centre on busy road. Lounge. 8 bedrooms (1 on ground floor). B&B: single £52–£62, double £80–£90, suite £90–£100.

Malmaison 3 Oxford Castle, New Road OX1 1AY. *Tel* 01865-268400, www.malmaison.com. Stylish incarceration in converted Victorian castle prison. Atmospheric: original landings, cell doors, keys, spyholes (reversed). *Visitors' Room* lounge, 2 bars, brasserie; outside seating. No parking. 94 rooms (16 in *House of Correction*; some in former *Governor's House*; some suitable for &). B&B: double from £140, suite from £195.

The Randolph Beaumont Street OX1 2LN. *Tel* 0870-400 8200, www. randolph-hotel.com. Oxford institution, by Ashmolean Museum, now high-comfort chain hotel (Macdonald group), but with 'privately run feel'. Lounges, *Morse* bar, restaurant. 151 bedrooms. B&B double from £120.

PADSTOW Cornwall   Map 1:D2

Tregea Hotel 16–18 High Street PL28 8BB. *Tel* 01841-532455, www. tregea.co.uk. In quiet street 300 yds from harbour: family-run hotel in 16th-century, creeper-covered building. New England-style decor. 2 lounges, bar (late entertainments sometimes), dining room; background music. Off-street parking. Sandy beaches ¼ mile. No smoking. No dogs. 8 bedrooms. B&B double £120.

PENRITH Cumbria   Map 4: inset C2

The George Devonshire Street CA11 7SU. *Tel* 01768-862696, www. georgehotelpenrith.co.uk. Family-owned, 300-year-old coaching inn, 4 miles from Lake Ullswater. Traditional decor. Lounges, bar, restaurant; function/wedding facilities. Parking. 32 bedrooms. B&B £50–£82 per person; D,B&B £76–£99.

PLYMOUTH Devon   Map 1:D4

Bowling Green Hotel 9–10 Osborne Place, Lockyer St, The Hoe PL1 2PU. *Tel* 01752-209090, www.bowlingreenhotel.co.uk. 5 mins' walk from Barbican, Tom Roberts's B&B: Georgian house facing Drake's Bowling Green. Lounge, TV room, conservatory, breakfast room. Parking. 12 bed-rooms. B&B: single £45, double £62, family £66.

Cliff House Kingsand, nr Torpoint, Cornwall PL10 1NJ. *Tel* 01752-823110, www.cliffhouse-kingsand.co.uk. On steep hill in quiet Cornish fishing village SW of Plymouth, near Mount Edgcumbe Country Park: Ann Heasman's no-smoking Grade II listed guest house, conversion of 2 cot-tages. Lounge, dining room (evening meal by arrangement). Garden/courtyard; small car park. 3 bedrooms (good views). B&B: single £35–£55, double £52–£75.

Plantation House Totnes Road, Ermington PL21 9NS. *Tel* 01548-831100, www.plantationhouseivybridge.co.uk. Richard and Magdalena Hendey's restaurant-with-rooms in Grade II-listed rectory; on sunny side of River Erme valley: fine views; 11¼ miles E of Plymouth. Lounge, bar, dining room (6-course gourmet menus), terrace; 1-acre garden. 10 rooms. B&B: single £55–£59.50, double £79.50–£110.

POOLE Dorset   Map 2:E1
Harbour Heights 73 Haven Road, Sandbanks BH13 7LW. *Tel* 01202-707272, www.harbourheights.net. Chic, white 1920s hotel (Best Western) above harbour (stunning views). Elegant, contemporary interior: 'comfy room, great bed'. 'Fabulous breakfast.' Lounge, *harbar* and brasserie; dining terrace; function facilities. Parking. 38 bedrooms. B&B £120–£140 per person.

The Mansion House Thames Street BH15 1JN. *Tel* 01202-685666, www.themansionhouse.co.uk. Jackie and Gerry Godden's Georgian building (1779), originally mayor's house, in Old Town near quayside. Modern cooking in panelled dining room; simpler menu in bistro. Lounge, bar. Conference/function/wedding facilities. 32 bedrooms. B&B: single £75–£96, double £135–£145.

READING Berkshire   Map 2:D3
The Forbury 26 The Forbury RG1 3EJ. *Tel* 08000 789 789, www.theforburyhotel.co.uk. Civic grandeur meets designer chic at this 100-year-old County Hall building opposite gardens, now transformed into stylish hotel. Artwork by French and British painters and sculptors. Bar, *Cerise* restaurant; cinema; courtyard garden; function facilities. 24 bedrooms: double £195–£295, suite £295–£440.

ROSS-ON-WYE Herefordshire   Map 3:D5
The Hill House Howle Hill HR9 5ST. *Tel* 01989-562033, www.thehowlinghillhouse.com. Above Forest of Dean: Duncan and Alex Stayton's 'most relaxed' house (views over Black Mountains), 17th century in origin. Organic, Aga-cooked, vegetarian-friendly breakfasts; packed lunch/evening meal by arrangement. Morning room, lounge. Cinema (DVD film library), bar. Hot tub. Garden. 4½-acre woodland. 5 bedrooms. B&B £25–£29 per person; D,B&B £35–£50.

Pencraig Court Pencraig HR9 6HR. *Tel* 01989-770306, www.pencraig-court.co.uk. Georgian house in 3½-acre garden and woodlands overlooking River Wye, 4 miles SW of town. Family owned (Liz and Malcolm Dobson, their daughter Katie and friends Shirley and Peter Jelliss). Home-grown fruit, vegetables, herbs. Lounge, dining room. 10 bedrooms. B&B £42–£54 per person. Dinner £25.

RYE East Sussex   **Map 2:E5**
White Vine House 24 High Street TN31 7JF. *Tel* 01797-224748, www.whitevinehouse.co.uk. Once the mayor's home: 16th-century terraced building: with creeper-covered Georgian facade. 2 reception rooms, oak-panelled dining room, crisp, white bedrooms; covered courtyard; small function/wedding facilities. 7 bedrooms. B&B: single £70, double/family £115–£175.

ST IVES Cornwall   **Map 1:D1**
The Garrack Burthallan Lane TR26 3AA. *Tel* 01736-796199, www.garrack. com. Creeper-clad stone building on hill above Porthmeor beach, a short, steep walk from town. Owned for over 40 years by Kilby family. Lounge, restaurant (Cornish produce); leisure centre (gym, sauna, indoor swimming pool); 2-acre garden; sun terrace. Parking. 18 bedrooms (3 suitable for &). B&B £65–£87 per person.
Porthminster Hotel TR26 2BN. *Tel* 01736-795221, www.porthminster-hotel.co.uk. In subtropical gardens overlooking bay; direct access to Porthminster beach: 100-year-old family-run hotel. Traditional interior. Lift. Lounge, bar, cocktail bar, restaurant (seafood/fish specialities). Leisure club: indoor/outdoor swimming pool. Function/wedding facilities. 43 bedrooms (some family). B&B £60–£125 per person.

SALISBURY Wiltshire   **Map 2:D2**
Leena's 50 Castle Road SP1 3RL. *Tel* 01722-335419. 15 mins' riverside walk from centre: Leena and Malcolm Street's budget no-smoking B&B: Edwardian house on busy Amesbury road (double glazing). Lounge, breakfast room. Garden. Parking. 6 bedrooms (1 on ground floor). B&B: single from £30, double £61.
Milford Hall 206 Castle Street SP1 3TE. *Tel* 01722-417411, www.milfordhallhotel.com. Georgian mansion with modern extension, now 3-star hotel. Lounge, bar, *brasserie@206*; conference/business/wedding facilities. Parking. Traditional decor. 35 bedrooms. B&B: single £106–£116, double £116–£136.

SANDWICH Kent   **Map 2:D5**
The Bell Hotel The Quay CT13 9EF. *Tel* 01304-613388, www. bellhotelsandwich.co.uk. Smart, modern refurbishment of 19th-century listed building by Barbican Gate and Toll, overlooking River Stour; in same ownership as *The Place* (see Camber, full entry). 2 bars. Brasserie (local, organic produce); function facilities. 34 bedrooms. B&B: single £85, double £105–£150, suite £165–£185.

SCARBOROUGH North Yorkshire   Map 4:C5

Interludes 32 Princess Street YO11 1QR. *Tel* 01723-360513, www. interludeshotel.co.uk. Listed Georgian building in Old Town conservation area. Run by theatre buffs, Ian Grundy and Bob Harris. Lots of thespian memorabilia, 'beautifully furnished and decorated, and spotlessly clean'. No smoking. 2 resident cats. Lounge, dining room; small patio. 5 bedrooms (4 with sea views). B&B ('and what a breakfast!'): £31.50–£35 per person. Evening meal (6 pm) £15.

SEAHOUSES Northumberland   Map 4:A4

The Olde Ship NE68 7RD. *Tel* 01665-720200, www.seahouses.co.uk. Overlooking tiny harbour, with view to islands: old building full of seafaring memorabilia. 2 lounges, 2 bars, dining room; function room. Boat trips, beaches nearby. 18 bedrooms (some facilities for &). B&B £48–£55 per person.

SHREWSBURY Shropshire   Map 3:B4

Albright Hussey Ellesmere Road SY4 3AF. *Tel* 01939-290523, www. albrighthussey.co.uk. 2½ miles N of centre, Subbiani family's hotel/ restaurant: much extended Grade II listed Tudor house. 'Great attention to detail.' Antiques, panelling, open fires, beams. Lounge, bar, restaurant; function facilities. 4-acre garden with moat and black swans. 26 bedrooms. B&B: single £79–£135, double £110–£180.

SIDMOUTH Devon   Map 1:C5

Victoria Hotel The Esplanade EX10 8RY. *Tel* 01395-512651, www. victoriahotel.co.uk. At western end of esplanade (views across the bay), large hotel (Brend Group) in 5-acre grounds. Snooker, gym, outdoor/ indoor swimming pool, spa bath, sauna, solarium, tennis, putting. 61 bedrooms (some with sea views). B&B £85–£130 per person.

SOUTHWOLD Suffolk   Map 2:B6

The Swan Market Place IP18 6EG. *Tel* 01502-722186, www.adnamshotels. co.uk. 300-year-old building on market square: 'excellent location and service'. 2 lounges, bar, restaurant; function facilities. Traditional decor; 'breakfast very good'. Garden. Parking. Beach 200 yds. 42 bedrooms (1 suitable for &; dog-friendly garden rooms round old bowling green). B&B: single from £80, double from £140.

STAMFORD Lincolnshire   Map 2:B3

The Crown All Saints Place PE9 2AG. *Tel* 01780-763136, www. thecrownhotelstamford.co.uk. Contemporary boutique hotel ('fresh, well designed') created by brother and sister Michael and Sue Thurlby, in old stone building in town centre. 2 lounges, bar, restaurant (local produce, lamb from owner's farm nearby, game in season). Parking. No smoking. 24 bedrooms. B&B: single from £85, double £100–£110.

STANSTED Essex   Map 2:C4
New Barn Hall Holder's Green, Lindsell, Great Dunmow CM6 3QH. *Tel* 01371-870720, www.newbarnhall.co.uk. Peter and Pamela Goodman's no-smoking B&B: spacious country house in 7-acre grounds (clear of flight path), 8 miles from airport. Snooker room. Parking. 3 bedrooms. B&B £30–£55 per person.
Oak Lodge Jacks Lane, Smiths Green, Takeley CM22 6NT. *Tel* 01279-871667, www.oaklodgebb.com. In village 2 miles SE of airport: Jan and Ron Griffiths's 'highly recommended' no-smoking 16th-century B&B. Evening meal by arrangement. Lounge/TV room, dining room. 2-acre garden. Parking. No credit cards. 3 bedrooms. B&B: single from £45, double from £55.

STOCKBRIDGE Hampshire   Map 2:D2
The Greyhound 31 High Street SO20 6EY. *Tel* 01264-810833. Popular with fishermen, 15th-century inn backing on to tributary of River Test, now restaurant-with-rooms with modern interior. Lounge (beams, open fire, leather sofas). Small riverside garden (fishing rights). 8 bedrooms ('ours had no hanging space'). B&B double £75–£100.

STOKE CANON Devon   Map 1:C5
Barton Cross Hotel Huxham EX5 4EJ. *Tel* 01392-841245, *email* bartonxhuxham@aol.com. 5 miles N of Exeter, off A396: Brian Hamilton's part-thatched 17th-century house: wooden beams, gallery, inglenook fireplace. 'Very friendly. Great fun. Good value. Sensational English breakfast.' Lounge, bar, muzak-free restaurant. 1-acre garden. Parking. 9 bedrooms (some suitable for &). B&B: single £69.50, double £98–£110.

STRATFORD-UPON-AVON Warwickshire   Map 3:D6
Parkfield 3 Broad Walk CV37 6HS. *Tel* 01789-293313, www.parkfieldbandb. co.uk. Roger and Joanna Pettitt's 'welcoming' no-smoking B&B in Victorian house near centre. Vegetarians catered for; help with theatre tickets. Large car park. 7 bedrooms. B&B: single £30, double £55.

STUDLAND Dorset   Map 2:E1
Manor House Hotel Studland Bay BH19 3AU. *Tel* 01929-450288, www. themanorhousehotel.com. 'Lovely old hotel in superb location overlooking

bay.' 18th-century National Trust property in 20 acres of private grounds, run by Andrew Purkis. Restaurant; picnic hampers; 2 tennis courts. 21 bedrooms (sea/garden/country views). D,B&B £82–£127 per person.

SUTTON COLDFIELD Warwickshire   Map 3:C6

New Hall Hotel Walmley Rd B76 1QX. *Tel* 0121-378 2442. www. newhalluk.com. Former hunting lodge for Earls of Warwick (Grade I listed): oldest inhabited moated manor house in England, owned by Bridgehouse Hotels. 20 mins' drive from Birmingham. Oak-panelled *Bridge* restaurant, *Terrace* room; leisure facilities (swimming pool, spa bath, steam room, beauty treatments, fitness room); function facilities. 26-acre grounds: tennis court, 9-hole par 3 golf course. 60 bedrooms: double from £160, D,B&B from £108 per person.

SWINDON Wiltshire   Map 2:C2

Blunsdon House Blunsdon SN26 7AS. *Tel* 01793-721701, www. blunsdonhouse.co.uk. Clifford family's creeper-clad 4-star hotel (Best Western). Lift. 2 lounges, 3 bars, 2 restaurants (*The Ridge* and *Christopher's*); beauty salon, gym, indoor swimming pool; function/wedding facilities. 30-acre grounds: 2 squash courts; 9-hole par 3 golf course. 118 bedrooms (48 in adjacent *Pavilion*). B&B: double from £135, suite £270.

The Saracens Head Market Place, Highworth SN6 7AG. *Tel* 01793-762284, www.saracenshead.co.uk. In market town 6 miles NE of Swindon: friendly pub with long history, owned by Arkells Brewery. Bars, restaurant. Patio garden (alfresco meals). 12 double bedrooms: from £50.

TEIGNMOUTH Devon   Map 1:D5

Britannia House 26 Teign Street TQ14 8EG. *Tel* 01626-770051, www. britanniahouse.org. 'A breath of fresh air to find a good, well-run English seaside B&B.' Reputedly built by 16th-century sea captain: Jennifer and Michael Gillett's 'welcoming' home, in maze of small streets, 5 mins' walk from seafront. Lounge, dining room. Small garden. 3 bedrooms. B&B £30–£60 per person.

TETBURY Gloucestershire   Map 3:E5

The Close 8 Long Street GL8 8AQ. *Tel* 01666-502272, www.theclose-hotel.com. 16th-century yeoman's house, hotel since 1974 (Greene King group), in centre. 'Rambling interior… comfortable, well maintained.' Elegant restaurant with Adam ceiling; panelled rooms; function/wedding facilities. Walled garden, terrace (alfresco meals), fountain. Parking. 15 bedrooms. B&B: single £100, double £120–£180. Set dinner £29.95.

THIRSK North Yorkshire   Map 4:C4

Oswalds Front Street YO7 1JF. *Tel* 01845-523655, www.oswaldsrestaurant
withrooms.co.uk. Graham and Heather Raine's restaurant-with-rooms on
quiet street a short walk from centre of market town. Lounge, bar,
restaurant, function room; indoor hot tub; patio (meal service). 8 bedrooms
(3 in stable block). B&B: single £75, double £95.

TORQUAY Devon   Map 1:D5

Mulberry House 1 Scarborough Road TQ2 5UJ. *Tel* 01803-213639,
www.mulberryhousetorquay.co.uk. 'A gem': family-run B&B and restaurant
in Victorian house (Grade II listed) on corner, close to sea and town centre.
Fresh, bright rooms; 'superb' breakfast. Children welcomed. 3 bedrooms.
B&B £30–£45 per person.

TOTNES Devon   Map 1:D4

Royal Seven Stars The Plains TQ9 5DD. *Tel* 01803-862125, www.royal
sevenstars.co.uk. 17th-century coaching inn, renovated in 2006 in contemporary style. 2 bars (log fires in winter); alfresco dining. Parking. No smoking. 16 bedrooms (quieter at back). B&B: single £79–£110, double £89–£120.

TROUTBECK Cumbria   Map 4: inset C2

Broadoaks Bridge Lane LA23 1LA. *Tel* 015394 45566, www.
broadoaks-lake-district.co.uk. Trevor and Joan Pavelyn 'are to be congratu-
lated on their attention to detail' at their Victorian country house 2 miles
N of Windermere. Lounge, music room with barrel-vaulted acoustic
ceiling, restaurant; function facilities. 7-acre grounds: bowling, pitch and
putt, fishing, rifle and clay-pigeon range. Access to leisure club, 1½ miles.
14 bedrooms (1 suitable for &; 3 in coach house). B&B £45.50–£105 per
person; D,B&B £75–£130.

TUNBRIDGE WELLS Kent   Map 2:D4

Spa Hotel Mount Ephraim TN4 8XJ. *Tel* 01892-520331, www.spahotel.
co.uk. 18th-century mansion in 14-acre grounds overlooking town. Owned
by Goring family (see *The Goring*, London). 'Enthusiastic well-trained staff.
Mix of nationalities.' Traditional country house decor. Lounge, dining
room; health/leisure centre (sauna, swimming pool). 69 bedrooms. B&B
double £140–£168.

ULLSWATER Cumbria   Map 4: inset C2

The Inn on the Lake Glenridding CA11 0PE. *Tel* 017684-82444, www.
lakedistricthotels.net. At rugged end of Lake Ullswater, large, 3-star hotel

(Lake District group). Lounge, 2 bars, *Lake View* restaurant; extensive conference/function/wedding facilities. 15-acre grounds leading to shore. 46 bedrooms. B&B £64–£92 per person.

VENTNOR Isle of Wight   Map 2:E2

The Royal Hotel Belgrave Road PO38 1JJ. *Tel* 01983-852186, www. royalhoteliow.co.uk. Classic seaside hotel (largest on island), used by Queen Victoria as annexe to Osborne House. 'Loved our stay; excellent food.' 2 lounges, bar, restaurant, conservatory. Landscaped gardens: terrace, heated swimming pool, children's play area. Sandy beach nearby (hilly walk). Parking. 55 bedrooms (some suitable for &). B&B: single £75–£115, double £130–£200.

WARMINSTER Wiltshire   Map 2:D1

Bishopstrow House Boreham Road BA12 9HH. *Tel* 01985-212312, www.bishopstrow.co.uk. Von Essen hotels' late Georgian country house, 2 miles E of Warminster in 27-acre grounds with River Wylye. Children and dogs welcomed. Drawing room, library, conservatory, bar, *Mulberry* restaurant; games room; function/wedding/conference facilities; spa (gym, etc); heated indoor/outdoor swimming pools, tennis. 32 bedrooms (some up steep stairs). B&B double £160–£330.

WARWICK Warwickshire   Map 3:C6

Northleigh House Five Ways Road, Hatton CV35 7HZ. *Tel* 01926-484203, www.northleigh.co.uk. In countryside (5 mins' drive from the M42, M40, A45 and A46 – Warwick, Birmingham, Coventry), Viv and Fred Morgan's 'delightful' white-painted B&B. 'Warm welcome.' Dog friendly. Garden. 7 rooms. B&B: single £50, double £70.

WATFORD Hertfordshire   Map 2:C3

The Grove Chandler's Cross WD3 4TG. *Tel* 01923-807807, www.thegrove. co.uk. Former home of Earl of Clarendon: 18th-century brick building, now luxury hotel much used for corporate events. Some noise from M25 motorway. Lounges, 3 restaurants; terrace, 300-acre grounds: spa, swimming pool, tennis, golf course, croquet, children's play area, high-tech gadgetry. 227 bedrooms: £240–£1,000.

WESTON-SUPER-MARE Somerset   Map 1:B6

Beachlands 17 Uphill Road North BS23 4NG. *Tel* 01934-621401, www. beachlandshotel.com. 'A real oasis' 300 yds from sandy beach, family-run hotel facing sand dunes and 18-hole links golf course. Bar/lounge, restaurant; 33-ft indoor swimming pool, sauna; function facilities. Garden. Parking. 23 bedrooms. B&B: single £44.50–£62.50, double £89–£109.50.

WHITBY North Yorkshire   Map 4:C5
Bagdale Hall 1 Bagdale YO21 1QL. *Tel* 01947-602958, www.bagdale.co.uk. Central, near harbour: Tudor manor house, 'genuinely olde-worldly' (mullioned windows, beamed ceilings, carved wooden overmantels). Lounge, bar, restaurant. 27 bedrooms. B&B double £118–£138.
Dunsley Hall Dunsley YO21 3TL. *Tel* 01947-893437, www.dunsleyhall. com. Carol and Bill Ward's Victorian mansion (oak panelling, stained-glass window with seafaring scene, inglenook fireplace), in hamlet 2½ miles NW of Whitby. Lounge/bar, 2 restaurants ('sensational dinner'); fitness room: swimming pool. 4-acre garden: putting, croquet, tennis, peacocks. Sea 1 mile. Parking. 18 bedrooms (some suitable for &). B&B: single £87.50–£115, double £165–£185, suite £200.
White Horse & Griffin 87 Church Street YO22 4BH. *Tel* 01947-604857, www.whitehorseandgriffin.co.uk. Chef/proprietor Stewart Perkins's welcoming restaurant-with-rooms in 320-year-old building (lots of stairs). Function facilities. Street parking only (charge). 10 rooms: single £35, double £60, family £85. Breakfast from £4.95

WILLINGTON Cheshire   Map 3:A5
Willington Hall CW6 0NB. *Tel* 01829-752321, www.willingtonhall.co.uk. Diana and Stuart Begbie's 19th-century hotel in 17-acre grounds at foot of Willington hills, 3½ miles NW of Tarporley, 10 miles E of Chester. Original features, antiques, family portraits. Lounge, 2 bars, restaurant; terrace; function facilities. 10 bedrooms. B&B: single from £70, double from £110.

WINCHESTER Hampshire   Map 2:D2
Lainston House Sparsholt SO21 2LT. *Tel* 01962-863588, www.exclusive hotels.co.uk. 17th-century country house, 3½ miles NW of city by B3049, in 63-acre park (tennis). Wood panelling; four-poster beds; smart bathrooms; elegant traditional style. Drawing room, *Cedar* bar, *Avenue* restaurant; gym; function facilities; croquet. 'Beautifully maintained grounds.' 50 bedrooms (4 in courtyard or stables; some suitable for &): single £125, double £130–£195, suite £330–£395. Breakfast £17.50.
The Wykeham Arms 75 Kingsgate Street SO23 9PE. *Tel* 01962-853834, *email* wykehamarms@accommodating-inns.co.uk. South of cathedral, 250-year-old inn (owned by George Gale & Co. Ltd), spruced into attractive, bustling restaurant-with-rooms. Oak desks, pew and curios salvaged from

Winchester College. Bar, restaurant. 14 bedrooms (7 in annexe). B&B: single from £57, double from £85.

WOBURN Bedfordshire   Map 2:C3
The Inn at Woburn George Street MK17 9PX. *Tel* 1525-290441, www.theinnatwoburn.com. Modern comforts at refurbished 18th-century coaching inn, on Woburn estate, 8 miles SE of Milton Keynes. 'Friendly, helpful service.' *Tavistock* bar, *Olivier's* restaurant; function facilities. 50 bedrooms (plus 7 cottages). B&B: single £110–£130, double £125–£180.

WYE Kent   Map 2:D5
The New Flying Horse Inn Upper Bridge Street TN25 5AN. *Tel* 01233-812297. Pub with spacious, updated rooms in 17th-century roadside posting house off A28 between Canterbury and Ashford. Garden, patio. 9 rooms (some in coach house). B&B: single from £55, double from £80.
The Wife of Bath 4 Upper Bridge Street TN25 5AF. *Tel* 01233-812540, www.wifeofbath.com. Timber-framed restaurant-with-rooms in Wye's main street which leads to River Stour. Bar, restaurant. Small garden. 5 bedrooms (2 in stables). B&B: single £55–£65, double £75–£95. Dinner from £24.50.

YARMOUTH Isle of Wight   Map 2:E2
The George Quay Street PO41 0PE. *Tel* 01983-760331, www.thegeorge. co.uk. By water's edge: 'highly recommended' 17th-century house with panelled walls, flagstone floors. Lounge, bar, brasserie, restaurant; ¾-acre garden facing sea; private pebble beach; safe bathing nearby. 17 bedrooms (2 share a balcony). B&B double £130–£255; D,B&B £235–£310.

YEOVIL Somerset   Map 1:C6
Yeovil Court Hotel West Coker Road BA20 2HE. *Tel* 01935-863746, www.yeovilhotel.com. In rolling countryside: spacious white-painted hotel. Stylish, modern interior. Lounge, restaurant; conference facilities. 30 bedrooms. B&B: single from £65, double £105–£160; D,B&B double from £165.

YORK North Yorkshire   Map 4:D4
The Bloomsbury 127 Clifton YO30 6BL. *Tel* 01904-634031, www. bloomsburyhotel.co.uk. Paul Andrew's no-smoking B&B: Victorian house in leafy area, 12 mins' walk from York Minster. Bright, sunny dining room. Vegetarians catered for. Parking. 9 bedrooms. B&B: single £40–£60, double £60–£90.

Dean Court Duncombe Place YO1 7EF. *Tel* 01904-625082, www. deancourt-york.co.uk. 'A special treat': opposite minster, award-winning Best Western hotel with mix of traditional and dramatic modern decor. 'Breakfasts without comparison'. Children welcomed. 2 lounges, bar, *The Court* café/bistro, *D.C.H.* restaurant; conference/function facilities. Valet parking. 37 bedrooms (some family). B&B: single £95, double £125–£205.

St Denys Hotel St Deny's Road YO1 9QD. *Tel* 01904-622207, www. stdenyshotel.co.uk. Owned by Marsh family for over 20 years: B&B in former rectory, 5 mins' walk from centre. Car park. 12 bedrooms. B&B: single £45–£65, double £65–£85.

SCOTLAND

ABERDEEN   Map 5:C3
Ardoe House South Deeside Road, Blairs AB12 5YP. *Tel* 01224-860600, www.ardoehouse.com. 4 miles E of centre: 19th-century baronial granite mansion, much extended (Macdonald group). Lounge, *Laird's* bar, restaurant; conference/banqueting facilities; leisure club (swimming pool, beauty salon, etc). 30-acre park. Views of River Dee. 109 bedrooms: single £62.50–£99, double £110–£130.

Marcliffe at Pitfodels North Deeside Road, Pitfodels AB15 9YA. *Tel* 01224-861000, www.marcliffe.com. Spence family's large, white hotel in lower Dee valley, 20 mins' drive from airport/centre. Drawing room bar and lounge (display of Scottish artists; 140 cheese dishes); conservatory restaurant; banqueting/conference facilities; health spa. No background music. 11-acre landscaped grounds: putting. 42 bedrooms (1 adapted for &). B&B: single £135–£185, double £145–£205, suite £245–£295.

ARDUAINE Argyll and Bute   Map 5:D1
Loch Melfort Hotel PA34 4XG. *Tel* 01852-200233, www.lochmelfort. co.uk. Nigel and Kyle Schofield's white-painted hotel overlooking Asknish Bay, with views to Jura, Shuna and Scarba. 'Fully justified' in claim to have finest location on the west coast of Scotland. 'Splendid seascapes.' Dining room, wood-panelled library; conference facilities. Close to Arduaine Gardens. 23 bedrooms (some in modern Cedar Wing via covered walkway). B&B £69–£89 per person.

ARISAIG Highland   Map 5:C1
Cnoc-Na-Faíre Back of Keppoch PH39 4NS. *Tel* 01687-450249, www. cnoc-na-faire.co.uk. 1 mile from village, on Road to the Isles: small hotel with 'gorgeous views' (Skye, Rum, Eigg). Lounge, bar, café with Internet,

restaurant (Scottish theme). 6 simple bedrooms (plaid fabrics). B&B from £52 per person.

BALLOCH West Dunbartonshire   Map 5:D2

Cameron House Loch Lomond G83 8QZ. *Tel* 01389-755565, www.cameronhouse.co.uk. 'Breathtaking views' from luxurious mansion on Loch Lomond (De Vere group). Lounge, 2 bars, 2 restaurants. Leisure centre with lagoon pool; water sports marina; health and beauty treatments. 96 no-smoking bedrooms (most in annexe). B&B: double £179–£339, suite £309–£479.

BANCHORY Aberdeenshire   Map 5:C3

The Learney Arms The Square, Torphins AB31 4GP. *Tel* 01339-882202, www.learneyarmshotel.com. Imposing Victorian building in landscaped gardens, overlooking Torphins village (6 miles NW of Banchory). *Golfers' Return* lounge bar (over 100 whiskies), restaurant. Garden: 9-hole golf course, bowling green. 8 bedrooms. B&B: single from £38, double from £48.

BRODICK North Ayrshire   Map 5:E1

Kilmichael Glen Cloy, Isle of Arran KA27 8BY. *Tel* 01770-302219, www.kilmichael.com. At end of unmade road in 5-acre grounds (ducks, peacocks, spectacular views of mountains): Geoffrey Botterill's 17th-century listed building (reputed to be oldest on Arran). Country house atmosphere. 2 drawing rooms, dining room. 7 bedrooms (3 in stable block). B&B £60–£95 per person.

CAMPTOWN Borders   Map 5:E3

Jedforest Hotel Jedburgh TD8 6PJ. *Tel* 01835-840222, www.jedforesthotel.com. 'In stunning countryside and blissfully quiet': small country house run by Robert Boddington and Audrey Craig (new owners in May 2005). Lounge, bar, restaurant, library; 35 acres of landscaped gardens and grounds; fishing. 'Superb dinner, exceptional service.' 12 bedrooms (4 in River Cottage; 1 adapted for ♿). B&B: single £65–£90, double £100–£140, suite £160; D,B&B from £75 per person.

DUNDEE   Map 5:D3

Apex City Quay 1 West Victoria Dock Road DD1 3JP. *Tel* 01382-202404, www.apexhotels.co.uk. 5-storey modern hotel on dockside (views over River Tay). 'Four-zone' bedrooms – for sleeping, working, relaxing, bathing. Metro bar, Metro brasserie, *Alchemy* restaurant; spa: gym, sauna, hot tubs, treatments. 153 bedrooms. B&B single/double from £120.

Invercarse 371 Perth Road DD2 1PG. *Tel* 01382-669231, www.bestwestern. co.uk. 3 miles from centre, 1 mile from airport: extended Victorian mansion (Best Western) in large wooded grounds on hill. Public rooms face River Tay. 2 bars, restaurant; large function facilities. Parking. 44 bedrooms (some no-smoking). B&B: single £72–£82, double £92–£102.

EDINBURGH   Map 5:D2

Borough Hotel 72–80 Causewayside EH9 1PY. *Tel* 0131-668 2255, www.boroughhotel.com. Blue-fronted former snooker club near Royal Mile, now privately owned, informal boutique hotel with minimalist decor. Bar, restaurant. 11 small bedrooms (large warehouse windows). B&B: double £80–£125, family £105–£190.

Channings 15 South Learmonth Gardens EH4 1EZ. *Tel* 0131-332 3232, www.channings.co.uk. Conversion of 5 Edwardian town houses in quiet cobbled street, ten mins' walk from city centre. (Part of Peter Taylor's Town House Company.) Elegant public rooms (wood panelling, period features); log fires. 3 lounges, bar, restaurant. Internet, DVD-player, video games, etc. Access to private gardens. Children welcomed. 41 bedrooms: single £101–£140, double £131–£230, suite £187–£275. Breakfast £7.50–£12.50.

The Howard 34 Great King Street EH3 6QH. *Tel* 0131-557 3500, www.thehoward.com. 3 Georgian houses in cobbled New Town street, now rather sophisticated hotel (Town House Company). Drawing room, restaurant (traditional; local produce); room-service meals; personal butlers. Parking. 18 bedrooms: single £108–£145, double £180–£295, suite £243–£395. Breakfast £10.50–£16.50.

The Lairg 11 Coates Gardens EH12 5LG. *Tel* 0131-337 1050, www. thelairghotel.co.uk. Family-run guest house with tartan touches, on quiet street near Haymarket station; 25 mins' walk from Waverley station. 'Helpful owner, excellent breakfast, lovely staff.' No smoking. 10 bedrooms. B&B £30–£70 per person.

Malmaison 1 Tower Place, Leith EH6 7DB. *Tel* 0131-468 5000, www. malmaison.com. Overlooking Leith harbour: stylishly converted 19th-century seamen's mission. Café/bar, brasserie; meeting/function facilities; fitness room. Free parking. 100 bedrooms: double £140–£160, suite £195. Breakfast £9.95–£12.75.

Prestonfield Priestfield Road EH16 5UT. *Tel* 0131-225 7800, www. prestonfield.com. Restaurateur James Thomson's 17th-century mansion with opulent interior (see also *The Witchery*, full entry). 1½ miles from centre, by Arthur's Seat, surrounded by golf course, in 20-acre garden and parkland. 3 drawing rooms, 2 bars, *Rhubarb* restaurant, 3 private dining rooms; function facilities. Parking. 22 bedrooms (2 suitable for &). B&B: double from £195, suite from £295.

Rick's 55a Frederick Street EH2 1LH. *Tel* 0131-622 7800, www. ricksedinburgh.co.uk. Fashionable bar/restaurant-with-rooms in basement of neo-classical house in Georgian New Town. Eclectic modern cooking; background 'soul/funk' music. 10 bedrooms (state-of-the-art; across covered courtyard). B&B double £129.25.

ELGIN Moray   Map 5:C2

Mansion House The Haugh IV30 1AW. *Tel* 01343-548811, www. mansionhousehotel.co.uk. On River Lossie in mature woodland, 5 mins' walk from centre: privately owned 19th-century Scots baronial mansion. Period decor. Piano lounge, snooker room, bar, restaurant, bistro; small function facilities; leisure club (indoor swimming pool, gym, etc). Fishing (permits available). Parking. 23 bedrooms. B&B: single £90–£104, double £143–£175.

FORT WILLIAM Highland   Map 5:C1

Glenlochy Nevis Bridge PH33 6LP. *Tel* 01397-702909, www. glenlochyguesthouse.co.uk. In large grounds on River Nevis, 10 mins' walk from centre: Hugh and Catherine MacPherson's guest house. Children welcomed. Lounge, breakfast room. Parking. 12 bedrooms. B&B £25–£38 per person.

Inverlochy Castle Torlundy PH33 6SN. *Tel* 01397-702177, www. inverlochycastlehotel.com. Baronial pile in foothills of Ben Nevis, 3 miles NE of Fort William. Opulent interior: Great Hall (Venetian chandeliers, frescoed ceiling); 2 lounges, restaurant, billiard room; 500-acre grounds: tennis, loch, fishing. 17 bedrooms. B&B: single £220–£310, double £300–£575, suite £470–£645.

Tornevis Banavie PH33 7LX. *Tel* 01397-772868, www.scotland2000. com/tornevis. Rob and Pat Kiff's B&B accommodation with views of Ben Nevis and Loch Linnhe, 3 miles from town centre. Lounge. Small garden. Parking. 3 bedrooms. B&B £30–£35 per person.

FORTROSE Highland   Map 5:C2

The Anderson Union Street, by Inverness IV10 8TD. *Tel* 01381-620236, www.theanderson.co.uk. In seaside village on Black Isle, lively restaurant-with-rooms owned by Americans Jim and Anne Anderson. Public bar, *Whisky* bar (over 160 single-malt whiskies; live Scottish music in summer), dining room. Beer garden. Sandy beach 1¼ miles. Parking. 9 bedrooms. B&B £42.50–£45 per person.

GATEHOUSE OF FLEET Dumfries and Galloway   Map 5:E2

The Bank of Fleet 47 High Street DG7 2HR. *Tel* 01557-814302, www.bankoffleet.co.uk. Small, family-run hotel on edge of Galloway Forest Park. Much blue in decoration. Bar/restaurant (inglenook fireplace) overlooking walled garden; dining room; small function facilities. 'Excellent value for money.' 4 bedrooms. B&B £30–£35 per person.

GLASGOW   Map 5:D2

Cathedral House 28–32 Cathedral Square G4 0XA. *Tel* 0141-552 3519, www.cathedralhouse.com. In leafy suburb, by cathedral, 1 mile from centre: 19th-century red brick mansion. Restaurant, café/bar; conference/function facilities. Beer garden. Parking. 8 bedrooms (via spiral staircase). B&B double £65–£85.

Saint Jude's 190 Bath Street G2 4HG. *Tel* 0141-352 8800, www.saintjudes. com. Chef/*patronne* Jenny Burns's contemporary boutique hotel in Victorian town house on busy street in business district. Bar, restaurant; function rooms. 6 bedrooms. B&B: single £90, double £115, suite £185.

The Town House 4 Hughenden Terrace G12 9XR. 0141-357 0862, www. thetownhouseglasgow.com. In handsome terrace: Victorian villa in quiet conservation area in West End area. Old-fashioned ambience. Lounge, breakfast room; room service. Easy street parking. 10 bedrooms. B&B £36–£60 per person.

GRANTOWN-ON-SPEY Highland   Map 5:C2

The Pines Woodside Avenue PH26 3JR. *Tel* 01479-872092, www. thepinesgrantown.co.uk. Michael and Gwen Stewart's Victorian Highland home in large landscaped gardens and woodland, down quiet country lane. Elegant decor; family portraits, original watercolours, oil paintings, antiques and *objets d'art*. 2 lounges, dining room, garden room, library. 'A real find that we were sad to leave.' 8 bedrooms. B&B £45–£58 per person.

INVERNESS Highland   Map 5:C2

Glenmoriston Town House 20 Ness Bank IV2 4SF. *Tel* 01463-223777, www.glenmoriston.com. 'Stunning' position near centre, with views of River Ness. Lounge bar (182 malt whiskies), *Abstract* restaurant; function facilities. Cooked breakfast 'exceptional'. 30 bedrooms. B&B double £130–£160.

Millwood House 36 Old Mill Road IV2 3HR. *Tel* 01463-237254, www.millwoodhouse.co.uk. Gillian and Bill Lee's B&B of 'cosy cottage charm' in secluded gardens, 20 mins' walk from centre. Lounge (log fire), breakfast room. No smoking. Parking. 3 bedrooms. B&B double £83–£89.

KINROSS Perth and Kinross   **Map 5:D2**

Roxburghe Guest House 126 High Street KY13 8DA. *Tel* 01577-862498, www.roxburgheguesthouse.co.uk. Sandy Ferguson and Steve Wrigley provide 'beautifully cooked' dinners at this modest guest house on high street of old market town. Dining room; garden. Loch fishing 10 mins' walk. Limited parking. 4 bedrooms (2 smoking); 'lots of notices'. B&B £20 per person.

LOCKERBIE Dumfries and Galloway   **Map 5:E2**

The Dryfesdale Dryfebridge DG11 2SF. *Tel* 01576-202427, www. dryfesdalehotel.co.uk. Handy staging post just over the border: family-run former manse, 1 mile from centre, near M74, exit 17. Lounges, bar, *Kirkhill* restaurant; conference/function facilities. 5-acre grounds. 16 bedrooms (5 family; 1 suitable for &). B&B: single £75, double £100–£125.

LYBSTER Highland   **Map 5:B3**

The Portland Arms KW3 6BS. *Tel* 01593-721721, www.portlandarms. co.uk. On A99 south of Wick, handsome granite coaching inn (1850s), owned by Swallow Hotels, on outskirts of fishing village, ½ mile from sea. Convenient stopover for Orkney ferry. Lounge, bistro/bar, *Kitchen* restaurant (local produce); function facilities; library. Small front garden. 22 bedrooms. B&B £43–£70 per person.

MELROSE Borders   **Map 5:E3**

The Townhouse Market Square TD6 9PQ. *Tel* 01896-822645, www. thetownhousemelrose.co.uk. Smartly renovated house with white-painted exterior in town square, opposite Henderson family's other hotel, *Burts* (see main entry). Brasserie, restaurant; function facilities. 11 bedrooms. B&B: single £65–£75, double £96–£100, suite £116–£130.

OBAN Argyll and Bute   **Map 5:D1**

Hawthornbank Dalriach Road PA34 5JE. *Tel* 01631-562041, *email* hawthornbank@aol.com. Brian and Valerie McGee's guest house: Victorian villa in elevated position 5 mins' walk from centre. Lounge, dining room. Patio. 8 bedrooms. B&B £27–£40 per person.

PEEBLES Borders   **Map 5:E2**

Caddon View 14 Pirn Road, Innerleithen EH44 6HH. *Tel* 01896-830208, www.caddonview.co.uk. 6 miles SE of Peebles: Bob and Gail Syratt's smart B&B in converted Victorian doctor's house. Lounge, conservatory. Garden. Parking. 8 bedrooms (2 on ground floor). B&B £47–£55 per person.

Park Hotel Innerleithen Road EH45 8BA. *Tel* 01721-720451, www.parkpeebles.co.uk. Turreted, gabled, white building (McMillan Hotels group), with views of hills. Lounges, bar, restaurant. Garden, putting, croquet; access to sports/health facilities at large sister, *Peebles Hotel Hydro* (700 yds: swimming pool, sauna; tennis, etc). 24 bedrooms. B&B: single from £62.50, double £39.50–£100.50.

PERTH   Map 5:D2

The Parklands 2 St Leonard's Banks PH2 8EB. *Tel* 01738-622451, www.theparklandshotel.com. 'Way beyond expectations.' Scott and Penny Edwards's contemporary hotel overlooking South Inch Park, stunning views across River Tay to Kinnoull Hill. 5 mins' walk to town. Lounge, bar, *Acanthus* restaurant, *Number 1 The Bank* bistro 'excellent quality ingredients, freshly cooked'; terrace, garden; function facilities. 14 bedrooms. B&B: single £69–£109, double £89–£149.

Sunbank House 50 Dundee Road PH2 7BA. *Tel* 01738-624882, www. sunbankhouse.com. By banks of River Tay, Victorian house in 'beautifully landscaped gardens', short walk to city centre. Remo (the chef) and Georgina Zane are 'attentive' owners. Restaurant serves Italian-influenced dishes using Scottish produce. Lounge, dining room. Traditional decor. 9 bedrooms. B&B £40–£79 per person.

PITLOCHRY Perth and Kinross   Map 5:D2

Green Park Clunie Bridge Road PH16 5JY. *Tel* 01796-473248, www. thegreenpark.co.uk. 'Perthshire's best-kept secret.' McMenemie family's 'very welcoming' country house, extensively refurbished, near theatre. In 3-acre garden on Loch Faskally (putting, fishing, boat hire). 3 lounges, library, bar, restaurant. 51 bedrooms (16 on ground floor; suitable for &). B&B £40–£57 per person; D,B&B £48–£81.

RODEL Western Isles   Map 5:B1

Rodel Hotel HS5 3TW. *Tel* 01859 520210, www.rodelhotel.co.uk. Donnie and Dena MacDonald 'want guests to enjoy themselves' at their much extended small hotel on picturesque harbour of tiny, historic village looking across to Skye. Tastefully decorated; works by local artists on display. 'Great food. Breakfast was as good as dinner.' 4 bedrooms. Double £100–£130. Breakfast £10.

ST ANDREWS Fife   Map 5:D3

The Inn at Lathones by Largoward KY9 1JE. *Tel* 01334-840494, www.theinn.co.uk. Outside village 5 miles from St Andrews, Nick White's

400-year-old single-storey coaching inn ('with ghosts'). Lounge, bar, function room. Award-winning modern European cooking in restaurant. 13 bedrooms. B&B double £80–£130; D,B&B (min. 2 nights) double £85–£130.

SCOURIE Highland   Map 5:B2
Eddrachilles Badcall Bay IV27 4TH. *Tel* 01971-502477, www.eddrachilles. com. On large estate at head of Badcall Bay, small hotel owned by Isabelle and Richard Flannery since 2005. Lounge, conservatory, 2 bars, restaurant. 'They are making the most of an old favourite; her French rural style cooking is the best there has been here.' 11 bedrooms. Closed Oct–mid-Mar. D,B&B £59.90–£63.95 per person.
Scourie Hotel IV27 4SX. *Tel* 01971-502396, www.scourie-hotel.co.uk. Overlooking Scourie Bay: Patrick and Judy Price's fishing hotel in old village coaching inn. 2 lounges, 2 bars, *table d'hôte* restaurant. 9-acre grounds leading to sea (5 mins' walk to sandy beach); 25,000 acres of brown trout, salmon, sea trout fishing. 20 bedrooms (2 garden rooms). B&B £32–£48 per person; D,B&B £46–£66.

SWINTON Borders   Map 5:E3
The Wheatsheaf Main Street TD11 3JJ. *Tel* 01890-860257, www. wheatsheaf-swinton.co.uk. 'First-class restaurant with well-prepared and presented food' at Chris and Jan Wilson's flower-bedecked country inn, in quiet village SE of Berwick-upon-Tweed. Easy access to coastal walks, forest walks, village walks, serious hill walking. 7 bedrooms. B&B £51–£92 per person.

TAYNUILT Argyll and Bute   Map 5:D1
Roineabhal Country House Kilchrenan PA35 1HD. *Tel* 01866-833207, www.roineabhal.com. Stone-built country house near Loch Awe. Owned by Roger and Maria Soep. 'Exceptional' B&B accommodation; 'amazing' home-cooked breakfasts, afternoon teas and 5-course dinners (vegetarian and dietary needs catered for). Lounge, dining room; garden. Pick-up service from Oban or Taynuilt if required. 3 bedrooms. B&B £37.50–£50 per person; D,B&B £67.50–£80.

WALKERBURN Borders   Map 5:E2
Windlestraw Lodge Tweed Valley EH43 6AA. *Tel* 01896-870636, www. windlestraw.co.uk. In elevated position with views down the Tweed valley and over the Elibank Forest: elegant Edwardian home of chef Alan Reid and his wife, Julie, formerly of *The Wheatsheaf*, Swinton (*qv*). Locally

sourced food in wood-panelled restaurant. Lounge, bar, dining room; garden. 6 bedrooms. B&B £60–£90 per person; D,B&B from £95.

WALES

ABERGAVENNY Monmouthshire   Map 3:D4
The Abbey Hotel NP7 7NN. *Tel* 01873-890487, www.llanthony.co.uk/ accommodation. 9 miles N of Abergavenny: quirky guest house (former domestic accommodation and towers of ruined medieval priory), in Brecon Beacons national park, near Offa's Dyke Path. Stone spiral stairs, antiques. Bar, dining room. Parking. 5 bedrooms (shared bathroom and loo). B&B £32.50–£36.25 per person.

BRECON Powys   Map 3:D3
Cantre Selyf 5 Lion Street LD3 7AU. *Tel* 01874-622904, www.cantreselyf. co.uk. Near St Mary's church: Mr and Mrs Roberts's yellow-painted 17th-century no-smoking town house. Lounge, dining room (traditional Welsh/ continental breakfast; evening meal by arrangement). Walled garden: summer house. Parking. 3 bedrooms (moulded, beamed ceilings, Georgian fireplaces, cast iron beds). B&B £62–£72 per person.

BRIDGEND   Map 3:E3
The Great House Laleston CF32 0HP. *Tel* 01656-657644, www. great-house-laleston.co.uk. 2 miles W of Bridgend: 16th-century Grade II* listed hunting lodge, restored by 'hands-on' owners, Stephen and Norma Bond. Many historical/architectural features. Lounge, bar, bistro, *Leicester's* restaurant; health suite; conference/wedding facilities. 1-acre walled garden: dovecote. 16 bedrooms (some suitable for &). B&B: single from £75, double £120.

CAERNARFON Gwynedd   Map 3:A2
Seiont Manor Llanrug LL55 2AQ. *Tel* 01286-673366, www.handpicked hotels.co.uk. 3 miles E of centre: Georgian farmstead in 150-acre farmland, with 1½-mile stretch of River Seiont. Lounge, library, bar, restaurant, conservatory; conference/leisure facilities (swimming pool, gym, sauna, etc); fishing. 28 bedrooms (8 no-smoking, some family). B&B double from £95.

CARDIFF   Map 3:E4
The Big Sleep Bute Terrace CF10 2FE. *Tel* 029-2063 6363, www. thebigsleephotel.com. Friendly budget designer B&B hotel (former British

Gas office building), owned by Cosmo Fry with consortium including John Malkovich. ½ mile from station. 'Minimalist kitsch' decor (much formica). Residents' bar, breakfast room; lift. Limited parking. 81 bedrooms. B&B (continental): double £45–£120, suite £99–£150.

HARLECH Gwynedd   Map 3:B3
Castle Cottage Y Llech LL46 2YL. *Tel* 01766-780479, www. castlecottageharlech.co.uk. Just off high street, Jacqueline and Glyn Roberts's informal restaurant-with-rooms in 2 adjoining buildings (16th/ 17th-century origins). Wooden beams, log fires; modern bathrooms. Lounge, bar, dining room. 7 bedrooms (4 in annexe; 2 on ground floor). B&B: single from £70, double £90–£120.

HAVERFORDWEST Pembrokeshire   Map 3:D1
Crug-Glas Abereiddy, Solva SA62 6XX. *Tel* 01348-831302, www. crug-glas.co.uk. 1¼ miles inland from Pembrokeshire coast: Evans family's no-smoking guest house on 600-acre working farm. Traditional decor (family heirlooms). Lounge (videos, books), bar; restaurant. 1-acre garden. 5 bedrooms. B&B £40–£65 per person.
College Guest House 93 Hill Street, St Thomas' Green SA61 1QL. *Tel* 01437-763710, www.collegeguesthouse.com. In Georgian town house (Grade II listed), 5 mins' walk from town centre: B&B run by Colin Larby and Pauline Good. Lounge. Beach 6 miles. Parking. 8 bedrooms. B&B: single £40–£45, double/family £55–£107.

LLANARMON DYFFRYN CEIRIOG Denbighshire Map 3:B4
The West Arms nr Llangollen LL20 7LD. *Tel* 01691-600665, www. thewestarms.co.uk. In hamlet 7 miles SW of Llangollen: 16th-century country hotel by River Ceiriog. Lounge, 2 bars (meal service), restaurant, conservatory; conference/function facilities. Garden facing Berwyn mountains. 15 bedrooms (some suitable for &). B&B: single £43.50–£95, double £87–£179.

MUMBLES Swansea   Map 3:E3
Norton House Hotel Norton Road SA3 5TQ. *Tel* 01792-404891, www. nortonhousehotel.co.uk. 3 miles SW of Swansea: 18th-century former mariner's house 100 yds from seafront. Run by Jan and John Power, and son Mark. Lounge, cocktail bar, restaurant. 1-acre grounds. 15 bedrooms (some on ground floor; 8 in stable block). B&B: single £85–£95, double £95–£120.
Patricks 638 Mumbles Road SA3 4EA. *Tel* 01792-360199, www. patrickswithrooms.com. 'Warm welcome; outstanding food'; 'spacious

bedrooms, uniquely styled' at Catherine and Patrick Walsh's restaurant-with-rooms on Swansea Bay. Fresh fish; vegetarian options. Lounge/bar. Beach 100 yds. 8 colourful bedrooms (some suitable for &). B&B double £155.

RUTHIN Denbighshire   Map 3:A4

The Wynnstay Arms Well Street LL15 1AN. *Tel* 01824-703147, www.wynnstayarms.com. Black-and-white half-timbered coaching inn (established 1549). Refurbished with contemporary comforts. Lounge, bar, café bar, *fusions* brasserie. Parking. No smoking. 6 bedrooms. B&B (continental) £45–£65 per person.

ST DAVID'S Pembrokeshire   Map 3:D1

Old Cross Hotel Cross Square SA62 6SP. *Tel* 01437-720387, www.oldcrosshotel.co.uk. In centre, 'simple, unspoilt' stone-built hotel, owned by Alex and Julie Babis. 'Good food, well cooked and served; enormous Welsh breakfast.' Lounge, bar (popular with locals), restaurant (alfresco in summer). Parking. 8 bedrooms. B&B: single £38–£62, double £68–£105.

The Waterings Anchor Drive, High Street SA62 6QH. *Tel* 01437-720876, www.waterings.co.uk. In quiet area on edge of city: Chant family's B&B with wide sea views. Dining room. Welsh breakfasts. No smoking. 2-acre grounds (picnic area, 9-hole putting green, water garden). Sand and rock beach ½ mile. 5 bedrooms (all on ground floor, round sheltered courtyard; some family). B&B £37.50–£40 per person.

SWANSEA   Map 3:E3

Morgans Somerset Place SA1 1RR. *Tel* 01792-484848, www.morganshotel.co.uk. Martin and Louisa Morgan's hotel in 'superbly transformed' converted Port Authority building (Grade II* star listed): modernised, with many impressive features. Bar, *Plimsoll* café/bar restaurant; function facilities; courtyard. 20 bedrooms. No smoking except in 'decking' area. B&B double £125–£250.

CHANNEL ISLANDS

ST MARTIN'S Guernsey   Map 1:E5

Hotel Bella Luce La Fosse GY4 6EB. *Tel* 01481-238764, www.bellalucehotel.guernsey.net. Manor house with 11th-century origins, 2 miles SW of St Peter Port. Oak-beamed lounge, bar (light meals available), restaurant. Garden: solar-heated swimming pool. Rock beach 5 mins' walk. 31 bedrooms (some family, one suitable for &). B&B £42–£60 per person.

IRELAND

BELFAST   Map 6:B6
Culloden Hotel Bangor Road, Holywood BT18 0EX. *Tel* 028-9042 1066,
www.slh.com/culloden. Former bishop's palace, now 5-star hotel (member
of Small Luxury Hotels of the World), overlooking Belfast Lough, 5 miles
NE of centre. Antiques, fine paintings, chandeliers; 'lots of comfortable
lounge areas', restaurant; spa; 12-acre grounds. 79 bedrooms. B&B: single
from £160, double from £200, suite from £275.
Malmaison 34–38 Victoria Street BT1 3GH. *Tel* 028-9022 0200, www.
malmaison-belfast.com. Former *McCausland Hotel*, converted 1860s red
brick warehouses near River Lagan in Cathedral Quarter (edge of centre),
smartly refurbished (bold colours). Lounges, bar, brasserie; small business
centre; gym. 64 bedrooms: double £125–£155, suite £295–£375. Breakfast
from £12.
Old Inn 15 Main Street, Crawfordsburn, Co. Down BT19 1JH. *Tel* 028-
9185 3255, www.theoldinn.com. 10 miles E of centre, on edge of wooded
country park that sweeps down to the sea: ancient coaching inn (1640:
thatched roof, beamed ceilings, wood-panelled walls). Gallery lounge, bar,
conservatory-style *1614* restaurant, *Churn* bistro; conference/function
facilities; 'marrying hot spot'. Small garden. 32 bedrooms (1 suitable for &).
B&B double £75–£200.
TENsq 10 Donegal Square South BT1 5JD. *Tel* 028-9024 1001, www.
tensquare.co.uk. Behind City Hall: Nicholas Hill's boutique hotel (former
linen warehouse). Oriental-influenced decor (reds, creams, whites; dark
wood). Bar/grill room; events suite. 23 bedrooms. B&B: single/double
£160, suite from £240.

DINGLE Co. Kerry   Map 6:D4
Milltown House *Tel* 00 353 66-915 1372, www.milltownhousedingle.com.
On peninsula, Tara Kerry's friendly, no-smoking B&B: white 19th-century
gabled house. Lounge, conservatory. 2-acre garden. Golf driving range,
pitch and putt behind house. 10 bedrooms. B&B double €100–€150.

DONEGAL Co. Donegal   Map 6:B5
Harvey's Point *Tel* 00 353 74-972 2208, www.harveyspoint.com. 3 miles
NE of Donegal on Lough Eske, at foot of Blue Stack mountains:
Gysling family's much extended country hotel. Spacious accommodation
(lavish penthouse suites). Lounge, bar, restaurant; conference/wedding
facilities; frequent events. 20-acre grounds. 42 bedrooms. B&B €99–
€250 per person.

DUBLIN   Map 6:C6

Brownes 22 St Stephen's Green, Dublin 2. *Tel* 00 353 1-638 3939, www.brownesdublin.com. Boutique hotel in Georgian town house (Stein group). Drawing room, brasserie; function/meeting facilities. 11 bedrooms: single €185–€200, double €240–€270, suite €425. Breakfast from €12.50–€20.

Buswells 25–29 Molesworth St, Dublin 2. *Tel* 00 353 1-614 6500, www.quinn-hotels.com. A hotel since 1882, in 5 Georgian town houses, next to Dáil (Irish Parliament). Part of Quinn group but 'feels like a privately run hotel'. Lounge, bar, *Trumans* restaurant; leisure centre; function facilities. 'Agreeable atmosphere; excellent breakfasts.' 67 rooms. B&B: single €125–€140, double €135–€190.

Leixlip House Captain's Hill, Leixlip, Co. Kildare. *Tel* 00 353 1-624 2268, www.leixliphouse.com. Overlooking village, 8 miles NW of Dublin (20 mins by motorway to centre/airport), Frank Towey's Georgian house. Traditional decor. Lounge, *Bradaun* restaurant (modern Irish cuisine); conference/function facilities; wireless Internet access; golf packages. Parking. 19 bedrooms (4 in coach house). B&B: single €140, double €170, suite €200.

Longfields 10 Fitzwilliam Street Lower, Dublin 2. *Tel* 00 353 1-676 1367, www.longfields.ie. Conversion of 2 Georgian terraced houses. Lounge, reading room, bar, *Longchamp@No.10* restaurant. 26 bedrooms (quietest at rear). B&B: single €99–€135, double €99–€165.

Raglan Lodge 10 Raglan Road (off Pembroke Road), Ballsbridge, Dublin 4. *Tel* 00 353 1-660 6697. Helen Moran's B&B: Victorian house in tree-lined residential street, 1 mile SE of centre. Parking. 7 bedrooms (some family). B&B double €100–€150.

DUNGARVAN Co. Waterford   Map 6:D5

Powersfield House Ballinamuck West. *Tel* 00 353 58-45594, www.powersfield.com. 1 mile outside Dungarvan, Edmund and Eunice (an award-winning cook) Power's B&B in symmetrical white house. Dinner by arrangement (€25-€35). Cookery courses. 6 bedrooms (1 suitable for &). B&B €50–€65 per person.

KILKENNY Co. Kilkenny   Map 6:D5

Kilkenny River Court Hotel The Bridge, John Street. *Tel* 00 353 56-772 3388, www.kilrivercourt.com. On River Nore, with views of castle: 4-star hotel/conference/leisure centre. Lounge, bar, riverside restaurant; leisure club: indoor swimming pool, etc. 90 bedrooms. B&B €45–€130 per person.

KILLARNEY Co. Kerry   Map 6:D4

Dunloe Castle *Tel* 00 353 64-71350, www.killarneyhotels.ie. Owned by German consortium: modern 5-star hotel facing Gap of Dunloe and River Laune (salmon fishing): 'The view in rain or shine is magical.' Lounge, bar, café, *Oak Room* restaurant; spa: huge indoor pool; conference/wedding facilities. 20-acre subtropical garden, castle ruins, Haflinger horses, 2 indoor tennis courts, putting, croquet, fishing. 110 bedrooms. B&B: double from €194, suite €350–€1,500.

KILLYBEGS Co. Donegal   Map 6:B5

Bay View Main Street. *Tel* 00 353 74-973 1950, www.bayviewhotel.ie. Modern 3-star hotel in town centre, by pier and harbour. Lounge (snacks served), *Wheelhouse* bar/carvery, *Captain's Table* restaurant; conference facilities; leisure centre: swimming pool, gym, sauna etc. 40 bedrooms. B&B from €79 per person.

WATERFORD Co. Waterford   Map 6:D5

Granville Hotel The Quay. *Tel* 00 353 51-305555, www.granville-hotel.ie. Large, family-run 4-star hotel: Georgian building by River Suir. Lounge bar, *Bianconi* restaurant; conference/wedding facilities. 100 bedrooms (penthouse suites have wide views). B&B €55–€135 per person.

WEXFORD Co. Wexford   Map 6:D6

The Blue Door 18 Lower George Street. *Tel* 00 353 53-21047, www.thebluedoorwexford.com. Imelda Scallan's B&B: Georgian town house 3 km from sea. Lounge, breakfast room (Irish or vegetarian breakfast). Street parking. 5 bedrooms (1 family). B&B €35–€45 per person.

Alphabetical list of hotels

(S) indicates a Shortlist entry

A

Abbey Abergavenny (S) 546
Abbey Penzance 262
Abbey House Abbotsbury 80
Aberdeen Lodge Dublin 470
Admiralty Lodge Miltown Malbay 491
Aghadoe Heights Killarney 481
Airds Port Appin 395
Albannach Lochinver 385
Albright Hussey Shrewsbury (S) 531
Alexandra Lyme Regis (S) 523
Allington Manor Grantham (S) 518
Amberley Castle Amberley 82
Amerdale House Arncliffe 85
Anchor Hotel & Ship Inn Porlock Weir 267
Anderson Fortrose (S) 541
Angel Inn Hetton 193
Angel Posting House Guildford (S) 518
Angel & Royal Grantham (S) 518
Annesley House Norwich (S) 527
Apex City of London London (S) 504
Apex City Quay Dundee (S) 539
Apple Lodge Lochranza 386
Apsley House Bath 96
Aquae Sulis Bath (S) 508
Ardanaiseig Kilchrenan 378
Ardeonaig Killin 379
Ardoch Lodge Strathyre 405
Ardoe House Aberdeen (S) 538
Argyll Iona 377
Arundel House Arundel 86

Arundell Arms Lifton 215
Ascot House Harrogate (S) 519
Ashbrook House Dublin 471
Ash-Rowan Belfast 459
At the Sign of the Angel Lacock 206
Auchendean Lodge Dulnain Bridge 360
Austwick Traddock Austwick 89
Aynsome Manor Cartmel 137
Ayrlington Bath (S) 508

B

Bagdale Hall Whitby (S) 536
Bailiffscourt Climping 148
Balfour Castle Shapinsay 402
Balgonie Country House Ballater 350
Ballachulish House Ballachulish 348
Ballathie House Kinclaven 380
Ballinkeele House Enniscorthy 474
Ballymakeigh House Killeagh 483
Ballymaloe House Shanagarry 500
Ballyvolane House Castlelyons 466
Ballywarren House Cong 468
Bank of Fleet Gatehouse of Fleet (S) 542
Barcelona Exeter 166
Barclay House Looe 221
Bark House Bampton 92
Barnham Broom Norwich (S) 527
Barton Cross Stoke Canon (S) 532
Bath Priory Bath 97
Bay Horse Ulverston 323
Bay View Killybegs (S) 551
Bayview Ballycotton 457
B+B Belgravia London (S) 504
Beach House Looe 221
Beachlands Weston-Super-Mare (S) 535

Champagne winners: Report of the Year competition

Readers' contributions are the lifeblood of the *Good Hotel Guide*. Each year we award a dozen bottles of champagne for the best reports. A bottle, a copy of the *Guide*, and an invitation to our launch party will go to the following generous readers for their contributions.

Dennis and Janet Allom of Torpoint, Cornwall
Conrad Barnard of Stowe Maries, Essex
Richard Barrett of Whiteparish, Wiltshire
Patricia and David Elliott of Barnes, London
Michael Lewis of High Barnet, Hertfordshire
Margaret Mallett of Bickley, Kent
Mark Purcell of Charlbury, Oxfordshire
Anne and Denis Tate of Mansfield, Nottinghamshire
Nikki Wild of Hook, Hampshire
Maggie Washington of Horley, Surrey
WG Watkins of Liphook, Hampshire
John Rowlands of Caernarfon, Wales

Hotel reports

The report forms on the following pages may be used to endorse or criticise an existing entry or to nominate a hotel for inclusion in the *Guide*. But it is not essential that you use our forms or restrict yourself to the space available.

All reports (*each on a separate piece of paper, please*) should include your name and address, the name and location of the hotel, and the date and length of your stay. Please nominate only places that you have visited in the past 12 months, unless friends tell you that standards have been maintained. Please be as specific as possible, and critical where appropriate, about the building, the public rooms and bedrooms, the meals, the service, the nightlife, the grounds.

If you describe the location as well as the hotel, particularly in less familiar regions, that is helpful. So are comments about worthwhile places to visit in the neighbourhood and, in the case of B&B hotels, recommendable restaurants.

We want the *Guide* to convey the special flavour of its hotels, and any details that you provide will give life to the description. We mind having to pass up a potentially attractive place because the report is too brief. Do not bother with prices and routine information about number of rooms and facilities; we get such details from the hotels. We want readers to supply information that is not accessible elsewhere. In the case of a new nomination, it helps if you include a brochure or mention a website.

Please never tell a hotel that you intend to file a report. Anonymity is essential to objectivity.

The 2008 edition of this volume will be written between mid-March and the end of May 2007, and published in early October 2007. Nominations should reach us not later than 15 May 2007. The latest date for comments on existing entries is 1 June 2007.

Please let us know if you would like us to send you more report forms. Our address for UK correspondents (no stamp needed) is: *Good Hotel Guide*, Freepost PAM 2931, London W11 4BR.

Reports can be faxed to us on 020-7602 4182, or they can be emailed to Goodhotel@aol.com. Reports posted outside the UK should be stamped normally and addressed to: *Good Hotel Guide*, 50 Addison Avenue, London W11 4QP, England.

[2007]

To: *The Good Hotel Guide*, Freepost PAM 2931, London W11 4BR

NOTE: No stamps needed in UK, but letters posted outside the UK should be addressed to 50 Addison Avenue, London W11 4QP, England, and stamped normally. Unless asked not to, we shall assume that we may publish your name. If you would like more report forms please tick ☐

Name of Hotel_____

Address _____

_____

Date of most recent visit   Duration of visit
☐ New recommendation   ☐ Comment on existing entry
Report:

I am not connected directly or indirectly with the management or proprietors

Signed _____

Name (CAPITALS PLEASE)

Address _____

_____

Email address _____

[2007]

To: *The Good Hotel Guide*, Freepost PAM 2931, London W11 4BR

NOTE: No stamps needed in UK, but letters posted outside the UK should be addressed to 50 Addison Avenue, London W11 4QP, England, and stamped normally. Unless asked not to, we shall assume that we may publish your name. If you would like more report forms please tick ☐

Name of Hotel_____

Address _____

_____

Date of most recent visit   Duration of visit
☐ New recommendation   ☐ Comment on existing entry
Report:

Please continue overleaf

I am not connected directly or indirectly with the management or proprietors

Signed _____

Name (CAPITALS PLEASE)

Address _____

_____

Email address _____

[2007]

To: *The Good Hotel Guide*, Freepost PAM 2931, London W11 4BR

NOTE: No stamps needed in UK, but letters posted outside the UK should be addressed to 50 Addison Avenue, London W11 4QP, England, and stamped normally. Unless asked not to, we shall assume that we may publish your name. If you would like more report forms please tick ☐

Name of Hotel_____

Address _____

_____

Date of most recent visit   Duration of visit
☐ New recommendation   ☐ Comment on existing entry
Report:

Please continue overleaf

I am not connected directly or indirectly with the management or proprietors

Signed _____

Name (CAPITALS PLEASE)

Address _____

_____

Email address _____

[2007]

To: *The Good Hotel Guide*, Freepost PAM 2931, London W11 4BR

NOTE: No stamps needed in UK, but letters posted outside the UK should be addressed to 50 Addison Avenue, London W11 4QP, England, and stamped normally. Unless asked not to, we shall assume that we may publish your name. If you would like more report forms please tick ☐

Name of Hotel _____

Address _____

_____

Date of most recent visit   Duration of visit

☐ New recommendation   ☐ Comment on existing entry

Report:

Please continue overleaf

I am not connected directly or indirectly with the management or proprietors

Signed _____

Name (CAPITALS PLEASE)

Address _____

_____

Email address _____